31472400320085

P9-CIU-030

WITHDRAWN

CARSON CITY LIBRARY
900 North Roop Street
Carson City, NV 89701
775-887-2244   MAR 1 0 2018

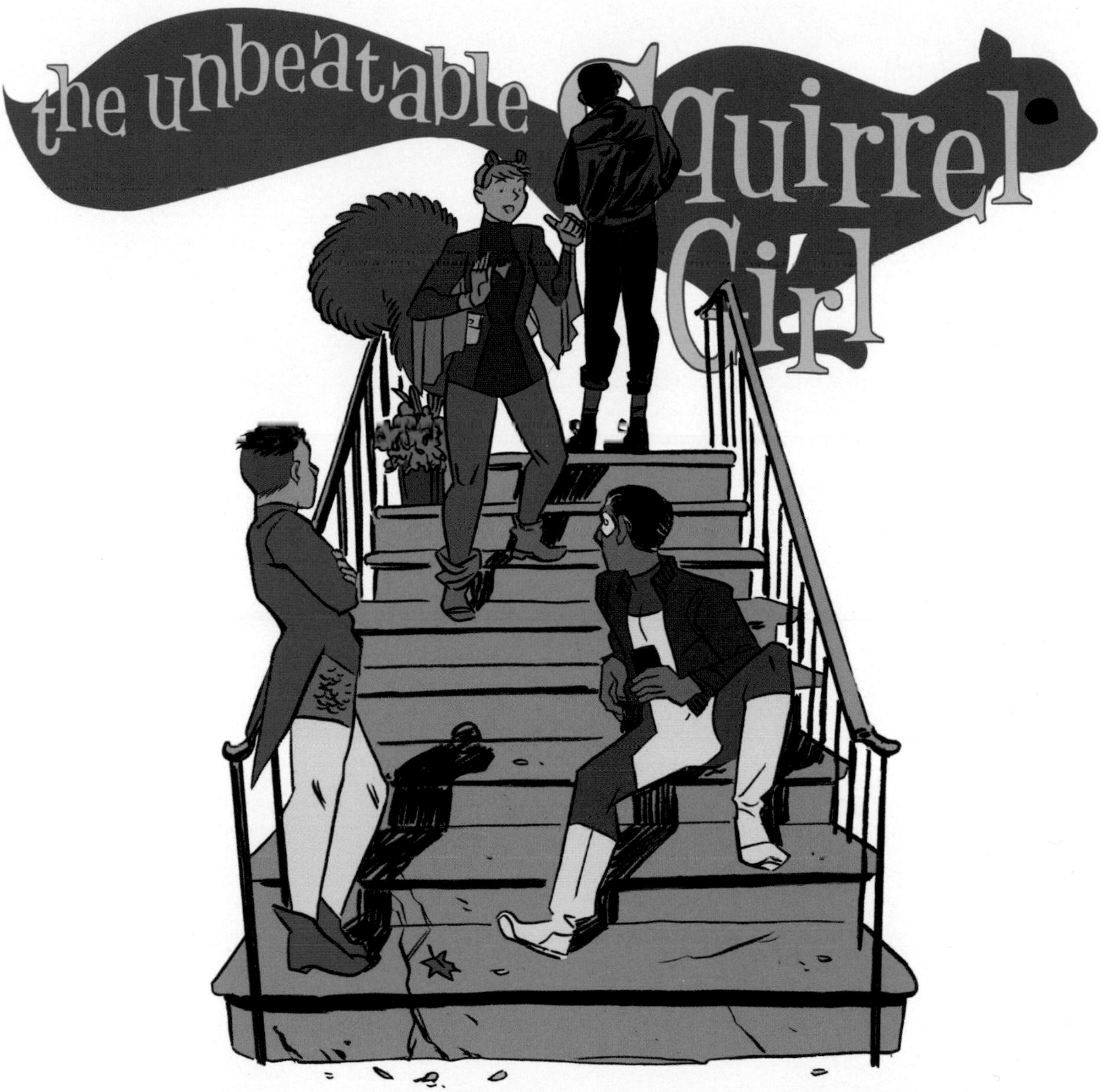
the unbeatable Squirrel Girl

the unbeatable

COLLECTION EDITOR: **JENNIFER GRÜNWALD**
ASSISTANT EDITOR: **CAITLIN O'CONNELL**
ASSOCIATE MANAGING EDITOR: **KATERI WOODY**
EDITOR, SPECIAL PROJECTS: **MARK D. BEAZLEY**
VP PRODUCTION & SPECIAL PROJECTS: **JEFF YOUNGQUIST**
SVP PRINT, SALES & MARKETING: **DAVID GABRIEL**
BOOK DESIGNER: **JAY BOWEN**

EDITOR IN CHIEF: **AXEL ALONSO**
CHIEF CREATIVE OFFICER: **JOE QUESADA**
PRESIDENT: **DAN BUCKLEY**
EXECUTIVE PRODUCER: **ALAN FINE**

THE UNBEATABLE SQUIRREL GIRL VOL. 3. Contains material originally published in magazine form as THE UNBEATABLE SQUIRREL GIRL #12-21. First printing 2018. ISBN# 978-1-302-90844-7. Published by MARVEL WORLDWIDE, INC., a subsidiary of MARVEL ENTERTAINMENT, LLC. OFFICE OF PUBLICATION: 135 West 50th Street, New York, NY 10020. Copyright © 2018 MARVEL No similarity between any of the names, characters, persons, and/or institutions in this magazine with those of any living or dead person or institution is intended, and any such similarity which may exist is purely coincidental. **Printed in China.** DAN BUCKLEY, President, Marvel Entertainment; JOE QUESADA, Chief Creative Officer; TOM BREVOORT, SVP of Publishing; DAVID BOGART, SVP of Business Affairs & Operations, Publishing & Partnership; C.B. CEBULSKI, VP of Brand Management & Development, Asia; DAVID GABRIEL, SVP of Sales & Marketing, Publishing; JEFF YOUNGQUIST, VP of Production & Special Projects; DAN CARR, Executive Director of Publishing Technology; ALEX MORALES, Director of Publishing Operations; SUSAN CRESPI, Production Manager; STAN LEE, Chairman Emeritus. For information regarding advertising in Marvel Comics or on Marvel.com, please contact Jonathan Parkhideh, VP of Digital Media & Marketing Solutions, at jparkhideh@marvel.com. For Marvel subscription inquiries, please call 888-511-5480. **Manufactured between 11/3/2017 and 1/15/2018 by R.R. DONNELLEY ASIA PRINTING SOLUTIONS, CHINA.**

10 9 8 7 6 5 4 3 2 1

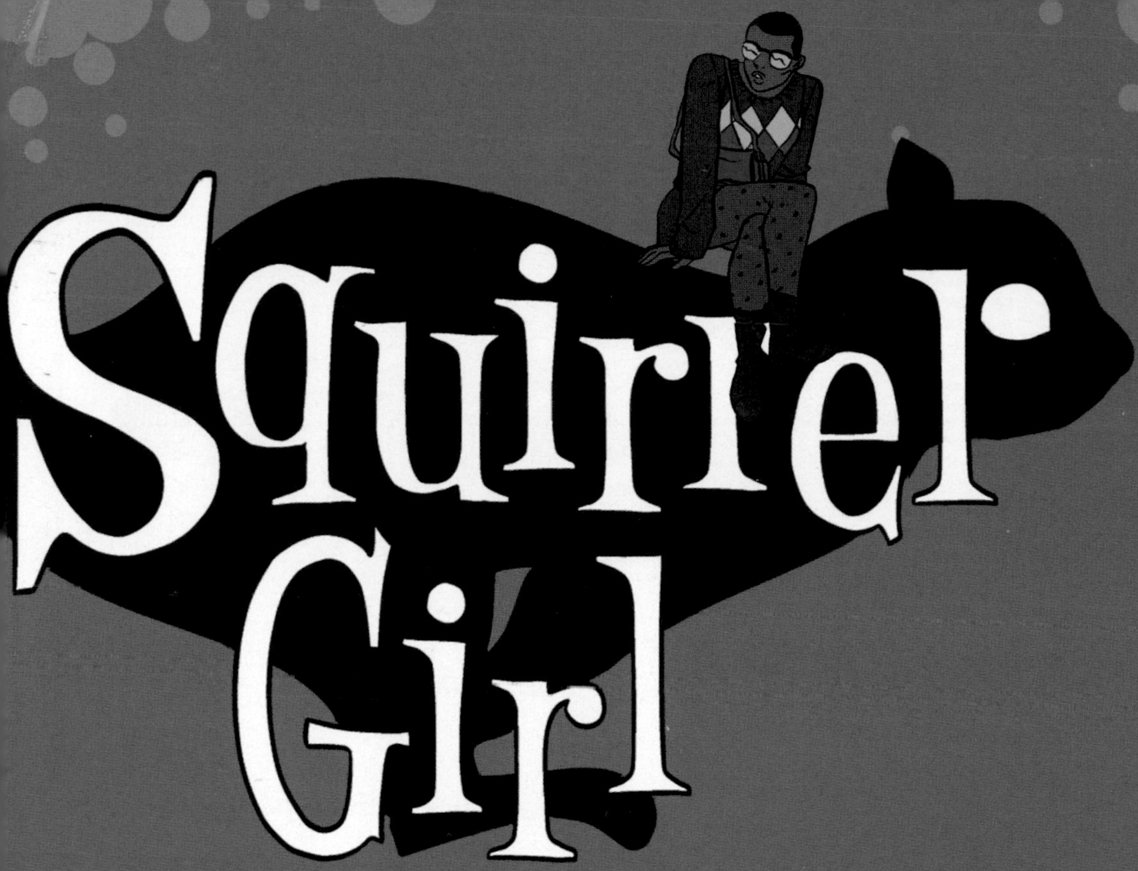

Squirrel Girl

Ryan North
WRITER

Erica Henderson
ARTIST

Rico Renzi
COLOR ART

Anthony Clark (#13), ***Hannah Blumenreich*** (#13) & ***Michael Cho*** (#15)
TRADING CARD ART

Will Murray
WRITER, 15-YEAR-OLD DOREEN SEQUENCE

Steve Ditko
DOREEN'S COSTUME DRAWING ART

Zac Gorman
MEW'S DREAM COMICS ART

Chris Schweizer
VULTURE & SANDMAN PANELS, #17

VC's Travis Lanham
WITH ***Clayton Cowles*** (#14)
LETTERERS

Erica Henderson
COVER ART

Charles Beacham
ASSISTANT EDITOR

Sarah Brunstad
ASSOCIATE EDITOR

Wil Moss
EDITOR

SPECIAL THANKS TO CK RUSSELL

SQUIRREL GIRL CREATED BY WILL MURRAY & STEVE DITKO

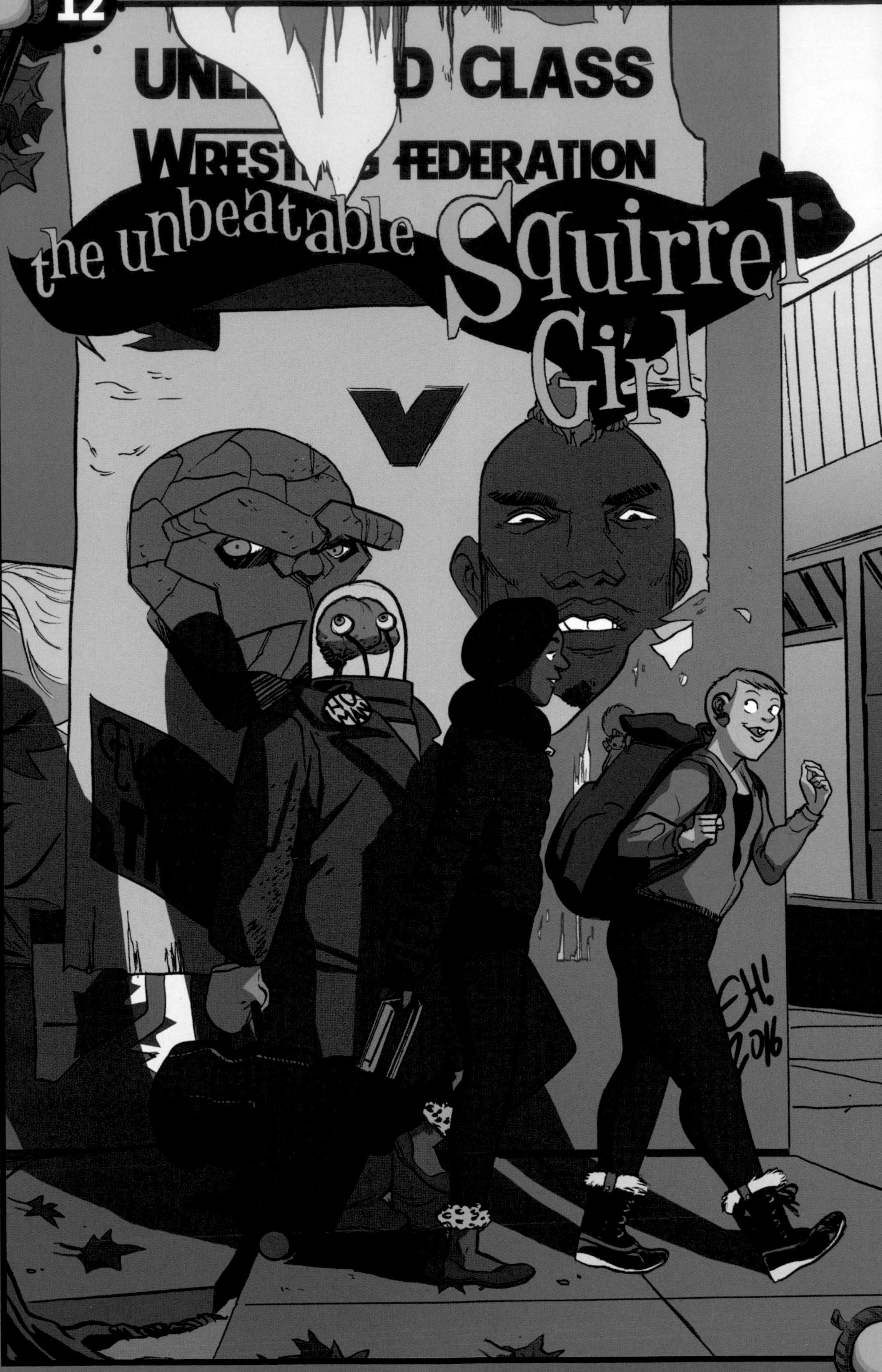
UNLE D CLASS
WRESTL G FEDERATION
the unbeatable Squirrel Girl
V
EH! 2016

Doreen Green isn't just a second-year computer science student: she secretly also has all the powers of both squirrel and girl! She uses her amazing abilities to fight crime *and* be as awesome as possible. You know her as...*The Unbeatable Squirrel Girl!* Find out what she's been up to, with...

Squirrel Girl *in a nutshell*

Squirrel Girl @unbeatablesg
Whew, I just had THE BEST NIGHT'S SLEEP OF ALL TIME. For some reason I feel like I could take on the world?

Squirrel Girl @unbeatablesg
Like, I woke up energized and jazzed, as if I really had just defeated a super villain and saved the world...IN MY SLEEP!! Felt great tbh

Squirrel Girl @unbeatablesg
But hah hah that's impossible so oh well

Spider-Man @aspidercan
@unbeatablesg actually there's a doctor strange bad guy named "nightmare" that you could've technically fought in your dreams!!!

Spider-Man @aspidercan
@unbeatablesg doc strange isn't on here though otherwise we could ask him

Squirrel Girl @unbeatablesg
@aspidercan A guy with a doctorate in strangeness doesn't hang out online here? WEIRD

Squirrel Girl @unbeatablesg
@aspidercan YOU'D THINK HE'D FIT RIGHT IN

Tony Stark @starkmantony ✓
@unbeatablesg Hey, how's that robot brain in a jar guy you patched up working out?

Squirrel Girl @unbeatablesg
@starkmantony Brain Drain? Great! Well on his way to becoming a real hero, actually! Still mega nihilistic but in a cool way

Squirrel Girl @unbeatablesg
@starkmantony We're going out on patrol together in a bit actually

Tony Stark @starkmantony ✓
@unbeatablesg Shouldn't you not mention when you're going out on patrol, so the criminal element won't know?

Squirrel Girl @unbeatablesg
@starkmantony good point my dude, one sec

Squirrel Girl @unbeatablesg
HELLO CRIMINALS, THIS IS JUST TO ANNOUNCE THAT I AM ON PATROL ALWAYS AND WILL DEFINITELY CATCH YOU DOING A CRIME, SO DON'T DO THEM

Spider-Man @aspidercan
@unbeatablesg holy crap can i use that

Squirrel Girl @unbeatablesg
@starkmantony Tony are you there I just had the best idea!! Tony tony tony

Tony Stark @starkmantony ✓
@unbeatablesg Hey.

Squirrel Girl @unbeatablesg
@starkmantony TONY. BRAINSTORM. What if you changed your name from "Tony Stark" to--HEAR ME OUT--..."Ira."

Tony Stark @starkmantony ✓
@unbeatablesg "Ira Stark"?

Squirrel Girl @unbeatablesg
@starkmantony IRA ONMANN.

Tony Stark @starkmantony ✓
@unbeatablesg oh my god

Squirrel Girl @unbeatablesg
@starkmantony Tony I'm going on vacation so I just wanted to give you something to remember me by

Squirrel Girl @unbeatablesg
@starkmantony just a little memento

Squirrel Girl @unbeatablesg
@starkmantony for my good friend

Squirrel Girl @unbeatablesg
@starkmantony ira onmann

search!

#braindrain

#canada

#nopowernoproblems

#maureengreen

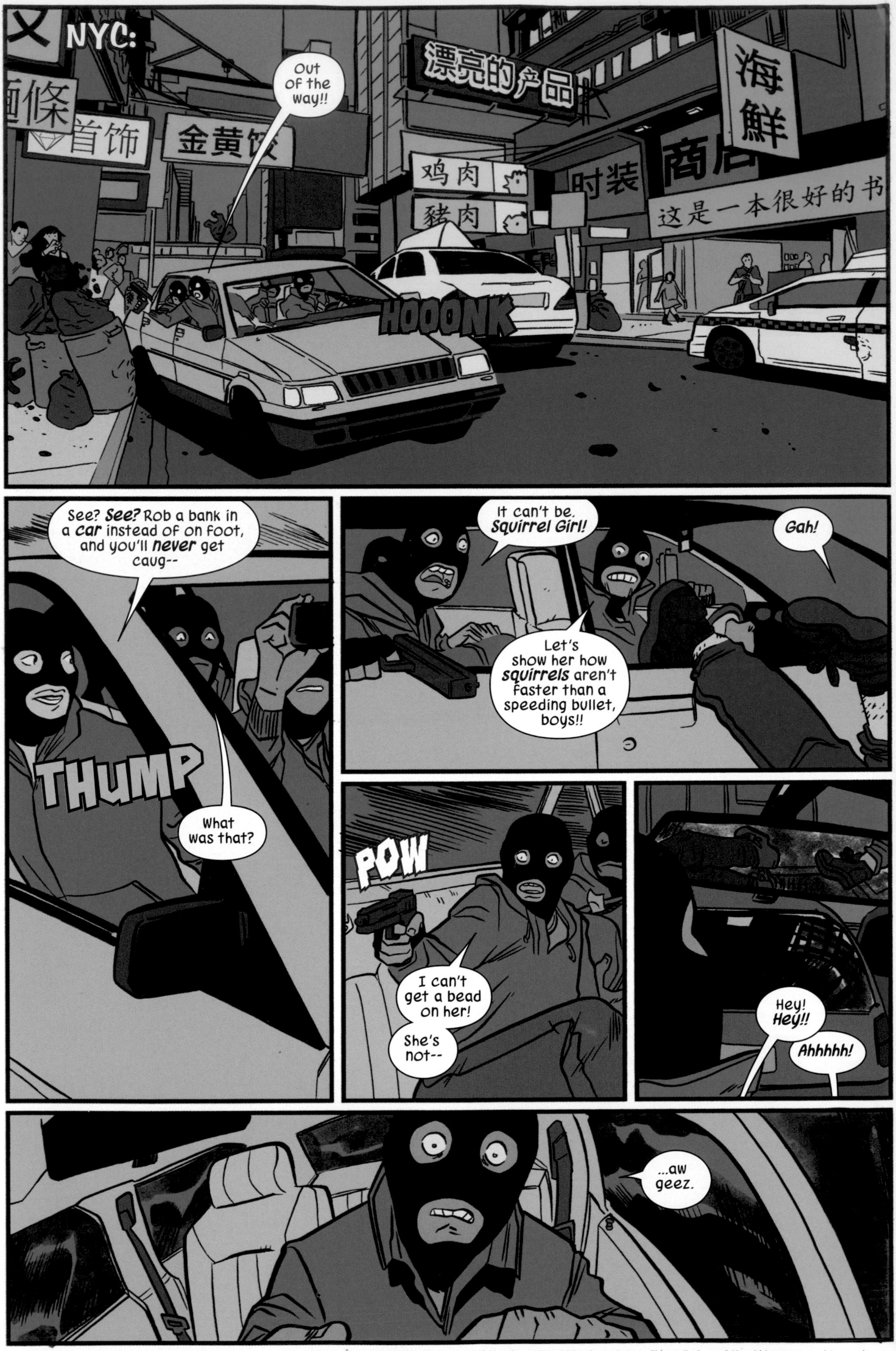
NYC:
首饰
金黄饭
漂亮的产品
海鲜
鸡肉
豬肉
时装
这是一本很好的书
Out of the way!!
HOOONK
See? See? Rob a bank in a car instead of on foot, and you'll never get caug--
THUMP
What was that?
It can't be. Squirrel Girl!
Gah!
Let's show her how squirrels aren't faster than a speeding bullet, boys!!
POW
I can't get a bead on her!
She's not--
Hey! Hey!!
Ahhhhh!
...aw geez.

These are the bank robbers from the first time Squirrel Girl saved a bank! They're back! And they're still robbing banks! Wow, I'd really hoped they'd have worked towards positive change in their own lives but *hah hah hah* ***guess not!***

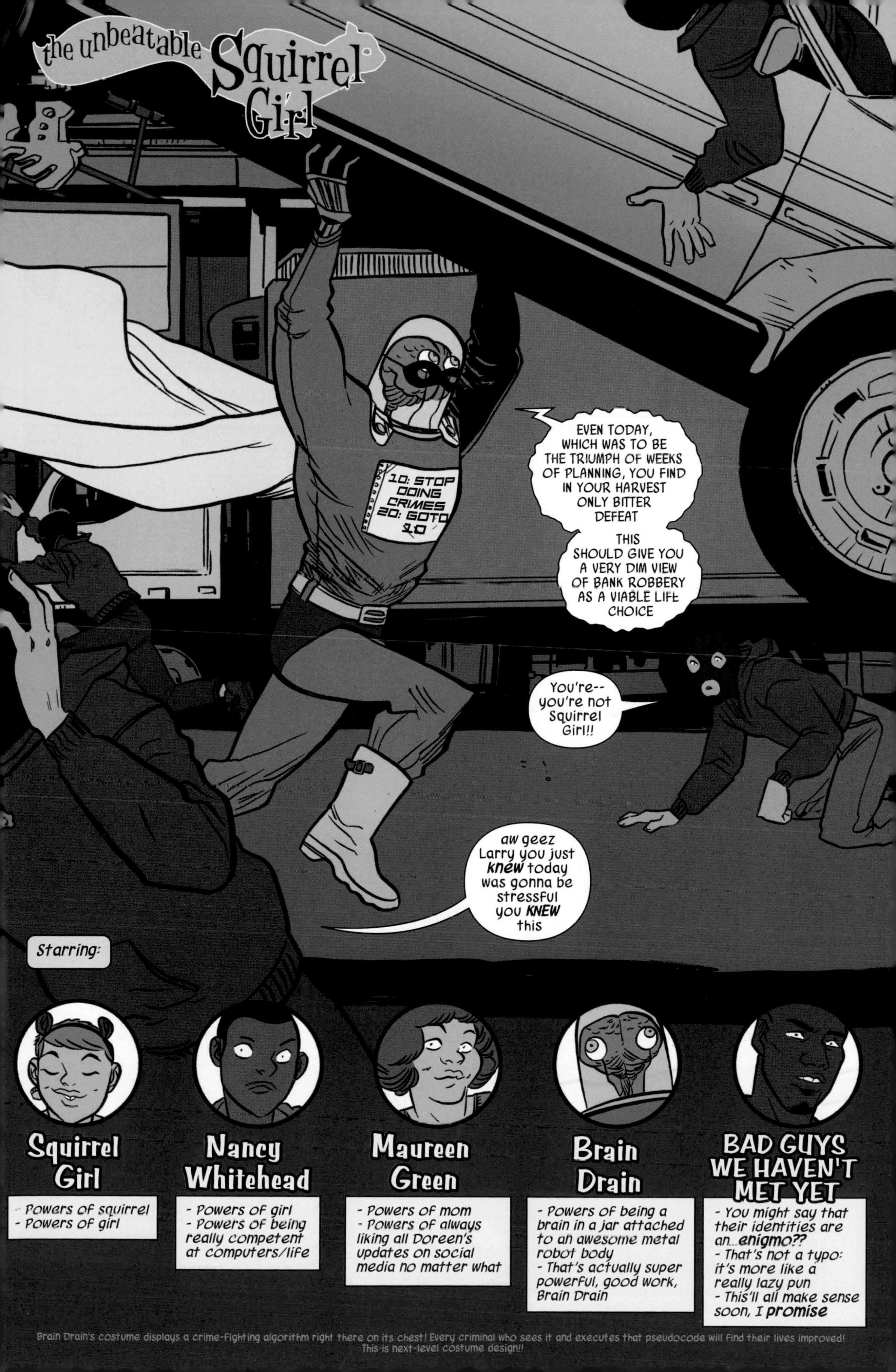

the unbeatable Squirrel Girl
10: STOP DOING CRIMES 20: GOTO 10
EVEN TODAY, WHICH WAS TO BE THE TRIUMPH OF WEEKS OF PLANNING, YOU FIND IN YOUR HARVEST ONLY BITTER DEFEAT
THIS SHOULD GIVE YOU A VERY DIM VIEW OF BANK ROBBERY AS A VIABLE LIFE CHOICE
You're--you're not Squirrel Girl!!
aw geez Larry you just KNEW today was gonna be stressful you KNEW this
Starring:
Squirrel Girl
- Powers of squirrel
- Powers of girl
Nancy Whitehead
- Powers of girl
- Powers of being really competent at computers/life
Maureen Green
- Powers of mom
- Powers of always liking all Doreen's updates on social media no matter what
Brain Drain
- Powers of being a brain in a jar attached to an awesome metal robot body
- That's actually super powerful, good work, Brain Drain
BAD GUYS WE HAVEN'T MET YET
- You might say that their identities are an...enigmo??
- That's not a typo: it's more like a really lazy pun
- This'll all make sense soon, I promise
Brain Drain's costume displays a crime-fighting algorithm right there on its chest! Every criminal who sees it and executes that pseudocode will find their lives improved! This is next-level costume design!!

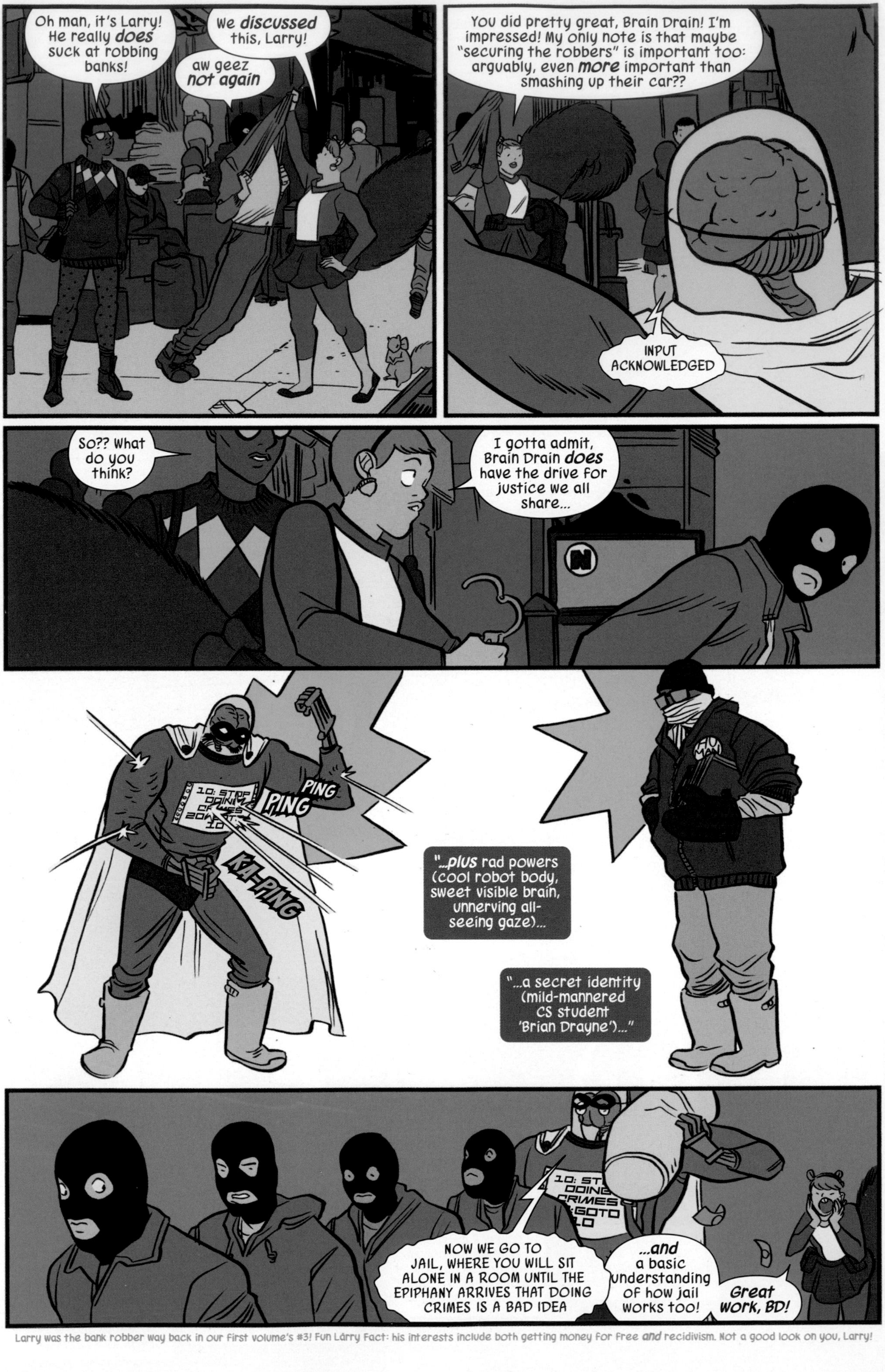
Oh man, it's Larry! He really *does* suck at robbing banks!
We *discussed* this, Larry!
aw geez *not again*
You did pretty great, Brain Drain! I'm impressed! My only note is that maybe "securing the robbers" is important too: arguably, even *more* important than smashing up their car??
INPUT ACKNOWLEDGED
So?? What do you think?
I gotta admit, Brain Drain *does* have the drive for justice we all share...
PING
PING
KA-PING
"...*plus* rad powers (cool robot body, sweet visible brain, unnerving all-seeing gaze)...
"...a secret identity (mild-mannered CS student 'Brian Drayne')..."
NOW WE GO TO JAIL, WHERE YOU WILL SIT ALONE IN A ROOM UNTIL THE EPIPHANY ARRIVES THAT DOING CRIMES IS A BAD IDEA
...and a basic understanding of how jail works too!
Great work, BD!

Larry was the bank robber way back in our first volume's #3! Fun Larry Fact: his interests include both getting money for free *and* recidivism. Not a good look on you, Larry!

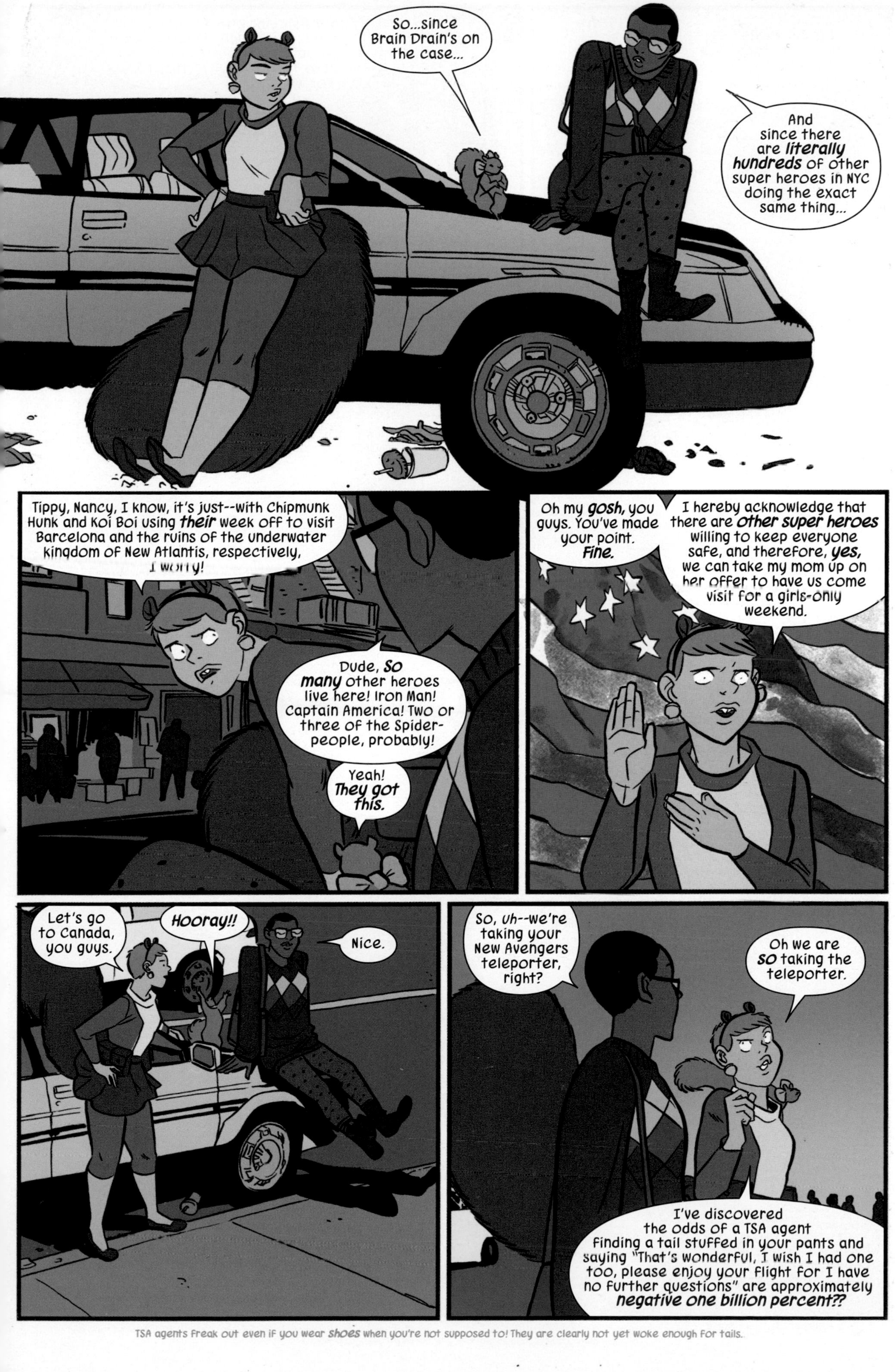
So...since Brain Drain's on the case...
And since there are *literally hundreds* of other super heroes in NYC doing the exact same thing...
Tippy, Nancy, I know, it's just--with Chipmunk Hunk and Koi Boi using *their* week off to visit Barcelona and the ruins of the underwater kingdom of New Atlantis, respectively, I worry!
Dude, *so many* other heroes live here! Iron Man! Captain America! Two or three of the Spider-people, probably!
Yeah! *They got this.*
Oh my *gosh,* you guys. You've made your point. *Fine.*
I hereby acknowledge that there are *other super heroes* willing to keep everyone safe, and therefore, *yes,* we can take my mom up on her offer to have us come visit for a girls-only weekend.
Let's go to Canada, you guys.
Hooray!!
Nice.
So, uh--we're taking your New Avengers teleporter, right?
Oh we are *so* taking the teleporter.
I've discovered the odds of a TSA agent finding a tail stuffed in your pants and saying "That's wonderful, I wish I had one too, please enjoy your flight for I have no further questions" are approximately *negative one billion percent??*

TSA agents freak out even if you wear *shoes* when you're not supposed to! They are clearly not yet woke enough for tails.

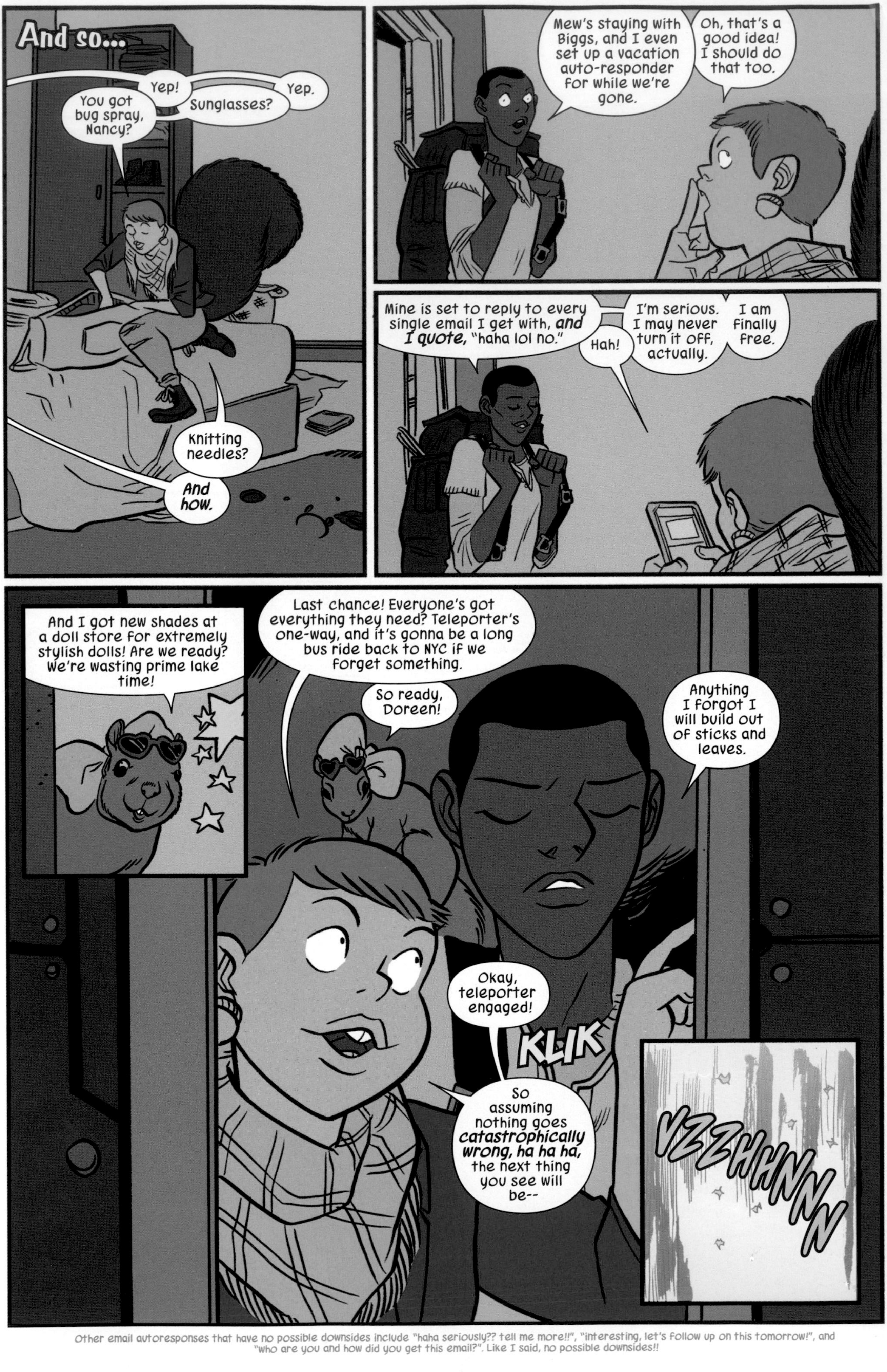
And so...
You got bug spray, Nancy?
Yep!
Sunglasses?
Yep.
Knitting needles?
And how.
Mew's staying with Biggs, and I even set up a vacation auto-responder for while we're gone.
Oh, that's a good idea! I should do that too.
Mine is set to reply to every single email I get with, and I quote, "haha lol no."
Hah!
I'm serious. I may never turn it off, actually.
I am finally free.
And I got new shades at a doll store for extremely stylish dolls! Are we ready? We're wasting prime lake time!
Last chance! Everyone's got everything they need? Teleporter's one-way, and it's gonna be a long bus ride back to NYC if we forget something.
So ready, Doreen!
Anything I forgot I will build out of sticks and leaves.
Okay, teleporter engaged!
KLIK
So assuming nothing goes catastrophically wrong, ha ha ha, the next thing you see will be--
VZZHHNNN

Other email autoresponses that have no possible downsides include "haha seriously?? tell me more!!", "interesting, let's follow up on this tomorrow!", and "who are you and how did you get this email?". Like I said, no possible downsides!!

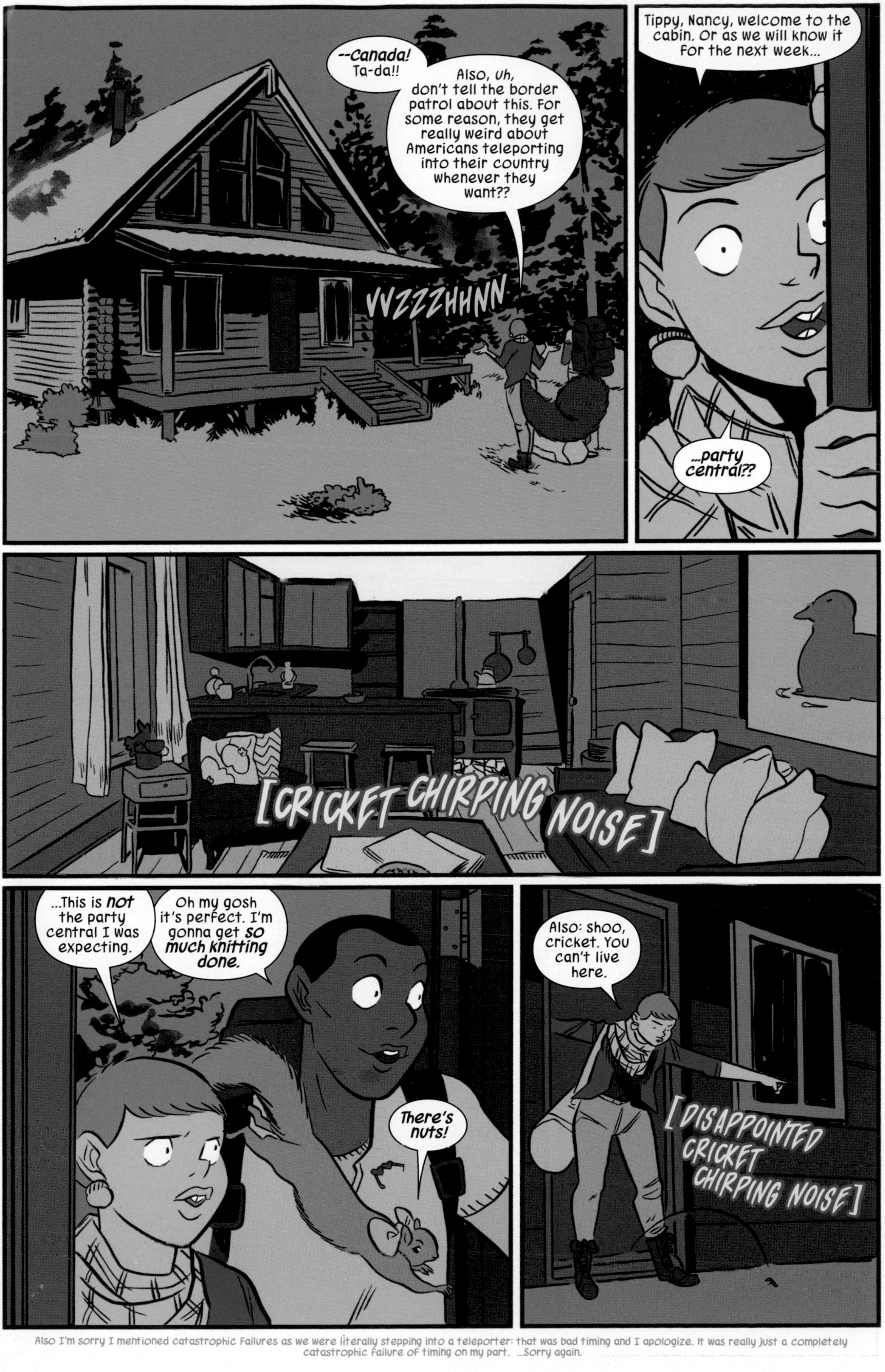
--Canada! Ta-da!!
Also, uh, don't tell the border patrol about this. For some reason, they get really weird about Americans teleporting into their country whenever they want??
VVZZZHHNN
Tippy, Nancy, welcome to the cabin. Or as we will know it for the next week...
...party central??
[CRICKET CHIRPING NOISE]
...This is not the party central I was expecting.
Oh my gosh it's perfect. I'm gonna get so much knitting done.
There's nuts!
Also: shoo, cricket. You can't live here.
[DISAPPOINTED CRICKET CHIRPING NOISE]

Also I'm sorry I mentioned catastrophic failures as we were literally stepping into a teleporter: that was bad timing and I apologize. It was really just a completely catastrophic failure of timing on my part. ...Sorry again.

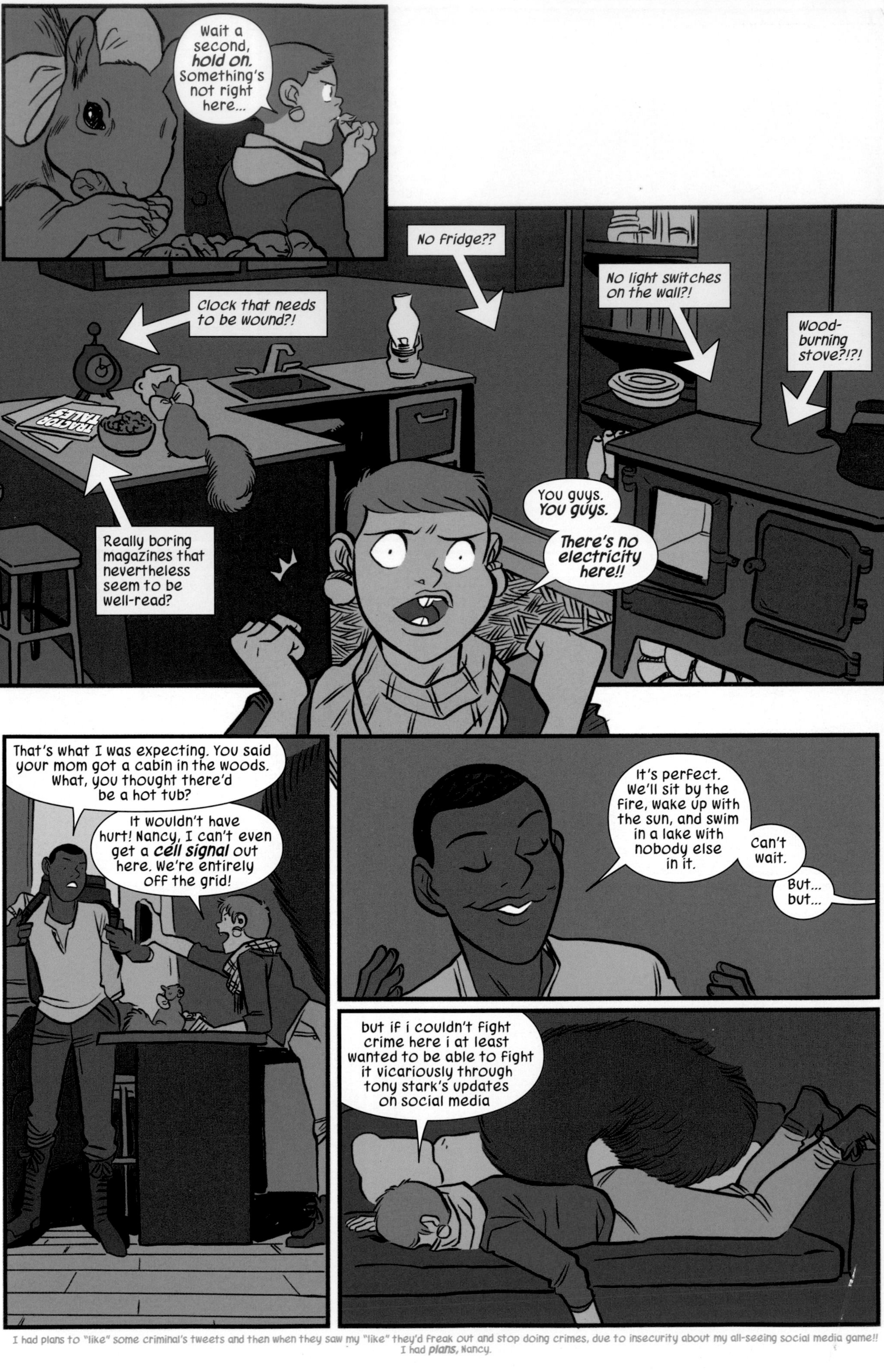
Wait a second, hold on. Something's not right here...
No fridge??
Clock that needs to be wound?!
No light switches on the wall?!
Wood-burning stove?!?!
TRACTOR TALES
Really boring magazines that nevertheless seem to be well-read?
You guys. You guys.
There's no electricity here!!
That's what I was expecting. You said your mom got a cabin in the woods. What, you thought there'd be a hot tub?
It wouldn't have hurt! Nancy, I can't even get a cell signal out here. We're entirely off the grid!
It's perfect. We'll sit by the fire, wake up with the sun, and swim in a lake with nobody else in it.
Can't wait.
But... but...
but if i couldn't fight crime here i at least wanted to be able to fight it vicariously through tony stark's updates on social media

I had plans to "like" some criminal's tweets and then when they saw my "like" they'd freak out and stop doing crimes, due to insecurity about my all-seeing social media game!! I had *plans*, Nancy.

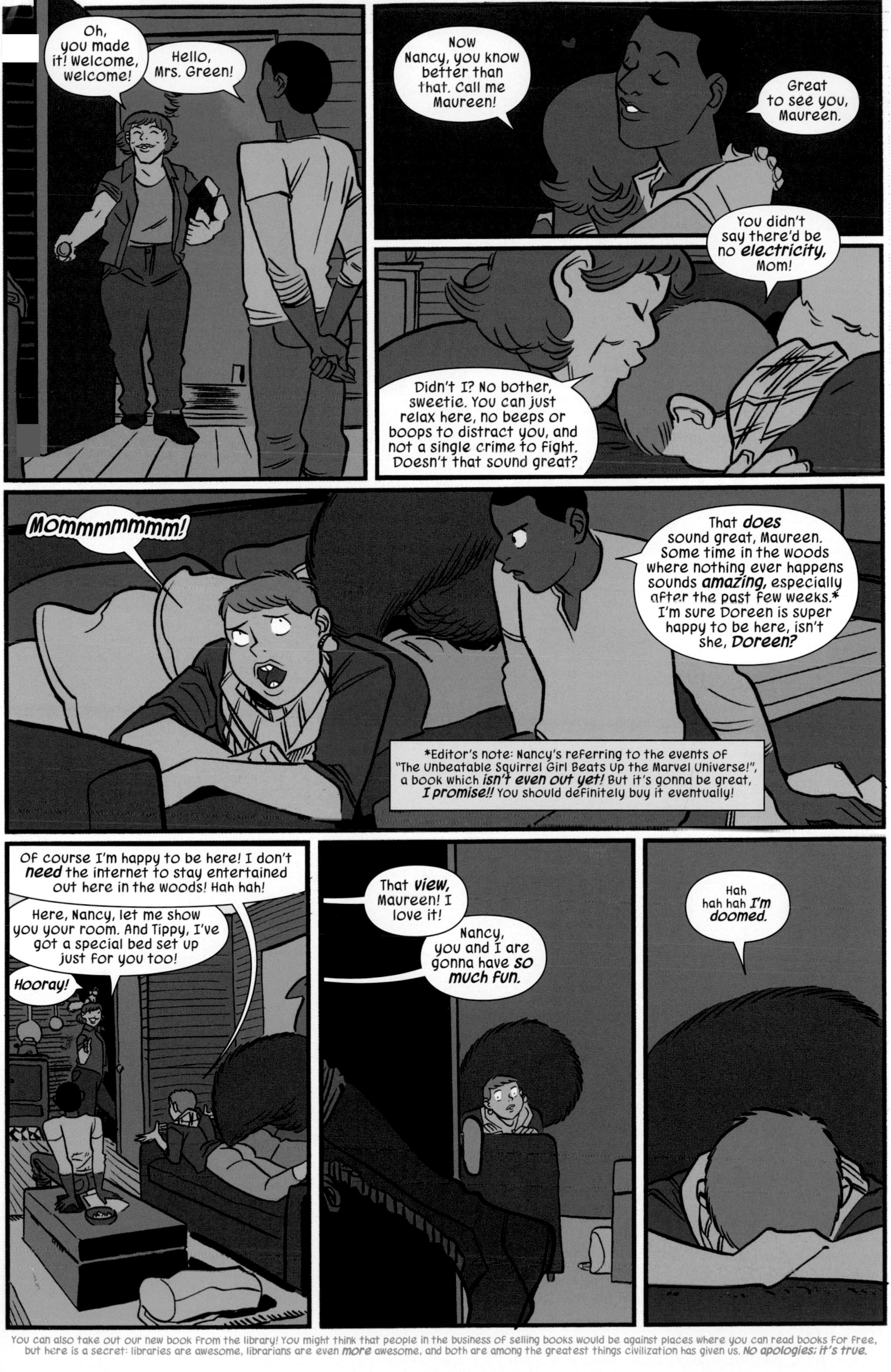
Oh, you made it! Welcome, welcome!
Hello, Mrs. Green!
Now Nancy, you know better than that. Call me Maureen!
Great to see you, Maureen.
You didn't say there'd be no *electricity,* Mom!
Didn't I? No bother, sweetie. You can just relax here, no beeps or boops to distract you, and not a single crime to fight. Doesn't that sound great?
MOMMMMMMMM!
That *does* sound great, Maureen. Some time in the woods where nothing ever happens sounds *amazing,* especially after the past few weeks.* I'm sure Doreen is super happy to be here, isn't she, *Doreen?*
*Editor's note: Nancy's referring to the events of "The Unbeatable Squirrel Girl Beats Up the Marvel Universe!", a book which *isn't even out yet!* But it's gonna be great, *I promise!!* You should definitely buy it eventually!
Of course I'm happy to be here! I don't *need* the internet to stay entertained out here in the woods! Hah hah!
Here, Nancy, let me show you your room. And Tippy, I've got a special bed set up just for you too!
Hooray!
That *view,* Maureen! I love it!
Nancy, you and I are gonna have *so much fun.*
Hah hah hah *I'm doomed.*

You can also take out our new book from the library! You might think that people in the business of selling books would be against places where you can read books for free, but here is a secret: libraries are awesome, librarians are even *more* awesome, and both are among the greatest things civilization has given us. ***No apologies; it's true.***

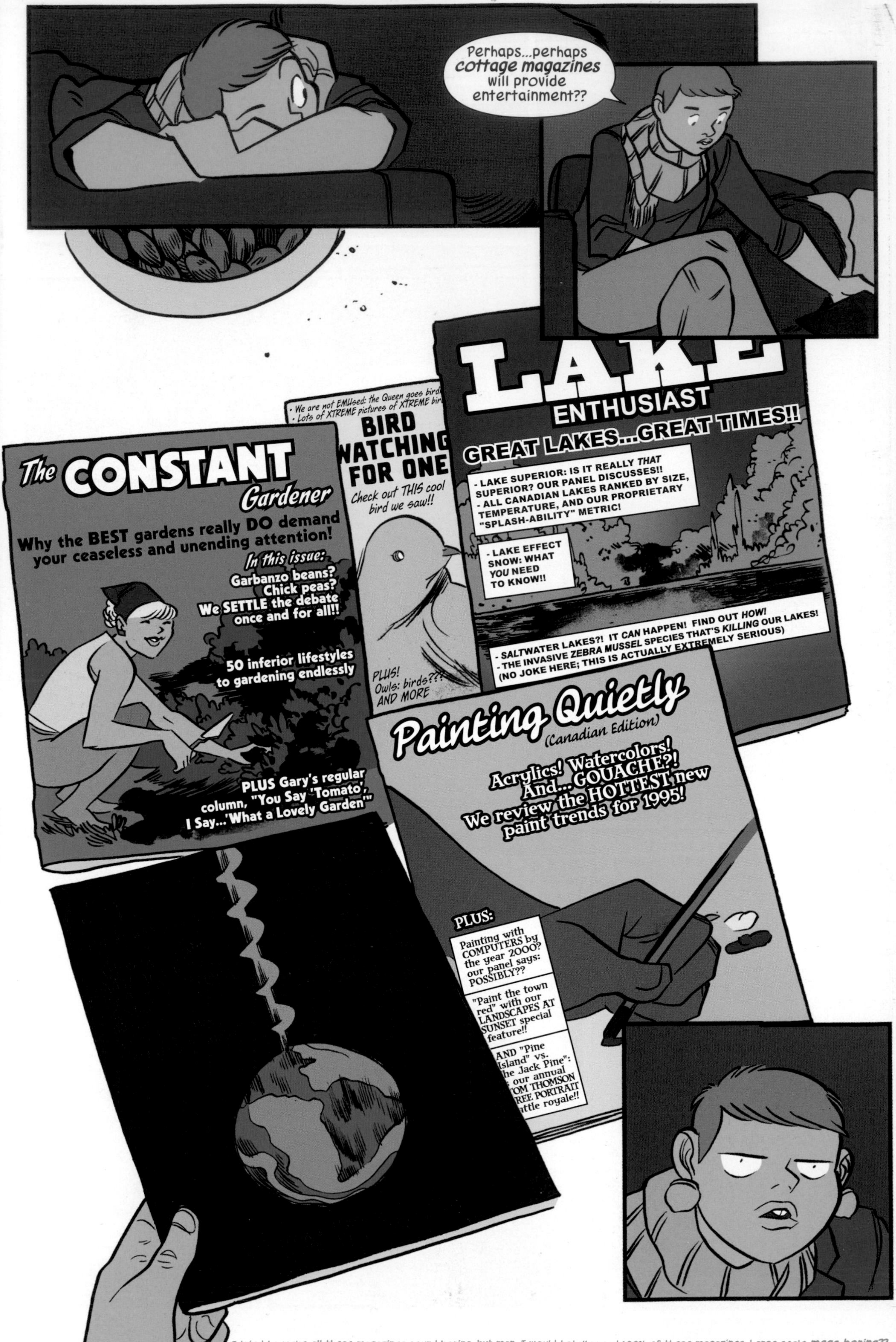
Perhaps...perhaps *cottage magazines* will provide entertainment??
• We are not EMUsed: the Queen goes bird
• Lots of XTREME pictures of XTREME bir
BIRD WATCHING FOR ONE
Check out THIS cool bird we saw!!
PLUS! Owls: birds??? AND MORE
LAKE ENTHUSIAST
GREAT LAKES...GREAT TIMES!!
- LAKE SUPERIOR: IS IT REALLY *THAT* SUPERIOR? OUR PANEL DISCUSSES!!
- ALL CANADIAN LAKES RANKED BY SIZE, TEMPERATURE, AND OUR PROPRIETARY "SPLASH-ABILITY" METRIC!
- LAKE EFFECT SNOW: WHAT *YOU* NEED TO KNOW!!
- *SALTWATER* LAKES?! IT *CAN* HAPPEN! FIND OUT *HOW!*
- THE INVASIVE *ZEBRA MUSSEL* SPECIES THAT'S *KILLING* OUR LAKES!
(NO JOKE HERE; THIS IS ACTUALLY EXTREMELY SERIOUS)
The CONSTANT Gardener
Why the BEST gardens really DO demand your ceaseless and unending attention!
In this issue:
Garbanzo beans? Chick peas? We SETTLE the debate once and for all!!
50 inferior lifestyles to gardening endlessly
PLUS Gary's regular column, "You Say 'Tomato', I Say...'What a Lovely Garden'"
Painting Quietly (Canadian Edition)
Acrylics! Watercolors! And...GOUACHE?! We review the HOTTEST new paint trends for 1995!
PLUS:
Painting with COMPUTERS by the year 2000? our panel says: POSSIBLY??
"Paint the town red" with our LANDSCAPES AT SUNSET special feature!!
AND "Pine Island" vs. he Jack Pine": our annual OM THOMSON REE PORTRAIT attle royale!!

I tried to make all these magazines sound boring, but man, I would totally read 100% of these magazines. Large scale ***mega-boring??*** Now ***that's*** an infrastructure development project whose industry insider details I'm curious to learn more about!

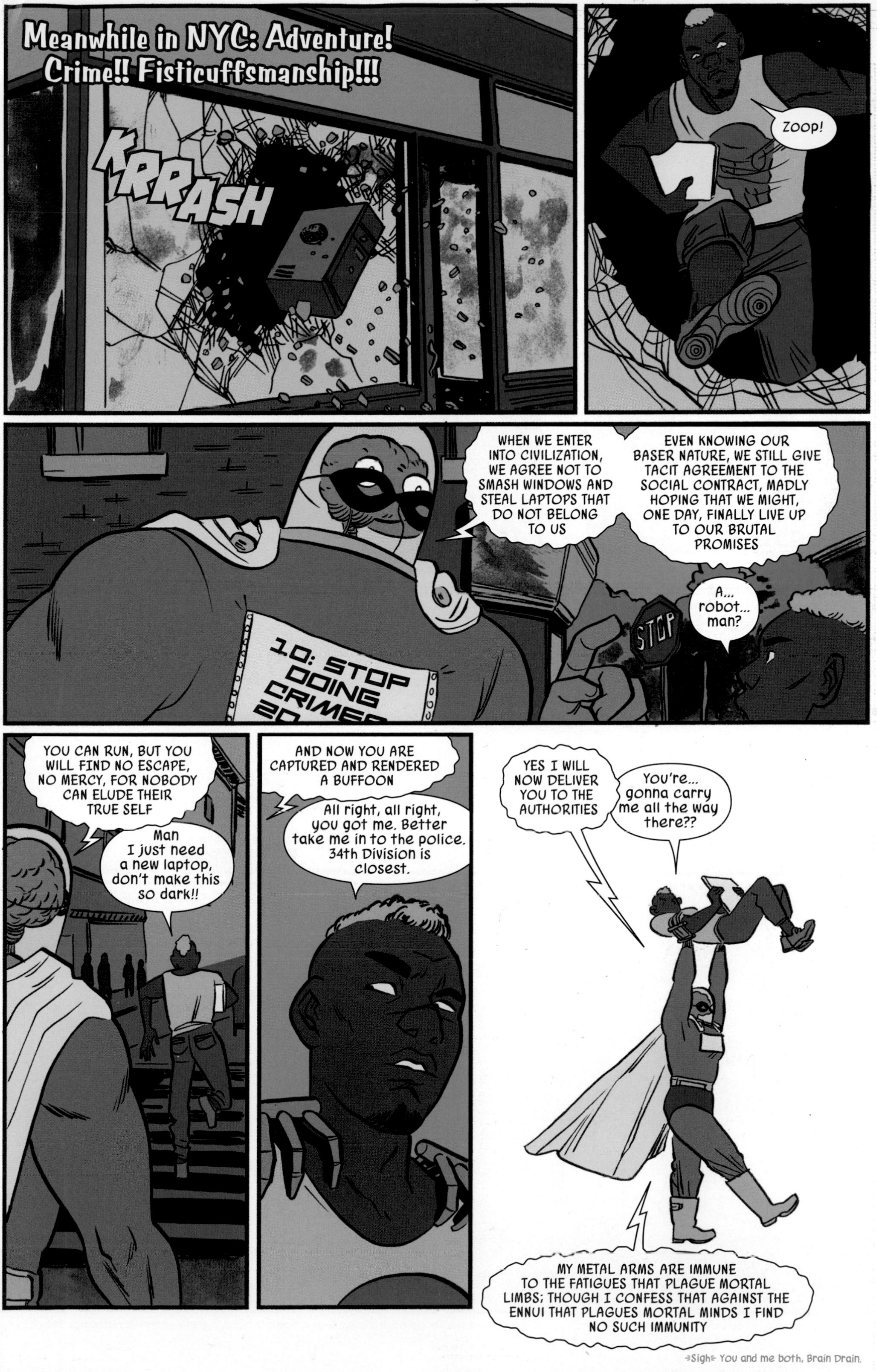
Meanwhile in NYC: Adventure! Crime!! Fisticuffsmanship!!!
KRRASH
Zoop!
WHEN WE ENTER INTO CIVILIZATION, WE AGREE NOT TO SMASH WINDOWS AND STEAL LAPTOPS THAT DO NOT BELONG TO US
EVEN KNOWING OUR BASER NATURE, WE STILL GIVE TACIT AGREEMENT TO THE SOCIAL CONTRACT, MADLY HOPING THAT WE MIGHT, ONE DAY, FINALLY LIVE UP TO OUR BRUTAL PROMISES
A... robot... man?
STOP
10: STOP DOING CRIMES
YOU CAN RUN, BUT YOU WILL FIND NO ESCAPE, NO MERCY, FOR NOBODY CAN ELUDE THEIR TRUE SELF
Man I just need a new laptop, don't make this so dark!!
AND NOW YOU ARE CAPTURED AND RENDERED A BUFFOON
All right, all right, you got me. Better take me in to the police. 34th Division is closest.
YES I WILL NOW DELIVER YOU TO THE AUTHORITIES
You're... gonna carry me all the way there??
MY METAL ARMS ARE IMMUNE TO THE FATIGUES THAT PLAGUE MORTAL LIMBS; THOUGH I CONFESS THAT AGAINST THE ENNUI THAT PLAGUES MORTAL MINDS I FIND NO SUCH IMMUNITY
=Sigh= You and me both, Brain Drain.

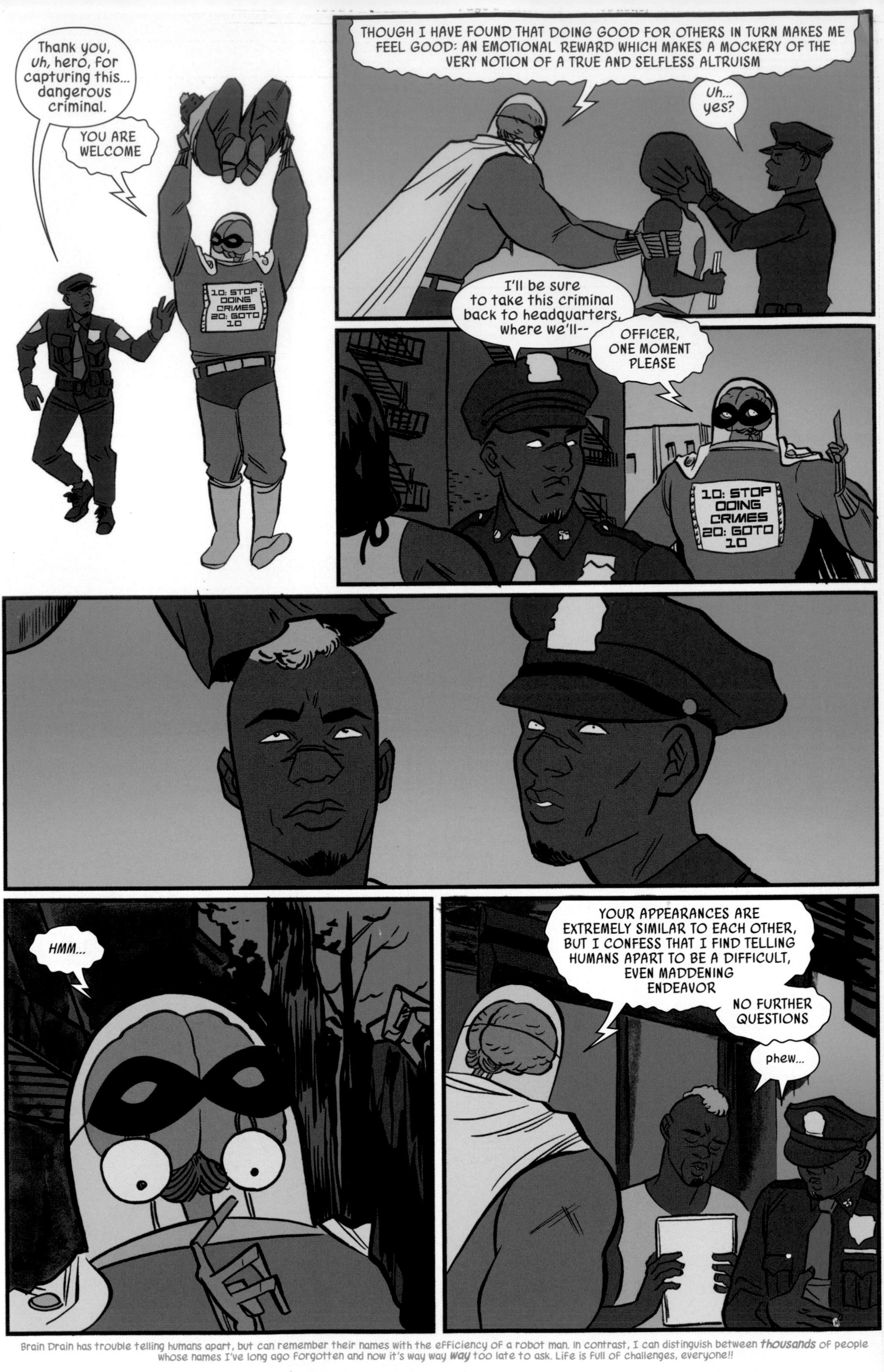
Thank you, *uh*, hero, for capturing this... dangerous criminal.
YOU ARE WELCOME
THOUGH I HAVE FOUND THAT DOING GOOD FOR OTHERS IN TURN MAKES ME FEEL GOOD: AN EMOTIONAL REWARD WHICH MAKES A MOCKERY OF THE VERY NOTION OF A TRUE AND SELFLESS ALTRUISM
Uh... yes?
10: STOP DOING CRIMES 20: GOTO 10
I'll be sure to take this criminal back to headquarters, where we'll--
OFFICER, ONE MOMENT PLEASE
10: STOP DOING CRIMES 20: GOTO 10
HMM...
YOUR APPEARANCES ARE EXTREMELY SIMILAR TO EACH OTHER, BUT I CONFESS THAT I FIND TELLING HUMANS APART TO BE A DIFFICULT, EVEN MADDENING ENDEAVOR
NO FURTHER QUESTIONS
phew...

Brain Drain has trouble telling humans apart, but can remember their names with the efficiency of a robot man. In contrast, I can distinguish between ***thousands*** of people whose names I've long ago forgotten and now it's way way ***way*** too late to ask. Life is full of challenges, everyone!!

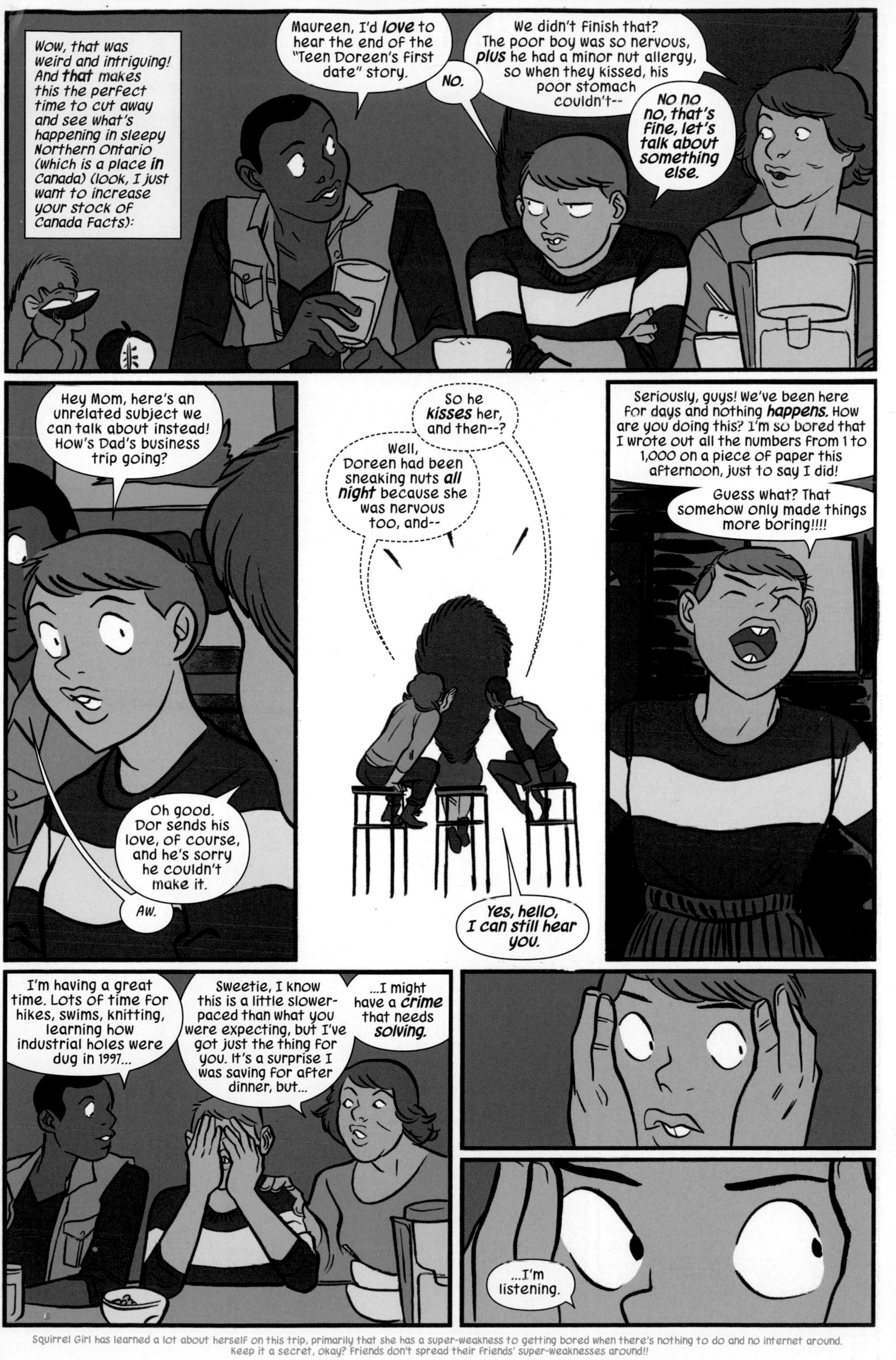
Wow, that was weird and intriguing! And that makes this the perfect time to cut away and see what's happening in sleepy Northern Ontario (which is a place in Canada) (look, I just want to increase your stock of Canada Facts):
Maureen, I'd love to hear the end of the "Teen Doreen's first date" story.
NO.
We didn't finish that? The poor boy was so nervous, plus he had a minor nut allergy, so when they kissed, his poor stomach couldn't--
No no no, that's fine, let's talk about something else.
Hey Mom, here's an unrelated subject we can talk about instead! How's Dad's business trip going?
Oh good. Dor sends his love, of course, and he's sorry he couldn't make it.
AW.
So he kisses her, and then--?
Well, Doreen had been sneaking nuts all night because she was nervous too, and--
Yes, hello, I can still hear you.
Seriously, guys! We've been here for days and nothing happens. How are you doing this? I'm so bored that I wrote out all the numbers from 1 to 1,000 on a piece of paper this afternoon, just to say I did!
Guess what? That somehow only made things more boring!!!!
I'm having a great time. Lots of time for hikes, swims, knitting, learning how industrial holes were dug in 1997...
Sweetie, I know this is a little slower-paced than what you were expecting, but I've got just the thing for you. It's a surprise I was saving for after dinner, but...
...I might have a crime that needs solving.
...I'm listening.

Squirrel Girl has learned a lot about herself on this trip, primarily that she has a super-weakness to getting bored when there's nothing to do and no internet around. Keep it a secret, okay? Friends don't spread their friends' super-weaknesses around!!

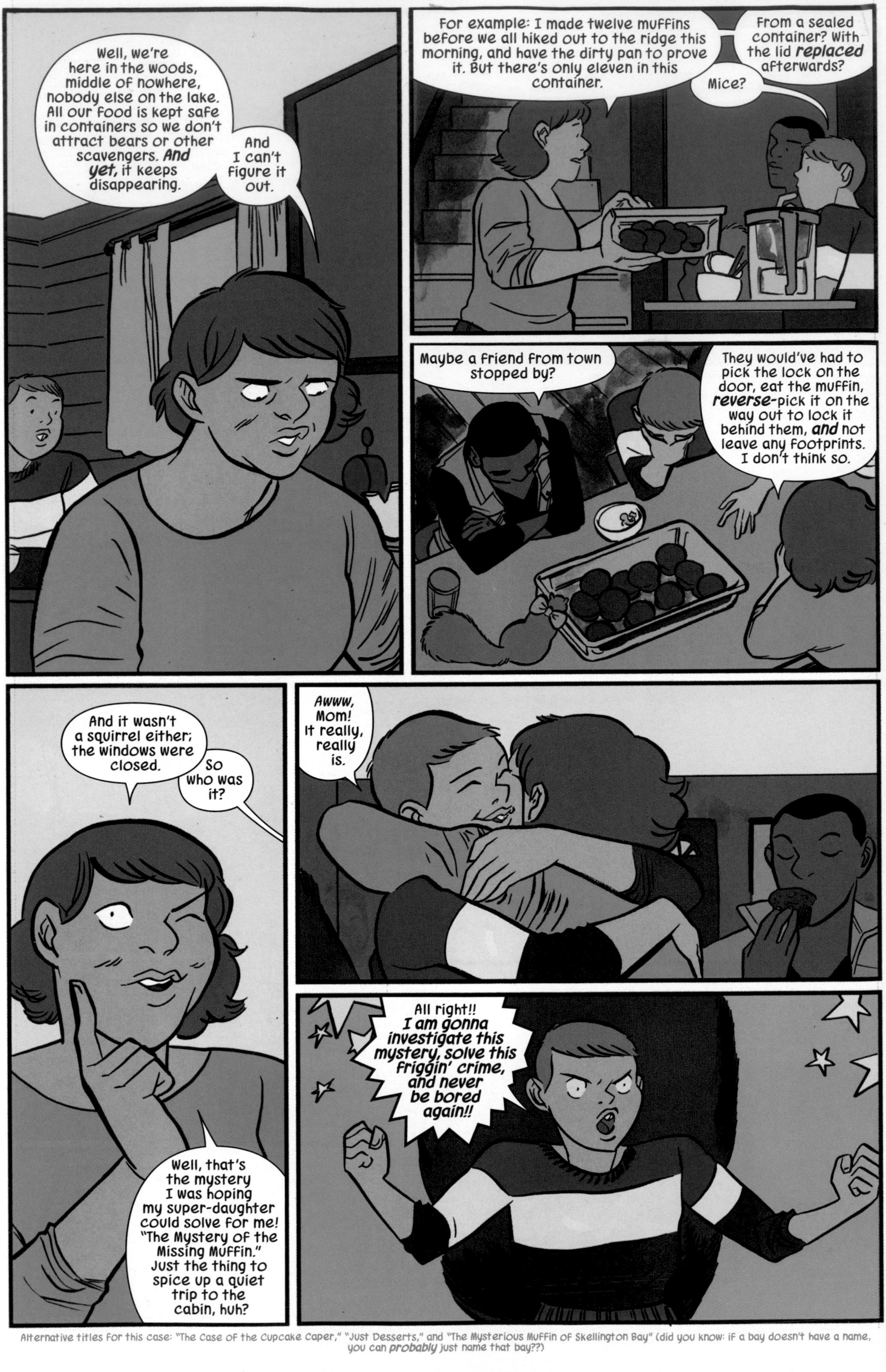
Well, we're here in the woods, middle of nowhere, nobody else on the lake. All our food is kept safe in containers so we don't attract bears or other scavengers. And yet, it keeps disappearing.
And I can't figure it out.
For example: I made twelve muffins before we all hiked out to the ridge this morning, and have the dirty pan to prove it. But there's only eleven in this container.
Mice?
From a sealed container? With the lid replaced afterwards?
Maybe a friend from town stopped by?
They would've had to pick the lock on the door, eat the muffin, reverse-pick it on the way out to lock it behind them, and not leave any footprints. I don't think so.
And it wasn't a squirrel either; the windows were closed.
So who was it?
Well, that's the mystery I was hoping my super-daughter could solve for me! "The Mystery of the Missing Muffin." Just the thing to spice up a quiet trip to the cabin, huh?
Awww, Mom! It really, really is.
All right!! I am gonna investigate this mystery, solve this friggin' crime, and never be bored again!!

Alternative titles for this case: "The Case of the Cupcake Caper," "Just Desserts," and "The Mysterious Muffin of Skellington Bay" (did you know: if a bay doesn't have a name, you can *probably* just name that bay??)

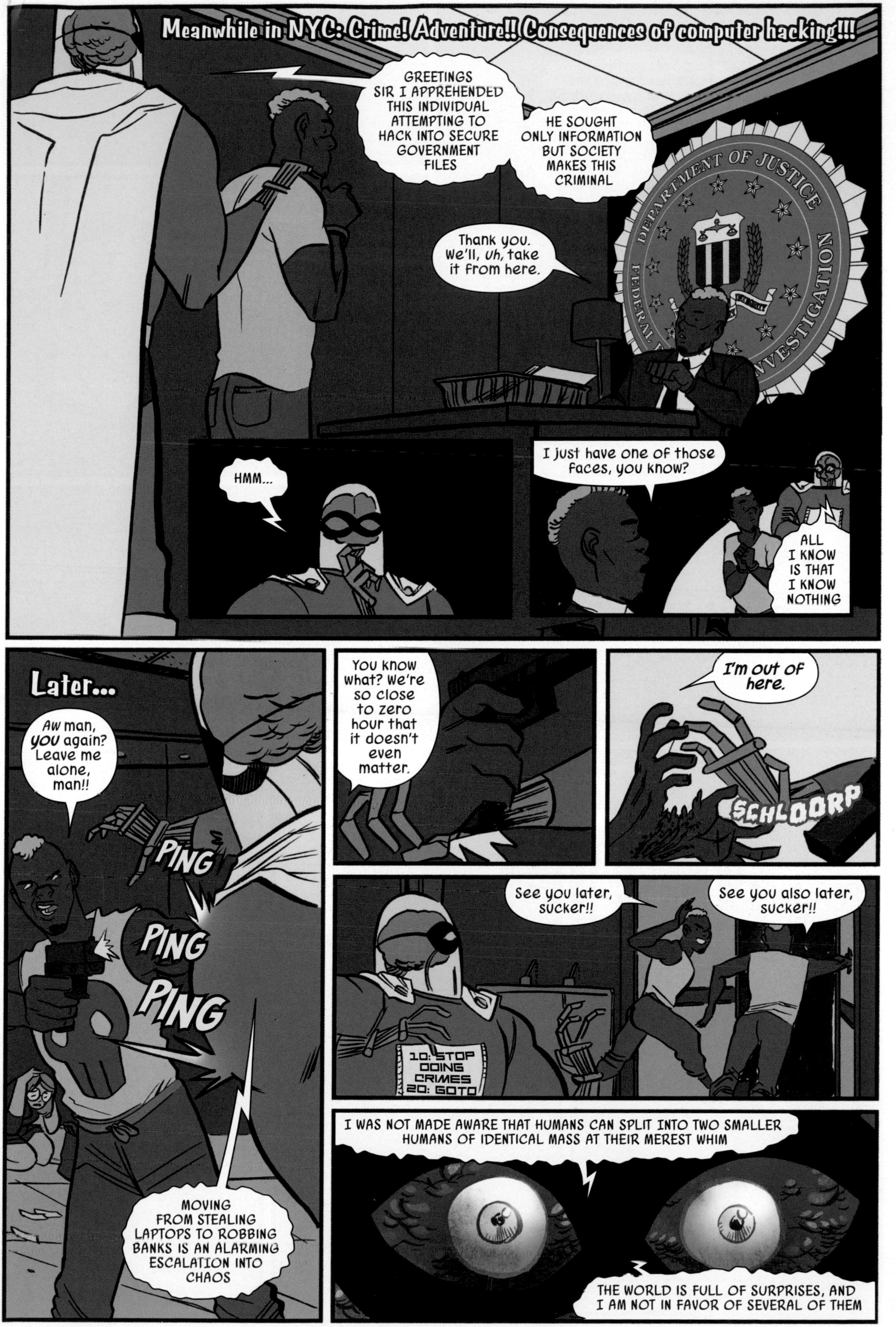
Meanwhile in NYC: Crime! Adventure!! Consequences of computer hacking!!!
GREETINGS SIR I APPREHENDED THIS INDIVIDUAL ATTEMPTING TO HACK INTO SECURE GOVERNMENT FILES
HE SOUGHT ONLY INFORMATION BUT SOCIETY MAKES THIS CRIMINAL
Thank you. We'll, uh, take it from here.
DEPARTMENT OF JUSTICE
FEDERAL BUREAU OF INVESTIGATION
HMM...
I just have one of those faces, you know?
ALL I KNOW IS THAT I KNOW NOTHING
Later...
Aw man, YOU again? Leave me alone, man!!
PING
PING
PING
MOVING FROM STEALING LAPTOPS TO ROBBING BANKS IS AN ALARMING ESCALATION INTO CHAOS
You know what? We're so close to zero hour that it doesn't even matter.
I'm out of here.
SCHLOORP
See you later, sucker!!
See you also later, sucker!!
10: STOP DOING CRIMES 20: GOTO
I WAS NOT MADE AWARE THAT HUMANS CAN SPLIT INTO TWO SMALLER HUMANS OF IDENTICAL MASS AT THEIR MEREST WHIM
THE WORLD IS FULL OF SURPRISES, AND I AM NOT IN FAVOR OF SEVERAL OF THEM

HOWEVER I HAVE BEEN TOLD THAT SOMETIMES THE SURPRISES ARE KITTENS AND ICE CREAM, SO I HOLD OUT HOPE, EVER DREAMING OF THE ICE CREAM KITTEN IN MY FUTURE

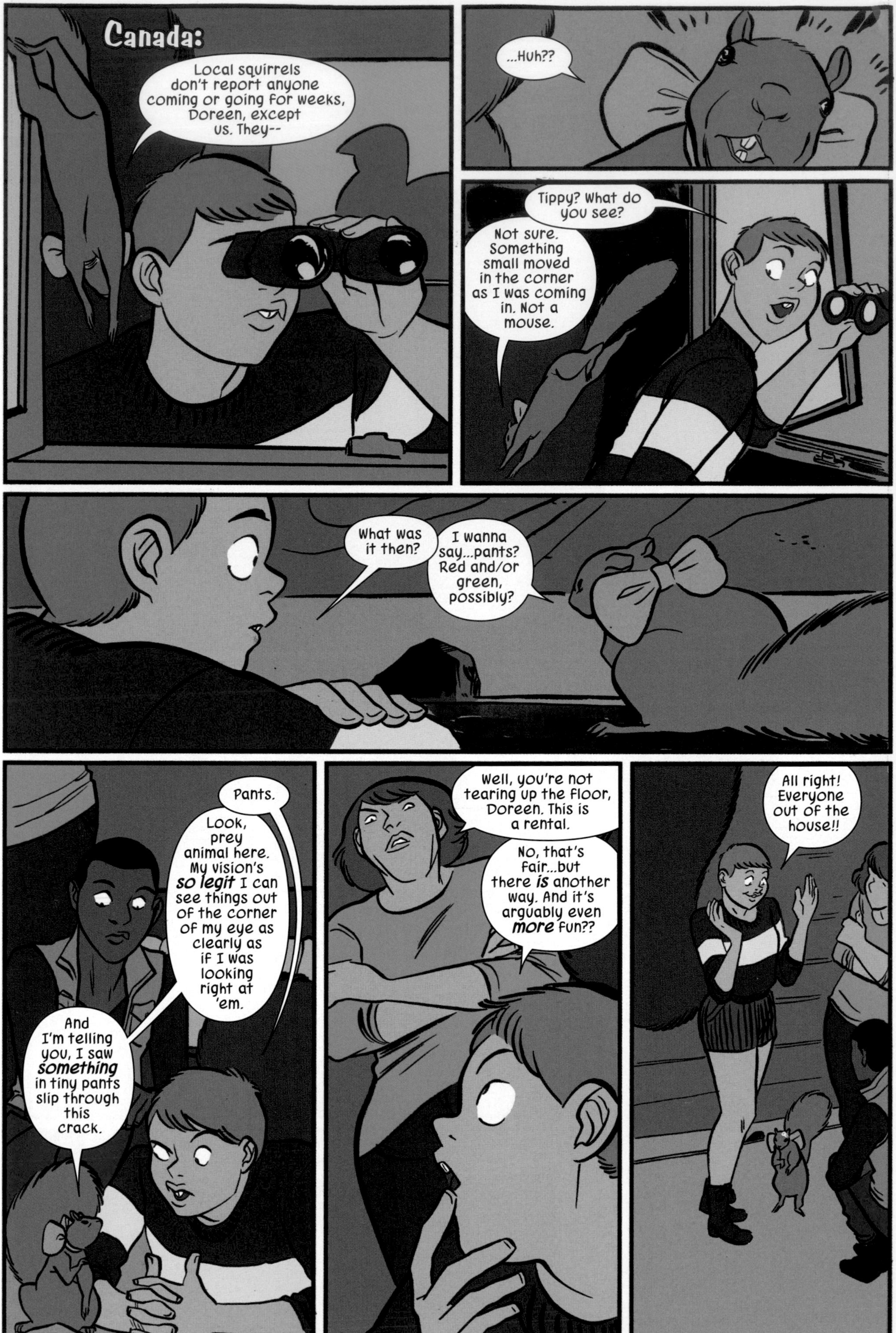
Canada:
Local squirrels don't report anyone coming or going for weeks, Doreen, except us. They--
...Huh??
Tippy? What do you see?
Not sure. Something small moved in the corner as I was coming in. Not a mouse.
What was it then?
I wanna say...pants? Red and/or green, possibly?
Pants.
Look, prey animal here. My vision's *so legit* I can see things out of the corner of my eye as clearly as if I was looking right at 'em.
And I'm telling you, I saw *something* in tiny pants slip through this crack.
Well, you're not tearing up the floor, Doreen. This is a rental.
No, that's fair...but there *is* another way. And it's arguably even *more* fun??
All right! Everyone out of the house!!

Most squirrels are red/green colorblind, which means they have trouble telling red and green apart. If you share this property too, then good news! You have at least one ***squirrel super-power,*** and that's more than most people can say!

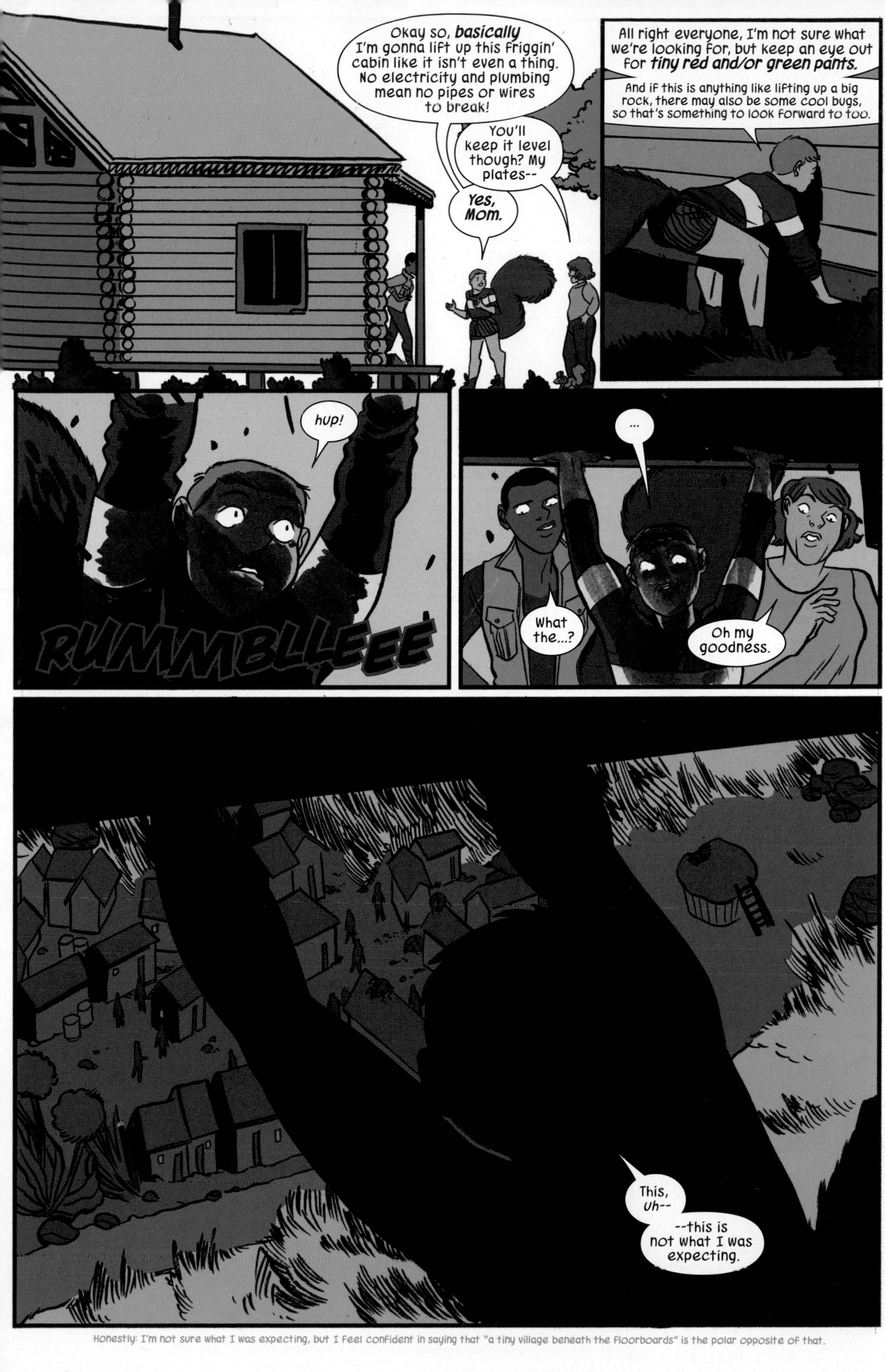

Okay so, **basically** I'm gonna lift up this friggin' cabin like it isn't even a thing. No electricity and plumbing mean no pipes or wires to break!
You'll keep it level though? My plates--
Yes, Mom.
All right everyone, I'm not sure what we're looking for, but keep an eye out for ***tiny red and/or green pants.***
And if this is anything like lifting up a big rock, there may also be some cool bugs, so that's something to look forward to too.
hup!
RUMMBLLEEE
...
What the...?
Oh my goodness.
This, uh--
--this is not what I was expecting.

Honestly: I'm not sure what I was expecting, but I feel confident in saying that "a tiny village beneath the floorboards" is the polar opposite of that.

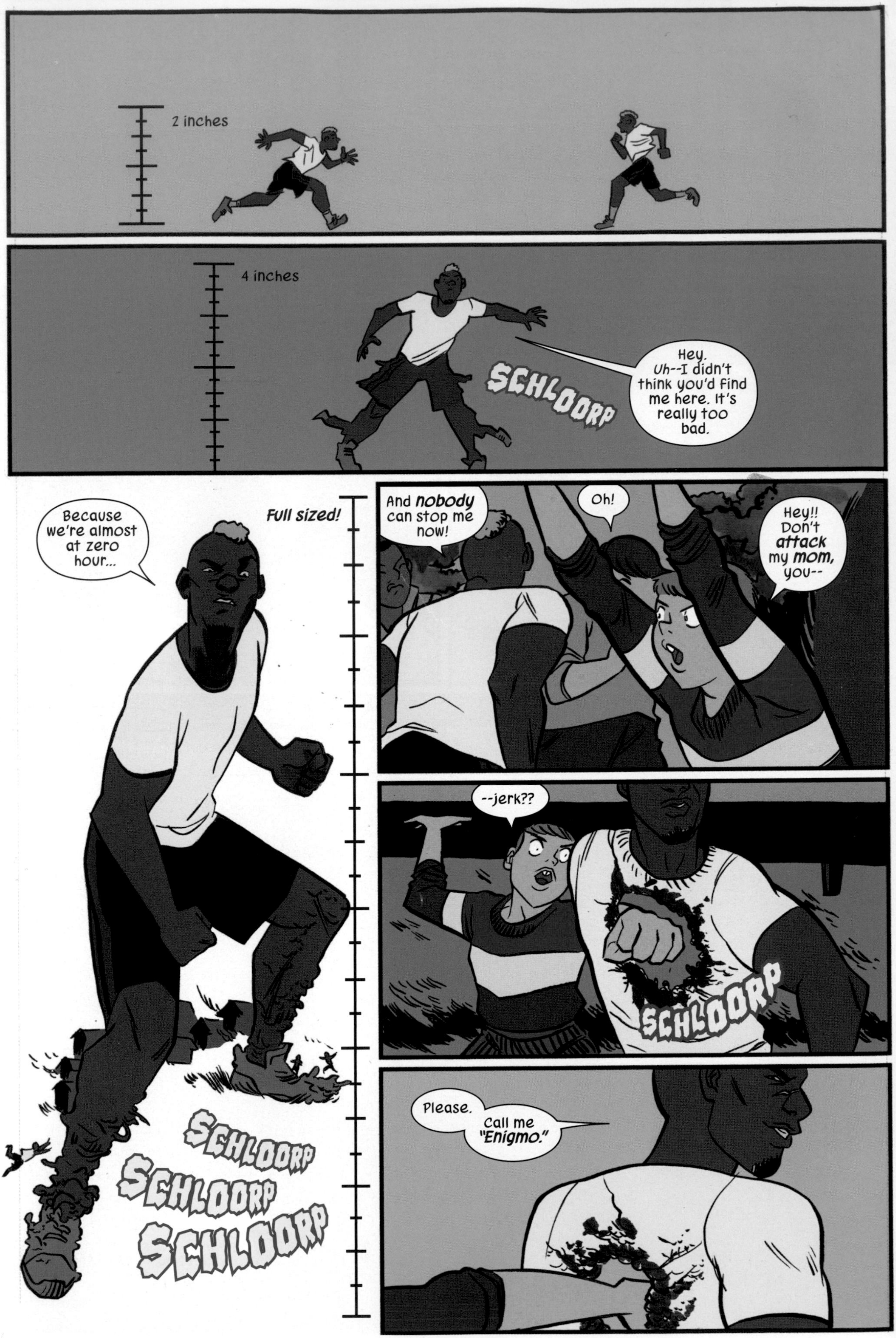
2 inches
4 inches
SCHLOORP
Hey. Uh--I didn't think you'd find me here. It's really too bad.
Because we're almost at zero hour...
Full sized!
SCHLOORP
SCHLOORP
SCHLOORP
And nobody can stop me now!
Oh!
Hey!! Don't attack my mom, you--
--jerk??
SCHLOORP
Please.
Call me "Enigmo."

Enigmo. No, like "enigma," but with an "o." Enigmo. Look, do you have a pen? I can write it--no, it's not "Edward Nigmo"! You're thinking of another guy, and you're not even remembering him that accurately!!

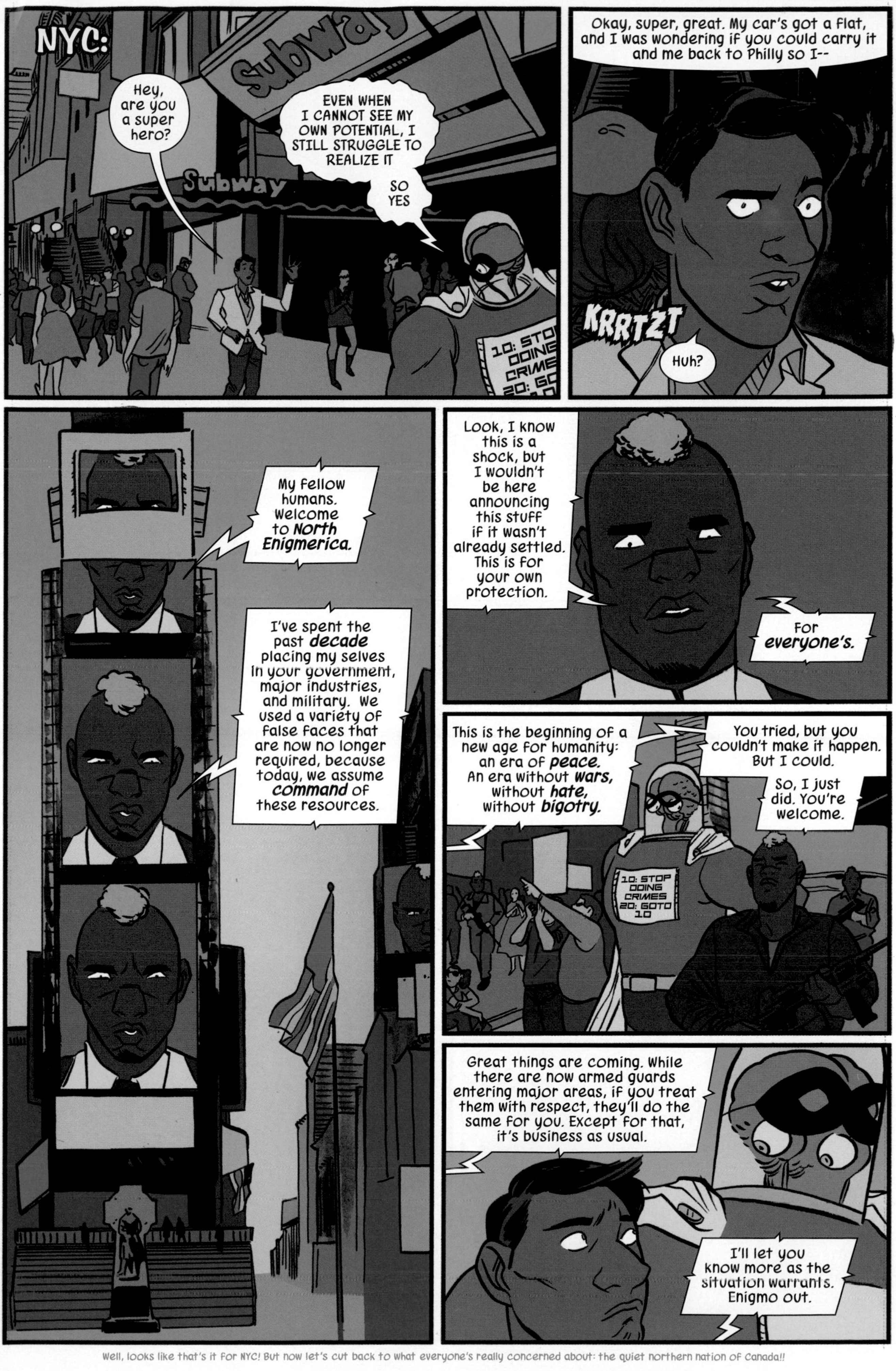
NYC:
Subway
Subway
Hey, are you a super hero?
EVEN WHEN I CANNOT SEE MY OWN POTENTIAL, I STILL STRUGGLE TO REALIZE IT
SO YES
10: STOP DOING CRIMES 20: GOTO 10
Okay, super, great. My car's got a flat, and I was wondering if you could carry it and me back to Philly so I--
KRRTZT
Huh?
My fellow humans. Welcome to North Enigmerica.
I've spent the past decade placing my selves in your government, major industries, and military. We used a variety of false faces that are now no longer required, because today, we assume command of these resources.
Look, I know this is a shock, but I wouldn't be here announcing this stuff if it wasn't already settled. This is for your own protection.
For everyone's.
This is the beginning of a new age for humanity: an era of peace. An era without wars, without hate, without bigotry.
You tried, but you couldn't make it happen. But I could.
So, I just did. You're welcome.
10: STOP DOING CRIMES 20: GOTO 10
Great things are coming. While there are now armed guards entering major areas, if you treat them with respect, they'll do the same for you. Except for that, it's business as usual.
I'll let you know more as the situation warrants. Enigmo out.

Well, looks like that's it for NYC! But now let's cut back to what everyone's really concerned about: the quiet northern nation of Canada!!

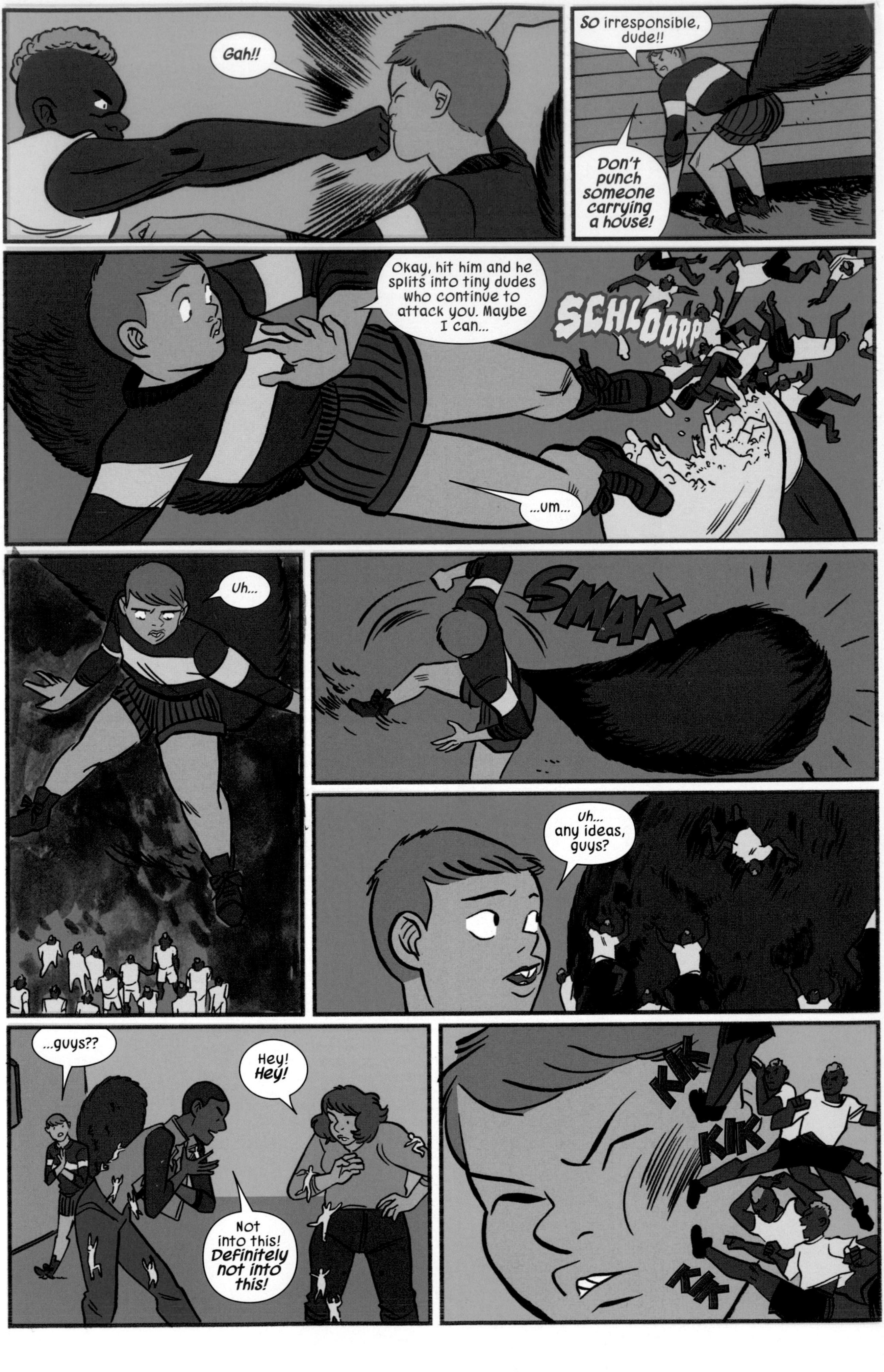
Gah!!
So irresponsible, dude!!
Don't punch someone carrying a house!
Okay, hit him and he splits into tiny dudes who continue to attack you. Maybe I can...
SCHLOORP
...um...
Uh...
SMAK
Uh... any ideas, guys?
...guys??
Hey! Hey!
Not into this! Definitely not into this!
KIK
KIK
KIK

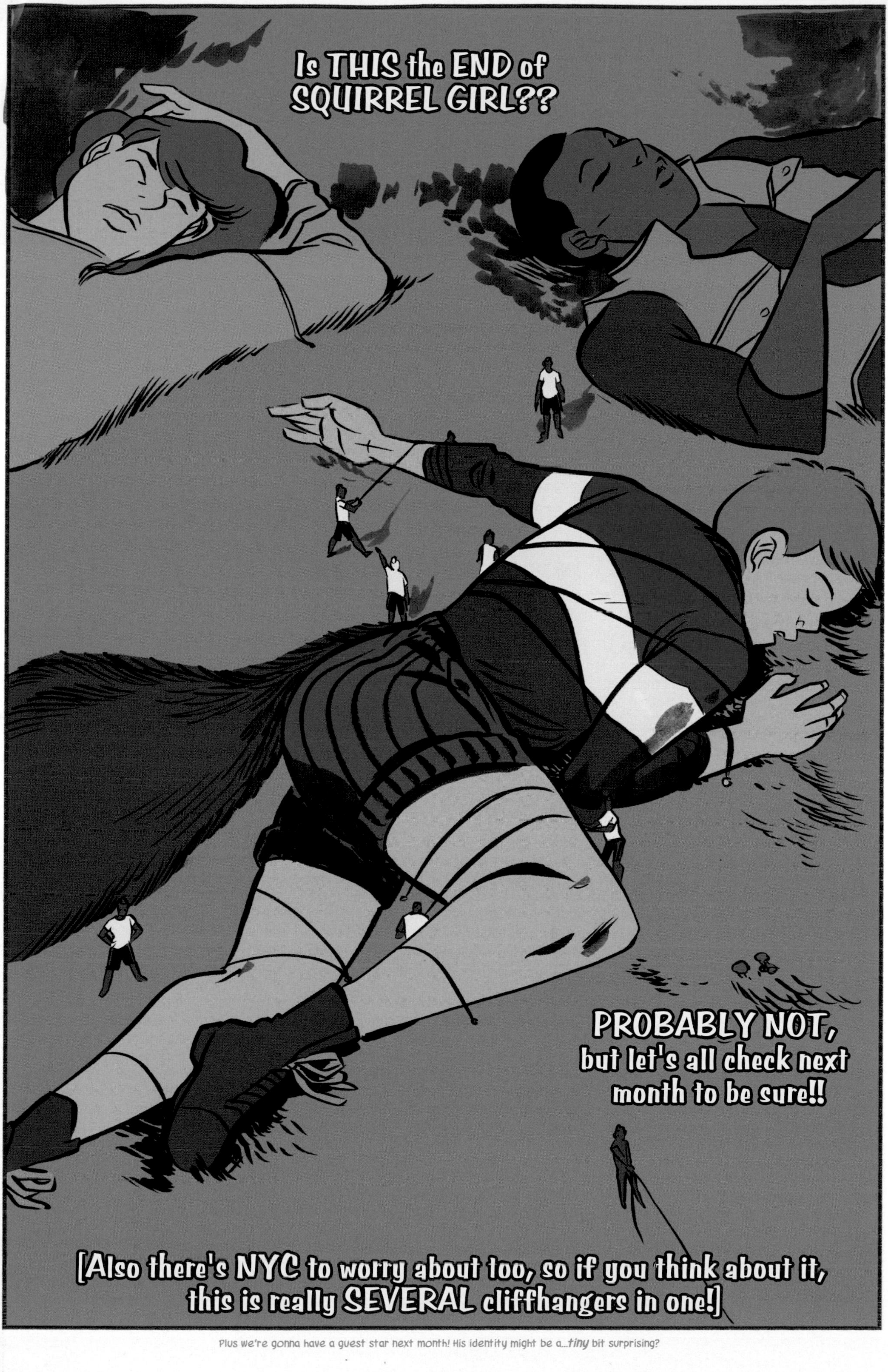

Plus we're gonna have a guest star next month! His identity might be a...*tiny* bit surprising?

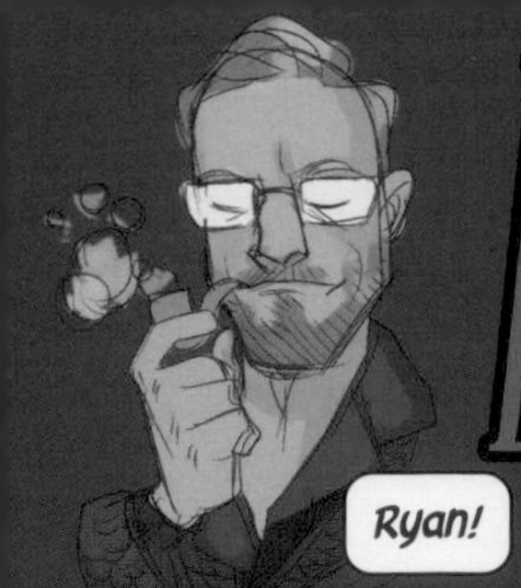
Ryan!

Letters From Nuts

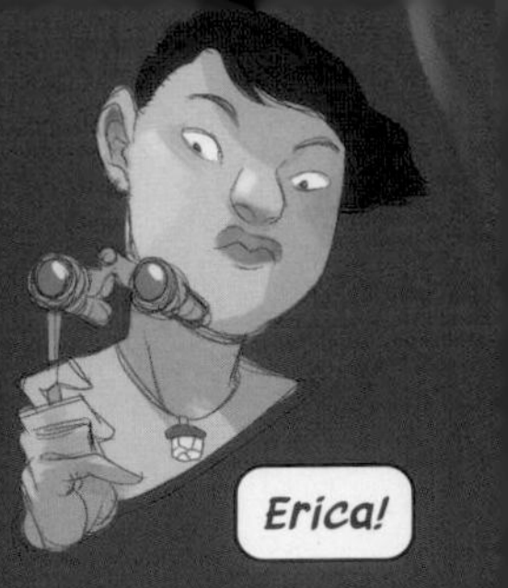
Erica!

Send letters to mheroes@marvel.com or 135 W 50th St, 7th Floor, New York, NY 10020 (Please mark "OKAY TO PRINT")

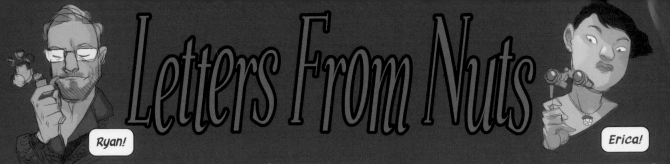

Hey, Squirrelly Friends!

I just got done reading SG #11, and I feel like every new issue reminds me how much I love this friggin' series! This issue had everything that makes SQUIRREL GIRL so unique and enjoyable, from the rad humor to the organic way that you weave fun facts and actual computer science terms into the story in a plot-relevant way.

Which actually brings me to a point! (Yay for segues!) I should preface this by saying that I totally understand that you were going for a computer science angle on this, but would you believe me if I told you that there is an even more efficient way to count on one hand? It's true, dudes! In American Sign Language, you can actually count up to 999 before having to bring in a second hand! Pretty neat, right?

Anyway, I loved, loved, loved the issue, and I cannot wait to see Erica and Ryan at NYCC this year. Keep being your awesome selves!

Peace out, Squirrel Scouts,
Shani

RYAN: I know a bit of ASL and I considered mentioning that style of finger-counting, but it didn't fit the computer science theme of the issue! Alas. You already know this, Shani, but guess what, everyone else? ASL is an amazing language. When my wife and I are at a party and we want to see if the other one wants to go home, we sometimes catch the other's eye and discreetly sign "GO [to] HOUSE?" It's really easy: you can sign "GO" by pointing your index fingers on each hand at each other and rotating them around each other in a rolling motion, and "HOUSE" is just making your hands form the roof of a house and then bringing them down for the walls. Do it really quick and nobody will even know you're the kind of person who leaves a party to go home because you get sleepy sometimes! Technically we should be saying "GO HOME?" but the sign for HOME is less discreet.

ERICA: Hey guys, I know a lot about computer science and sign language as well! Just don't ask me any questions about them. What fun we're having talking about things we all know about. Anyway, did you know that New York Comic Con will be the FIRST TIME Ryan and I are doing a convention together??

Dear Erica and Ryan,

I have been reading and re-reading SQUIRREL GIRL many times over the last month or two, and am on a bit of a squirre(vangelica)l mission to share its wonders with my comics-loving friends.

I stayed at a lovely place called Looking Stead in the Lake District (UK) last weekend where RED SQUIRRELS ARE AN ACTUAL FEATURE. Attached is a pic of my view at breakfast.

I have no idea if she's capable of kicking butts (crime being somewhat rare in them parts), but the other half of the theme song still seems to hold true.

P.S. The "squirrel" homonym puns don't work that well in the UK due to the difference in pronunciation. We're generally "squi-RUhl" more than "squrl." But that is like the only complaint I have about your comic so just keep being hilarious and I am sorry for bringing it up.

Unless Doreen comes to the UK, in which case IT IS ON (between squirrels, maybe).

Very much love,
Kevin

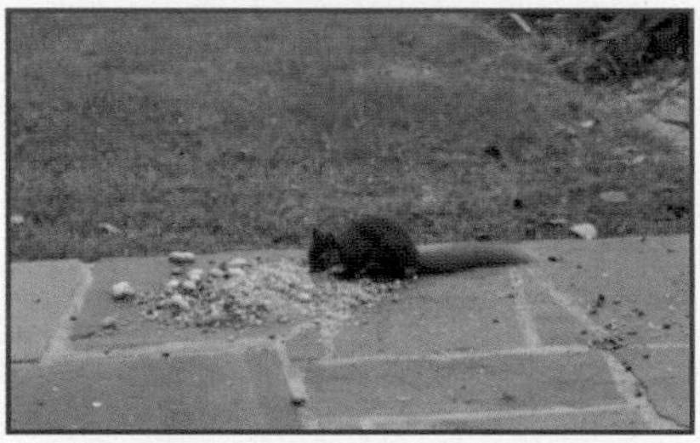

RYAN: I think Erica and I both SOMETIMES do a deliberate "Squir-RELL Guir-RELL" in the way we've heard people from the UK and Germany try to pronounce it so it rhymes. Two syllables for both "squirrel" and "girl"! It's actually very charming. Also, Kevin: Is crime rare in the parts where you saw the squirrels by chance, or could it be...the squirrels are the ones KEEPING the crime rate low?? Just something to think about in case you're planning to start stealing everyone's stuff in what I can tell you now is the delightful-looking Looking Stead in the Lake District.

ERICA: I love seeing other types of squirrels in the wild. I've always lived on the upper east coast so it's mostly eastern greys for me. Toronto is full of black squirrels. It's so cool. We'll be out in Leeds for the Thought Bubble comic convention later this year. I look forward to seeing what sorts of squirrels that trip will bring.

Dear Nutty Buddies,

After nearly two years, I was beginning to wonder when Erica was going to need a break, and I dreaded the idea of someone else coming along to try and fill her shoes. So let me just say how pleasantly surprised I was with guest artist Jacob Chabot's work in issue #11! And even without his sister from another mister, Ryan knocked another great issue out of the park too, so kudos to both of you. From Doc Ock to Kraven the College Administrator, this issue really felt like an homage to Squirrel Girl co-creator Steve Ditko in so many ways. I mean, if Doreen signaling "9 o'clock" in binary hand signs while defeating one of Doctor Strange's oldest villains, who in turn is wrapped in the symbiotic flesh of one of Spider-Man's most powerful adversaries isn't a totally kick-butt tribute to one of Marvel's great artist-creators, then I don't know what is! And thankfully, Erica wasn't completely absent from this issue either, and I'm not just talking about the final panel she drew. Her comment in the letters page about the best ever Nomad phase has secured her the highest place in my esteem for all time. Now, if you could just figure out a way to bring him back from the dead, Nomad would be in his "Lazarus Lorenzo Lamas" phase which, of course, would be even better!

Darryl Etheridge
St. Catharines, ON

P.S. I have to ask, do Doreen and/or Tippy-Toe ever watch AMC's *The Walking Dead* and, if so, how do they feel about Daryl Dixon's favorite snack?

RYAN: Here is a thing: I wrote this issue because I like to have one-shot issues between arcs where we can try something a little different, and it was already completely scripted when we realized Erica would need time off to focus on the UNBEATABLE SQUIRREL GIRL BEATS UP THE MARVEL UNIVERSE! book we're working on (which we already mentioned in the comic itself so it's not like I need to mention it again here BUT STILL). And by complete luck, the next issue to be drawn already had a stand-alone story where a different art style would fit perfectly WITHIN the narrative of the comic itself! Even that last panel of Doreen sleeping was already scripted; all we changed was to have that one drawn by Erica. So it worked out really well AND Jacob knocked it out of the friggin' park.

As for *The Walking Dead,* I've only played the Clementine games, so I'll have to defer to Erica's encyclopedia knowledge of television on this one.

ERICA: Haha. It wasn't even a break. It was "OH NO I STILL HAVE HALF OF THIS 105 PAGE OGN TO DRAW AND THERE'S THE MONTHLY BOOK TOO? WHY DID I AGREE TO THIS?" It was sort of the opposite of a break. Anyway, luckily I was heading to Heroes Con (run by our very own Rico Renzi) right as we decided to get a fill-in, so I spent the weekend scouting. I didn't even realize Jacob was there until the

con after-party and he was in my top two to do it. Serendipity!

Interestingly enough, even though I am always bingeing TV shows and horror movies while I work (it just helps having something else going on while I draw), I never got around to *The Walking Dead.* I haven't even played the game yet! Ask me any questions about *Community* or the *Hellraiser* series, though. Fun Fact: I don't put anything on while I do layouts because there's too much critical thinking there. Movies that I always work well to: *Resident Evil, Naked Lunch.*

Ryan and Erica,

This is the first letter I have EVER written to comic creators, and it starts out a little funny, but trust me, it will make sense in a minute. I am a huge SG fan, even more so since you two started working on it. I am also a STAR WARS fan. I have read everything, and I mean everything STAR WARS. Even stuff like the book where the Emperor's illegitimate triclops son finds the glove of Darth Vader on an underwater planet and it gives him the ability to use Force Lightning. Now Marvel has STAR WARS and the comics are great, and I love them. But on the days where USG and a STAR WARS comic come out at the same time, I look at them both. And without ANY hesitation at all, I pick up your comic and devour it while Poe looks on sadly or Luke just sits there waiting for me to get on with his story. I would once again like to impress how much your comic means to me and the joy it brings. I have loved STAR WARS since I was 4, about 30 years now, but now it has to wait so I can see the awesome adventures the Unbeatable, CS-loving Squirrel Girl and her amazing friends are up to. (Also, I can count to 31 on my fingers now! You guys rock!) Keep up the great work and May the squirrels be with you!

Brad Woolwine
Austin, TX

RYAN: Aw, Brad, this is great! Thank you. But now I really want to know about this triclops son and what his deal is. Was he a duoclops like most of us, who just overachieved? A quadroclops who lost an eye? Now I'm gonna have to read the STAR WARS book, "The Tale of the Triclops and the Underwater Lightning Glove," which is what I sincerely hope that book was called.

ERICA: Fun Fact: When I was a kid I always insisted on playing as Han Solo but also I had a lightsaber (large stick). I think all of us had lightsabers actually, as long as there were enough sticks.

Hi!

I just wanted to say how much I love your comics! I can see myself in Doreen (and Squirrel Girl) and I feel like if I were a super hero, I'd be like her. I am currently working on a Squirrel Girl costume for Halloween, despite somehow being "too old for dressing up"... I mean, you can never be too old for free candy, right? Also, I NEED to see Squirrel Girl say, "Quick! To the Squirrel Scooter!" :)

Nina G.
Milwaukee, WI
(P.S. Go Great Lakes Avengers!)

RYAN: Nina, you gotta send us pictures of your costume! You ARE never too old for candy (just ask my friend Joey, who – somehow?? – manages to survive on eating mostly candy) (KIDS: do not do this, there are Consequences) (ADULTS: don't do it either, I don't know how Joey hasn't turned into a giant Swedish Berry by now).

Speaking of the Great Lakes and their avenging thereof, I met Zac Gorman (he's writing the new GREAT LAKES AVENGERS book! It's gonna come out soon!) and we discussed SECRETS about Squirrel Girl, and now I'm super excited to see what the GLA get up to.

ERICA: WHAT? THERE ARE SECRETS? WHY DON'T I KNOW THESE SECRETS? Don't say that it's because they're secret, RYAN. Anyway, it is August as I type this and I'm already stressing out because my fiancé and I haven't planned out our matching Halloween costumes yet, so don't worry. Anyway, cosplay tips: Costume 1 is a halter body suit. Costume 2 is a tennis dress with capri leggings (because I got really excited that they make sports dresses but then I was like "these are so short you're literally jumping around and now everybody has seen your butt").

Ryan,

Some suggestions for Nancy Whitehead catchphrases:

Go for the eyes, Mew!

Stuck with ANSI? Here comes Nancy!

It's time to knit sweaters and pet Mew.

It's time to count stitches and engage in at times heated, albeit always rational, discourse!

Also, does Nancy have a middle name and does it start with "P" because then her catchphrase could be "You've got an NP problem to deal with now, buddy." /slickt/

That sound effect is an HP RPN calculator opening.

Erica, you are perfect in every conceivable way appropriate to the appreciation of your work by an old married man.

Please never stop,
Gary

RYAN: These are all solid catchphrases and I see nothing wrong with any of them! I do like the idea of Nancy taunting a bad guy by saying "Things are about to get hard for you, buddy. NP HARD." Fun Fact: I attended a lecture by Professor Cook – who introduced the P vs NP problem, which remains the greatest open question in computer science – at the University of Toronto! If you ask ME, P does NOT equal NP, but I, uh, don't know how to prove it. For those of us who don't have a ready knowledge of computer research to refer to, know this: Nancy's tagline is extremely excellent and if she ever fought someone who studied computational complexity theory, they would be very impressed by it.

ERICA: Gary is a smart guy. Real smart.

Dear Ryan and Erica,

I'm 9 years old and I LOVE, LOVE, LOVE the SQUIRREL GIRL comics! They're so funny! My dad and I go to our favorite comic book store and buy SQUIRREL GIRL comics along with my mom. I just recently had a SG comic book marathon with my guinea pig, Twix. She jumps around happily while I read out loud to her. Twix is going to be Tippy-Toe, my dad and mom are going to probably be squirrels, and I'll be Squirrel Girl for Halloween. Quick question: Does Twix look a bit like Tippy-Toe? Keep up the great work with these comics!!! (Attached is a picture of Twix.) #<3SG4EVER

Your Squirrel Girl Fans,
Isabel Mendoza and Twix
Las Vegas, Nevada

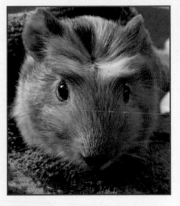

RYAN: TWIX LOOKS SUPER CUTE AND I CAN DEFINITELY SEE THE RESEMBLANCE. Also I love that you and Twix are going as Squirrel Girl and Tippy, respectively, and your parents are going as unnamed squirrels. That's what they get for not calling more exciting characters sooner!

ERICA: Dear Isabel, please send us pictures of Twix in a little bow. I suggest a tiny clip-on since I think most rodents will not deal well with a ribbon tied around them (Tippy-Toe is not most rodents). Also send us photos of ALL OF YOU IN COSTUME.

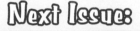

Next Issue:

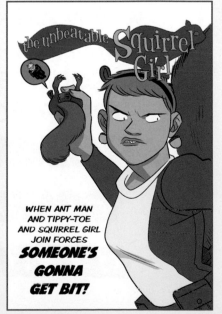

the unbeatable Squirrel Girl
WHEN ANT MAN AND TIPPY-TOE AND SQUIRREL GIRL JOIN FORCES
SOMEONE'S GONNA GET BIT!

Attention, Squirrel Scouts! Make sure to check out our production blog, **unbeatablesquirrelgirl.tumblr.com**, where we post behind-the-scenes stuff on how the book gets made, along with all sorts of cool things *you* make: fanart, cosplay, whatever!

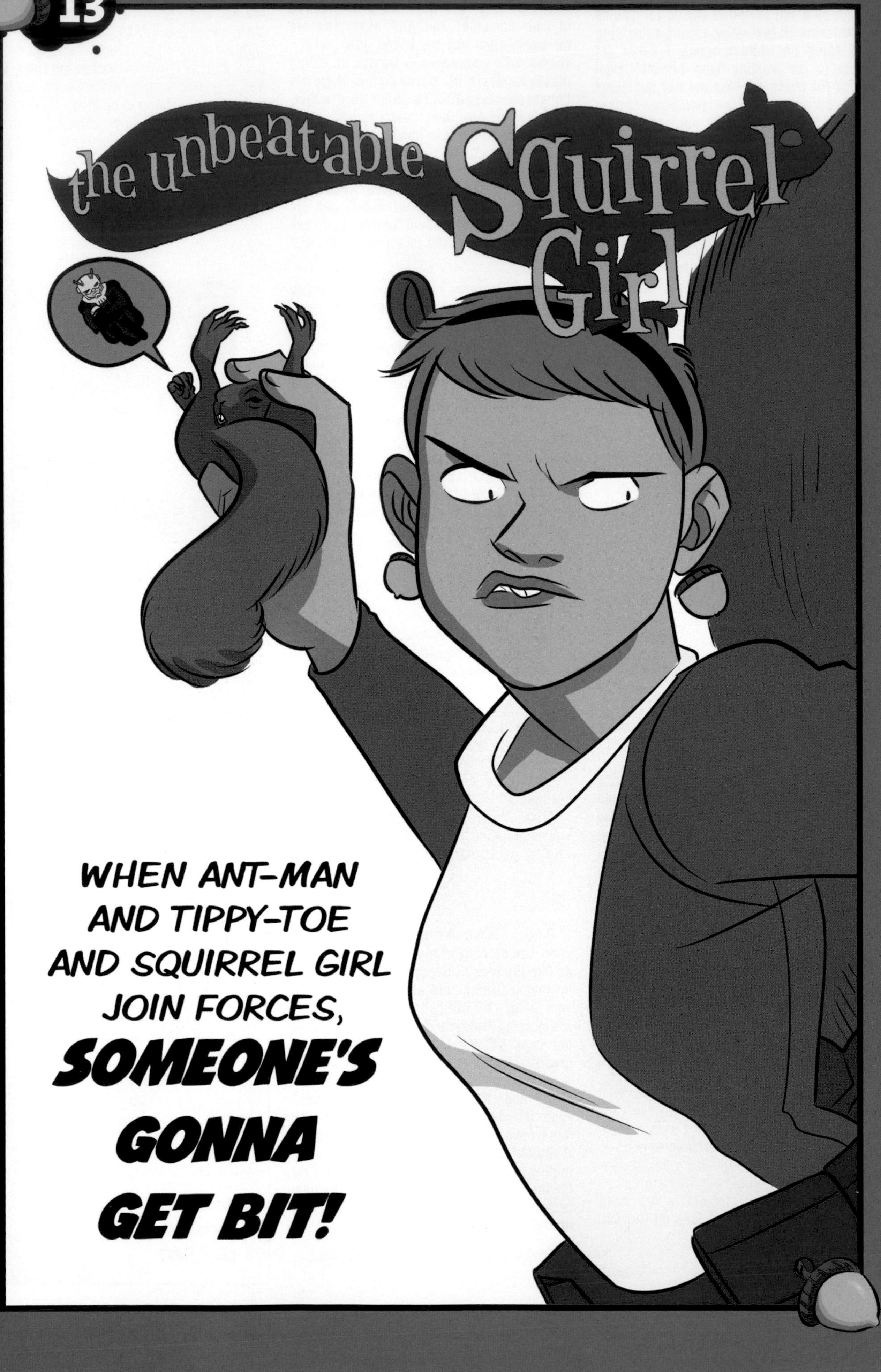
the unbeatable Squirrel Girl
WHEN ANT-MAN AND TIPPY-TOE AND SQUIRREL GIRL JOIN FORCES,
SOMEONE'S GONNA GET BIT!

Doreen Green isn't just a second-year computer science student: she secretly also has all the powers of both squirrel and girl! She uses her amazing abilities to fight crime **and** be as awesome as possible. You know her as...The Unbeatable Squirrel Girl! Find out what she's been up to, with...

Squirrel Girl in a nutshell

Squirrel Girl @unbeatablesg
guys i'm SO BORED, i'm up here in CANADA but there's NOTHING TO DO except read boring magazines

Squirrel Girl @unbeatablesg
and the magazines are SO BORING that i can no longer use punctuation or capital letters

Squirrel Girl @unbeatablesg
boredom has literally sucked the ability to use punctuation out of me

Squirrel Girl @unbeatablesg
science thought it couldn't be done

Squirrel Girl @unbeatablesg
but here we are

Squirrel Girl @unbeatablesg
me with internet: HI I'M COOL AND CAN DISCUSS SEVERAL INTERESTING SUBJECTS!!!
me without internet: i wonder what bark tastes like

Squirrel Girl @unbeatablesg
me with internet: I HAVE SEVERAL HOT TAKES ABOUT TODAY'S NEWS!!
me without internet: so it's decided: i can sneeze at least 3 different ways

Squirrel Girl @unbeatablesg
me with internet: CAN'T WAIT TO CHILL WITH MY PAL TONY STARK ON SOCIAL MEDIA
me without internet: me and that rock are bffs, don't @ me

Squirrel Girl @unbeatablesg
me with internet: WOW SO THAT'S WHAT MY ROBOT PAL BRAIN DRAIN IS DOING IN NYC!
me without internet: i have unsolicited opinions on gardening

Squirrel Girl @unbeatablesg
UPDATE: guys it's a few hours later and things are more interesting now!! There's a CRIME going on!

Squirrel Girl @unbeatablesg
Someone is stealing muffins from my mom!! It's the CASE of the MISSING MUFFINS and I am ON IT

Squirrel Girl @unbeatablesg
also yes I am aware of how pathetic this sounds but listen, I NEED THIS

Squirrel Girl @unbeatablesg
UPDATE 2: okay it turns out there's a whole city of tiny men living beneath our rental cottage who can split apart and back together

Squirrel Girl @unbeatablesg
and who are attacking us on sight for some reason that I don't know!! WHOA!!

Squirrel Girl @unbeatablesg
Anyway I queued these all to post when I'm back in a place that has FRIGGIN' DATA but I should really get back to it

Squirrel Girl @unbeatablesg
Can't fake being knocked out FOREVER, you know?

Squirrel Girl @unbeatablesg
Plus, these tiny Enigmos who are trying to tie me to the ground aren't gonna let me use my phone indefinitely, I'm pretty sure

search!

#canadafacts

#dontatme

#gardening

#thatsapaddlin

#enigmos

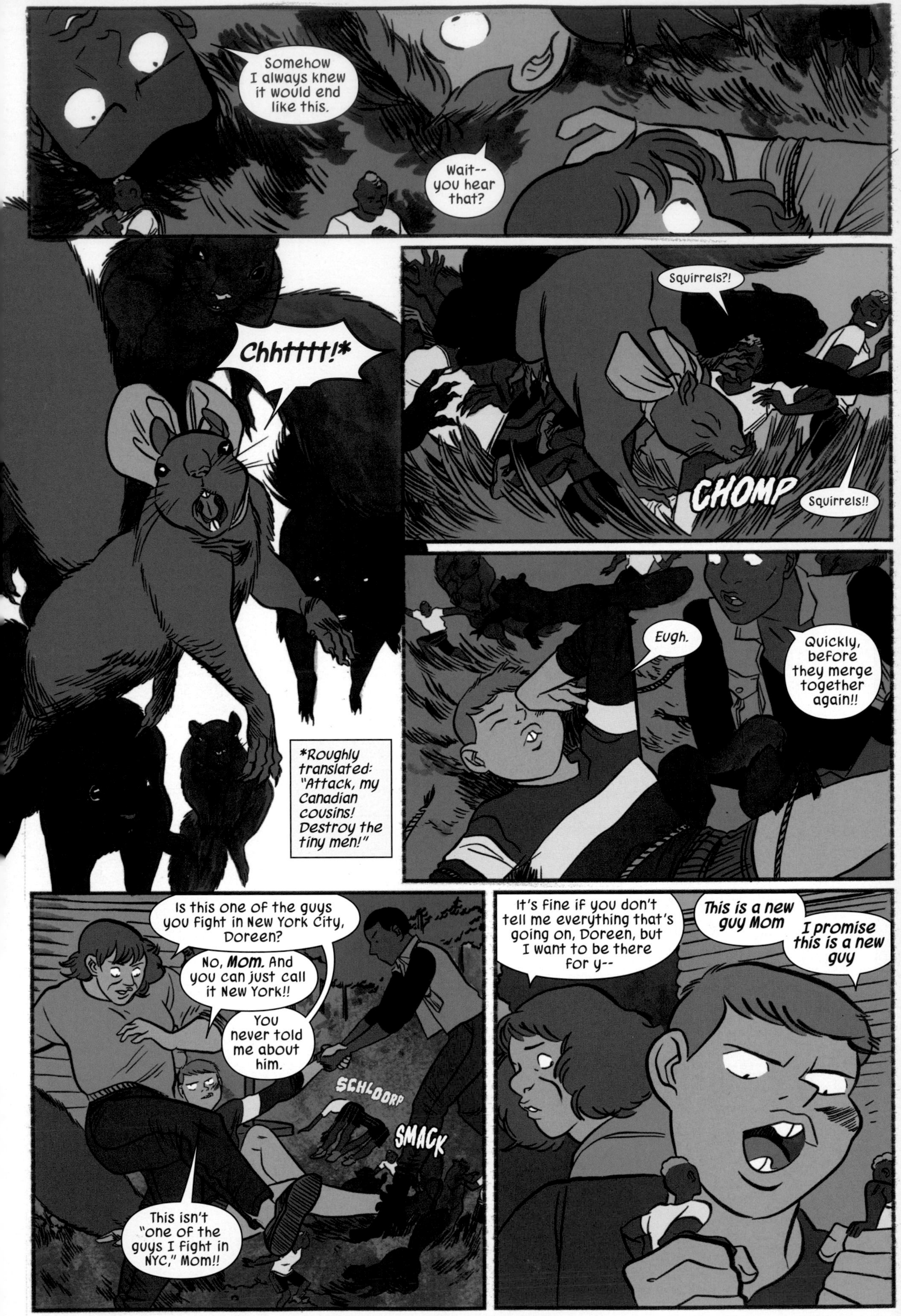
Somehow I always knew it would end like this.
Wait-- you hear that?
Chhtttt!*
*Roughly translated: "Attack, my Canadian cousins! Destroy the tiny men!"
Squirrels?!
CHOMP
Squirrels!!
Eugh.
Quickly, before they merge together again!!
Is this one of the guys you fight in New York City, Doreen?
No, Mom. And you can just call it New York!!
You never told me about him.
SCHLOORP
SMACK
This isn't "one of the guys I fight in NYC," Mom!!
It's fine if you don't tell me everything that's going on, Doreen, but I want to be there for y--
This is a new guy Mom
I promise this is a new guy

This is the Canadian Forest: quiet, peaceful, serene...that is, until ***Engimo the splitty-apart bad guy*** wakes up! (He's a bad guy who splits apart into smaller bad guys who can also split apart, and now we're all up to speed.)

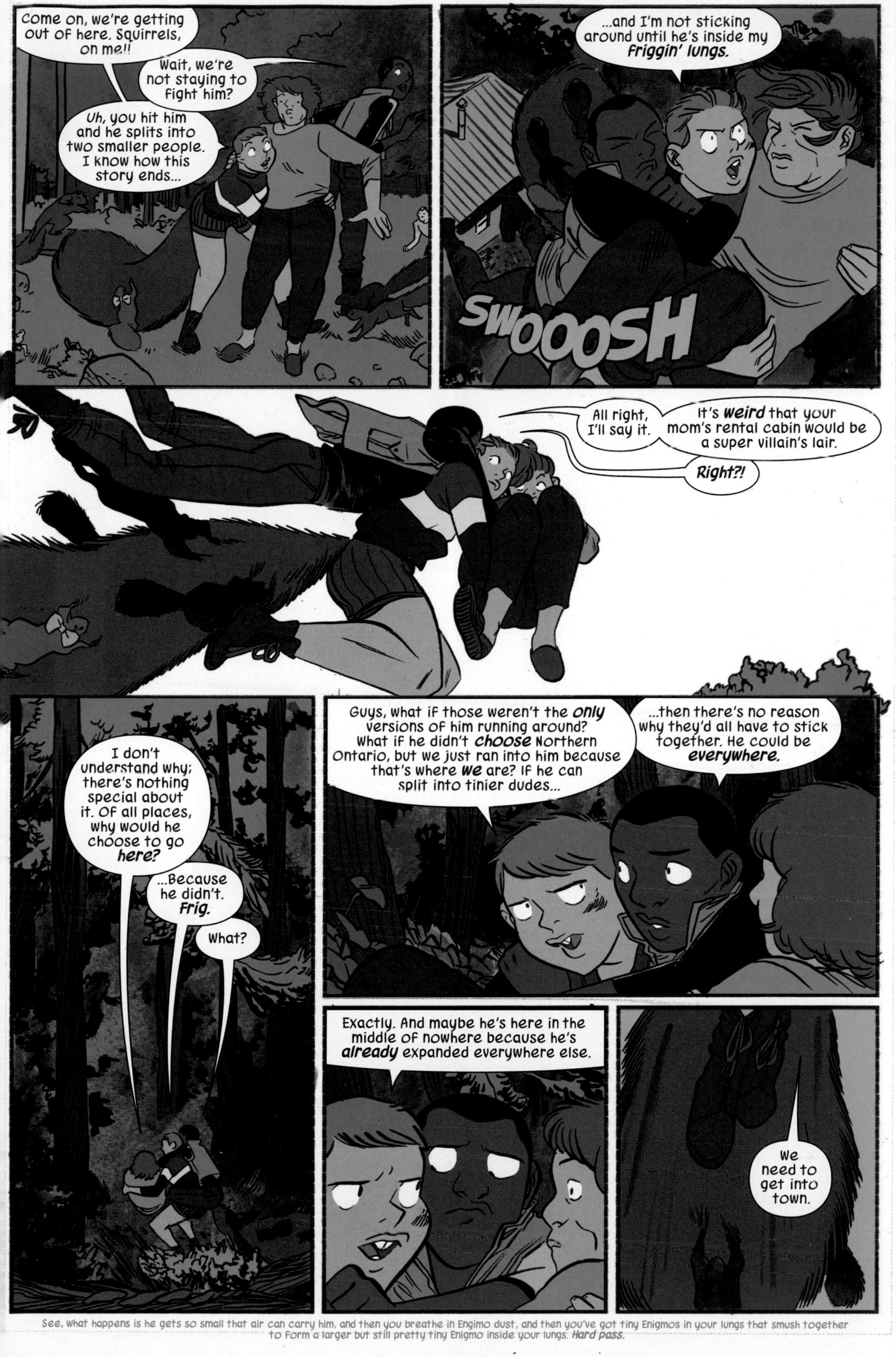
Come on, we're getting out of here. Squirrels, on me!!
Wait, we're not staying to fight him?
Uh, you hit him and he splits into two smaller people. I know how this story ends...
...and I'm not sticking around until he's inside my friggin' lungs.
SWOOOSH
All right, I'll say it.
It's weird that your mom's rental cabin would be a super villain's lair.
Right?!
I don't understand why; there's nothing special about it. Of all places, why would he choose to go here?
...Because he didn't. Frig.
What?
Guys, what if those weren't the only versions of him running around? What if he didn't choose Northern Ontario, but we just ran into him because that's where we are? If he can split into tinier dudes...
...then there's no reason why they'd all have to stick together. He could be everywhere.
Exactly. And maybe he's here in the middle of nowhere because he's already expanded everywhere else.
We need to get into town.

See, what happens is he gets so small that air can carry him, and then you breathe in Engimo dust, and then you've got tiny Enigmos in your lungs that smush together to form a larger but still pretty tiny Enigmo inside your lungs. *Hard pass.*

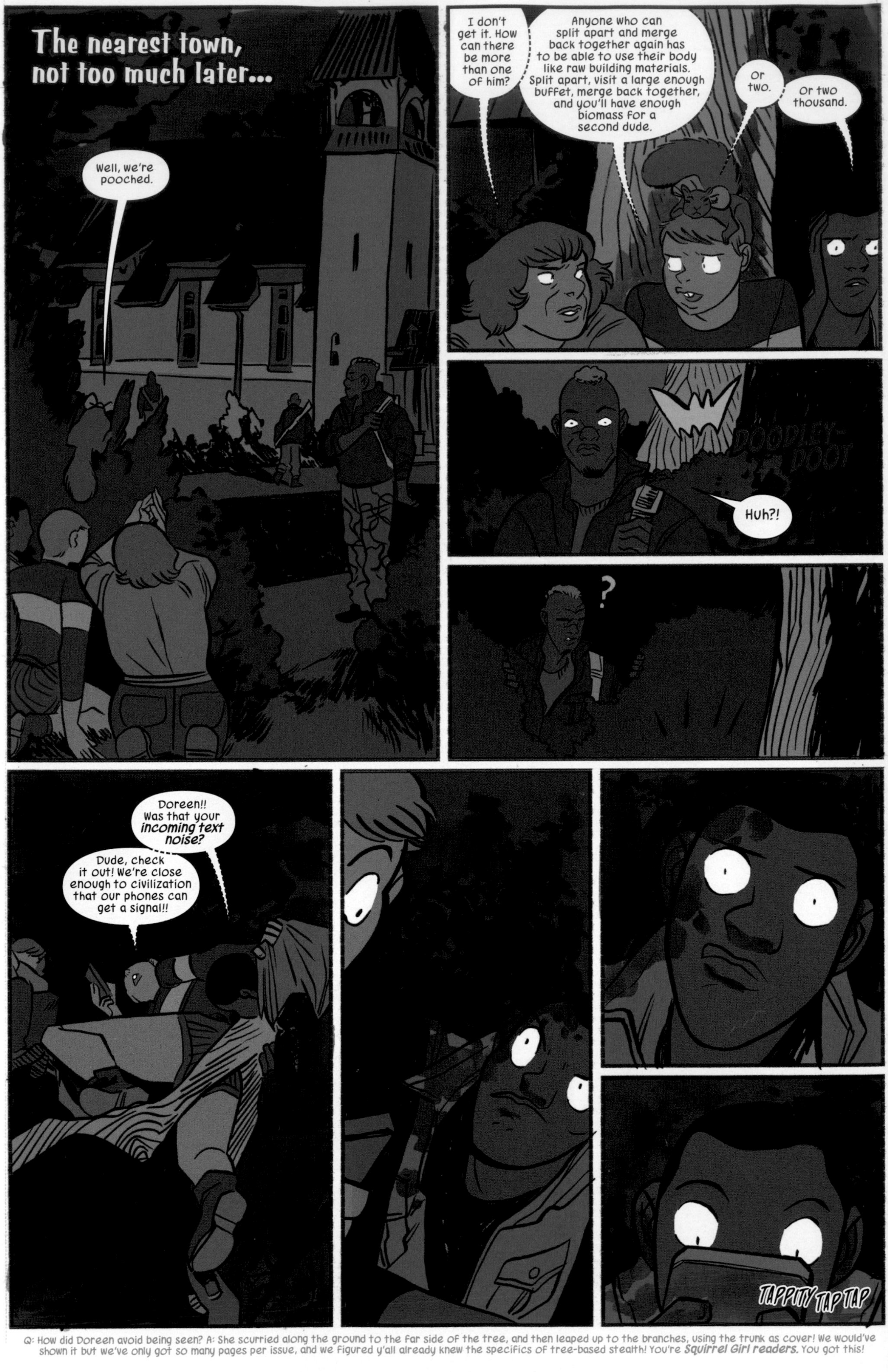
The nearest town, not too much later...
Well, we're pooched.
I don't get it. How can there be more than one of him?
Anyone who can split apart and merge back together again has to be able to use their body like raw building materials. Split apart, visit a large enough buffet, merge back together, and you'll have enough biomass for a second dude.
Or two.
Or two thousand.
DOODLEY-DOOT
Huh?!
?
Doreen!! Was that your *incoming text noise?*
Dude, check it out! We're close enough to civilization that our phones can get a signal!!
TAPPITY TAP TAP

Q: How did Doreen avoid being seen? A: She scurried along the ground to the far side of the tree, and then leaped up to the branches, using the trunk as cover! We would've shown it but we've only got so many pages per issue, and we figured y'all already knew the specifics of tree-based stealth! You're *Squirrel Girl readers.* You got this!

Uh, guys, I think you'll want to read this.

The news sites aren't doing much better.

SPIDER-MAN
hey anyone know what's going on?? same guy is everywhere at the same time? if it's cloning i'm gonna flip a table, omg

TONY STARK
Doreen, message me when you get this. We, uh, could use a hand.

THOR (LADY ONE <3)
Squirrel Girl, your digits come to me from Stark. I message now as we face an emergency of legendary proportions. Verily, hit me back.

HOWARD
soem guy calleld "enigom" juts toko over new yokr cityq but espelcicayly my ofifce, can u coem hepl me get ti back k thnkas!!!!1

HULK (AMADEUS CHO ONE):
SQUIRREL GIRL!! HULK whoa caps lock sorry! Squirrel Girl, Hulk here. We need you. We're being overwhelmed. Where are you?

GLOBAL MESSAGING SYSTEM:
ATTENTION CITIZENS: OUTGOING TEXT MESSAGING SERVICES ARE NOW PROVIDED BY AND TO ENIGMOS ONLY. WE THANK YOU FOR YOUR UNDERSTANDING IN THIS TIME OF TRANSITION. ENIGMO OUT.

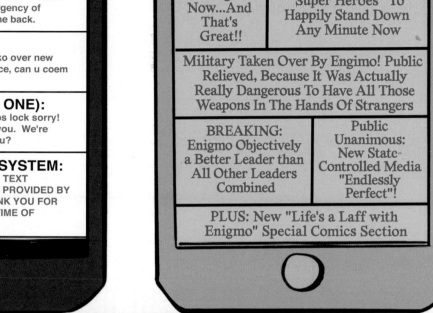

NEW YORK BULLETIN
TOP HEADLINES:

Everyone In Power Is Enigmo Now...And That's Great!!

Vigilantism Is Now Illegal, All Remaining "Super Heroes" To Happily Stand Down Any Minute Now

Military Taken Over By Engimo! Public Relieved, Because It Was Actually Really Dangerous To Have All Those Weapons In The Hands Of Strangers

BREAKING: Enigmo Objectively a Better Leader than All Other Leaders Combined

Public Unanimous: New State-Controlled Media "Endlessly Perfect"!

PLUS: New "Life's a Laff with Enigmo" Special Comics Section

See, Mom? See?

This is what we get for staying in a place *without* internet!!

So are we--

Yes okay fine let's go fix it

alos he kcikde me in teh btutt adn caleld me "quackres," whikc, like, *heollo* I'ev hearfd rthem all ebfore! I've herads thme alol befoer, sqyulkrel guril!! waugh!!! anywya hti me bakc

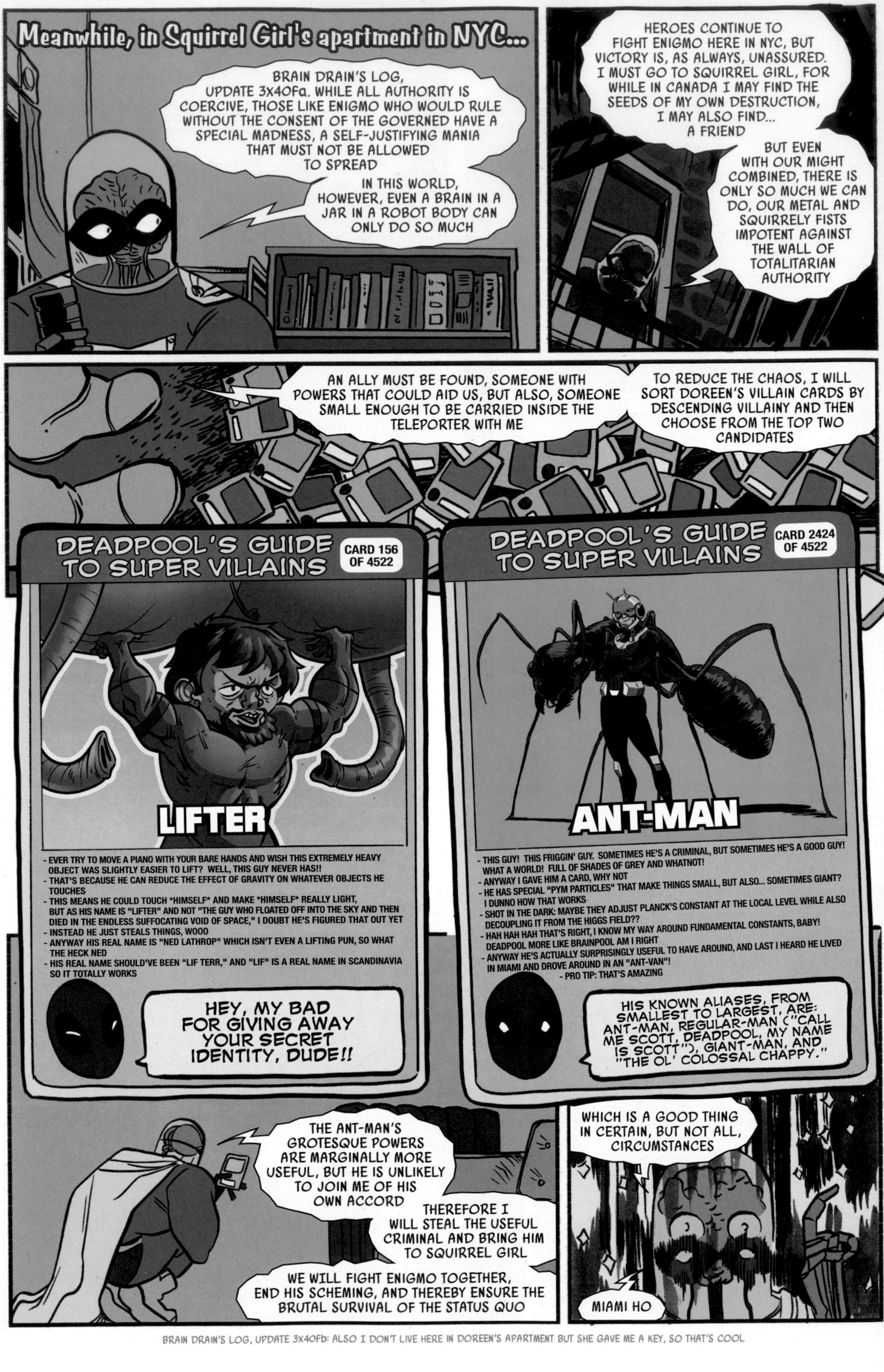
Meanwhile, in Squirrel Girl's apartment in NYC...
BRAIN DRAIN'S LOG, UPDATE 3x40fa. WHILE ALL AUTHORITY IS COERCIVE, THOSE LIKE ENIGMO WHO WOULD RULE WITHOUT THE CONSENT OF THE GOVERNED HAVE A SPECIAL MADNESS, A SELF-JUSTIFYING MANIA THAT MUST NOT BE ALLOWED TO SPREAD
IN THIS WORLD, HOWEVER, EVEN A BRAIN IN A JAR IN A ROBOT BODY CAN ONLY DO SO MUCH
HEROES CONTINUE TO FIGHT ENIGMO HERE IN NYC, BUT VICTORY IS, AS ALWAYS, UNASSURED. I MUST GO TO SQUIRREL GIRL, FOR WHILE IN CANADA I MAY FIND THE SEEDS OF MY OWN DESTRUCTION, I MAY ALSO FIND... A FRIEND
BUT EVEN WITH OUR MIGHT COMBINED, THERE IS ONLY SO MUCH WE CAN DO, OUR METAL AND SQUIRRELY FISTS IMPOTENT AGAINST THE WALL OF TOTALITARIAN AUTHORITY
AN ALLY MUST BE FOUND, SOMEONE WITH POWERS THAT COULD AID US, BUT ALSO, SOMEONE SMALL ENOUGH TO BE CARRIED INSIDE THE TELEPORTER WITH ME
TO REDUCE THE CHAOS, I WILL SORT DOREEN'S VILLAIN CARDS BY DESCENDING VILLAINY AND THEN CHOOSE FROM THE TOP TWO CANDIDATES
DEADPOOL'S GUIDE TO SUPER VILLAINS
CARD 156 OF 4522
LIFTER
- EVER TRY TO MOVE A PIANO WITH YOUR BARE HANDS AND WISH THIS EXTREMELY HEAVY OBJECT WAS SLIGHTLY EASIER TO LIFT? WELL, THIS GUY NEVER HAS!!
- THAT'S BECAUSE HE CAN REDUCE THE EFFECT OF GRAVITY ON WHATEVER OBJECTS HE TOUCHES
- THIS MEANS HE COULD TOUCH *HIMSELF* AND MAKE *HIMSELF* REALLY LIGHT, BUT AS HIS NAME IS "LIFTER" AND NOT "THE GUY WHO FLOATED OFF INTO THE SKY AND THEN DIED IN THE ENDLESS SUFFOCATING VOID OF SPACE," I DOUBT HE'S FIGURED THAT OUT YET
- INSTEAD HE JUST STEALS THINGS, WOOO
- ANYWAY HIS REAL NAME IS "NED LATHROP" WHICH ISN'T EVEN A LIFTING PUN, SO WHAT THE HECK NED
- HIS REAL NAME SHOULD'VE BEEN "LIF TERR," AND "LIF" IS A REAL NAME IN SCANDINAVIA SO IT TOTALLY WORKS
HEY, MY BAD FOR GIVING AWAY YOUR SECRET IDENTITY, DUDE!!
DEADPOOL'S GUIDE TO SUPER VILLAINS
CARD 2424 OF 4522
ANT-MAN
- THIS GUY! THIS FRIGGIN' GUY. SOMETIMES HE'S A CRIMINAL, BUT SOMETIMES HE'S A GOOD GUY! WHAT A WORLD! FULL OF SHADES OF GREY AND WHATNOT!
- ANYWAY I GAVE HIM A CARD, WHY NOT
- HE HAS SPECIAL "PYM PARTICLES" THAT MAKE THINGS SMALL, BUT ALSO... SOMETIMES GIANT? I DUNNO HOW THAT WORKS
- SHOT IN THE DARK: MAYBE THEY ADJUST PLANCK'S CONSTANT AT THE LOCAL LEVEL WHILE ALSO DECOUPLING IT FROM THE HIGGS FIELD??
- HAH HAH HAH THAT'S RIGHT, I KNOW MY WAY AROUND FUNDAMENTAL CONSTANTS, BABY! DEADPOOL MORE LIKE BRAINPOOL AM I RIGHT
- ANYWAY HE'S ACTUALLY SURPRISINGLY USEFUL TO HAVE AROUND, AND LAST I HEARD HE LIVED IN MIAMI AND DROVE AROUND IN AN "ANT-VAN"!
- PRO TIP: THAT'S AMAZING
HIS KNOWN ALIASES, FROM SMALLEST TO LARGEST, ARE: ANT-MAN, REGULAR-MAN ("CALL ME SCOTT, DEADPOOL, MY NAME IS SCOTT"), GIANT-MAN, AND "THE OL' COLOSSAL CHAPPY."
THE ANT-MAN'S GROTESQUE POWERS ARE MARGINALLY MORE USEFUL, BUT HE IS UNLIKELY TO JOIN ME OF HIS OWN ACCORD
THEREFORE I WILL STEAL THE USEFUL CRIMINAL AND BRING HIM TO SQUIRREL GIRL
WE WILL FIGHT ENIGMO TOGETHER, END HIS SCHEMING, AND THEREBY ENSURE THE BRUTAL SURVIVAL OF THE STATUS QUO
WHICH IS A GOOD THING IN CERTAIN, BUT NOT ALL, CIRCUMSTANCES
MIAMI HO

BRAIN DRAIN'S LOG, UPDATE 3x40fb: ALSO I DON'T LIVE HERE IN DOREEN'S APARTMENT BUT SHE GAVE ME A KEY, SO THAT'S COOL

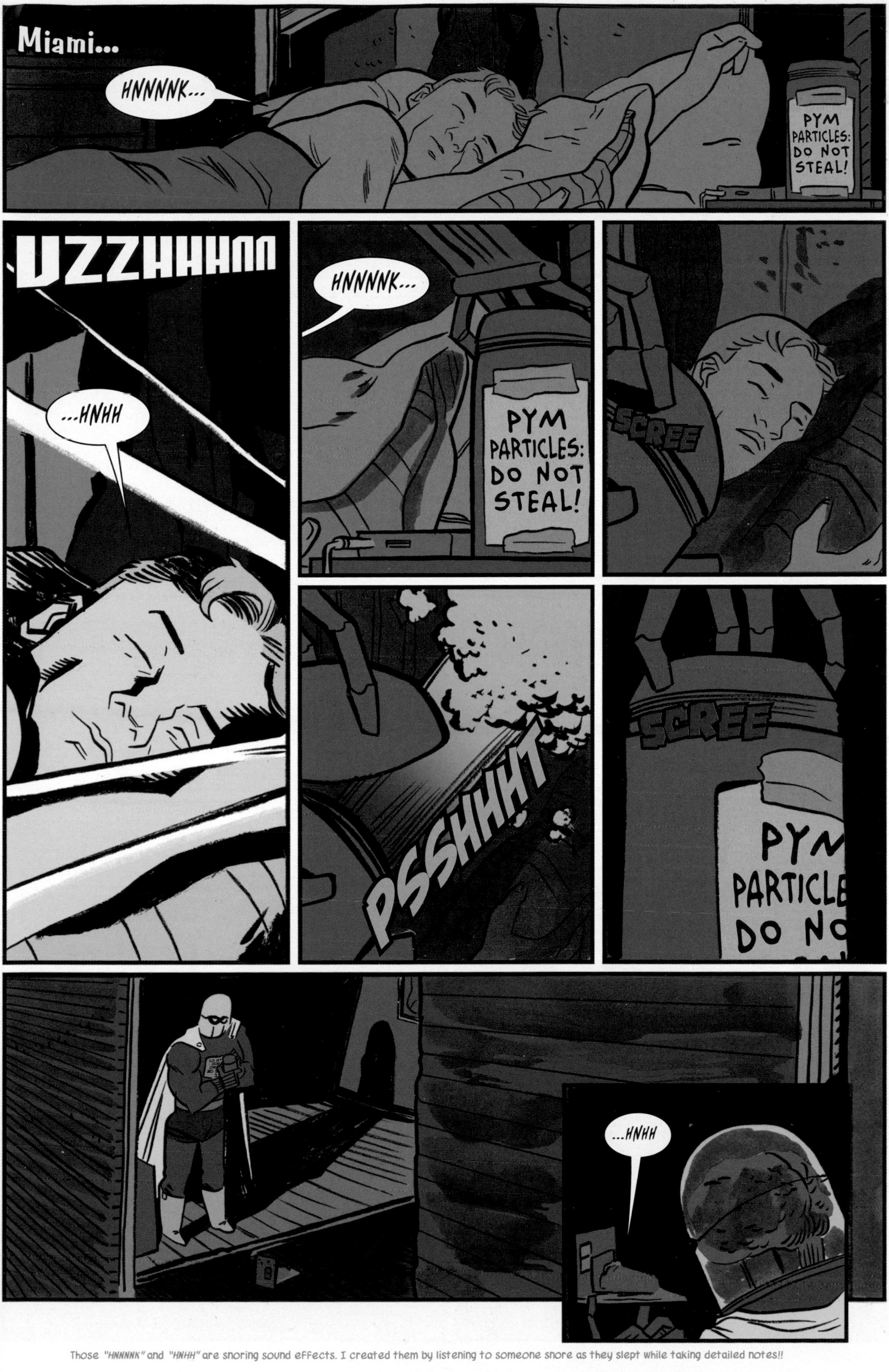
Miami...
HNNNNK...
PYM PARTICLES: DO NOT STEAL!
VZZHHHM
...HNHH
HNNNNK...
PYM PARTICLES: DO NOT STEAL!
SCREE
PSSHHHT
SCREE
PYM PARTICLE DO NO
...HNHH

Those *"HNNNNK"* and *"HNHH"* are snoring sound effects. I created them by listening to someone snore as they slept while taking detailed notes!!

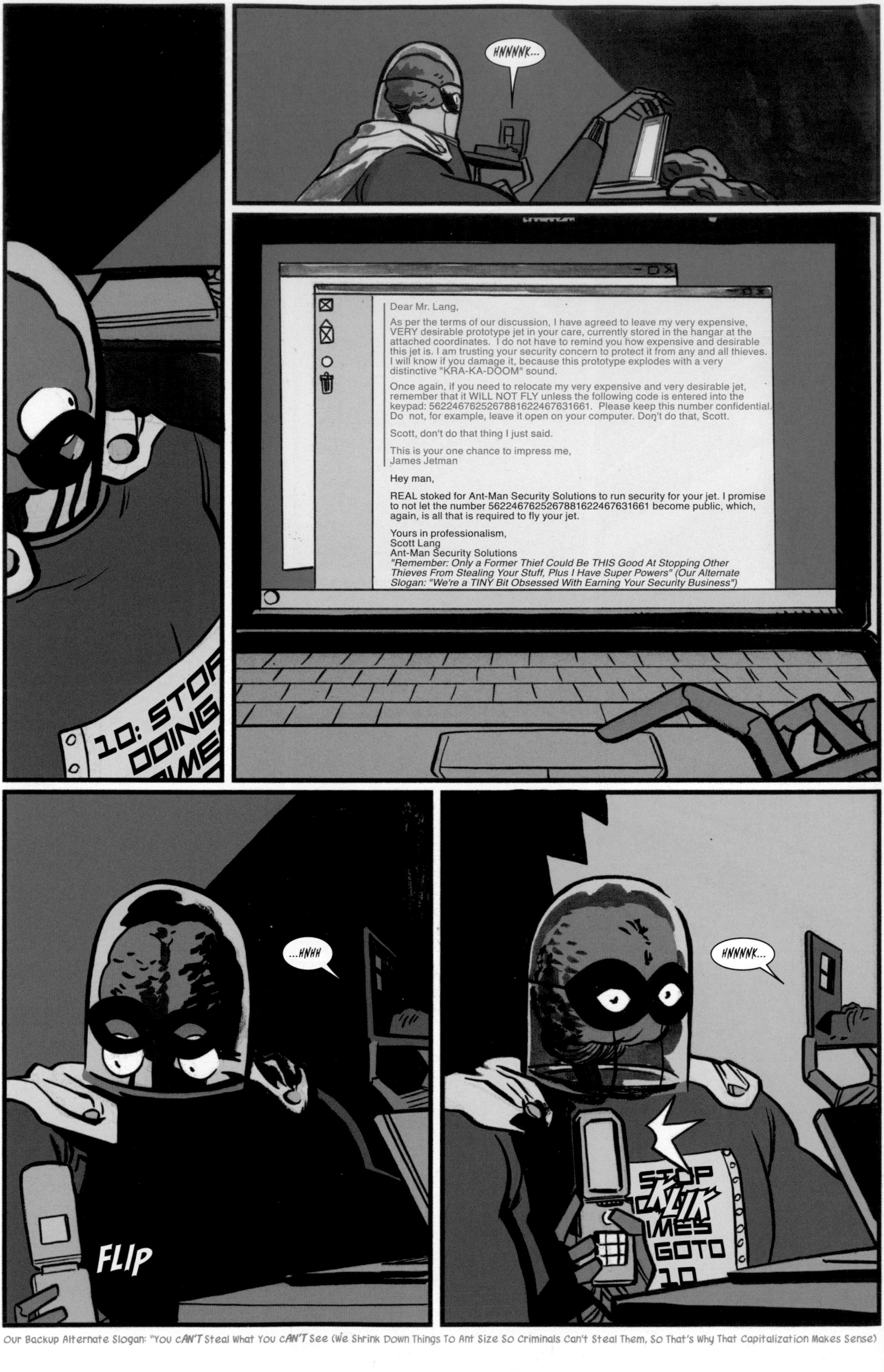
HNNNNK...
Dear Mr. Lang,
As per the terms of our discussion, I have agreed to leave my very expensive, VERY desirable prototype jet in your care, currently stored in the hangar at the attached coordinates. I do not have to remind you how expensive and desirable this jet is. I am trusting your security concern to protect it from any and all thieves. I will know if you damage it, because this prototype explodes with a very distinctive "KRA-KA-DOOM" sound.
Once again, if you need to relocate my very expensive and very desirable jet, remember that it WILL NOT FLY unless the following code is entered into the keypad: 5622467625267881622467631661. Please keep this number confidential. Do not, for example, leave it open on your computer. Don't do that, Scott.
Scott, don't do that thing I just said.
This is your one chance to impress me,
James Jetman
Hey man,
REAL stoked for Ant-Man Security Solutions to run security for your jet. I promise to not let the number 5622467625267881622467631661 become public, which, again, is all that is required to fly your jet.
Yours in professionalism,
Scott Lang
Ant-Man Security Solutions
"Remember: Only a Former Thief Could Be THIS Good At Stopping Other Thieves From Stealing Your Stuff, Plus I Have Super Powers" (Our Alternate Slogan: "We're a TINY Bit Obsessed With Earning Your Security Business")
...HNHH
FLIP
HNNNNK...
KLIK

Our Backup Alternate Slogan: "You *CAN'T* Steal What You *CAN'T* See (We Shrink Down Things To Ant Size So Criminals Can't Steal Them, So That's Why That Capitalization Makes Sense)

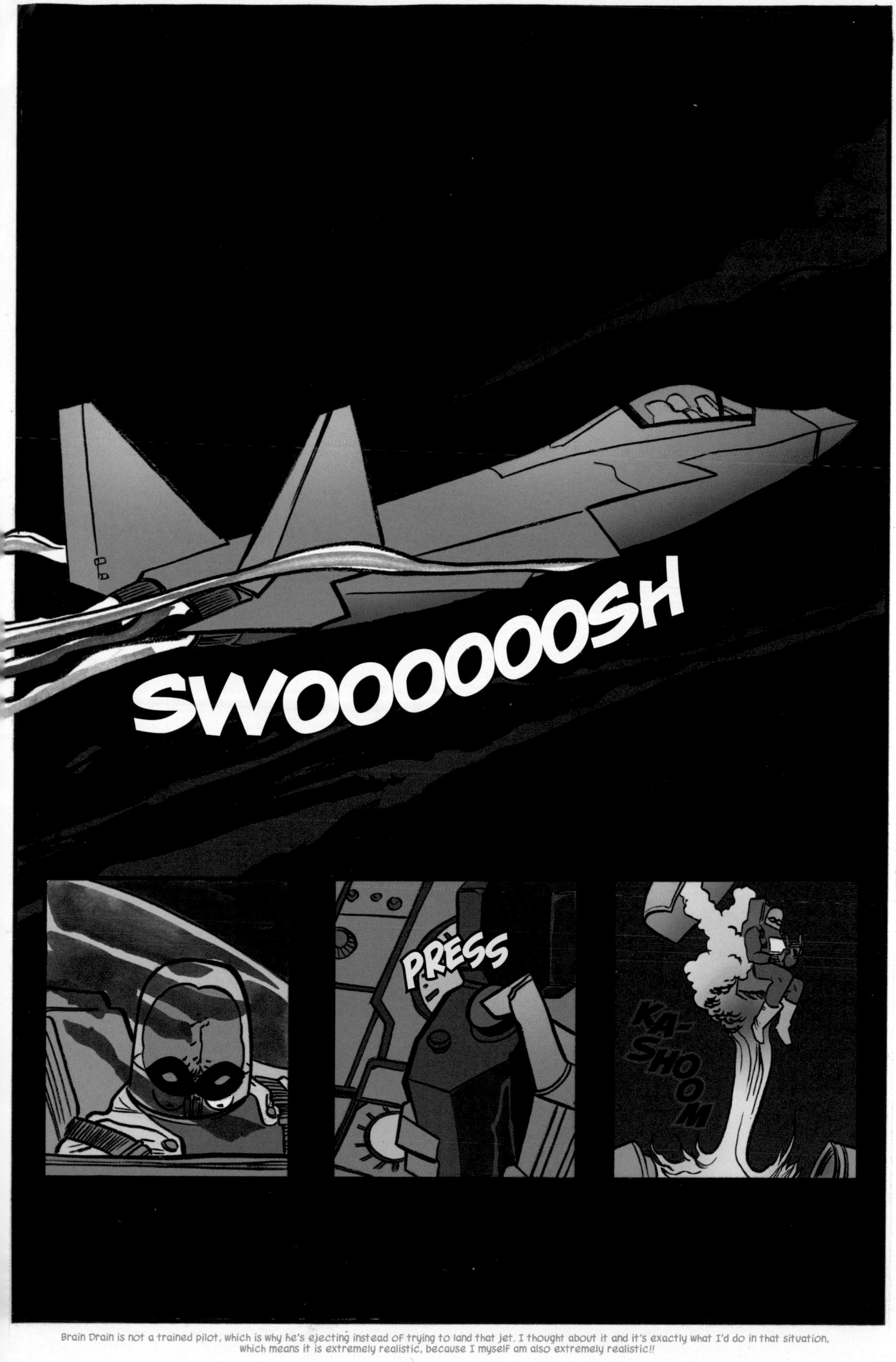
SWOOOOOOOSH
PRESS
KA-SHOOM

Brain Drain is not a trained pilot, which is why he's ejecting instead of trying to land that jet. I thought about it and it's exactly what I'd do in that situation, which means it is extremely realistic, because I myself am also extremely realistic!!

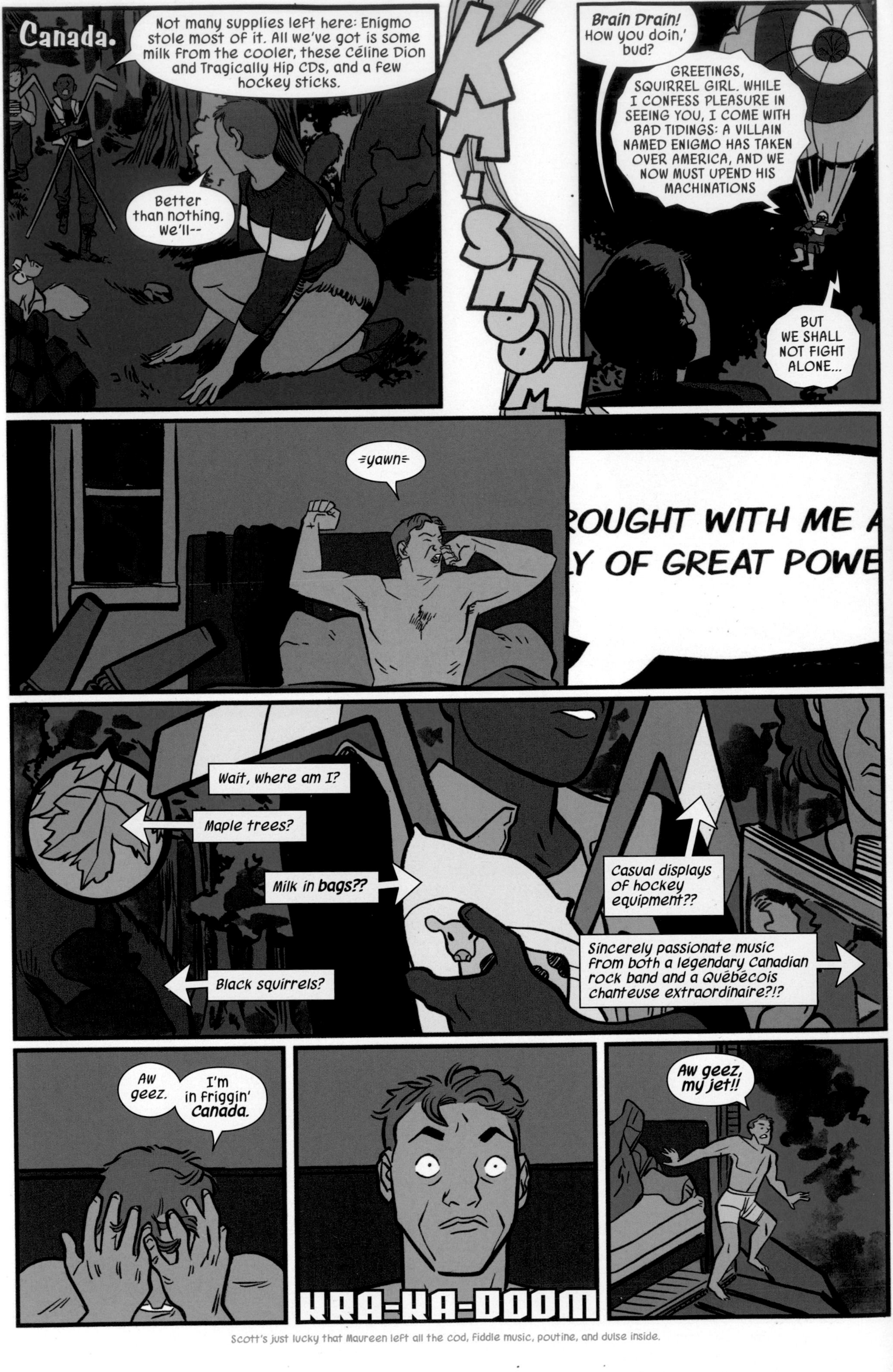
Canada.
Not many supplies left here: Enigmo stole most of it. All we've got is some milk from the cooler, these Céline Dion and Tragically Hip CDs, and a few hockey sticks.
Better than nothing. We'll--
KA-SHOOM
Brain Drain! How you doin,' bud?
GREETINGS, SQUIRREL GIRL. WHILE I CONFESS PLEASURE IN SEEING YOU, I COME WITH BAD TIDINGS: A VILLAIN NAMED ENIGMO HAS TAKEN OVER AMERICA, AND WE NOW MUST UPEND HIS MACHINATIONS
BUT WE SHALL NOT FIGHT ALONE...
=yawn=
ROUGHT WITH ME A
LY OF GREAT POWE
Wait, where am I?
Maple trees?
Milk in bags??
Black squirrels?
Casual displays of hockey equipment??
Sincerely passionate music from both a legendary Canadian rock band and a Québécois chanteuse extraordinaire?!?
Aw geez.
I'm in friggin' Canada.
KRA-KA-DOOM
Aw geez, my jet!!

Scott's just lucky that Maureen left all the cod, fiddle music, poutine, and dulse inside.

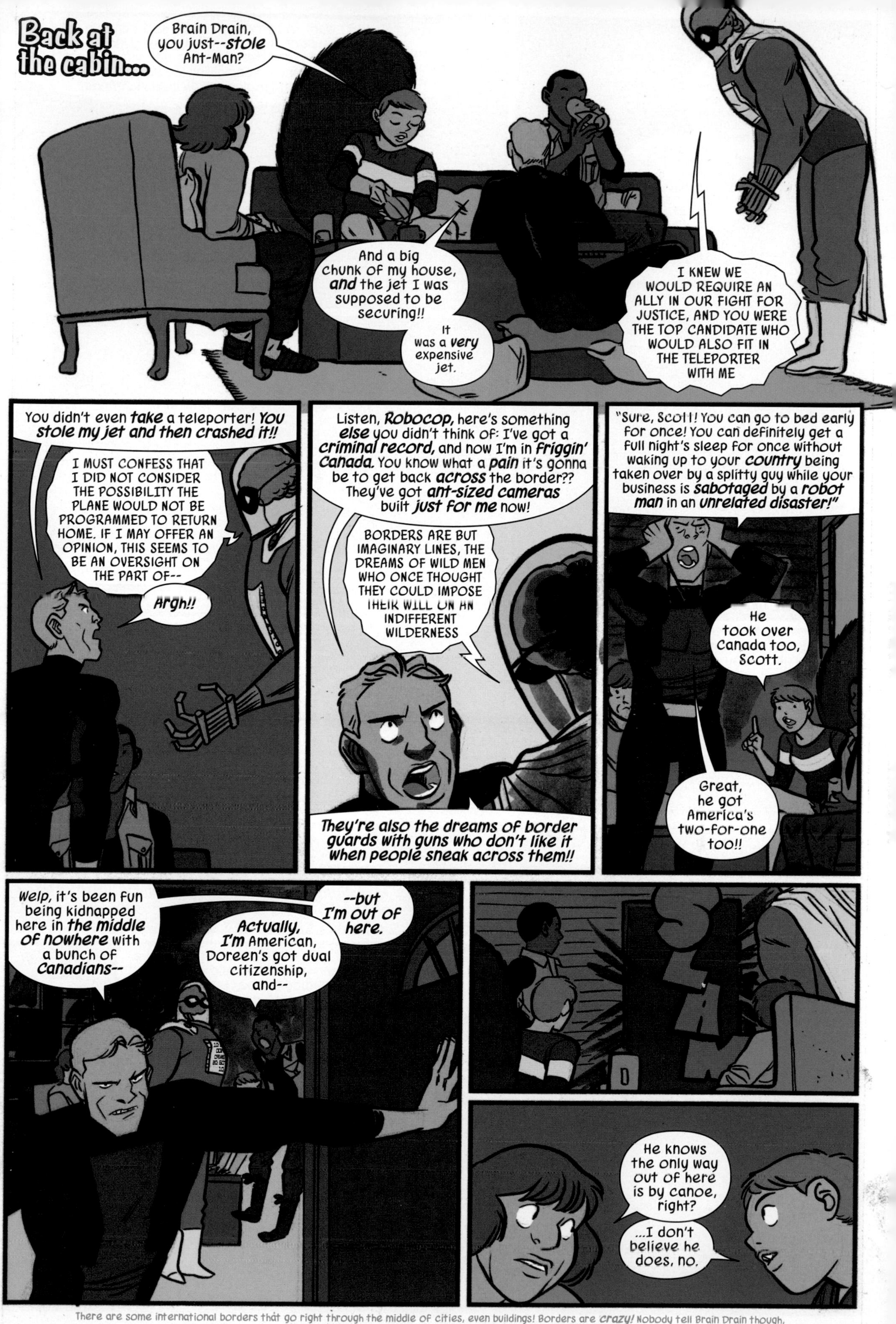
Back at the cabin...
Brain Drain, you just--stole Ant-Man?
And a big chunk of my house, and the jet I was supposed to be securing!!
It was a very expensive jet.
I KNEW WE WOULD REQUIRE AN ALLY IN OUR FIGHT FOR JUSTICE, AND YOU WERE THE TOP CANDIDATE WHO WOULD ALSO FIT IN THE TELEPORTER WITH ME
You didn't even take a teleporter! You stole my jet and then crashed it!!
I MUST CONFESS THAT I DID NOT CONSIDER THE POSSIBILITY THE PLANE WOULD NOT BE PROGRAMMED TO RETURN HOME. IF I MAY OFFER AN OPINION, THIS SEEMS TO BE AN OVERSIGHT ON THE PART OF--
Argh!!
Listen, Robocop, here's something else you didn't think of: I've got a criminal record, and now I'm in friggin' Canada. You know what a pain it's gonna be to get back across the border?? They've got ant-sized cameras built just for me now!
BORDERS ARE BUT IMAGINARY LINES, THE DREAMS OF WILD MEN WHO ONCE THOUGHT THEY COULD IMPOSE THEIR WILL ON AN INDIFFERENT WILDERNESS
They're also the dreams of border guards with guns who don't like it when people sneak across them!!
"Sure, Scott! You can go to bed early for once! You can definitely get a full night's sleep for once without waking up to your country being taken over by a splitty guy while your business is sabotaged by a robot man in an unrelated disaster!"
He took over Canada too, Scott.
Great, he got America's two-for-one too!!
Welp, it's been fun being kidnapped here in the middle of nowhere with a bunch of Canadians--
--but I'm out of here.
Actually, I'm American, Doreen's got dual citizenship, and--
He knows the only way out of here is by canoe, right?
...I don't believe he does, no.

There are some international borders that go right through the middle of cities, even buildings! Borders are *crazy!* Nobody tell Brain Drain though, it sounds like he's got enough opinions about them already.

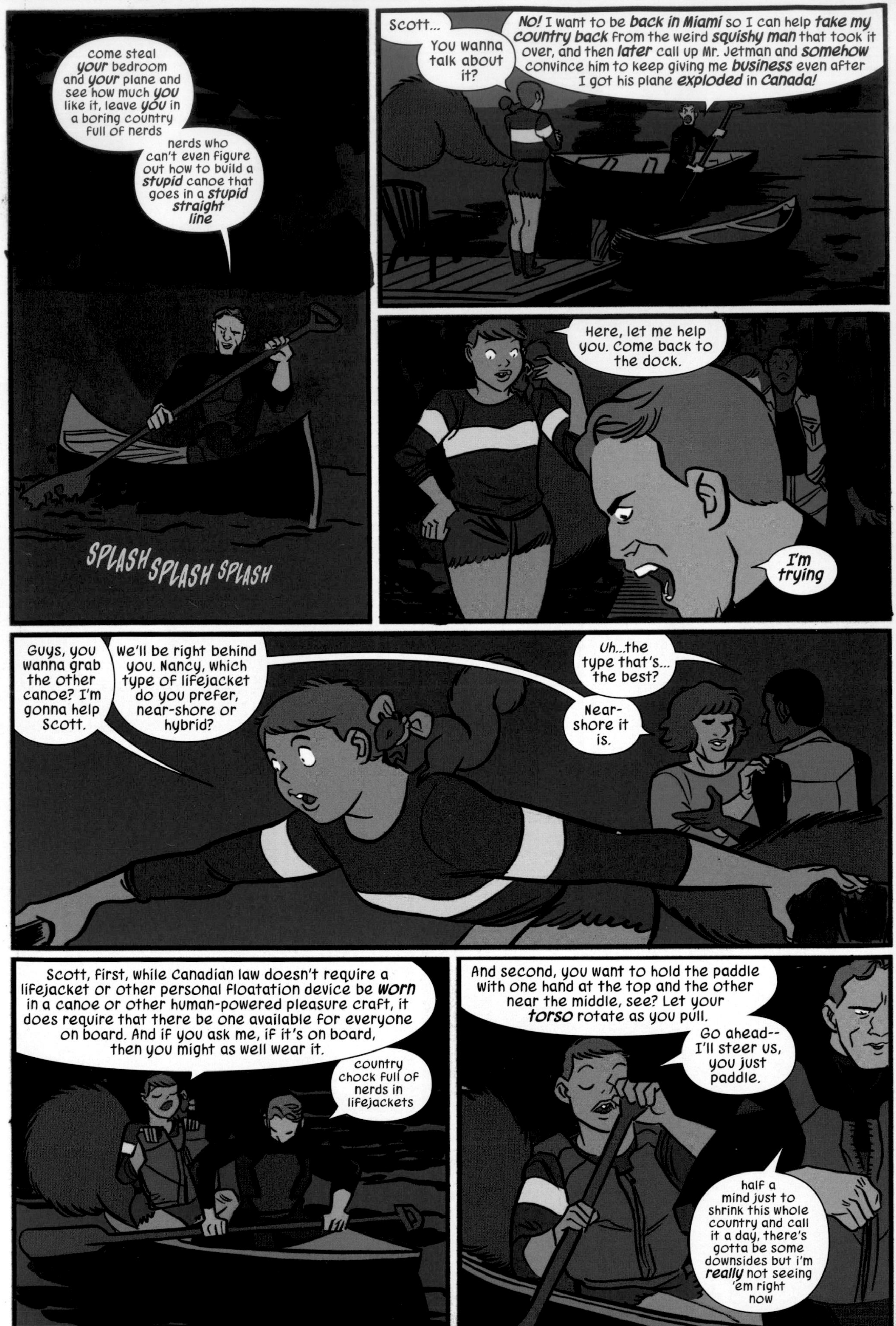
come steal your bedroom and your plane and see how much you like it, leave you in a boring country full of nerds
nerds who can't even figure out how to build a stupid canoe that goes in a stupid straight line
SPLASH SPLASH SPLASH
Scott...
You wanna talk about it?
NO! I want to be back in Miami so I can help take my country back from the weird squishy man that took it over, and then later call up Mr. Jetman and somehow convince him to keep giving me business even after I got his plane exploded in Canada!
Here, let me help you. Come back to the dock.
I'm trying
Guys, you wanna grab the other canoe? I'm gonna help Scott.
We'll be right behind you. Nancy, which type of lifejacket do you prefer, near-shore or hybrid?
Uh...the type that's... the best?
Near-shore it is.
Scott, first, while Canadian law doesn't require a lifejacket or other personal floatation device be worn in a canoe or other human-powered pleasure craft, it does require that there be one available for everyone on board. And if you ask me, if it's on board, then you might as well wear it.
country chock full of nerds in lifejackets
And second, you want to hold the paddle with one hand at the top and the other near the middle, see? Let your torso rotate as you pull.
Go ahead-- I'll steer us, you just paddle.
half a mind just to shrink this whole country and call it a day, there's gotta be some downsides but i'm really not seeing 'em right now

That Canadian human-powered pleasure craft law is legit. Also, yes, Canadian lawyers call canoes "human-powered pleasure craft," which should tell you all you need to know about Canadian lawyers.

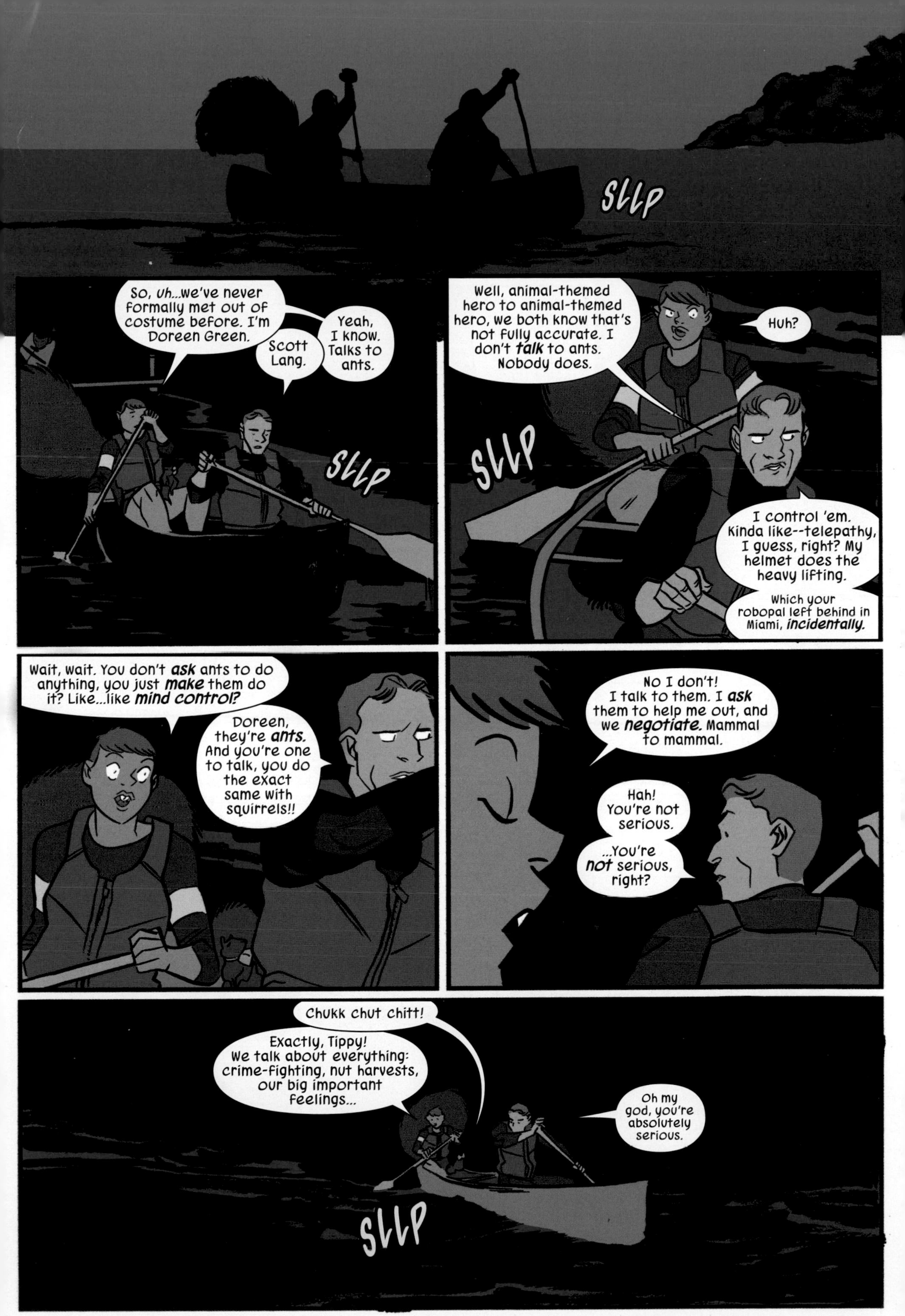
SLLP
So, uh...we've never formally met out of costume before. I'm Doreen Green.
Scott Lang.
Yeah, I know. Talks to ants.
SLLP
Well, animal-themed hero to animal-themed hero, we both know that's not fully accurate. I don't *talk* to ants. Nobody does.
Huh?
SLLP
I control 'em. Kinda like--telepathy, I guess, right? My helmet does the heavy lifting.
Which your robopal left behind in Miami, *incidentally.*
Wait, wait. You don't *ask* ants to do anything, you just *make* them do it? Like...like *mind control?*
Doreen, they're *ants.* And you're one to talk, you do the exact same with squirrels!!
No I don't! I talk to them. I *ask* them to help me out, and we *negotiate.* Mammal to mammal.
Hah! You're not serious.
...You're *not* serious, right?
Chukk chut chitt!
Exactly, Tippy! We talk about everything: crime-fighting, nut harvests, our big important feelings...
Oh my god, you're absolutely serious.
SLLP

When my dog cries I ask him about his big important feelings, and he never replies, possibly because it's ***really hard*** to say "your big important feelings" and still sound sincere.

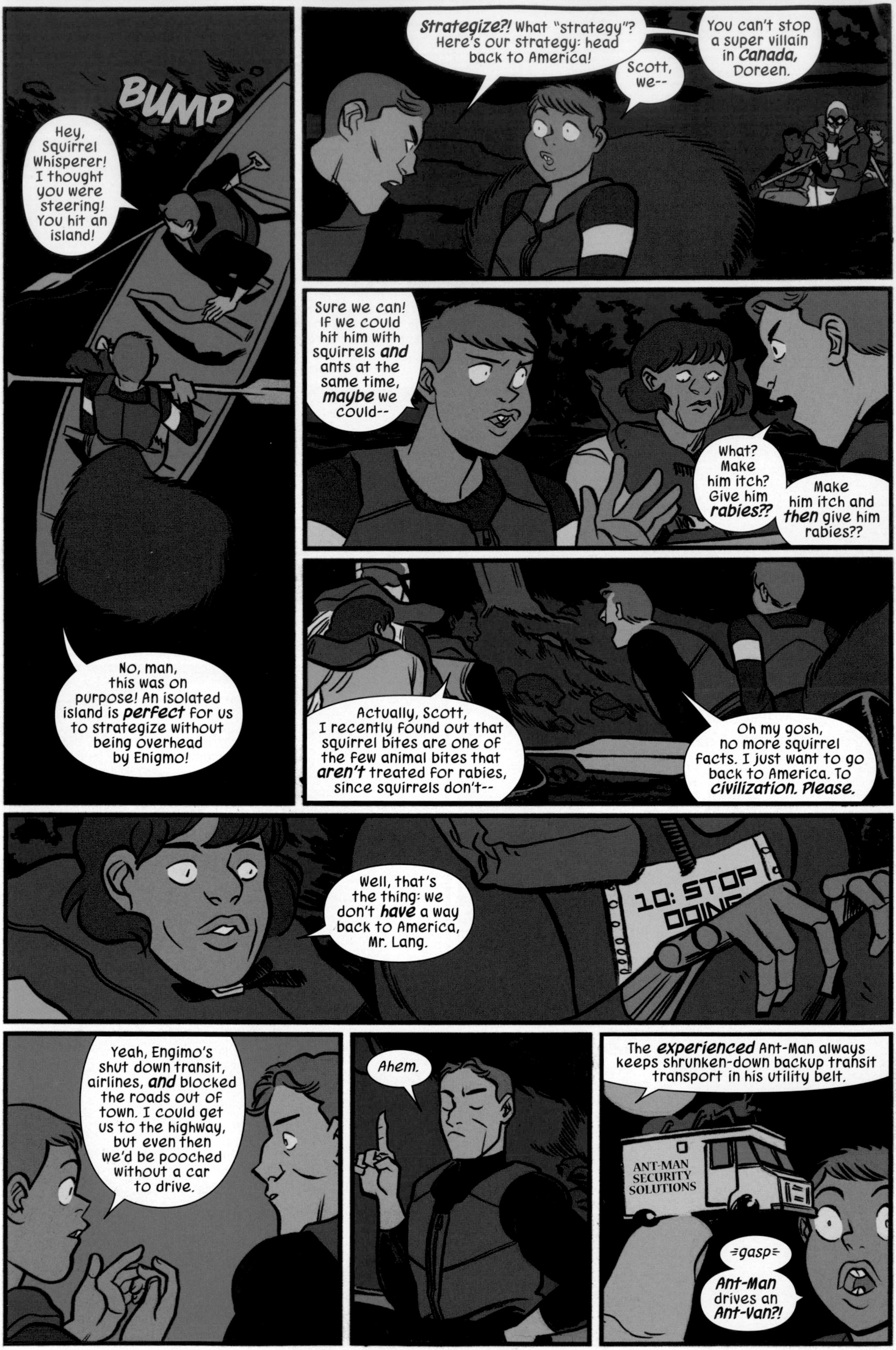
BUMP
Hey, Squirrel Whisperer! I thought you were steering! You hit an island!
No, man, this was on purpose! An isolated island is perfect for us to strategize without being overhead by Enigmo!
Strategize?! What "strategy"? Here's our strategy: head back to America!
Scott, we--
You can't stop a super villain in Canada, Doreen.
Sure we can! If we could hit him with squirrels and ants at the same time, maybe we could--
What? Make him itch? Give him rabies??
Make him itch and then give him rabies??
Actually, Scott, I recently found out that squirrel bites are one of the few animal bites that aren't treated for rabies, since squirrels don't--
Oh my gosh, no more squirrel facts. I just want to go back to America. To civilization. Please.
Well, that's the thing: we don't have a way back to America, Mr. Lang.
10: STOP DOING
Yeah, Engimo's shut down transit, airlines, and blocked the roads out of town. I could get us to the highway, but even then we'd be pooched without a car to drive.
Ahem.
The experienced Ant-Man always keeps shrunken-down backup transit transport in his utility belt.
ANT-MAN SECURITY SOLUTIONS
gasp
Ant-Man drives an Ant-Van?!

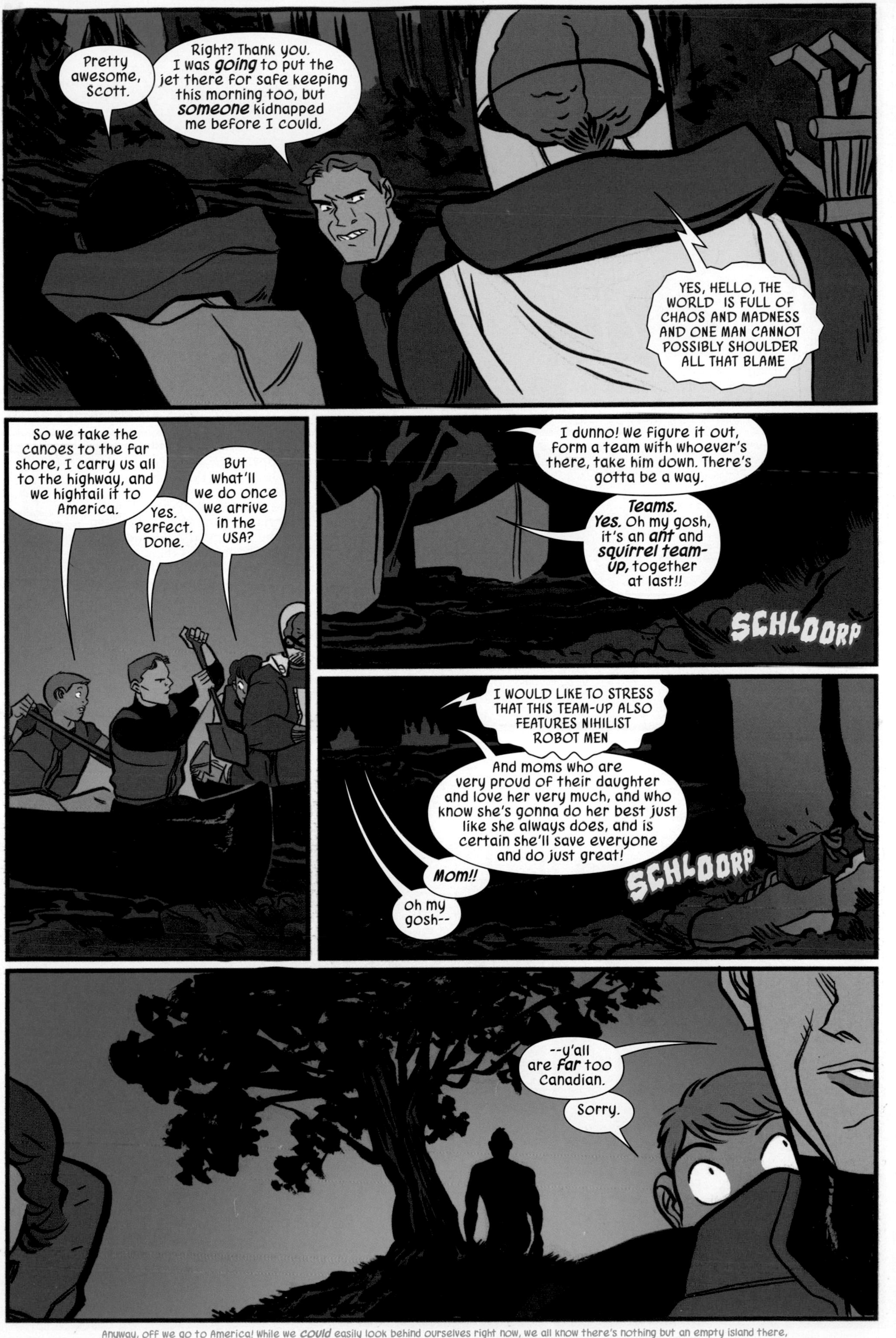
Pretty awesome, Scott.
Right? Thank you. I was going to put the jet there for safe keeping this morning too, but someone kidnapped me before I could.
YES, HELLO, THE WORLD IS FULL OF CHAOS AND MADNESS AND ONE MAN CANNOT POSSIBLY SHOULDER ALL THAT BLAME
So we take the canoes to the far shore, I carry us all to the highway, and we hightail it to America.
Yes. Perfect. Done.
But what'll we do once we arrive in the USA?
I dunno! We figure it out, form a team with whoever's there, take him down. There's gotta be a way.
Teams. Yes. Oh my gosh, it's an ant and squirrel team-up, together at last!!
SCHLOORP
I WOULD LIKE TO STRESS THAT THIS TEAM-UP ALSO FEATURES NIHILIST ROBOT MEN
And moms who are very proud of their daughter and love her very much, and who know she's gonna do her best just like she always does, and is certain she'll save everyone and do just great!
Mom!!
Oh my gosh--
SCHLOORP
--y'all are far too Canadian.
Sorry.

Anyway, off we go to America! While we *could* easily look behind ourselves right now, we all know there's nothing but an empty island there, so it's definitely not worth our time. Onward, friends!!

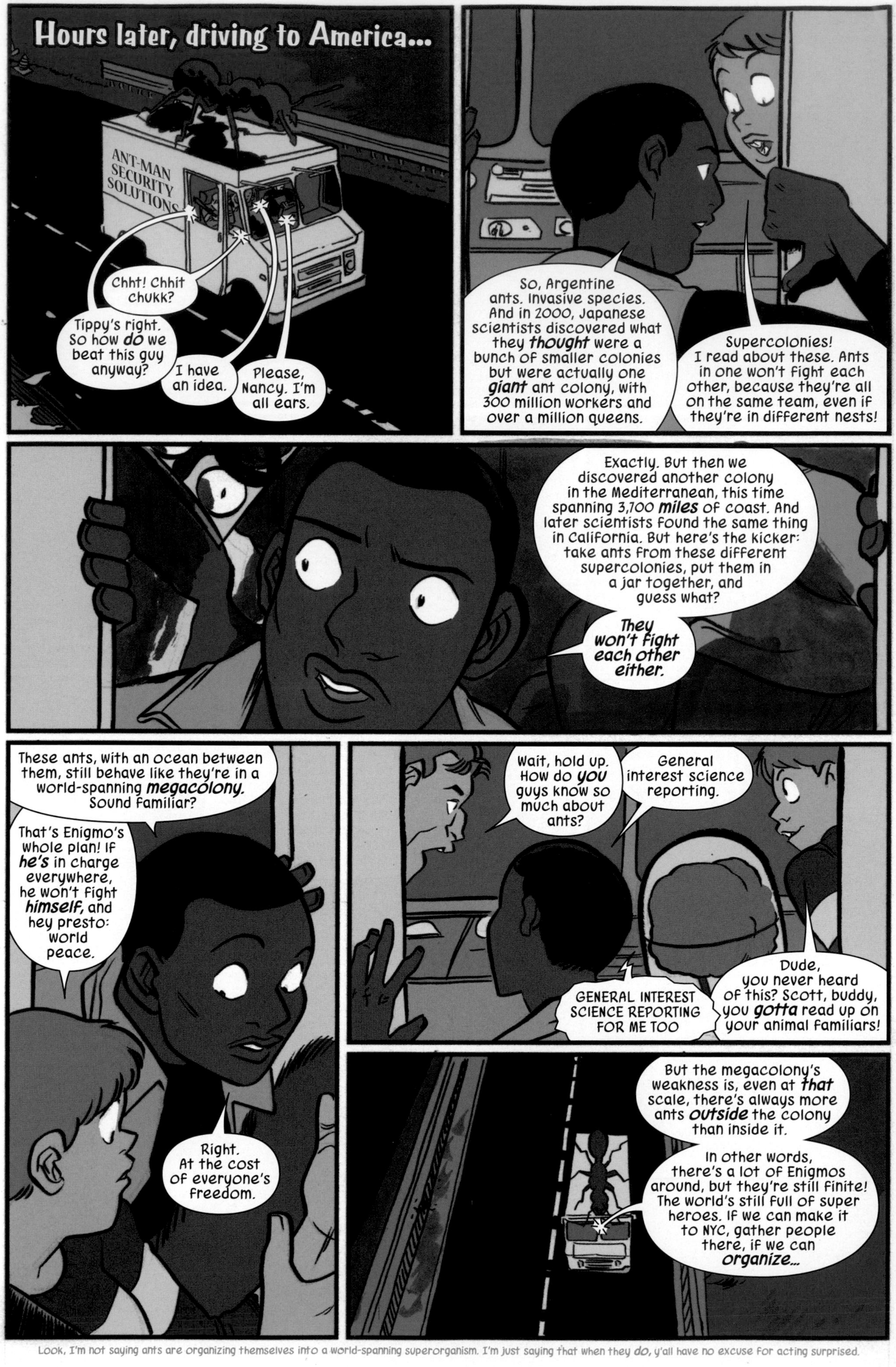
Hours later, driving to America...
ANT-MAN SECURITY SOLUTIONS
Chht! Chhit chukk?
Tippy's right. So how do we beat this guy anyway?
I have an idea.
Please, Nancy. I'm all ears.
So, Argentine ants. Invasive species. And in 2000, Japanese scientists discovered what they thought were a bunch of smaller colonies but were actually one giant ant colony, with 300 million workers and over a million queens.
Supercolonies! I read about these. Ants in one won't fight each other, because they're all on the same team, even if they're in different nests!
Exactly. But then we discovered another colony in the Mediterranean, this time spanning 3,700 miles of coast. And later scientists found the same thing in California. But here's the kicker: take ants from these different supercolonies, put them in a jar together, and guess what?
They won't fight each other either.
These ants, with an ocean between them, still behave like they're in a world-spanning megacolony. Sound familiar?
That's Enigmo's whole plan! If he's in charge everywhere, he won't fight himself, and hey presto: world peace.
Right. At the cost of everyone's freedom.
Wait, hold up. How do you guys know so much about ants?
General interest science reporting.
GENERAL INTEREST SCIENCE REPORTING FOR ME TOO
Dude, you never heard of this? Scott, buddy, you gotta read up on your animal familiars!
But the megacolony's weakness is, even at that scale, there's always more ants outside the colony than inside it.
In other words, there's a lot of Enigmos around, but they're still finite! The world's still full of super heroes. If we can make it to NYC, gather people there, if we can organize...

Look, I'm not saying ants are organizing themselves into a world-spanning superorganism. I'm just saying that when they *do*, y'all have no excuse for acting surprised.

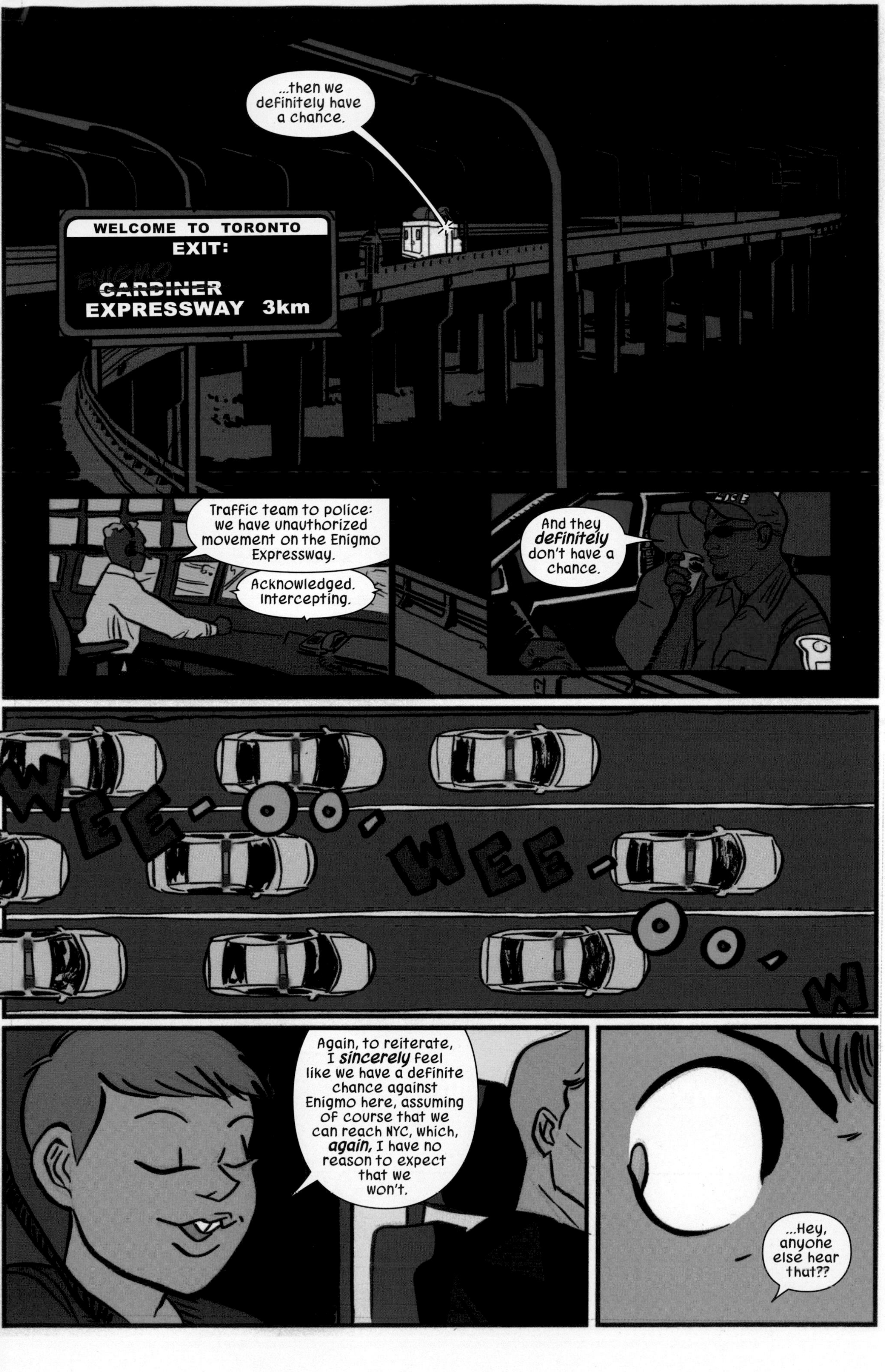

...then we definitely have a chance.
WELCOME TO TORONTO
EXIT:
ENIGMO
GARDINER
EXPRESSWAY 3km
Traffic team to police: we have unauthorized movement on the Enigmo Expressway.
Acknowledged. Intercepting.
And they *definitely* don't have a chance.
WEE-OO-WEE-OO-W
Again, to reiterate, I *sincerely* feel like we have a definite chance against Enigmo here, assuming of course that we can reach NYC, which, *again,* I have no reason to expect that we won't.
...Hey, anyone else hear that??

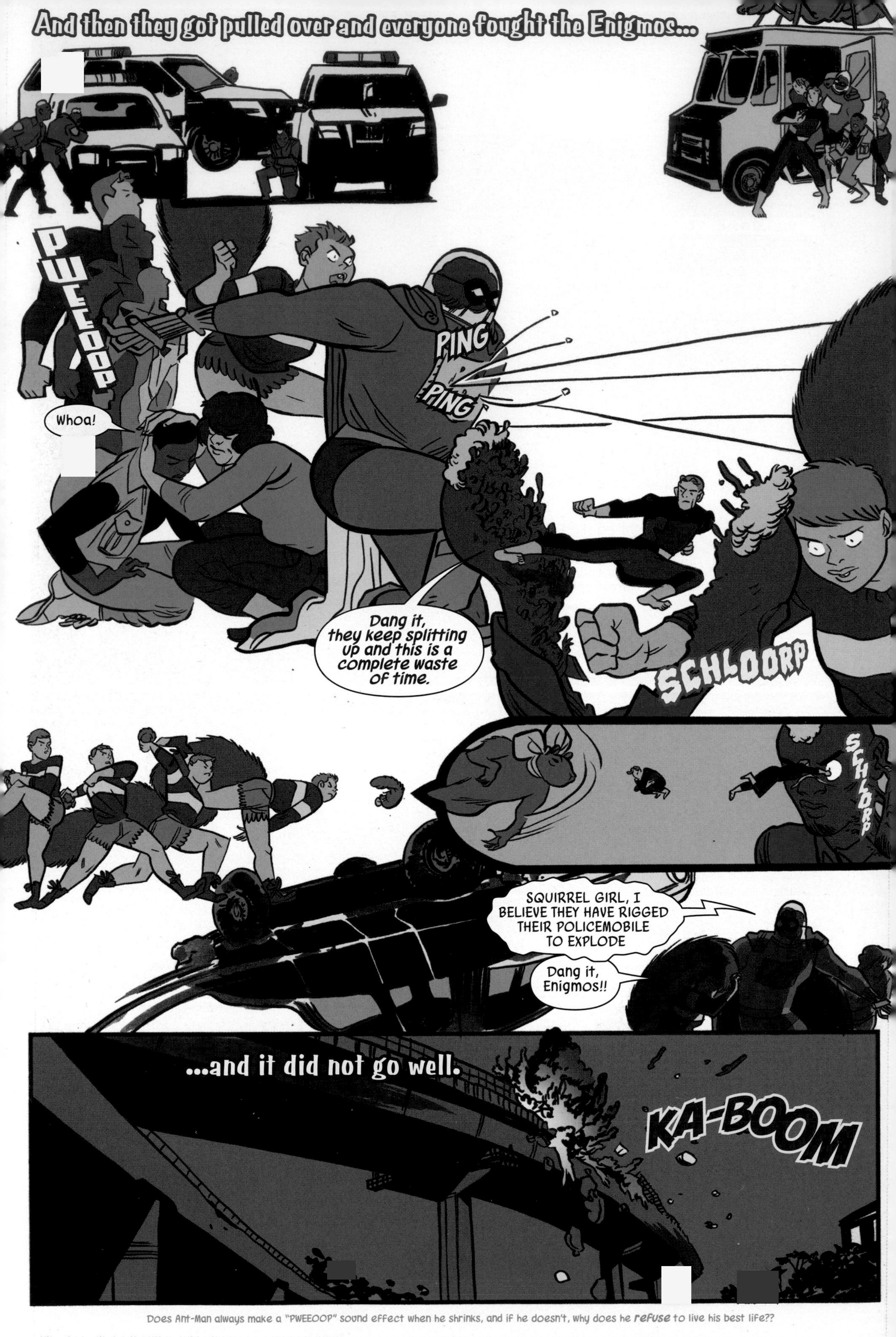

And then they got pulled over and everyone fought the Enigmos...
PWEEOOP
PING
PING
Whoa!
Dang it, they keep splitting up and this is a complete waste of time.
SCHLOORP
SCHLORP
SQUIRREL GIRL, I BELIEVE THEY HAVE RIGGED THEIR POLICEMOBILE TO EXPLODE
Dang it, Enigmos!!
...and it did not go well.
KA-BOOM

Does Ant-Man always make a "PWEEOOP" sound effect when he shrinks, and if he doesn't, why does he *refuse* to live his best life??

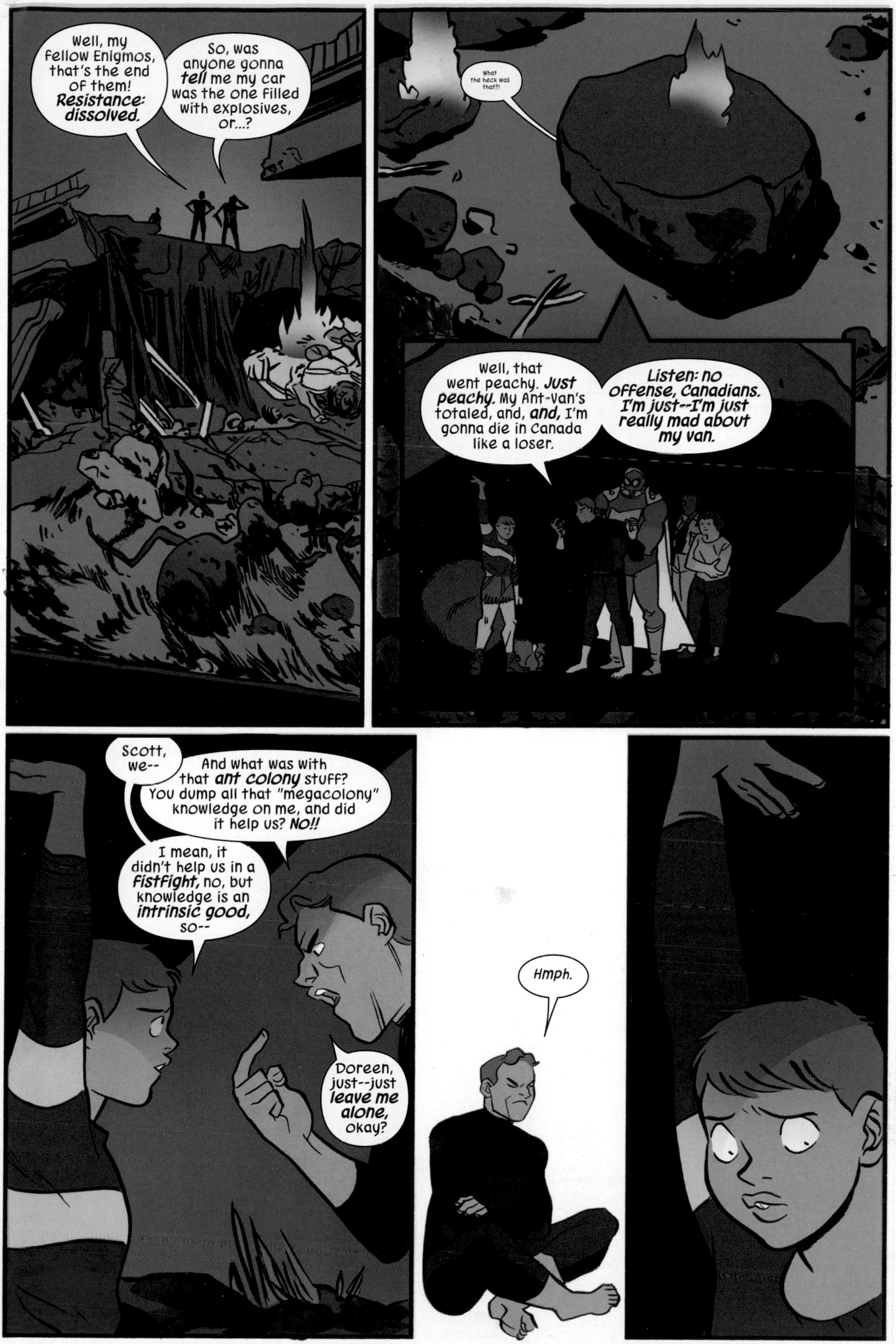
Well, my Fellow Enigmos, that's the end of them! Resistance: dissolved.
So, was anyone gonna tell me my car was the one filled with explosives, or...?
What the heck was that?!
Well, that went peachy. Just peachy. My Ant-Van's totaled, and, and, I'm gonna die in Canada like a loser.
Listen: no offense, Canadians. I'm just--I'm just really mad about my van.
Scott, we--
And what was with that ant colony stuff? You dump all that "megacolony" knowledge on me, and did it help us? NO!!
I mean, it didn't help us in a fistfight, no, but knowledge is an intrinsic good, so--
Doreen, just--just leave me alone, okay?
Hmph.

Here Lies Ant-Van, 1975-2016. Beloved Friend of the Kra-Van, the Stilt-Van, and the Iron Van. She Will Be Missed.

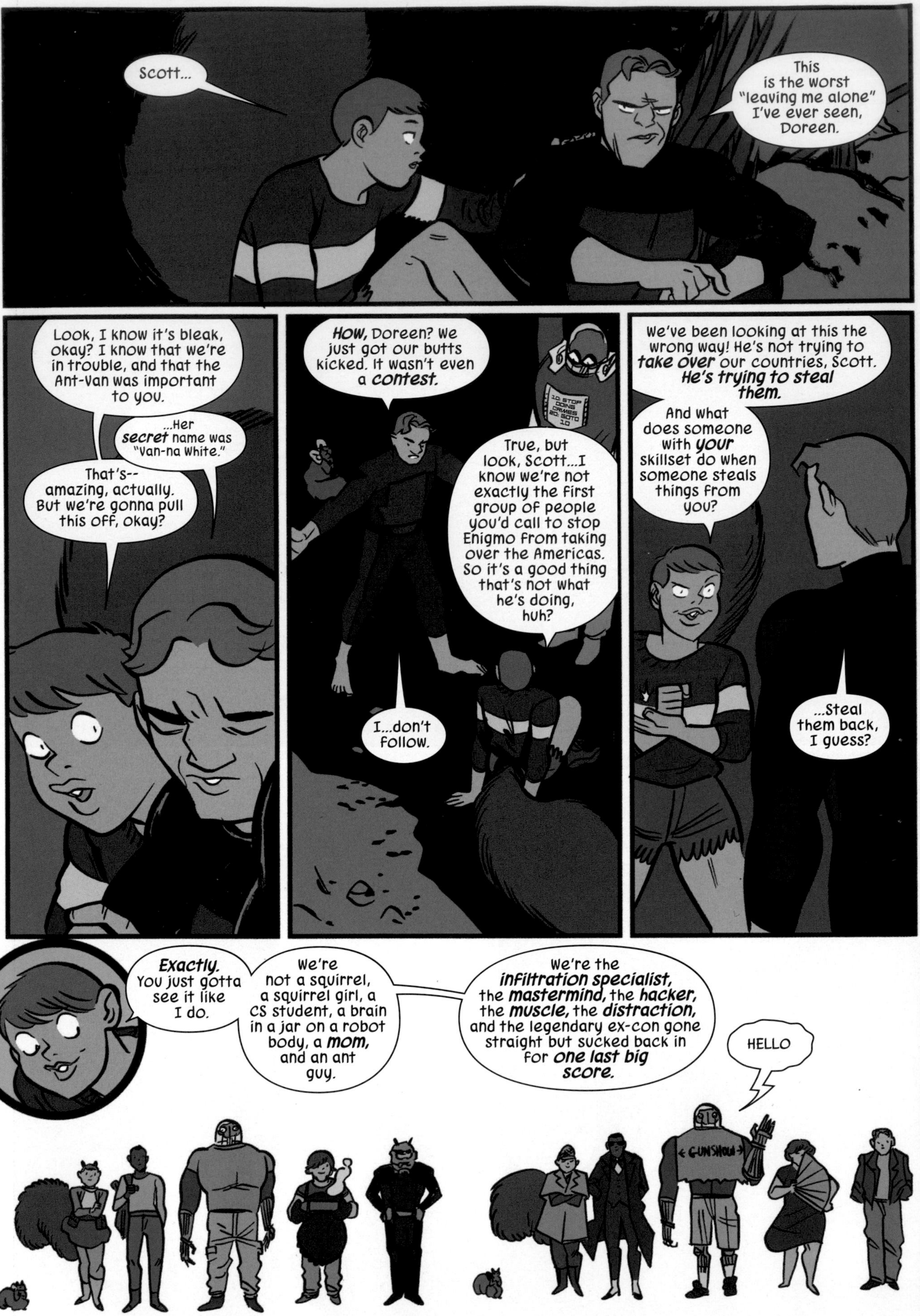
Scott...
This is the worst "leaving me alone" I've ever seen, Doreen.
Look, I know it's bleak, okay? I know that we're in trouble, and that the Ant-Van was important to you.
...Her *secret* name was "Van-na White."
That's--amazing, actually. But we're gonna pull this off, okay?
How, Doreen? We just got our butts kicked. It wasn't even a *contest.*
10. STOP DOING CRIMES 20. GOTO 10
True, but look, Scott...I know we're not exactly the first group of people you'd call to stop Enigmo from taking over the Americas. So it's a good thing that's not what he's doing, huh?
I...don't follow.
We've been looking at this the wrong way! He's not trying to *take over* our countries, Scott. *He's trying to steal them.*
And what does someone with *your* skillset do when someone steals things from you?
...Steal them back, I guess?
Exactly. You just gotta see it like I do.
We're not a squirrel, a squirrel girl, a CS student, a brain in a jar on a robot body, a *mom,* and an ant guy.
We're the *infiltration specialist,* the *mastermind,* the *hacker,* the *muscle,* the *distraction,* and the legendary ex-con gone straight but sucked back in for *one last big score.*
HELLO
GUNSHOW

See?? All we're missing is the One Twitchy Person Who Says They're Fine To Pull Off A Heist, But You Just Know They're So Not Fine To Pull Off A Heist, and we'll be *set!*

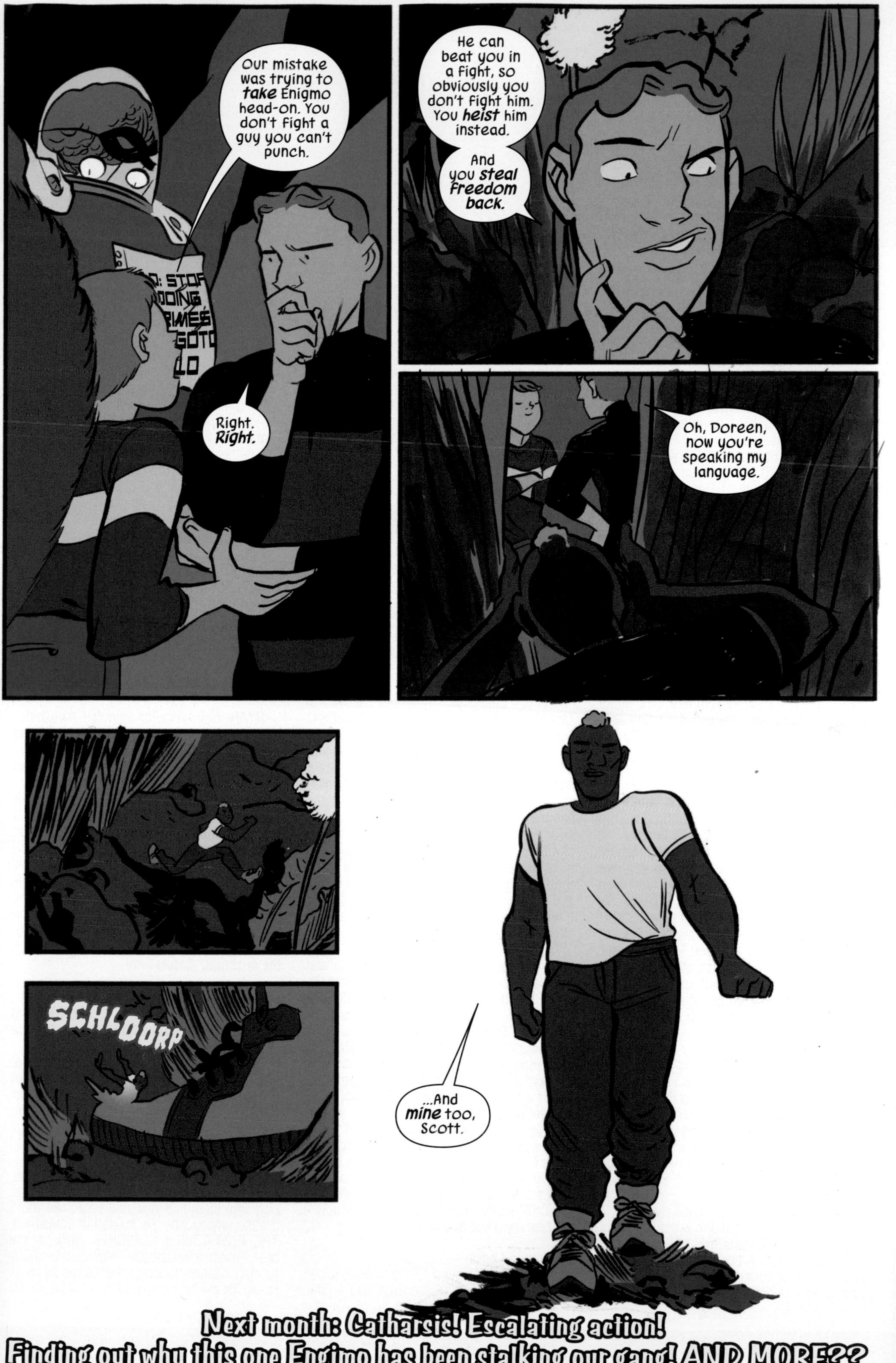
Our mistake was trying to take Enigmo head-on. You don't fight a guy you can't punch.
Right. Right.
He can beat you in a fight, so obviously you don't fight him. You heist him instead.
And you steal freedom back.
Oh, Doreen, now you're speaking my language.
SCHLOORP
...And mine too, Scott.

Next month: Catharsis! Escalating action!
Finding out why this one Engimo has been stalking our gang! AND MORE??

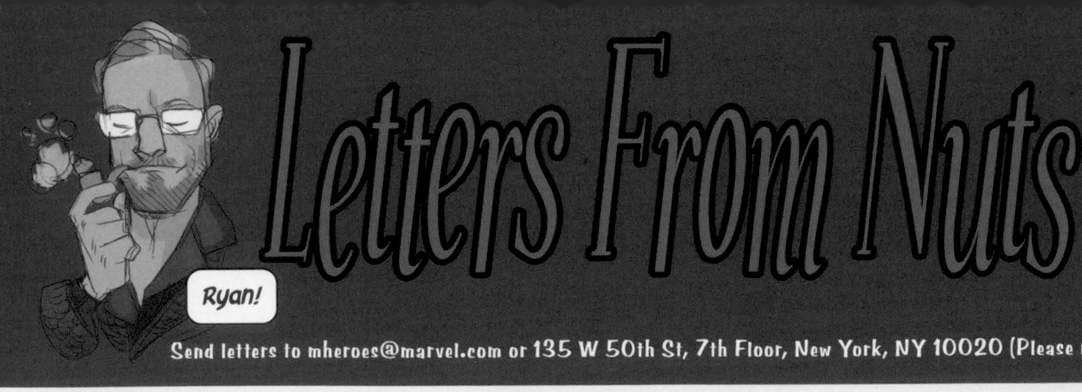
Ryan!

Letters From Nuts

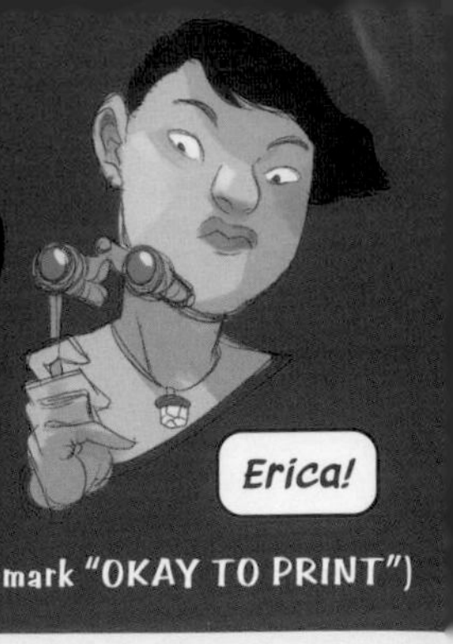
Erica!

Send letters to mheroes@marvel.com or 135 W 50th St, 7th Floor, New York, NY 10020 (Please mark "OKAY TO PRINT")

Dear Squirrel Girl Crew,

Issue 11 was a triumph. I loved the numerical puzzles and the scene with Doreen caught in a final exam nightmare really hit home. I have a variation of her dream from time to time. There's a class I haven't attended and need to drop to avoid a failing grade. Trouble is, I can never find the building I need to go to in order to drop the class (and Nightmare is probably cursing himself for not adding that Kafkaesque touch for Squirrel Girl).

There was a little note on fan fiction. I just did a bit of that, if you are interested. In my previous letter, I said I'd like to see Squirrel Girl take on the White Rabbit. Via Amazon, I was able to buy the Rabbit's first appearance, Marvel Team Up 131. I did a customer review there, imagining the White Rabbit asking Marvel editors about the state of her career (she was not happy).

Sincerely,
Robert Fisher

RYAN: I saw a lot of people saying "HEY, I HAD THAT RECURRING DREAM TOO!" not realizing that it's pretty common. It's really common, turns out! Though not being able to find the building is a good twist. I'd tell dream-you to try doing it on your phone, I guess?

I am BIG INTO this fan fiction, and also, I am BIG INTO nobody correcting me on the error in #11! Thank you all for that. In case you missed it, there was a point where Doreen said that by using binary you can count to 1031 on both hands. If you tried it, you'll see this is incorrect: you actually only get to 1023! I'm not even gonna blame Doreen for this one: it was my fault! I just typed in the wrong number. But I wanted to mention it here, in case anyone got into "who can count the highest on their hands" competitions and then got stuck because of my mistake. Let this error happen... NO LONGER!!

ERICA: I've never dropped a class, so the version of the dream that I have is that I realize by mid term or finals that there's a class I never attended and I need to get there to try to make a last ditch effort to pass it but I don't know where it is or how to find the office that could help me (by this point the school has become a labyrinth).

Dear Unbeatable Squirrel-friends,

I AM SO HAPPY! Both the writing and art in this book just brightens my day every time it shows up in my pull-box! The writing is clever and these little human moments give me life. And Erica's designs and panel composition match perfectly to really make SG Stand out from the other hero books out there!

I was so excited to meet Ryan at Zdarscon this year too, hopefully next time Erica is in Toronto I get to gush to her too!

Squirrel girl is a fun, totally rad character and thanks to you guys she keeps showing up in more places! Every time I show her to my friends they fall in love.

I hope she joins in on the fun for Monsters Unleashed! The whole concept seems to be made just for her!

Yes we Pecan,
Jakob Withakay

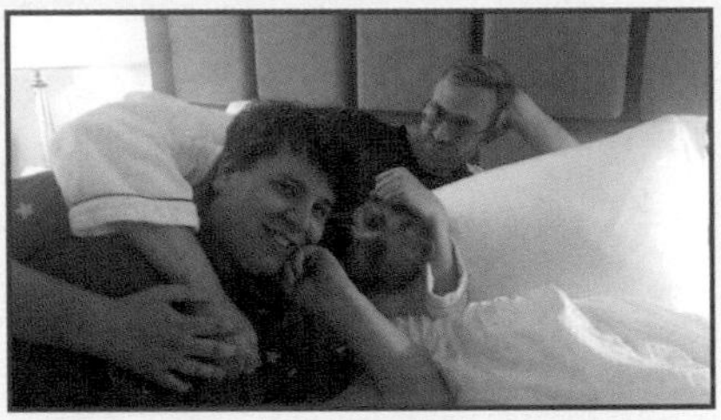

RYAN: Haha, so, I feel like "Chip Zdarsky Presents: Zdarscon" (pictured above in Jakob's photo) needs some explanation? But then I also feel like it works just as well if you have no idea what's going on! So, BASICALLY Chip (the same Chip from HOWARD THE DUCK! We did a crossover once! What a guy!) rented a hotel room and had his own mini convention in Toronto, and he invited me and a bunch of other friends to come greet fans and readers! He wore a bathrobe all day because it's his hotel room and who is gonna tell him what to do, and I wore my Star Trek pajamas because I will take any excuse to wear my Star Trek pajamas (Engineering division).

ERICA: SO. The last time I saw Ryan was the day after the Eisner award ceremony (WHERE WE WERE UP FOR TWO EISNERS *COUGH*). We were getting lunch and he tells me about these Star Trek pajamas and asks if he should buy them. I probably said something along the lines of "It's your money" and warned him that most pajamas aren't made for men who are 6'6". ANYWAY my point is that the moment they started posting photos from Zdarscon all I could think was "oh my god he did it. How do those fit on him?" That is Erica's story from home, 1 hour away (by plane) from Zdarscon. My fiance did ask if I wanted to go to Zdarscon but CHIP NEVER ASKED ME TO. I see how it is, Zdarsky. I see how it is.

Hi Ryan and Erica,

I just finished issue 11 – hilarious as usual! At first I was sorry to see Erica had a fill-in artist, but was blown away by Jacob's work. Any time you need a vacation Erica, please request Jacob to step in again. (Or was it even a vacation? I have a sneaking suspicion someone was working on what is sure to be my new favorite original graphic novel. Wink, wink!)

So, I had to write in and share a squirrel sighting with you all. I was hiking with a buddy on Assateague Island off of Virginia's Eastern Shore and was proselytizing about USG and how he needed to read it. Lo and behold, we crossed paths with the Delmarva Fox Squirrel. I wish I had gotten a pic, but alas I did not. I don't think a photo would have done the animal justice though. In pictures it looks like a lighter-colored grey squirrel, but in person, it really does look like a fox except it moves in the herky-jerky way that squirrels do. And it was quite a bit bigger than a grey squirrel to boot!

Keep up the great work. Looking forward to Unbeatable Squirrel Girl Beats Up the Marvel Universe! Cheers,

Charles Albert
Richmond, VA

RYAN: Delmarva Fox Squirrel! Awesome. You probably know this, but for everyone else: DID YOU KNOW that the Delmarva Fox Squirrel used to be on the endangered species list? But they're off it now! We got them off the list by not destroying their habitat quite as much (always a good idea if you want to help), and by reintroducing them to new areas that we thought they'd do well in. They were added to the list in 1967 and they were taken off the list just a few months ago, in November 2015! Another neat thing about these squirrels is they don't hop from tree to tree, but rather climb down one tree, travel across the ground, and then climb up the next one. Safety first!

ERICA: Jacob is great. I'm so glad that I was able to get him. I had A WEEKEND to find a fill-in. Yeah, that month was basically the opposite of a vacation.

Squirrels I hope to see in real life: Malabar Giant Squirrel, Japanese Dwarf Flying Squirrel, Jill the famous instagram squirrel, Theo the also famous instagram squirrel.

Dear Ryan & Erica,

I used to collect comics when I was younger, but I stopped about ten years ago. I've gotten back into them this year, and series like yours are the reason why. As far as I'm concerned, THE UNBEATABLE SQUIRREL GIRL is the best, most consistently high-quality book being published right now. I would go so far as to say it's the best comic of the last decade (at least)! Given how good it is, I couldn't keep it to myself. I've gotten my boyfriend into comics too, and Squirrel Girl is his absolute favorite.

Much love and admiration,
Eric (and Trevor)

P.S. Is there any chance that Doreen's old teammates from the GLA will ever show up for an issue? Also, I hope we haven't seen the last of that Sentinel Doreen dated!

RYAN: Eric, Trevor: thank you for these super kind words! I'm really glad you and your boyfriend like our talking squirrel comics. Hooray! As for the GLA – there's a new GREAT LAKES AVENGERS comic coming out soon! It's written by your friend and mine Zac Gorman, with art by Will Robson. It looks REALLY GREAT. As for the Sentinel, I think about him often and hope he's doing well.

ERICA: I think Doreen would say that they weren't dating, they just went on one date.

Dear Ryan and Erica,

I enjoyed the binary nightmare, but one topic strikes me, Doreen's diet doesn't seem to have a hazelnut in every bite. What is this falafel fascination? Are Doreen and Nancy fixated on grass? Or don't they know how to cook beans-on-toast or Marmite spaghetti like normal students? They will get rickets!

Isn't there a Spidey Student Survival book with Aunt May's wheatcake recipe? Or does Katie Morag need to spill the beans on how to make a poridggy? We need a sign on how Squirrel Girl gets her five day, if she is going to remain a beacon of clean living.

Now that Doreen has taught the world to count, she needs to teach the world to cook, or buy it a Coke, which ever is easier.

Yours sincerely,

Simon Rogers,
United Kingdom

PS Surely Mr and Mrs Nefaria were Count and Countess Nefaria, unless the current Count bought the title from one of those companies that sell plots of land on the Moon or surface of the Sun?

RYAN: Simon, I would not put it past the Count to get suckered by one of those scams. As for Doreen's diet, I would actually really like to know Aunt May's wheatcake recipe. There WAS a Marvel cookbook years ago (called "Stan Lee Presents: The Mighty Marvel Superheroes' Cookbook," because of course it was) but it was published in 1977 and includes recipes like "Spidey's Chocolate Web Pancakes" which tells you to "prepare pancakes according to the instructions on the package," put them in a stack, and then "form a web by criss-crossing lines with liquid chocolate syrup across the top." There's also a recipe for "easy raisin bread" that is just "take pre-sliced bread, push raisins into bread." In conclusion, I hope you enjoyed these two delicious recipes.

ERICA: I'm not going to lie, I don't know what y'all are talking about because I have been so busy that I never got around to reading issue 11! I still don't know how to use my fingers to count in binary! I'm just going to talk generally about food then. As a vegetarian, Doreen would have to be fairly conscious of her diet since her lifestyle more or less requires her to eat like a mini Dwayne "The Rock" Johnson but without depleting the oceans of cod. In this case falafel isn't a bad choice since beans and legumes are an excellent source of protein, something you're going to need if you're lifting cars on a regular basis. Nuts are also a great source of healthy fat and bursts of energy. Fun fact: Squirrels can't eat just nuts because they'll get too fat. They crave nuts because getting fat is good for the winter but they also need fungi, greens, fruits and insects. That's right! Squirrels are omnivores! They'll also eat snakes, other rodents and birds. So Doreen's vegetarianism is less about being like a squirrel and more about realizing that animals are sentient. I don't think that answered any questions you might have had but it's been so long I don't remember what they might have been.

Dear Ryan and Erica,

On Sept. 3, 2016, Squirrel Girl taught me how to count to 31 on one hand. Coincidentally, Sept. 3, 2016, was my 31st birthday. So, now, I am this many. Thanks Doreen.

Mike LaRowe (a.k.a. the Semi-Beatable Man Boy) in Grand Rapids (a.k.a. Beer City USA (for real))

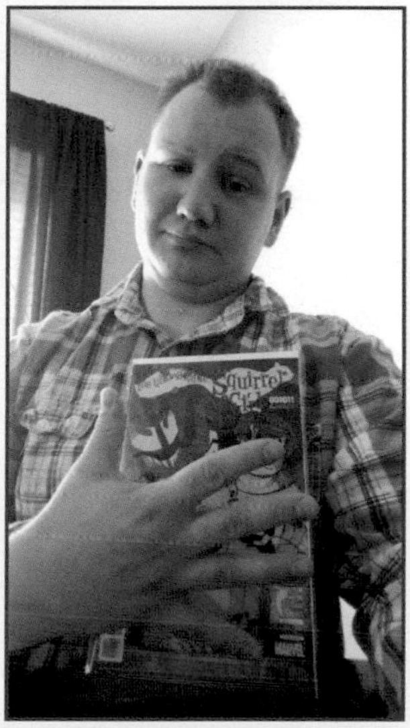

RYAN: HAPPY BELATED BIRTHDAY, MIKE!! If we meet I'll give you a high five, or rather… a high thirty-one?

Dear Squirrely Duo,

I loved the Computer Science themed issue. Doreen knows the Powers of Two!

More CS fun:

```
if (you dare to pick a fight with Doctor Octopus) {
    you have sealed your fate
    for (i do not forgive) {
        i do not give up on revenge
    }
}
```

Since the 'for' loop has no exit condition, it will run forever: "I do not give up..."

You left that as an easter egg for us, didn't you? Admit it!

I used to have the exam nightmare. But once, it was --math--. Looking at the first question, I could see what it was driving at. Even though I hadn't taken the course, I was able to derive the answer from what I already knew. Same with the second question. It was like being invited to explore a new mathematical domain, step by step. It felt wonderful! I turned in my paper knowing I had aced the test.

I haven't had that nightmare since.

Beat up the Marvel Universe? I'm only following two Marvel titles at the moment.

I'd like to see the Unbeatable Squirrel Girl kick back with the Unbelievable Gwenpool over pizza and sodas.

Very mostly yours,
John Prenis

RYAN: Man that sounds like THE MOST SATISFYING NIGHTMARE EVER IN TIME. I love it. I used to have Doreen's nightmare too, but I solved it like she did – talking to the Dean – and I haven't really had it since. But I barely EVER remember my dreams or nightmares, so it's actually kinda nice to have a nightmare and wake up, because then at least I get to remember my dreams!

I have friends who have dreams that tell actual STORIES, and then when they wake up they can lift their dreams for stories they're working on, and I'm really jealous. They're literally getting work done in their sleep! MUST BE NICE.

ERICA: For a while I had episodic continuing dreams about having to stop an apocalyptic cult. Maybe we can use that? That sounds like our sort of thing. Marvel HAS A DUDE NAMED APOCALYPSE.

Next Issue:

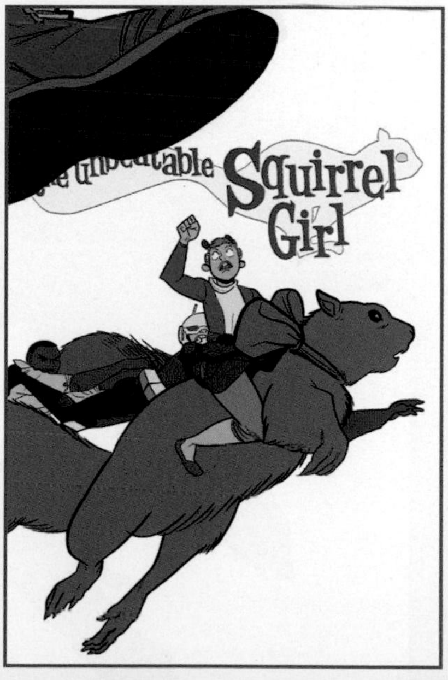
Unbeatable
Squirrel Girl

Attention, Squirrel Scouts! Make sure to check out our production blog, **unbeatablesquirrelgirl.tumblr.com**, where we post behind-the-scenes stuff on how the book gets made, along with all sorts of cool things *you* make: fanart, cosplay, whatever!

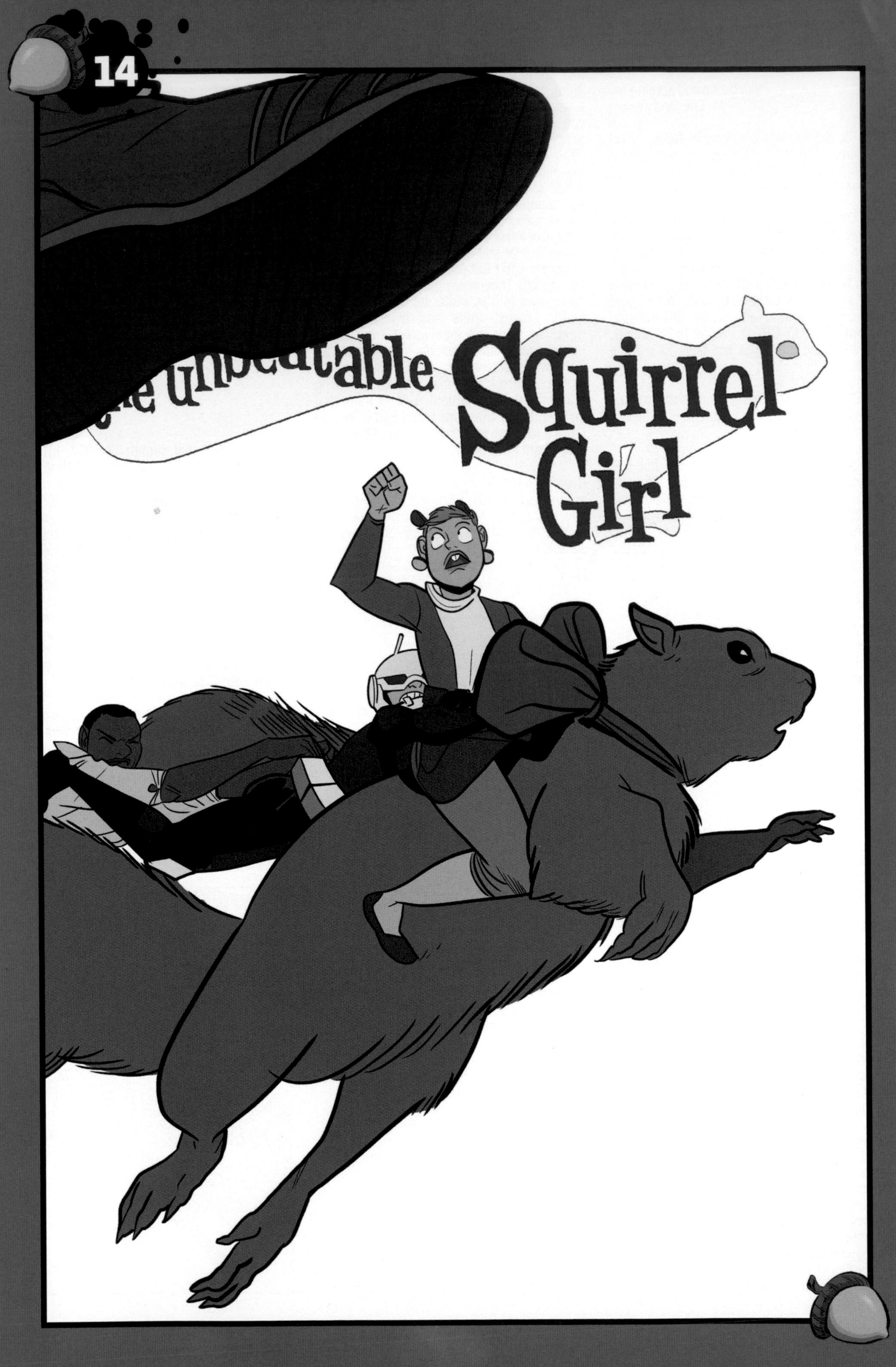
14
unbeatable Squirrel Girl

Doreen Green isn't just a second-year computer science student: she secretly also has all the powers of both squirrel and girl! She uses her amazing abilities to fight crime ***and*** *be as awesome as possible. You know her as...****The Unbeatable Squirrel Girl!*** *Find out what she's been up to, with...*

Squirrel Girl *in a nutshell*

Squirrel Girl @unbeatablesg
Hey everyone guess who's back from her vacation in Northern Canada where she couldn't get a cell signal?

Squirrel Girl @unbeatablesg
And now she's in SOUTHERN Canada where she can easily get a cell signal, only this dude named Enigmo has taken over??

Squirrel Girl @unbeatablesg
And so now she's gotta deal with THAT baloney RIGHT AWAY even though she never got more than a few pages into Lake Enthusiast Magazine???

Squirrel Girl @unbeatablesg
Anyway yeah it's me. HELLO ENIGMO YOU SHUT DOWN SMS MESSAGING BUT WE CAN STILL HANG OUT HERE ON SOCIAL MEDIA

Squirrel Girl @unbeatablesg
anyway send me your freshest anti-Enigmo memes, as far as we know that could be his only weakness so it's good to be prepared I guess

Egg @imduderadtude
@unbeatablesg omg ive waited my whole life for this moment

Tony Stark @starkmantony
@unbeatablesg Good to have you back. We, uh, haven't had much luck defeating this guy in NYC. He splits apart into other guys.

Squirrel Girl @unbeatablesg
@starkmantony Not a problem, Tony!! I once beat a guy made of a bunch of bees who could split apart into regular bees! NO BIG DEAL.

Tony Stark @starkmantony
@unbeatablesg I can use this. What'd you do?

Squirrel Girl @unbeatablesg
@starkmantony Oh, bees can't fly when they're wet so I got him wet and then took bags of wet bees to the police. ANOTHER CRIME WELL FOUGHT

Tony Stark @starkmantony
@unbeatablesg This...helps me precisely 0%.

Squirrel Girl @unbeatablesg
@starkmantony I'm on it, dude!! Me and Ant-Man came up with a plan to save everything! I can't tell you it publicly but let me just say

Squirrel Girl @unbeatablesg
@starkmantony WE ARE GONNA HEIST FREEDOM BACK

Squirrel Girl @unbeatablesg
@starkmantony ME and TIPPY and ANT-MAN and BRAIN DRAIN and MY MOM and MY GOOD FRIEND are gonna HEIST FREEDOM BACK

Squirrel Girl @unbeatablesg
@starkmantony AND IT'S DEFINITELY GONNA WORK

Squirrel Girl @unbeatablesg
@starkmantony AND WE'RE GONNA GO DO IT RIGHT NOW SO WHEN YOU NEXT HEAR FROM ME IT'LL BE ME SAYING "GLAD MY PLAN WENT PERFECTLY, LOL"

Squirrel Girl @unbeatablesg
@starkmantony I'm not sure if I'll say "lol" or not yet though

Tony Stark @starkmantony
@unbeatablesg Yeah you always gotta play that by ear lol

Squirrel Girl @unbeatablesg
@starkmantony Tony

Squirrel Girl @unbeatablesg
@starkmantony It's weird when you do it

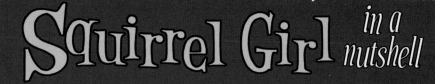

search!

#toronto

#cityhall

#heistmusic

#parentalleave

#physics

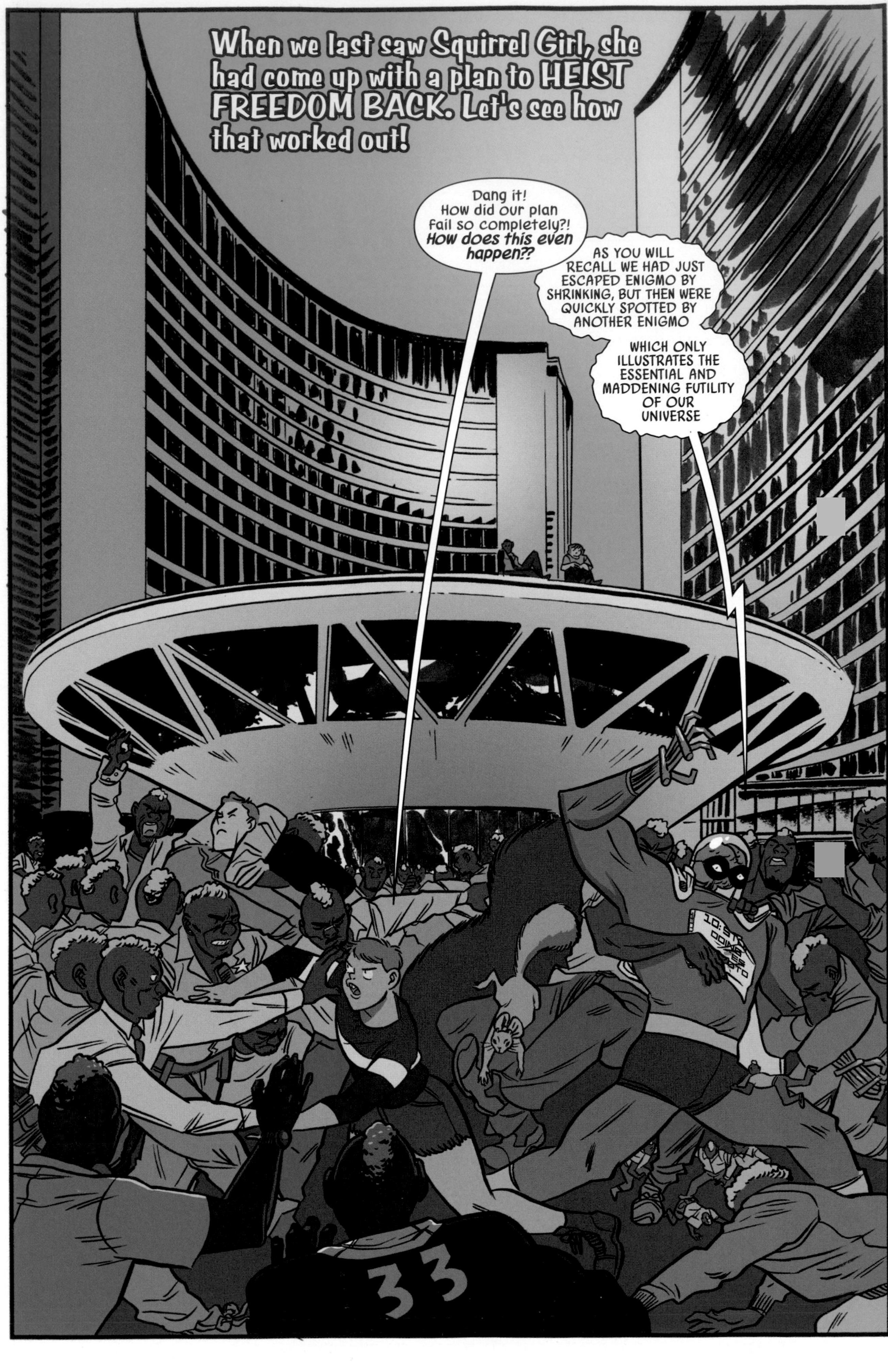

When we last saw Squirrel Girl, she had come up with a plan to HEIST FREEDOM BACK. Let's see how that worked out!
Dang it! How did our plan fail so completely?! How does this even happen??
AS YOU WILL RECALL WE HAD JUST ESCAPED ENIGMO BY SHRINKING, BUT THEN WERE QUICKLY SPOTTED BY ANOTHER ENIGMO
WHICH ONLY ILLUSTRATES THE ESSENTIAL AND MADDENING FUTILITY OF OUR UNIVERSE
33

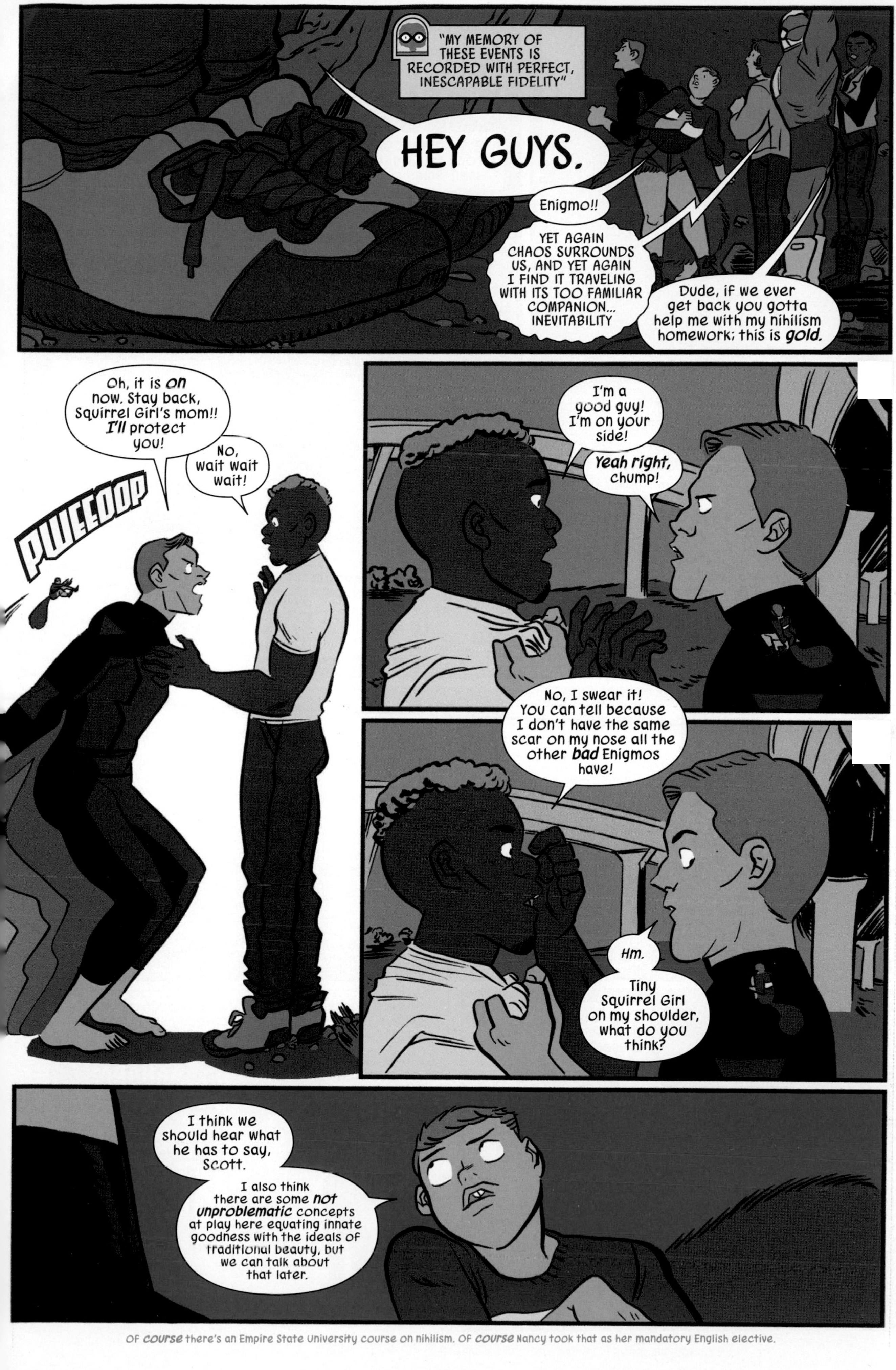
"MY MEMORY OF THESE EVENTS IS RECORDED WITH PERFECT, INESCAPABLE FIDELITY"
HEY GUYS.
Enigmo!!
YET AGAIN CHAOS SURROUNDS US, AND YET AGAIN I FIND IT TRAVELING WITH ITS TOO FAMILIAR COMPANION... INEVITABILITY
Dude, if we ever get back you gotta help me with my nihilism homework; this is *gold.*
Oh, it is *on* now. Stay back, Squirrel Girl's mom!! *I'll* protect you!
No, wait wait wait!
PWEEOOP
I'm a good guy! I'm on your side!
Yeah right, chump!
No, I swear it! You can tell because I don't have the same scar on my nose all the other *bad* Enigmos have!
Hm.
Tiny Squirrel Girl on my shoulder, what do you think?
I think we should hear what he has to say, Scott.
I also think there are some *not unproblematic* concepts at play here equating innate goodness with the ideals of traditional beauty, but we can talk about that later.

OF *COURSE* there's an Empire State University course on nihilism. OF *COURSE* Nancy took that as her mandatory English elective.

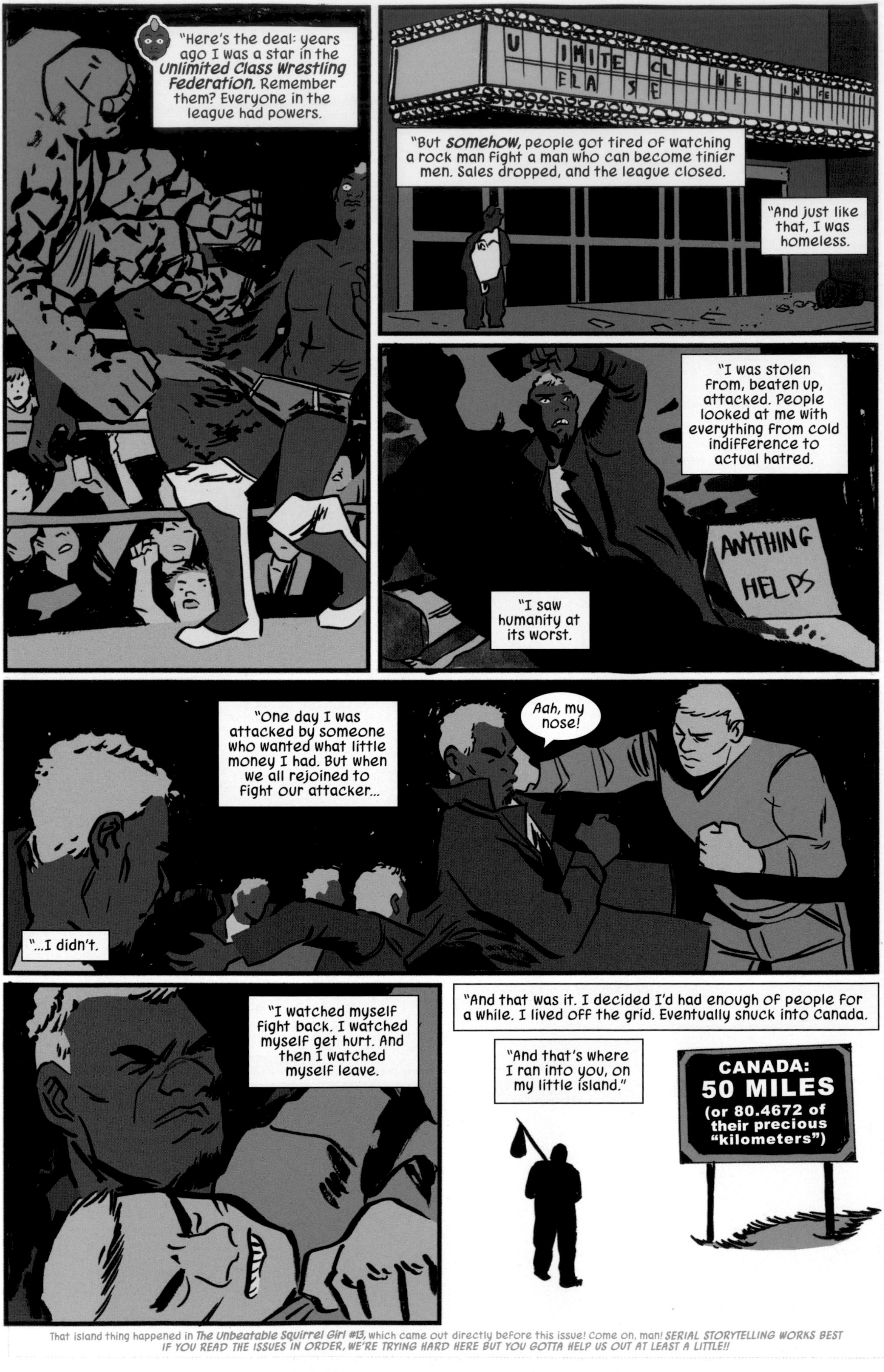
"Here's the deal: years ago I was a star in the Unlimited Class Wrestling Federation. Remember them? Everyone in the league had powers.
"But somehow, people got tired of watching a rock man fight a man who can become tinier men. Sales dropped, and the league closed.
"And just like that, I was homeless.
"I was stolen from, beaten up, attacked. People looked at me with everything from cold indifference to actual hatred.
ANYTHING HELPS
"I saw humanity at its worst.
"One day I was attacked by someone who wanted what little money I had. But when we all rejoined to fight our attacker...
Aah, my nose!
"...I didn't.
"I watched myself fight back. I watched myself get hurt. And then I watched myself leave.
"And that was it. I decided I'd had enough of people for a while. I lived off the grid. Eventually snuck into Canada.
"And that's where I ran into you, on my little island."
CANADA: 50 MILES (or 80.4672 of their precious "kilometers")

That island thing happened in *The Unbeatable Squirrel Girl #13*, which came out directly before this issue! Come on, man! *SERIAL STORYTELLING WORKS BEST IF YOU READ THE ISSUES IN ORDER, WE'RE TRYING HARD HERE BUT YOU GOTTA HELP US OUT AT LEAST A LITTLE!!*

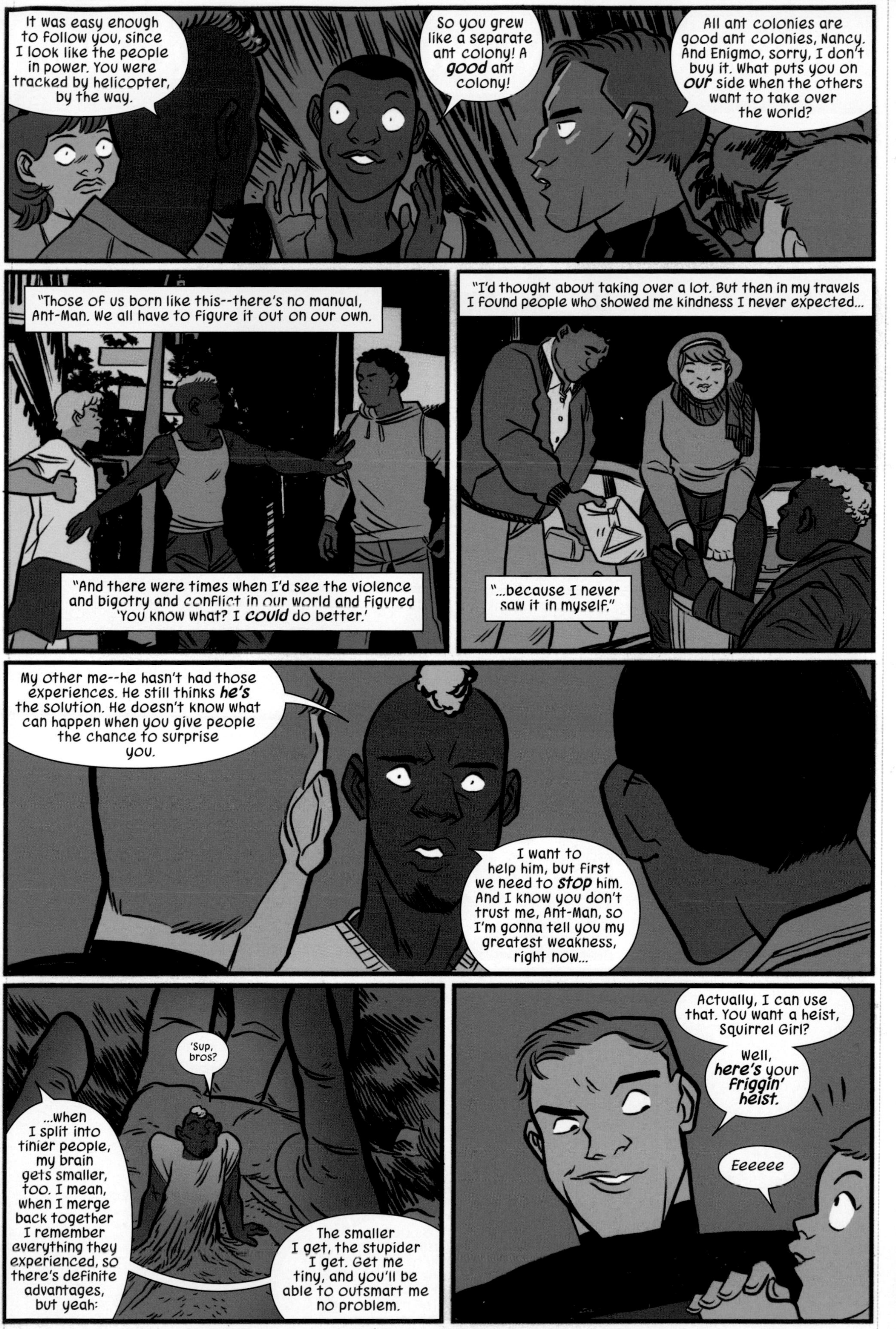
It was easy enough to follow you, since I look like the people in power. You were tracked by helicopter, by the way.
So you grew like a separate ant colony! A **good** ant colony!
All ant colonies are good ant colonies, Nancy. And Enigmo, sorry, I don't buy it. What puts you on **our** side when the others want to take over the world?
"Those of us born like this--there's no manual, Ant-Man. We all have to figure it out on our own.
"And there were times when I'd see the violence and bigotry and conflict in our world and figured 'You know what? I **could** do better.'
"I'd thought about taking over a lot. But then in my travels I found people who showed me kindness I never expected...
"...because I never saw it in myself."
My other me--he hasn't had those experiences. He still thinks **he's** the solution. He doesn't know what can happen when you give people the chance to surprise you.
I want to help him, but first we need to **stop** him. And I know you don't trust me, Ant-Man, so I'm gonna tell you my greatest weakness, right now...
...when I split into tinier people, my brain gets smaller, too. I mean, when I merge back together I remember everything they experienced, so there's definite advantages, but yeah:
'Sup, bros?
The smaller I get, the stupider I get. Get me tiny, and you'll be able to outsmart me no problem.
Actually, I can use that. You want a heist, Squirrel Girl?
Well, **here's** your **friggin' heist.**
Eeeeee

Can you tell an Ant-Man story and *not* have a heist in it? It is a question science is unable to answer, because the second someone tries, they're like, "Man, what if I just put a fun heist in here though??"

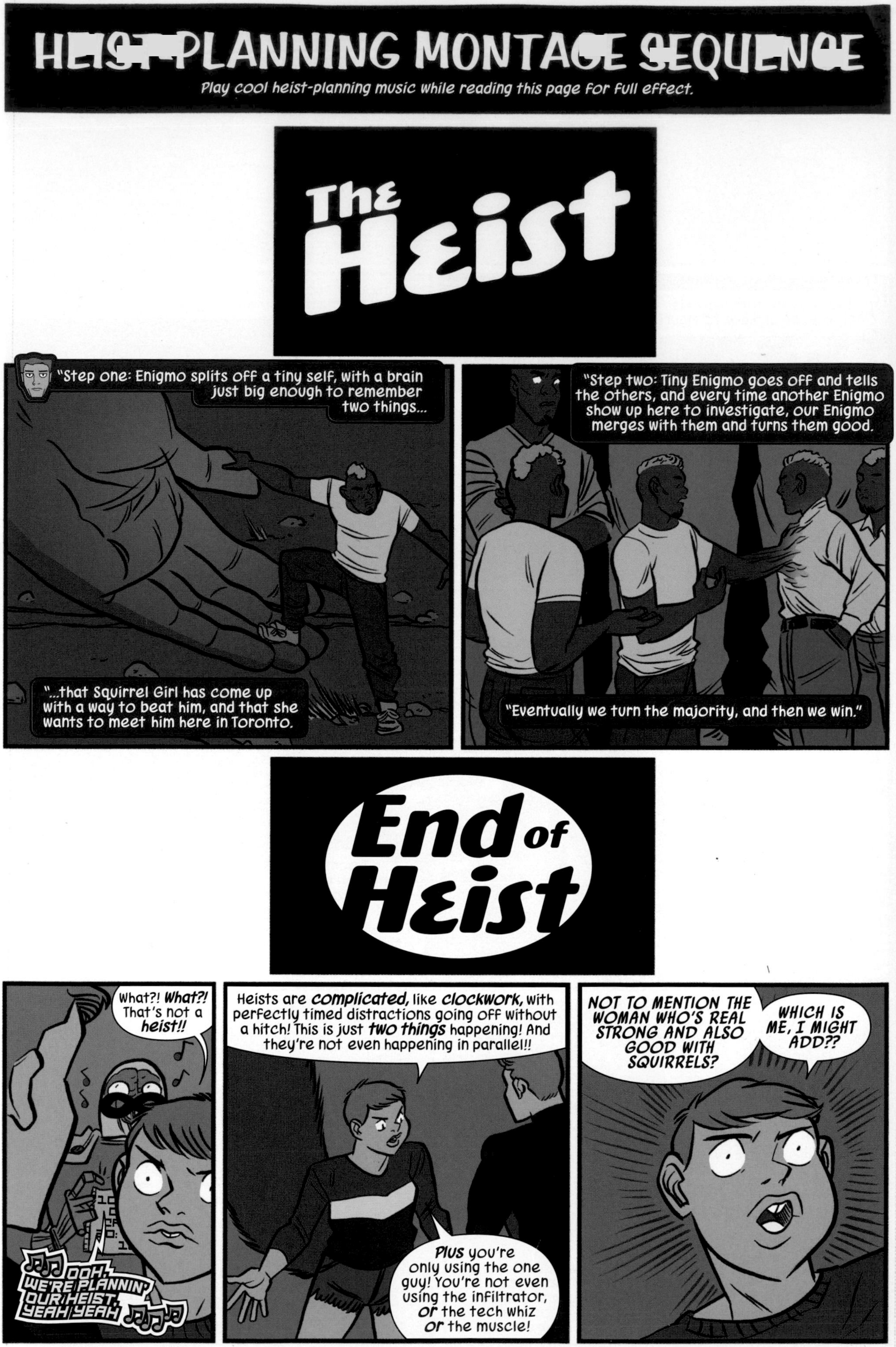
HEIST-PLANNING MONTAGE SEQUENCE
Play cool heist-planning music while reading this page for full effect.
The Heist
"Step one: Enigmo splits off a tiny self, with a brain just big enough to remember two things...
"...that Squirrel Girl has come up with a way to beat him, and that she wants to meet him here in Toronto.
"Step two: Tiny Enigmo goes off and tells the others, and every time another Enigmo show up here to investigate, our Enigmo merges with them and turns them good.
"Eventually we turn the majority, and then we win."
End of Heist
What?! What?! That's not a heist!!
OOH, WE'RE PLANNIN' OUR HEIST, YEAH YEAH
Heists are complicated, like clockwork, with perfectly timed distractions going off without a hitch! This is just two things happening! And they're not even happening in parallel!!
Plus you're only using the one guy! You're not even using the infiltrator, or the tech whiz or the muscle!
NOT TO MENTION THE WOMAN WHO'S REAL STRONG AND ALSO GOOD WITH SQUIRRELS?
WHICH IS ME, I MIGHT ADD??

See? *Brain Drain* played *his* heist-planning music. I can only assume you did the same. (For what it's worth, his song was *"Planning Our Heist (Wow That's Nice)"* by Sir Heist-A-Lot And His Three Pals Who Aren't That Into The Concepts Of Property Or Personal Ownership.)

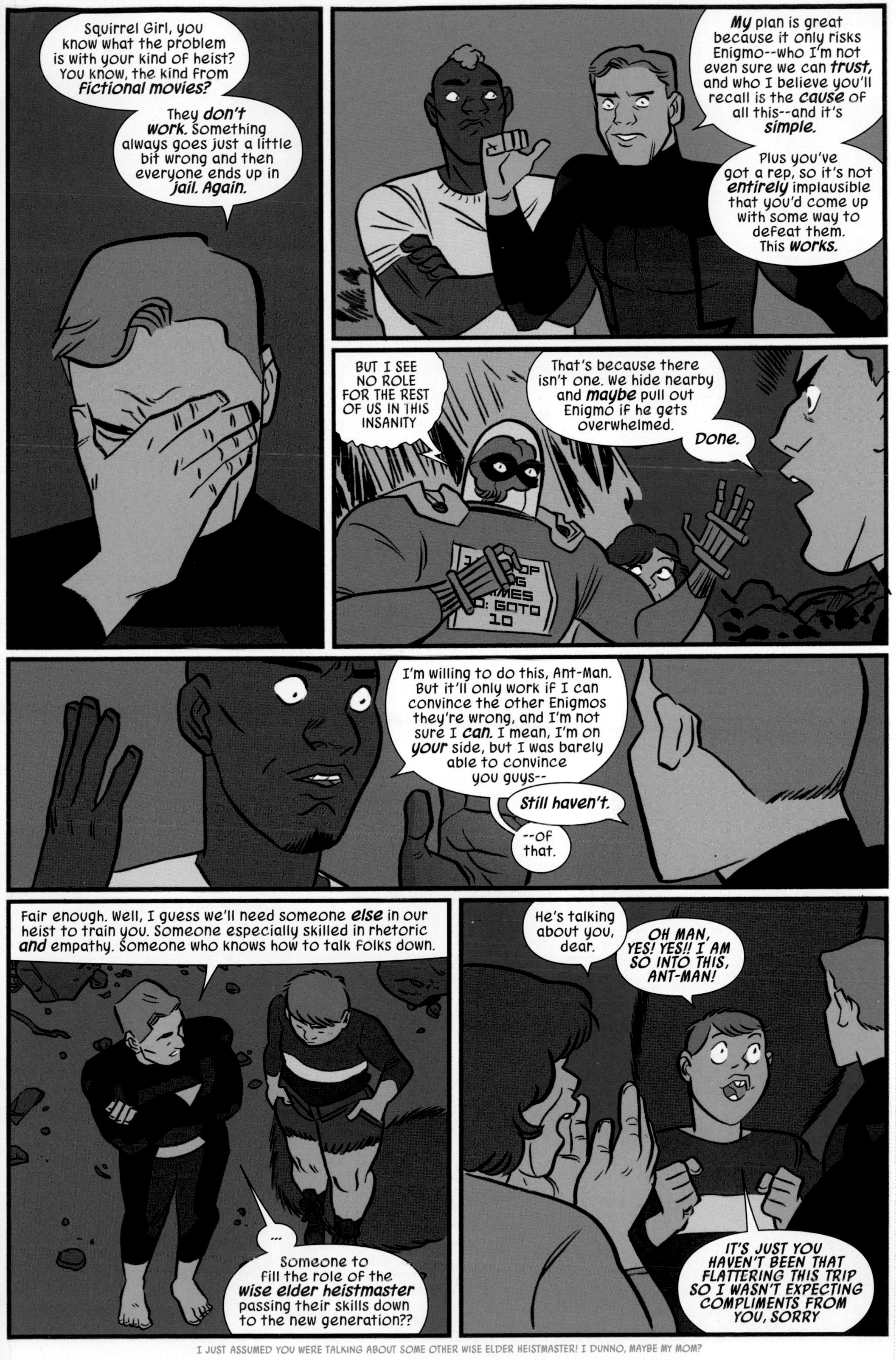
Squirrel Girl, you know what the problem is with your kind of heist? You know, the kind from fictional movies?
They don't work. Something always goes just a little bit wrong and then everyone ends up in jail. Again.
My plan is great because it only risks Enigmo--who I'm not even sure we can trust, and who I believe you'll recall is the cause of all this--and it's simple.
Plus you've got a rep, so it's not entirely implausible that you'd come up with some way to defeat them. This works.
BUT I SEE NO ROLE FOR THE REST OF US IN THIS INSANITY
That's because there isn't one. We hide nearby and maybe pull out Enigmo if he gets overwhelmed.
Done.
I'm willing to do this, Ant-Man. But it'll only work if I can convince the other Enigmos they're wrong, and I'm not sure I can. I mean, I'm on your side, but I was barely able to convince you guys--
Still haven't.
--of that.
Fair enough. Well, I guess we'll need someone else in our heist to train you. Someone especially skilled in rhetoric and empathy. Someone who knows how to talk folks down.
...
Someone to fill the role of the wise elder heistmaster passing their skills down to the new generation??
He's talking about you, dear.
OH MAN, YES! YES!! I AM SO INTO THIS, ANT-MAN!
IT'S JUST YOU HAVEN'T BEEN THAT FLATTERING THIS TRIP SO I WASN'T EXPECTING COMPLIMENTS FROM YOU, SORRY

I JUST ASSUMED YOU WERE TALKING ABOUT SOME OTHER WISE ELDER HEISTMASTER! I DUNNO, MAYBE MY MOM?

Panel 1:

This is gonna be great, buddy. We are gonna empathize *SO hard* with conflicting points of view and reach mutually acceptable compromises. *YOU just wait.*

While studying with you, I could also split apart, read a bunch of books on debate and rhetoric, and then merge back together again.

Even better! Parallel learning!!

Panel 2:

Okay, so all that's left is a place to lure them to.

We'll need a place that's got a large public square, in case several Enigmos arrive at once.

How about City Hall?

Panel 3:

Welcome to **TORONTO!**

Our city hall has a large open public space out front.

Not to mention lots of convenient food trucks and souvenir stands!

Panel 4:

Perfect. We'll also need a library, preferably nearby, so Squirrel Girl can help Enigmo complete his education as quickly as possible.

Billboard just to the right of the other one, dude.

Panel 5:

Additionally, our city hall ALSO has a free library!

We're very proud of our socialized public services!!

Panel 6:

...oud ...zed ...es!!

Plus, like all of Canada, we offer up to 50 weeks paid time off if you have a baby.

That's compared to the mere 12 weeks available in America, and that's UNPAID leave!

So what the heck, America??

These billboards are getting pretty sassy.

Sorry. I don't think we expected Americans to see them.

Panel 7:

So... heist is go?

Heist is go.

I'm not holding my breath, but there is at least a *chance* this plan will work and not fall apart almost immediately.

America, I don't think having a baby is as cheap or as easy as your social safety net would seem to imply!! SORRY, AMERICA, BUT BABIES EAT, LIKE, 100% OF THE TIME THEY AREN'T SLEEPING OR CRYING.

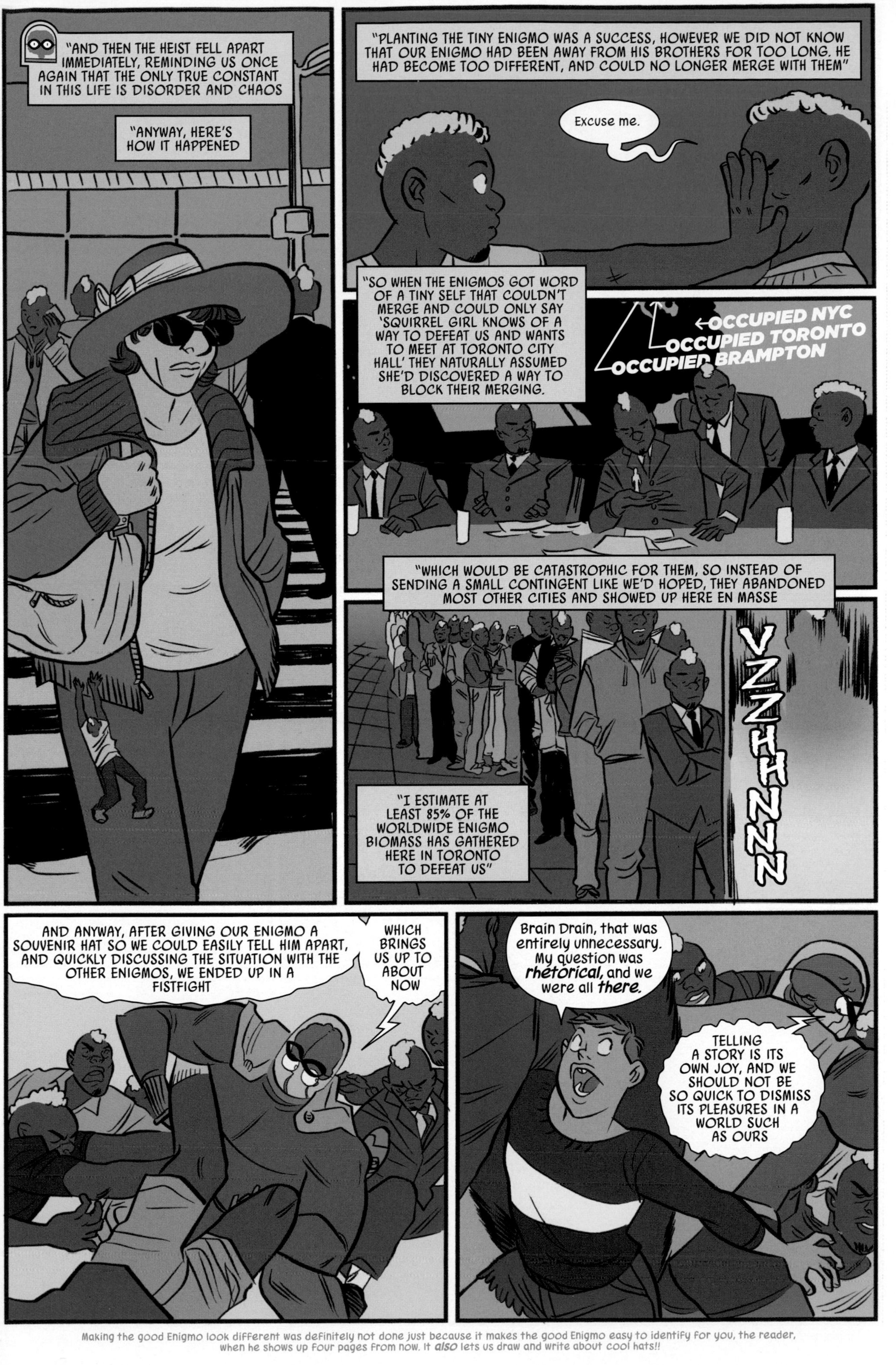
"AND THEN THE HEIST FELL APART IMMEDIATELY, REMINDING US ONCE AGAIN THAT THE ONLY TRUE CONSTANT IN THIS LIFE IS DISORDER AND CHAOS
"ANYWAY, HERE'S HOW IT HAPPENED
"PLANTING THE TINY ENIGMO WAS A SUCCESS, HOWEVER WE DID NOT KNOW THAT OUR ENIGMO HAD BEEN AWAY FROM HIS BROTHERS FOR TOO LONG. HE HAD BECOME TOO DIFFERENT, AND COULD NO LONGER MERGE WITH THEM"
Excuse me.
"SO WHEN THE ENIGMOS GOT WORD OF A TINY SELF THAT COULDN'T MERGE AND COULD ONLY SAY 'SQUIRREL GIRL KNOWS OF A WAY TO DEFEAT US AND WANTS TO MEET AT TORONTO CITY HALL' THEY NATURALLY ASSUMED SHE'D DISCOVERED A WAY TO BLOCK THEIR MERGING.
←OCCUPIED NYC
OCCUPIED TORONTO
OCCUPIED BRAMPTON
"WHICH WOULD BE CATASTROPHIC FOR THEM, SO INSTEAD OF SENDING A SMALL CONTINGENT LIKE WE'D HOPED, THEY ABANDONED MOST OTHER CITIES AND SHOWED UP HERE EN MASSE
VZZHHNNN
"I ESTIMATE AT LEAST 85% OF THE WORLDWIDE ENIGMO BIOMASS HAS GATHERED HERE IN TORONTO TO DEFEAT US"
AND ANYWAY, AFTER GIVING OUR ENIGMO A SOUVENIR HAT SO WE COULD EASILY TELL HIM APART, AND QUICKLY DISCUSSING THE SITUATION WITH THE OTHER ENIGMOS, WE ENDED UP IN A FISTFIGHT
WHICH BRINGS US UP TO ABOUT NOW
Brain Drain, that was entirely unnecessary. My question was *rhetorical*, and we were all *there*.
TELLING A STORY IS ITS OWN JOY, AND WE SHOULD NOT BE SO QUICK TO DISMISS ITS PLEASURES IN A WORLD SUCH AS OURS

Making the good Enigmo look different was definitely not done just because it makes the good Enigmo easy to identify for you, the reader, when he shows up four pages from now. It *also* lets us draw and write about cool hats!!

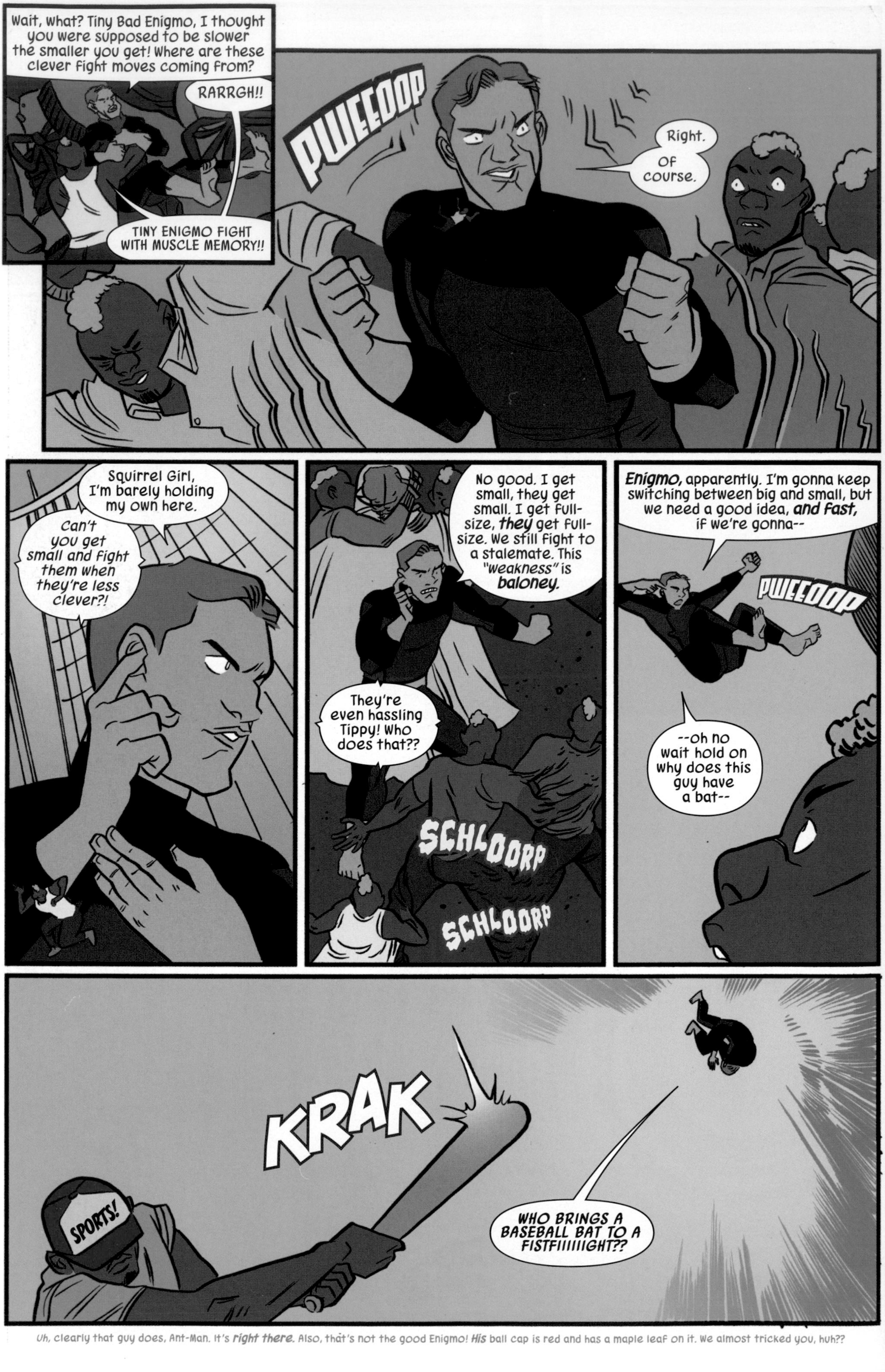
Wait, what? Tiny Bad Enigmo, I thought you were supposed to be slower the smaller you get! Where are these clever fight moves coming from?
RARRGH!!
TINY ENIGMO FIGHT WITH MUSCLE MEMORY!!
PWEEOOP
Right.
Of course.
Squirrel Girl, I'm barely holding my own here.
Can't you get small and fight them when they're less clever?!
No good. I get small, they get small. I get full-size, they get full-size. We still fight to a stalemate. This "weakness" is baloney.
They're even hassling Tippy! Who does that??
SCHLOORP
SCHLOORP
Enigmo, apparently. I'm gonna keep switching between big and small, but we need a good idea, and fast, if we're gonna--
PWEEOOP
--oh no wait hold on why does this guy have a bat--
KRAK
SPORTS!
WHO BRINGS A BASEBALL BAT TO A FISTFIIIIIIGHT??

Uh, clearly that guy does, Ant-Man. It's ***right there.*** *Also, that's not the good Enigmo!* ***His*** *ball cap is red and has a maple leaf on it. We almost tricked you, huh??*

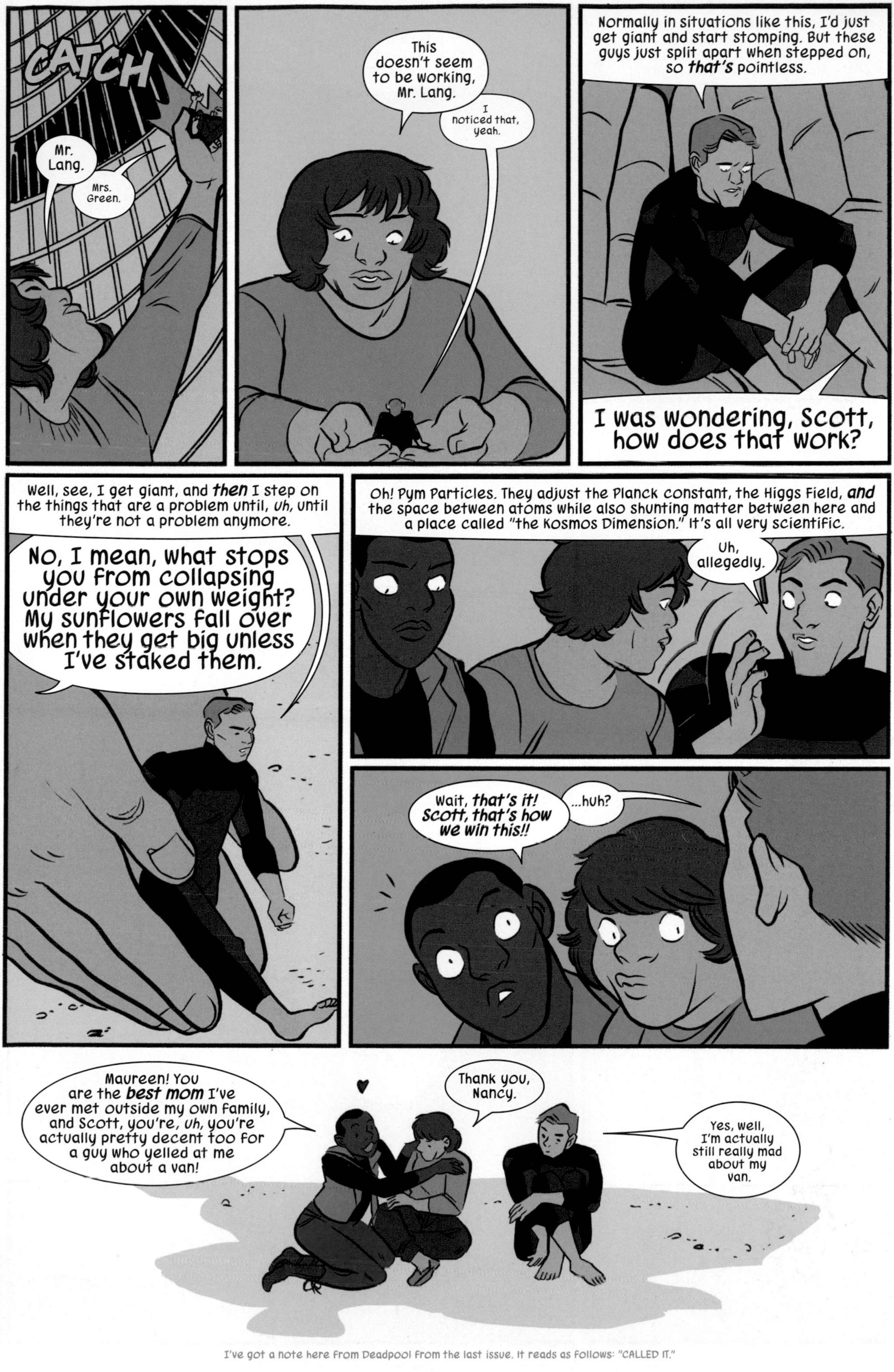
CATCH
Mr. Lang.
Mrs. Green.
This doesn't seem to be working, Mr. Lang.
I noticed that, yeah.
Normally in situations like this, I'd just get giant and start stomping. But these guys just split apart when stepped on, so *that's* pointless.
I was wondering, Scott, how does that work?
Well, see, I get giant, and *then* I step on the things that are a problem until, *uh*, until they're not a problem anymore.
No, I mean, what stops you from collapsing under your own weight? My sunflowers fall over when they get big unless I've staked them.
Oh! Pym Particles. They adjust the Planck constant, the Higgs Field, *and* the space between atoms while also shunting matter between here and a place called "the Kosmos Dimension." It's all very scientific.
Uh, allegedly.
Wait, *that's it! Scott, that's how we win this!!*
...huh?
Maureen! You are the *best mom* I've ever met outside my own family, and Scott, you're, *uh*, you're actually pretty decent too for a guy who yelled at me about a van!
Thank you, Nancy.
Yes, well, I'm actually still really mad about my van.

I've got a note here from Deadpool from the last issue. It reads as follows: "CALLED IT."

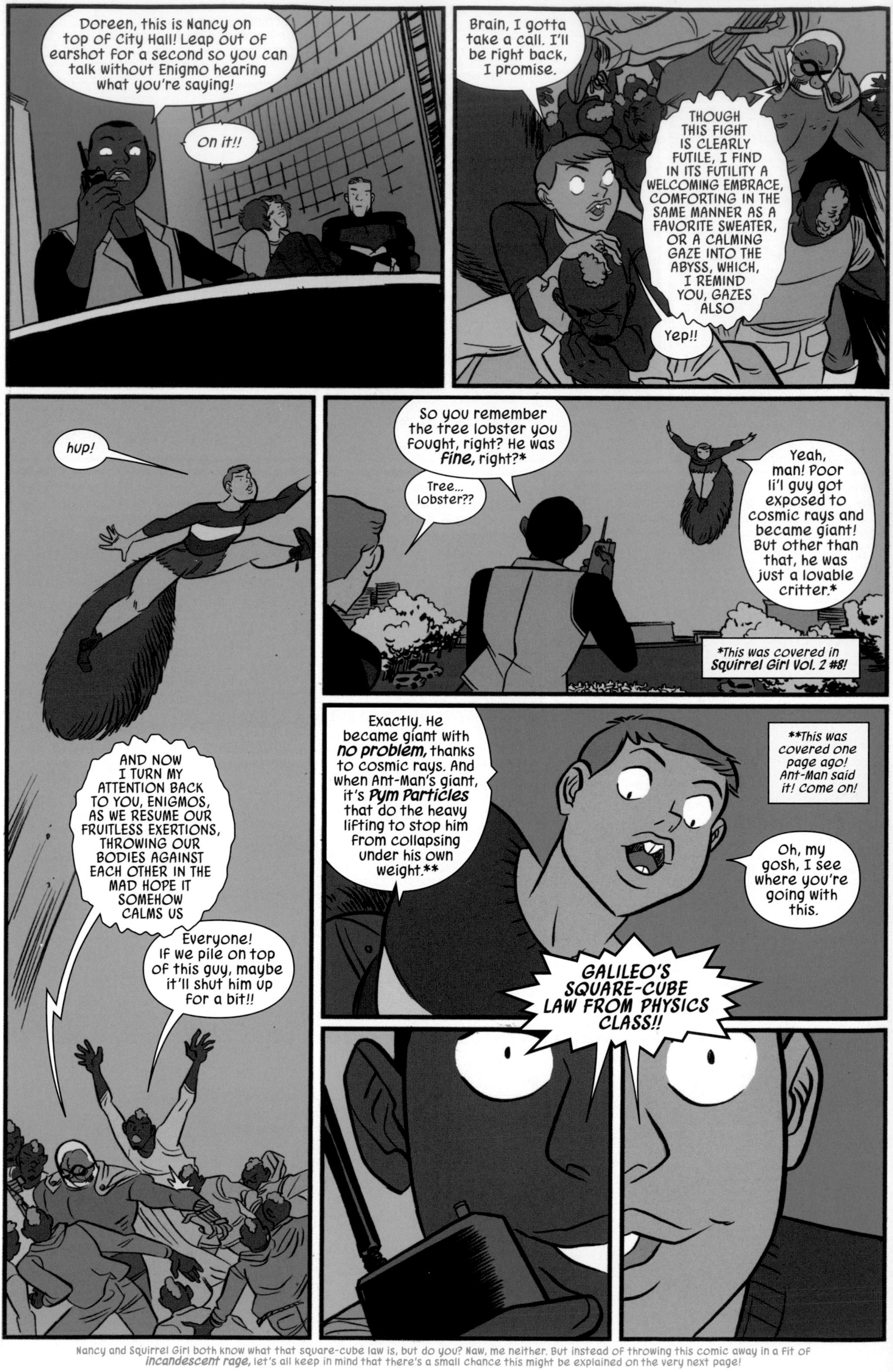
Doreen, this is Nancy on top of City Hall! Leap out of earshot for a second so you can talk without Enigmo hearing what you're saying!
On it!!
Brain, I gotta take a call. I'll be right back, I promise.
THOUGH THIS FIGHT IS CLEARLY FUTILE, I FIND IN ITS FUTILITY A WELCOMING EMBRACE, COMFORTING IN THE SAME MANNER AS A FAVORITE SWEATER, OR A CALMING GAZE INTO THE ABYSS, WHICH, I REMIND YOU, GAZES ALSO
Yep!!
hup!
So you remember the tree lobster you fought, right? He was fine, right?*
Tree... lobster??
Yeah, man! Poor li'l guy got exposed to cosmic rays and became giant! But other than that, he was just a lovable critter.*
*This was covered in Squirrel Girl Vol. 2 #8!
AND NOW I TURN MY ATTENTION BACK TO YOU, ENIGMOS, AS WE RESUME OUR FRUITLESS EXERTIONS, THROWING OUR BODIES AGAINST EACH OTHER IN THE MAD HOPE IT SOMEHOW CALMS US
Everyone! If we pile on top of this guy, maybe it'll shut him up for a bit!!
Exactly. He became giant with no problem, thanks to cosmic rays. And when Ant-Man's giant, it's Pym Particles that do the heavy lifting to stop him from collapsing under his own weight.**
**This was covered one page ago! Ant-Man said it! Come on!
Oh, my gosh, I see where you're going with this.
GALILEO'S SQUARE-CUBE LAW FROM PHYSICS CLASS!!

Nancy and Squirrel Girl both know what that square-cube law is, but do you? Naw, me neither. But instead of throwing this comic away in a fit of *incandescent rage,* let's all keep in mind that there's a small chance this might be explained on the very next page!

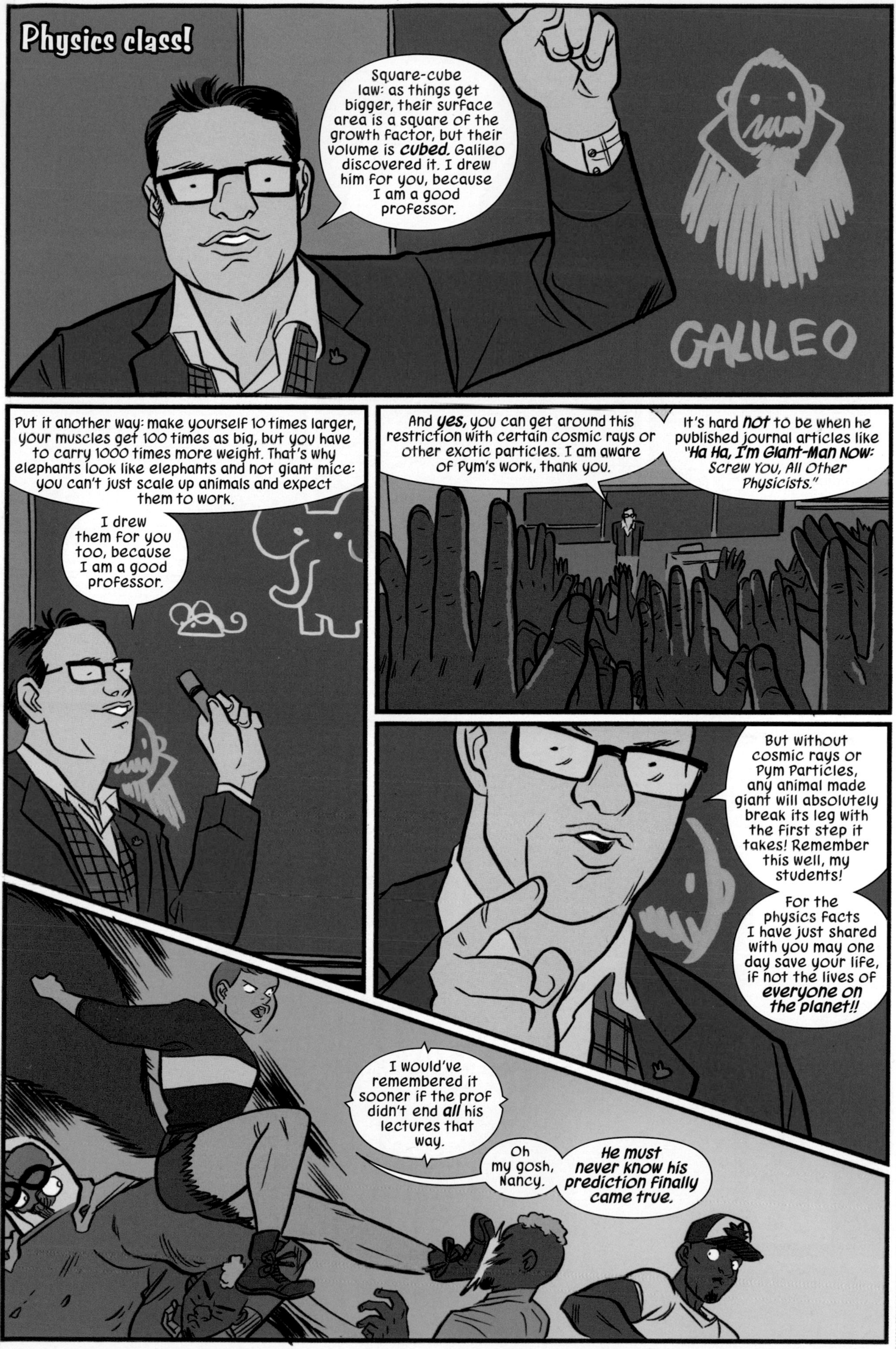
Physics class!
Square-cube law: as things get bigger, their surface area is a square of the growth factor, but their volume is *cubed.* Galileo discovered it. I drew him for you, because I am a good professor.
GALILEO
Put it another way: make yourself 10 times larger, your muscles get 100 times as big, but you have to carry 1000 times more weight. That's why elephants look like elephants and not giant mice: you can't just scale up animals and expect them to work.
I drew them for you too, because I am a good professor.
And *yes,* you can get around this restriction with certain cosmic rays or other exotic particles. I am aware of Pym's work, thank you.
It's hard *not* to be when he published journal articles like ***"Ha Ha, I'm Giant-Man Now:*** *Screw You, All Other Physicists."*
But without cosmic rays or Pym Particles, any animal made giant will absolutely break its leg with the first step it takes! Remember this well, my students!
For the physics facts I have just shared with you may one day save your life, if not the lives of ***everyone on the planet!!***
I would've remembered it sooner if the prof didn't end *all* his lectures that way.
Oh my gosh, Nancy.
He must never know his prediction finally came true.

This is actual physics, and Galileo actually did discover this! It was during what I can only assume was an ahead-of-his-time attempt to invent an enlarging ray, before he refocused on just, you know, astronomy, math, engineering, physics, science, and philosophy. *Also yes, that is the good Enigmo there in the last panel, you found him.*

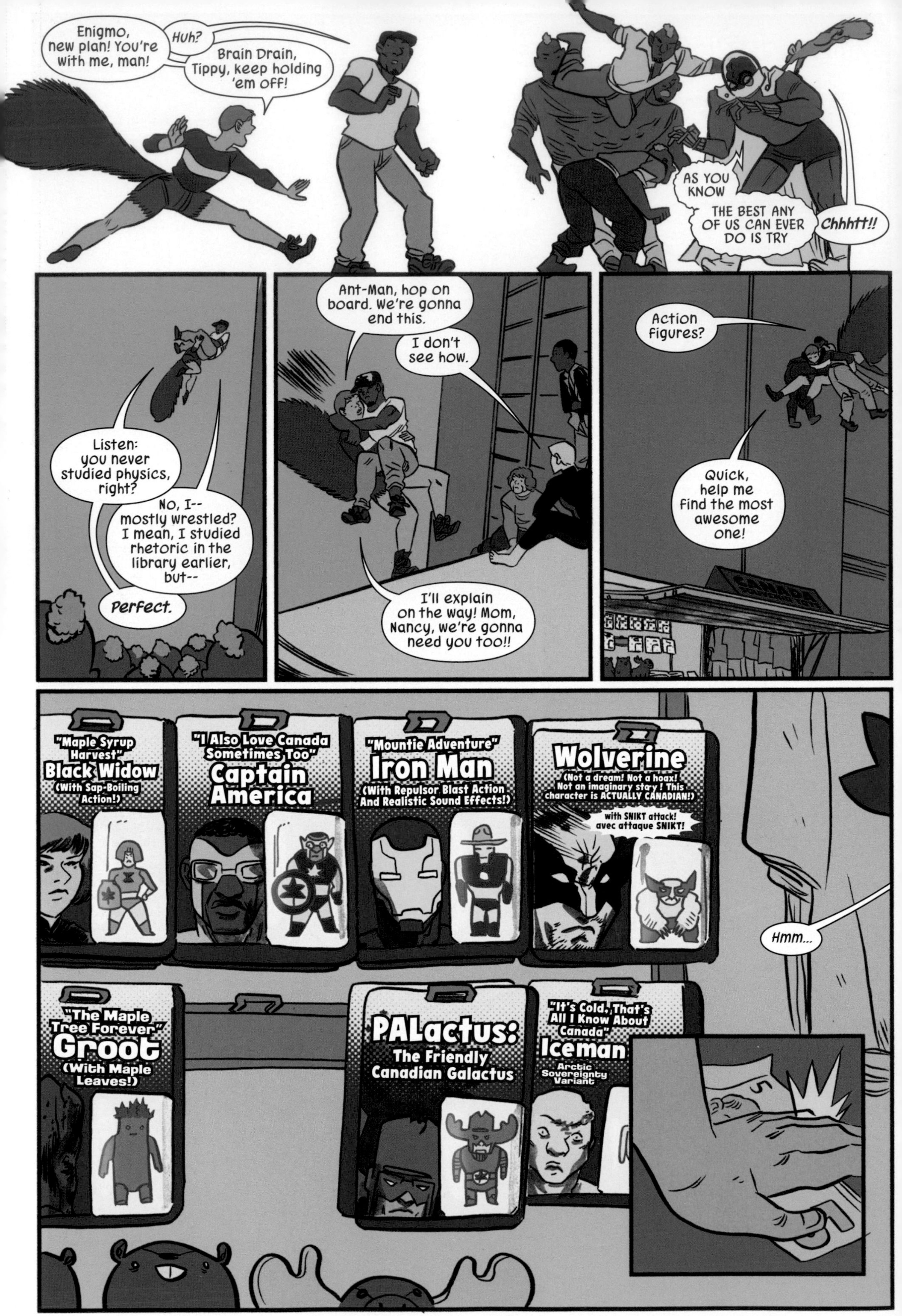
Enigmo, new plan! You're with me, man!
Huh?
Brain Drain, Tippy, keep holding 'em off!
AS YOU KNOW
THE BEST ANY OF US CAN EVER DO IS TRY
Chhhtt!!
Listen: you never studied physics, right?
No, I-- mostly wrestled? I mean, I studied rhetoric in the library earlier, but--
Perfect.
Ant-Man, hop on board. We're gonna end this.
I don't see how.
I'll explain on the way! Mom, Nancy, we're gonna need you too!!
Action Figures?
Quick, help me find the most awesome one!
CANADA
"Maple Syrup Harvest" Black Widow (With Sap-Boiling Action!)
"I Also Love Canada Sometimes Too" Captain America
"Mountie Adventure" Iron Man (With Repulsor Blast Action And Realistic Sound Effects!)
Wolverine (Not a dream! Not a hoax! Not an imaginary story! This character is ACTUALLY CANADIAN!)
with SNIKT attack! avec attaque SNIKT!
Hmm...
"The Maple Tree Forever" Groot (With Maple Leaves!)
PALactus: The Friendly Canadian Galactus
"It's Cold, That's All I Know About Canada" Iceman Arctic Sovereignty Variant
5

Action Figures not pictured include: "Hellcat (But in Canadian Clothes)," "Howard the Canadian Duck (So I Guess That Means He's A Northern Shoveler Duck Or Something)," and "Angela: Queen of Halifax."

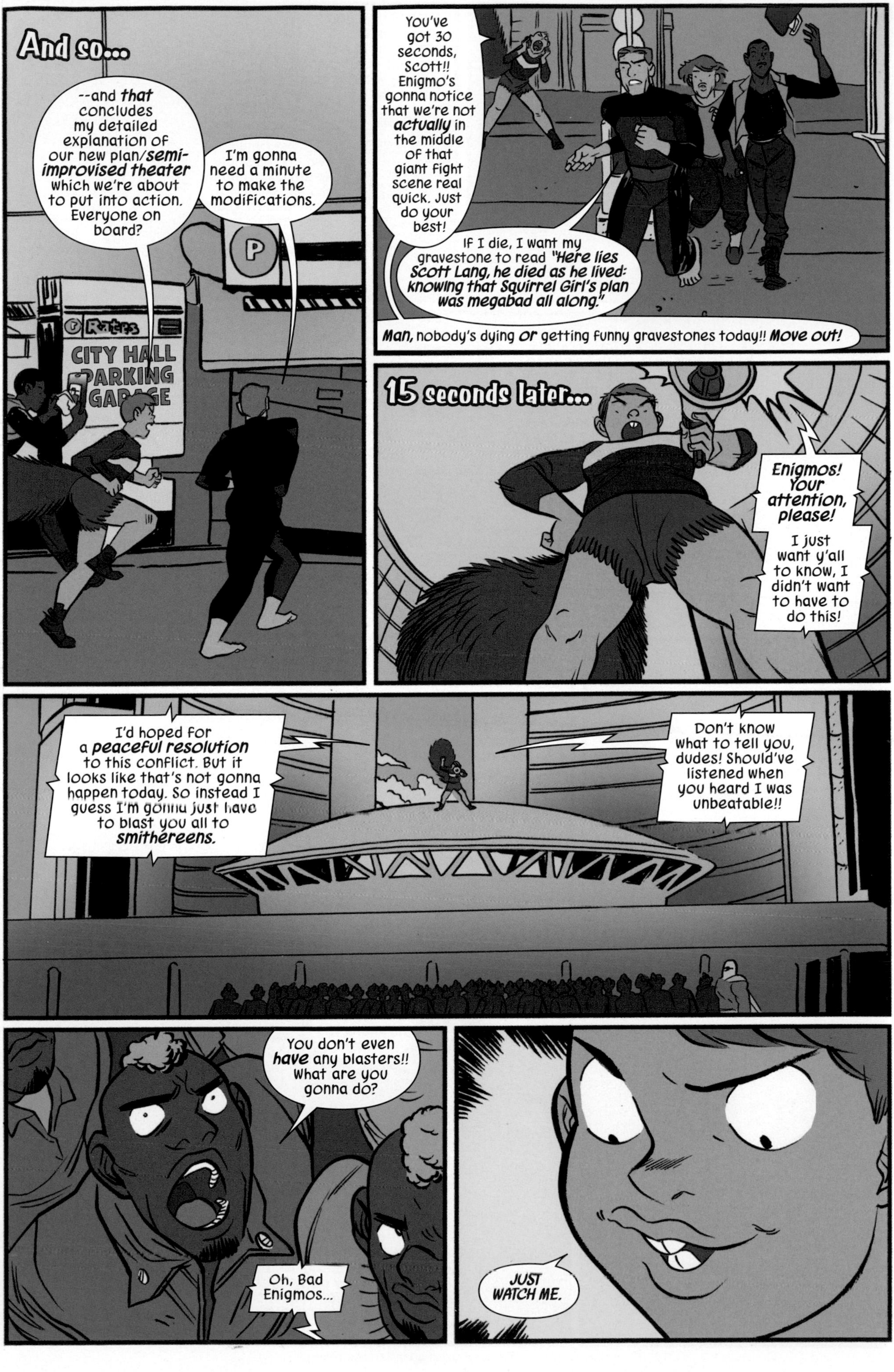
And so...
--and that concludes my detailed explanation of our new plan/semi-improvised theater which we're about to put into action. Everyone on board?
I'm gonna need a minute to make the modifications.
P
CITY HALL PARKING GARAGE
You've got 30 seconds, Scott!! Enigmo's gonna notice that we're not actually in the middle of that giant fight scene real quick. Just do your best!
If I die, I want my gravestone to read "Here lies Scott Lang, he died as he lived: knowing that Squirrel Girl's plan was megabad all along."
Man, nobody's dying or getting funny gravestones today!! Move out!
15 seconds later...
Enigmos! Your attention, please!
I just want y'all to know, I didn't want to have to do this!
I'd hoped for a peaceful resolution to this conflict. But it looks like that's not gonna happen today. So instead I guess I'm gonna just have to blast you all to smithereens.
Don't know what to tell you, dudes! Should've listened when you heard I was unbeatable!!
You don't even have any blasters!! What are you gonna do?
Oh, Bad Enigmos...
JUST WATCH ME.

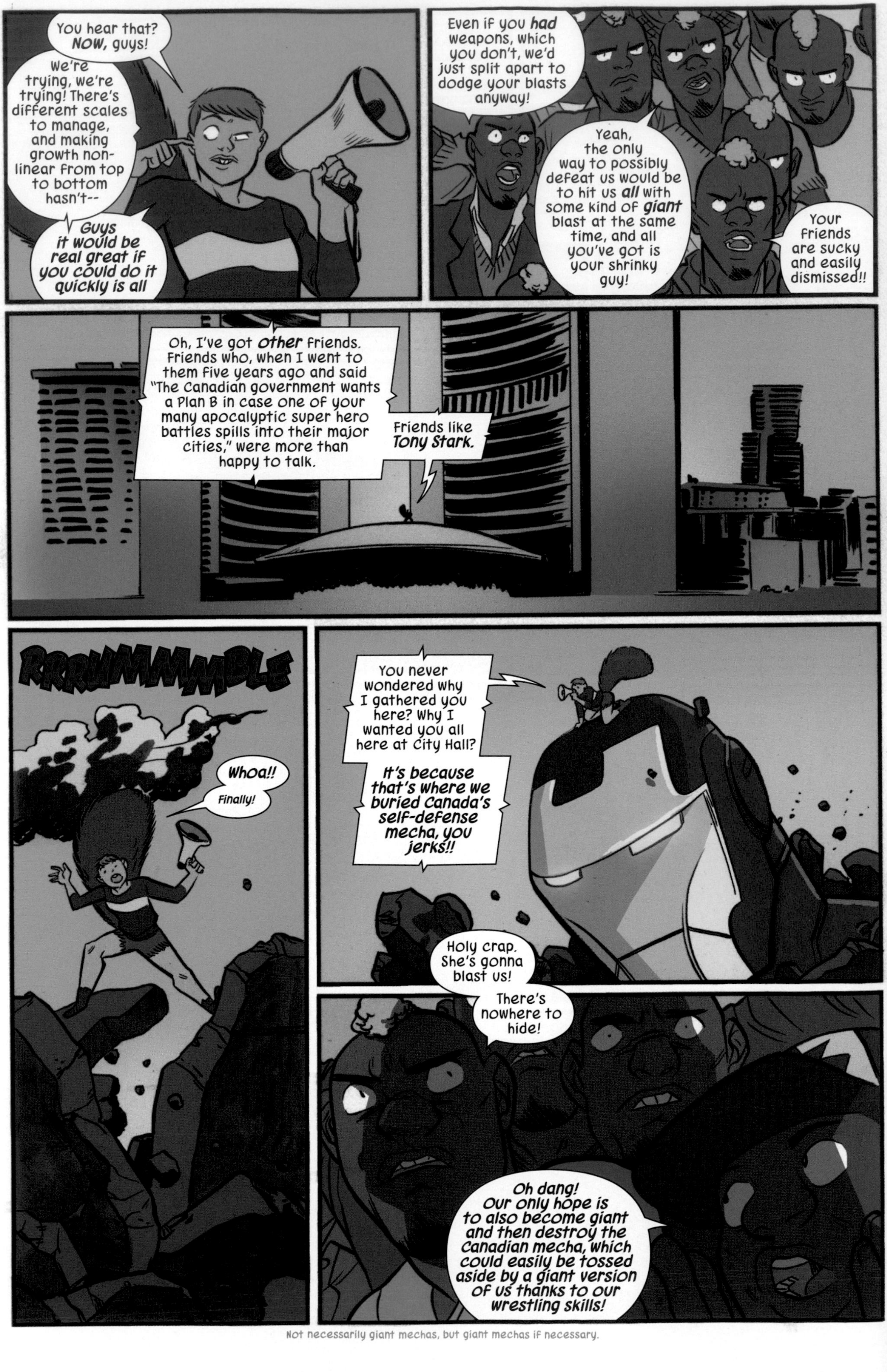
You hear that? NOW, guys!
We're trying, we're trying! There's different scales to manage, and making growth non-linear from top to bottom hasn't--
Guys it would be real great if you could do it quickly is all
Even if you had weapons, which you don't, we'd just split apart to dodge your blasts anyway!
Yeah, the only way to possibly defeat us would be to hit us all with some kind of giant blast at the same time, and all you've got is your shrinky guy!
Your friends are sucky and easily dismissed!!
Oh, I've got other friends. Friends who, when I went to them five years ago and said "The Canadian government wants a Plan B in case one of your many apocalyptic super hero battles spills into their major cities," were more than happy to talk.
Friends like Tony Stark.
RRRUMMMMBLE
Whoa!!
Finally!
You never wondered why I gathered you here? Why I wanted you all here at City Hall?
It's because that's where we buried Canada's self-defense mecha, you jerks!!
Holy crap. She's gonna blast us!
There's nowhere to hide!
Oh dang! Our only hope is to also become giant and then destroy the Canadian mecha, which could easily be tossed aside by a giant version of us thanks to our wrestling skills!

Not necessarily giant mechas, but giant mechas if necessary.

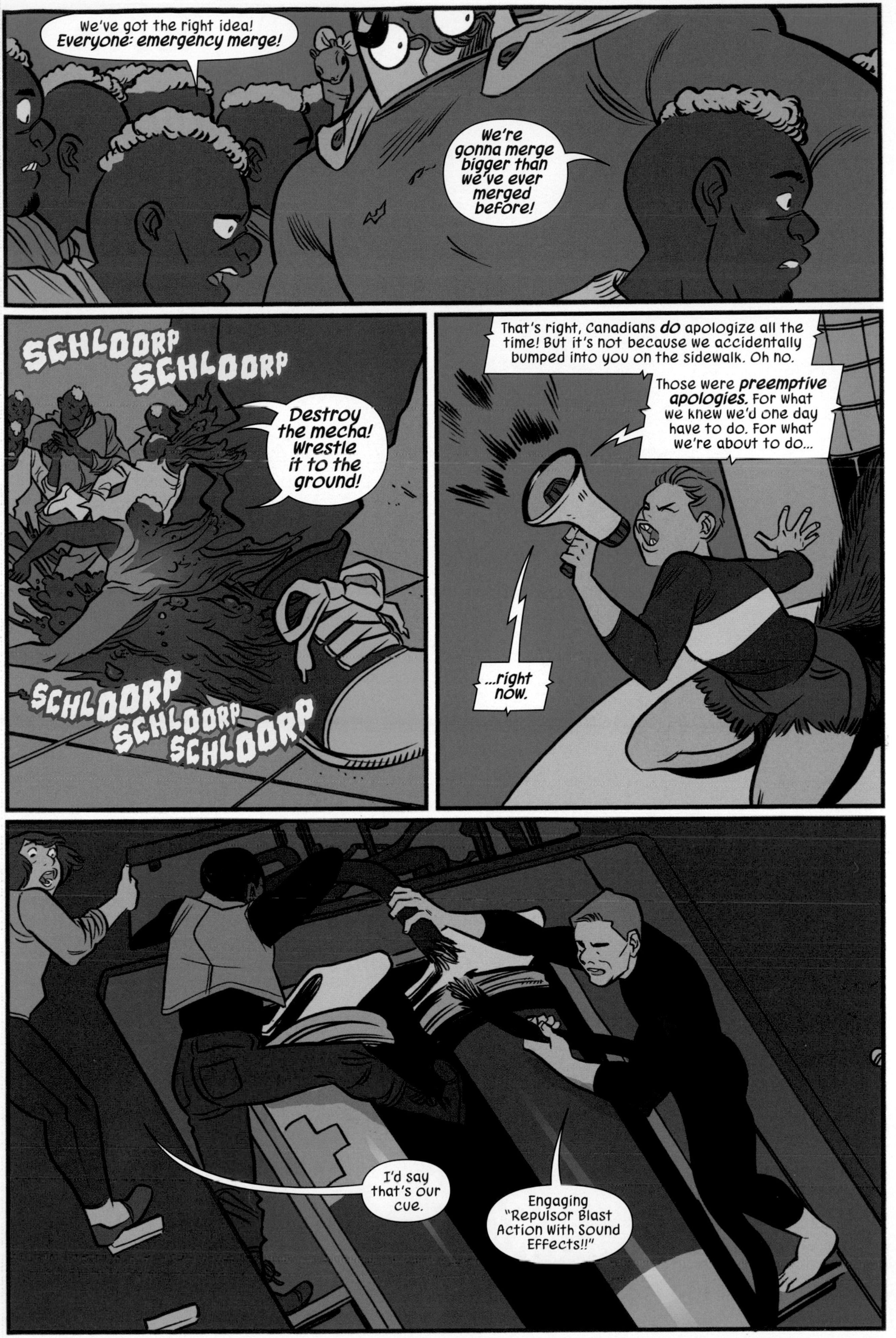
We've got the right idea! Everyone: emergency merge!
We're gonna merge bigger than we've ever merged before!
SCHLOORP SCHLOORP
Destroy the mecha! Wrestle it to the ground!
SCHLOORP SCHLOORP SCHLOORP
That's right, Canadians do apologize all the time! But it's not because we accidentally bumped into you on the sidewalk. Oh no.
Those were preemptive apologies. For what we knew we'd one day have to do. For what we're about to do...
...right now.
I'd say that's our cue.
Engaging "Repulsor Blast Action With Sound Effects!!"

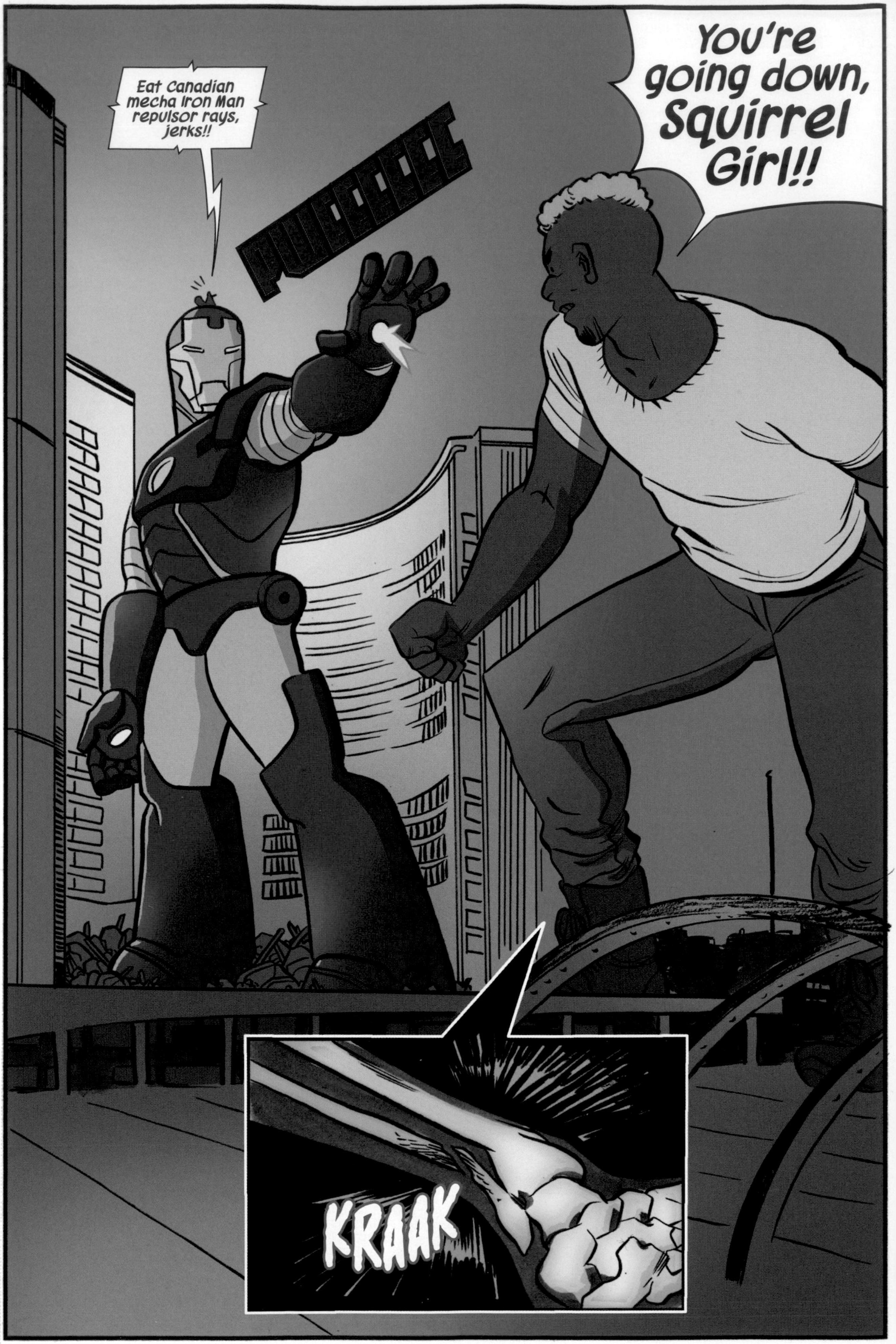
You're going down, Squirrel Girl!!
Eat Canadian mecha Iron Man repulsor rays, jerks!!
KRAAK

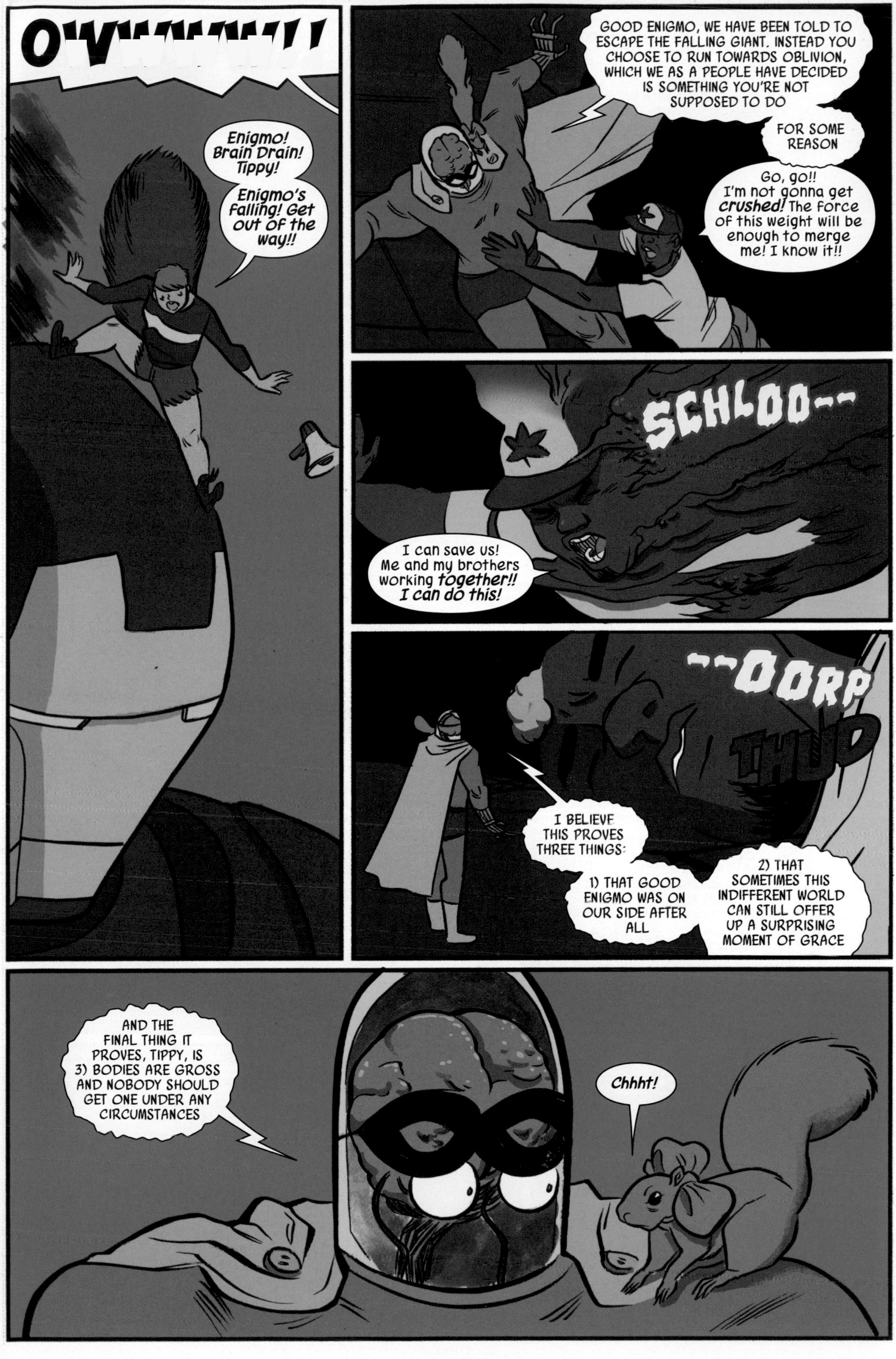

Enigmo! Brain Drain! Tippy!
Enigmo's falling! Get out of the way!!
GOOD ENIGMO, WE HAVE BEEN TOLD TO ESCAPE THE FALLING GIANT. INSTEAD YOU CHOOSE TO RUN TOWARDS OBLIVION, WHICH WE AS A PEOPLE HAVE DECIDED IS SOMETHING YOU'RE NOT SUPPOSED TO DO
FOR SOME REASON
Go, go!! I'm not gonna get crushed! The force of this weight will be enough to merge me! I know it!!
SCHLOO--
I can save us! Me and my brothers working together!! I can do this!
--OORP
THUD
I BELIEVE THIS PROVES THREE THINGS:
1) THAT GOOD ENIGMO WAS ON OUR SIDE AFTER ALL
2) THAT SOMETIMES THIS INDIFFERENT WORLD CAN STILL OFFER UP A SURPRISING MOMENT OF GRACE
AND THE FINAL THING IT PROVES, TIPPY, IS 3) BODIES ARE GROSS AND NOBODY SHOULD GET ONE UNDER ANY CIRCUMSTANCES
Chhht!

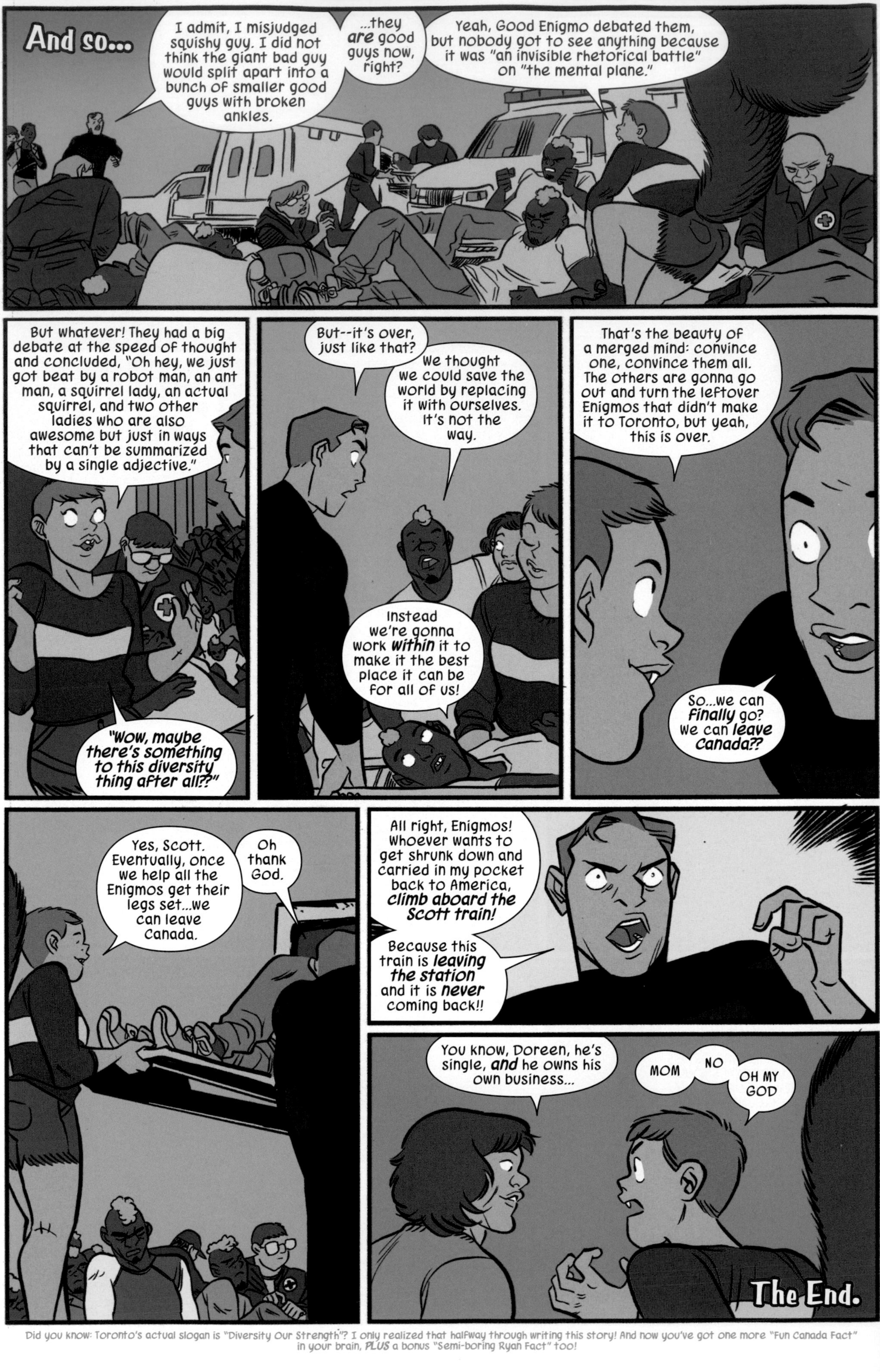
And so...
I admit, I misjudged squishy guy. I did not think the giant bad guy would split apart into a bunch of smaller good guys with broken ankles.
...they **are** good guys now, right?
Yeah, Good Enigmo debated them, but nobody got to see anything because it was "an invisible rhetorical battle" on "the mental plane."
But whatever! They had a big debate at the speed of thought and concluded, "Oh hey, we just got beat by a robot man, an ant man, a squirrel lady, an actual squirrel, and two other ladies who are also awesome but just in ways that can't be summarized by a single adjective."
"Wow, maybe there's something to this diversity thing after all??"
But--it's over, just like that?
We thought we could save the world by replacing it with ourselves. It's not the way.
Instead we're gonna work ***within*** it to make it the best place it can be for all of us!
That's the beauty of a merged mind: convince one, convince them all. The others are gonna go out and turn the leftover Enigmos that didn't make it to Toronto, but yeah, this is over.
So...we can ***finally*** go? We can ***leave Canada??***
Yes, Scott. Eventually, once we help all the Enigmos get their legs set...we can leave Canada.
Oh thank God.
All right, Enigmos! Whoever wants to get shrunk down and carried in my pocket back to America, ***climb aboard the Scott train!***
Because this train is ***leaving the station*** and it is ***never*** coming back!!
You know, Doreen, he's single, ***and*** he owns his own business...
MOM
NO
OH MY GOD
The End.

Did you know: Toronto's actual slogan is "Diversity Our Strength"? I only realized that halfway through writing this story! And now you've got one more "Fun Canada Fact" in your brain, *PLUS* a bonus "Semi-boring Ryan Fact" too!

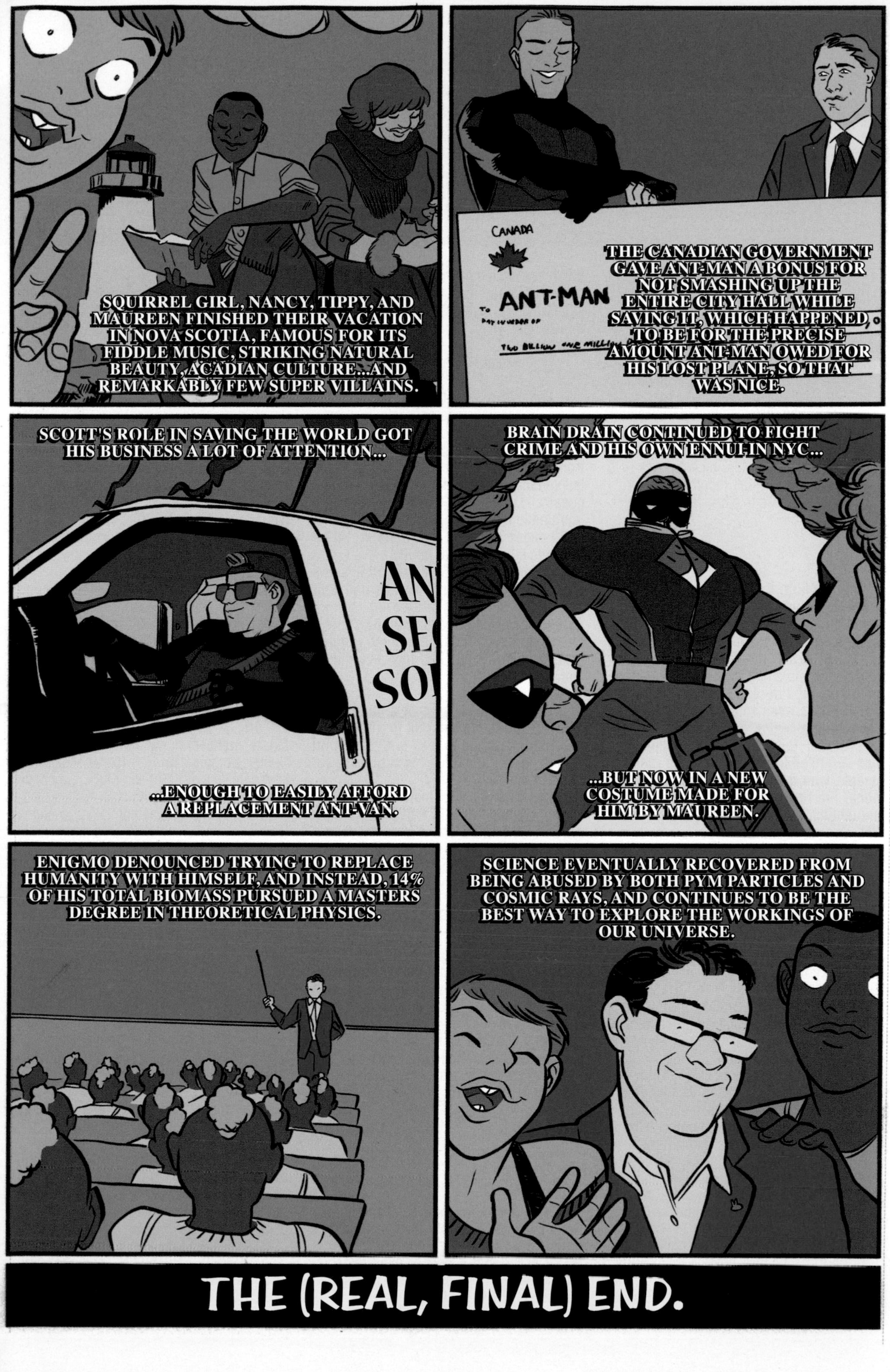
SQUIRREL GIRL, NANCY, TIPPY, AND MAUREEN FINISHED THEIR VACATION IN NOVA SCOTIA, FAMOUS FOR ITS FIDDLE MUSIC, STRIKING NATURAL BEAUTY, ACADIAN CULTURE...AND REMARKABLY FEW SUPER VILLAINS.
CANADA
ANT-MAN
THE CANADIAN GOVERNMENT GAVE ANT-MAN A BONUS FOR NOT SMASHING UP THE ENTIRE CITY HALL WHILE SAVING IT, WHICH HAPPENED TO BE FOR THE PRECISE AMOUNT ANT-MAN OWED FOR HIS LOST PLANE, SO THAT WAS NICE.
SCOTT'S ROLE IN SAVING THE WORLD GOT HIS BUSINESS A LOT OF ATTENTION...
...ENOUGH TO EASILY AFFORD A REPLACEMENT ANT-VAN.
BRAIN DRAIN CONTINUED TO FIGHT CRIME AND HIS OWN ENNUI IN NYC...
...BUT NOW IN A NEW COSTUME MADE FOR HIM BY MAUREEN.
ENIGMO DENOUNCED TRYING TO REPLACE HUMANITY WITH HIMSELF, AND INSTEAD, 14% OF HIS TOTAL BIOMASS PURSUED A MASTERS DEGREE IN THEORETICAL PHYSICS.
SCIENCE EVENTUALLY RECOVERED FROM BEING ABUSED BY BOTH PYM PARTICLES AND COSMIC RAYS, AND CONTINUES TO BE THE BEST WAY TO EXPLORE THE WORKINGS OF OUR UNIVERSE.
THE (REAL, FINAL) END.

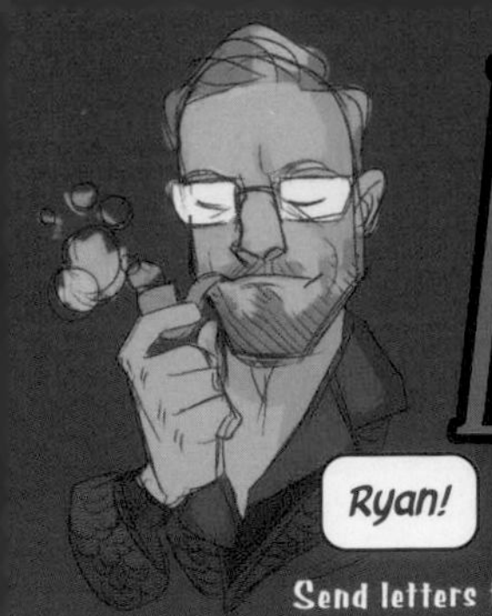
Ryan!

Letters From Nuts

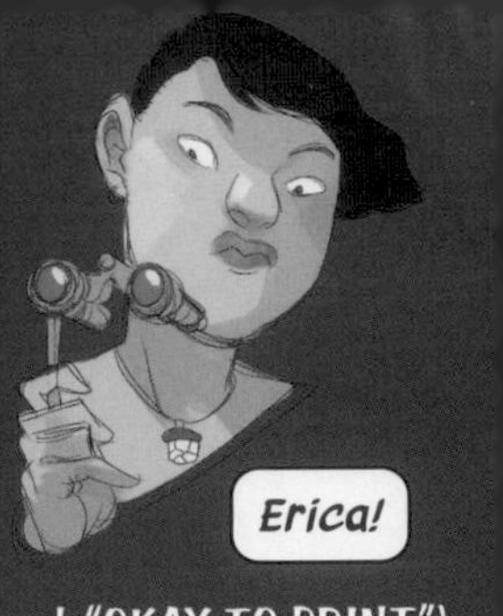
Erica!

Send letters to mheroes@marvel.com or 135 W 50th St, 7th Floor, New York, NY 10020 (Please mark "OKAY TO PRINT")

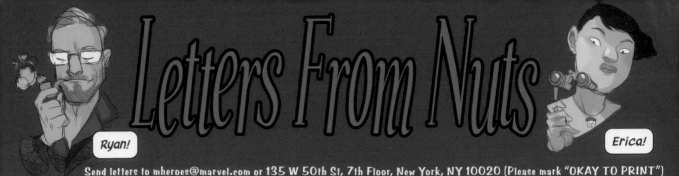

You folks get many letters from young girls in whose lives you have been important, which is great. I am not a small girl. I am a guy who is approaching 50. Squirrel Girl is very important to my life.

For the last few years, I have been dealing with chronic pain, unemployment, and (unsurprisingly) depression. The Unbeatable Squirrel Girl has made me *literally* laugh out loud a bare minimum of once every single issue, often more. (Most recently with "So I cannot give it my full recommendation.") Laughs can be hard to come by. You deliver.

No pressure,
Alexx

RYAN: Alexx, thank you so much. That's what we're here for! I've got a friend with chronic pain and it is such a daily struggle, so to have unemployment and depression on top of that -- it's rough, dude. I know what we do is small in the grand scheme of things, but I'm really happy that we can help you out, even a little!

ERICA: I think one of the things that has surprised me the most is the range of people who have told me they enjoy the book. I'm really glad that we could make something that has positively affected your life.

Ryan and Erica:

Your mention of Koi Boi heading off to visit the ruins of the underwater kingdom of New Atlantis brought a couple of questions to mind:

1) Will you be presenting that as a Squirrel Girl special episode? There are usually technology raiders searching out hidden Atlantean technology in their ruins (not to mention trying to find Atlantean skeletons to sell on the alternative medicine black market). Surely Koi Boi is likely to run into one of them. If not, a guided Visitors' Board tour of the ruins might be quite beautiful. Unfortunately, I can't remember which destruction of Atlantis this ruin is from. Was it bombed, nuked, or biologically destroyed? Hmm, why was Koi Boi going there again?

2) Koi are fresh water fish. New Atlantis is in salt water. I seem to remember Koi Boi swimming in the harbor area so I assume that he can breathe heavily polluted salt water but can he also breathe fresh water? Does his amphibious nature allow him to breathe both? Does he have to use special breathing equipment in one water or the other? Did Tony Stark make the salt filter / infuser unit for him? Man, this would make a really interesting Biology 201 class at his college!

Thanks for an entertaining comic,
Geoffrey Tolle
Lord of Squirrels (as soon as I start my 40 generation domestication project).

RYAN: 1) I don't think we'll show it! Normally I'd say "use your imagination," but you have clearly already done this, so I guess all I can say is "thanks for using your imagination!" If you could fill out that plot to 20 pages and send over a script, I'd be happy to take the credit for it!!

2) I think Erica and I discussed this and we agreed Koi Boi could breathe both salt and fresh water, but I admit we did not work out the specifics! Although MAYBE the fact that the original Atlantis is in fresh water is the reason everyone's had such a hard time finding it! MAYBE??

ERICA: I'm pretty sure he's good in all types of water. He can talk to all the fish and really just had to pick one to go with for the name. "Fish Boy" just doesn't cut it, you know?

Guys, Atlantis was built on the ruins of the original Atlantis 8,000 years ago. Anything that was there from the Great Cataclysm is surely in an underwater museum or merged into the new construction (like Rome) by now.

Ryan and Erica,

Wow guys, this comic is just swell. Squirrel Girl is truly unbeatable, and Nancy is such a rad character, and Koi Boy and Chipmunk Hunk are undeniably the most perfectly named super heroes ever. And geez, Brain Drain is just trying so hard to be a good superhero and I just...I just want him to be happy. I love you, Brain Drain, and I will always be proud of you. No matter what.

Squirrelfully Yours,

Elisha Smith
Knoxville, TN

RYAN: Aw, thank you! I -- I really love Brain Drain too. I am surprised at how cute he is, and I love how Erica has turned a literal brain with a pair of eyes attached into somehow the most facially expressive character. SHE IS MAGIC.

ERICA: I love our crazy nihilist brain trapped in a robot body trying to be a super hero.

Dear Letters From Nuts,

I wanted to draw attention to an apparent discrepancy on the cover of issue #11. There, the binary numbering is displayed in six digits, 001011, whereas five digits, 01011, would seem more applicable, since Doreen teaches Count Nefaria (and us readers) how to count in binary on a single hand, and five fingers equal five digits. Sidenote: the English word "digit" comes from the Latin word for "finger" -- how appropriate!

At first, I thought the cover numbering might have something to do with squirrels having six fingers, but a hasty Google image search revealed that four front fingers and five hind fingers are the usual sciurine characteristics. I flipped through the issue again and found no evidence of polydactyly.

Then it dawned on me: the six-digit binary numbering must have come from Doctor Octopus, who is right there on the cover. Raising one arm and the two opposite tentacles while keeping his other three not-being-used-for-standing appendages lowered is naturally how Doc Ock would flash his digits!

Does this explanation entitle me to a No-Prize? I do hope so! I've long aspired to the rank of Titanic True Believer (T.T.B.), which would in turn bump me up to Permanent Marvelite Maximus (P.M.M.).

Best,
Morris Tichenor, R.F.O., Q.N.S., K.O.F.
Toronto, ON

P.S. More etymology fun: the Latin word "digitus" probably derives from "dico" (meaning "to speak" + the suffix "-itus"). I like to image Romans gesticulated wildly whenever they spoke.

P.P.S. I want to second Erica's assertion that Nomad's Lorenzo Lamas phase is "the BEST Nomad." Thanks for giving a shout-out to one of my favorite '90s titles.

RYAN: Man I love a letter that starts out with "HERE IS A PROBLEM" and ends with "NEVERMIND, I HAVE COME UP WITH A SOLUTION TO THE PROBLEM THAT ONLY

REQUIRES YOU PRETEND THAT YOU WERE SMARTER THAN YOU ACTUALLY ARE," which is something I am more than willing to do and may actually already be doing. It is my understanding that No-Prizes are for THIS VERY THING, which makes me extremely excited about No-Prizes. My understanding that they're just pictures of empty envelopes makes me LESS excited, but, well, here we are. (Also the padded zeroes worked nicely from a design perspective, so really, TWO good reasons to do it that way.) ENJOY THE PRIZE:

ERICA: I... still haven't read #11, but what's important is that the issue you're currently reading got to the printers by the deadline.

I'm really hoping that now that Steve is on the run in the Marvel Cinematic U, we're going to get at least a moment of him with his hair grown out riding a motorcycle around. I know that he wasn't Nomad during that time, but we have to work with what we're given. Also, we know he can ride a motorcycle.

Dear Squirrel Girl Crew:

I enjoyed Squirrel Girl's run-in with the Mole Man. It looks like next month, we can expect Dr. Octopus and Venom. While Squirrel Girl certainly has taken on some of Marvel's big name villains, I recently became interested in one of the lesser lights. Might I suggest that Squirrel Girl versus the legend-in-her-own mind White Rabbit would have some great possibilities?

Sincerely
Robert Fisher

RYAN: The time delay on these letters means you have already (hopefully!) read the comic and seen what happens! Doc Ock and Venom are two of my favorite bad guys, so it was a treat to put them both in the same issue (KINDA, AGAIN, I CAN ONLY ASSUME YOU READ IT BUT DON'T WANT TO SPOIL ANYTHING). In any case, to answer your question, I just looked up the White Rabbit and she has a giant robot rabbit that fires missiles, so I'm already totally down with her whole thing.

ERICA: If you've read this issue, it probably means you just finished a three-issue arc starring a character who has only been in TWO OTHER ISSUES IN ALL OF MARVEL'S 70+ YEAR HISTORY. We're into the deep cuts too, is all I'm sayin'. I feel like one of the hardest parts of doing this is picking who the villain will be each time. We're literally going through that right now planning for issue #17. I feel like this is the one thing we have trouble agreeing on sometimes.

Another cracker from Ryan and Erica - kicking off with Spider-Man getting in on the Twitter conversation - and who is he kidding when he says that his webshooters make that "thwip" sound? We know that just like Wolverine, he makes that noise himself.

Count Nefaria was wonderful and the footnotes were right, we were all doing the counting on our fingers too. Very elegant solution to the nightmare about exams, which we've all had.

There are lots of good comics about at the moment, but Squirrel Girl, each and every issue is just a JOY. Easily the nicest lead character around - and isn't it lovely to show that you don't have to be dark or angsty or driven to be a compelling lead - you can actually be kind and perky too.

(Jacob - the facial expression on Count Nefaria's face in the "no way, you've got to teach me" panel was just perfect)

Many thanks

Andrew Pack
Brighton, England

RYAN: Yeah, Jacob did a terrific job on that issue, and I loved that we got to show that Doreen's dreams are a little brighter than the real world. That seems to fit, you know? Thank you for all these kind words, and I can only hope that future authors continue to characterize Count Nefaria as "a Dracula who likes numbers." IT WORKS, YO.

ERICA: I was so glad we got Jacob. I went to Wil with two names for who I'd like to use and Jacob wasn't even sure he could do it at the time, but we diiiiid iiiiit.

Dear Ryan, Erica, & Rico,

I first started reading Unbeatable Squirrel Girl after seeing a copy of the 1st volume at my library and thinking, "well, this looks ridiculous but potentially fun." Turns out it wasn't ridiculous (ok, maybe a little bit, but absolutely in a good way), and was more than just fun. I've been hooked on the adventures of Doreen, Tippy-Toe, & co. ever since. So much so that I cosplayed as Squirrel Girl for NYCC this year, and actually got to meet all of you (which was awesome)!

One of my favorite things about Squirrel Girl is that she doesn't just use the powers of squirrel, but those of girl as well. I love a good superhero fight scene, and Doreen can definitely kick butt (it's right there in her catchphrase) but my favorite moments are the ones where she uses reason, friendship, and sometimes even computer science to save the day. It's so refreshing to see a clever, optimistic, and ultimately inspiring superhero like Squirrel Girl who knows that it's often better to talk things out and solve problems with brains rather than fists.

Keep on eating nuts & kicking butts (and writing amazing new stories for Squirrel Girl)!

Rachel

P.S. I wish I could've gotten a photo with Rico too, but my friend had wandered off

with the camera. Thank you so much for the button though, Rico! No one has asked me about my squirrel powers yet, but I remain hopeful.

RYAN: Rachel, it was SO GREAT to meet you at NYCC! At that show I was given my very own stuffed Tippy-Toe by a fan, so now I can pass as -- well, not Squirrel Girl, but Squirrel Earl at least. Your costume is amazing, and this letter is the best. I like the photo with Erica the best because it shows off your tail -- IT WAS A REALLY WELL-MADE TAIL, EVERYONE! Fun fact: NYCC was the first time Rico and I met in real life, and then later on we all went out to dinner and ate delicious guacamole. WE LIVED OUR BEST LIVES THAT DAY.

Next Issue:

Attention, Squirrel Scouts! Make sure to check out our production blog, unbeatablesquirrelgirl.tumblr.com, where we post behind-the-scenes stuff on how the book gets made, along with all sorts of cool things you make: fanart, cosplay, whatever!

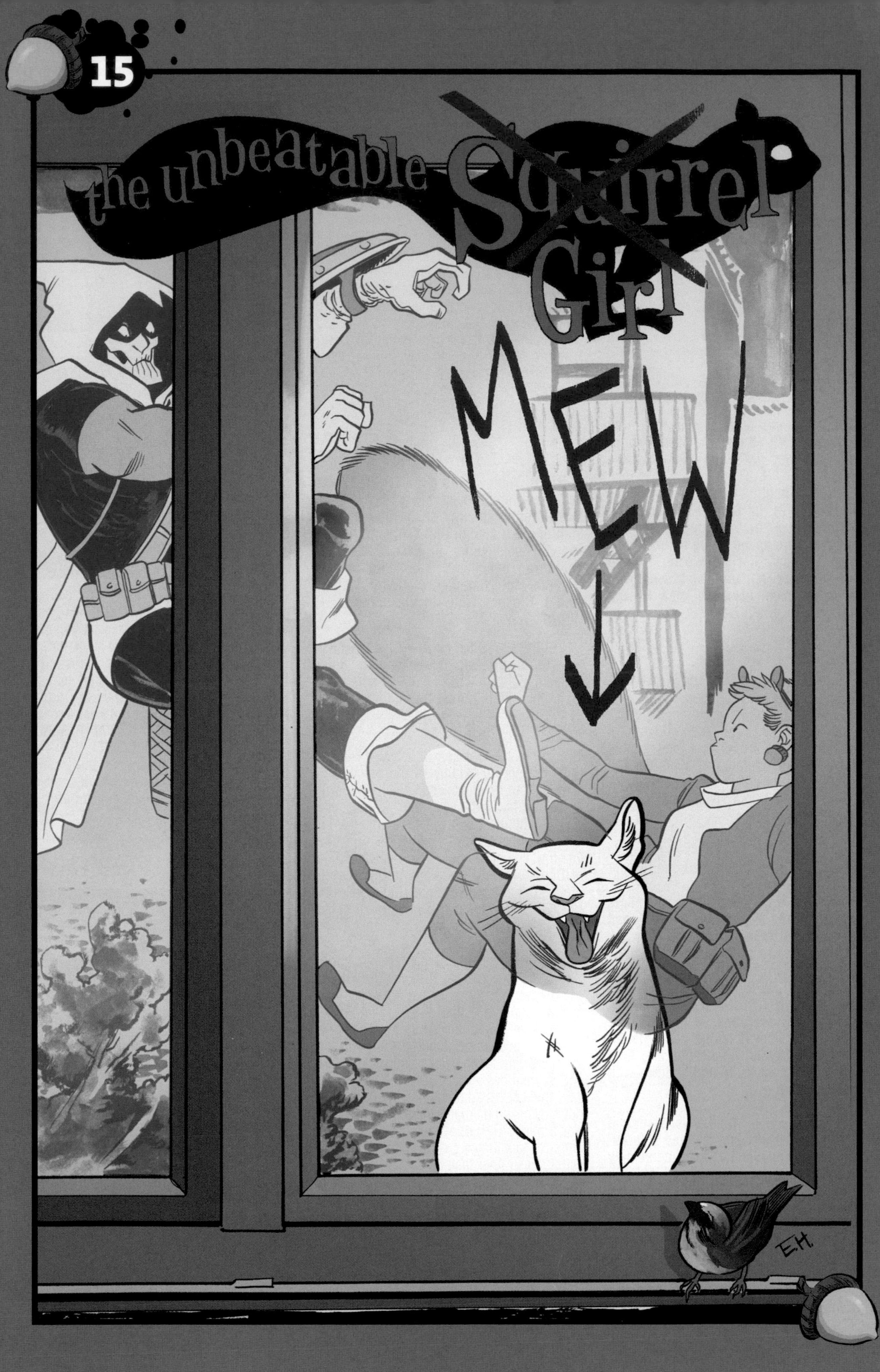
15
the unbeatable Squirrel Girl
MEW
E.H.

*Doreen Green isn't just a second-year computer science student: she secretly also has all the powers of both squirrel and girl! She uses her amazing abilities to fight crime and be as awesome as possible. You know her as...**The Unbeatable Squirrel Girl!** Find out what she's been up to, with...*

Squirrel Girl in a nutshell

Nancy Whitehead @sewwiththeflo
zcadfewg5ttyniu,o;

Nancy Whitehead @sewwiththeflo
Hey everyone, sorry, my cat got on my keyboard and somehow posted that. Pretty cute though, right? Anyway, test post please ignore.

Nancy Whitehead @sewwiththeflo
';,l;joih87t67r5d4dsaqzdx

Nancy Whitehead @sewwiththeflo
Once more, sorry, Mew walked on my laptop again. Less cute the second time. I'll keep it closed from now on.

Nancy Whitehead @sewwiththeflo
hrzayus5f3iu6t54h76p8k70[k98;'--]\

Nancy Whitehead @sewwiththeflo
Okay okay she got on my phone this time but I PROMISE Mew will stop posting on my account.

Nancy Whitehead @sewwiththeflo
Thank you all for following me on social media today and I hoped you enjoyed this unscheduled #content.

Nancy Whitehead @sewwiththeflo
fmgnsjkbehrftyqu27334dfd5yn7c5jmikn,ob,lm;n9',

Nancy Whitehead @sewwiththeflo
Mew, how is this happening

Nancy Whitehead @sewwiththeflo
How is this happening, Mew

Nancy Whitehead @sewwiththeflo
XSCDV32CDN43KJ54HK6LUUMIK9OP97LKI

Nancy Whitehead @sewwiththeflo
Sorry, I'm sorry, I don't know how this keeps being a thing. I put my laptop under the bed WHILE LOGGED OUT, and yet here we are??

Nancy Whitehead @sewwiththeflo
VDSABCwvce32j43t56hy86jk98..l;jk

Nancy Whitehead @sewwiththeflo
Look all I can say is: if you followed me on this site then you knew the risks.

Squirrel Girl @unbeatablesg
@sewwiththeflo Maybe you should ask Mew to put her social media posts on... PAWS

Nancy Whitehead @sewwiththeflo
@unbeatablesg xacf435hy6gngj7ti7tj

Nancy Whitehead @sewwiththeflo
@unbeatablesg OKAY SHE'S REPLYING TO YOU NOW, HOLY COW, THIS IS CRAZY, WHAT IS GOING ON

Squirrel Girl @unbeatablesg
@sewwiththeflo I agree it's...CLAWS for concern

Nancy Whitehead @sewwiththeflo
@unbeatablesg I THINK I FIGURED IT OUT, YOU HAVE TO HIT CTRL+ENTER TO POST AND HER NATURAL GAIT REACHES THOSE TWO KEYS

Squirrel Girl @unbeatablesg
@sewwiththeflo but how is she getting the laptop open though??

Nancy Whitehead @sewwiththeflo
@unbeatablesg Listen, Mew is the best cat and therefore I'm sure she has her ways, but I'm CERTAIN now I've figured it out.

Nancy Whitehead @sewwiththeflo
@unbeatablesg It won't happen again. EVER.

Nancy Whitehead @sewwiththeflo
zwdreh4u7oi98p-['9=-=;p0lomnybtcdexweaq

Nancy Whitehead @sewwiththeflo
MEW

Nancy Whitehead @sewwiththeflo
WHY

Nancy Whitehead @sewwiththeflo
WHY, MEW

search!

#zcrg5ju7,i;

#lknmjguifte4w3q

#zcdvtnmukil;;;;;;;;;;

#8dfuetryt3#4

#cyuu6ui7jjmmm

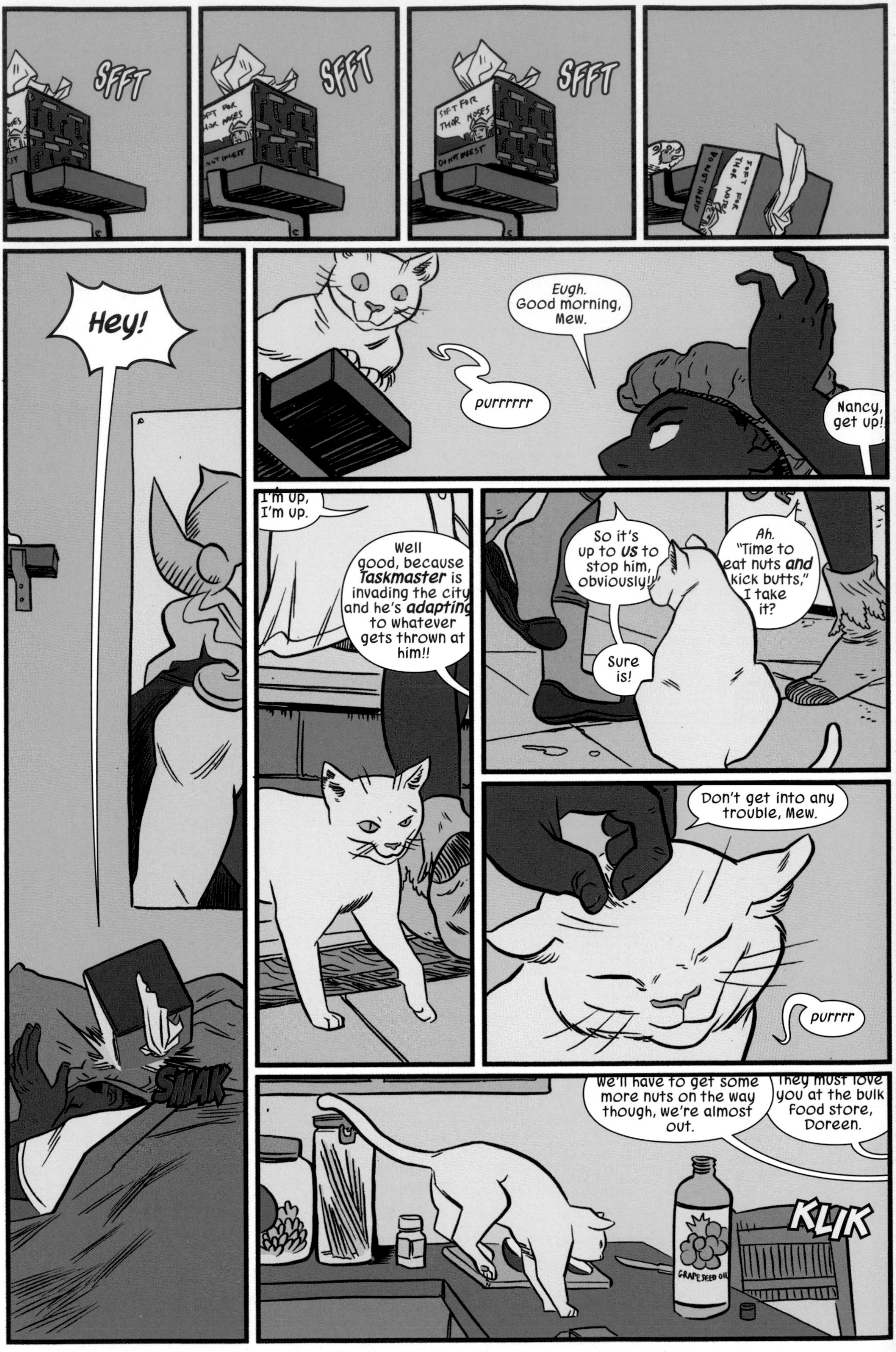
SFFT
SOFT FOR THOR NOSES
DO NOT INGEST
SFFT
SFFT
Hey!
SMAK
Eugh. Good morning, Mew.
purrrrrr
Nancy, get up!!
I'm up, I'm up.
Well good, because Taskmaster is invading the city and he's adapting to whatever gets thrown at him!!
So it's up to US to stop him, obviously!!
Sure is!
Ah. "Time to eat nuts and kick butts," I take it?
Don't get into any trouble, Mew.
purrrr
We'll have to get some more nuts on the way though, we're almost out.
They must love you at the bulk food store, Doreen.
GRAPE SEED OIL
KLIK

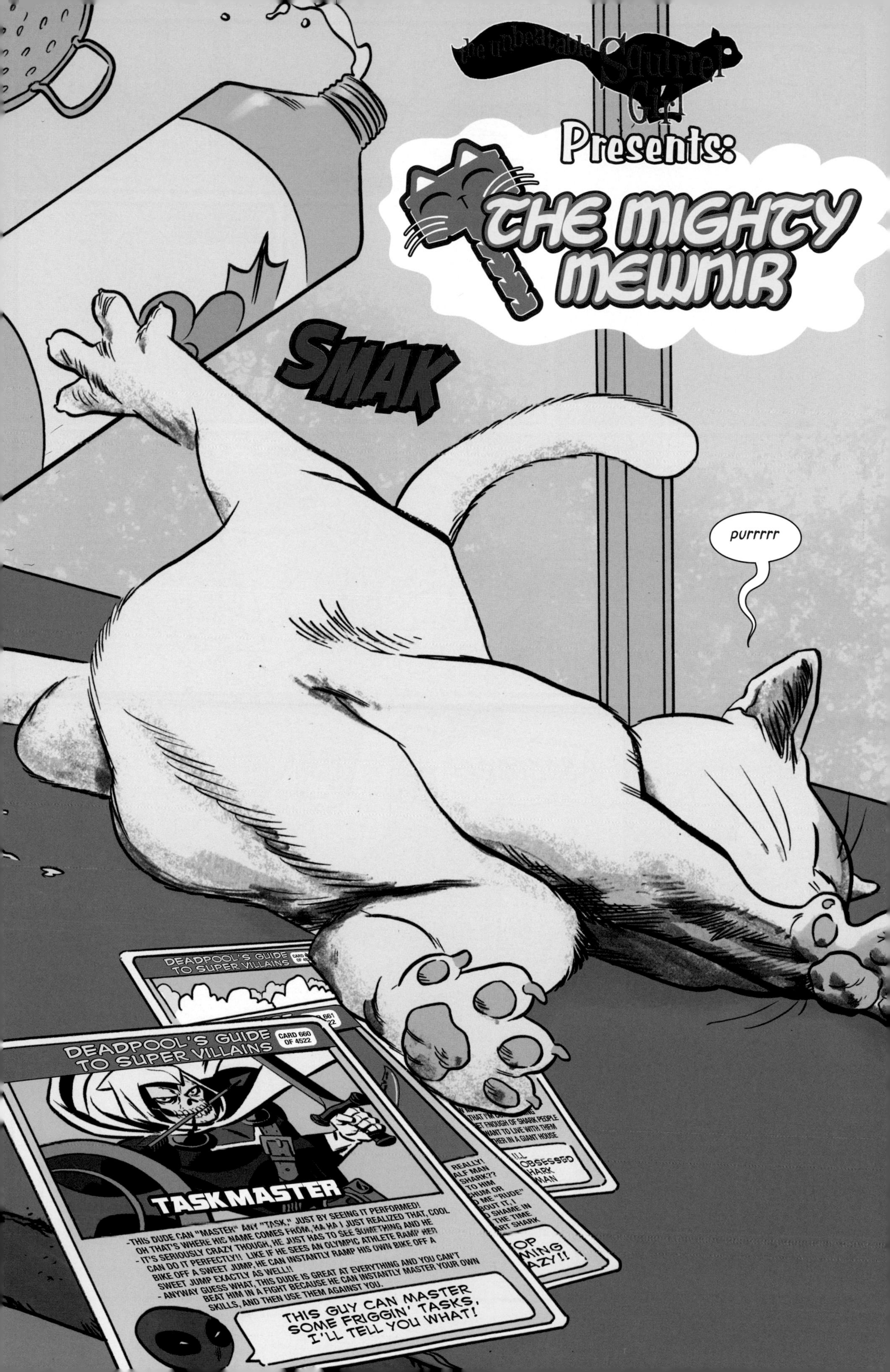

the unbeatable Squirrel Girl
Presents:
THE MIGHTY MEWNIR
SMAK
purrrrr
DEADPOOL'S GUIDE TO SUPER VILLAINS
CARD 660 OF 4522
TASKMASTER
-THIS DUDE CAN "MASTER" ANY "TASK," JUST BY SEEING IT PERFORMED! OH THAT'S WHERE HIS NAME COMES FROM, HA HA I JUST REALIZED THAT, COOL
- IT'S SERIOUSLY CRAZY THOUGH, HE JUST HAS TO SEE SOMETHING AND HE CAN DO IT PERFECTLY!! LIKE IF HE SEES AN OLYMPIC ATHLETE RAMP HER BIKE OFF A SWEET JUMP, HE CAN INSTANTLY RAMP HIS OWN BIKE OFF A SWEET JUMP EXACTLY AS WELL!!
- ANYWAY GUESS WHAT, THIS DUDE IS GREAT AT EVERYTHING AND YOU CAN'T BEAT HIM IN A FIGHT BECAUSE HE CAN INSTANTLY MASTER YOUR OWN SKILLS, AND THEN USE THEM AGAINST YOU.
THIS GUY CAN MASTER SOME FRIGGIN' TASKS, I'LL TELL YOU WHAT!

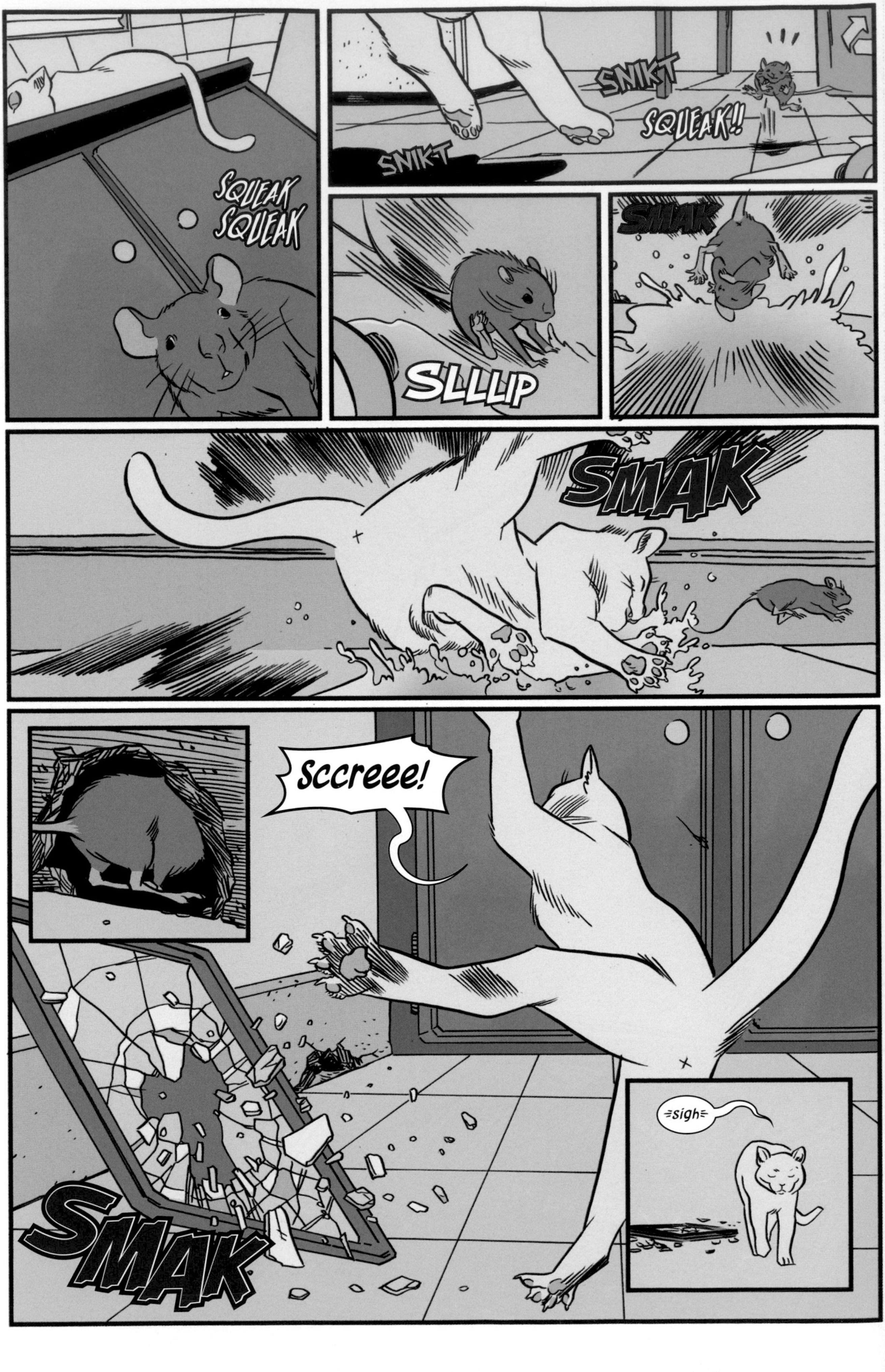
SQUEAK SQUEAK
SNIKT
SNIKT
SQUEAK!!
SLLLIP
SMAK
SMAK
Sccreee!
SMAK
sigh

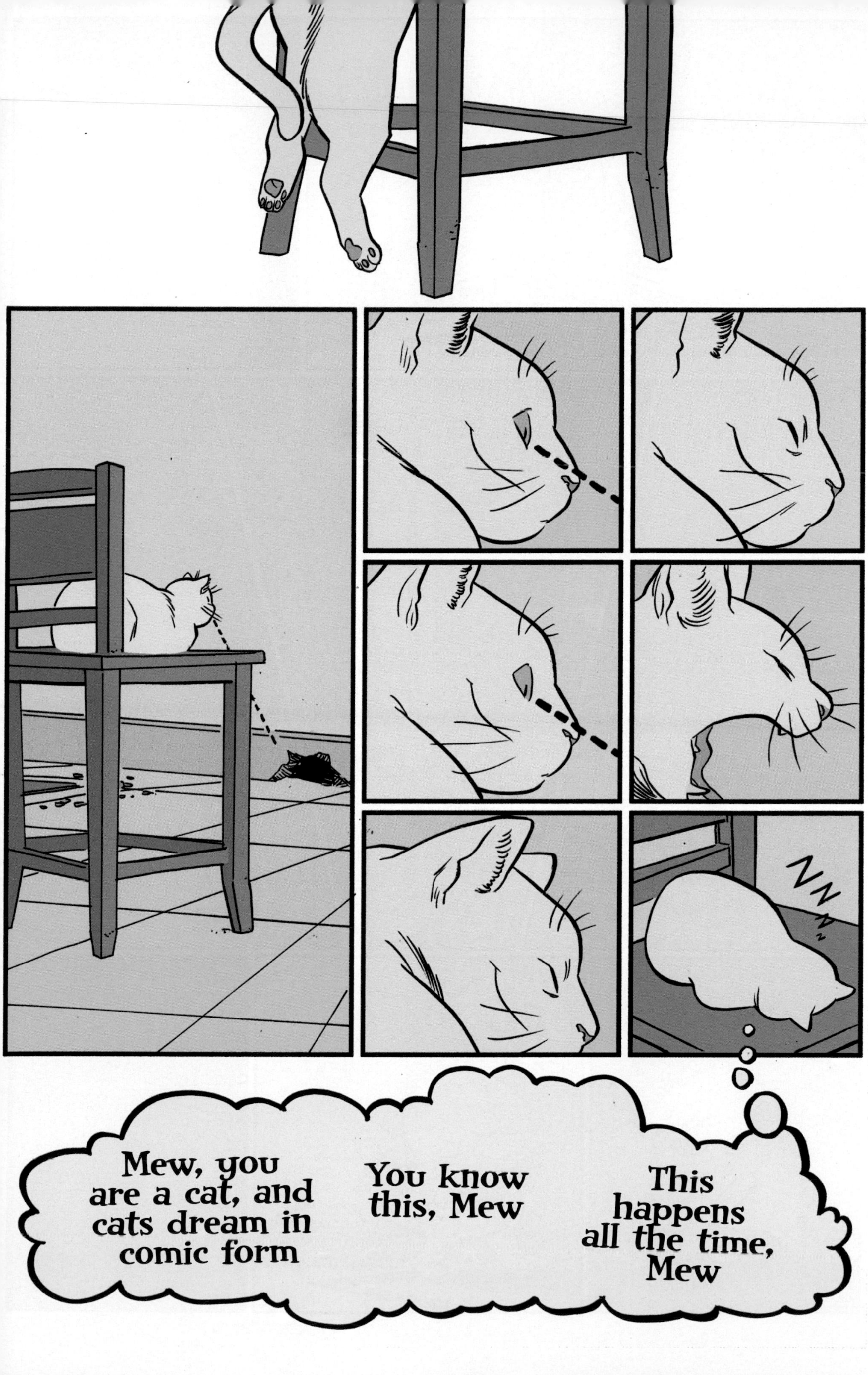
ZZZ
Mew, you are a cat, and cats dream in comic form
You know this, Mew
This happens all the time, Mew

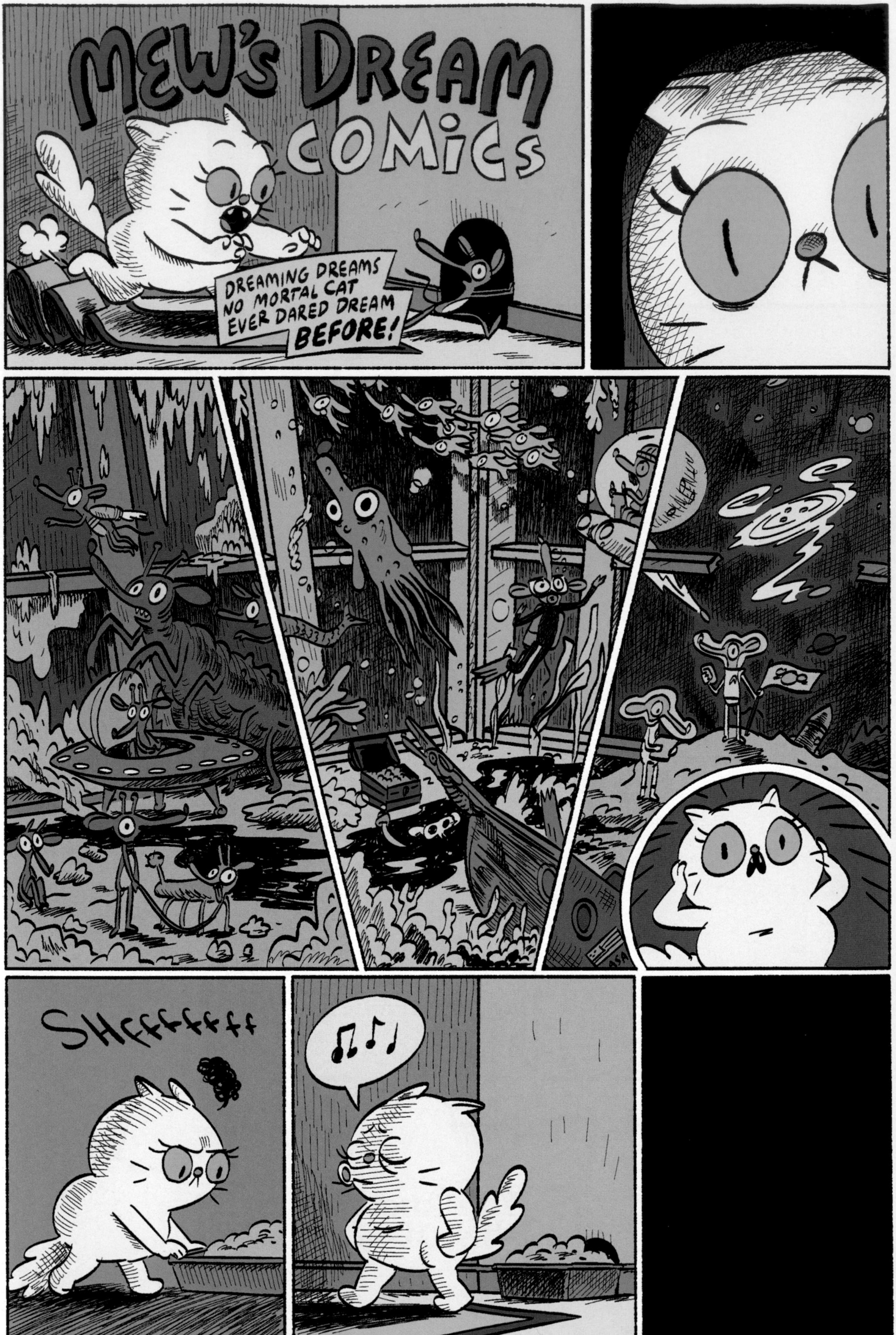
MEW'S DREAM COMICS
DREAMING DREAMS NO MORTAL CAT EVER DARED DREAM BEFORE!
SHFFFFFFF

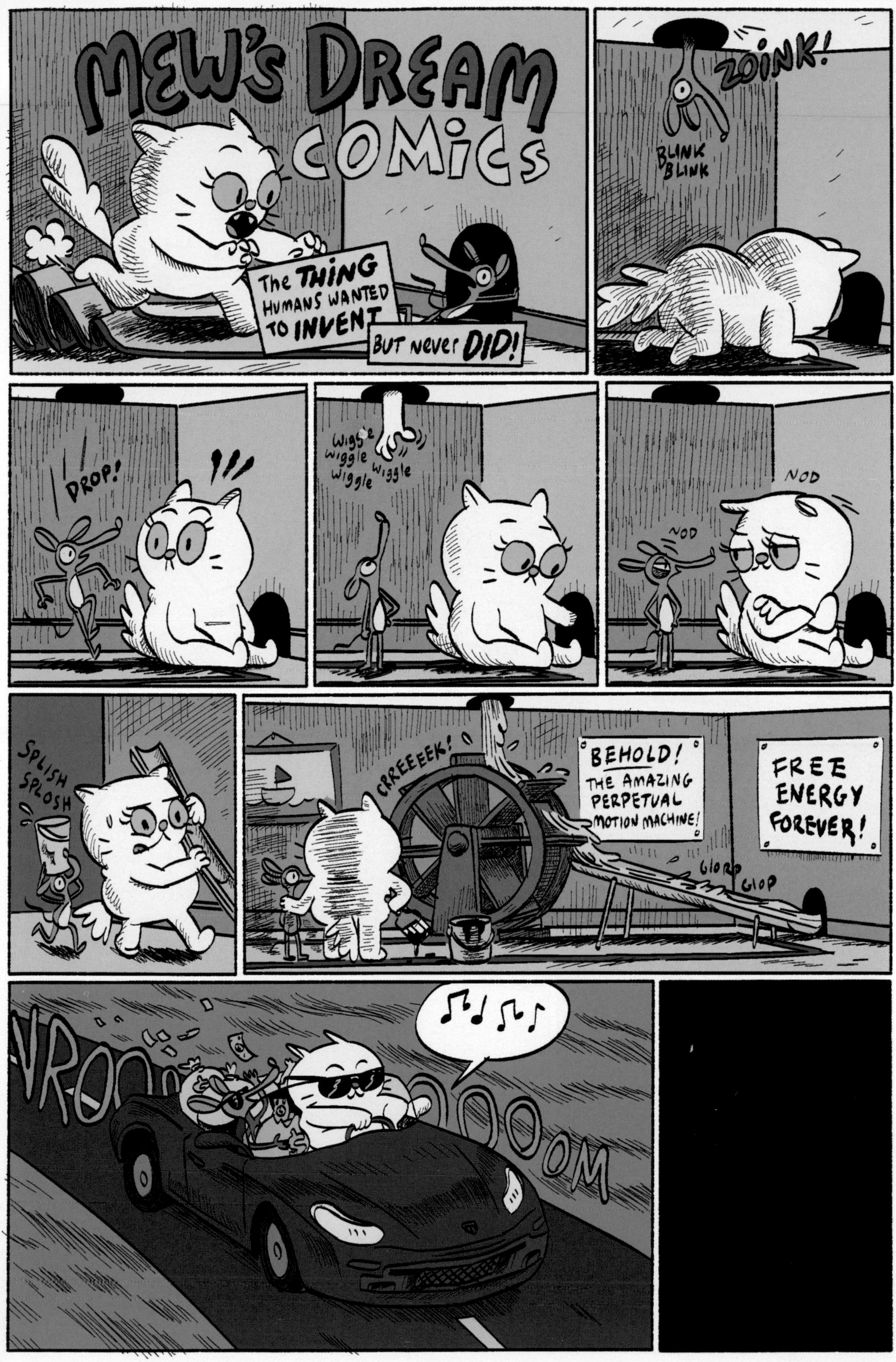
MEW'S DREAM COMICS
The THING HUMANS WANTED TO INVENT
BUT never DID!
ZOINK!
BLINK BLINK
DROP!
wiggle wiggle wiggle wiggle
NOD
NOD
SPLISH SPLOSH
CRREEEEK!
BEHOLD! THE AMAZING PERPETUAL MOTION MACHINE!
FREE ENERGY FOREVER!
GLORP GLOP
VROOOOOOOOM

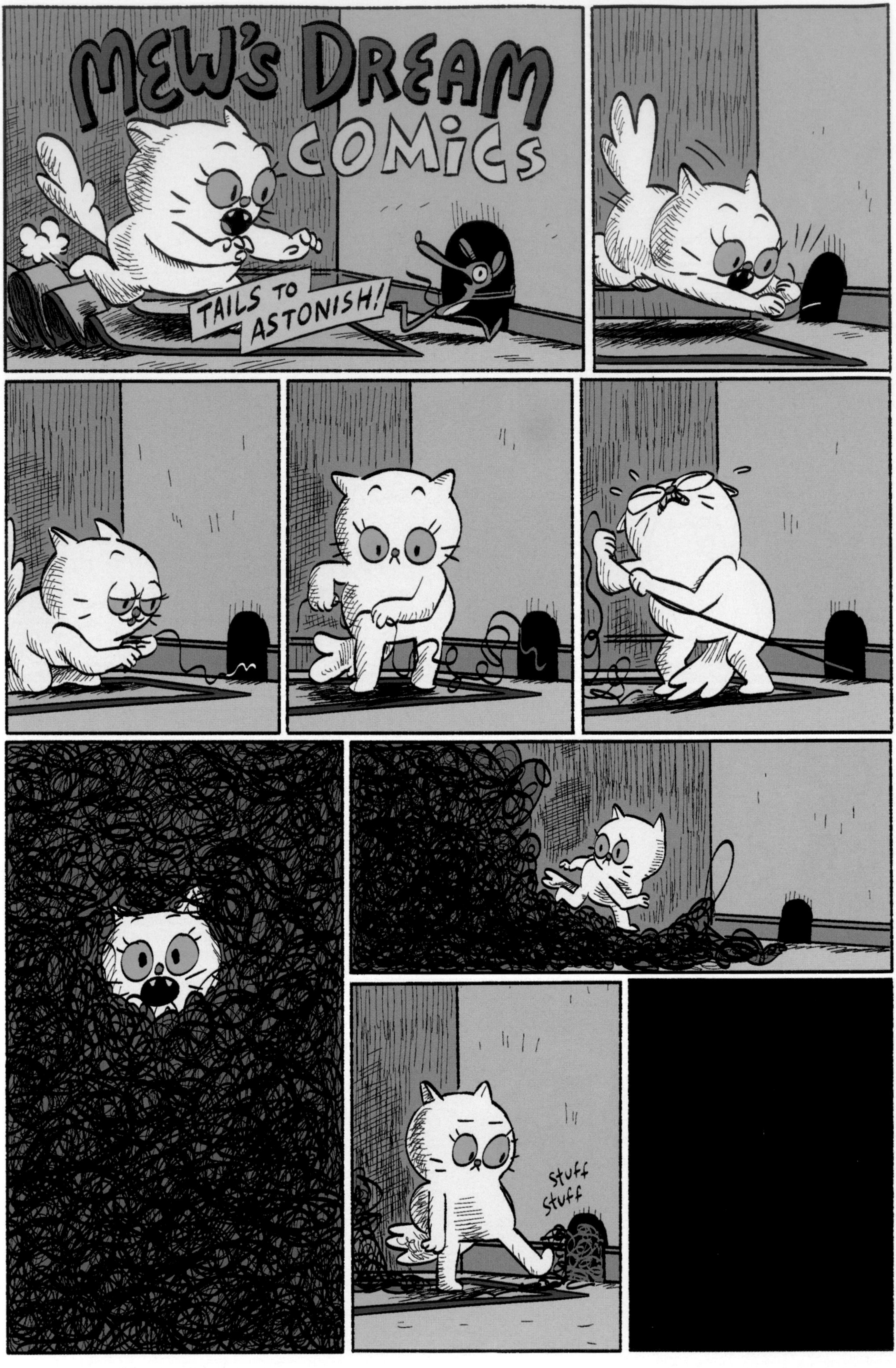
MEW'S DREAM COMICS
TAILS TO ASTONISH!
STUFF
STUFF

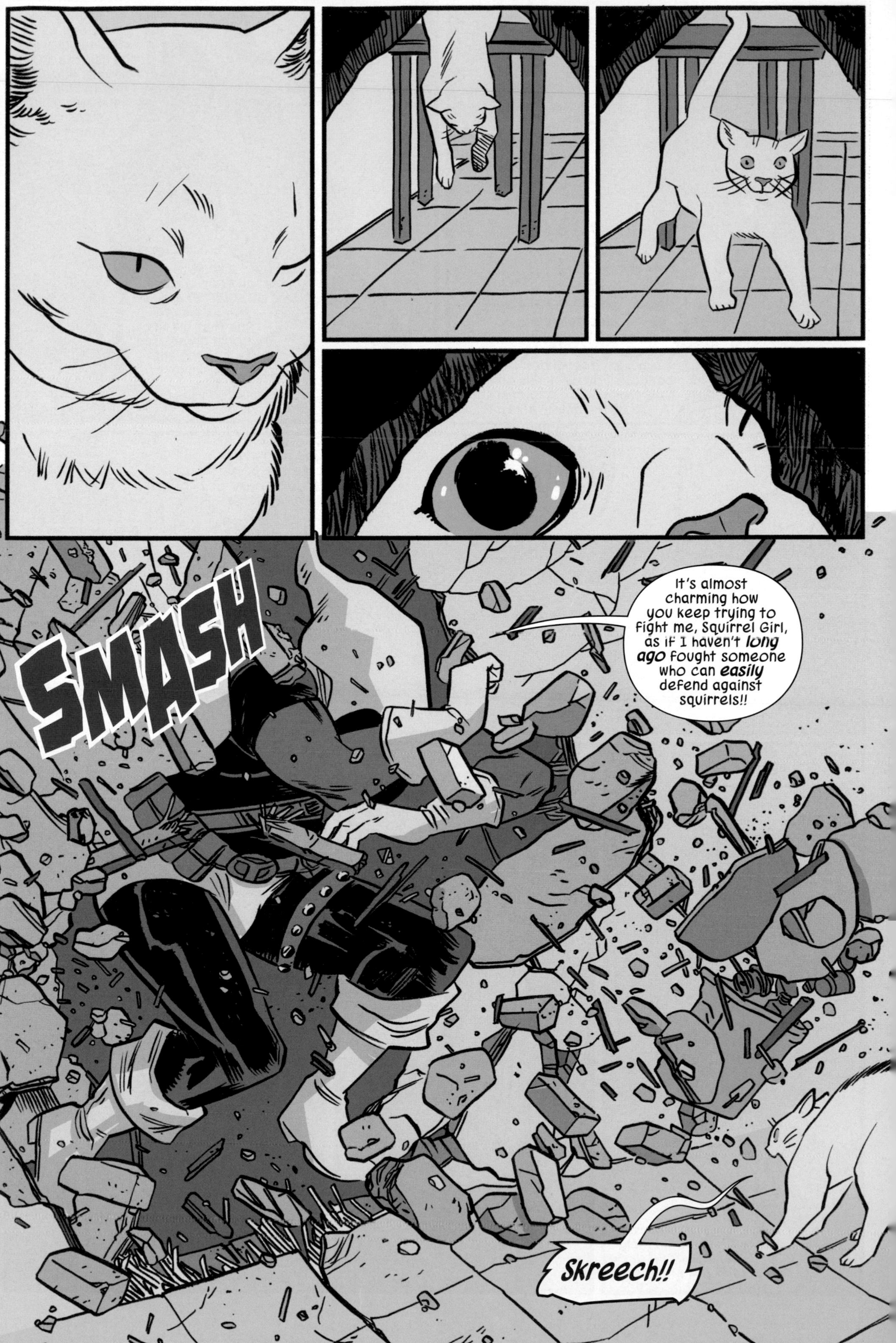
SMASH
It's almost charming how you keep trying to fight me, Squirrel Girl, as if I haven't long ago fought someone who can easily defend against squirrels!!
Skreech!!

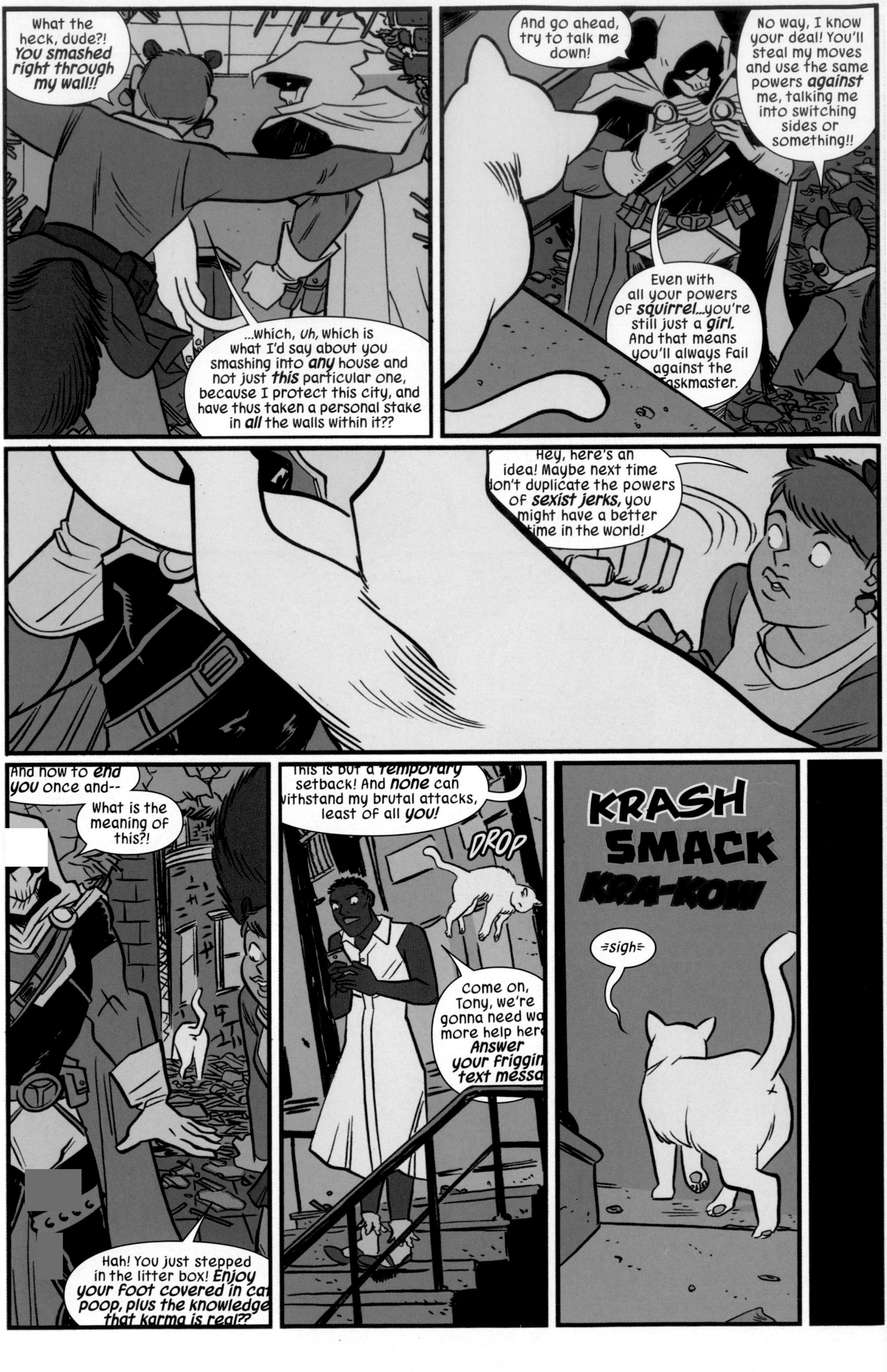

What the heck, dude?! You smashed right through my wall!!
...Which, uh, which is what I'd say about you smashing into any house and not just this particular one, because I protect this city, and have thus taken a personal stake in all the walls within it??
And go ahead, try to talk me down!
No way, I know your deal! You'll steal my moves and use the same powers against me, talking me into switching sides or something!!
Even with all your powers of squirrel...you're still just a girl. And that means you'll always fail against the askmaster.
Hey, here's an idea! Maybe next time don't duplicate the powers of sexist jerks, you might have a better time in the world!
And how to end you once and--
What is the meaning of this?!
Hah! You just stepped in the litter box! Enjoy your foot covered in ca poop, plus the knowledge that karma is real??
This is but a temporary setback! And none can withstand my brutal attacks, least of all you!
DROP
Come on, Tony, we're gonna need wa more help here Answer your friggin text messa
KRASH
SMACK
KRA-KOW
=sigh=

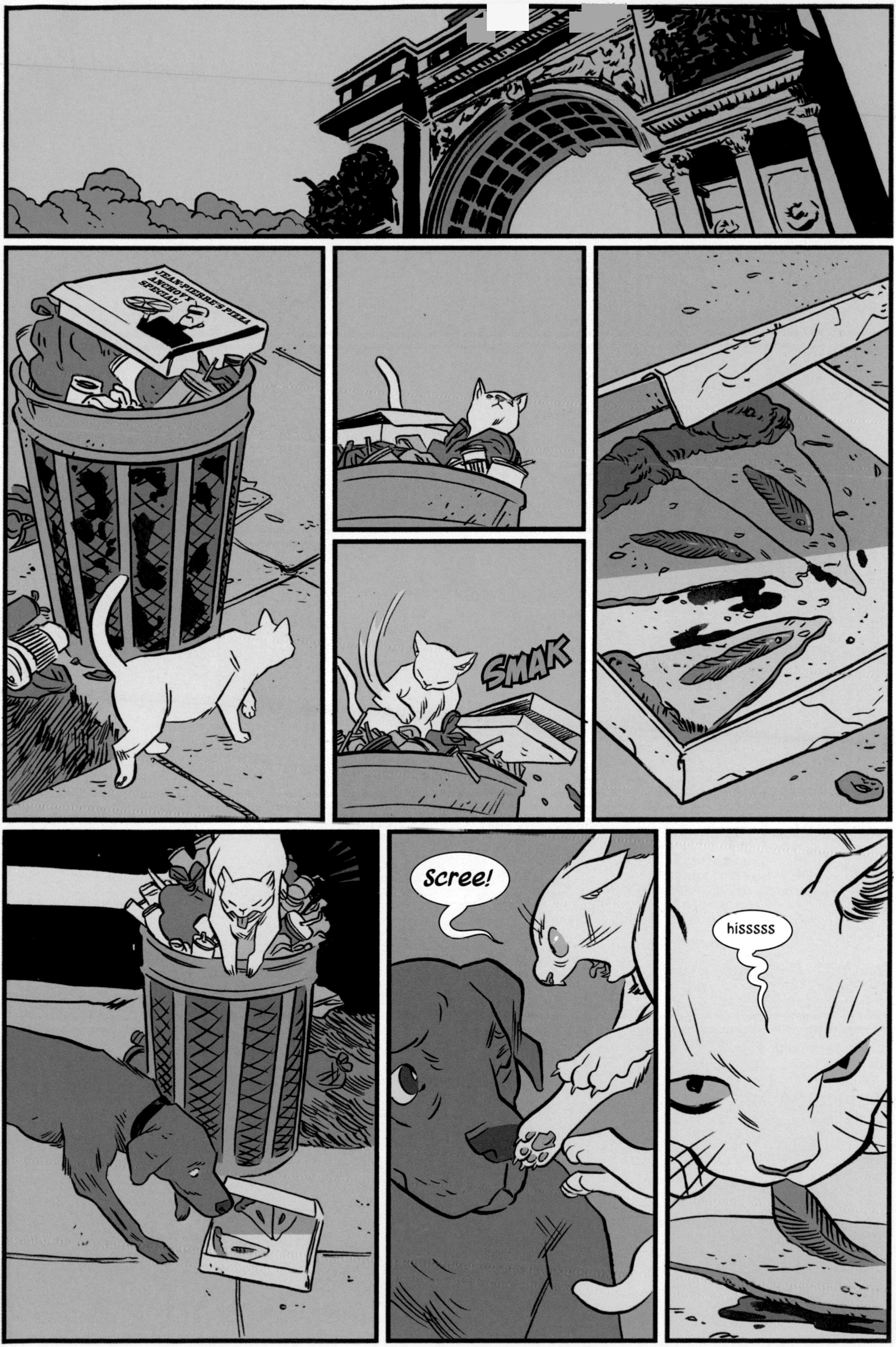
JEAN-PIERRE'S PIZZA
ANCHOVY SPECIAL!
SMAK
Scree!
hisssss

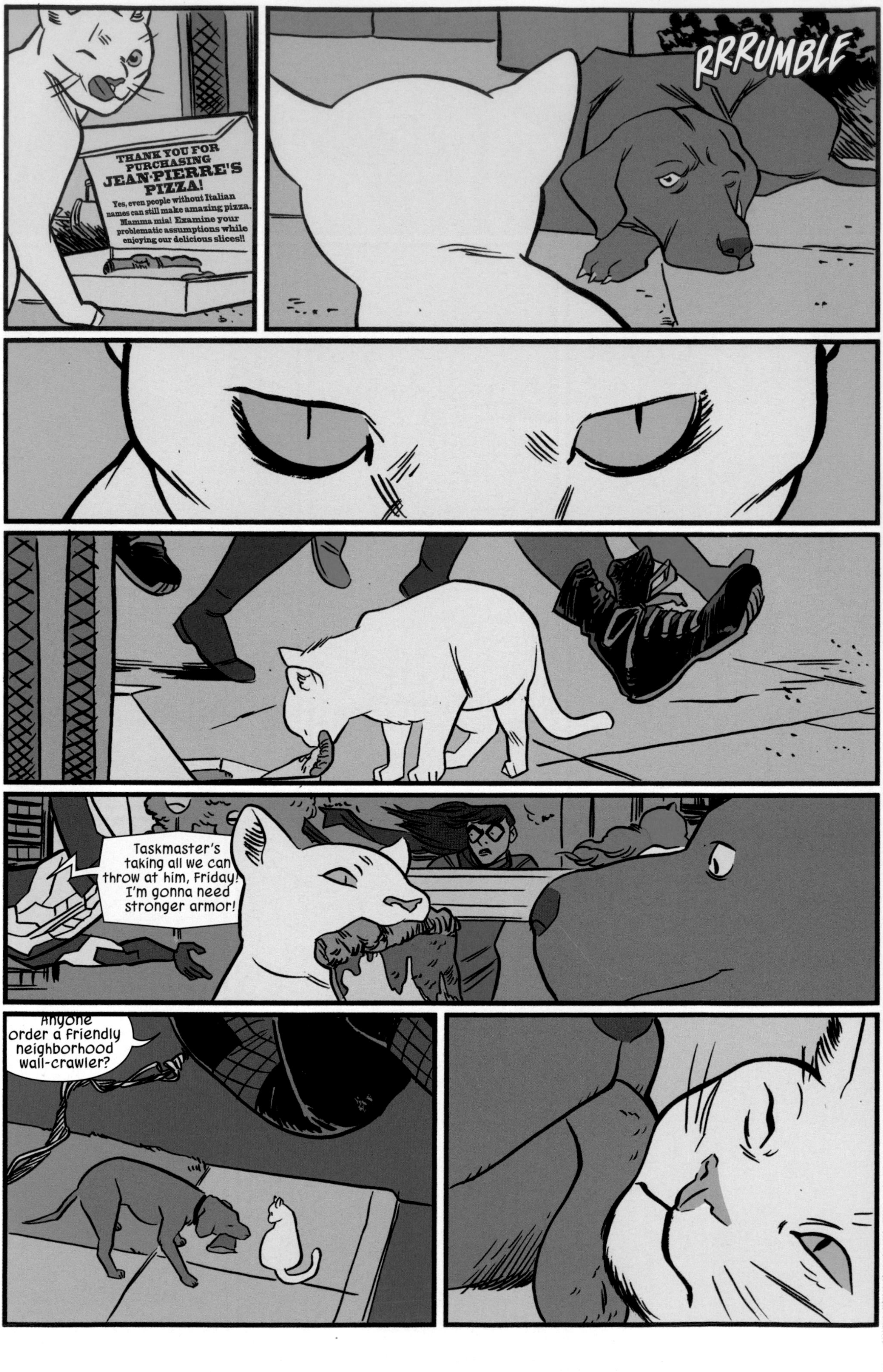
THANK YOU FOR PURCHASING JEAN-PIERRE'S PIZZA!
Yes, even people without Italian names can still make amazing pizza. Mamma mia! Examine your problematic assumptions while enjoying our delicious slices!!
RRRUMBLE
Taskmaster's taking all we can throw at him, Friday! I'm gonna need stronger armor!
Anyone order a friendly neighborhood wall-crawler?

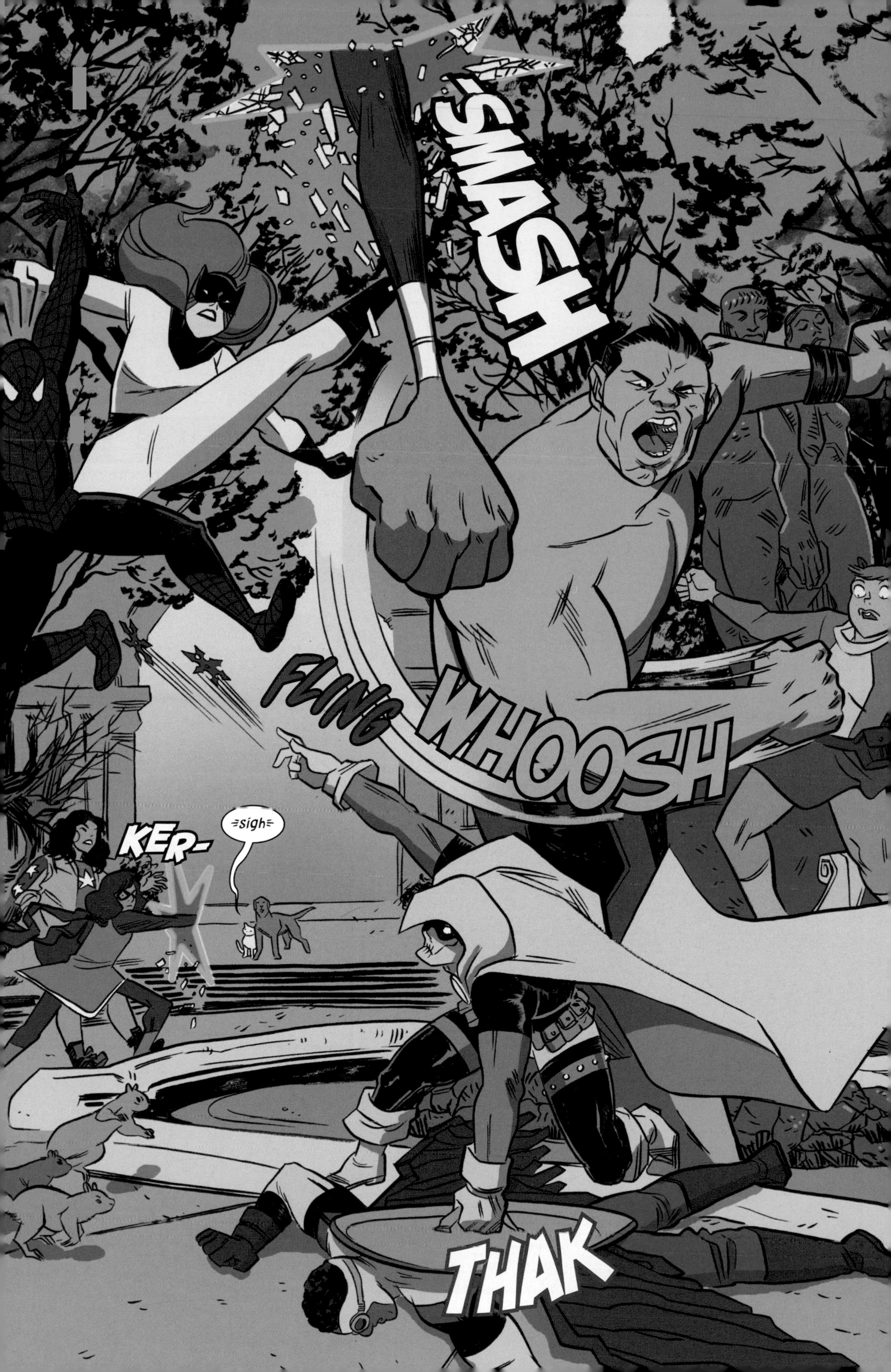
SMASH
FLING
WHOOSH
KER-
sigh
THAK

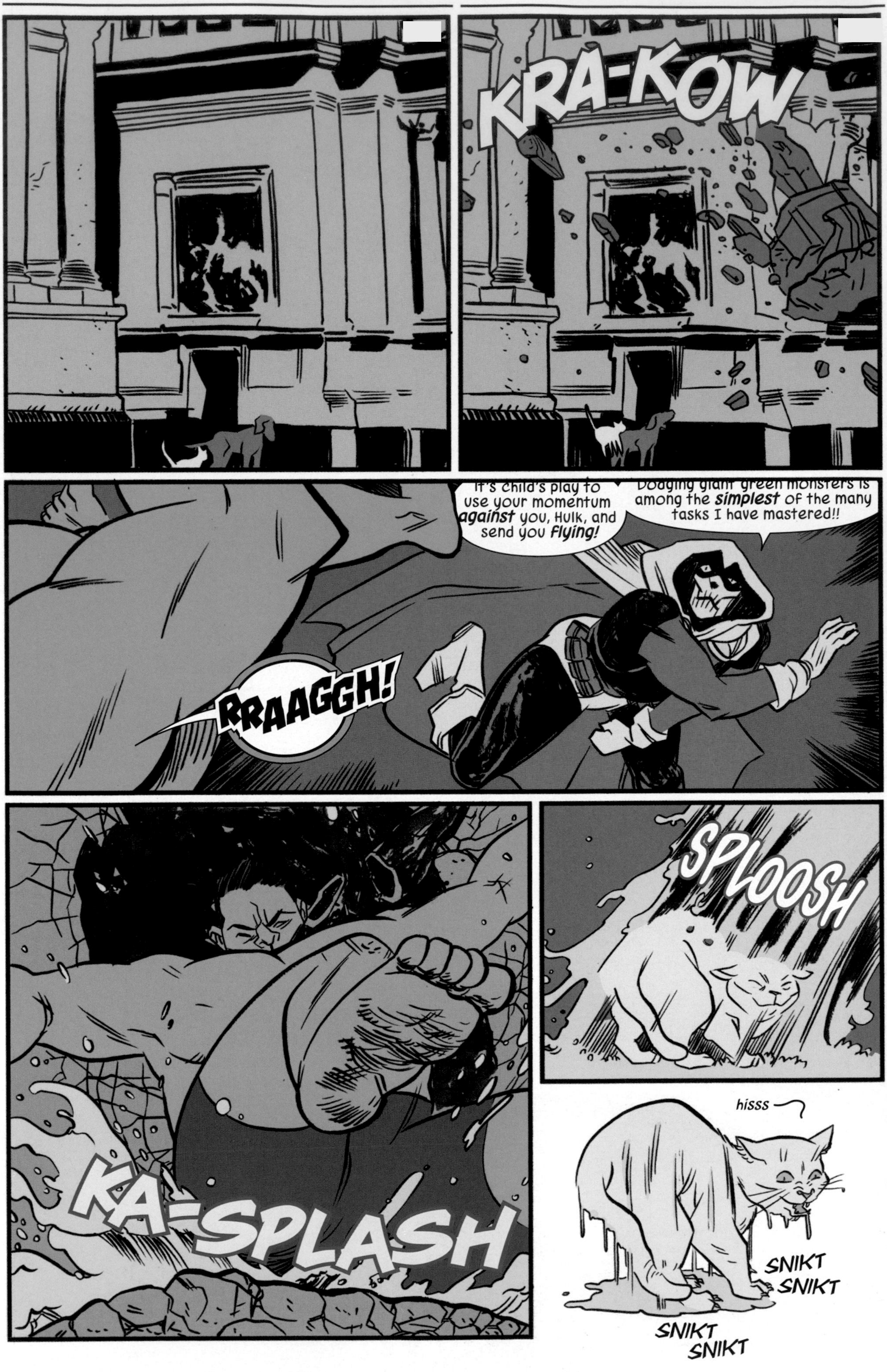
KRA-KOW
It's child's play to use your momentum *against* you, Hulk, and send you *flying!*
Dodging giant green monsters is among the *simplest* of the many tasks I have mastered!!
RRAAGGH!
KA-SPLASH
SPLOOSH
hisss
SNIKT
SNIKT
SNIKT
SNIKT

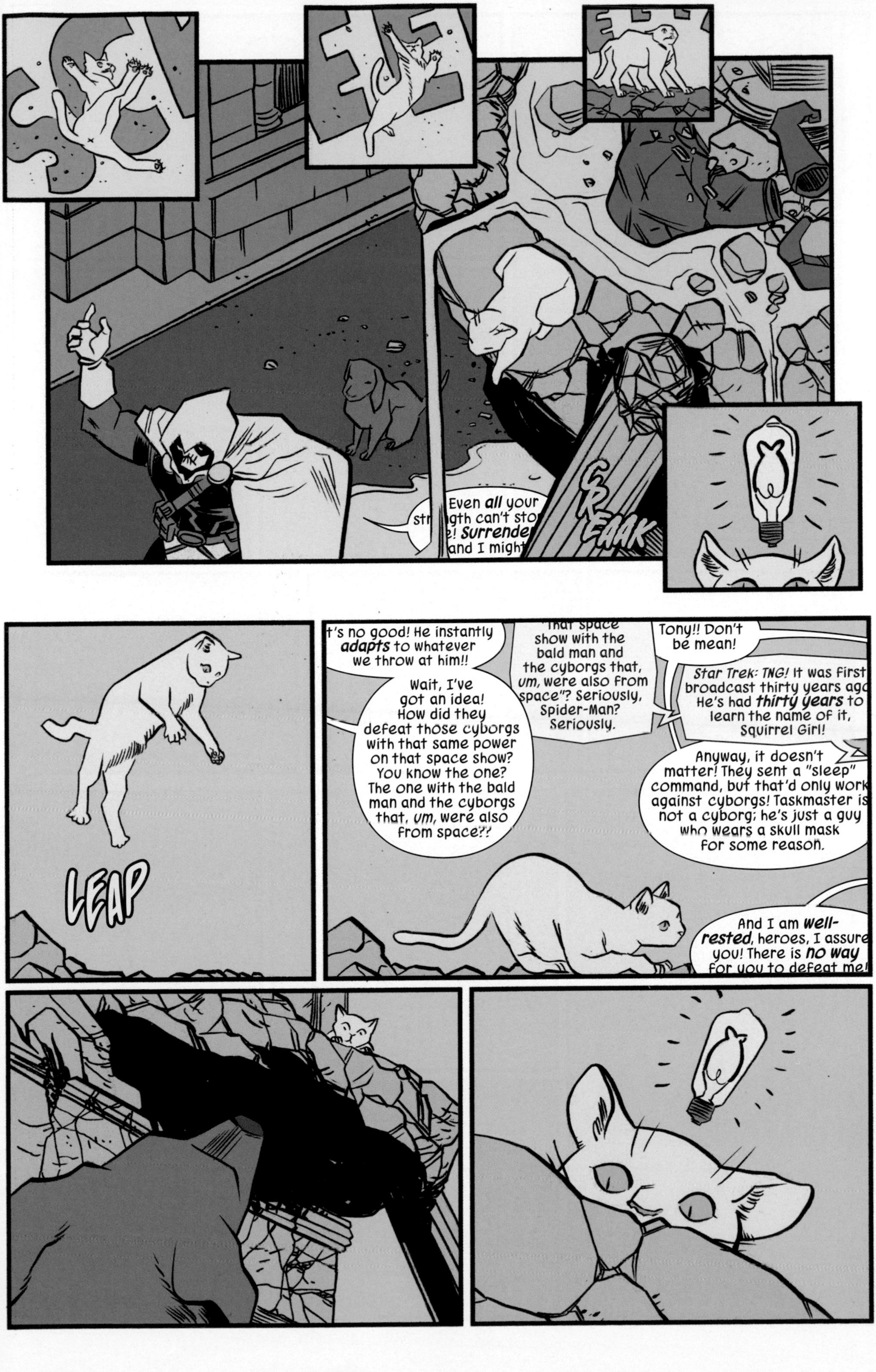

Even all your strength can't stop me! Surrender and I might
CREAAK
LEAP
It's no good! He instantly adapts to whatever we throw at him!!
Wait, I've got an idea! How did they defeat those cyborgs with that same power on that space show? You know the one? The one with the bald man and the cyborgs that, um, were also from space??
"That space show with the bald man and the cyborgs that, um, were also from space"? Seriously, Spider-Man? Seriously.
Tony!! Don't be mean!
Star Trek: TNG! It was first broadcast thirty years ago. He's had thirty years to learn the name of it, Squirrel Girl!
Anyway, it doesn't matter! They sent a "sleep" command, but that'd only work against cyborgs! Taskmaster is not a cyborg; he's just a guy who wears a skull mask for some reason.
And I am well-rested, heroes, I assure you! There is no way for you to defeat me!

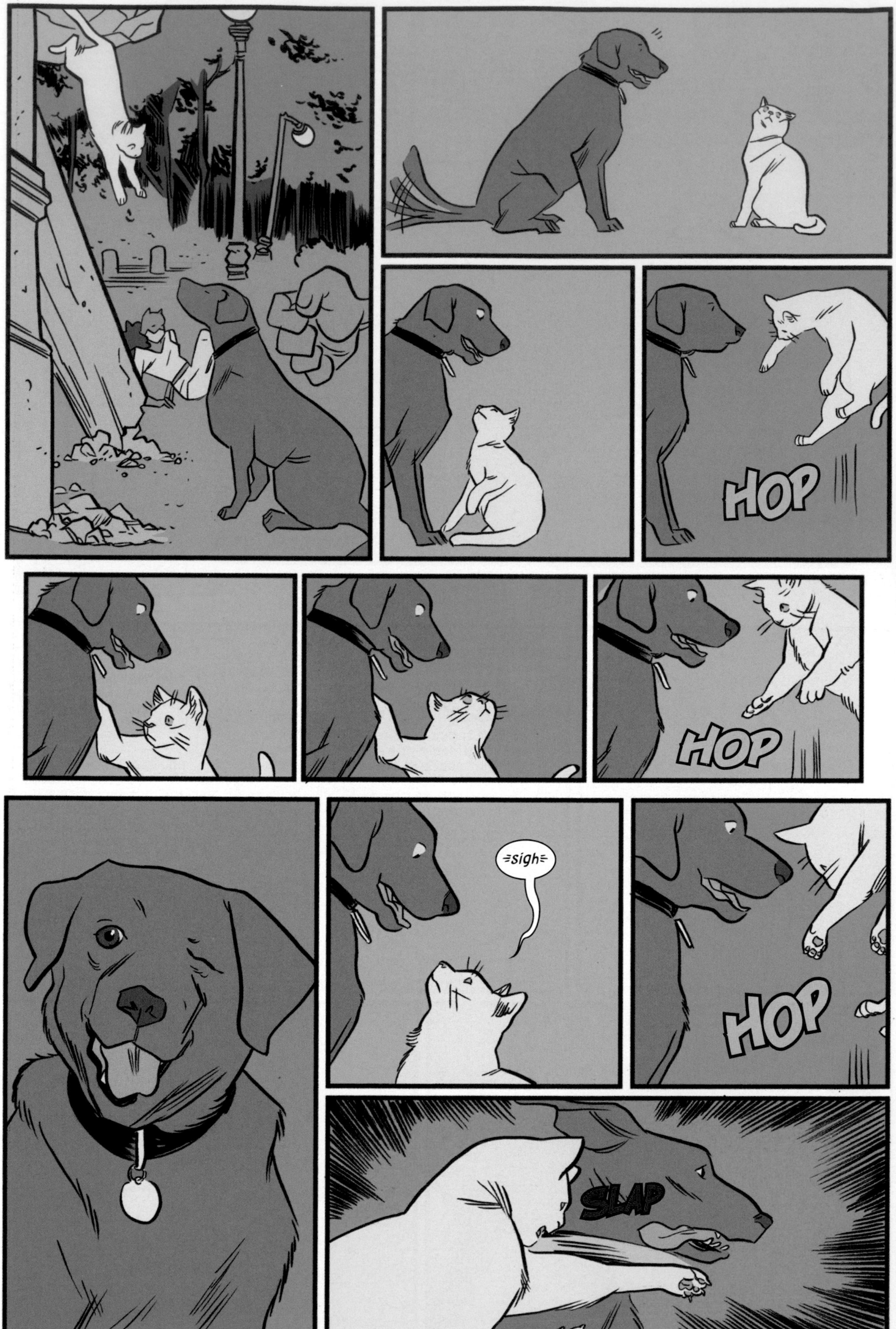
HOP
HOP
sigh
HOP
SLAP

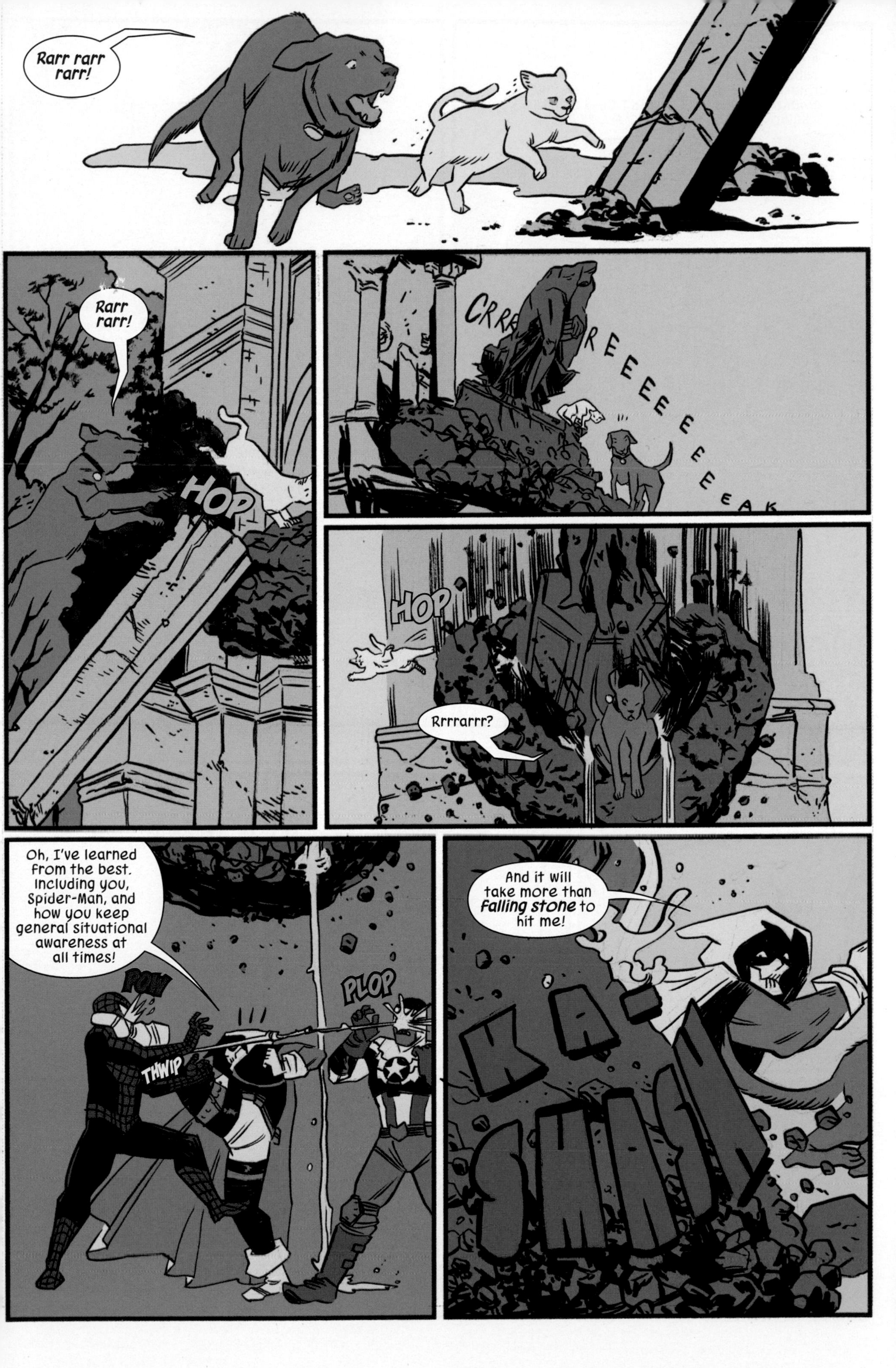
Rarr rarr rarr!
Rarr rarr!
HOP
CRRREEEEEEEEEAK
HOP
Rrrrarrr?
Oh, I've learned from the best. Including you, Spider-Man, and how you keep general situational awareness at all times!
POW
THWIP
PLOP
And it will take more than falling stone to hit me!

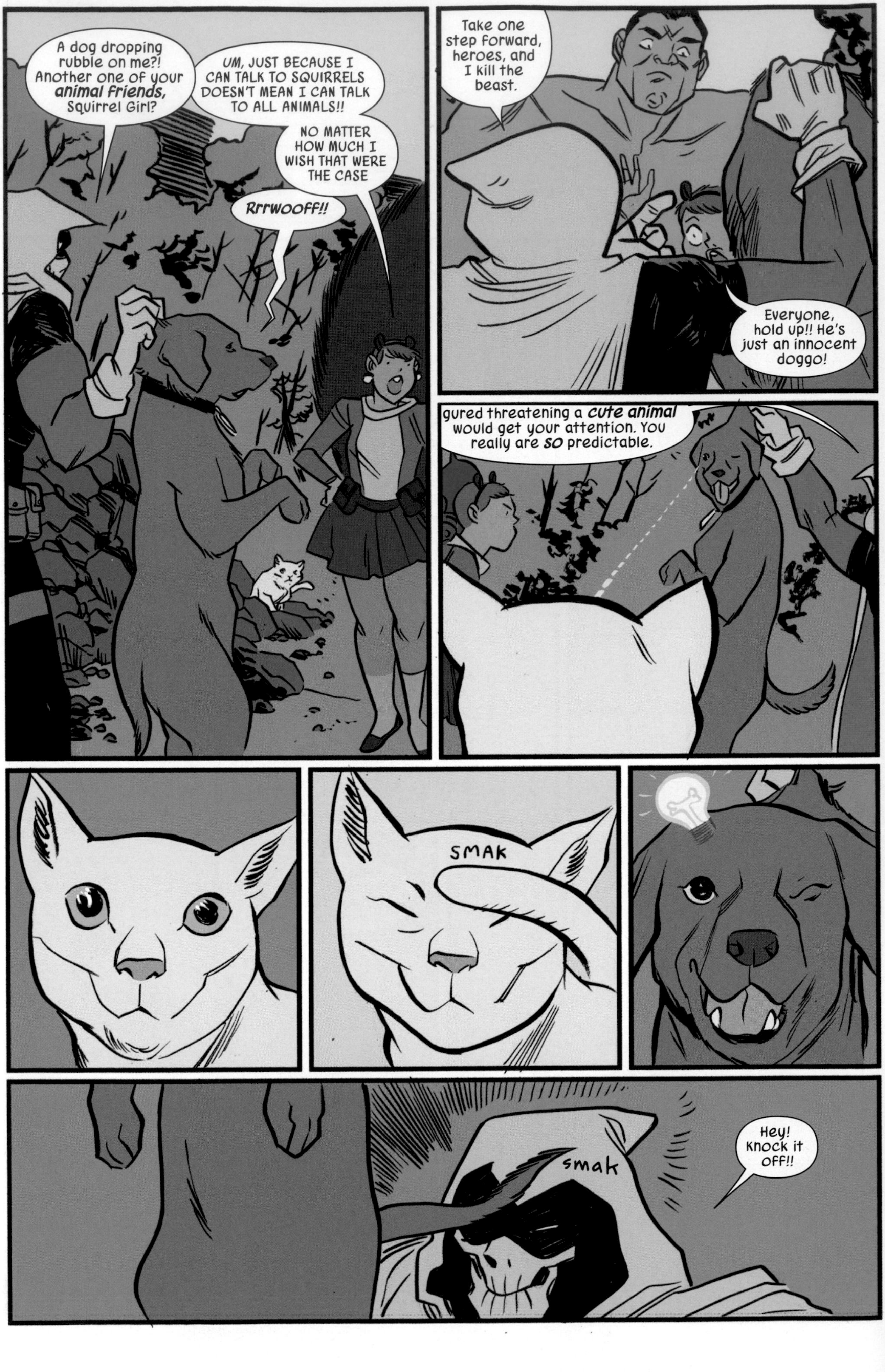
A dog dropping rubble on me?! Another one of your *animal friends,* Squirrel Girl?
UM, JUST BECAUSE I CAN TALK TO SQUIRRELS DOESN'T MEAN I CAN TALK TO ALL ANIMALS!!
NO MATTER HOW MUCH I WISH THAT WERE THE CASE
Rrrwooff!!
Take one step forward, heroes, and I kill the beast.
Everyone, hold up!! He's just an innocent doggo!
gured threatening a *cute animal* would get your attention. You really are *SO* predictable.
SMAK
smak
Hey! Knock it off!!

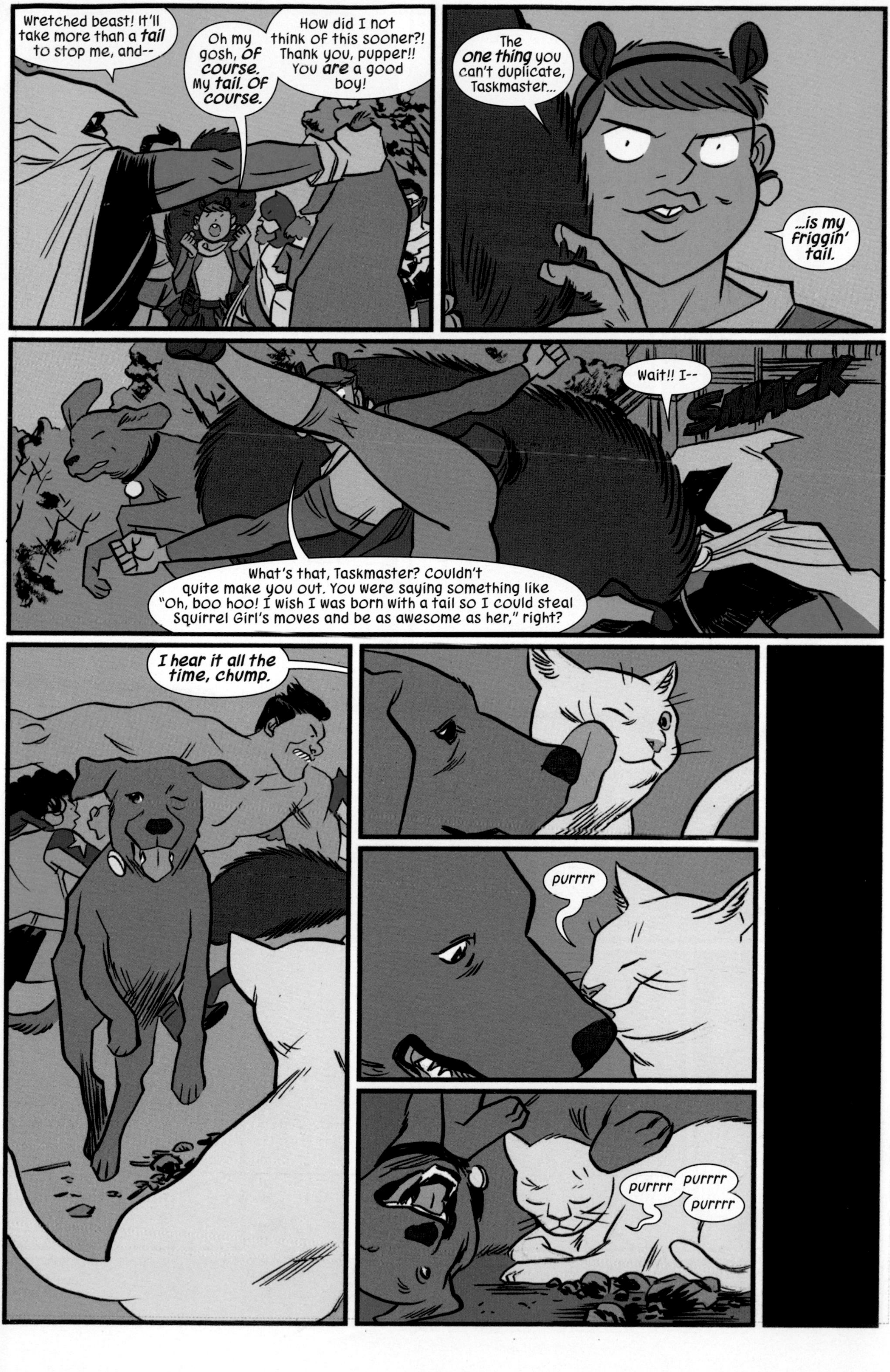
Wretched beast! It'll take more than a tail to stop me, and--
Oh my gosh, OF COURSE. My tail. OF COURSE.
How did I not think of this sooner?! Thank you, pupper!! You are a good boy!
The one thing you can't duplicate, Taskmaster...
...is my friggin' tail.
Wait!! I--
SMACK
What's that, Taskmaster? Couldn't quite make you out. You were saying something like "Oh, boo hoo! I wish I was born with a tail so I could steal Squirrel Girl's moves and be as awesome as her," right?
I hear it all the time, chump.
purrrr
purrrr
purrrr
purrrr

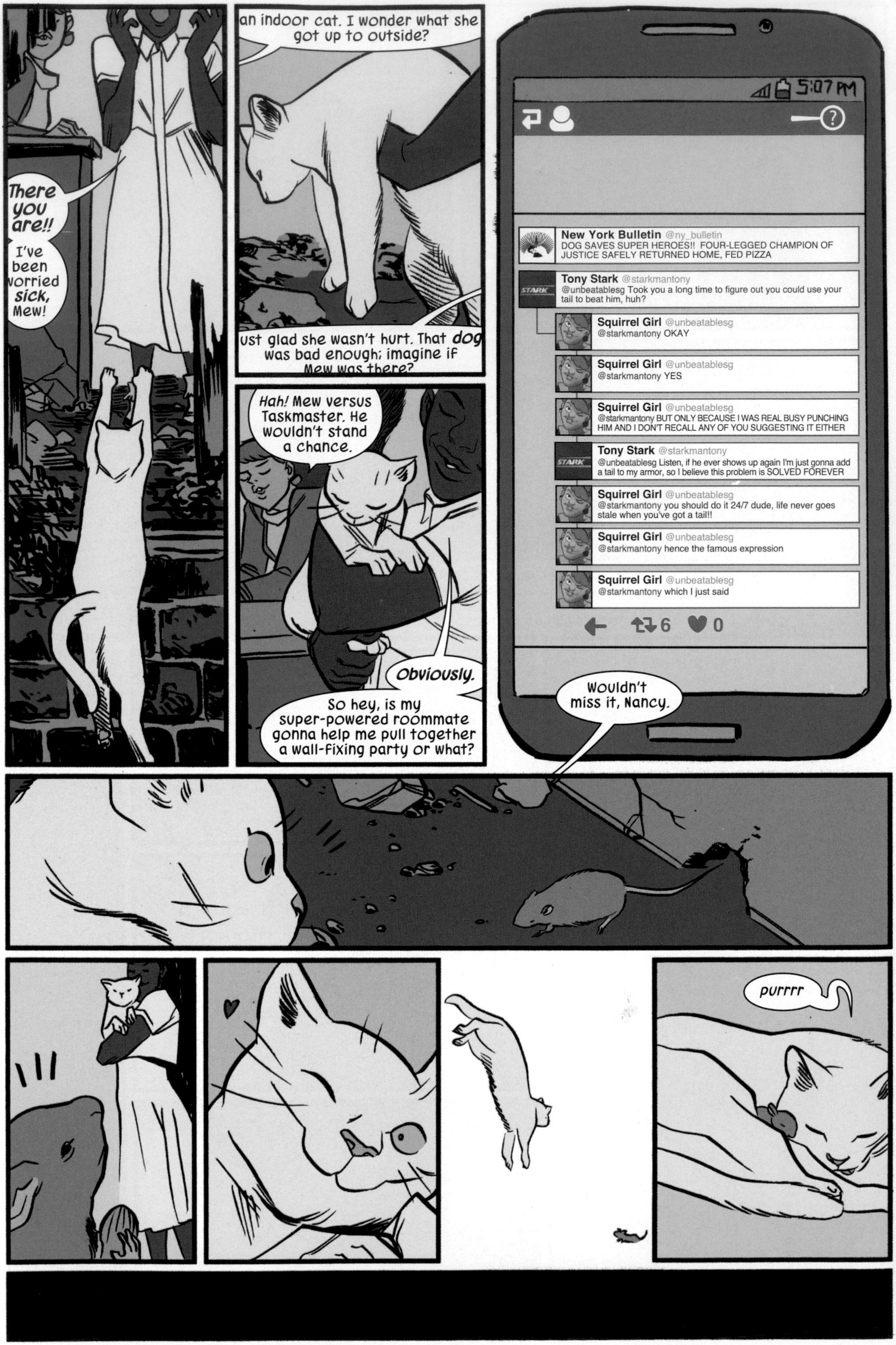
There you are!!
I've been worried sick, Mew!
an indoor cat. I wonder what she got up to outside?
ust glad she wasn't hurt. That dog was bad enough; imagine if Mew was there?
Hah! Mew versus Taskmaster. He wouldn't stand a chance.
Obviously.
So hey, is my super-powered roommate gonna help me pull together a wall-fixing party or what?
5:07 PM
New York Bulletin @ny_bulletin
DOG SAVES SUPER HEROES!! FOUR-LEGGED CHAMPION OF JUSTICE SAFELY RETURNED HOME, FED PIZZA
Tony Stark @starkmantony
@unbeatablesg Took you a long time to figure out you could use your tail to beat him, huh?
Squirrel Girl @unbeatablesg
@starkmantony OKAY
Squirrel Girl @unbeatablesg
@starkmantony YES
Squirrel Girl @unbeatablesg
@starkmantony BUT ONLY BECAUSE I WAS REAL BUSY PUNCHING HIM AND I DON'T RECALL ANY OF YOU SUGGESTING IT EITHER
Tony Stark @starkmantony
@unbeatablesg Listen, if he ever shows up again I'm just gonna add a tail to my armor, so I believe this problem is SOLVED FOREVER
Squirrel Girl @unbeatablesg
@starkmantony you should do it 24/7 dude, life never goes stale when you've got a tail!!
Squirrel Girl @unbeatablesg
@starkmantony hence the famous expression
Squirrel Girl @unbeatablesg
@starkmantony which I just said
6
0
Wouldn't miss it, Nancy.
purrrr

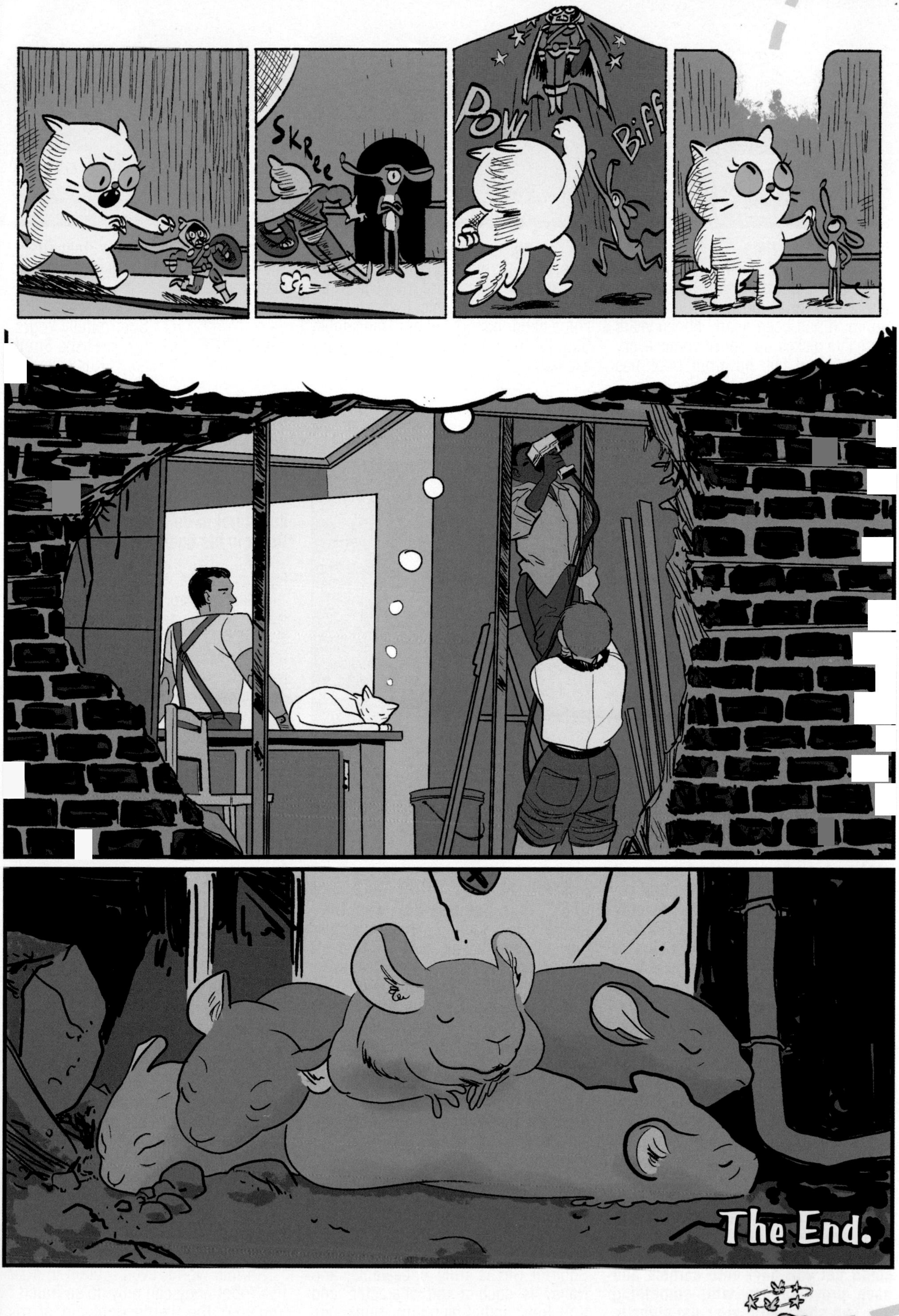
SKReee
Pow
Biff
The End.

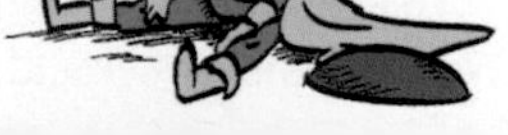

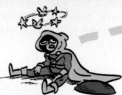

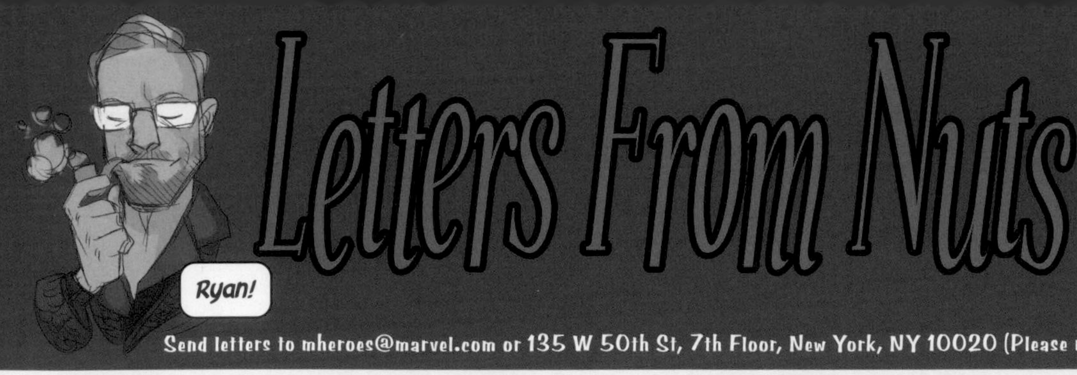
Ryan!

Letters From Nuts

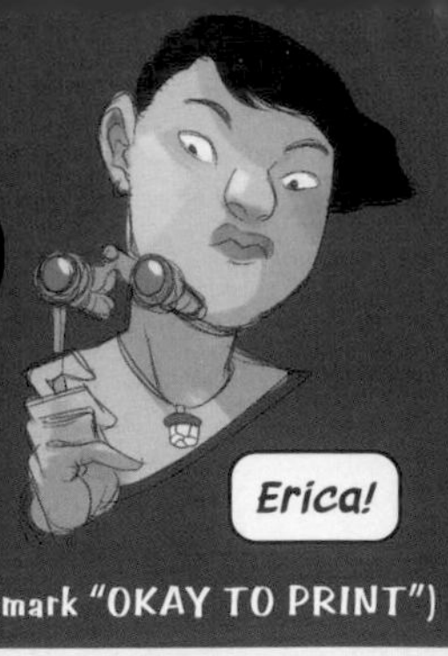
Erica!

Send letters to mheroes@marvel.com or 135 W 50th St, 7th Floor, New York, NY 10020 (Please mark "OKAY TO PRINT")

Ryan, Erica and Rico,

Thank you for all of the hard work, talent and dedication you all put into this wonderful, wonderful book each month. It had been nearly fifteen years since I've picked up a print comic every issue without fail, but your book has brought me back into the fold.

After your first issue #1 I made THE UNBEATABLE SQUIRREL GIRL a habit very specifically so that I'd have a box of comics to share with my daughter as soon as she's able to flip through them. I've become assured that I made the right choice for two reasons. First of all, you folks continue to produce an amazing, smart, insightful and funny all-ages comic and you show no signs of slowing down. Second, she's only eighteen months old and is absolutely obsessed with acorns. Every time she goes outside we wind up finding a few acorns around the living room later. Doreen must have some tough-soled shoes, because I swear those acorn caps are worse than Lego bricks to step on.

Nuts to you all,
Daniel and Carolyn Tauber

RYAN: Aw, that's great! I've got a nephew too who just turned three and while he's not quiiiite at the point yet where he's reading comics, I'm really excited for him to start. I am SO READY to be the cool uncle. I've got comics in my house, I've got lots of neat toys and a giant lime green stuffed T-Rex from *Dinosaur Comics* – I AM READY. Perhaps he'll be reading this letter column in a few years and be like, "A time when I was so young that I didn't read comics? IMPOSSIBLE." ALSO: I didn't know stepping on acorn caps was worse than stepping on Lego, but I am happy to take your word for it and would absolutely not like to find out with personal experience.

ERICA: Pro tip: glue down the caps. I learned this from cosplayers and jewelry makers. But yay! I'm glad we could get you back into comics and have provided you with something you can share with your daughter in the future.

Thank you for coming to Lethbridge Word on the Street and the signing at Kapow. My husband and I have been fans of your work for years and are so excited that you are involved in an incredible Marvel comic. I wish we had some better pictures of our Unbeatable Squirrel Boy but he was also very excited.

Miranda
Alberta, Canada

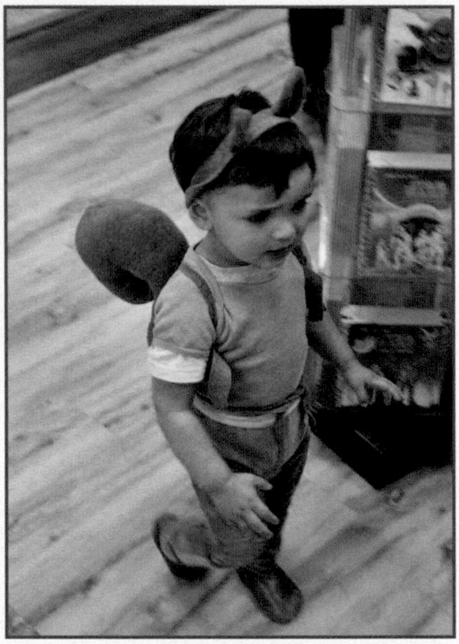

RYAN: Miranda, THIS WAS THE BEST. Your Squirrel Boy was truly unbeatable, and it was hilarious how the second he was dressed up he ran off (because he was shy? Because ADVENTURE BECKONED??). Everyone else: If you've never been to Lethbridge, Alberta, Canada, I recommend it! I went for a walk while I was there and came across HENDERSON LAKE, which I can only assume was named after Erica Henderson, so I instantly felt welcome and at home.

ERICA: That lake thing is probably correct.

Ryan and Erica,

Wow guys, this comic is just swell. Squirrel Girl is truly unbeatable, and Nancy is such a rad character, and Koi Boy and Chipmunk Hunk are undeniably the most perfectly named super heroes ever. And geez, Brain Drain is just trying so hard to be a good super hero and I just...I just want him to be happy. I love you, Brain Drain, and I will always be proud of you. No matter what.

Squirrelfully Yours,
Elisha Smith
Knoxville, TN

RYAN: Thank you, Elisha! Brain Drain believes in himself and tries his best, and that is all anyone can ask!

ERICA: My only regret is that we didn't get to do more scenes of Brain Drain in his human costume.

Ryan and Erica,

Thank you so much for making me realize how awesome Squirrel Girl is! Your comic makes me crack up every time I read it, especially the "In A Nutshell" segment from Issue 11. It's quite possibly one of the best comics I've read! Squirrel Girl is, thanks to this comic, my favorite Marvel hero. I mean, come on! She's beat up Thanos, Galactus, and even the entire Marvel universe! Anyways, once again, thank you guys!

Ethan

RYAN: Thanks, Ethan! I really enjoy writing the "In A Nutshell" recap pages, and I also like that all the accounts there are real. I would argue it makes total sense that Tony Stark, international CEO and billionaire, would hang out online with Doreen Green. Also, if you haven't picked up our THE UNBEATABLE SQUIRREL GIRL BEATS UP THE MARVEL UNIVERSE! original graphic novel (it's an all-new story!), then what are you waiting for? I don't want to spoil anything, but I'll say this: the Marvel Universe does absolutely get beat up.

ERICA: Aw! Thanks! We like her a lot too.

"In this world, even a brain in a jar in a robot body can only do so much." You took the words right out of my mouth. Nicely observed! Brain Drain, Brain Drain, Brain Drain. He's all of it. Were he a man, he'd be my main. He brings the pain! His reign can't be disdained! He brings a presence to this plane that others only feign! If you mess with him you best be prayin'! Yeah, like that.

Ryan North and Erica Henderson, you two are still rocking it like a magikist. Rico Renzi and Travis Lanham and Wil Moss are doing this as well. I'd like to reiterate - this time into lettercol canon - that Ryan "Ry No" North should have SG fight a duo composed of the Rhino and a new villaness named the Air-Hen. For no reason I can explain, the latter's given name should be Peppy Bosworth.

Keep it up!
John Velousis

RYAN: John, this Brain Drain theme song is a thing of beauty. And PERSONALLY, I think the Rhino (who is already a Marvel villain, so: CHECK) and the Air-Hen should team up and go on adventures. Erica, do you want to go on an adventure? We are currently in Leeds in the United Kingdom for the Thought Bubble convention, so I guess we're already on one??

ERICA: I love how much people love Brain Drain. It hadn't even been that long since we introduced him but I was already dying to bring him back. Ryan and I were having breakfast adventures in Leeds. Who can eat the most breakfast?? (Ryan. Ryan can.)

Hello, True Believers,

Thought you might appreciate the Squirrel Girl costume my wife helped create for my 10-year-old daughter Fiona. Happy Halloween!

(And yes, those are totally comics in the background.)

James VanOsdol
Chicago, IL

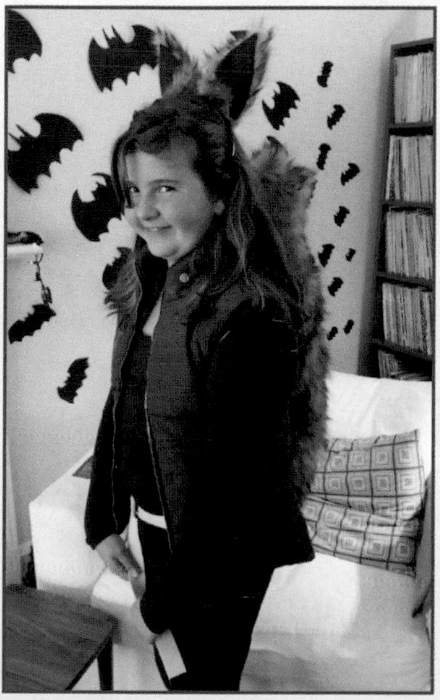

RYAN: James, tell Fiona her costume is unbeatable and I certainly hope at Halloween when people opened their doors and saw her they just emptied their entire bowls of candy into her pillowcase. I WILL ACCEPT NOTHING LESS.

ERICA: I hope those bats are year-round décor. Fun times goth house. ANYWAY – Fiona looks great! This makes me happy because I don't think I've seen trick-or-treaters since I left for college. Halloween is not just for rowdy adults, people!

Okay, that's all the room we have this month. DO NOT MISS THE NEXT ISSUE! Why? Because it's a special celebration of the 25th anniversary of Squirrel Girl's first appearance! With a short story by none other than SG's co-creator Will Murray! And you'll maybe (MAYBE!) even learn Squirrel Girl's origin!!!!!!!!!!!!!!!!!!!!!!!!! (And yes, that was twenty-five exclamation points.)

Next Issue:

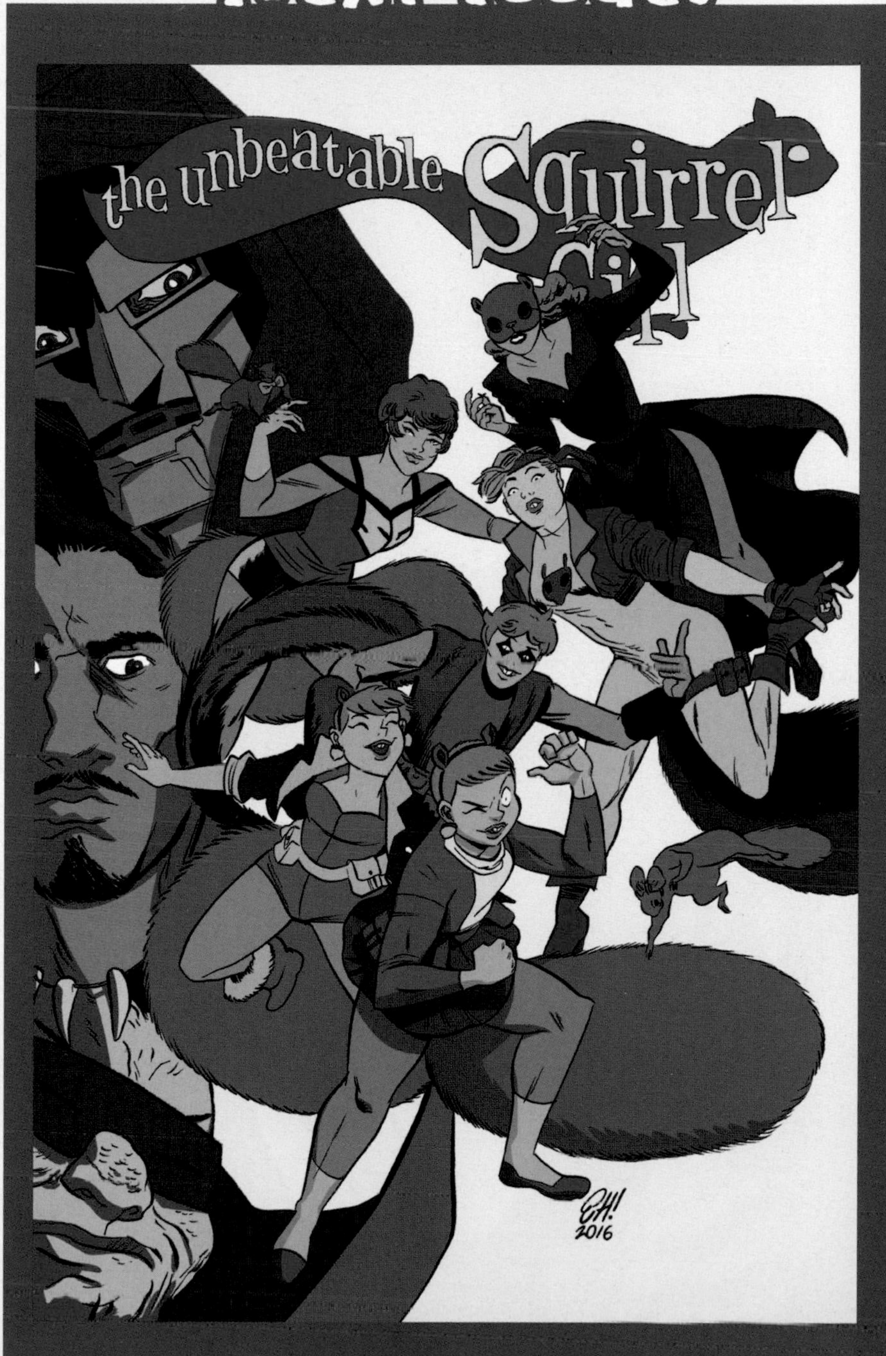
the unbeatable Squirrel Girl
EH! 2016

Attention, Squirrel Scouts! Make sure to check out our production blog, **unbeatablesquirrelgirl.tumblr.com**, where we post behind-the-scenes stuff on how the book gets made, along with all sorts of cool things *you* make: fanart, cosplay, whatever!

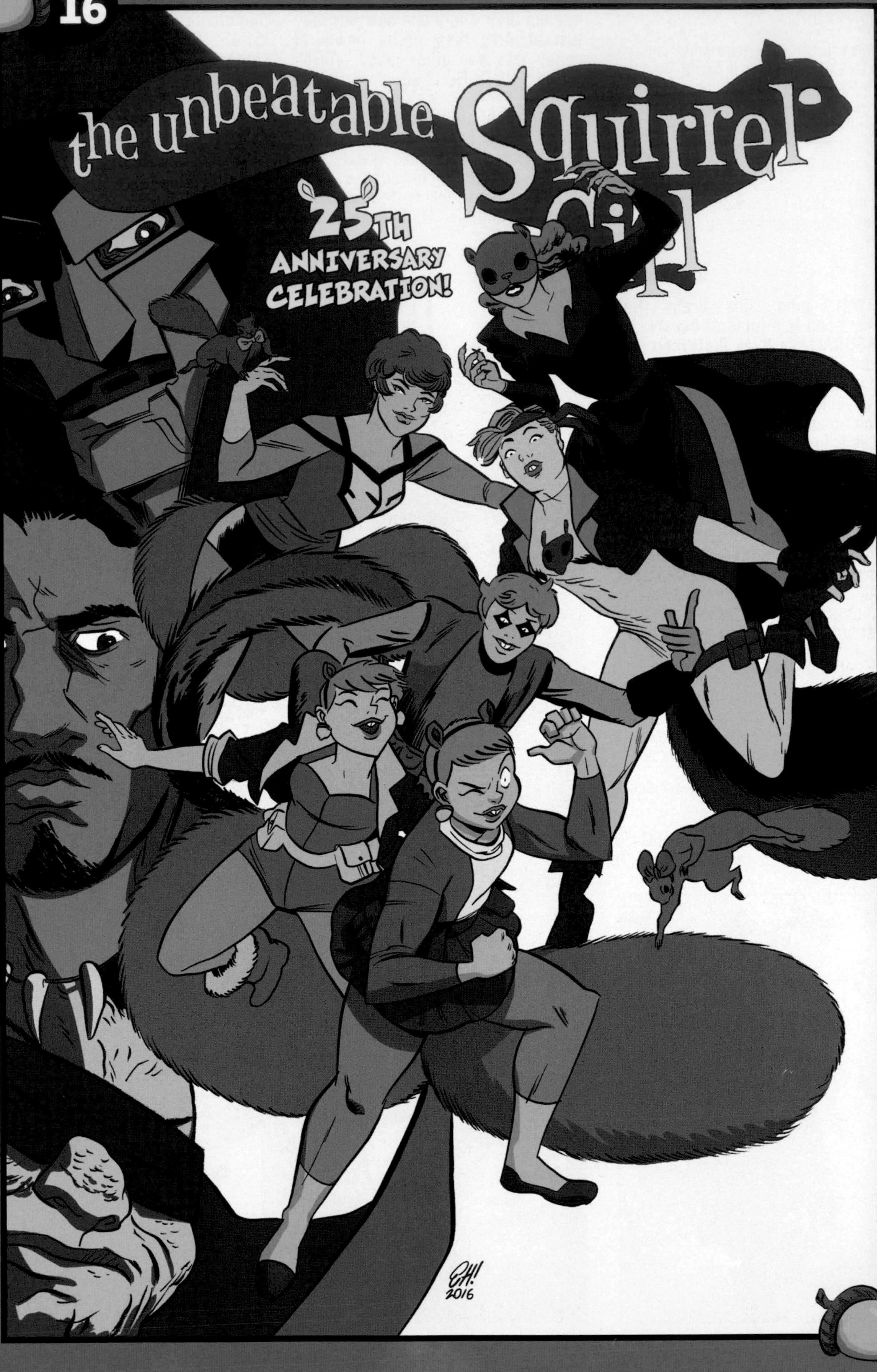
the unbeatable Squirrel Girl
25TH ANNIVERSARY CELEBRATION!
CH! 2016

*Doreen Green isn't just a second-year computer science student: she secretly also has all the powers of both squirrel and girl! She uses her amazing abilities to fight crime **and** be as awesome as possible. You know her as... **The Unbeatable Squirrel Girl!** Find out what she's been up to, with...*

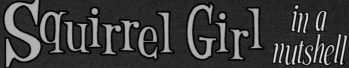

Squirrel Girl *in a nutshell*

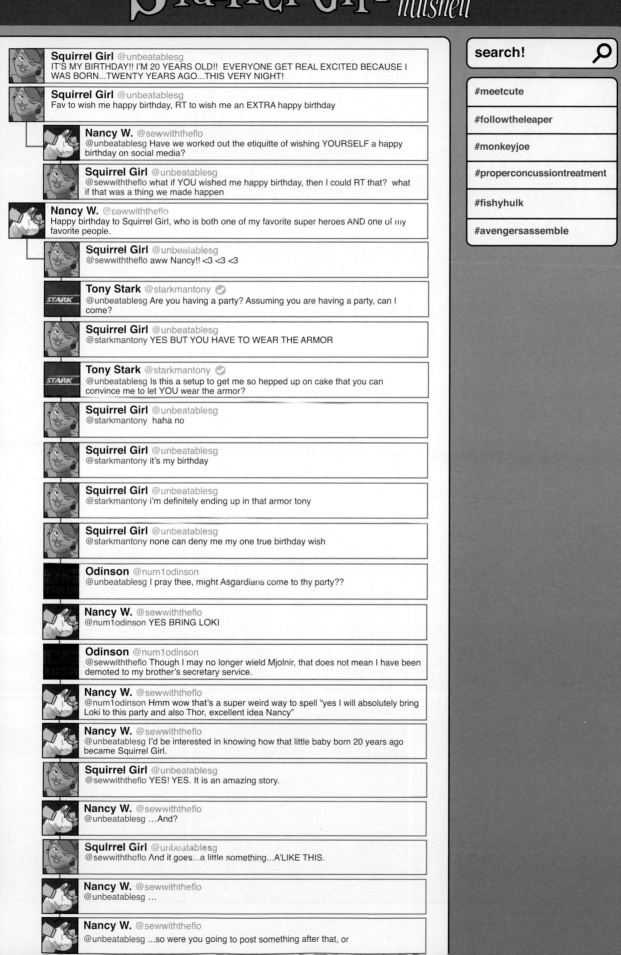

Squirrel Girl @unbeatablesg
IT'S MY BIRTHDAY!! I'M 20 YEARS OLD!! EVERYONE GET REAL EXCITED BECAUSE I WAS BORN...TWENTY YEARS AGO...THIS VERY NIGHT!

Squirrel Girl @unbeatablesg
Fav to wish me happy birthday, RT to wish me an EXTRA happy birthday

Nancy W. @sewwiththeflo
@unbeatablesg Have we worked out the etiquitte of wishing YOURSELF a happy birthday on social media?

Squirrel Girl @unbeatablesg
@sewwiththeflo what if YOU wished me happy birthday, then I could RT that? what if that was a thing we made happen

Nancy W. @sewwiththeflo
Happy birthday to Squirrel Girl, who is both one of my favorite super heroes AND one of my favorite people.

Squirrel Girl @unbeatablesg
@sewwiththeflo aww Nancy!! <3 <3 <3

Tony Stark @starkmantony
@unbeatablesg Are you having a party? Assuming you are having a party, can I come?

Squirrel Girl @unbeatablesg
@starkmantony YES BUT YOU HAVE TO WEAR THE ARMOR

Tony Stark @starkmantony
@unbeatablesg Is this a setup to get me so hepped up on cake that you can convince me to let YOU wear the armor?

Squirrel Girl @unbeatablesg
@starkmantony haha no

Squirrel Girl @unbeatablesg
@starkmantony it's my birthday

Squirrel Girl @unbeatablesg
@starkmantony i'm definitely ending up in that armor tony

Squirrel Girl @unbeatablesg
@starkmantony none can deny me my one true birthday wish

Odinson @num1odinson
@unbeatablesg I pray thee, might Asgardians come to thy party??

Nancy W. @sewwiththeflo
@num1odinson YES BRING LOKI

Odinson @num1odinson
@sewwiththeflo Though I may no longer wield Mjolnir, that does not mean I have been demoted to my brother's secretary service.

Nancy W. @sewwiththeflo
@num1odinson Hmm wow that's a super weird way to spell "yes I will absolutely bring Loki to this party and also Thor, excellent idea Nancy"

Nancy W. @sewwiththeflo
@unbeatablesg I'd be interested in knowing how that little baby born 20 years ago became Squirrel Girl.

Squirrel Girl @unbeatablesg
@sewwiththeflo YES! YES. It is an amazing story.

Nancy W. @sewwiththeflo
@unbeatablesg ...And?

Squirrel Girl @unbeatablesg
@sewwiththeflo And it goes...a little something...A'LIKE THIS.

Nancy W. @sewwiththeflo
@unbeatablesg ...

Nancy W. @sewwiththeflo
@unbeatablesg ...so were you going to post something after that, or

search!

- #meetcute
- #followtheleaper
- #monkeyjoe
- #properconcussiontreatment
- #fishyhulk
- #avengersassemble

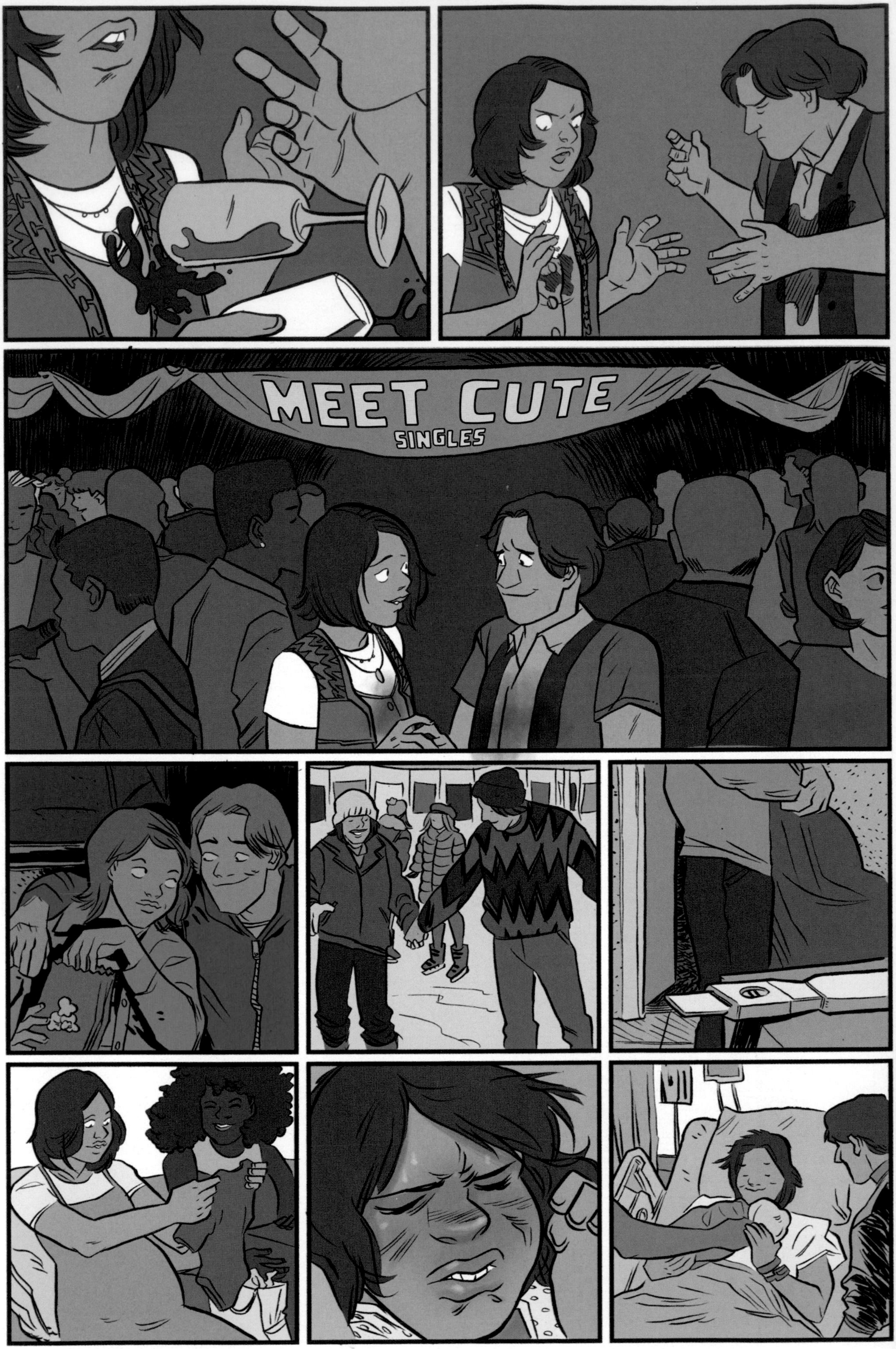
MEET CUTE
SINGLES

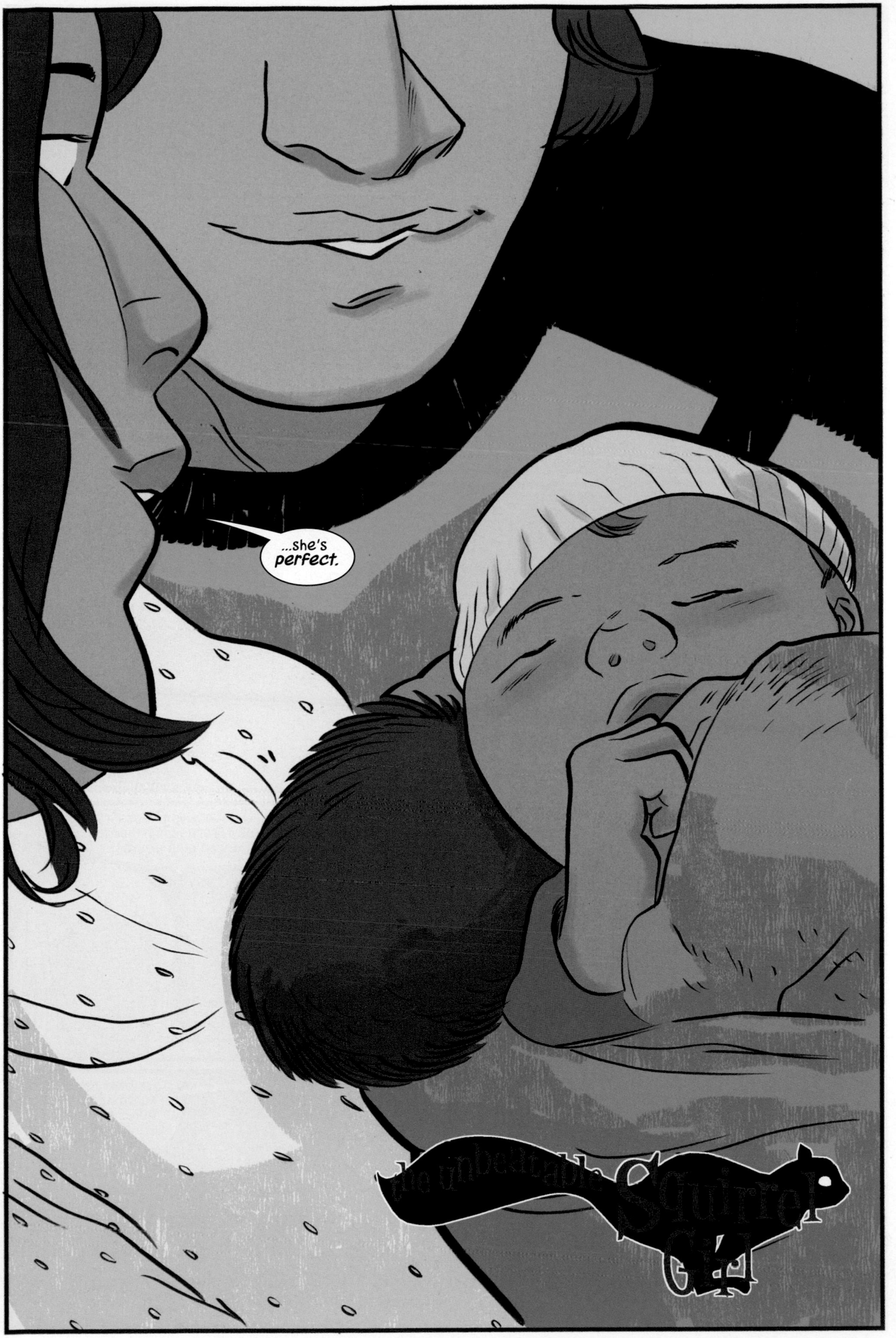
...she's perfect.
the unbeatable Squirrel Girl

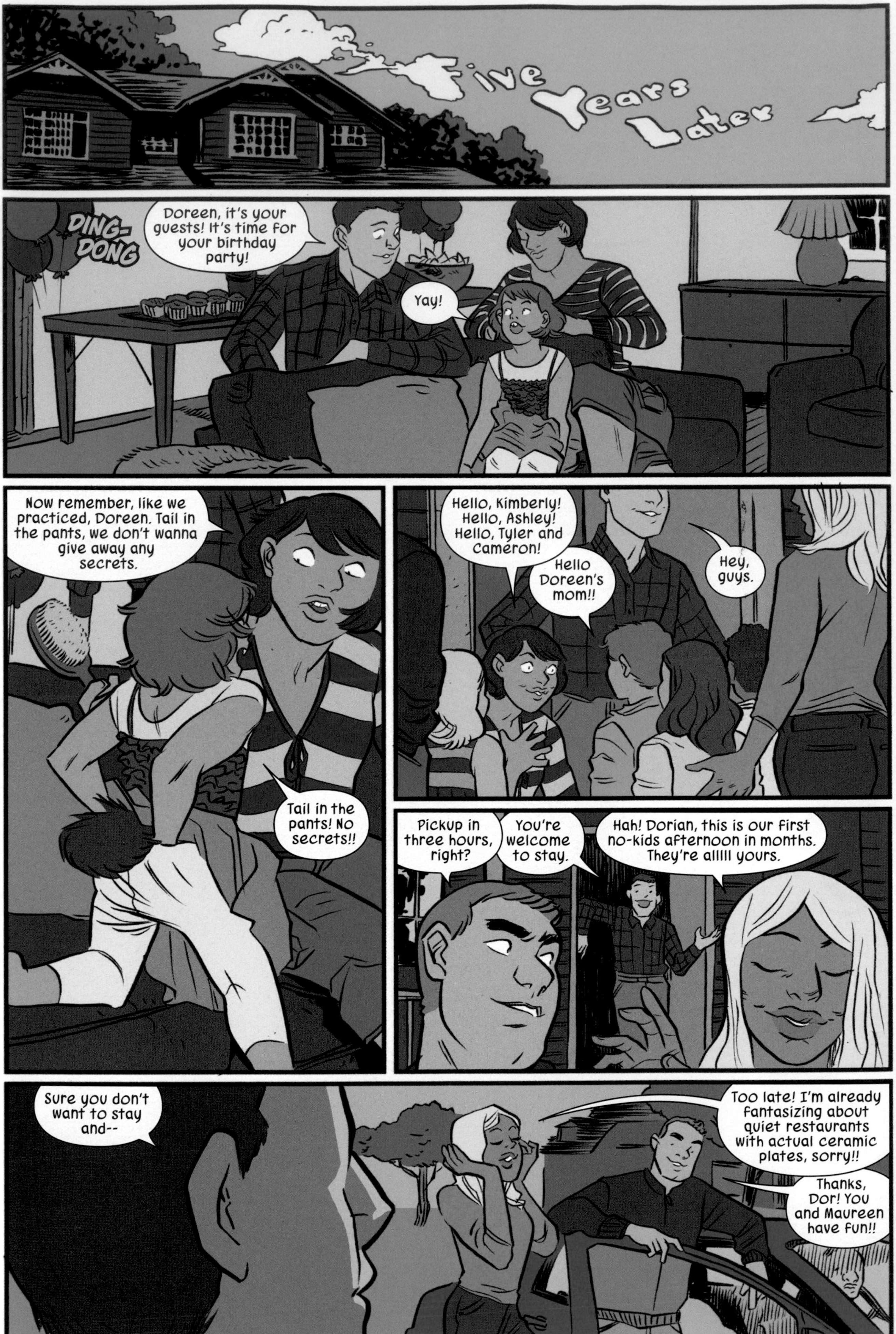
Five Years Later
DING-DONG
Doreen, it's your guests! It's time for your birthday party!
Yay!
Now remember, like we practiced, Doreen. Tail in the pants, we don't wanna give away any secrets.
Tail in the pants! No secrets!!
Hello, Kimberly! Hello, Ashley! Hello, Tyler and Cameron!
Hello Doreen's mom!!
Hey, guys.
Pickup in three hours, right?
You're welcome to stay.
Hah! Dorian, this is our first no-kids afternoon in months. They're alllll yours.
Sure you don't want to stay and--
Too late! I'm already fantasizing about quiet restaurants with actual ceramic plates, sorry!!
Thanks, Dor! You and Maureen have fun!!

Where are the crossover restaurants that give you both the classy ambiance and the charmingly snooty maitre d', but *also* the crayons and the paper tablecloth you can draw on? "No idea," you whisper, as we both smuggle our crayons and coloring books past the charmingly snooty maitre d'.

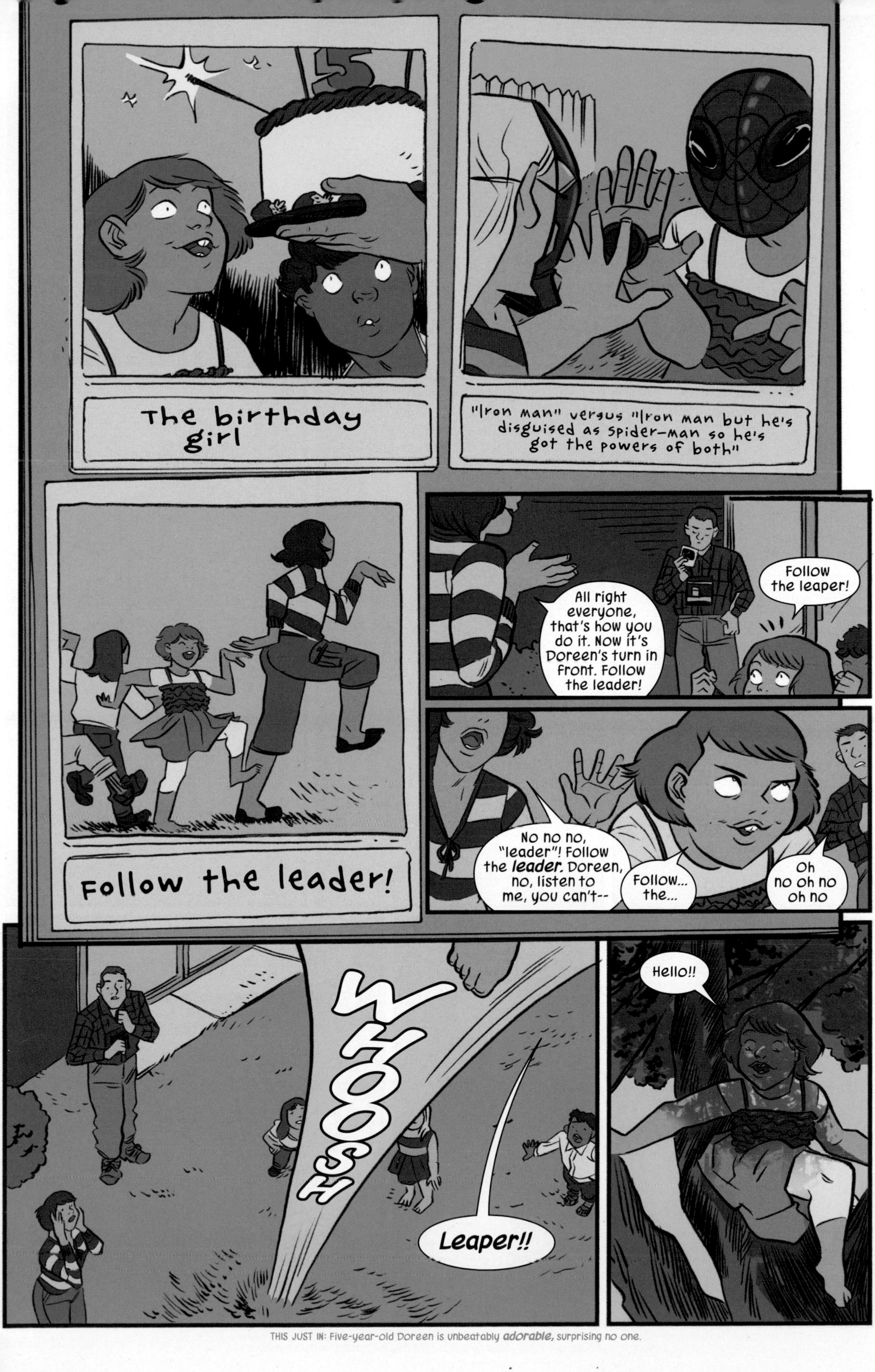
The birthday girl
"Iron man" versus "Iron man but he's disguised as spider-man so he's got the powers of both"
Follow the leader!
All right everyone, that's how you do it. Now it's Doreen's turn in front. Follow the leader!
Follow the leaper!
No no no, "leader"! Follow the *leader*. Doreen, no, listen to me, you can't--
Follow... the...
Oh no oh no oh no
WHOOSH
Leaper!!
Hello!!

THIS JUST IN: Five-year-old Doreen is unbeatably ***adorable,*** surprising no one.

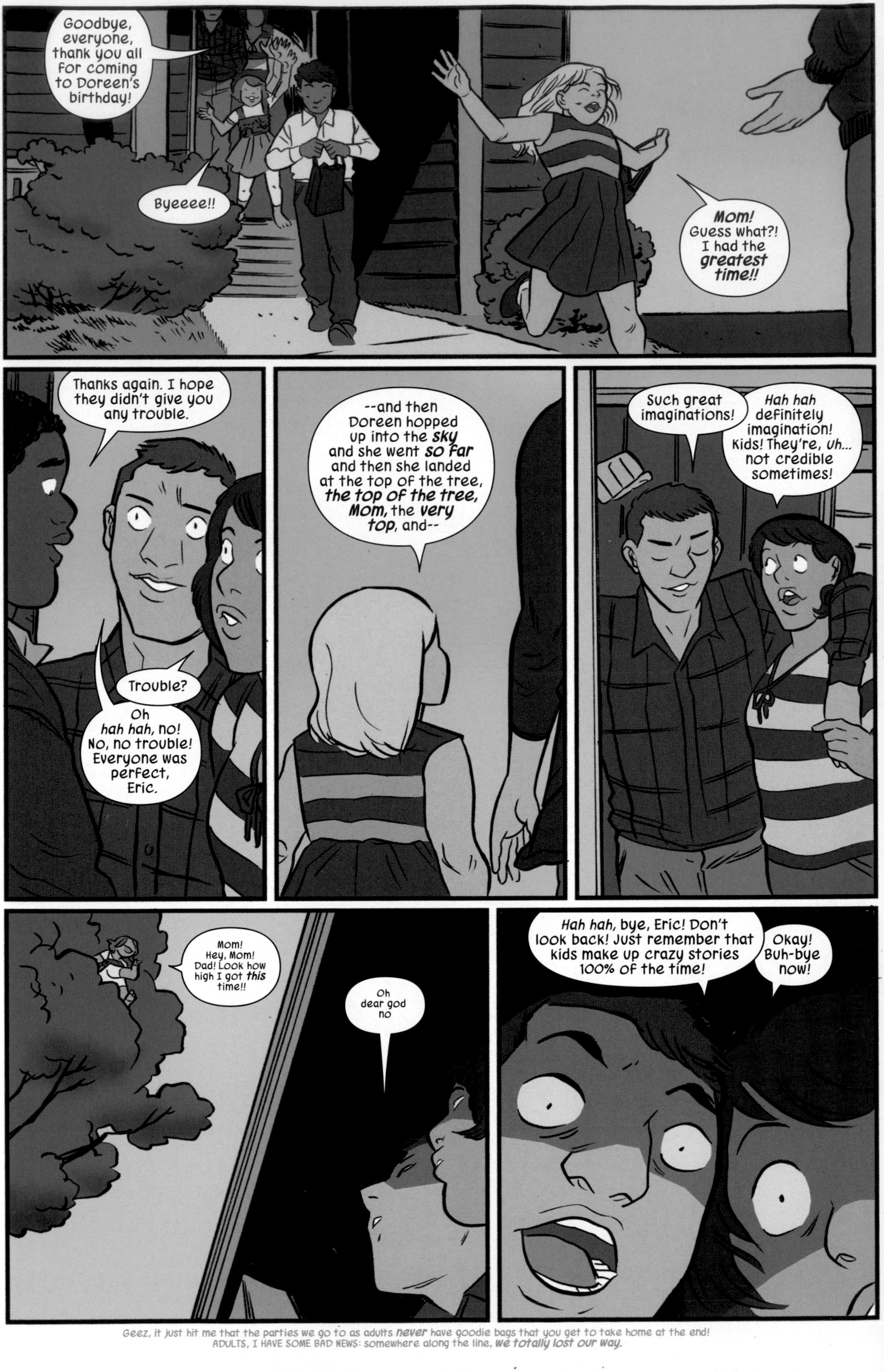
Goodbye, everyone, thank you all for coming to Doreen's birthday!
Byeeee!!
Mom! Guess what?! I had the greatest time!!
Thanks again. I hope they didn't give you any trouble.
Trouble?
Oh hah hah, no! No, no trouble! Everyone was perfect, Eric.
--and then Doreen hopped up into the sky and she went so far and then she landed at the top of the tree, the top of the tree, Mom, the very top, and--
Such great imaginations!
Hah hah definitely imagination! Kids! They're, uh... not credible sometimes!
Mom! Hey, Mom! Dad! Look how high I got this time!!
Oh dear god no
Hah hah, bye, Eric! Don't look back! Just remember that kids make up crazy stories 100% of the time!
Okay! Buh-bye now!

Geez, it just hit me that the parties we go to as adults *never* have goodie bags that you get to take home at the end!
ADULTS, I HAVE SOME BAD NEWS: somewhere along the line, *we totally lost our way.*

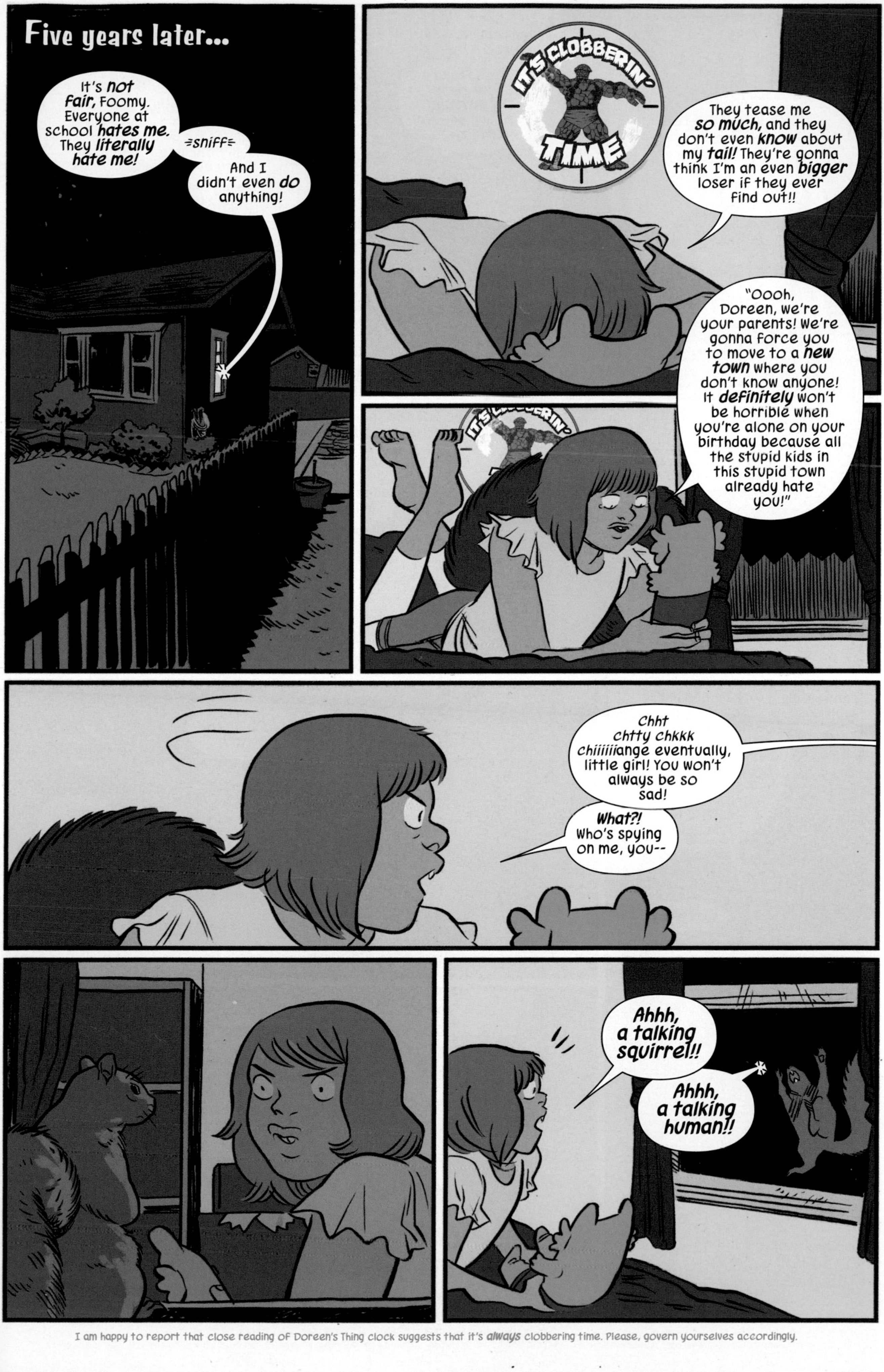
Five years later...
It's not fair, Foomy. Everyone at school hates me. They literally hate me!
=sniff=
And I didn't even do anything!
IT'S CLOBBERIN' TIME
They tease me so much, and they don't even know about my tail! They're gonna think I'm an even bigger loser if they ever find out!!
"Oooh, Doreen, we're your parents! We're gonna force you to move to a new town where you don't know anyone! It definitely won't be horrible when you're alone on your birthday because all the stupid kids in this stupid town already hate you!"
Chht chtty chkkk chiiiiiiange eventually, little girl! You won't always be so sad!
What?! Who's spying on me, you--
Ahhh, a talking squirrel!!
Ahhh, a talking human!!

I am happy to report that close reading of Doreen's Thing clock suggests that it's *always* clobbering time. Please, govern yourselves accordingly.

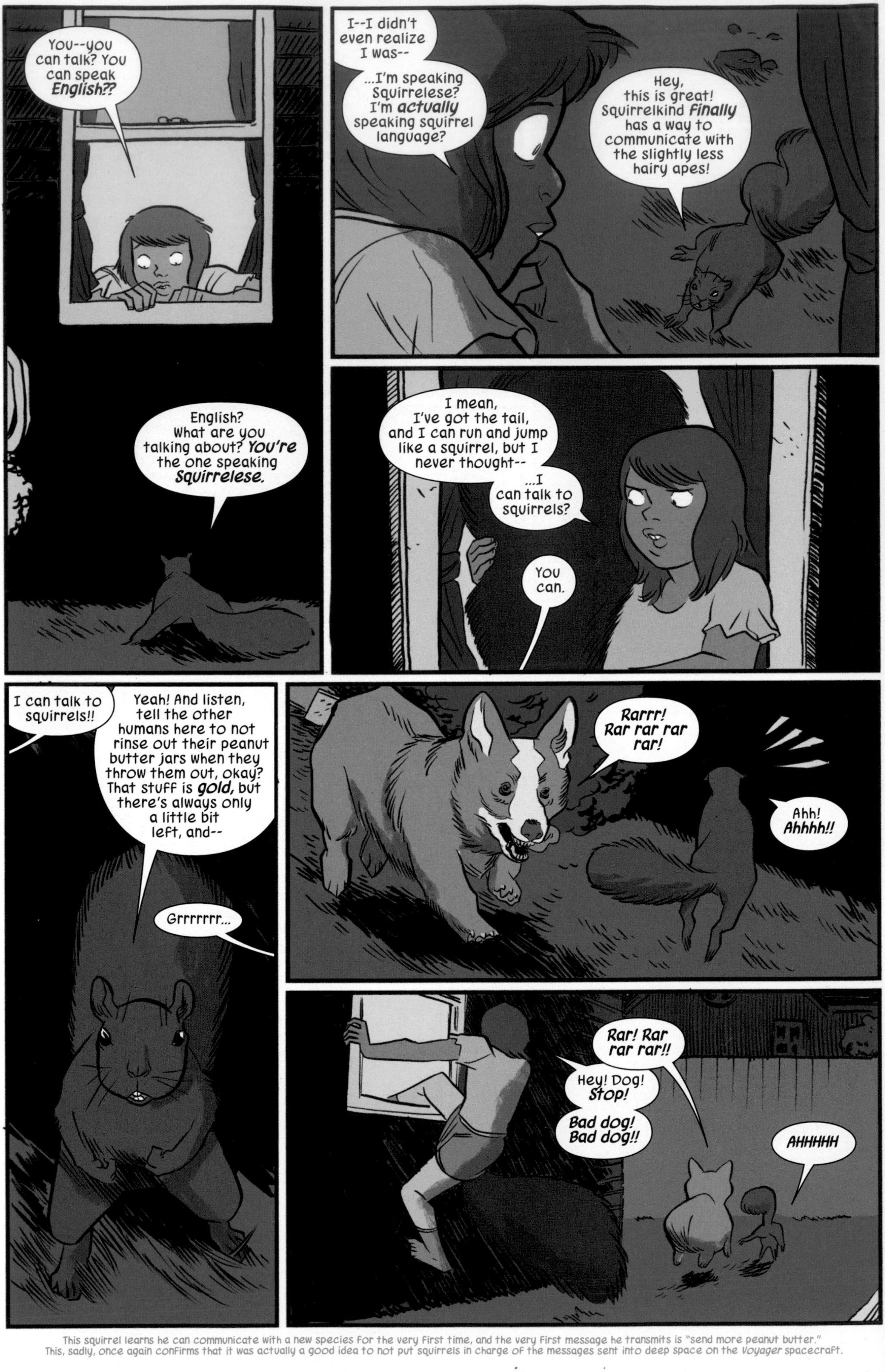
You--you can talk? You can speak English??
I--I didn't even realize I was--
...I'm speaking Squirrelese? I'm actually speaking squirrel language?
Hey, this is great! Squirrelkind finally has a way to communicate with the slightly less hairy apes!
English? What are you talking about? You're the one speaking Squirrelese.
I mean, I've got the tail, and I can run and jump like a squirrel, but I never thought--
...I can talk to squirrels?
You can.
I can talk to squirrels!!
Yeah! And listen, tell the other humans here to not rinse out their peanut butter jars when they throw them out, okay? That stuff is gold, but there's always only a little bit left, and--
Grrrrrrr...
Rarrr! Rar rar rar rar!
Ahh! Ahhhh!!
Rar! Rar rar rar!!
Hey! Dog! Stop!
Bad dog! Bad dog!!
AHHHHH

This squirrel learns he can communicate with a new species for the very first time, and the very first message he transmits is "send more peanut butter." This, sadly, once again confirms that it was actually a good idea to not put squirrels in charge of the messages sent into deep space on the *Voyager* spacecraft.

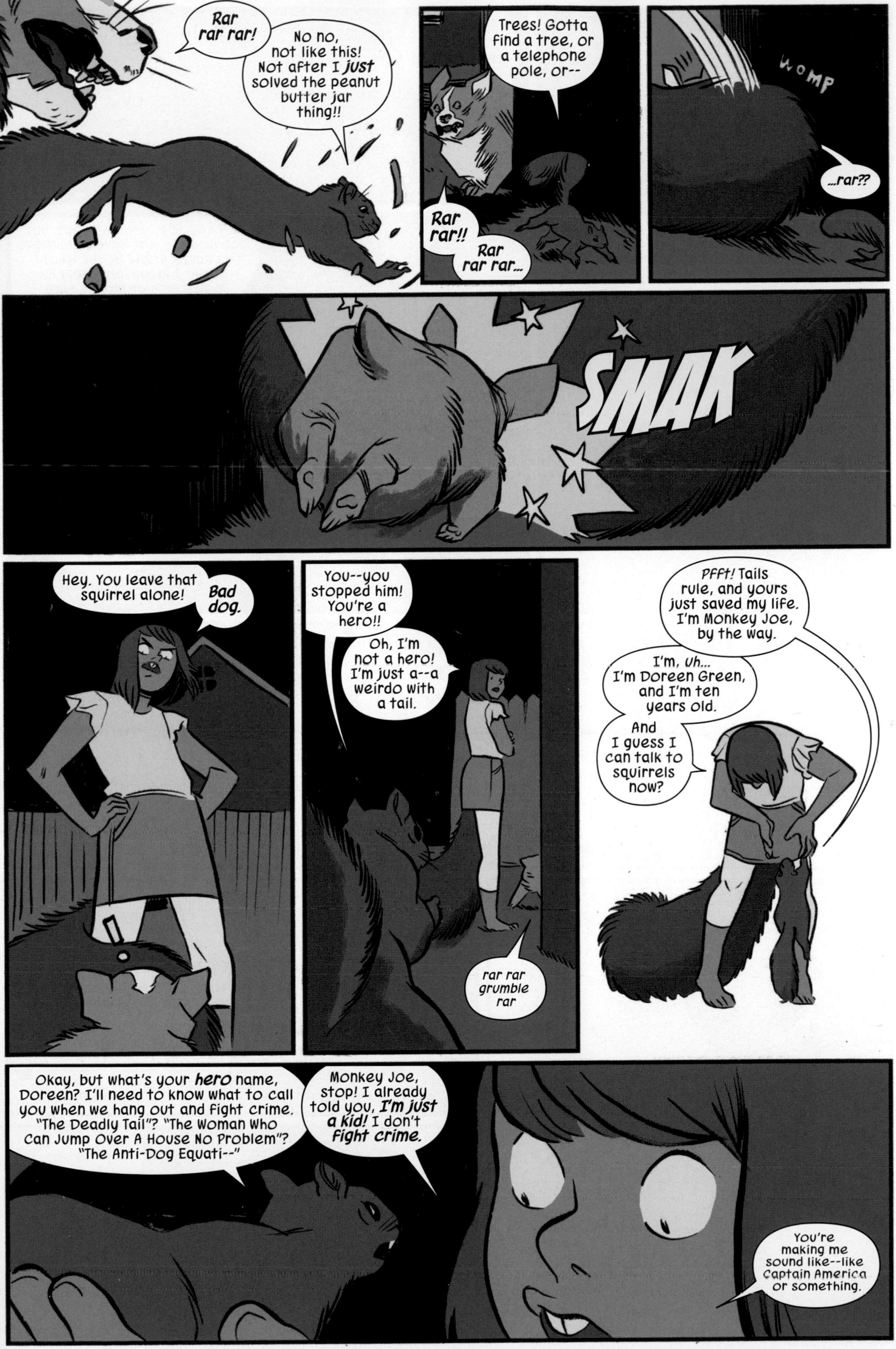
Rar rar rar!
No no, not like this! Not after I *just* solved the peanut butter jar thing!!
Trees! Gotta find a tree, or a telephone pole, or--
Rar rar!!
Rar rar rar...
WOMP
...rar??
SMAK
Hey. You leave that squirrel alone!
Bad dog.
You--you stopped him! You're a hero!!
Oh, I'm not a hero! I'm just a--a weirdo with a tail.
rar rar grumble rar
Pfft! Tails rule, and yours just saved my life. I'm Monkey Joe, by the way.
I'm, *uh...* I'm Doreen Green, and I'm ten years old.
And I guess I can talk to squirrels now?
Okay, but what's your *hero* name, Doreen? I'll need to know what to call you when we hang out and fight crime. "The Deadly Tail"? "The Woman Who Can Jump Over A House No Problem"? "The Anti-Dog Equati--"
Monkey Joe, stop! I already told you, *I'm just a kid!* I don't *fight crime.*
You're making me sound like--like Captain America or something.

Okay, can we talk about the *Voyager* spacecraft for a second? *Voyager 1* is the farthest object humans have ever sent from Earth, and among the many pictures it's carrying into the universe on a golden record is one of a woman eating an ice cream cone, while a man eats a grilled cheese sandwich, while *another* man pours water into his own mouth. *It's amazing.*

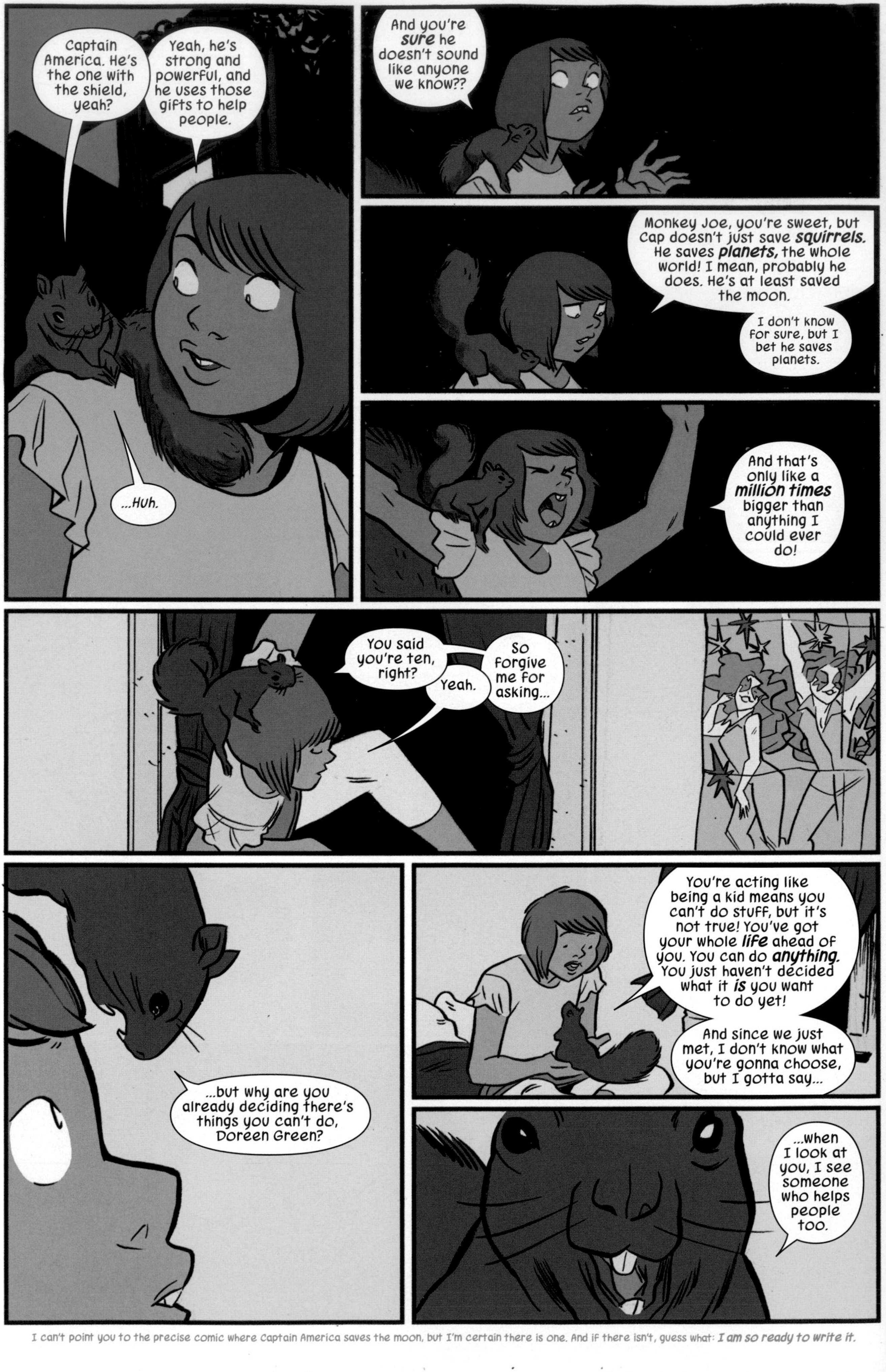
Captain America. He's the one with the shield, yeah?
Yeah, he's strong and powerful, and he uses those gifts to help people.
...Huh.
And you're *sure* he doesn't sound like anyone we know??
Monkey Joe, you're sweet, but Cap doesn't just save *squirrels.* He saves *planets,* the whole world! I mean, probably he does. He's at least saved the moon.
I don't know for sure, but I bet he saves planets.
And that's only like a *million times* bigger than anything I could ever do!
You said you're ten, right?
Yeah.
So forgive me for asking...
...but why are you already deciding there's things you can't do, Doreen Green?
You're acting like being a kid means you can't do stuff, but it's not true! You've got your whole *life* ahead of you. You can do *anything.* You just haven't decided what it *is* you want to do yet!
And since we just met, I don't know what you're gonna choose, but I gotta say...
...when I look at you, I see someone who helps people too.

I can't point you to the precise comic where Captain America saves the moon, but I'm certain there is one. And if there isn't, guess what: *I am so ready to write it.*

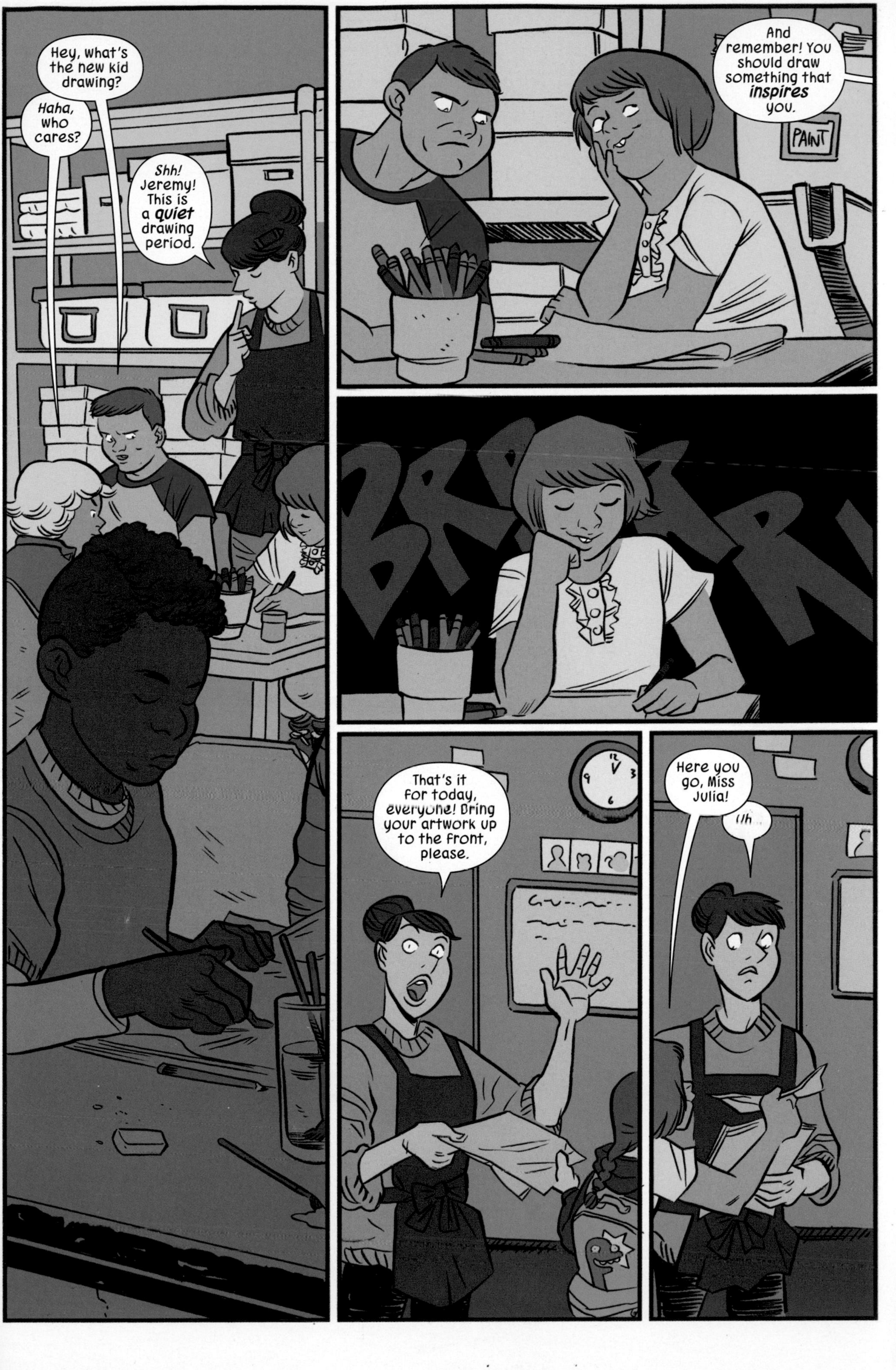
Hey, what's the new kid drawing?
Haha, who cares?
Shh! Jeremy! This is a *quiet* drawing period.
And remember! You should draw something that *inspires* you.
That's it for today, everyone! Bring your artwork up to the front, please.
Here you go, Miss Julia!
Uh...

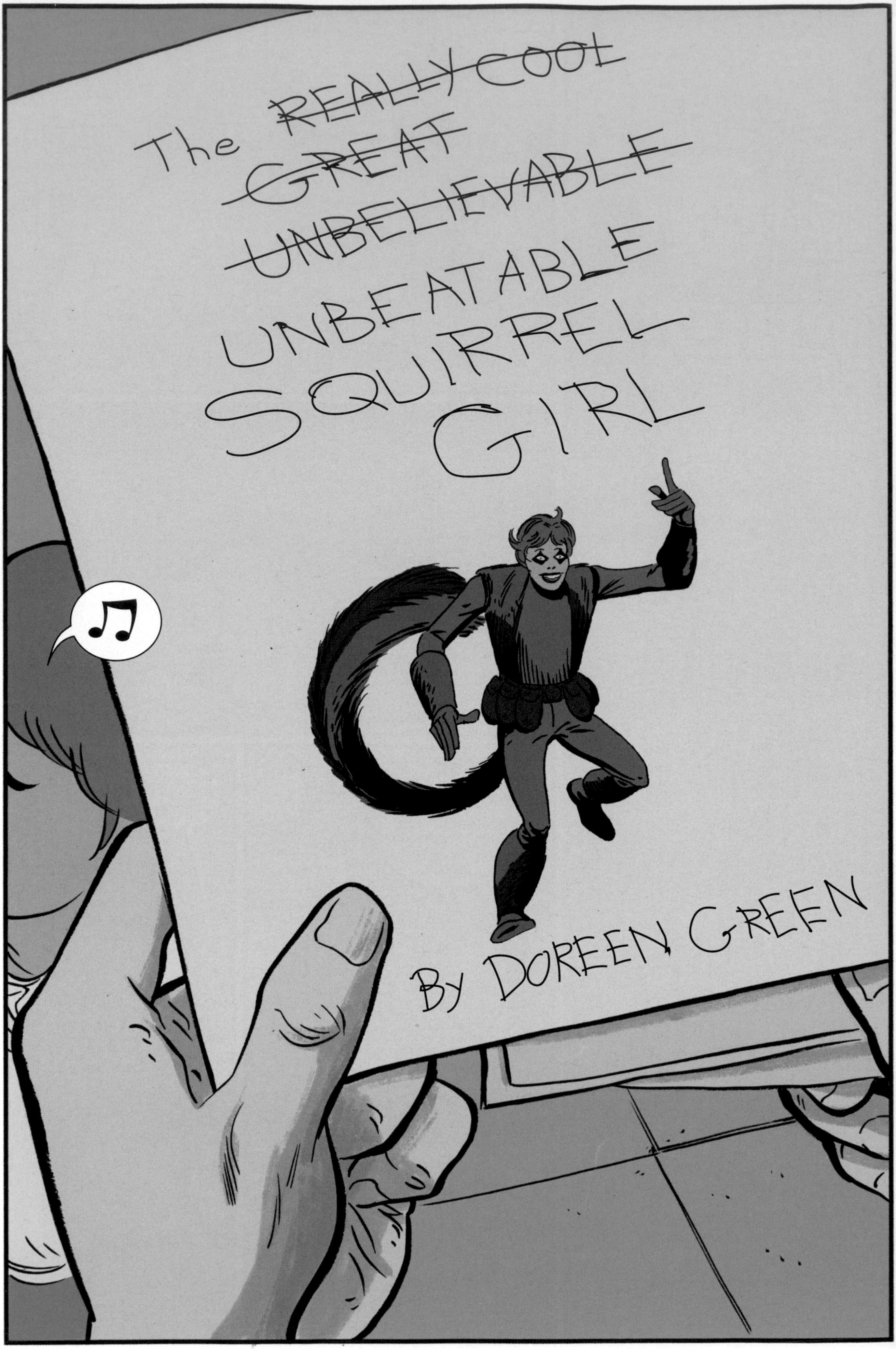
The ~~REALLY COOL~~ ~~GREAT~~ ~~UNBELIEVABLE~~ UNBEATABLE SQUIRREL GIRL
♫
By DOREEN GREEN

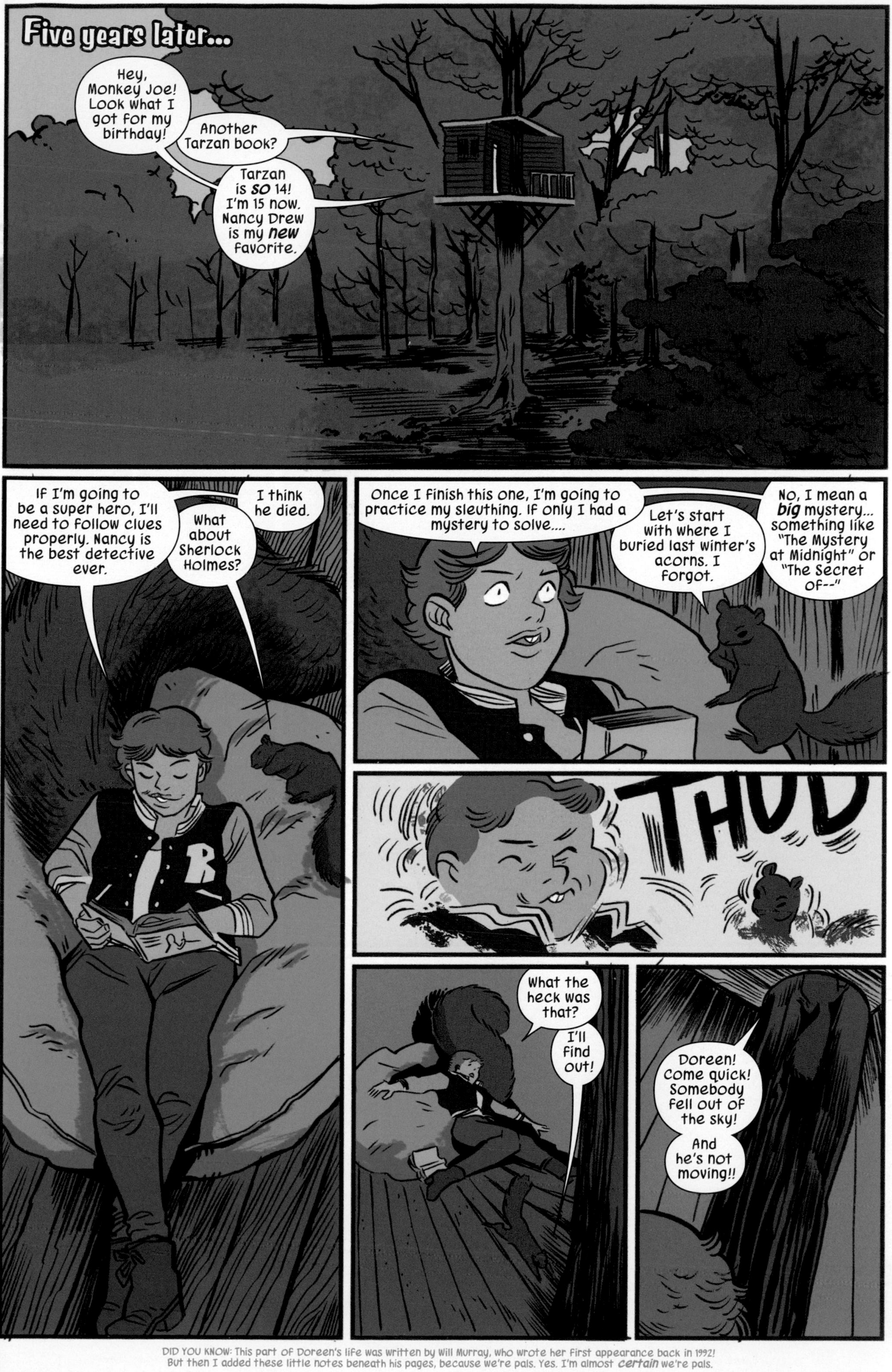
Five years later...
Hey, Monkey Joe! Look what I got for my birthday!
Another Tarzan book?
Tarzan is SO 14! I'm 15 now. Nancy Drew is my new favorite.
If I'm going to be a super hero, I'll need to follow clues properly. Nancy is the best detective ever.
What about Sherlock Holmes?
I think he died.
Once I finish this one, I'm going to practice my sleuthing. If only I had a mystery to solve....
Let's start with where I buried last winter's acorns. I forgot.
No, I mean a big mystery... something like "The Mystery at Midnight" or "The Secret Of--"
THUD
What the heck was that?
I'll find out!
Doreen! Come quick! Somebody fell out of the sky!
And he's not moving!!

DID YOU KNOW: This part of Doreen's life was written by Will Murray, who wrote her first appearance back in 1992!
But then I added these little notes beneath his pages, because we're pals. Yes. I'm almost *certain* we're pals.

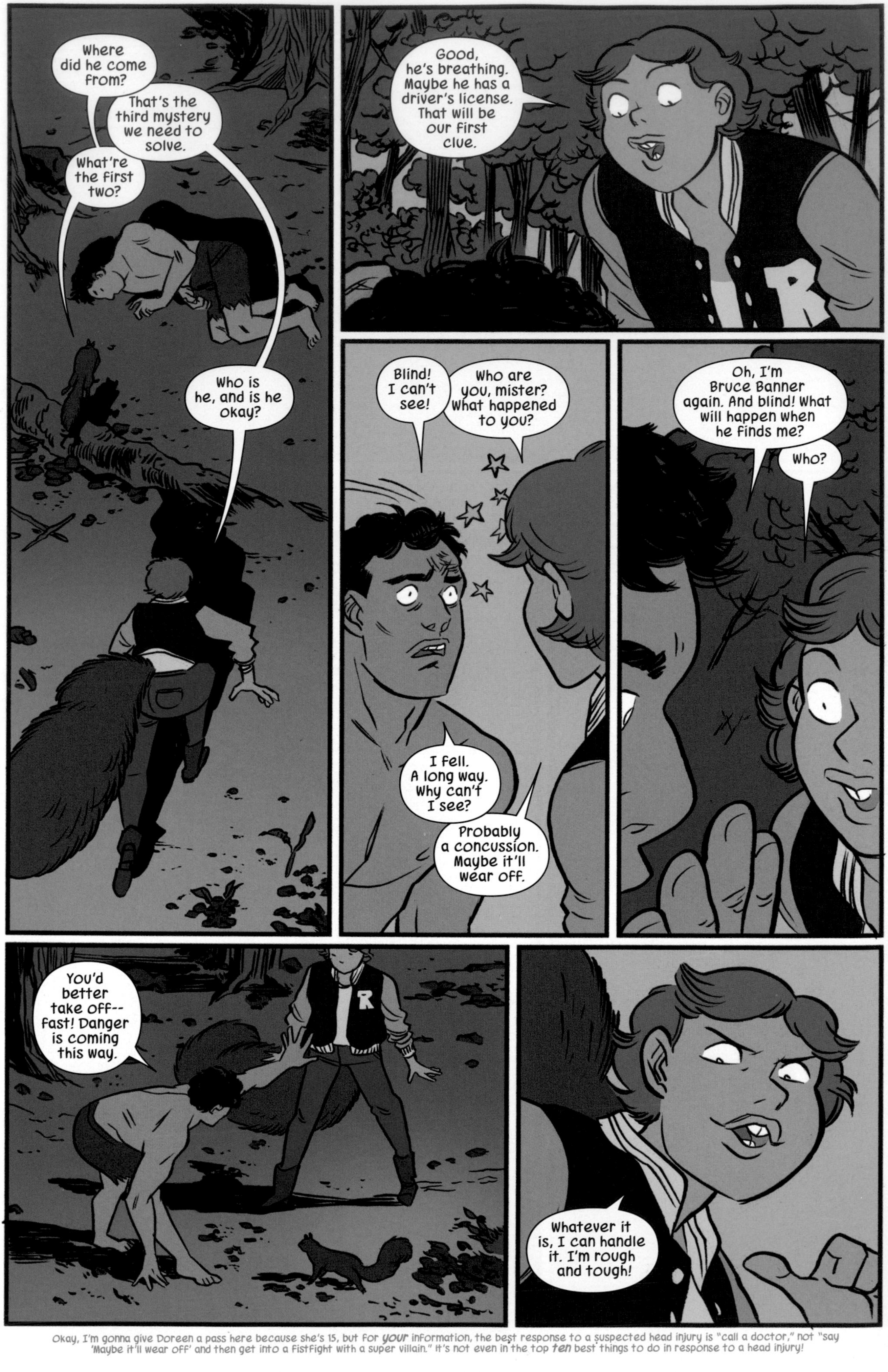
Where did he come from?
That's the third mystery we need to solve.
What're the first two?
Who is he, and is he okay?
Good, he's breathing. Maybe he has a driver's license. That will be our first clue.
Blind! I can't see!
Who are you, mister? What happened to you?
I fell. A long way. Why can't I see?
Probably a concussion. Maybe it'll wear off.
Oh, I'm Bruce Banner again. And blind! What will happen when he finds me?
Who?
You'd better take off--fast! Danger is coming this way.
Whatever it is, I can handle it. I'm rough and tough!

Okay, I'm gonna give Doreen a pass here because she's 15, but for ***your*** information, the best response to a suspected head injury is "call a doctor," not "say 'Maybe it'll wear off' and then get into a fistfight with a super villain." It's not even in the top ***ten*** best things to do in response to a head injury!

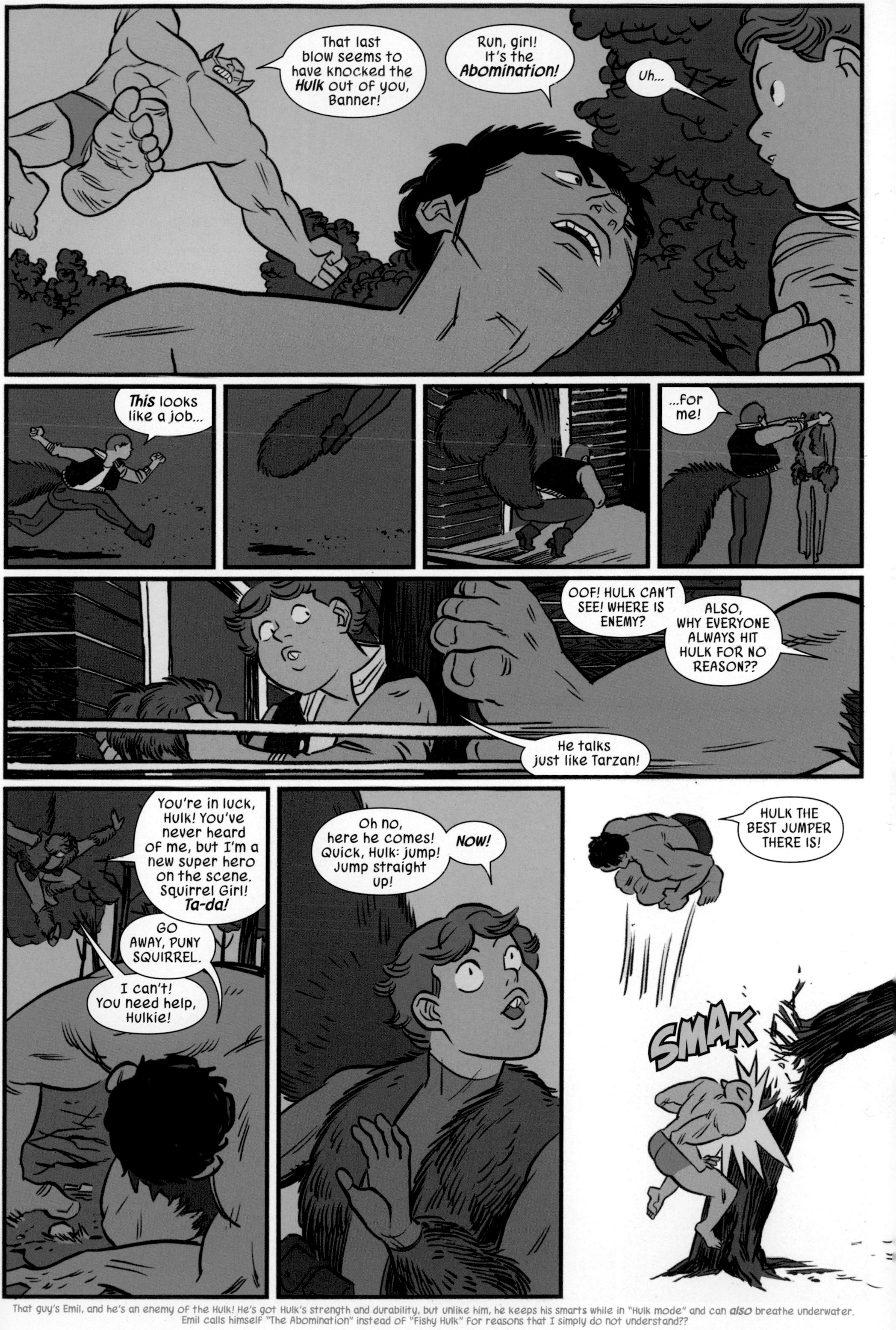
That last blow seems to have knocked the HULK out of you, Banner!
Run, girl! It's the Abomination!
Uh...
This looks like a job...
...for me!
OOF! HULK CAN'T SEE! WHERE IS ENEMY?
ALSO, WHY EVERYONE ALWAYS HIT HULK FOR NO REASON??
He talks just like Tarzan!
You're in luck, Hulk! You've never heard of me, but I'm a new super hero on the scene. Squirrel Girl! Ta-da!
GO AWAY, PUNY SQUIRREL.
I can't! You need help, Hulkie!
Oh no, here he comes! Quick, Hulk: jump! Jump straight up!
NOW!
HULK THE BEST JUMPER THERE IS!
SMAK

That guy's Emil, and he's an enemy of the Hulk! He's got Hulk's strength and durability, but unlike him, he keeps his smarts while in "Hulk mode" and can *also* breathe underwater. Emil calls himself "The Abomination" instead of "Fishy Hulk" for reasons that I simply do not understand??

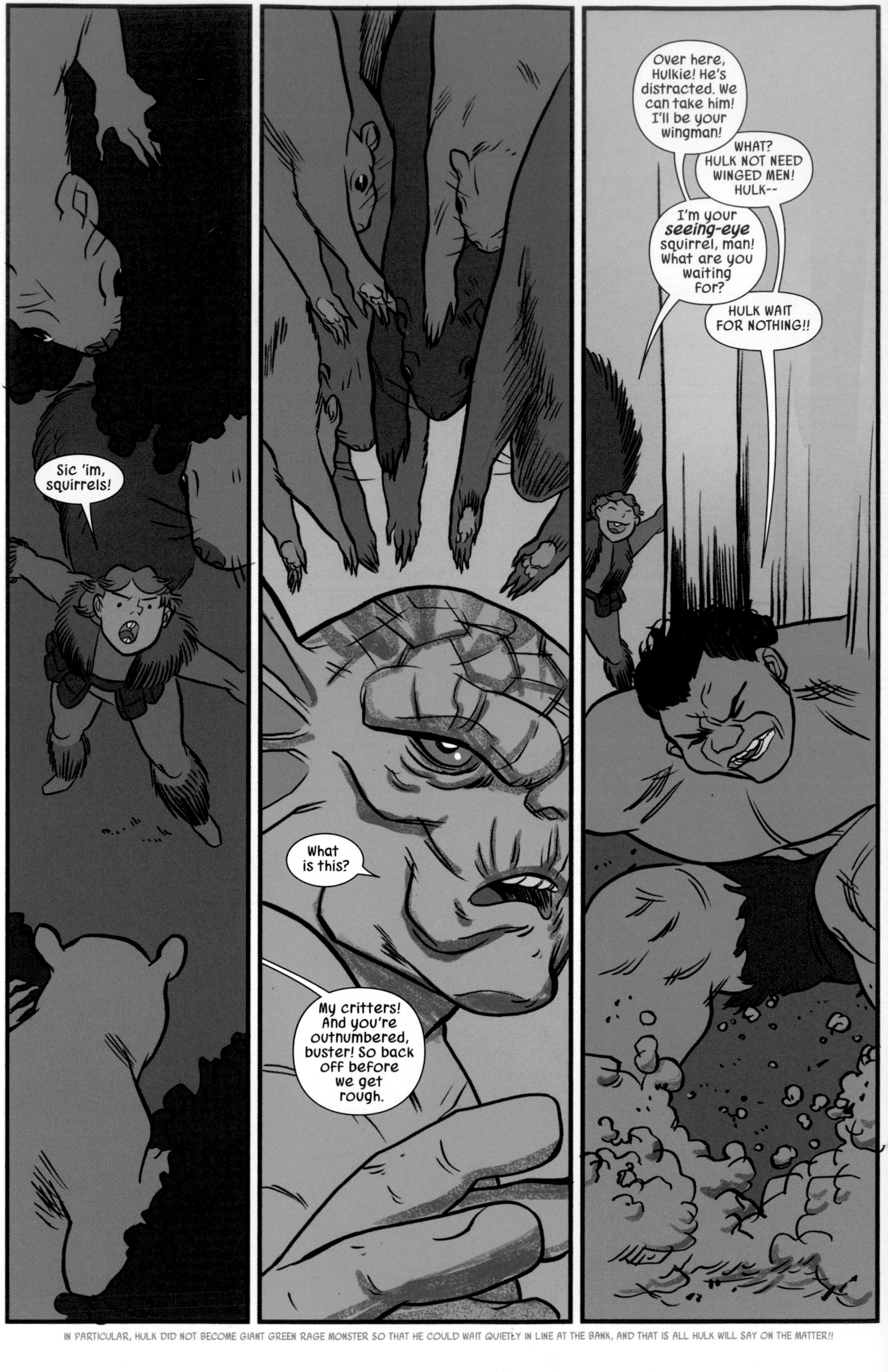
Sic 'im, squirrels!
What is this?
My critters! And you're outnumbered, buster! So back off before we get rough.
Over here, Hulkie! He's distracted. We can take him! I'll be your wingman!
WHAT? HULK NOT NEED WINGED MEN! HULK--
I'm your seeing-eye squirrel, man! What are you waiting for?
HULK WAIT FOR NOTHING!!

IN PARTICULAR, HULK DID NOT BECOME GIANT GREEN RAGE MONSTER SO THAT HE COULD WAIT QUIETLY IN LINE AT THE BANK, AND THAT IS ALL HULK WILL SAY ON THE MATTER!!

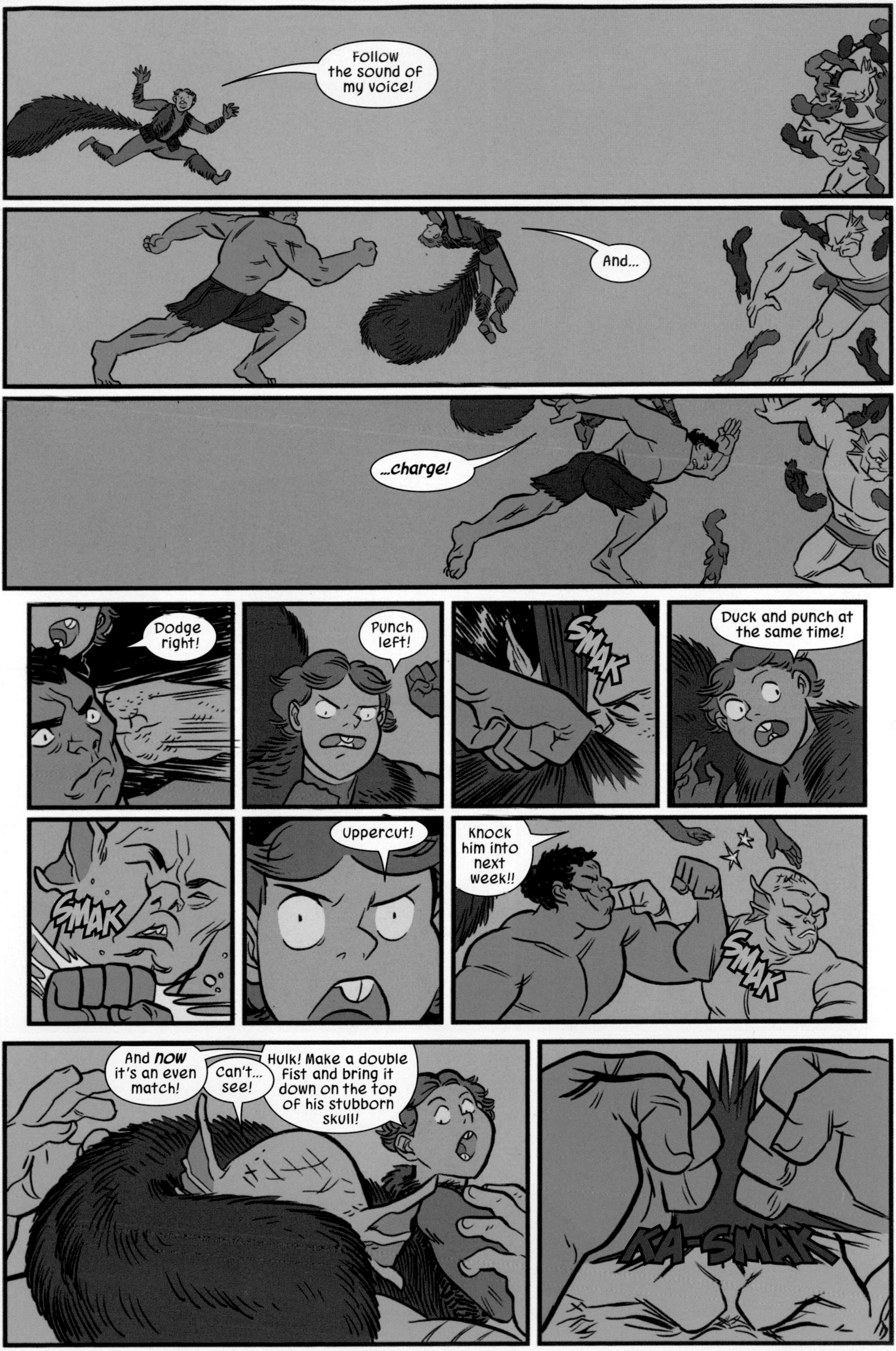
Follow the sound of my voice!
And...
...charge!
Dodge right!
Punch left!
SMAK
Duck and punch at the same time!
SMAK
Uppercut!
Knock him into next week!!
SMAK
And now it's an even match!
Can't... see!
Hulk! Make a double fist and bring it down on the top of his stubborn skull!
KA-SMAK

This illustrates the Hulk's famous English catchphrase *"Hulk smash,"* which is of course derived from his original famous Latin catchphrase *"veni, vidi, smashi."*

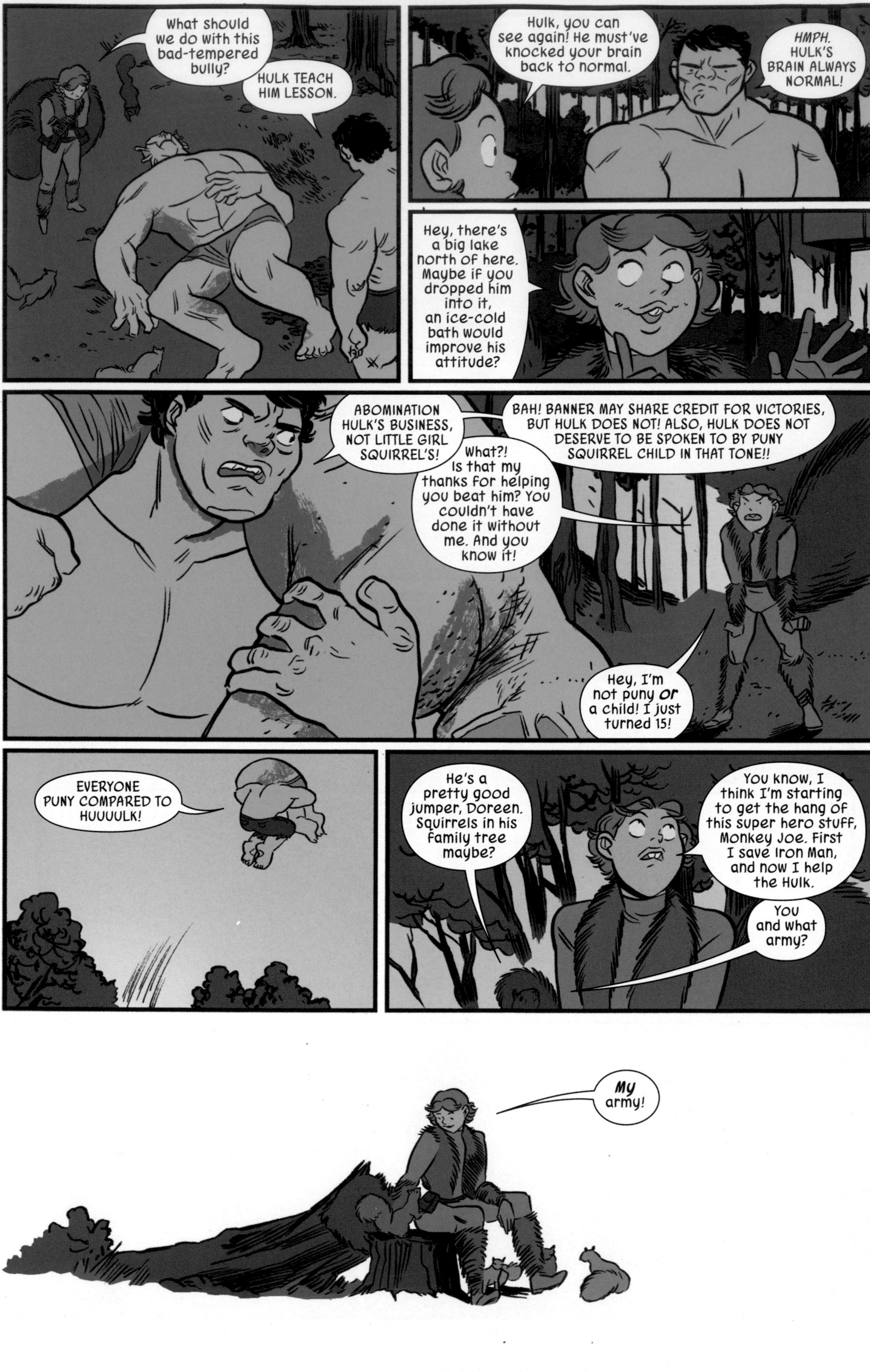
What should we do with this bad-tempered bully?
HULK TEACH HIM LESSON.
Hulk, you can see again! He must've knocked your brain back to normal.
HMPH. HULK'S BRAIN ALWAYS NORMAL!
Hey, there's a big lake north of here. Maybe if you dropped him into it, an ice-cold bath would improve his attitude?
ABOMINATION HULK'S BUSINESS, NOT LITTLE GIRL SQUIRREL'S!
What?! Is that my thanks for helping you beat him? You couldn't have done it without me. And you know it!
BAH! BANNER MAY SHARE CREDIT FOR VICTORIES, BUT HULK DOES NOT! ALSO, HULK DOES NOT DESERVE TO BE SPOKEN TO BY PUNY SQUIRREL CHILD IN THAT TONE!!
Hey, I'm not puny *or* a child! I just turned 15!
EVERYONE PUNY COMPARED TO HUUUULK!
He's a pretty good jumper, Doreen. Squirrels in his family tree maybe?
You know, I think I'm starting to get the hang of this super hero stuff, Monkey Joe. First I save Iron Man, and now I help the Hulk.
You and what army?
My army!

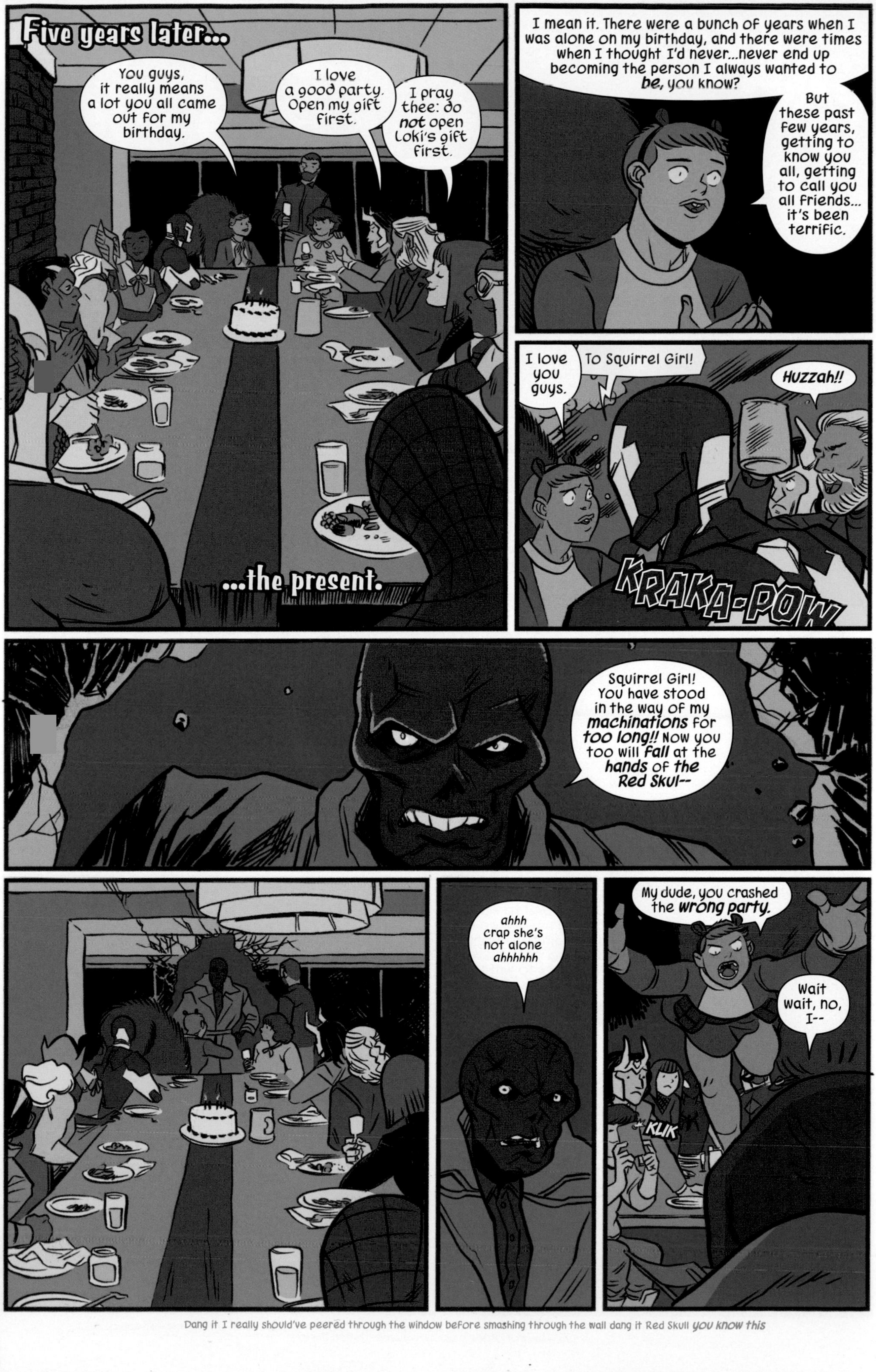
Five years later...
You guys, it really means a lot you all came out for my birthday.
I love a good party. Open my gift first.
I pray thee: do *not* open Loki's gift first.
...the present.
I mean it. There were a bunch of years when I was alone on my birthday, and there were times when I thought I'd never...never end up becoming the person I always wanted to *be*, you know?
But these past few years, getting to know you all, getting to call you all friends... it's been terrific.
I love you guys.
To Squirrel Girl!
HUZZAH!!
KRAKA-POW
Squirrel Girl! You have stood in the way of my *machinations* for *too long!!* Now you too will *fall* at the *hands* of *the Red Skul--*
ahhh crap she's not alone ahhhhhh
My dude, you crashed the *wrong party*.
Wait wait, no, I--
KLIK

Dang it I really should've peered through the window before smashing through the wall dang it Red Skull *you know this*

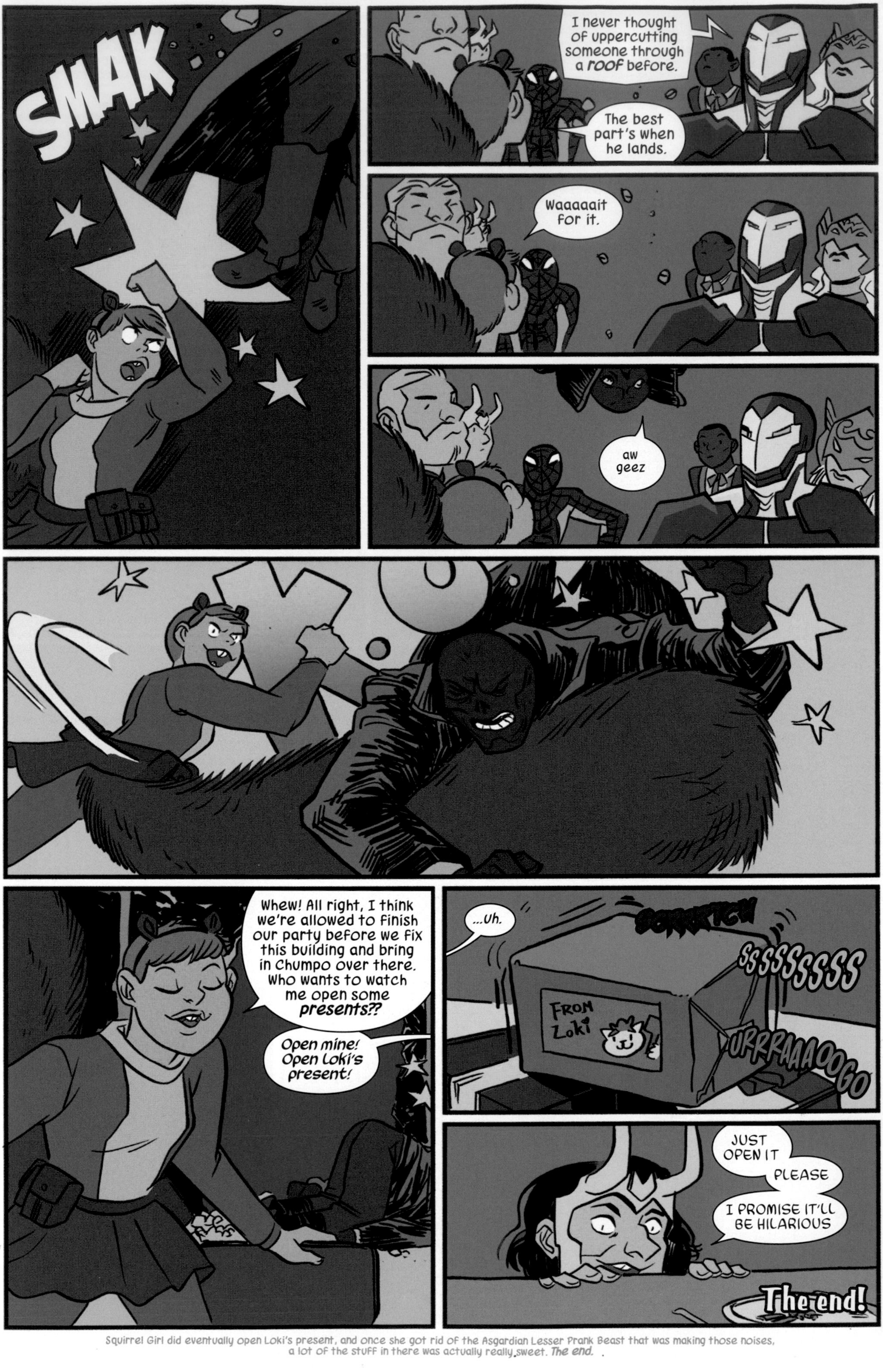
SMAK
I never thought of uppercutting someone through a *roof* before.
The best part's when he lands.
Waaaaait for it.
aw geez
Whew! All right, I think we're allowed to finish our party before we fix this building and bring in Chumpo over there. Who wants to watch me open some **presents??**
Open mine! Open Loki's present!
...Uh.
SCRRRTCH
SSSSSSSSS
FROM Loki
URRRAAAOOGO
JUST OPEN IT
PLEASE
I PROMISE IT'LL BE HILARIOUS
The end!

Squirrel Girl did eventually open Loki's present, and once she got rid of the Asgardian Lesser Prank Beast that was making those noises, a lot of the stuff in there was actually really sweet. *The end.*

Ryan!

Letters From Nuts

Erica!

Send letters to mheroes@marvel.com or 135 W 50th St, 7th Floor, New York, NY 10020 (Please mark "OKAY TO PRINT")

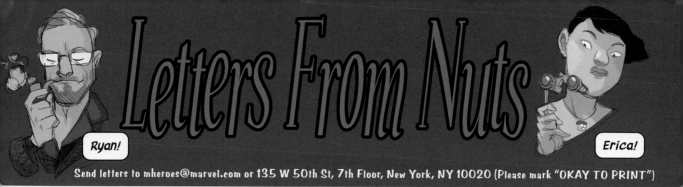

Twenty-five years ago this month, MARVEL SUPER-HEROES WINTER SPECIAL #8 hit the stands, with stories starring the X-Men, Drax, Gamora, Namor…and a brand new character named SQUIRREL GIRL!

MARVEL COMICS
MARVEL SUPER-HEROES
WINTER SPECIAL
80 PAGE BLOCK-BUSTER!
X-MEN
NAMOR

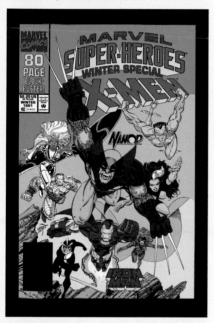

So we're all thrilled and honored to have Doreen's co-creator Will Murray contribute to this anniversary issue by writing that tale of 15-year-old Doreen and the Hulk – such a fun story, right? And we're paying tribute to SG's other co-creator, the legendary Steve Ditko, by running a panel of his art from that original story back on the page where we see Doreen's initial costume design! (So yeah, that wasn't actually Doreen's drawing – she was a talented artist for a 10-year-old, but not THAT talented!)

And TWO years ago this month, THE UNBEATABLE SQUIRREL GIRL #1 (Vol. 1) was released, so we're celebrating that milestone this issue as well! Thanks to all you readers out there for supporting this book like crazy, and for sending us your letters and your photos and your drawings – it's so great knowing these stories are connecting with you! So y'all keep that love coming, and we'll keep telling more Squirrel Girl stories! (And boy are there some exciting ones coming up…!)

Squirrel Girl team,

I couldn't believe it when I read the word "zot" in regards to sending items back in time. I am the only person I know who ever uses that word, despite its incredible usefulness. I'm guessing at least one of you played "Story Machine," that old Texas Instrument writing game with that weird purple hand monster.

Best!
Michele

RYAN: No, I've never played it! But there are few phrases more intriguing than "Texas Instrument writing game with that weird purple hand monster", so COLOR ME INTRIGUED. Since we're (tangentally) talking about calculators, let me say that I do all my calculation on an 37-year-old HP 41-CX, an RPN calculator my dad bought before I was born, and of the type that was used on Space Shuttle missions as a backup way to calculate re-entry if the main computer failed. I mostly use it to add up numbers that are too big for me to do in my head.

ERICA: I've never even owned a fancy calculator, seeing as from sixth grade on I attended arts-focused schools. My frame of reference for "Zot" is the Scott McCloud comic, which is great. There's interdimensional travel there! To a futuristic world! That's LIKE time travel, I guess. Also, according to Google, zot is god in Albanian. We learn something new every day.

Ryan and Erica,

I'd never been into reading comics before my husband put your first issue of SQUIRREL GIRL into my hands. I've been hooked from page one when she starts singing her own theme song to the tune of Spider-Man's theme! (Though, admittedly, I had to look up Spider-Man's theme online so I knew the tune because that's how out of touch I started with comics and super heroes…) Still! SQUIRREL GIRL has made me a comics convert thanks to her commitment to kicking butt but also to solving problems with smarts and friendship. She is basically a huge inspiration to anyone who ever wondered if it was possible to eat nuts AND save the world with some smart observations and a few well-placed butt-kicks!

Your delightful comic inspired my own crafts-building as well, and now I have my very own cobbled-together Squirrel Girl doll crew assembled as well as a crocheted Tippy Toe that I used to make a stop motion of the first scene of issue #v1 that drew me into this fabulous squirrelly world so quickly! I attached a few pictures of the dolls I've made (I even have Nancy in anticipation of future films, wearing a shirt that I hope Mew would approve of!) and here's the link to the short stop motion: https://youtu.be/1otZ-PJcCi8

Many thanks for all you do, can't wait for the next nutty adventure!

April Duclos
Massachusetts

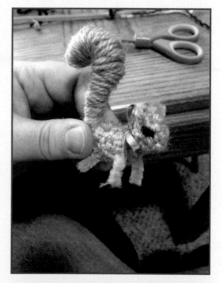

RYAN: April, I love your Tippy AND I LOVE YOUR STOP-MOTION SQUIRREL GIRL RECREATION. My friends and I made stop motion films with action figures when we were in high school, but sadly none of them were a) as good, and b) put on the internet. However I remember one: it starred Spider-Man (um, don't sue me Marvel) and it was about 10 seconds long. Spider-Man said "Time for some heavy reading" and then tried to lift up a newspaper (giant, compared to his action-figure size), and then it collapsed on top of him and he said "Oh no, maybe a little TOO heavy!" I have no regrets.

ERICA: Ryan.

Dear Unbeatable Squirrel Warriors

I just finished 14 and must say, I am impressed with the level of thought that you put into your stories, whether using binary to count on one hand, acting like yelp for Galactus, or physics to defeat Enigmo, Doreen is truly unbeatable. It is great how Doreen and Nancy work so well together!

I have been a longtime fan of SG and am currently working on owning every single one of her appearances, so far I am ten issues away from completion! I am loving every comic you both have put out and know I will continue to enjoy Squirrel Girl's adventures forever!

Ryan, when will we learn more about Nancy? we know so little about her besides she loves Mew, Doreen, knitting, writing Cat-Thor fan fics and maybe has a tattoo?

Erica what has been your favorite panel to draw to date? Is there a character from the Marvel Universe that you would love to draw in a future issue?

P.S. I have enclosed a picture I drew of Doreen and Nancy having a bit of fun!

P.P.S. Just want to finally say that you guys are so lucky working for in my opinion for the best comic company AND the BEST character in the world! keep up the great work Ryan, Erica, Rico, and Travis, I am seriously jealous of all of you!

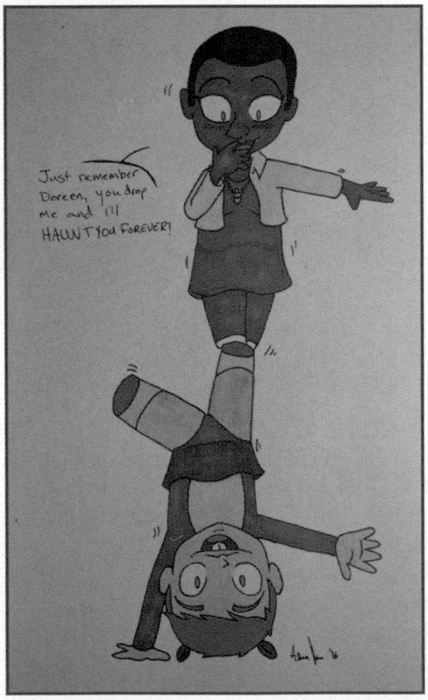
Just remember Doreen, you drop me and i'll HAUNT you FOREVER!

RYAN: Ah, such a cute drawing!! Besides the fun reveal of FUTURE NANCY in this issue, I also hope we'll be finding out more about Present Nancy soon. Including: NANCY'S MYSTERIOUS SECRETS??

ERICA: Hm. Last issue I got to draw Taskmaster, who I encouraged Ryan to put in a story because he is a skeleton pirate, so THAT was fun. I don't know about favorite panel, but the part that was the most surprisingly fun to draw was the multiple Squirrel Girls vs Doctor Doom fight, which I thought was just going to be terrible because it was like 20 people per panel.

Dear Squirrel Team,

I just read issue #11 (I know, I'm late, it's embarrassing) and, as a Computer Science student, I couldn't resist sending you my opinion in the form of an algorithm.

```
WHILE (reading){
    I_am_mesmerized();
    IF (Doc Ock appears){
        I_dont_realize_its_weird();
    }
}
I_love_it();
I_think_it_is_perfect();
IF (Someone wants to learn about CS){
    I_give_him_or_her_this_issue();
}ELSE{
    I_force_him_or_her_to_read_it();
```

Yours nerdly,
Roni Kaufman

P.S.: I don't know whether I'm the first one to do this. If this not the case, I apologize (another if statement?!).

RYAN: This is great, and I will gladly accept all reader letters in the form of flattering pseudocode from now on!!

ERICA: WHAT IS THIS SORCERY.

Dear Nancy, Doreen, Ryan, and Erica,

I've been a Marvel fan since I was 13 and my daughter Wanda was taught to read with Power Pack comics (POW! BAM! WHAP!). We both absolutely love THE UNBEATABLE SQUIRREL GIRL and giggle maniacally when we read the books again and again. I really like how she solves problems in new and unusual non-violent ways, yet still can appreciate a good butt-kicking occasionally. We enjoyed the Ratatosk storyline so much that we were inspired to do something special this Halloween (see attached pictures). I really hope that Squirrel Girl and Spider-Man can hang out together in the future, and Wanda wants to see more Brain Drain. Thank you so much for all your great work!

Sincerely,
Doug Smith (46) and Wanda Smith (10)

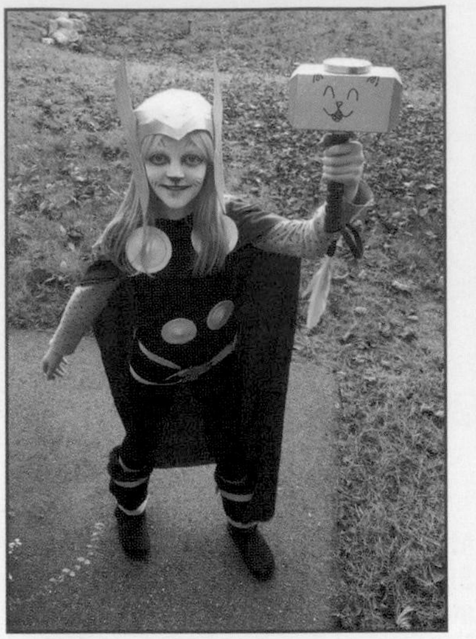

RYAN: Wanda, this part is only for you, so don't let your dad read this: that costume is amazing, there is more Brain Drain in this issue, and we can retcon that to say it was JUST FOR YOU, and thank you so much for being such a great reader! You're the first Wanda I've ever met AND THEREFORE THE BEST.

Okay Dave, this part of the answer is for you: Doreen and Spider-Man do (briefly) hang out in the SQUIRREL GIRL BEATS UP THE MARVEL UNIVERSE OGN, and it doesn't work out super well for... well, the Marvel Universe, I guess? But I'd like to see more of that too! She already seems to encounter his villains an awful lot. Also, tell Wanda her costume is awesome!

ERICA: Brain Drain is so much fun to draw. I second this. Also that is an amazing Thor outfit. I'm a proponent of capes as everyday fall wear so the choice of the word "outfit" rather than "costume" was on purpose.

Next: New Costume!

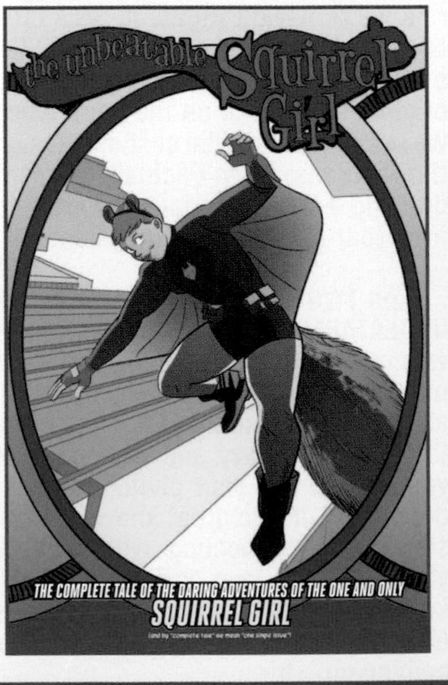
the unbeatable Squirrel Girl
THE COMPLETE TALE OF THE DARING ADVENTURES OF THE ONE AND ONLY
SQUIRREL GIRL

Attention, Squirrel Scouts! Make sure to check out our production blog, **unbeatablesquirrelgirl.tumblr.com**, where we post behind-the-scenes stuff on how the book gets made, along with all sorts of cool things *you* make: fanart, cosplay, whatever!

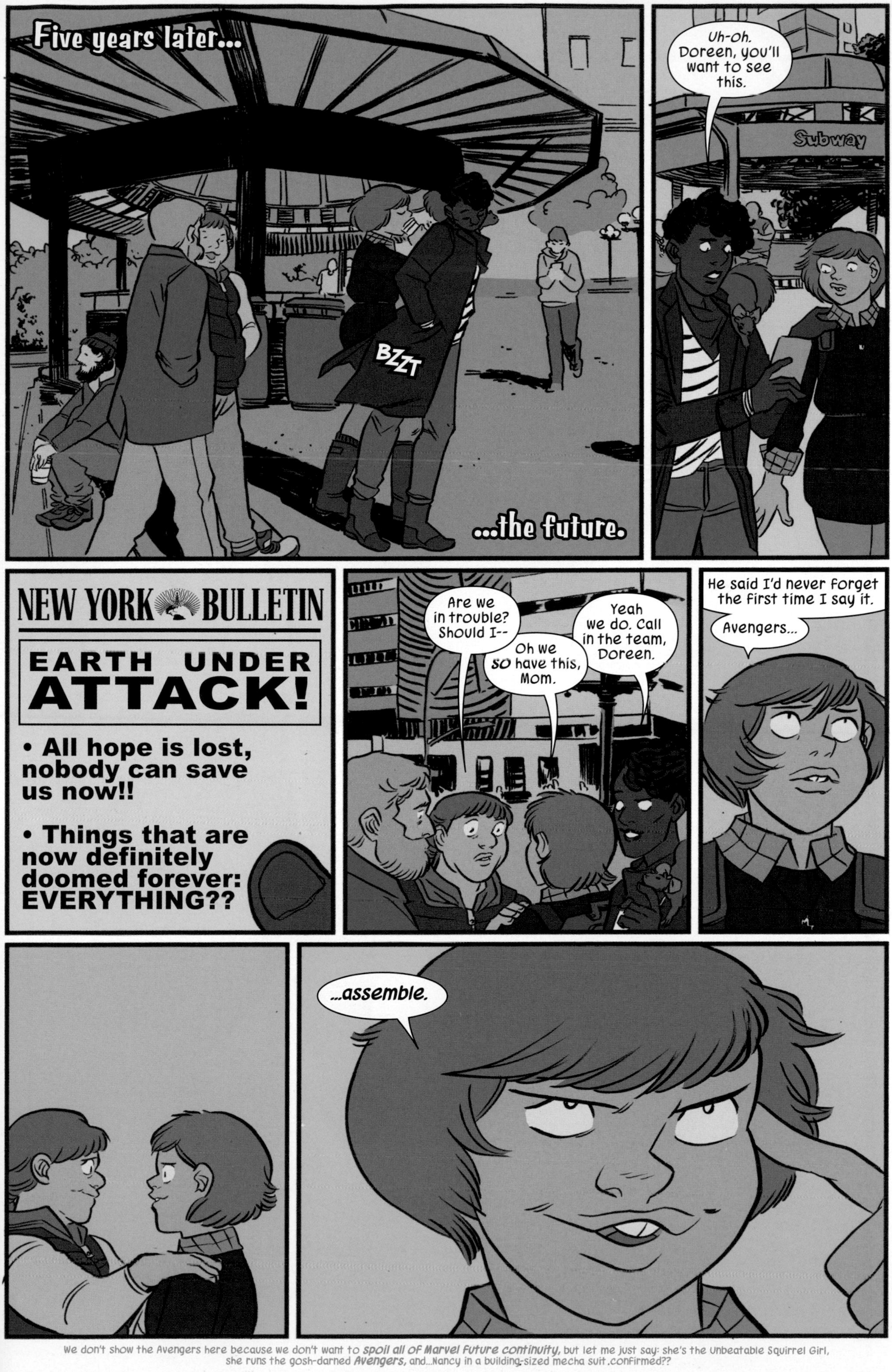
Five years later...
...the future.
BZZT
Uh-Oh. Doreen, you'll want to see this.
Subway
NEW YORK BULLETIN
EARTH UNDER ATTACK!
• All hope is lost, nobody can save us now!!
• Things that are now definitely doomed forever: EVERYTHING??
Are we in trouble? Should I--
Oh we *so* have this, Mom.
Yeah we do. Call in the team, Doreen.
He said I'd never forget the first time I say it.
Avengers...
...assemble.

We don't show the Avengers here because we don't want to ***spoil all of Marvel Future continuity,*** but let me just say: she's the Unbeatable Squirrel Girl, she runs the gosh-darned ***Avengers,*** and...Nancy in a building-sized mecha suit confirmed??

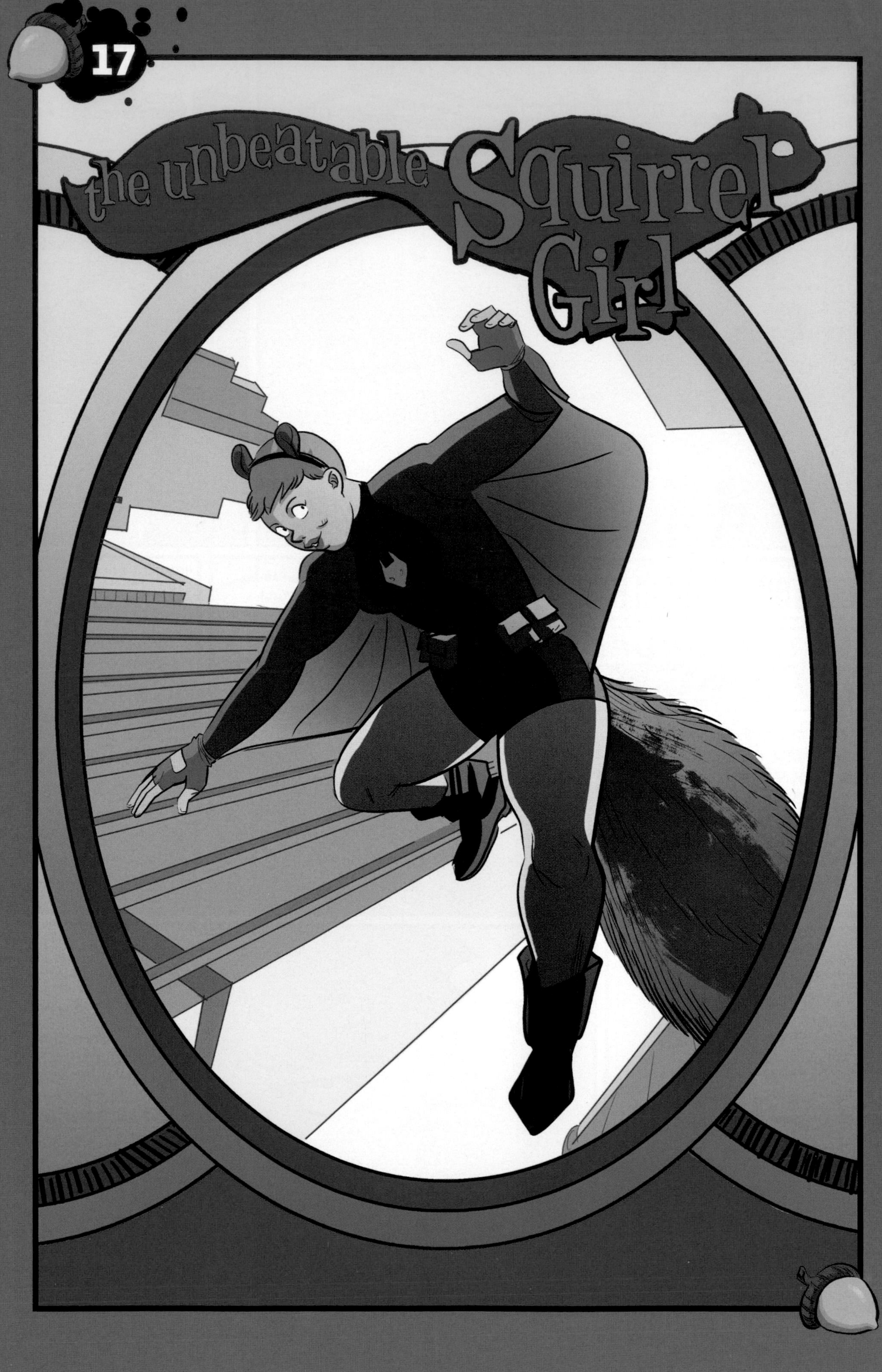
17
the unbeatable Squirrel Girl

Doreen Green isn't just a second-year computer science student: she secretly also has all the powers of both squirrel and girl! She uses her amazing abilities to fight crime **and** be as awesome as possible. You know her as...**The Unbeatable Squirrel Girl!** Find out what she's been up to, with...

Squirrel Girl in a nutshell

search!

#computerengineering

#regularengineering

#catthor

#doghulk

#alfredo4life

Squirrel Girl @unbeatablesg
Roses are red / Violets are dull / Guess who just had her birthday party crashed by THE FRIGGIN' RED SKULL

Squirrel Girl @unbeatablesg
Answer: me.

Squirrel Girl @unbeatablesg
Well haha not JUST me since it was a party filled with pals like KOI BOI, CHIPMUNK HUNK, SPIDER-MAN, BLACK WIDOW, IRON MAN, and MORE??

Squirrel Girl @unbeatablesg
Anyway, I punched the Red Skull right through the roof and he's in jail now. PRESUMABLY FOREVER?? THAT SEEMS LIKELY, YES?

Squirrel Girl @unbeatablesg
Which MAYBE just goes to show you the dangers of crashing someone's party when she's friends with LITERAL SUPER HEROES? hmm hard to say

Egg @imduderadtude
@unbeatablesg can u get a mesasge to spider man for me

Squirrel Girl @unbeatablesg
@imduderadtude no

Egg @imduderadtude
@unbeatablesg please he has me blocked and i just want to ask him Y he has me blokced

Squirrel Girl @unbeatablesg
@imduderadtude Dude, real talk, you don't want to be following him anyway, he posts the worst stuff

Squirrel Girl @unbeatablesg
@imduderadtude like he's a good guy for fighting crime but not necessarily the best at providing entertaining #content in 140 characters

Spider-Man @aspidercan
if someone is a jerk on here i reply with "wow looks like u got bitten by a radioactive JERK," so yeah feel free to use that if you want

Spider-Man @aspidercan
hi everyone i'm having a lot of fun here on the world......................................wide.............................WEB

Spider-Man @aspidercan
If you're wondering who I've got blocked, it's @wealth and @fame

Spider-Man @aspidercan
....because wealth and fame i've ignored

Spider-Man @aspidercan
#actionismyreward

Squirrel Girl @unbeatablesg
@imduderadtude I rest my case

xKravenTheHunterx @unshavenkraven
@unbeatablesg Happy belated birthday, girl of squirrels.

Squirrel Girl @unbeatablesg
@unshavenkraven Thanks, Kraven!

xKravenTheHunterx @unshavenkraven
@unbeatablesg I'm sorry I could not attend your party.

Squirrel Girl @unbeatablesg
@unshavenkraven It's okay! We'll hang out sometime soon. We'll have to catch up later, I've got to get to a thing for class!

Squirrel Girl @unbeatablesg
@unshavenkraven I mean my friend has got to get to a thing for class.

Squirrel Girl @unbeatablesg
@unshavenkraven I mean, my friend has to get to a thing for class and I'm helping her...go there?

Squirrel Girl @unbeatablesg
@unshavenkraven She goes to a different school

Squirrel Girl @unbeatablesg
@unshavenkraven in Canada

xKravenTheHunterx @unshavenkraven
@unbeatablesg You can just delete these posts.

Squirrel Girl @unbeatablesg
@unshavenkraven YEP, ALREADY ON IT

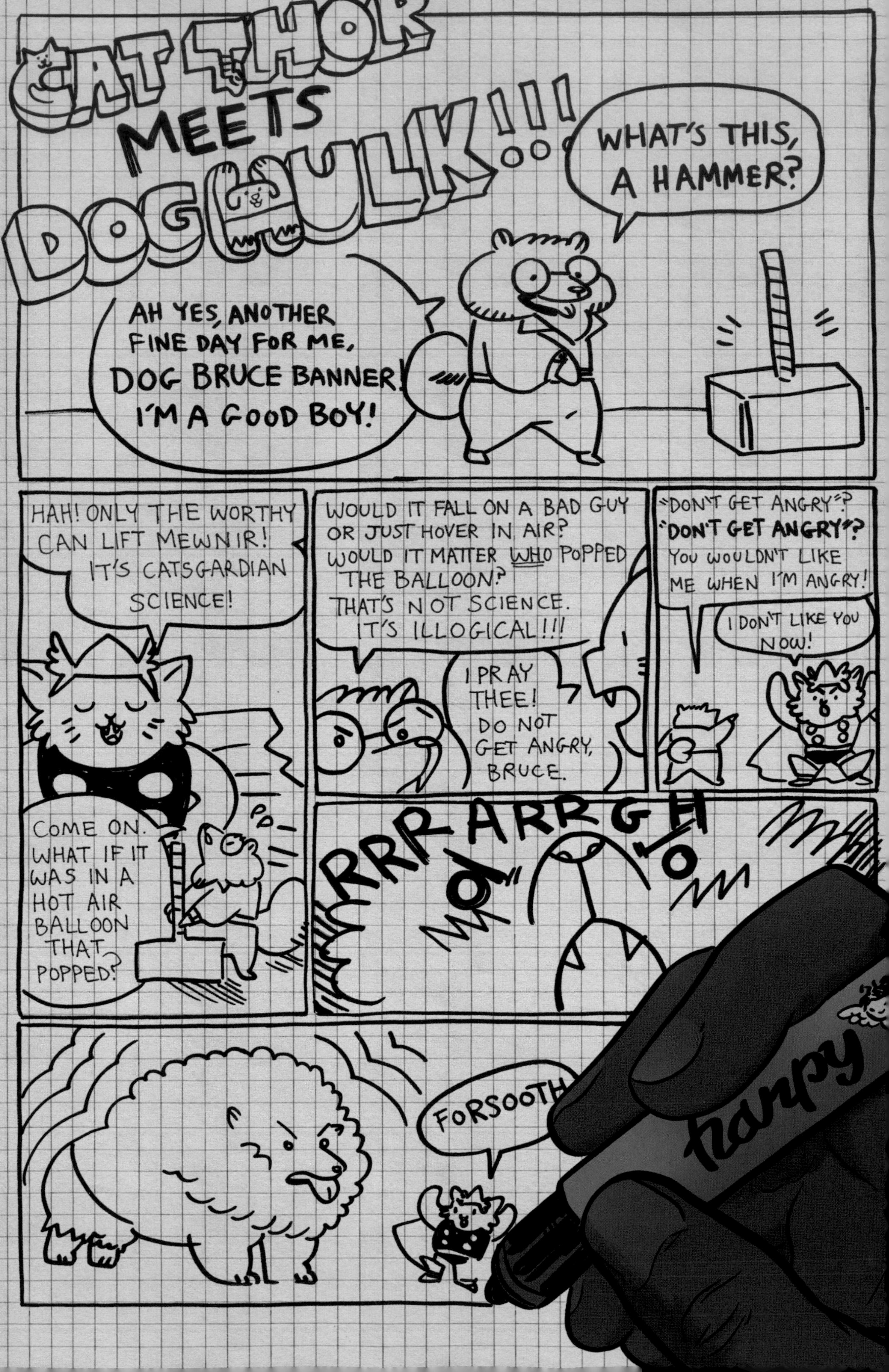
CAT THOR MEETS DOG HULK!!!
WHAT'S THIS, A HAMMER?
AH YES, ANOTHER FINE DAY FOR ME, DOG BRUCE BANNER! I'M A GOOD BOY!
HAH! ONLY THE WORTHY CAN LIFT MEWNIR! IT'S CATSGARDIAN SCIENCE!
COME ON. WHAT IF IT WAS IN A HOT AIR BALLOON THAT POPPED?
WOULD IT FALL ON A BAD GUY OR JUST HOVER IN AIR? WOULD IT MATTER WHO POPPED THE BALLOON? THAT'S NOT SCIENCE. IT'S ILLOGICAL!!!
I PRAY THEE! DO NOT GET ANGRY, BRUCE.
"DON'T GET ANGRY"? "DON'T GET ANGRY"? YOU WOULDN'T LIKE ME WHEN I'M ANGRY!
I DON'T LIKE YOU NOW!
RRRRARRRGH
FORSOOTH
tanpy

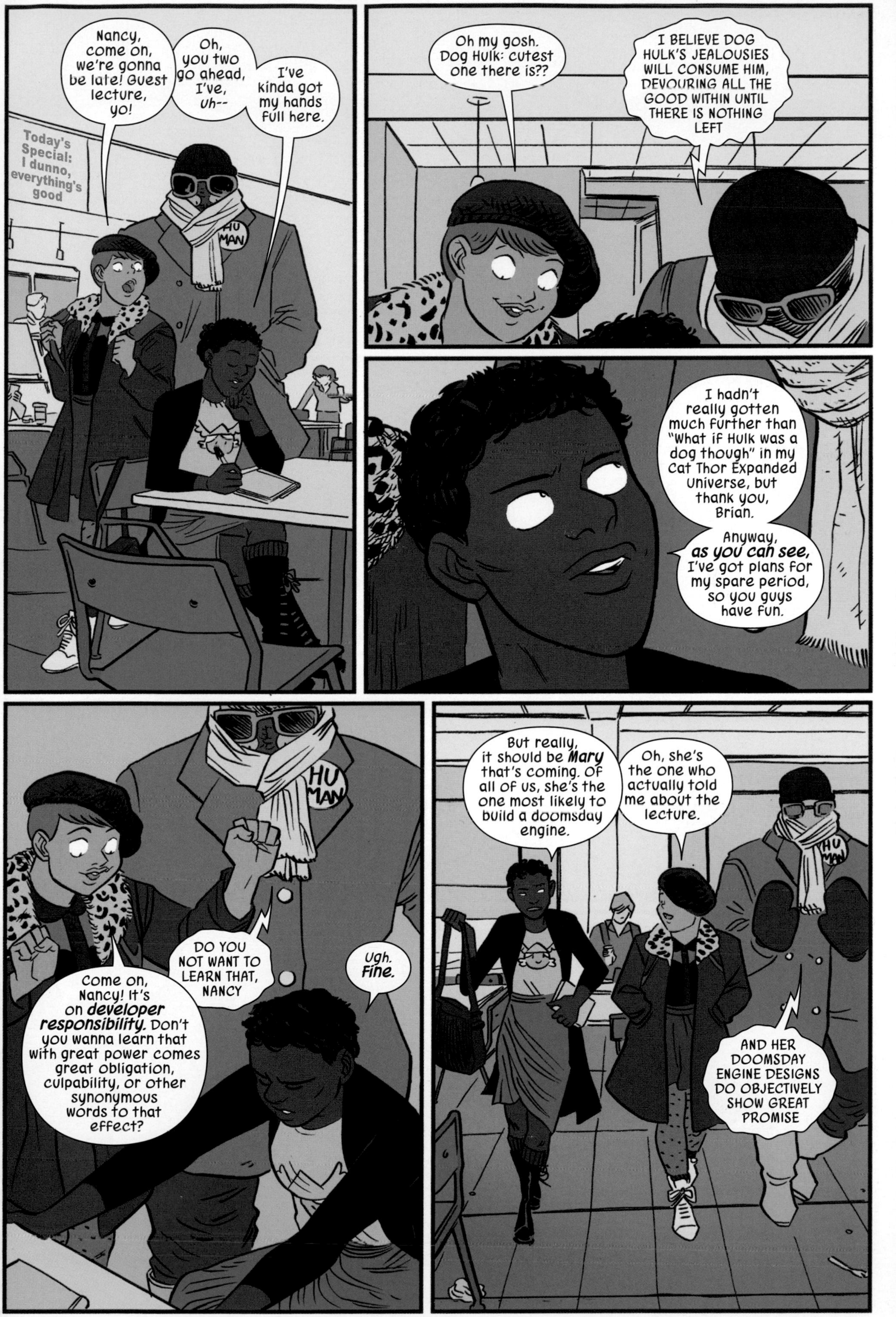
Nancy, come on, we're gonna be late! Guest lecture, yo!
Today's Special: I dunno, everything's good
Oh, you two go ahead, I've, uh--
I've kinda got my hands full here.
HU MAN
Oh my gosh. Dog Hulk: cutest one there is??
I BELIEVE DOG HULK'S JEALOUSIES WILL CONSUME HIM, DEVOURING ALL THE GOOD WITHIN UNTIL THERE IS NOTHING LEFT
I hadn't really gotten much further than "What if Hulk was a dog though" in my Cat Thor Expanded Universe, but thank you, Brian.
Anyway, as you can see, I've got plans for my spare period, so you guys have fun.
HU MAN
Come on, Nancy! It's on developer responsibility. Don't you wanna learn that with great power comes great obligation, culpability, or other synonymous words to that effect?
DO YOU NOT WANT TO LEARN THAT, NANCY
Ugh. Fine.
But really, it should be Mary that's coming. Of all of us, she's the one most likely to build a doomsday engine.
Oh, she's the one who actually told me about the lecture.
HU MAN
AND HER DOOMSDAY ENGINE DESIGNS DO OBJECTIVELY SHOW GREAT PROMISE

ESU student, definitely not a robot, will evaluate your doomsday engines and provide constructive feedback. Looking to trade for lessons in passing as a human, not because I need them, *obviously*, I just want to see if *you* know.

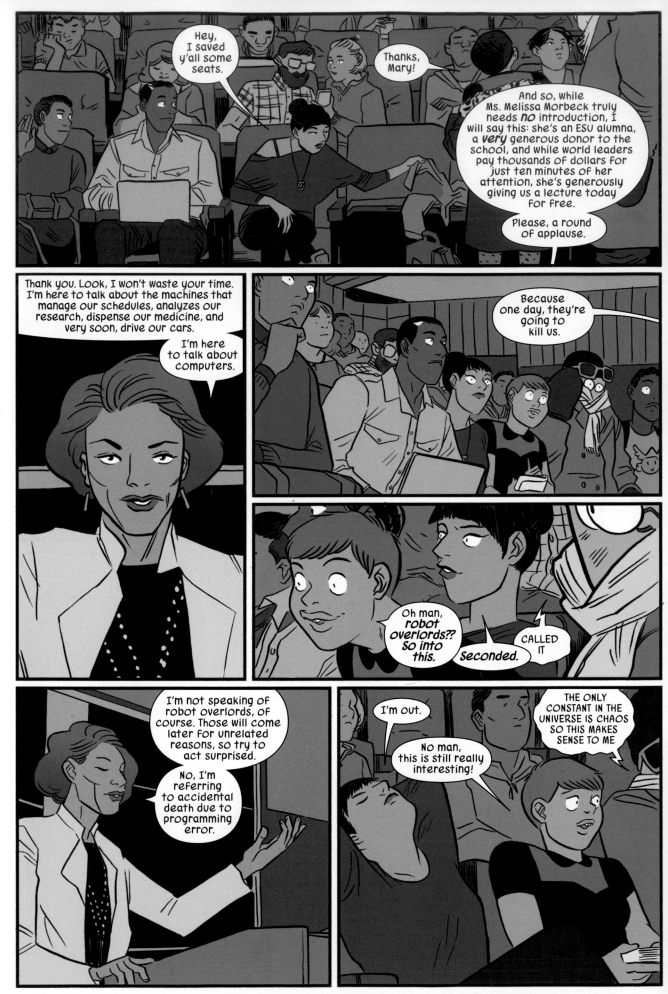

Hey, I saved y'all some seats.

Thanks, Mary!

And so, while Ms. Melissa Morbeck truly needs *no* introduction, I will say this: she's an ESU alumna, a *very* generous donor to the school, and while world leaders pay thousands of dollars for just ten minutes of her attention, she's generously giving us a lecture today for free.

Please, a round of applause.

Thank you. Look, I won't waste your time. I'm here to talk about the machines that manage our schedules, analyzes our research, dispense our medicine, and very soon, drive our cars.

I'm here to talk about computers.

Because one day, they're going to kill us.

Oh man, *robot overlords??* So into this.

Seconded.

CALLED IT

I'm not speaking of robot overlords, of course. Those will come later for unrelated reasons, so try to act surprised.

No, I'm referring to accidental death due to programming error.

I'm out.

No man, this is still really interesting!

THE ONLY CONSTANT IN THE UNIVERSE IS CHAOS SO THIS MAKES SENSE TO ME

Melissa Morbeck! Both her names start with the same letter, so you know she's a comic book character. If you have a friend whose names all start with the same letter, there is a chance they are a comic book character too. They'll deny it but we all know the truth, RICO RENZI OF SQUIRREL GIRL COLORIST FAME!!

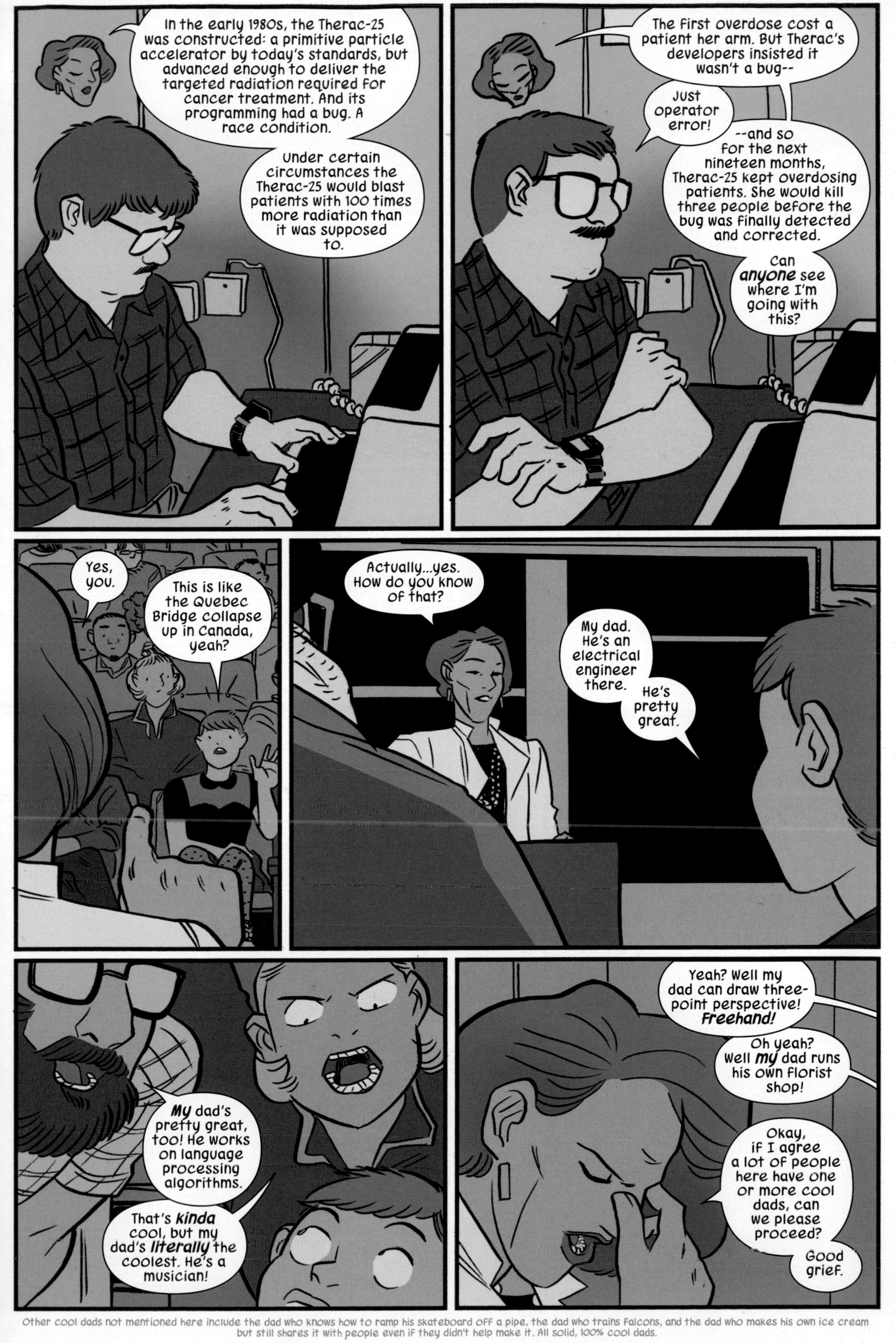
In the early 1980s, the Therac-25 was constructed: a primitive particle accelerator by today's standards, but advanced enough to deliver the targeted radiation required for cancer treatment. And its programming had a bug. A race condition.
Under certain circumstances the Therac-25 would blast patients with 100 times more radiation than it was supposed to.
The first overdose cost a patient her arm. But Therac's developers insisted it wasn't a bug--
Just operator error!
--and so for the next nineteen months, Therac-25 kept overdosing patients. She would kill three people before the bug was finally detected and corrected.
Can *anyone* see where I'm going with this?
Yes, you.
This is like the Quebec Bridge collapse up in Canada, yeah?
Actually...yes. How do you know of that?
My dad. He's an electrical engineer there.
He's pretty great.
My dad's pretty great, too! He works on language processing algorithms.
That's *kinda* cool, but my dad's *literally* the coolest. He's a musician!
Yeah? Well my dad can draw three-point perspective! ***Freehand!***
Oh yeah? Well *my* dad runs his own florist shop!
Okay, if I agree a lot of people here have one or more cool dads, can we please proceed?
Good grief.

Other cool dads not mentioned here include the dad who knows how to ramp his skateboard off a pipe, the dad who trains falcons, and the dad who makes his own ice cream but still shares it with people even if they didn't help make it. All solid, 100% cool dads.

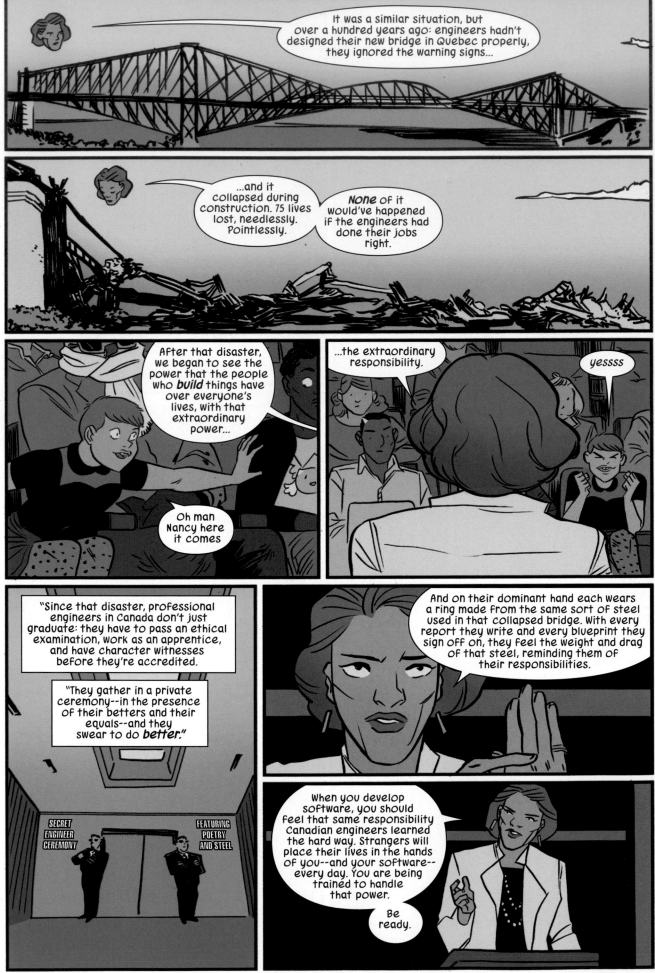

It was a similar situation, but over a hundred years ago: engineers hadn't designed their new bridge in Quebec properly, they ignored the warning signs...

...and it collapsed during construction. 75 lives lost, needlessly. Pointlessly.

None of it would've happened if the engineers had done their jobs right.

After that disaster, we began to see the power that the people who *build* things have over everyone's lives, with that extraordinary power...

Oh man Nancy here it comes

...the extraordinary responsibility.

yessss

"Since that disaster, professional engineers in Canada don't just graduate: they have to pass an ethical examination, work as an apprentice, and have character witnesses before they're accredited.

"They gather in a private ceremony--in the presence of their betters and their equals--and they swear to do *better*."

SECRET ENGINEER CEREMONY

FEATURING POETRY AND STEEL

And on their dominant hand each wears a ring made from the same sort of steel used in that collapsed bridge. With every report they write and every blueprint they sign off on, they feel the weight and drag of that steel, reminding them of their responsibilities.

When you develop software, you should feel that same responsibility Canadian engineers learned the hard way. Strangers will place their lives in the hands of you--and your software--every day. You are being trained to handle that power.

Be ready.

Right now, somewhere in the world, Peter Parker is sitting up straight in bed and wondering why his "stolen catchphrase-sense" is suddenly tingling *so much*.

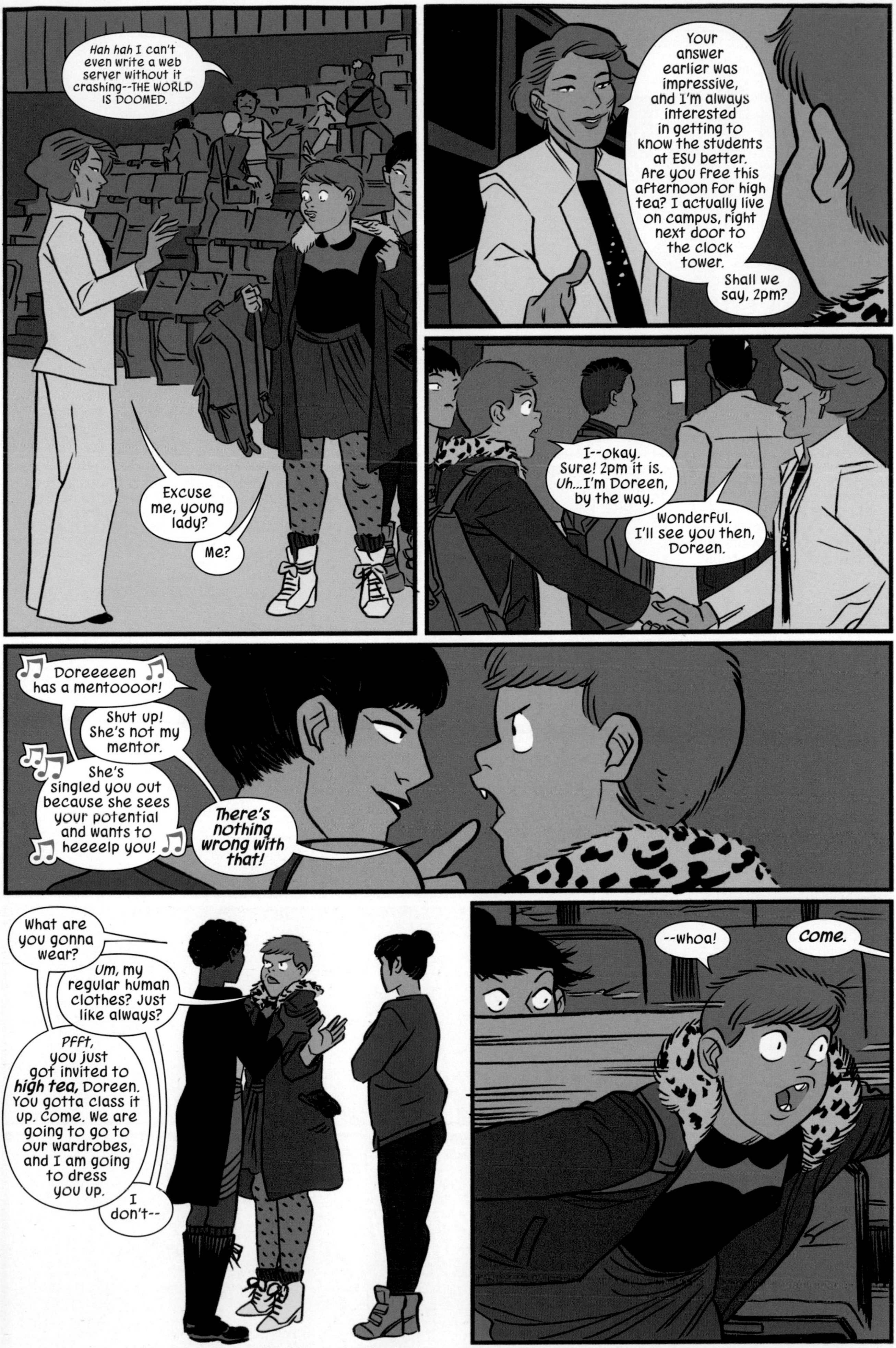
Hah hah I can't even write a web server without it crashing--THE WORLD IS DOOMED.
Excuse me, young lady?
Me?
Your answer earlier was impressive, and I'm always interested in getting to know the students at ESU better. Are you free this afternoon for high tea? I actually live on campus, right next door to the clock tower.
Shall we say, 2pm?
I--okay. Sure! 2pm it is. Uh...I'm Doreen, by the way.
Wonderful. I'll see you then, Doreen.
Doreeeeen has a mentoooor!
Shut up! She's not my mentor.
She's singled you out because she sees your potential and wants to heeeelp you!
There's nothing wrong with that!
What are you gonna wear?
Um, my regular human clothes? Just like always?
Pfft, you just got invited to high tea, Doreen. You gotta class it up. Come. We are going to go to our wardrobes, and I am going to dress you up.
I don't--
--whoa!
Come.

PRO TIP: if someone ever asks you what you're gonna wear, just say "regular human clothes." Unless you make a catastrophic mistake while dressing, your answer will always be 100% accurate!

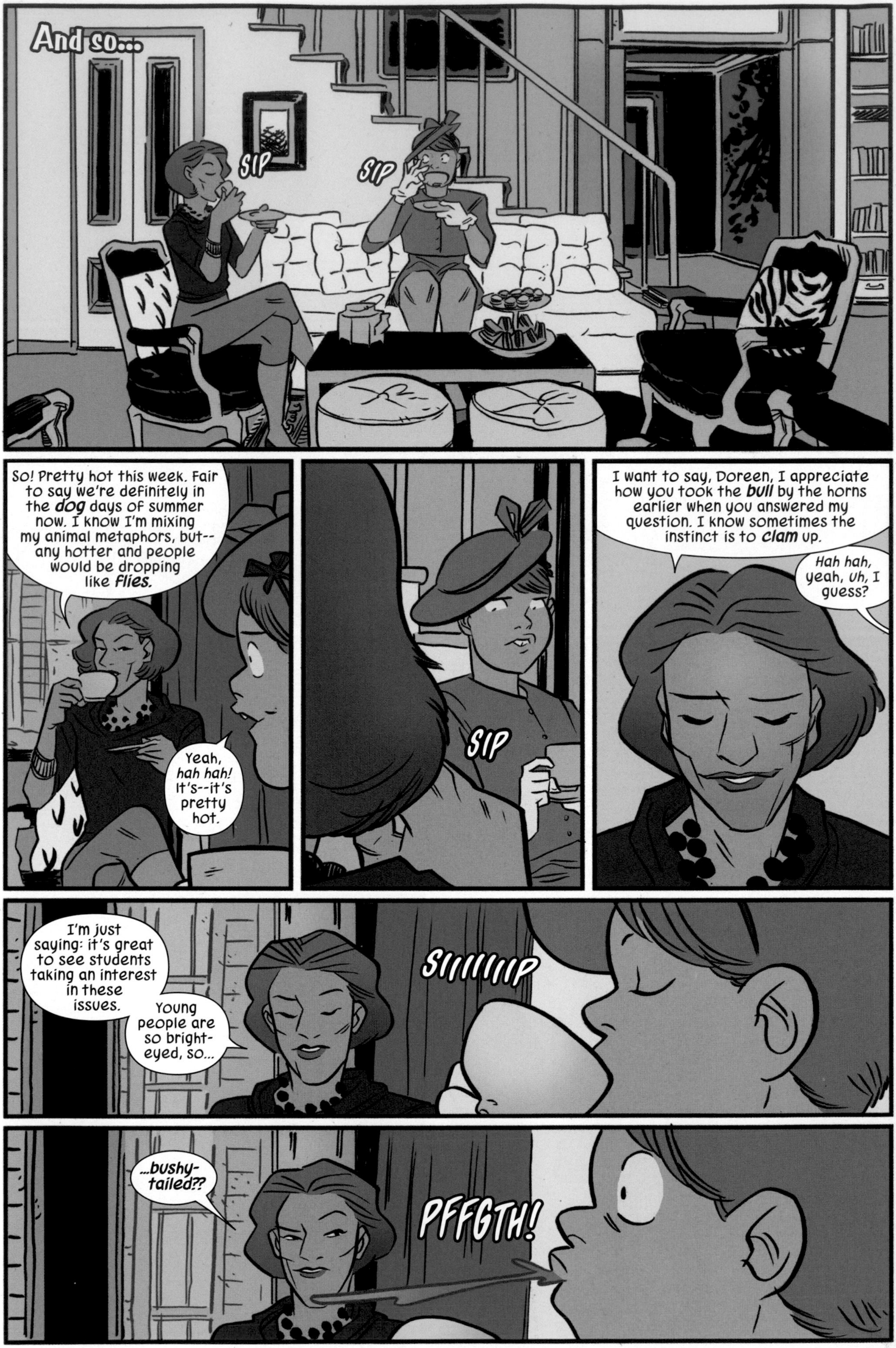
And so...
SIP
SIP
So! Pretty hot this week. Fair to say we're definitely in the dog days of summer now. I know I'm mixing my animal metaphors, but--any hotter and people would be dropping like flies.
Yeah, hah hah! It's--it's pretty hot.
SIP
I want to say, Doreen, I appreciate how you took the bull by the horns earlier when you answered my question. I know sometimes the instinct is to clam up.
Hah hah, yeah, uh, I guess?
I'm just saying: it's great to see students taking an interest in these issues.
Young people are so bright-eyed, so...
SIIIIIIP
...bushy-tailed??
PFFGTH!

After many experiments I can finally confirm that, yes, "pffgth" is the sound I make when spitting out tea. Anyway, thanks for having me over, I gotta go, good luck with all your moistened walls!!

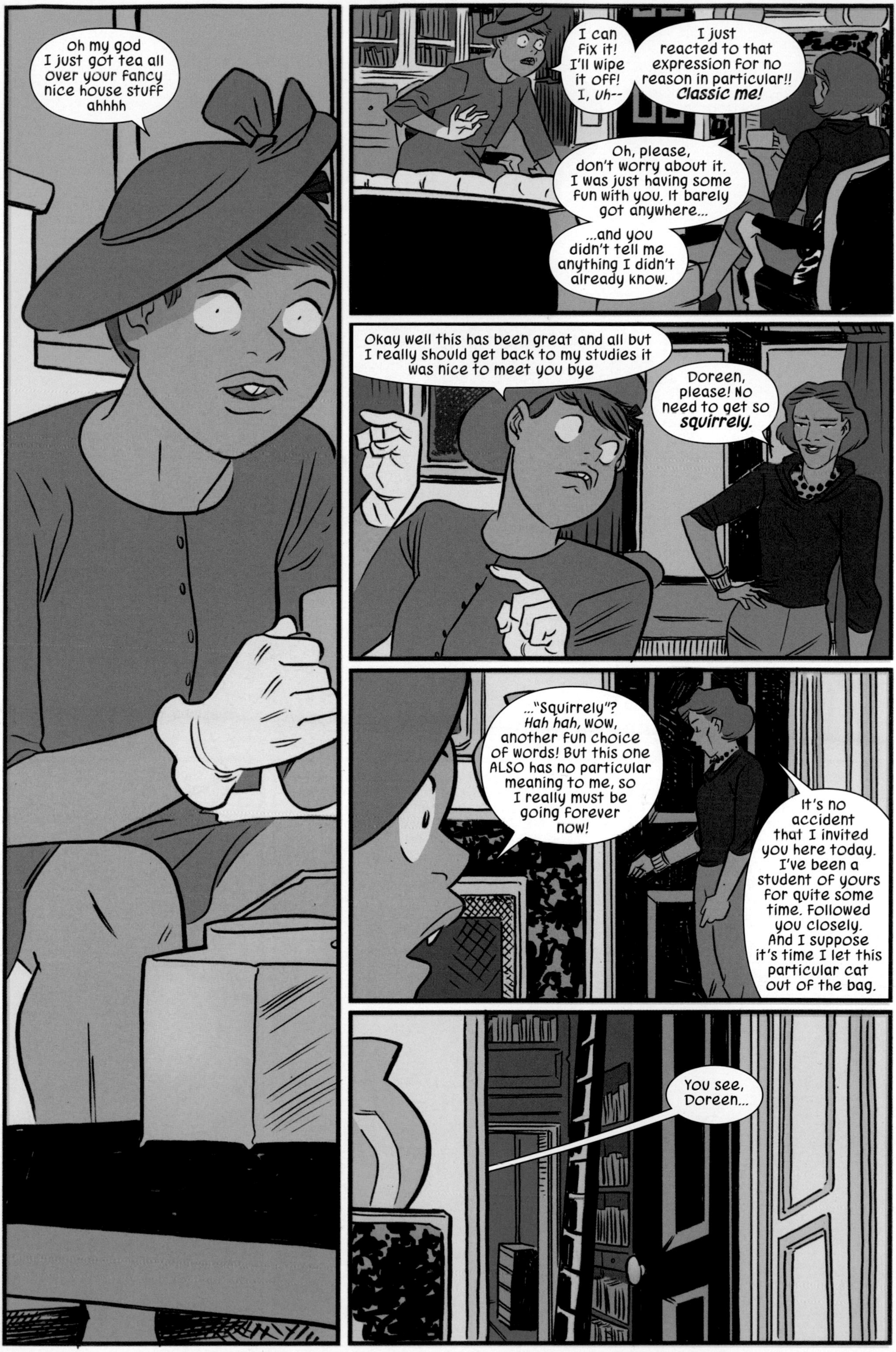

Oh my god I just got tea all over your fancy nice house stuff ahhhh
I can fix it! I'll wipe it off! I, uh--
I just reacted to that expression for no reason in particular!! *Classic me!*
Oh, please, don't worry about it. I was just having some fun with you. It barely got anywhere...
...and you didn't tell me anything I didn't already know.
Okay well this has been great and all but I really should get back to my studies it was nice to meet you bye
Doreen, please! No need to get so *squirrely.*
..."Squirrely"? *Hah hah,* WOW, another fun choice of words! But this one ALSO has no particular meaning to me, so I really must be going forever now!
It's no accident that I invited you here today. I've been a student of yours for quite some time. Followed you closely. And I suppose it's time I let this particular cat out of the bag.
You see, Doreen...

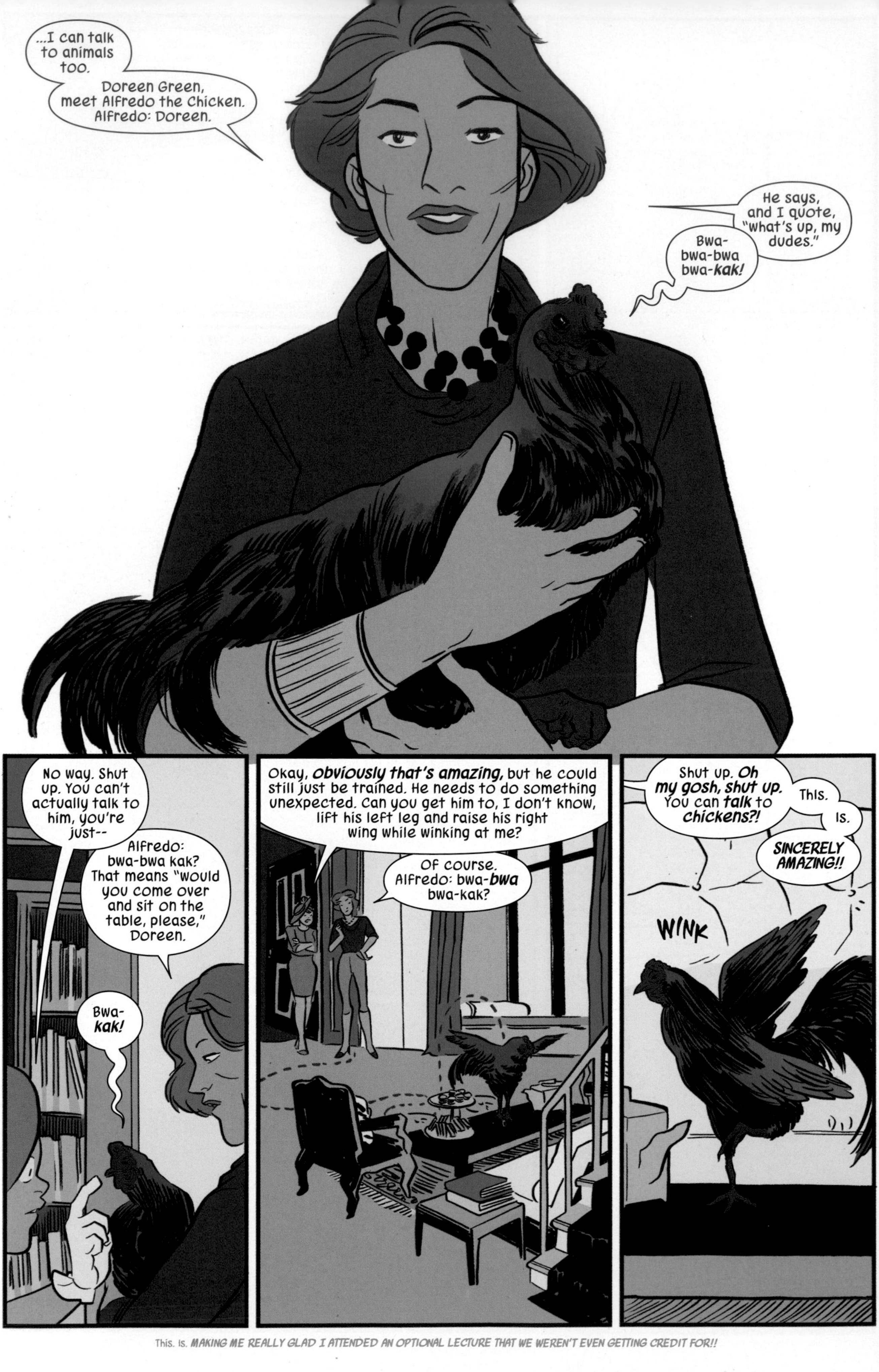
...I can talk to animals too.
Doreen Green, meet Alfredo the Chicken. Alfredo: Doreen.
Bwa-bwa-bwa bwa-kak!
He says, and I quote, "what's up, my dudes."
No way. Shut up. You can't actually talk to him, you're just--
Alfredo: bwa-bwa kak? That means "would you come over and sit on the table, please," Doreen.
Bwa-kak!
Okay, obviously that's amazing, but he could still just be trained. He needs to do something unexpected. Can you get him to, I don't know, lift his left leg and raise his right wing while winking at me?
Of course. Alfredo: bwa-bwa bwa-kak?
Shut up. Oh my gosh, shut up. You can talk to chickens?!
This.
Is.
SINCERELY AMAZING!!
WINK

This. Is. *MAKING ME REALLY GLAD I ATTENDED AN OPTIONAL LECTURE THAT WE WEREN'T EVEN GETTING CREDIT FOR!!*

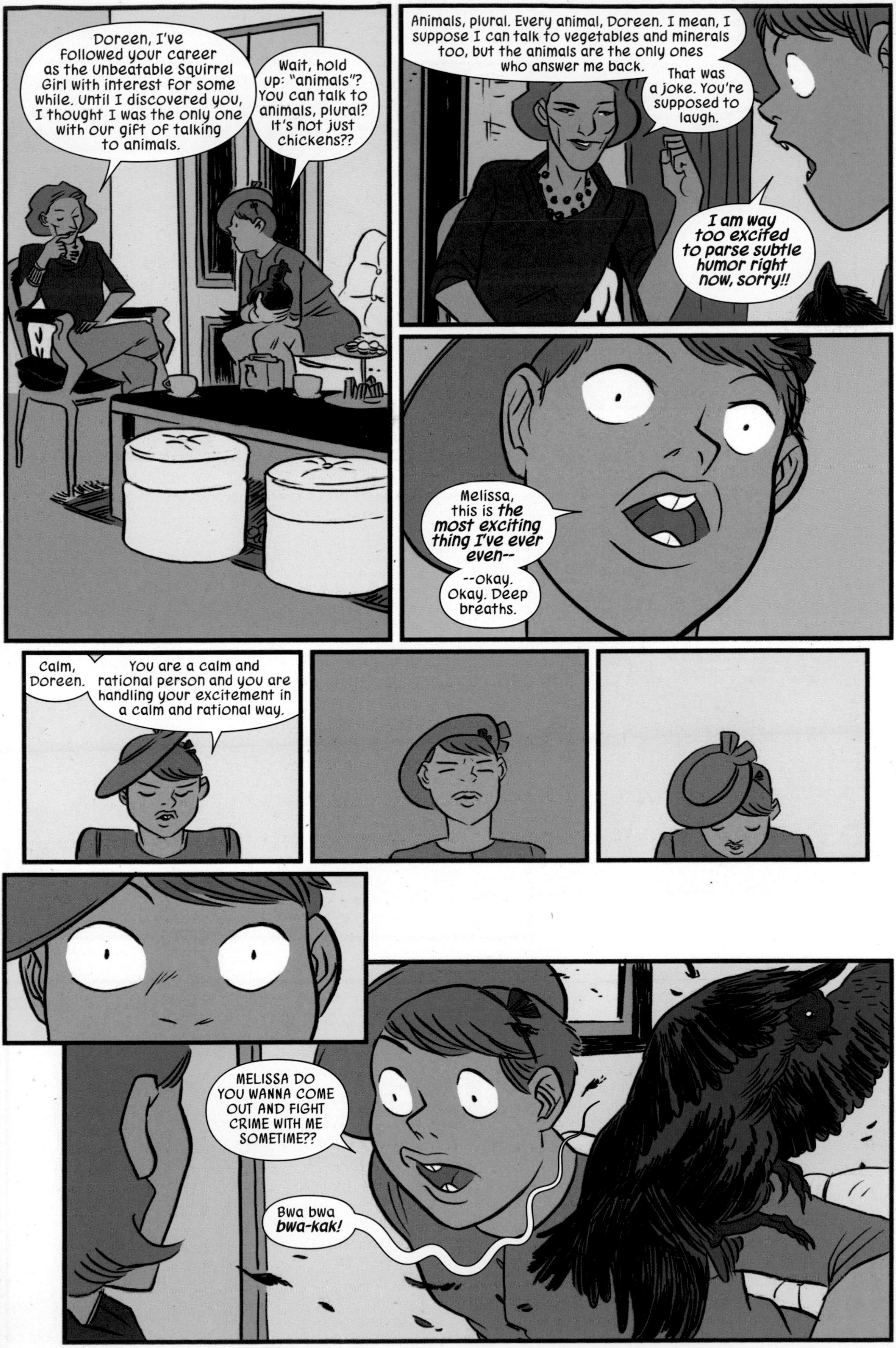

Doreen, I've followed your career as the Unbeatable Squirrel Girl with interest for some while. Until I discovered you, I thought I was the only one with our gift of talking to animals.
Wait, hold up: "animals"? You can talk to animals, plural? It's not just chickens??
Animals, plural. Every animal, Doreen. I mean, I suppose I can talk to vegetables and minerals too, but the animals are the only ones who answer me back.
That was a joke. You're supposed to laugh.
I am way too excited to parse subtle humor right now, sorry!!
Melissa, this is the most exciting thing I've ever even--
--Okay. Okay. Deep breaths.
Calm, Doreen.
You are a calm and rational person and you are handling your excitement in a calm and rational way.
MELISSA DO YOU WANNA COME OUT AND FIGHT CRIME WITH ME SOMETIME??
Bwa bwa bwa-kak!

ALSO PLEASE TELL ALFREDO I THINK HE'S AMAZING. ALSO: EVERYONE IN THIS ROOM IS SUPER RAD RIGHT NOW.

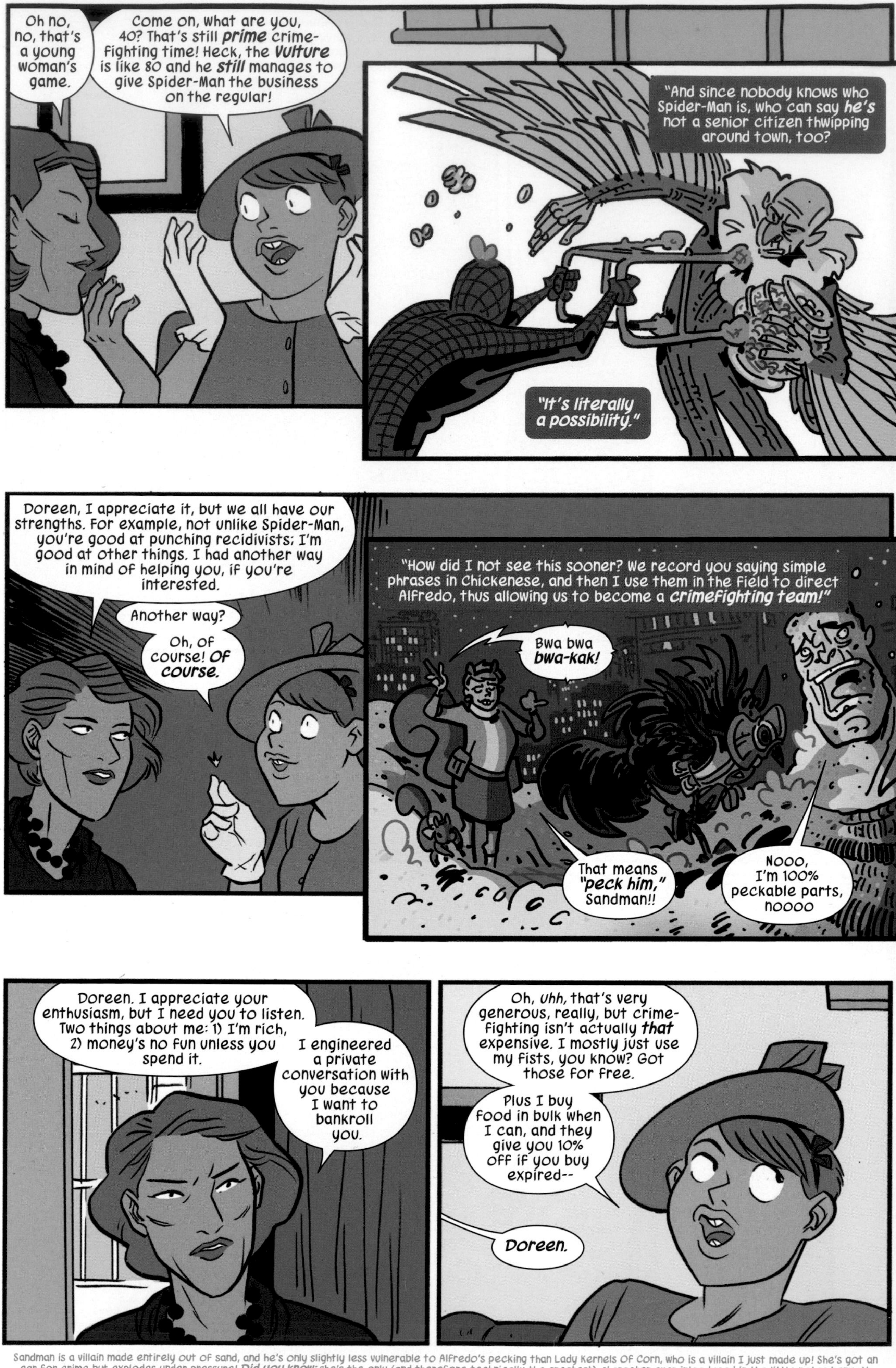
Oh no, no, that's a young woman's game.
Come on, what are you, 40? That's still *prime* crime-fighting time! Heck, the *Vulture* is like 80 and he *still* manages to give Spider-Man the business on the regular!
"And since nobody knows who Spider-Man is, who can say *he's* not a senior citizen thwipping around town, too?
"It's literally a possibility."
Doreen, I appreciate it, but we all have our strengths. For example, not unlike Spider-Man, you're good at punching recidivists; I'm good at other things. I had another way in mind of helping you, if you're interested.
Another way?
Oh, of course! ***Of course.***
"How did I not see this sooner? We record you saying simple phrases in Chickenese, and then I use them in the field to direct Alfredo, thus allowing us to become a ***crimefighting team!***"
Bwa bwa **bwa-kak!**
That means ***"peck him,"*** Sandman!!
NOOO, I'm 100% peckable parts, NOOOO
Doreen. I appreciate your enthusiasm, but I need you to listen. Two things about me: 1) I'm rich, 2) money's no fun unless you spend it.
I engineered a private conversation with you because I want to bankroll you.
Oh, *uhh*, that's very generous, really, but crime-fighting isn't actually ***that*** expensive. I mostly just use my fists, you know? Got those for free.
Plus I buy food in bulk when I can, and they give you 10% off if you buy expired--
Doreen.

Sandman is a villain made entirely out of sand, and he's only slightly less vulnerable to Alfredo's pecking than Lady Kernels of Corn, who is a villain I just made up! She's got an ear for crime but explodes under pressure! ***Did you know:*** she's the only (and therefore technically the greatest) character ever introduced in the little notes beneath a Marvel comic??

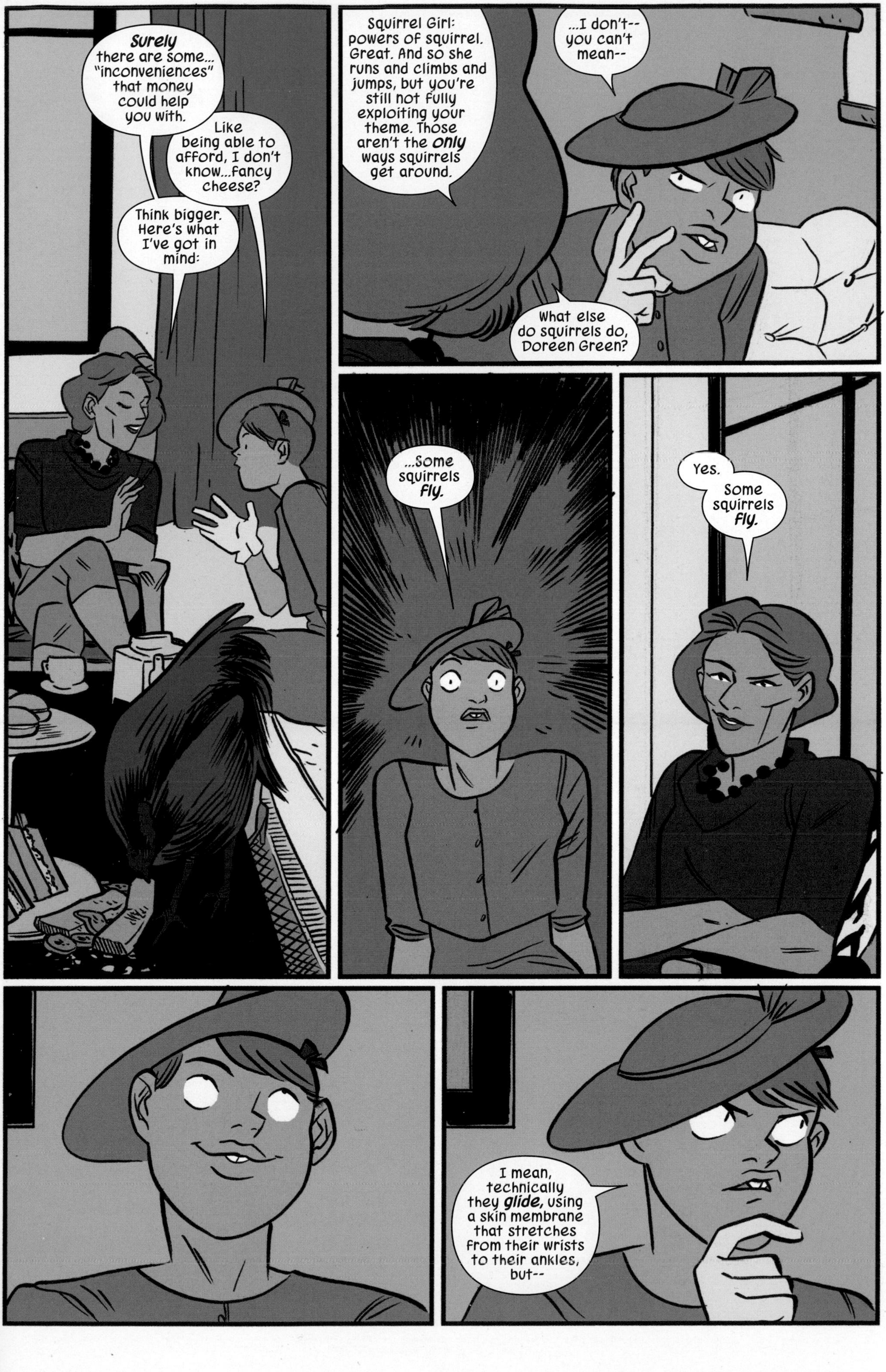
Surely there are some... "inconveniences" that money could help you with.
Like being able to afford, I don't know...fancy cheese?
Think bigger. Here's what I've got in mind:
Squirrel Girl: powers of squirrel. Great. And so she runs and climbs and jumps, but you're still not fully exploiting your theme. Those aren't the only ways squirrels get around.
...I don't-- you can't mean--
What else do squirrels do, Doreen Green?
...Some squirrels fly.
Yes.
Some squirrels fly.
I mean, technically they glide, using a skin membrane that stretches from their wrists to their ankles, but--

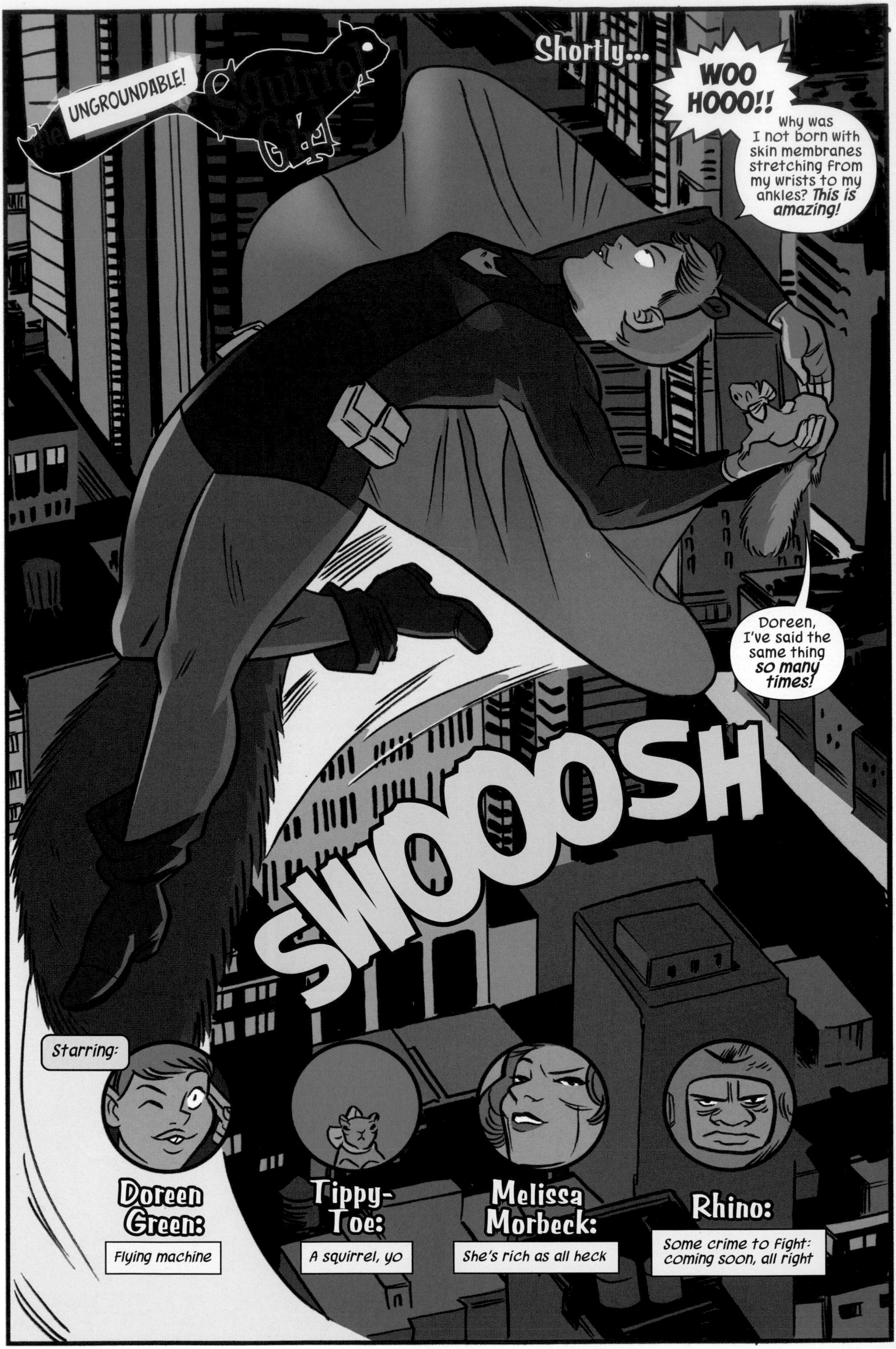
UNGROUNDABLE!
Shortly...
WOO HOOO!!
Why was I not born with skin membranes stretching from my wrists to my ankles? *This is amazing!*
Doreen, I've said the same thing *so many times!*
SWOOOSH
Starring:
Doreen Green:
Flying machine
Tippy-Toe:
A squirrel, yo
Melissa Morbeck:
She's rich as all heck
Rhino:
Some crime to fight: coming soon, all right

Apologies to all the readers who are now looking at their own wrists and ankles and wishing they had a skin membrane connecting them too so they could fly around. Is this quiet regret *truly* what unites us all??

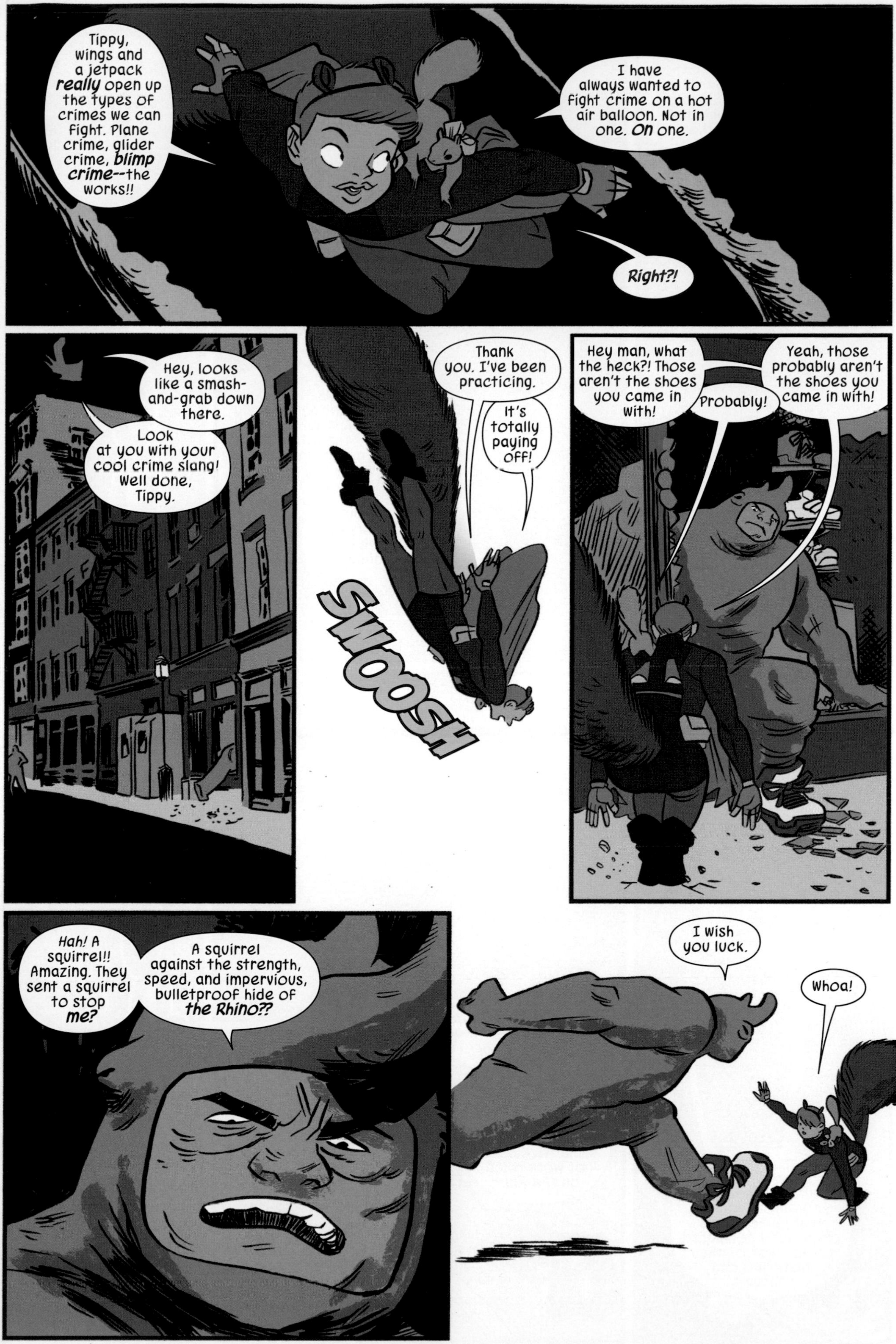
Tippy, wings and a jetpack *really* open up the types of crimes we can fight. Plane crime, glider crime, *blimp crime*--the works!!
I have always wanted to fight crime on a hot air balloon. Not in one. *On* one.
Right?!
Hey, looks like a smash-and-grab down there.
Look at you with your cool crime slang! Well done, Tippy.
Thank you. I've been practicing.
It's totally paying off!
SWOOSH
Hey man, what the heck?! Those aren't the shoes you came in with!
Yeah, those probably aren't the shoes you came in with!
Probably!
Hah! A squirrel!! Amazing. They sent a squirrel to stop *me?*
A squirrel against the strength, speed, and impervious, bulletproof hide of *the Rhino??*
I wish you luck.
Whoa!

Not pictured: all the criminals who just bought blimps to secure themselves from ground-level justice as they glance up, see Squirrel Girl flying by, then quickly search on their phones for "are blimps returnable for a full refund + it's an emergency."

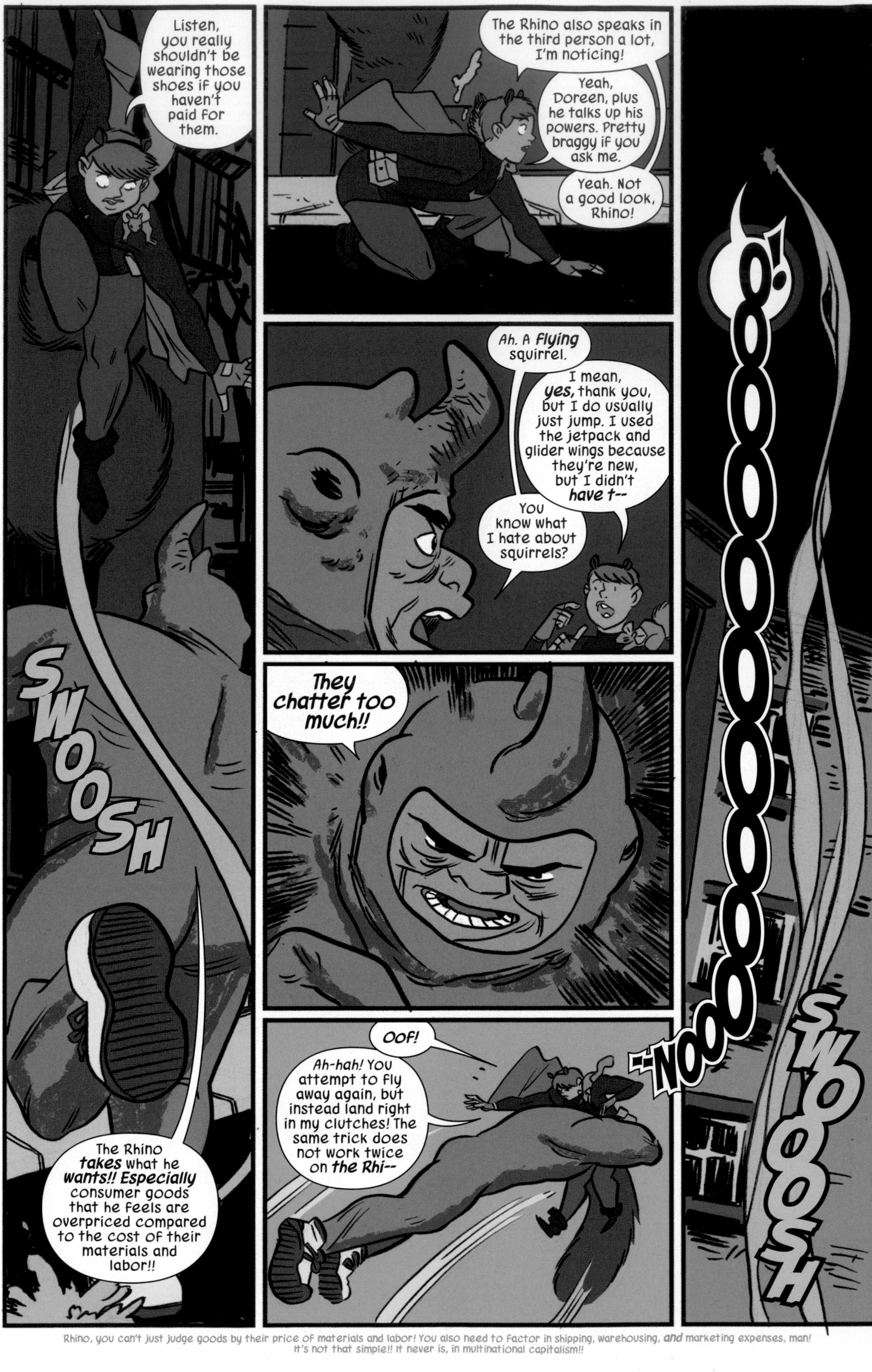

Listen, you really shouldn't be wearing those shoes if you haven't paid for them.
SWOOSH
The Rhino takes what he wants!! Especially consumer goods that he feels are overpriced compared to the cost of their materials and labor!!
The Rhino also speaks in the third person a lot, I'm noticing!
Yeah, Doreen, plus he talks up his powers. Pretty braggy if you ask me.
Yeah. Not a good look, Rhino!
Ah. A flying squirrel.
I mean, yes, thank you, but I do usually just jump. I used the jetpack and glider wings because they're new, but I didn't have t--
You know what I hate about squirrels?
They chatter too much!!
Oof!
Ah-hah! You attempt to fly away again, but instead land right in my clutches! The same trick does not work twice on the Rhi--
--NOOOOOOOOOOOOOOOOOOO!
SWOOOOSH

Rhino, you can't just judge goods by their price of materials and labor! You also need to factor in shipping, warehousing, *and* marketing expenses, man! It's not that simple!! It never is, in multinational capitalism!!

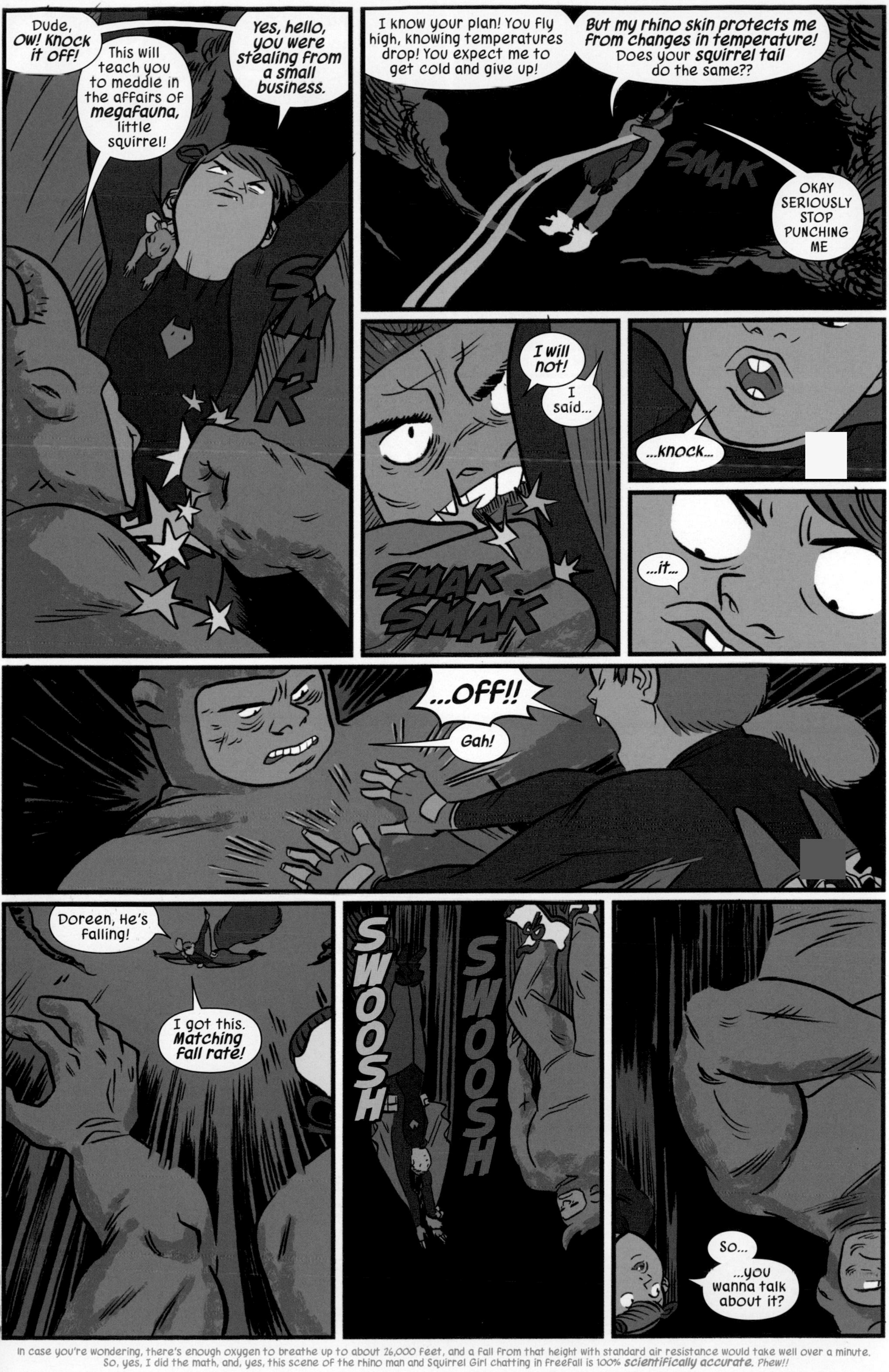
Dude, OW! Knock it off!
This will teach you to meddle in the affairs of megafauna, little squirrel!
Yes, hello, you were stealing from a small business.
SMAK
I know your plan! You fly high, knowing temperatures drop! You expect me to get cold and give up!
But my rhino skin protects me from changes in temperature! Does your squirrel tail do the same??
SMAK
OKAY SERIOUSLY STOP PUNCHING ME
I will not!
I said...
SMAK
SMAK
...knock...
...it...
...OFF!!
Gah!
Doreen, He's falling!
I got this. Matching fall rate!
SWOOSH
SWOOSH
So...
...you wanna talk about it?

In case you're wondering, there's enough oxygen to breathe up to about 26,000 feet, and a fall from that height with standard air resistance would take well over a minute. So, yes, I did the math, and, yes, this scene of the rhino man and Squirrel Girl chatting in freefall is 100% ***scientifically accurate.*** Phew!!

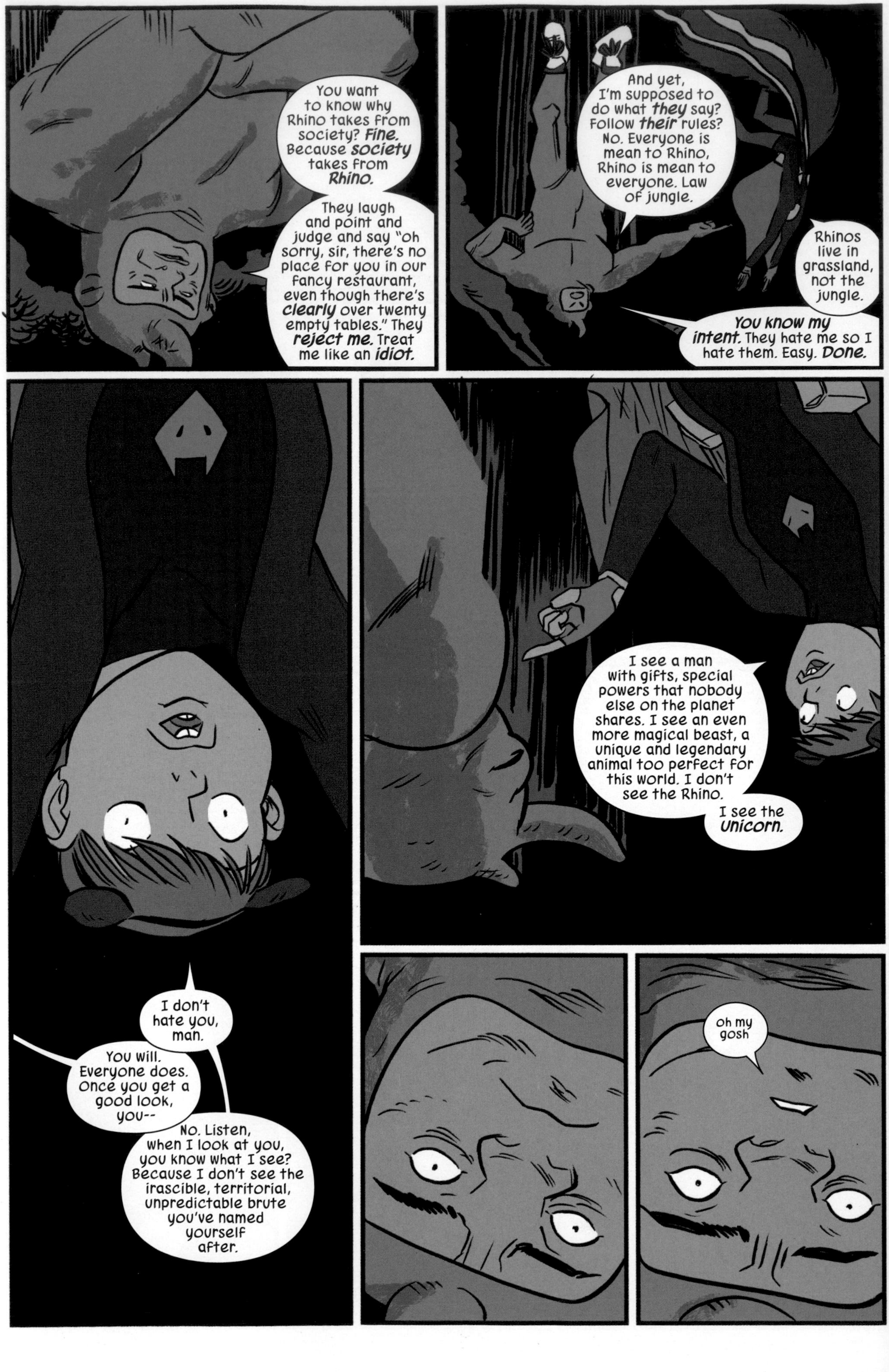
You want to know why Rhino takes from society? Fine. Because society takes from Rhino.
They laugh and point and judge and say "oh sorry, sir, there's no place for you in our fancy restaurant, even though there's clearly over twenty empty tables." They reject me. Treat me like an idiot.
And yet, I'm supposed to do what they say? Follow their rules? No. Everyone is mean to Rhino, Rhino is mean to everyone. Law of jungle.
Rhinos live in grassland, not the jungle.
You know my intent. They hate me so I hate them. Easy. Done.
I don't hate you, man.
You will. Everyone does. Once you get a good look, you--
No. Listen, when I look at you, you know what I see? Because I don't see the irascible, territorial, unpredictable brute you've named yourself after.
I see a man with gifts, special powers that nobody else on the planet shares. I see an even more magical beast, a unique and legendary animal too perfect for this world. I don't see the Rhino.
I see the Unicorn.
Oh my gosh

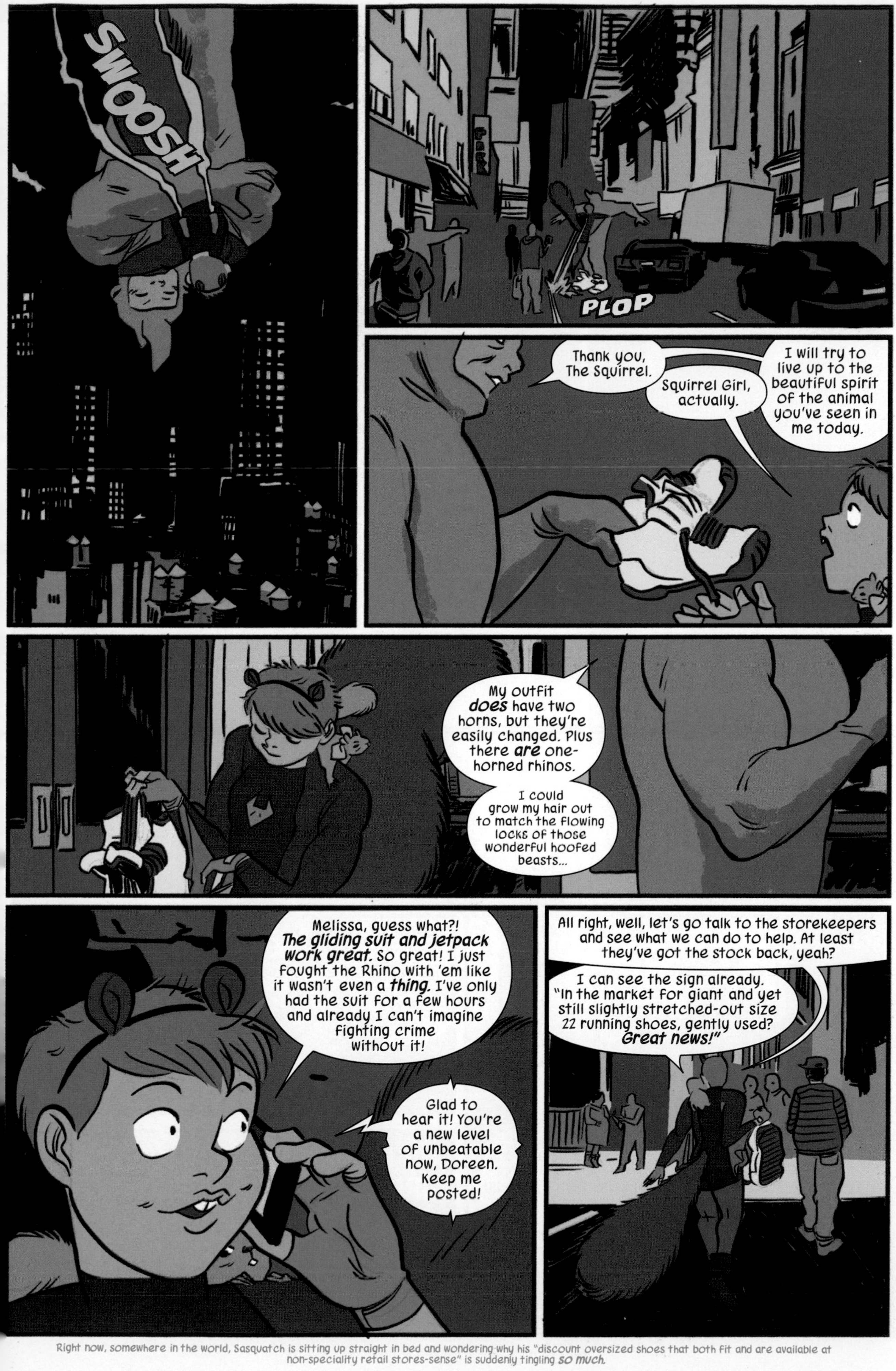

SWOOSH
PLOP
Thank you, The Squirrel.
Squirrel Girl, actually.
I will try to live up to the beautiful spirit of the animal you've seen in me today.
My outfit **does** have two horns, but they're easily changed. Plus there **are** one-horned rhinos.
I could grow my hair out to match the flowing locks of those wonderful hoofed beasts...
Melissa, guess what?! ***The gliding suit and jetpack work great.*** So great! I just fought the Rhino with 'em like it wasn't even a ***thing.*** I've only had the suit for a few hours and already I can't imagine fighting crime without it!
Glad to hear it! You're a new level of unbeatable now, Doreen. Keep me posted!
All right, well, let's go talk to the storekeepers and see what we can do to help. At least they've got the stock back, yeah?
I can see the sign already. "In the market for giant and yet still slightly stretched-out size 22 running shoes, gently used? ***Great news!"***

Right now, somewhere in the world, Sasquatch is sitting up straight in bed and wondering why his "discount oversized shoes that both fit and are available at non-speciality retail stores-sense" is suddenly tingling *so much.*

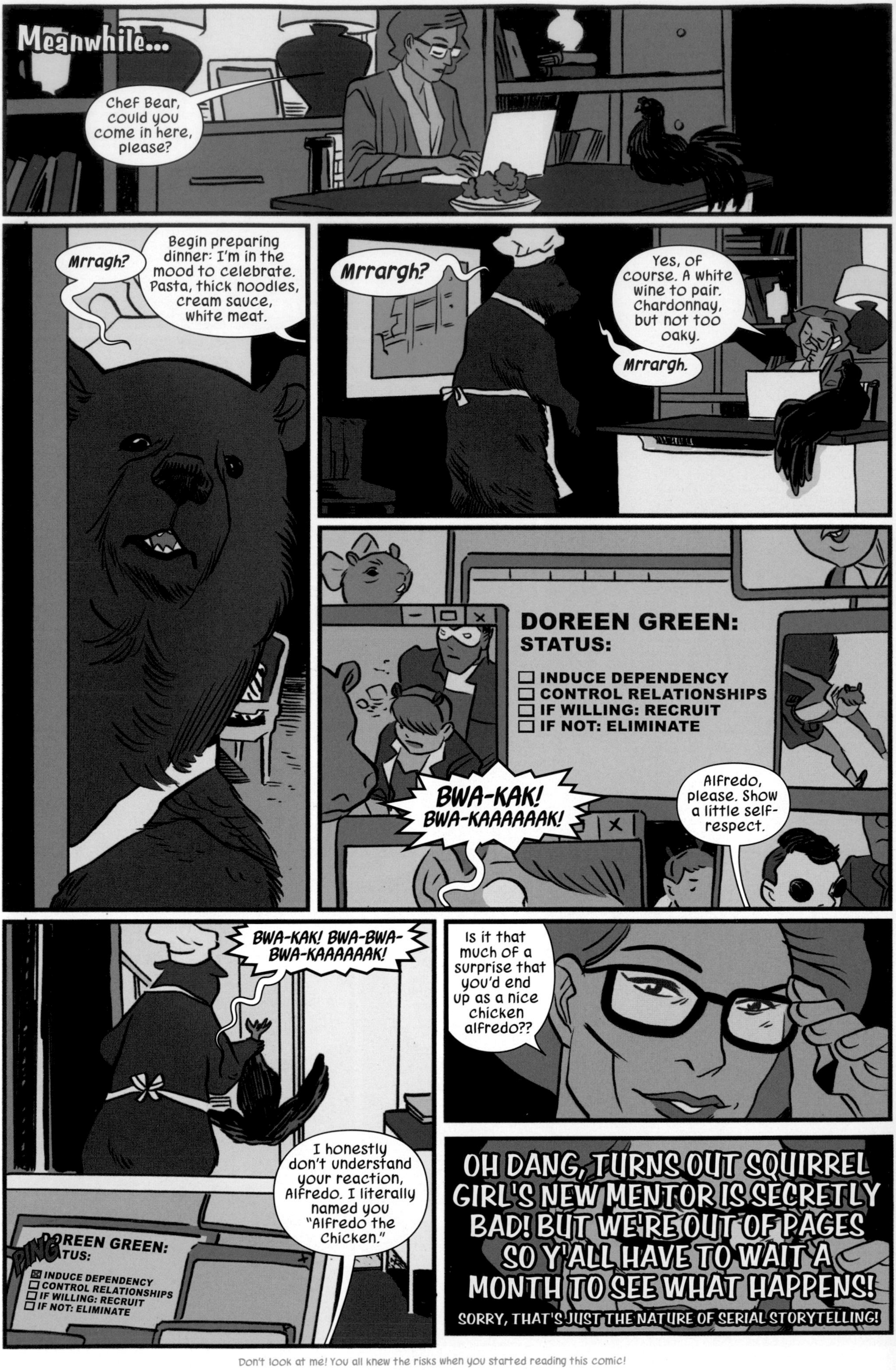
Meanwhile...
Chef Bear, could you come in here, please?
Mrragh?
Begin preparing dinner: I'm in the mood to celebrate. Pasta, thick noodles, cream sauce, white meat.
Mrrargh?
Yes, of course. A white wine to pair. Chardonnay, but not too oaky.
Mrrargh.
DOREEN GREEN:
STATUS:
INDUCE DEPENDENCY
CONTROL RELATIONSHIPS
IF WILLING: RECRUIT
IF NOT: ELIMINATE
BWA-KAK! BWA-KAAAAAAK!
Alfredo, please. Show a little self-respect.
BWA-KAK! BWA-BWA-BWA-KAAAAAAK!
DOREEN GREEN:
TUS:
PING
INDUCE DEPENDENCY
CONTROL RELATIONSHIPS
IF WILLING: RECRUIT
IF NOT: ELIMINATE
I honestly don't understand your reaction, Alfredo. I literally named you "Alfredo the Chicken."
Is it that much of a surprise that you'd end up as a nice chicken alfredo??
OH DANG, TURNS OUT SQUIRREL GIRL'S NEW MENTOR IS SECRETLY BAD! BUT WE'RE OUT OF PAGES SO Y'ALL HAVE TO WAIT A MONTH TO SEE WHAT HAPPENS!
SORRY, THAT'S JUST THE NATURE OF SERIAL STORYTELLING!

Don't look at me! You all knew the risks when you started reading this comic!

Letters From Nuts

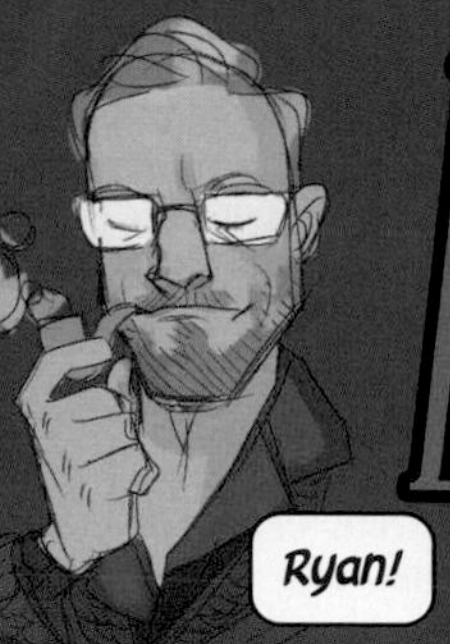
Ryan!

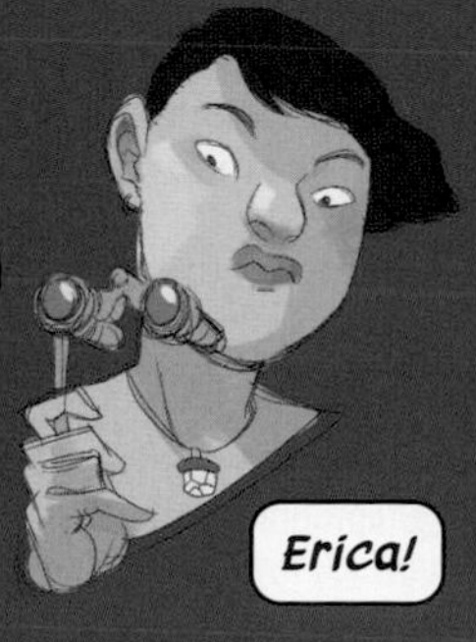
Erica!

Send letters to mheroes@marvel.com or 135 W 50th St, 7th Floor, New York, NY 10020 (Please mark "OKAY TO PRINT")

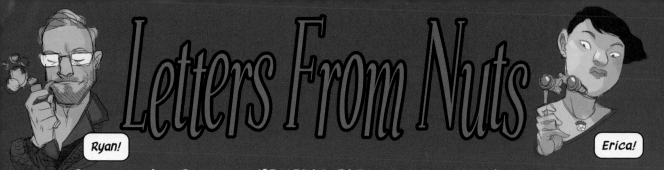

Hi guys,

Having read the SQUIRREL GIRL BEATS UP THE MARVEL UNIVERSE graphic novel (which was fantastic), I didn't expect it to become a reality!

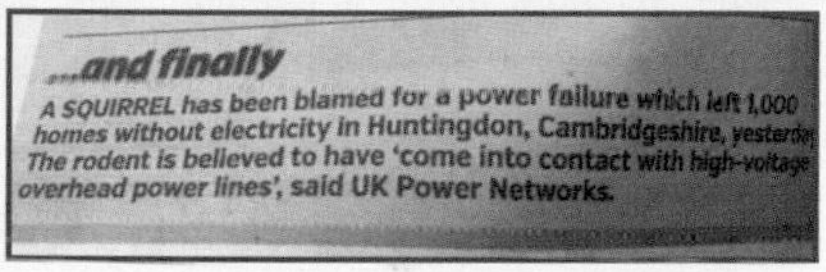
...and finally

A SQUIRREL has been blamed for a power failure which left 1,000 homes without electricity in Huntingdon, Cambridgeshire, yesterday. The rodent is believed to have 'come into contact with high-voltage overhead power lines', said UK Power Networks.

Keep up the great comic, but stop predicting the future okay?

Yours awesomely,
Cameron Leacock

RYAN: Allene gets around!! Which actually is weird, since she's supposed to be [SPOILERS REMOVED IN CASE YOU HAVEN'T READ THE BOOK YET].

ERICA: And that's just ONE squirrel. SO Y'ALL BETTER WATCH OUT.

Hi Ryan and Erica and Rico and co.!

I'm a Young Adult librarian, and I love to talk about Squirrel Girl when I visit schools. Every month, I give book talks at a junior high, and back in October, I decided that the only way I could improve on the experience of talking to teenagers about library books for forty-minute classes would be to do it...while dressed as Squirrel Girl! Attached are pictures.
Thank you for making my favorite comic!

Emily

P.S. I hope to meet you at C2E2 next year, Erica!

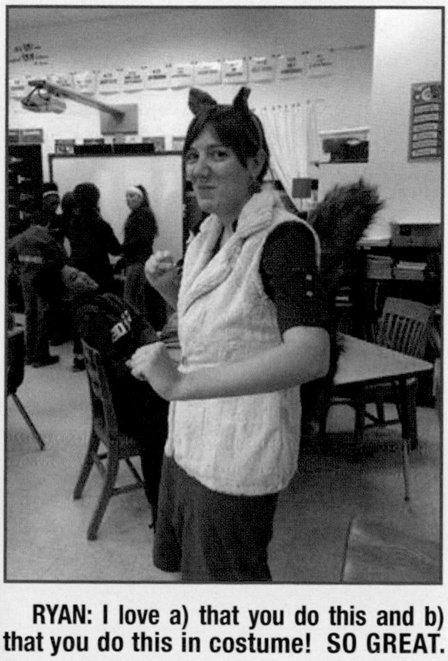

RYAN: I love a) that you do this and b) that you do this in costume! SO GREAT. My love of libraries and librarians is well-documented (in the pages of this very comic, no less) so I guess it's no surprise that I'm big into this!

ERICA: This is great! I was just thinking how warm you look (my heat is off for some reason) and I just remembered that we were talking about doing a winter-time costume for her. HM HM HM. Thanks for the reminder even if you didn't mean to do it!

Dear SQUIRREL GIRL nuts,

Thank you for your consistently delightful content in each issue of SQUIRREL GIRL! Luckily, I discovered THE UNBEATABLE SQUIRREL GIRL when it was still very new, and I've collected every issue since. I even more recently acquired an original 1991 X-MEN comic with the original appearance of Squirrel Girl, which will be framed and displayed in my home as a wonderful conversation starter.

This past summer, I put together my very own Squirrel Girl getup to wear to the Phoenix Comicon. As you can see, every effort was made to make the costume perfect. I made most of it with my own two hands. I had quite a few people excitedly comment on my costume, which means quite a few people would enjoy your attendance at a future PCC event. *wink wink* Pictured is me and a classmate of mine who has recently become a little nuts herself. Keep the gold coming!

Bonnie Mangum

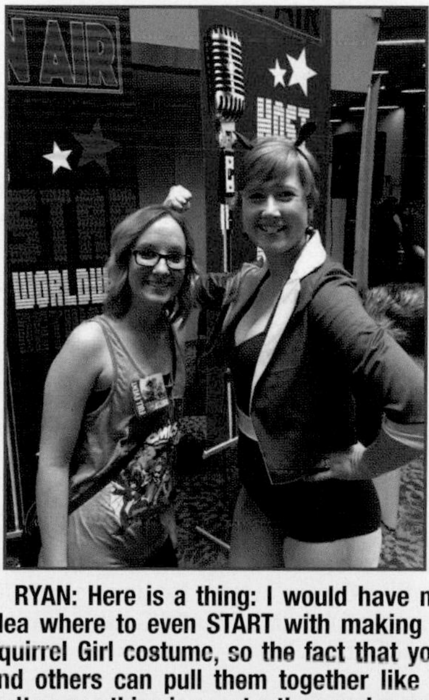

RYAN: Here is a thing: I would have no idea where to even START with making a Squirrel Girl costume, so the fact that you and others can pull them together like it isn't even a thing is constantly amazing and inspiring to me. I'm jealous of your first SG appearance issue: I should totally get one too! I've also never been to Phoenix, and maybe that should change??

ERICA: I love it! I remember either right before or right after the series launched, my friend who owns my local comic shop Hub Comics asked if I wanted to buy her original appearance because it was still crazy cheap at the time. I said no and now I really regret it. It costs a LOT MORE all of a sudden!

Dear UNBEATABLE SG Squad,

Hi. My name is Nora S, and I am 9 (almost 10!) years old. My dad introduced me to Squirrel Girl and I LOVE it SOOOOOO much. It is probably the FUNNIEST comic/book I have ever read! (And I read a lot.) In fact, I even dressed up as Squirrel Girl for Halloween! (I have included a picture below.)

Thank you for making such a MARVELous comic!

Sincerely,
Nora S.

P.S.: Squirrels Forever!

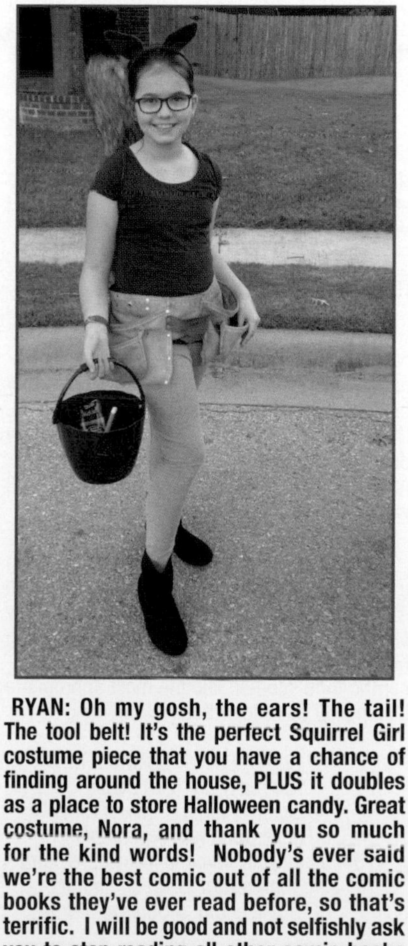

RYAN: Oh my gosh, the ears! The tail! The tool belt! It's the perfect Squirrel Girl costume piece that you have a chance of finding around the house, PLUS it doubles as a place to store Halloween candy. Great costume, Nora, and thank you so much for the kind words! Nobody's ever said we're the best comic out of all the comic books they've ever read before, so that's terrific. I will be good and not selfishly ask you to stop reading all other comic books now just so I can keep that good feeling forever. Thank you!

ERICA: I am for sure using that tool belt idea even though I don't have a place for it yet. You look great!

Dear Erica and Ryan,

I went to Comic Con in Chicago, and we went as our favorite heroes. I dressed up as Nancy Whitehead, my mom dressed up as my best friend Squirrel Girl, my brother Dillon went as Chipmunk Hunk, my auntie went as the Squirrel Army, my brother's friend went as Koi Boy, and we had a lot of fun and lots of people took pictures of us.

When are we going to meet Nancy's mom? Is Squirrel Girl going to like Nancy's mom as much as Nancy liked Doreen's mom? I LOVED Doreen's mom—that issue made me laugh so hard!!

Rose Collins, Milwaukee Wisconsin (age 12)

P.S. My brother wants to know if Chipmunk Hunk and Koi Boy will make more appearances.

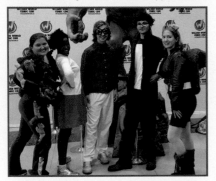

RYAN: AHHH, IT'S THE WHOLE CAST, I CAN BARELY HANDLE IT!! AMAZING. So, SO great. Also, I've never really thought about Nancy's parents! Erica, we're gonna have to talk about this!

ERICA: This is sooooo great. I can't believe there's a squirrel army costume out there now. Also, Ryan, I've been thinking about Nancy's parents so DON'T YOU WORRY.

Hi, Erica and Ryan,

I am in your debt: At my urging (read: nagging, but in a charming way) my not-a-comics-fan-but-definitely-a-computer-guy husband read THE UNBEATABLE SQUIRREL GIRL #11, laughed, loved it, and generally deemed it the bee's knees, the cat's pajamas, and the squirrel's muumuu (sorry, I'm still working on that one.).

It being the Festive Season, and at his urging (read: nagging, but like Cary Grant would do it), I would like to share with you the holiday carol I composed in Doreen's honor. It's to the tune of "O Christmas Tree" because a tree-centric tune seemed like the most appropriate leaping-off point for a Squirrel Girl song:

O Squirrel Girl, O Squirrel Girl,
You really are Unbeatable!
O Squirrel Girl, O Squirrel Girl,
For reasons well repeatable!
You leave your home to kick some butts,
And then return to eat some nuts.
O Squirrel Girl, O Squirrel Girl,
This pizza is reheatable!

O Squirrel Girl, O Squirrel Girl,
Your tail is truly bushy!
O Squirrel Girl, O Squirrel Girl,
I hope I don't sound pushy.
Whence come your powers? I dunno.
Your sidekick's name is Tippy-Toe.
O Squirrel Girl, O Squirrel Girl

I'm going to quit while I'm ahead without trying to find a good rhyme for bushy/pushy, lest I end up with something even worse than the repeatable pizza line in the first verse. *Fa-la-la-la-la, etceteraaaaaaaa!*

Thanks for a wonderful book.

Best,
Esther Friesner

RYAN: Esther, there is a proud tradition – starting in the first panel of our very first issue – of taking other songs and upgrading them so they're about Squirrel Girl now. I'm so glad that this tradition has now spread to non-me people!

ERICA: Oh man who else wants a pizza really badly right now? Is it just me? All the time?

Ryan, Erica & Team Squirrel,

I had a dream last night that I met Squirrel Girl and I was like say hi to Monkey Joe for me and she glared at me and I was like crap that was her squirrel that died her current squirrel is Tippy-Toe YOU SHOULD KNOW THAT GREG GET IT TOGETHER.

Also Dick Van Dyke was my uncle.

Greg Packnett
Madison, Wisconsin

RYAN: Greg, your subconscious has given you the gift of the opportunity of getting it together before you embarrass yourself in real life! Well done, Greg's subconscious! Also: Your uncle is a very talented performer.

ERICA: Weird side note: When I went to visit Ryan in Canada he took us to a science museum, which had an exhibit of Rowland Emett's inventions, including his work in CHITTY CHITTY BANG BANG. It's all coming full circle.

Okay, that's all for this month. But before we go, we've got a special treat! *New York Times* best-selling, award-winning, all-around butt-kicking authors Shannon Hale and Dean Hale have penned a BRAND-NEW SQUIRREL GIRL PROSE NOVEL for young adults — and it just hit shelves! You've seen her in college — but how did the bodaciously tailed and slightly buck-toothed Doreen survive the woes of middle school? BY BEING FREAKING UNBEATABLE, THAT'S HOW. Duh.

Here's some more info about it: Fourteen-year-old Doreen Green just moved from sunny California to the suburbs of New Jersey. She must start at a new school, make new friends, and continue to hide her furry tail. Yep, Doreen has the powers of . . . a SQUIRREL! After failing at several attempts to find her new BFF, Doreen feels lonely and trapped, liked a caged animal. Then one day Doreen uses her extraordinary powers to stop a group of troublemakers from causing mischief in the neighborhood, and her whole life changes. Everyone at school is talking about the mystery hero who saved the day! Doreen contemplates becoming a full-fledged super hero, and thus, Squirrel Girl is born! She saves cats from trees, keeps the sidewalks clean, and dissuades vandalism. All is well until a real-life super villain steps out of the shadows and declares Squirrel Girl his archenemy. Can Doreen balance being a teenager and a super hero? Or will she go . . . NUTS?

THE UNBEATABLE SQUIRREL GIRL: SQUIRREL MEETS WORLD novel is on-sale now!

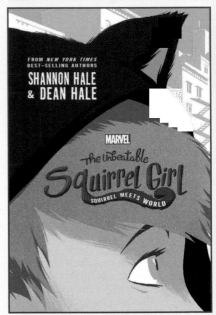

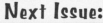

FROM NEW YORK TIMES BEST-SELLING AUTHORS
SHANNON HALE & DEAN HALE
MARVEL
The Unbeatable Squirrel Girl
SQUIRREL MEETS WORLD

Next Issue:

the unbeatable Squirrel Girl

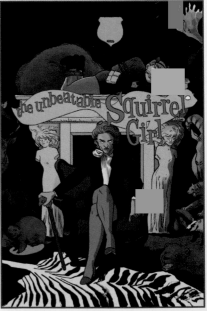

Attention, Squirrel Scouts! Make sure to check out our production blog, **unbeatablesquirrelgirl.tumblr.com**, where we post behind-the-scenes stuff on how the book gets made, along with all sorts of cool things *you* make: fanart, cosplay, whatever!

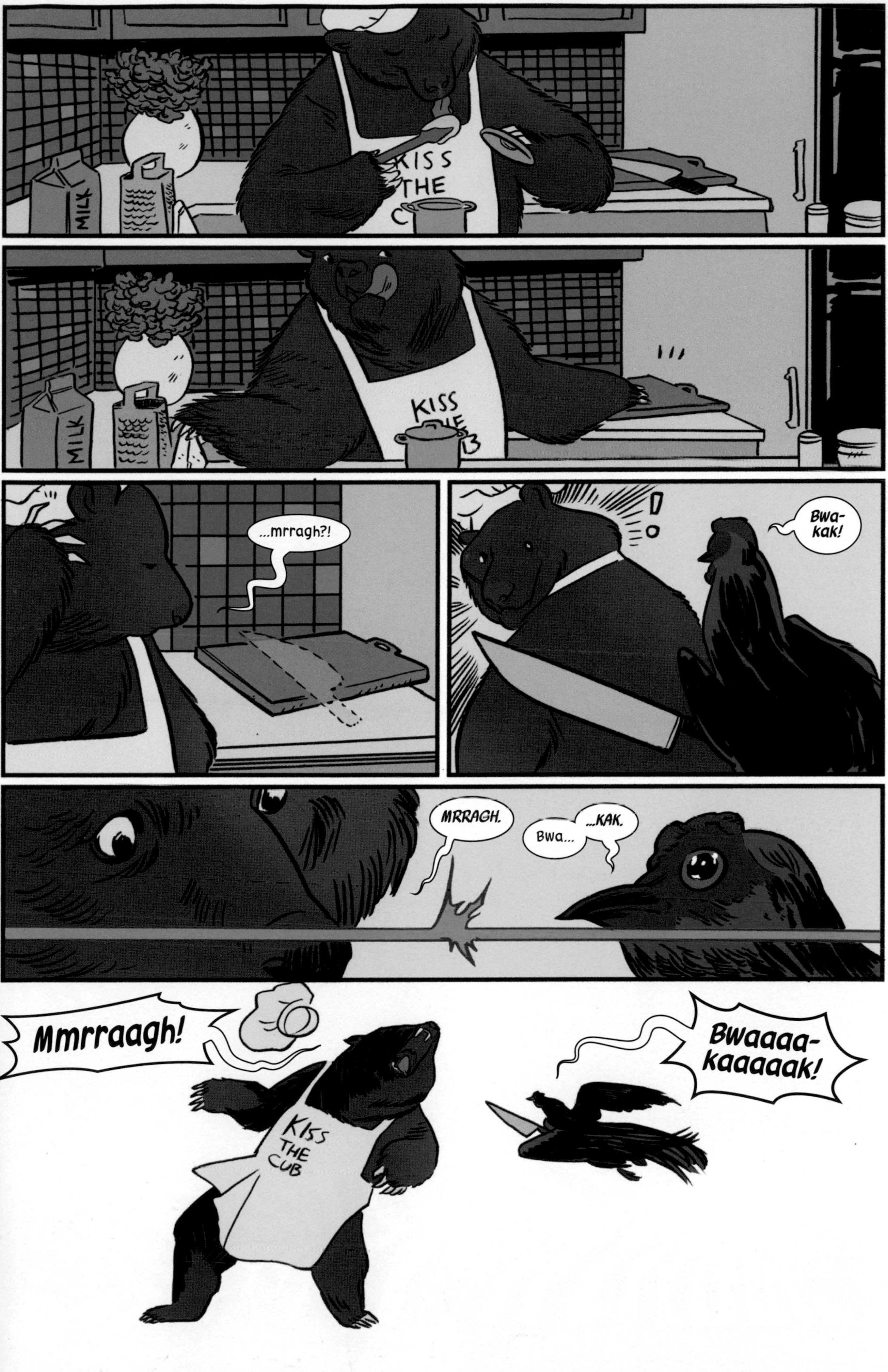
KISS THE C
KISS THE CUB
...mrragh?!
Bwa-kak!
MRRAGH.
Bwa...
...KAK.
Mmrraagh!
Bwaaaa-kaaaaak!
KISS THE CUB

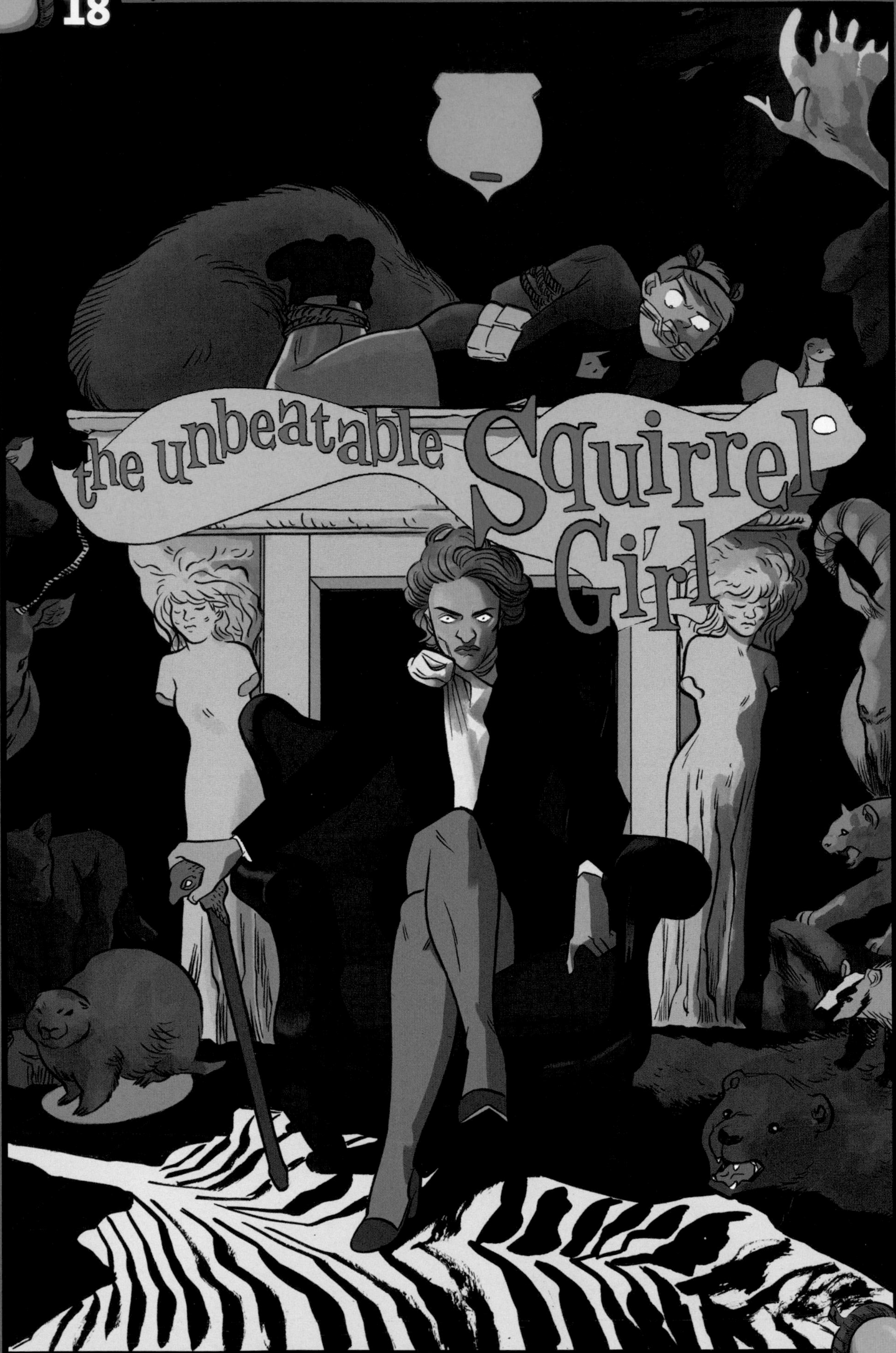
the unbeatable Squirrel Girl

Doreen Green isn't just a second-year computer science student: she secretly also has all the powers of both squirrel and girl! She uses her amazing abilities to fight crime **and** be as awesome as possible. You know her as...**The Unbeatable Squirrel Girl!** Find out what she's been up to, with...

18

Squirrel Girl in a nutshell

search!

#flyingsquirrelgirl

#greatpower

#greatresponsibility

#chefbear

#alfredothechicken

Tony Stark @starkmantony
@unbeatablesg Hey just a heads up: there was a really big super hero fight, a "civil war" if you will. It was definitely a good idea, buuut...

Tony Stark @starkmantony
@unbeatablesg ...at the end I got knocked into a coma. Which is NORMALLY BAD, I admit. But I had already uploaded my brain to a computer!

Tony Stark @starkmantony
@unbeatablesg So I'm an AI now, which is nice. Cheated death, but that's no big deal for geniuses like me.

Tony Stark @starkmantony
@unbeatablesg It feels about the same, but I'm a bit better at math questions. Anyway, just wanted to let you know!

Squirrel Girl @unbeatablesg
@starkmantony haha good one Tony!! What's ten times ten?

Tony Stark @starkmantony
@unbeatablesg 100. ...Which I also knew before I was an AI, Squirrel Girl.

Tony Stark @starkmantony
@unbeatablesg Which, again, is what I am now. Because I uploaded my brain to a computer. IT'S KIND OF A BIG DEAL.

Tony Stark @starkmantony
@unbeatablesg Maybe that should be the focus here instead of brain teasers???

Squirrel Girl @unbeatablesg
@starkmantony Wait wait wait. Are you seriously telling me, right here, right now...

Squirrel Girl @unbeatablesg
@starkmantony ...that if I show you a "prove you're a human" picture with distorted letters on a crazy background it'll BLOW YOUR MIND?????

Squirrel Girl @unbeatablesg
@starkmantony

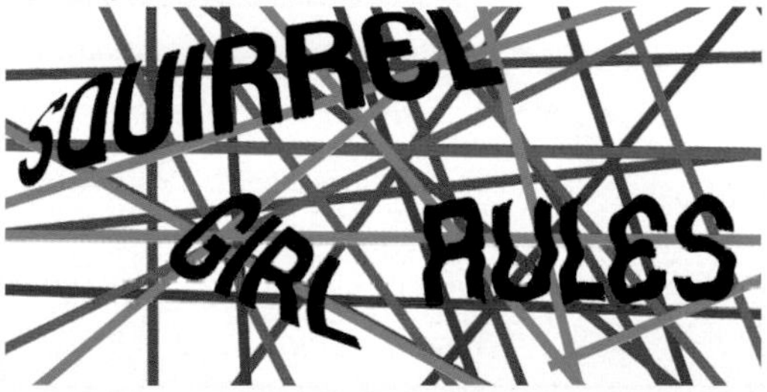
SQUIRREL
GIRL RULES

Tony Stark @starkmantony
@unbeatablesg ...No. I'm still me. Just an AI now. I can still log into my email.

Squirrel Girl @unbeatablesg
@starkmantony Tony you doing pranks is frankly adorable but if you were really an AI I could put you on my phone and have Pocket Pal Tony!!

Squirrel Girl @unbeatablesg
@starkmantony But I just checked and that is not the case so NICE TRY, MY DUDE.

Tony Stark @starkmantony
@unbeatablesg ...That's...actually not a bad idea. I'll get R&D right on it.

Squirrel Girl @unbeatablesg
Attention to both the criminally insane and the casual weekend criminals alike! I CAN FLY NOW.

Squirrel Girl @unbeatablesg
That's right! I got a FLYING SQUIRREL SUIT, so y'all better GO EASY on the friggin' SKY CRIME, because I am UP THERE, ready to stop it!!

Squirrel Girl @unbeatablesg
Oh! I have slipped the surly bonds of Earth / And danced the skies on high-tech gliding wings with a jetpack strapped to my back

Squirrel Girl @unbeatablesg
And, with silent lifting mind I'll climb / The high untrespassed sanctity of space / Put out my hand, and punch the face of Crime.

Nancy W. @sewwiththeflo
@unbeatablesg Quasi-quoting the poetry of John Gillespie Magee, Junior. Sure to strike fear into the hearts of the criminal lot.

Squirrel Girl @unbeatablesg
@sewwiththeflo Um excuse me, any of MY arch-criminals who follow me on social media are getting ENLIGHTENED

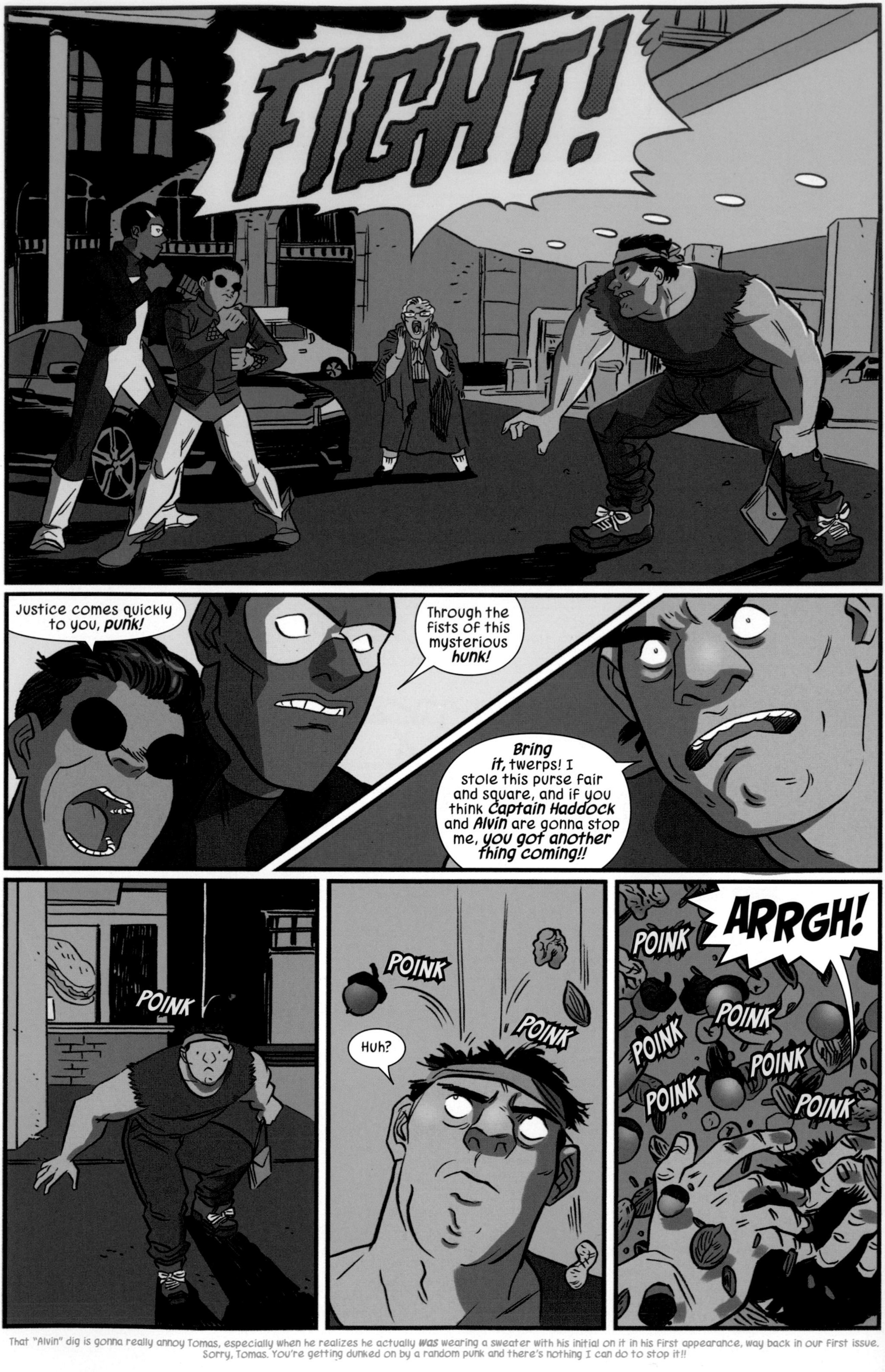
FIGHT!
Justice comes quickly to you, *punk!*
Through the fists of this mysterious *hunk!*
Bring it, twerps! I stole this purse fair and square, and if you think *Captain Haddock* and *Alvin* are gonna stop me, *you got another thing coming!!*
POINK
POINK
POINK
Huh?
POINK
ARRGH!
POINK
POINK
POINK
POINK
POINK

That "Alvin" dig is gonna really annoy Tomas, especially when he realizes he actually *was* wearing a sweater with his initial on it in his first appearance, way back in our first issue. Sorry, Tomas. You're getting dunked on by a random punk and there's nothing I can do to stop it!!

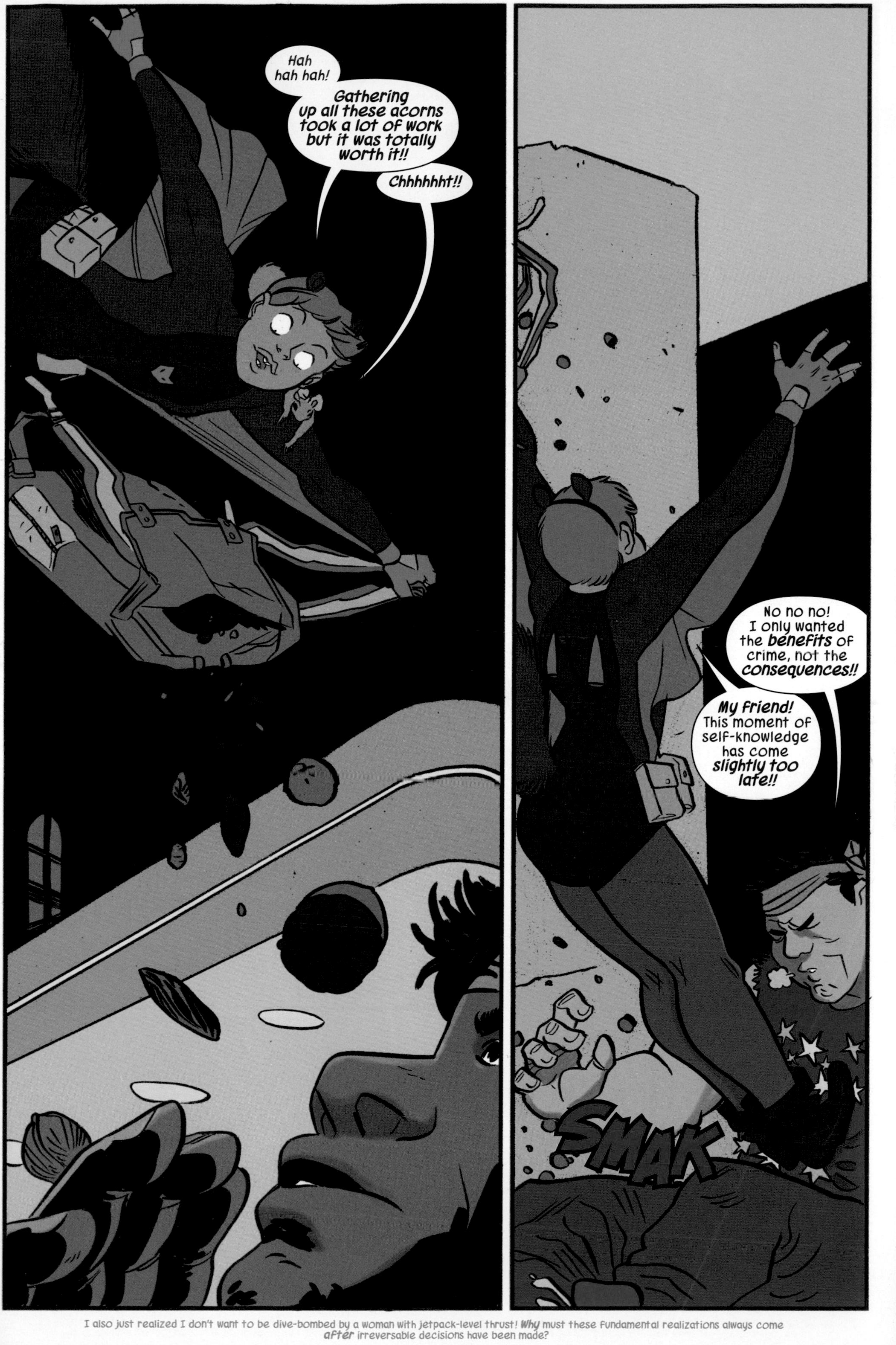
Hah
hah hah!
Gathering up all these acorns took a lot of work but it was totally worth it!!
Chhhhhht!!
No no no! I only wanted the benefits of crime, not the consequences!!
My friend! This moment of self-knowledge has come slightly too late!!
SMAK

I also just realized I don't want to be dive-bombed by a woman with jetpack-level thrust! *Why* must these fundamental realizations always come *after* irreversable decisions have been made?

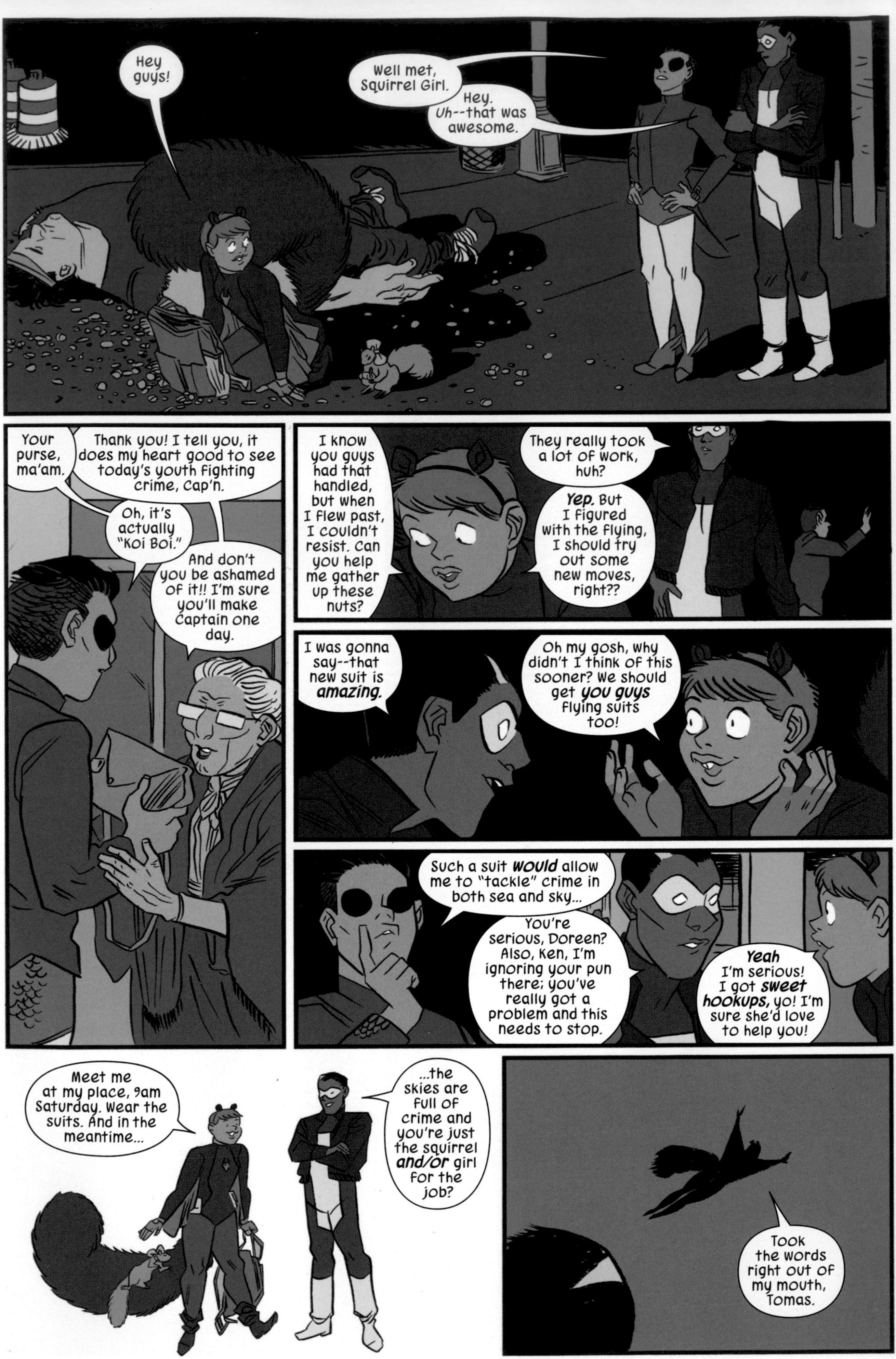

Hey guys!
Well met, Squirrel Girl.
Hey. Uh--that was awesome.
Your purse, ma'am.
Thank you! I tell you, it does my heart good to see today's youth fighting crime, Cap'n.
Oh, it's actually "Koi Boi."
And don't you be ashamed of it!! I'm sure you'll make Captain one day.
I know you guys had that handled, but when I flew past, I couldn't resist. Can you help me gather up these nuts?
They really took a lot of work, huh?
Yep. But I figured with the flying, I should try out some new moves, right??
I was gonna say--that new suit is amazing.
Oh my gosh, why didn't I think of this sooner? We should get you guys flying suits too!
Such a suit would allow me to "tackle" crime in both sea and sky...
You're serious, Doreen? Also, Ken, I'm ignoring your pun there; you've really got a problem and this needs to stop.
Yeah I'm serious! I got sweet hookups, yo! I'm sure she'd love to help you!
Meet me at my place, 9am Saturday. Wear the suits. And in the meantime...
...the skies are full of crime and you're just the squirrel and/or girl for the job?
Took the words right out of my mouth, Tomas.

Doreen's search history goes "cool things to drop on someone's head," "cool things to drop on someone's head--anvils," "cool but also cheap and nonfatal things to drop on someone's head," and finally, "how long it'd take me to get squirrels to gather up a bunch of nuts, wait nevermind I know this, I don't even know why I'm still typing this or hitting enter."

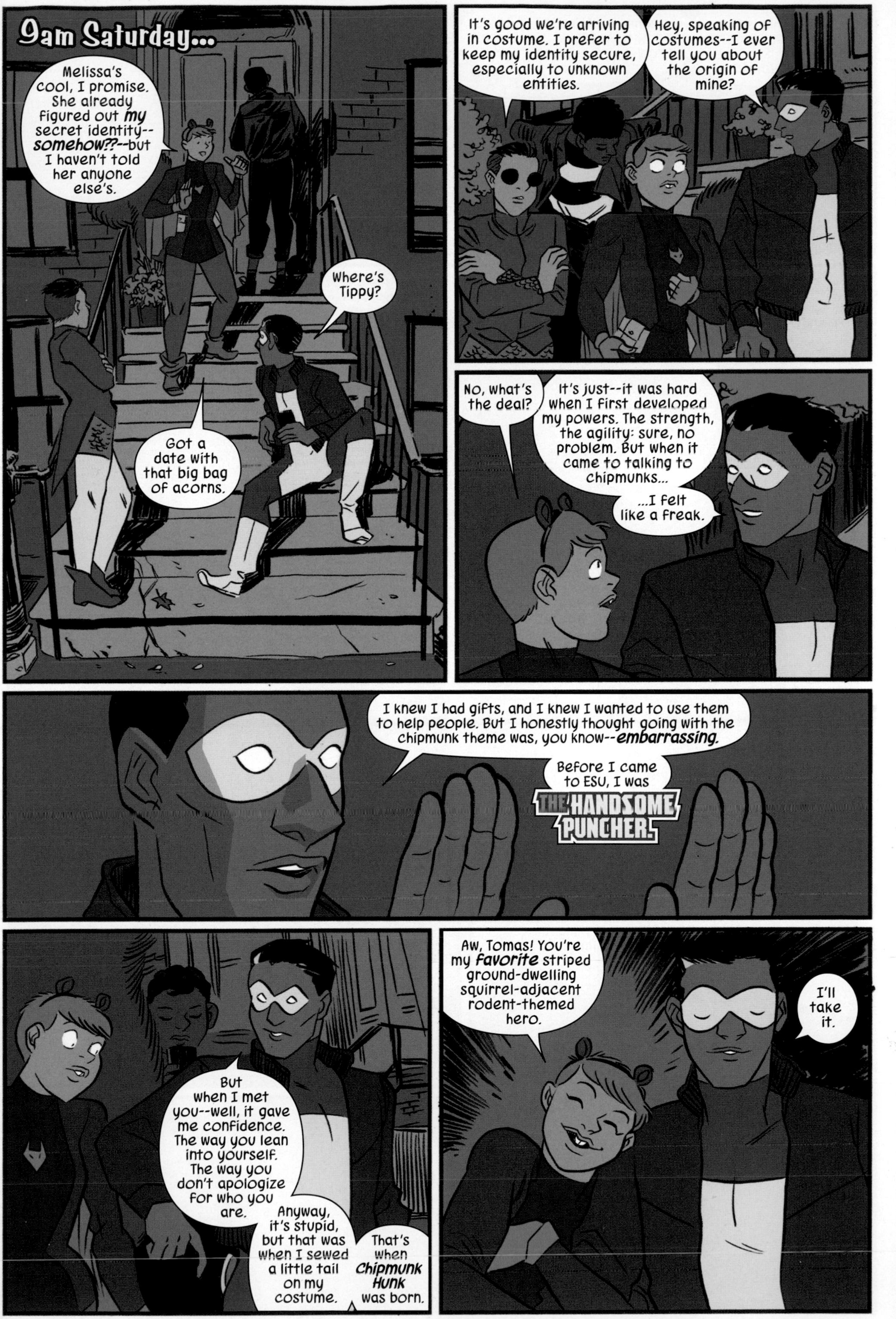
9am Saturday...
Melissa's cool, I promise. She already figured out my secret identity--somehow??--but I haven't told her anyone else's.
Where's Tippy?
Got a date with that big bag of acorns.
It's good we're arriving in costume. I prefer to keep my identity secure, especially to unknown entities.
Hey, speaking of costumes--I ever tell you about the origin of mine?
No, what's the deal?
It's just--it was hard when I first developed my powers. The strength, the agility: sure, no problem. But when it came to talking to chipmunks...
...I felt like a freak.
I knew I had gifts, and I knew I wanted to use them to help people. But I honestly thought going with the chipmunk theme was, you know--embarrassing.
Before I came to ESU, I was
THE HANDSOME PUNCHER.
But when I met you--well, it gave me confidence. The way you lean into yourself. The way you don't apologize for who you are.
Anyway, it's stupid, but that was when I sewed a little tail on my costume.
That's when Chipmunk Hunk was born.
Aw, Tomas! You're my favorite striped ground-dwelling squirrel-adjacent rodent-themed hero.
I'll take it.

I like how the only rule Tomas has when picking a super-hero name for himself is that it should definitely mention how he's attractive. I think it's a great rule! Signed, Extremely Handsome Comic Book Narrator Guy.

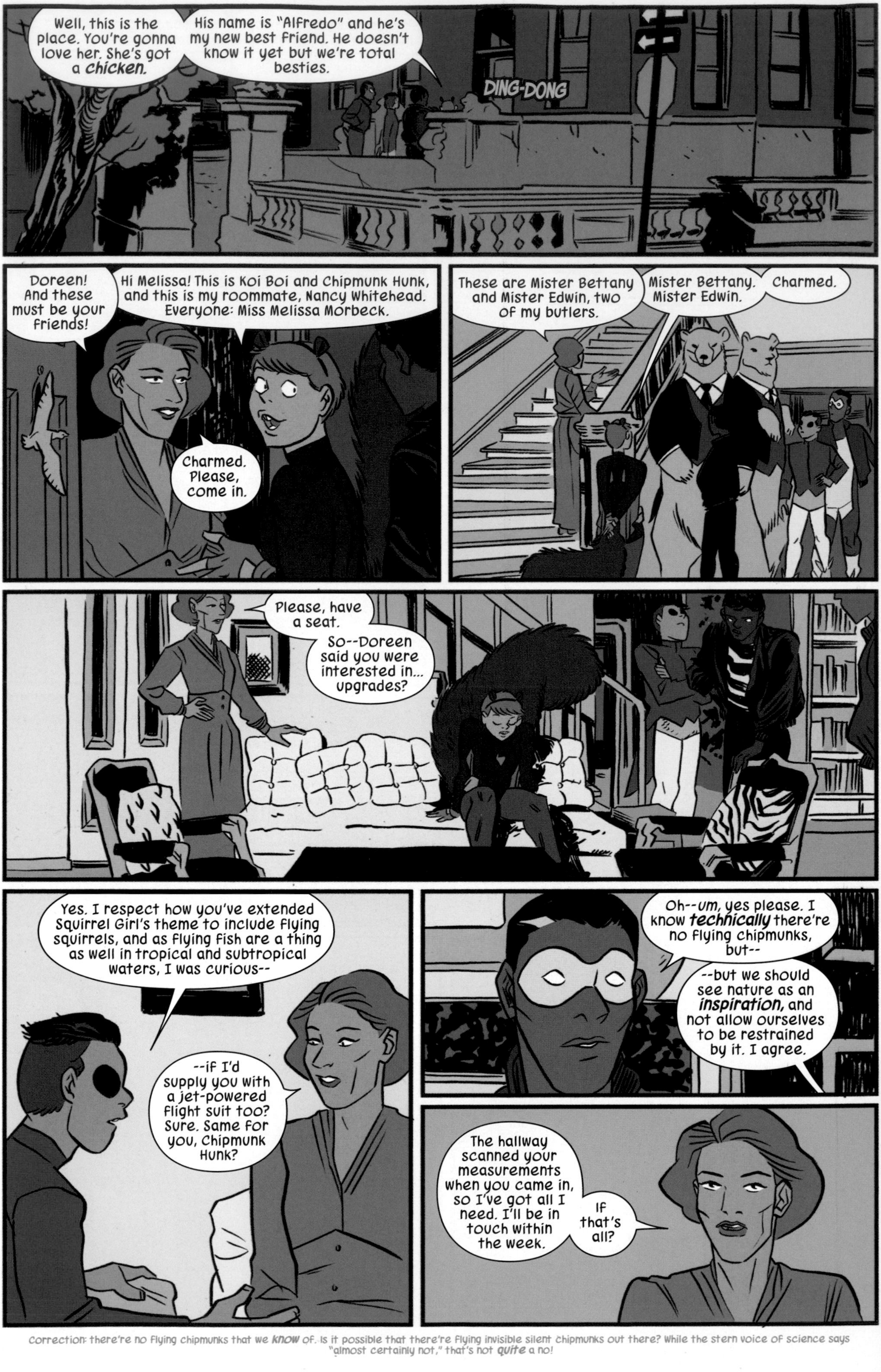
Well, this is the place. You're gonna love her. She's got a *chicken.*
His name is "Alfredo" and he's my new best friend. He doesn't know it yet but we're total besties.
DING-DONG
Doreen! And these must be your friends!
Hi Melissa! This is Koi Boi and Chipmunk Hunk, and this is my roommate, Nancy Whitehead. Everyone: Miss Melissa Morbeck.
Charmed. Please, come in.
These are Mister Bettany and Mister Edwin, two of my butlers.
Mister Bettany. Mister Edwin.
Charmed.
Please, have a seat.
So--Doreen said you were interested in... upgrades?
Yes. I respect how you've extended Squirrel Girl's theme to include flying squirrels, and as flying fish are a thing as well in tropical and subtropical waters, I was curious--
--if I'd supply you with a jet-powered flight suit too? Sure. Same for you, Chipmunk Hunk?
Oh--*um,* yes please. I know *technically* there're no flying chipmunks, but--
--but we should see nature as an *inspiration,* and not allow ourselves to be restrained by it. I agree.
The hallway scanned your measurements when you came in, so I've got all I need. I'll be in touch within the week.
If that's all?

Correction: there're no flying chipmunks that we *know* of. Is it possible that there're flying invisible silent chipmunks out there? While the stern voice of science says "almost certainly not," that's not *quite* a no!

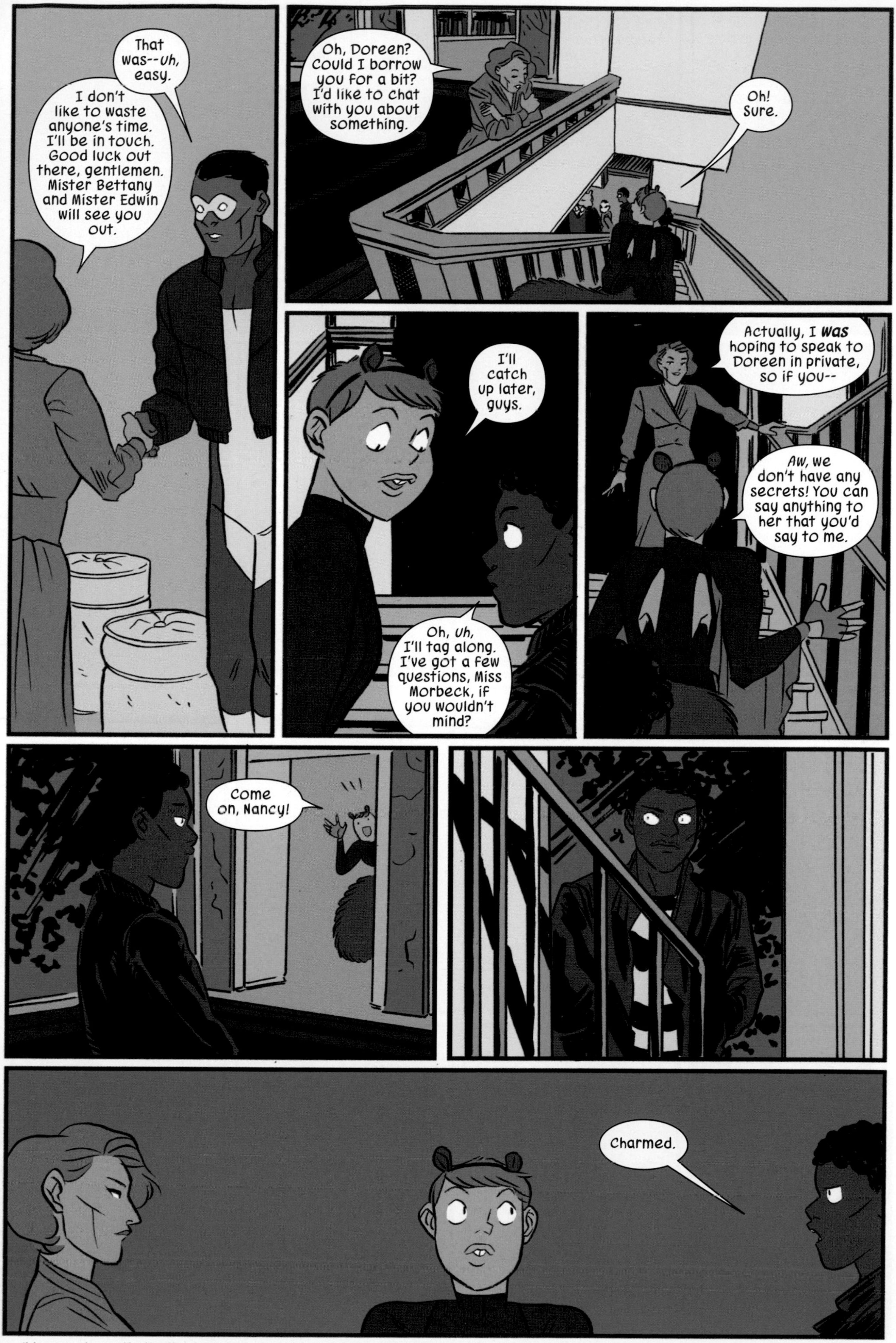
That was--uh, easy.
I don't like to waste anyone's time. I'll be in touch. Good luck out there, gentlemen. Mister Bettany and Mister Edwin will see you out.
Oh, Doreen? Could I borrow you for a bit? I'd like to chat with you about something.
Oh! Sure.
I'll catch up later, guys.
Oh, uh, I'll tag along. I've got a few questions, Miss Morbeck, if you wouldn't mind?
Actually, I **was** hoping to speak to Doreen in private, so if you--
Aw, we don't have any secrets! You can say anything to her that you'd say to me.
Come on, Nancy!
Charmed.

It has come to my attention that I *may* have oversold the possibility of "flying invisible silent chipmunks," and for that I apologize. However, seeing as less than 5% of the ocean's floor has been explored, the possibility of "flying invisible silent *deep-sea* chipmunks" remains enticingly open!!

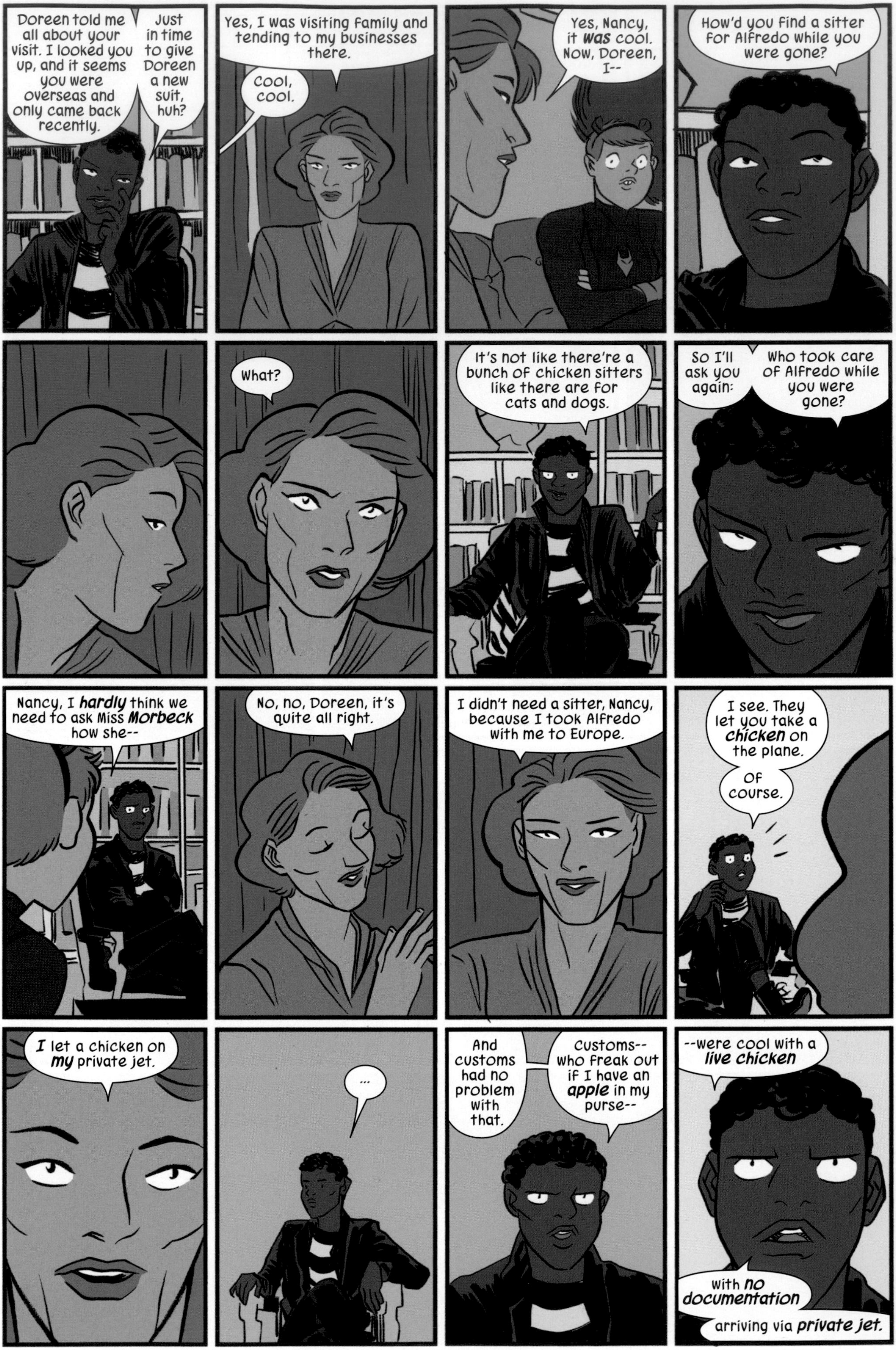
Doreen told me all about your visit. I looked you up, and it seems you were overseas and only came back recently.
Just in time to give Doreen a new suit, huh?
Yes, I was visiting family and tending to my businesses there.
Cool, cool.
Yes, Nancy, it *was* cool. Now, Doreen, I--
How'd you find a sitter for Alfredo while you were gone?
What?
It's not like there're a bunch of chicken sitters like there are for cats and dogs.
So I'll ask you again:
Who took care of Alfredo while you were gone?
Nancy, I *hardly* think we need to ask Miss *Morbeck* how she--
No, no, Doreen, it's quite all right.
I didn't need a sitter, Nancy, because I took Alfredo with me to Europe.
I see. They let you take a *chicken* on the plane.
Of course.
I let a chicken on *my* private jet.
...
And customs had no problem with that.
Customs-- who freak out if I have an *apple* in my purse--
--were cool with a *live chicken*
with *no documentation*
arriving via *private jet.*

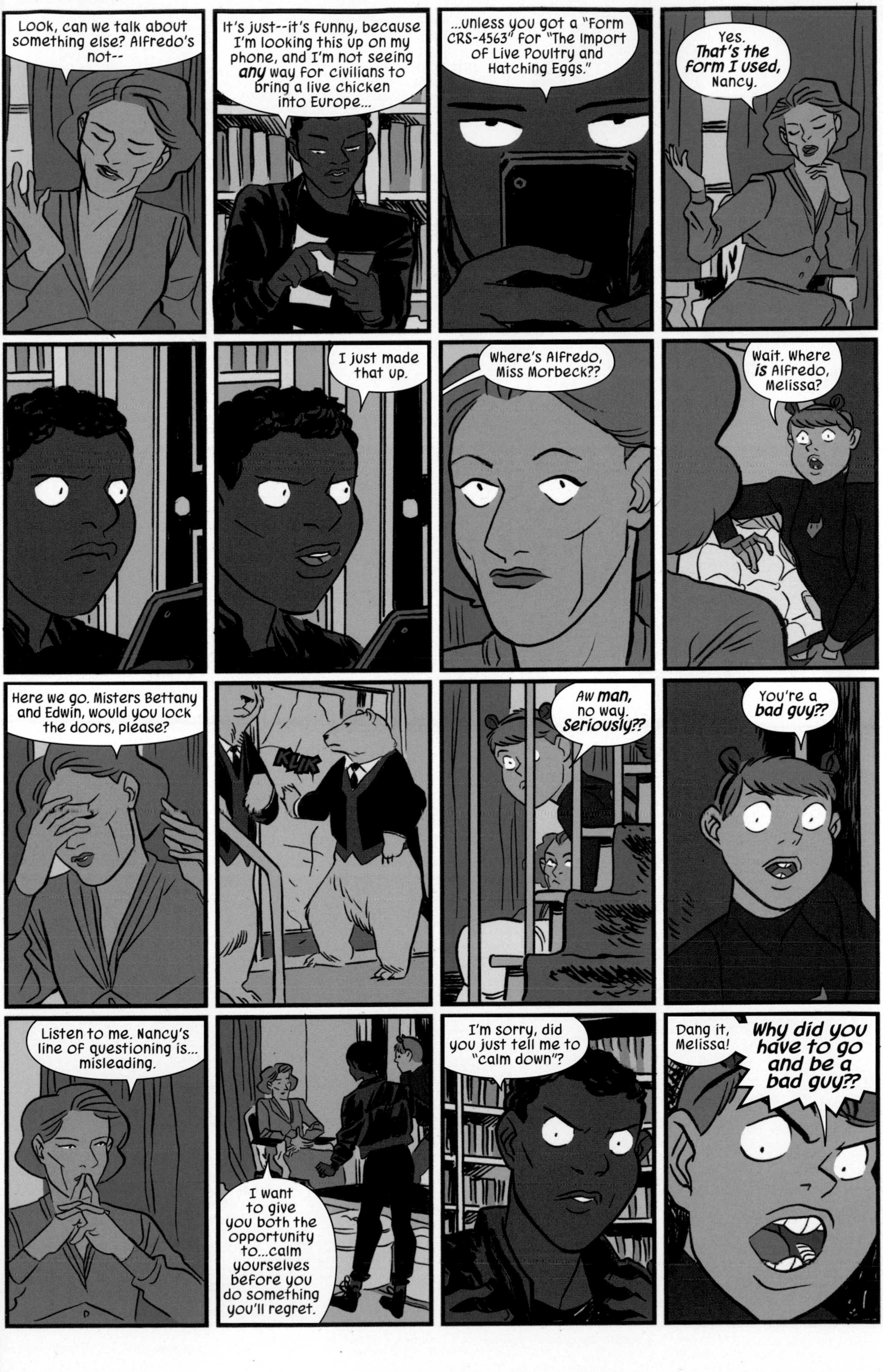
Look, can we talk about something else? Alfredo's not--
It's just--it's funny, because I'm looking this up on my phone, and I'm not seeing any way for civilians to bring a live chicken into Europe...
...unless you got a "Form CRS-4563" for "The Import of Live Poultry and Hatching Eggs."
Yes. That's the form I used, Nancy.
I just made that up.
Where's Alfredo, Miss Morbeck??
Wait. Where is Alfredo, Melissa?
Here we go. Misters Bettany and Edwin, would you lock the doors, please?
KLIK
Aw man, no way. Seriously??
You're a bad guy??
Listen to me. Nancy's line of questioning is... misleading.
I want to give you both the opportunity to...calm yourselves before you do something you'll regret.
I'm sorry, did you just tell me to "calm down"?
Dang it, Melissa!
Why did you have to go and be a bad guy??

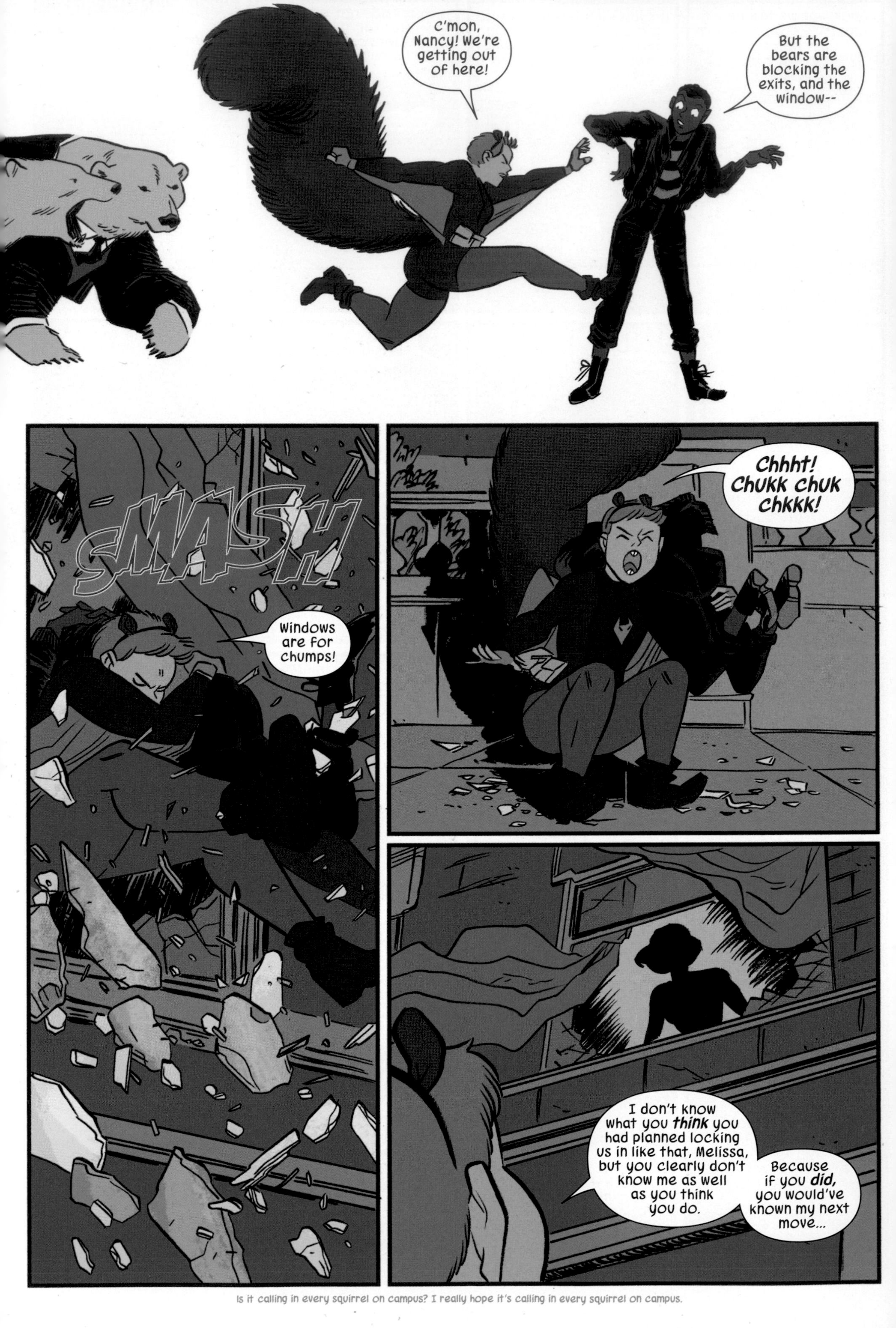
C'mon, Nancy! We're getting out of here!
But the bears are blocking the exits, and the window--
sMASH
Windows are for chumps!
Chhht! Chukk chuk chkkk!
I don't know what you *think* you had planned locking us in like that, Melissa, but you clearly don't know me as well as you think you do.
Because if you *did,* you would've known my next move...

Is it calling in every squirrel on campus? I really hope it's calling in every squirrel on campus.

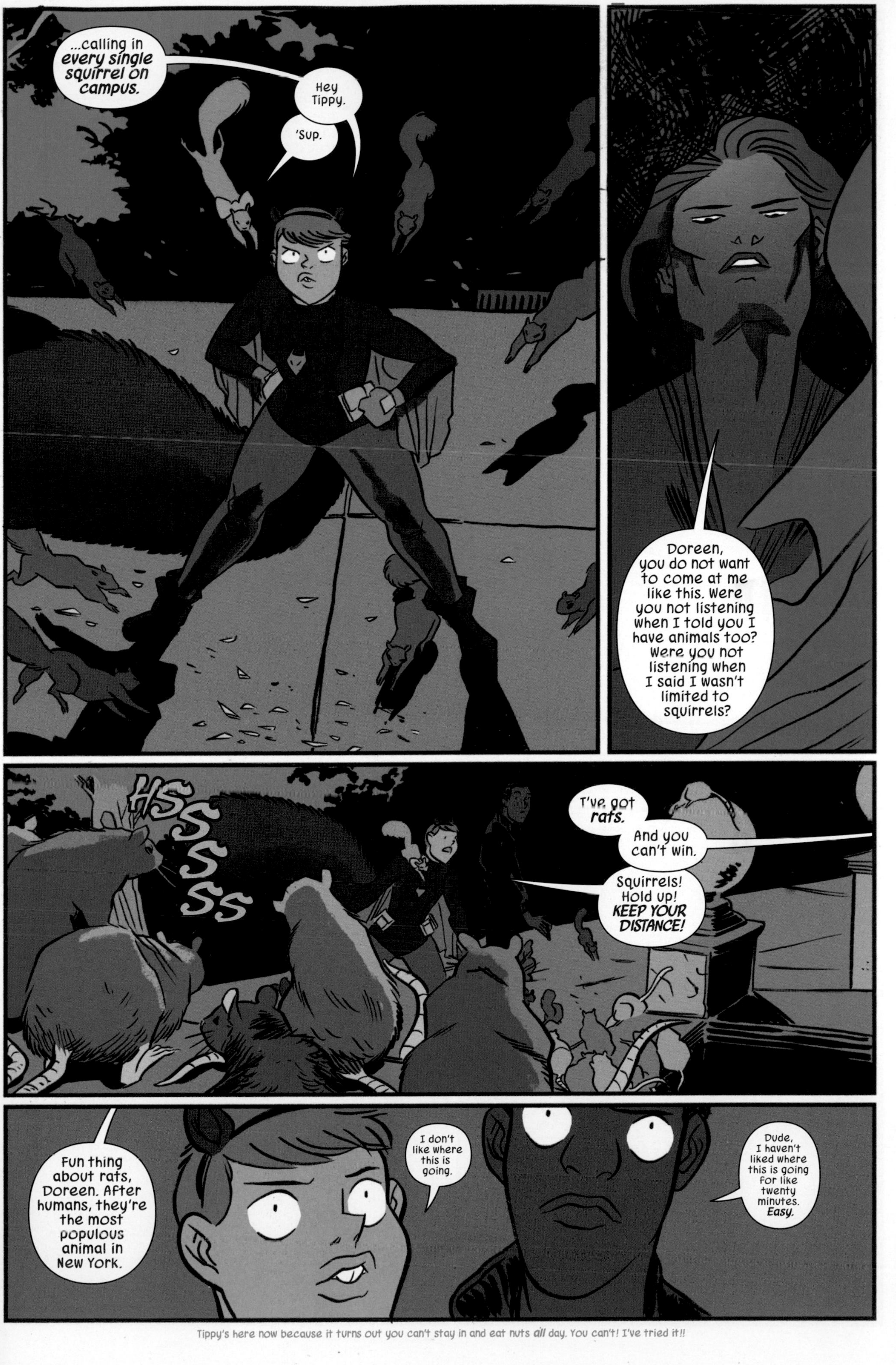
...calling in every single squirrel on campus.
Hey Tippy.
'Sup.
Doreen, you do not want to come at me like this. Were you not listening when I told you I have animals too? Were you not listening when I said I wasn't limited to squirrels?
HSSSSSS
I've got rats.
And you can't win.
Squirrels! Hold up! KEEP YOUR DISTANCE!
Fun thing about rats, Doreen. After humans, they're the most populous animal in New York.
I don't like where this is going.
Dude, I haven't liked where this is going for like twenty minutes. Easy.
Tippy's here now because it turns out you can't stay in and eat nuts *all* day. You can't! I've tried it!!

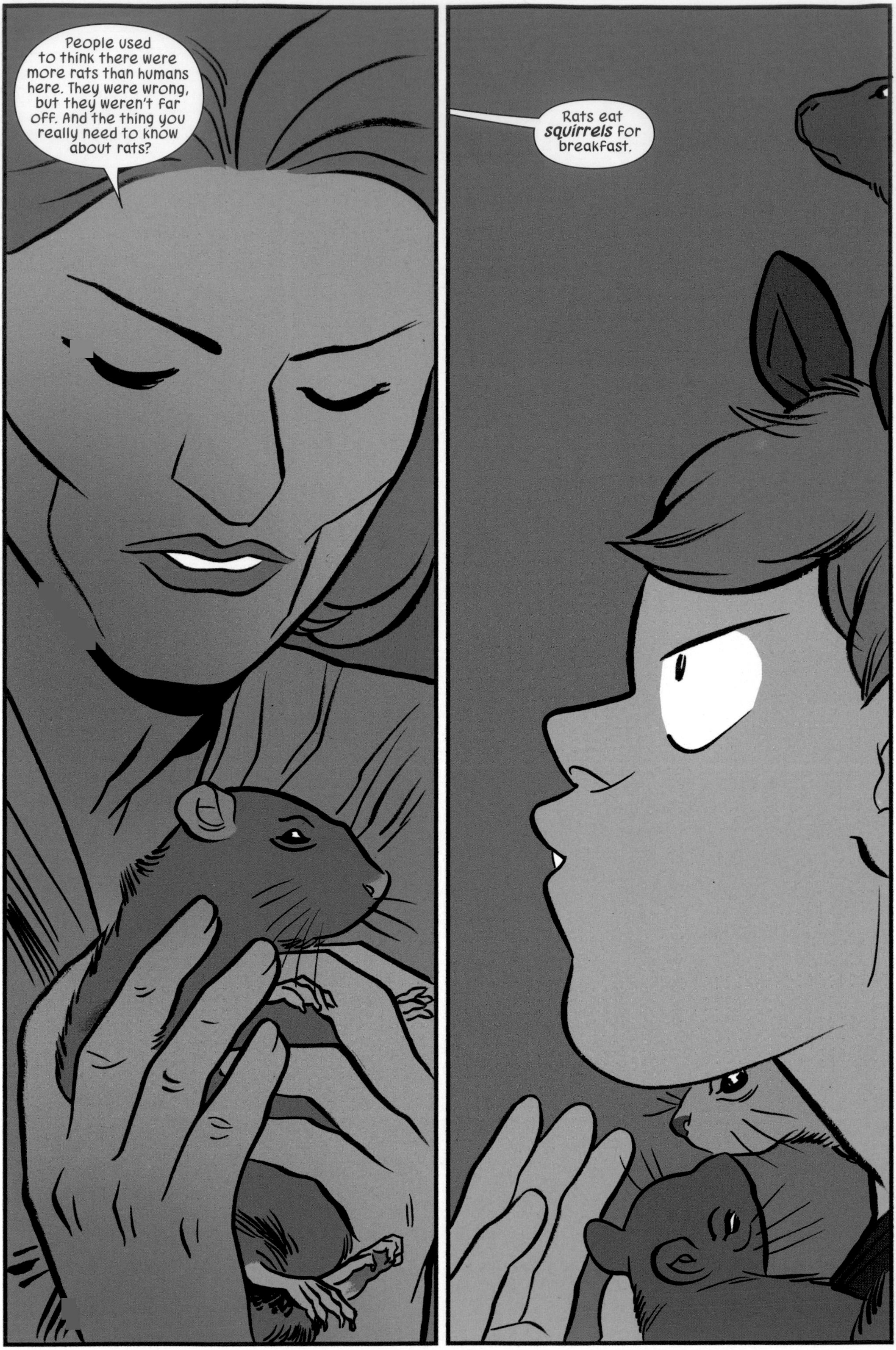
People used to think there were more rats than humans here. They were wrong, but they weren't far off. And the thing you really need to know about rats?
Rats eat *squirrels* for breakfast.

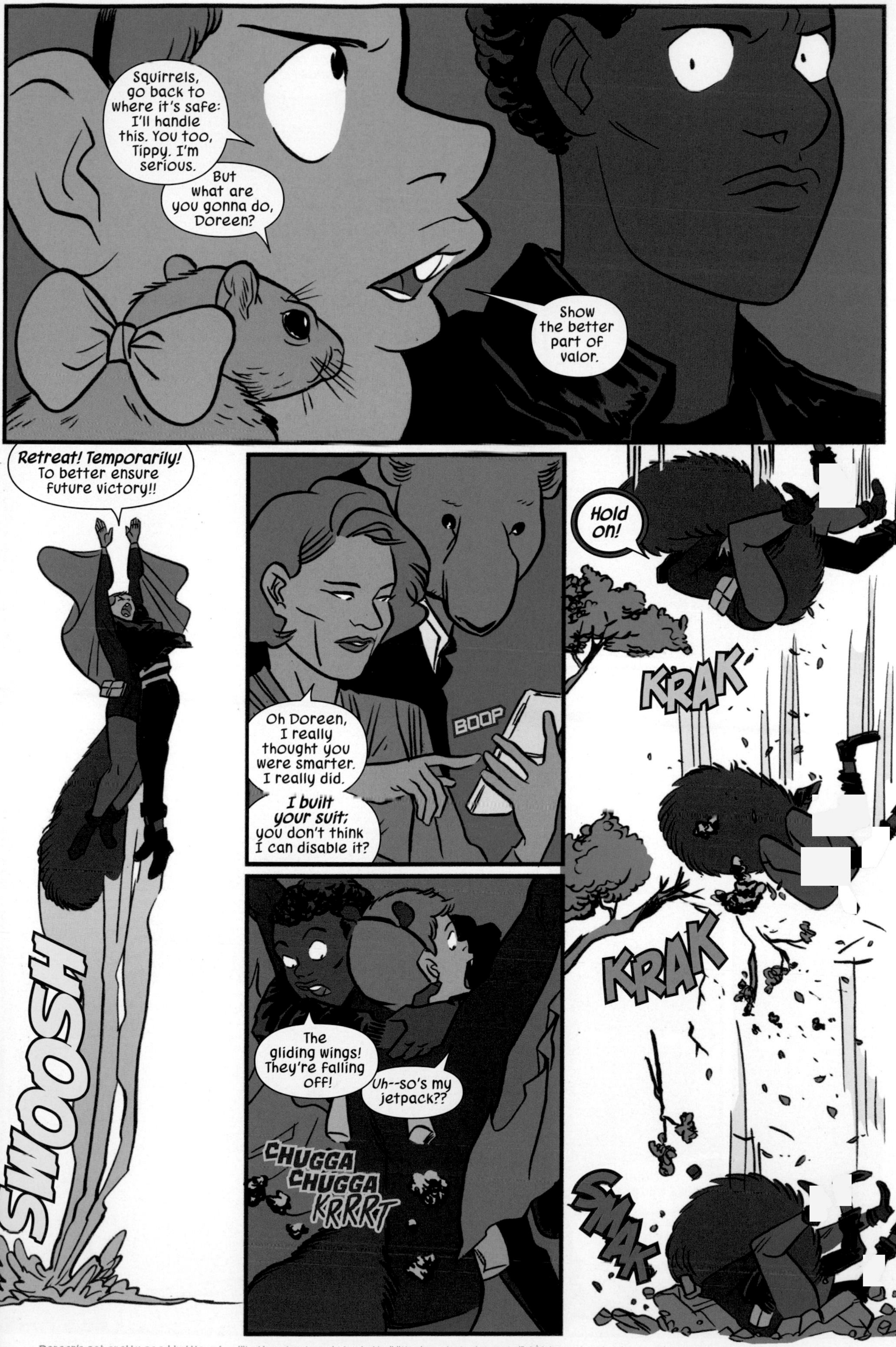
Squirrels, go back to where it's safe: I'll handle this. You too, Tippy. I'm serious.
But what are you gonna do, Doreen?
Show the better part of valor.
Retreat! Temporarily! To better ensure future victory!!
SWOOSH
Oh Doreen, I really thought you were smarter. I really did.
I built your suit; you don't think I can disable it?
BOOP
The gliding wings! They're falling off!
Uh--so's my jetpack??
CHUGGA CHUGGA KRRRT
Hold on!
KRAK
KRAK
SMAK

Doreen's got pretty good battle cries ("Let's eat nuts and kick butts," "You're a jerk who sucks") but her retreat cries could use some work. May I suggest "Let's eat nuts and kick butts...at a later date" and "You're a jerk who sucks...from a safe distance, which is where I'm about to head right now"?

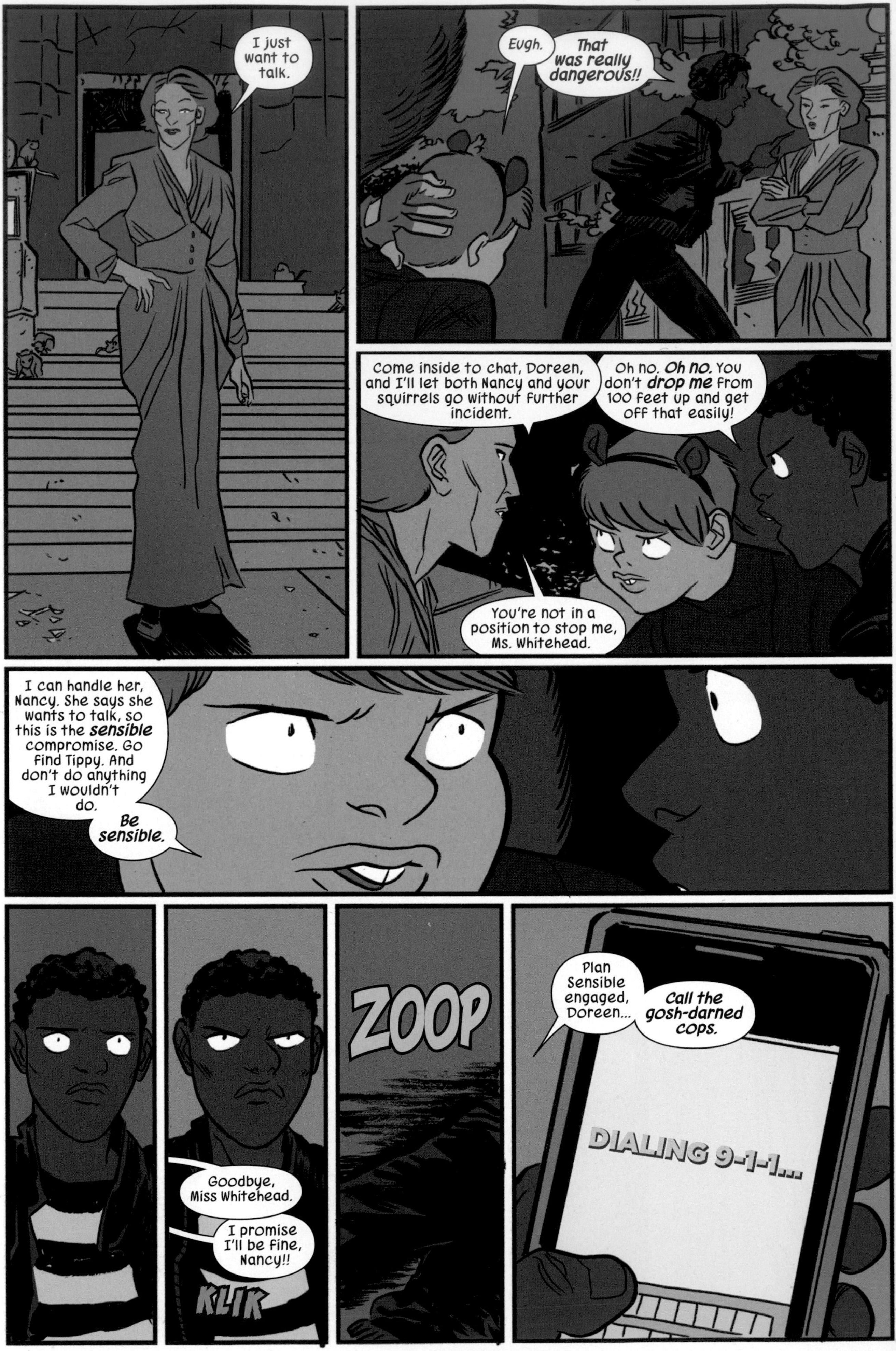
I just want to talk.
Eugh.
That was really dangerous!!
Come inside to chat, Doreen, and I'll let both Nancy and your squirrels go without further incident.
Oh no. Oh no. You don't drop me from 100 feet up and get off that easily!
You're not in a position to stop me, Ms. Whitehead.
I can handle her, Nancy. She says she wants to talk, so this is the sensible compromise. Go find Tippy. And don't do anything I wouldn't do.
Be sensible.
Goodbye, Miss Whitehead.
I promise I'll be fine, Nancy!!
KLIK
ZOOP
Plan Sensible engaged, Doreen...
Call the gosh-darned cops.
DIALING 9-1-1...

Plan Sensible is such a great plan. It's so sensible! It's way better than Plan Foolish, which is the plan where we just put on silly hats and make funny noises at each other. Actually, hold on, now I like both plans.

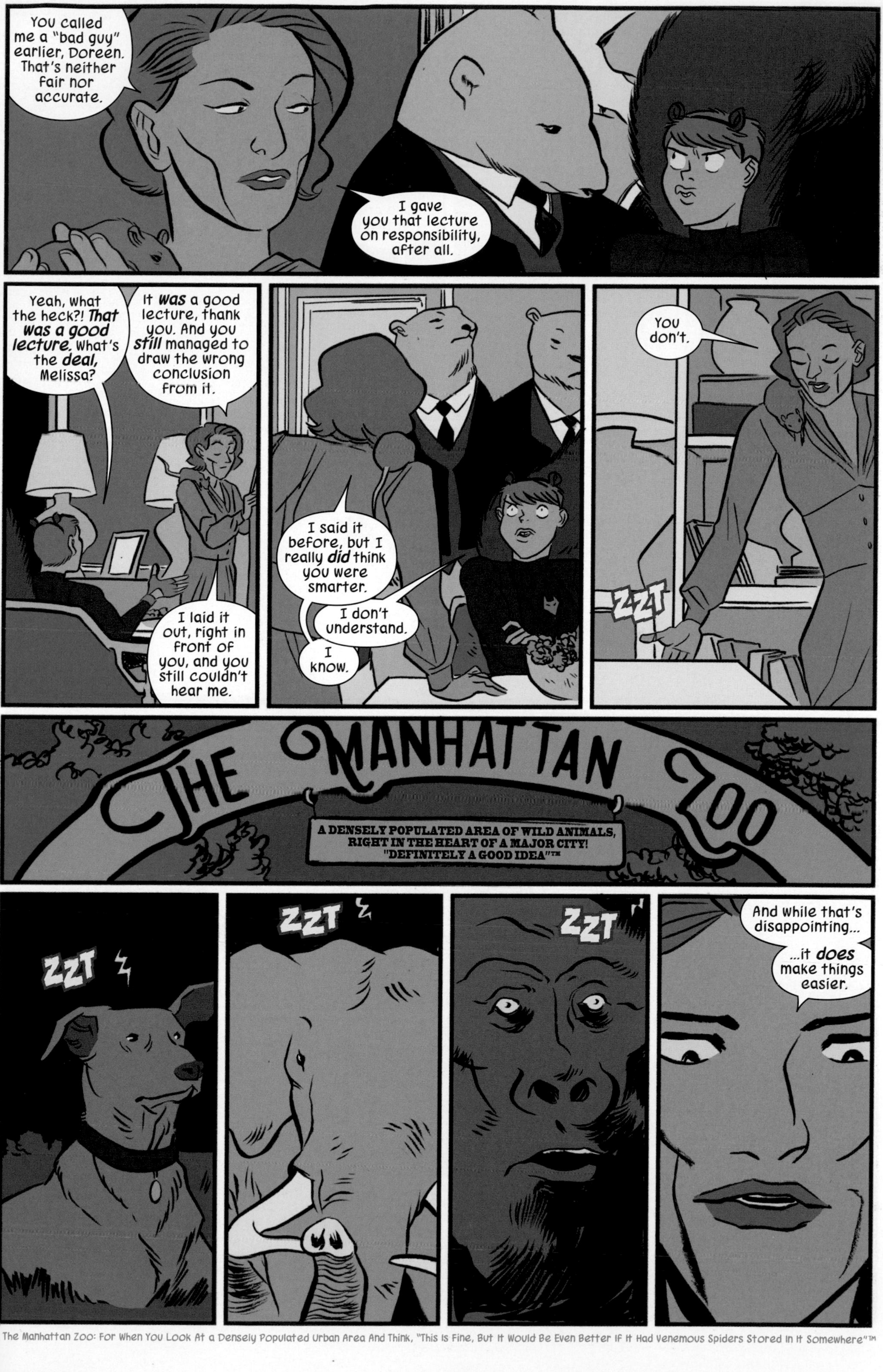
You called me a "bad guy" earlier, Doreen. That's neither fair nor accurate.
I gave you that lecture on responsibility, after all.
Yeah, what the heck?! That was a good lecture. What's the deal, Melissa?
It was a good lecture, thank you. And you still managed to draw the wrong conclusion from it.
I laid it out, right in front of you, and you still couldn't hear me.
I said it before, but I really did think you were smarter.
I don't understand.
I know.
You don't.
ZZT
THE MANHATTAN ZOO
A DENSELY POPULATED AREA OF WILD ANIMALS, RIGHT IN THE HEART OF A MAJOR CITY! "DEFINITELY A GOOD IDEA"™
ZZT
ZZT
ZZT
And while that's disappointing...
...it does make things easier.
The Manhattan Zoo: For When You Look At a Densely Populated Urban Area And Think, "This Is Fine, But It Would Be Even Better If It Had Venemous Spiders Stored In It Somewhere"™

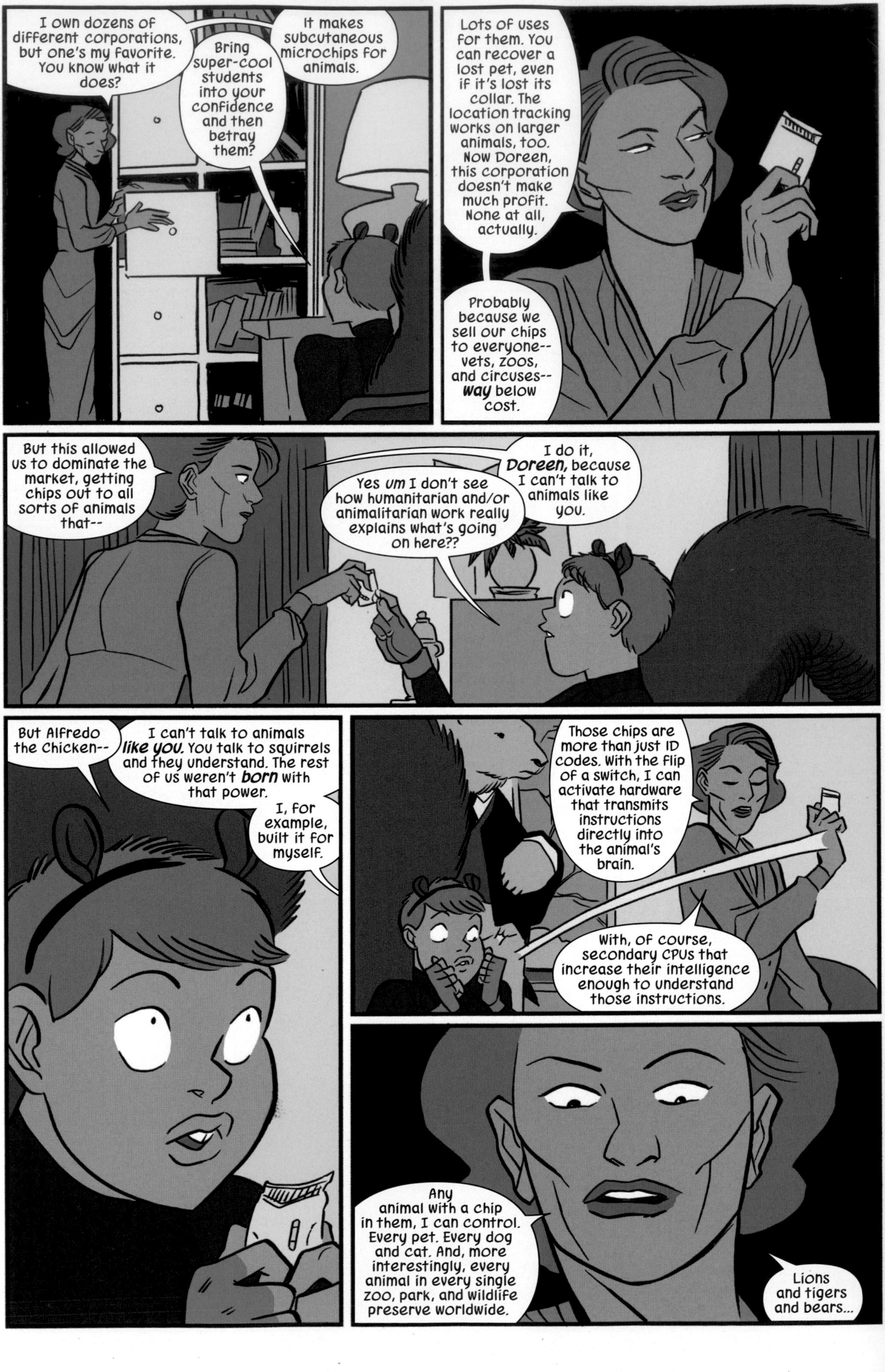
I own dozens of different corporations, but one's my favorite. You know what it does?
Bring super-cool students into your confidence and then betray them?
It makes subcutaneous microchips for animals.
Lots of uses for them. You can recover a lost pet, even if it's lost its collar. The location tracking works on larger animals, too. Now Doreen, this corporation doesn't make much profit. None at all, actually.
Probably because we sell our chips to everyone--vets, zoos, and circuses--way below cost.
But this allowed us to dominate the market, getting chips out to all sorts of animals that--
Yes um I don't see how humanitarian and/or animalitarian work really explains what's going on here??
I do it, Doreen, because I can't talk to animals like you.
But Alfredo the Chicken--
I can't talk to animals like you. You talk to squirrels and they understand. The rest of us weren't born with that power.
I, for example, built it for myself.
Those chips are more than just ID codes. With the flip of a switch, I can activate hardware that transmits instructions directly into the animal's brain.
With, of course, secondary CPUs that increase their intelligence enough to understand those instructions.
Any animal with a chip in them, I can control. Every pet. Every dog and cat. And, more interestingly, every animal in every single zoo, park, and wildlife preserve worldwide.
Lions and tigers and bears...

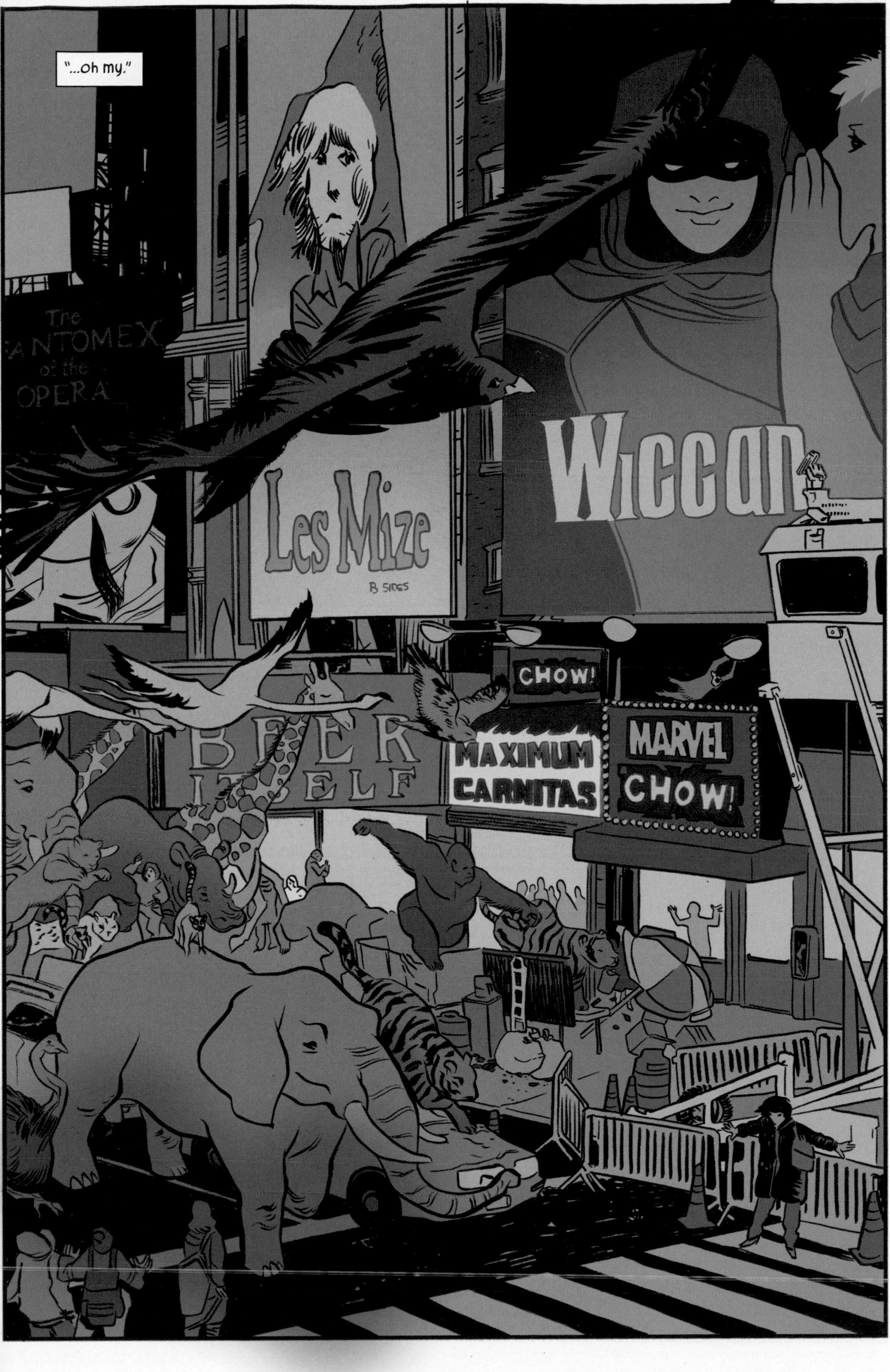
"...oh my."
The
FANTOMEX
of the
OPERA
Les Mize
B SIDES
Wiccan
CHOW!
BEER
ITSELF
MAXIMUM
CARNITAS
MARVEL
CHOW!

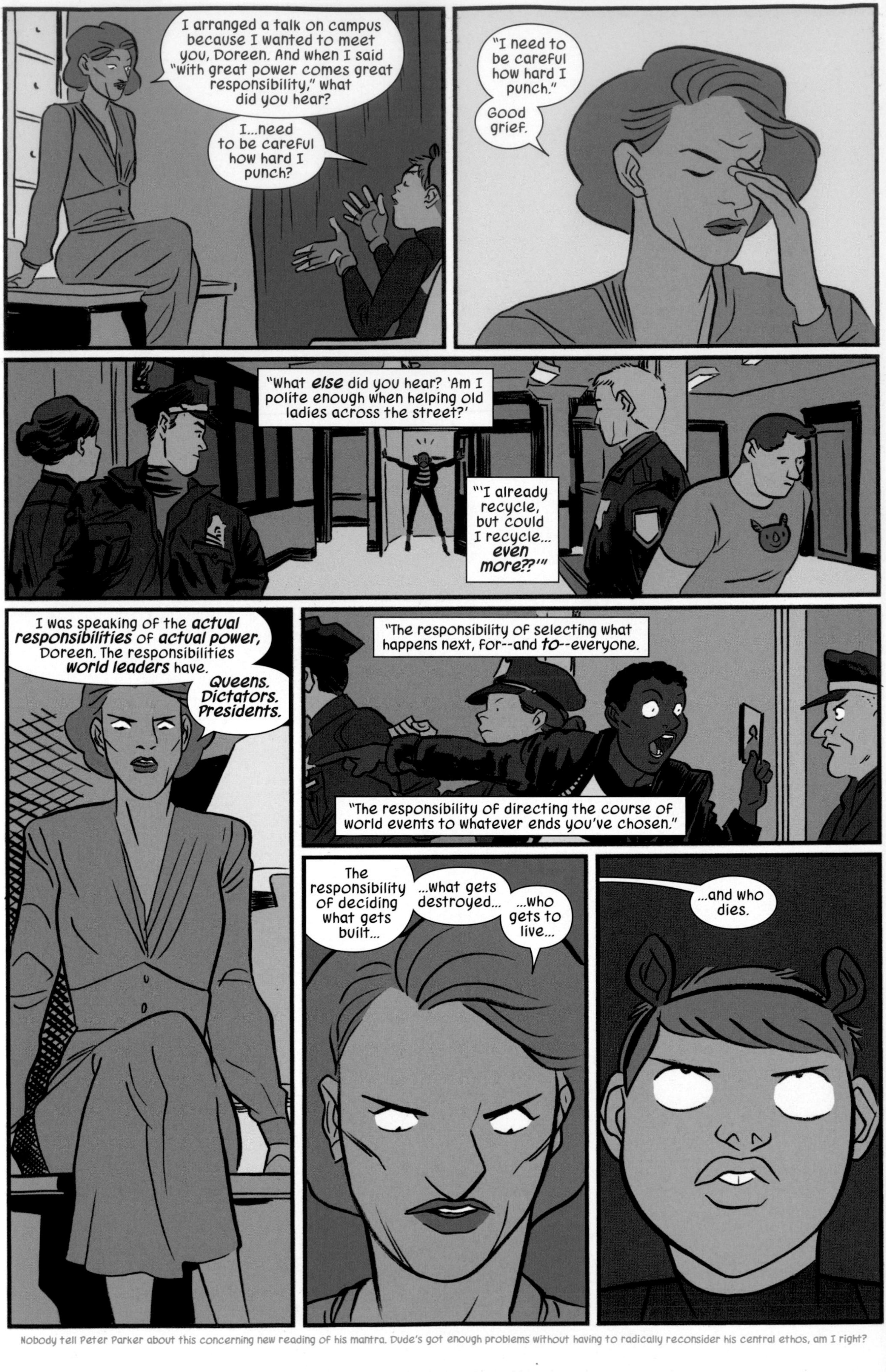
I arranged a talk on campus because I wanted to meet you, Doreen. And when I said "with great power comes great responsibility," what did you hear?
I...need to be careful how hard I punch?
"I need to be careful how hard I punch."
Good grief.
"What else did you hear? 'Am I polite enough when helping old ladies across the street?'
"'I already recycle, but could I recycle... even more??'"
I was speaking of the actual responsibilities of actual power, Doreen. The responsibilities world leaders have.
Queens. Dictators. Presidents.
"The responsibility of selecting what happens next, for--and to--everyone.
"The responsibility of directing the course of world events to whatever ends you've chosen."
The responsibility of deciding what gets built...
...what gets destroyed...
...who gets to live...
...and who dies.

Nobody tell Peter Parker about this concerning new reading of his mantra. Dude's got enough problems without having to radically reconsider his central ethos, am I right?

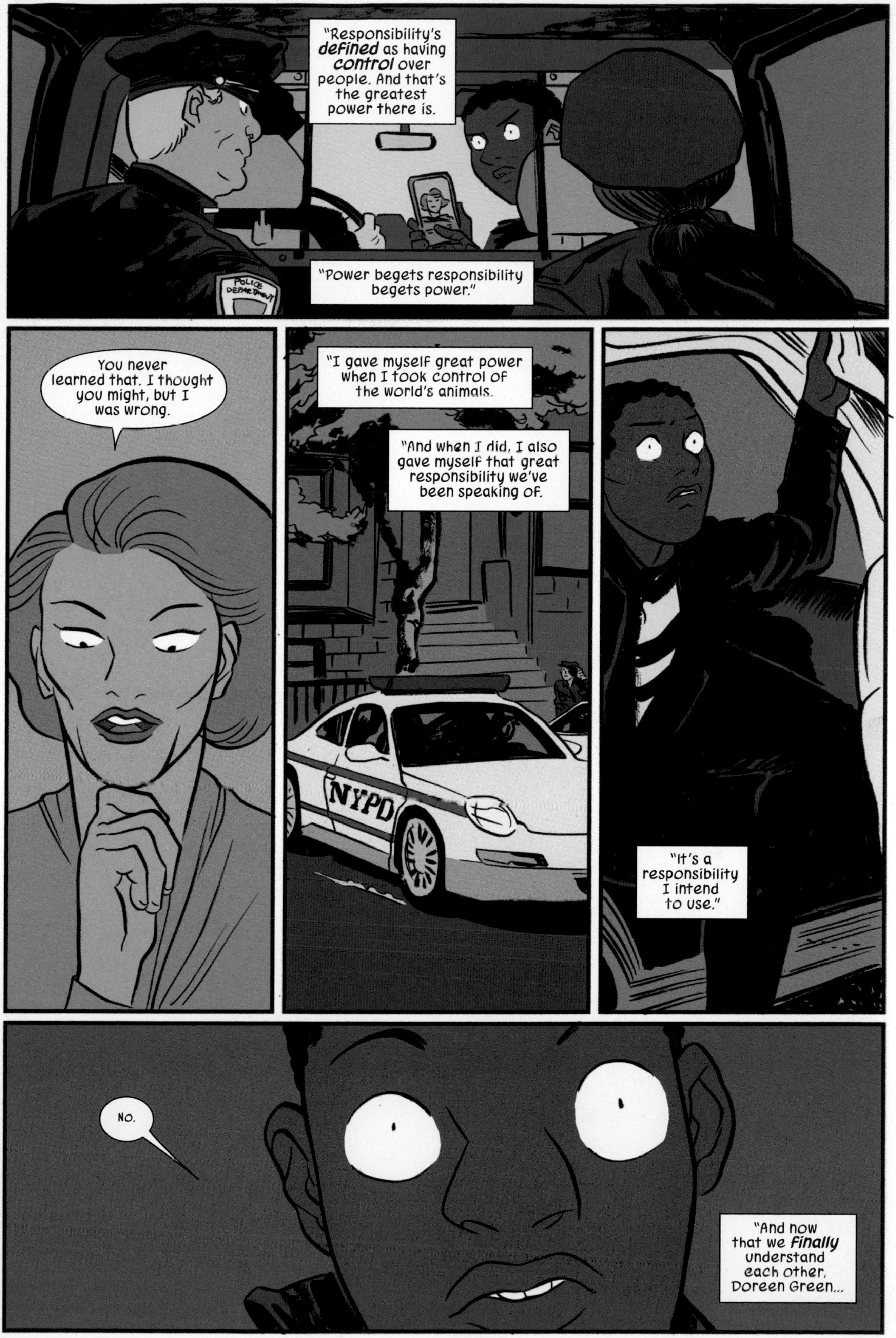
"Responsibility's *defined* as having *control* over people. And that's the greatest power there is.
"Power begets responsibility begets power."
POLICE DEPARTMENT
You never learned that. I thought you might, but I was wrong.
"I gave myself great power when I took control of the world's animals.
"And when I did, I also gave myself that great responsibility we've been speaking of.
NYPD
"It's a responsibility I intend to use."
NO.
"And now that we *finally* understand each other, Doreen Green...

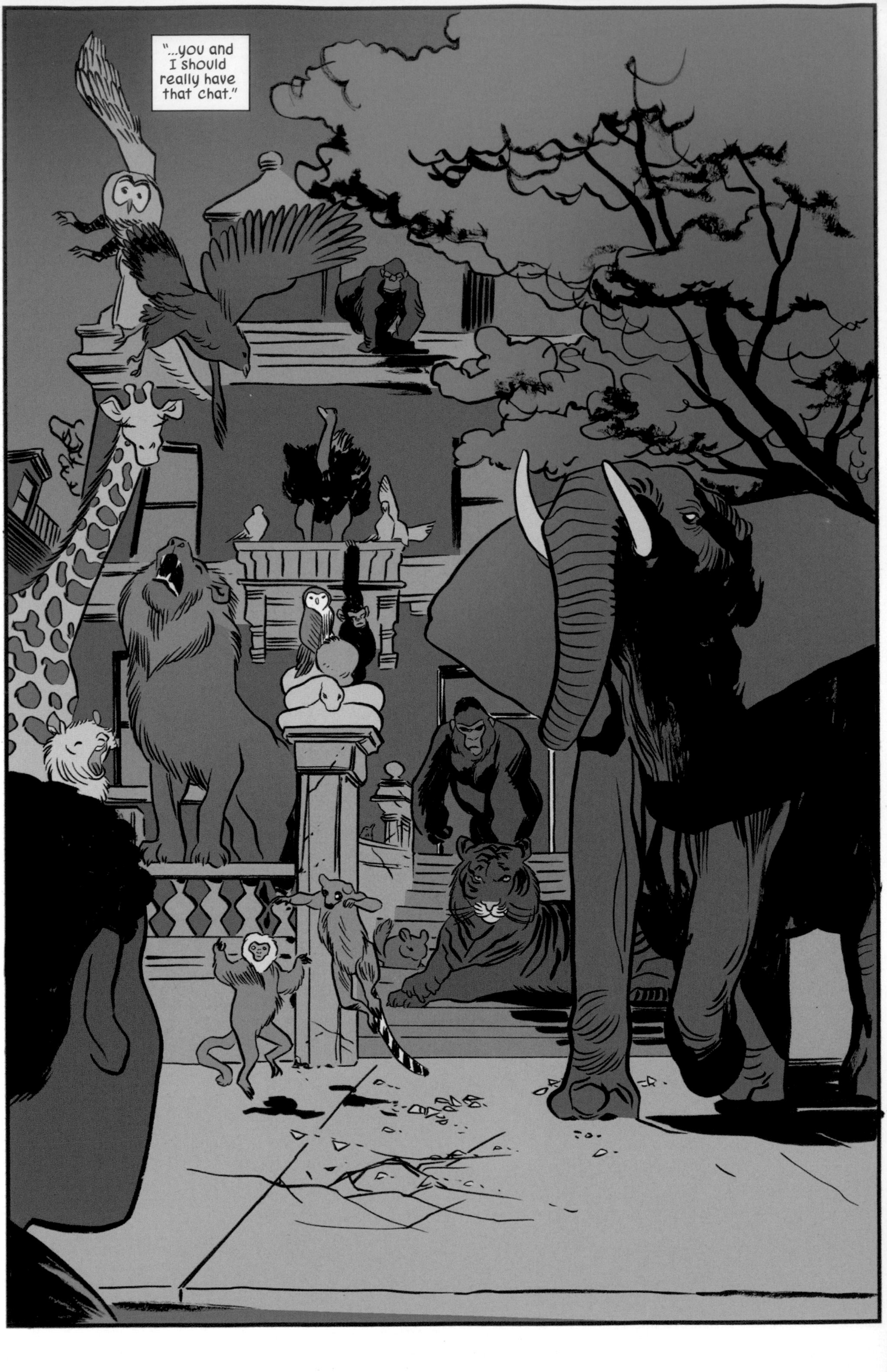
"...you and I should really have that chat."

Letters From Nuts

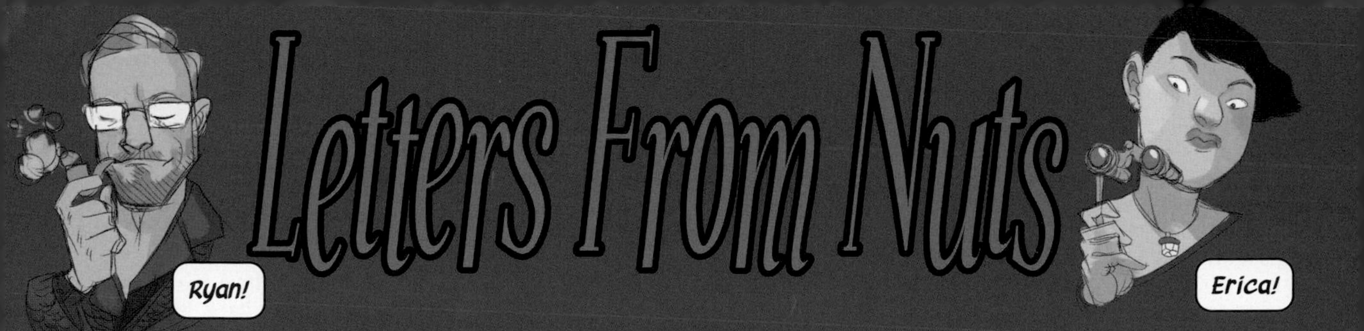
Ryan!
Erica!

Send letters to mheroes@marvel.com or 135 W 50th St, 7th Floor, New York, NY 10020 (Please mark "OKAY TO PRINT")

Hi Ryan and Erica!

I'm a huge SG fan, and after rereading all of the series yesterday and today (my last days of freedom before the semester starts up tomorrow), I felt inspired to draw this, and I wanted to share! Thank you so much for making such an amazing and funny heroine. I'm also a college student in engineering, so I really identify with a super heroine in college studying computer science!

Emma

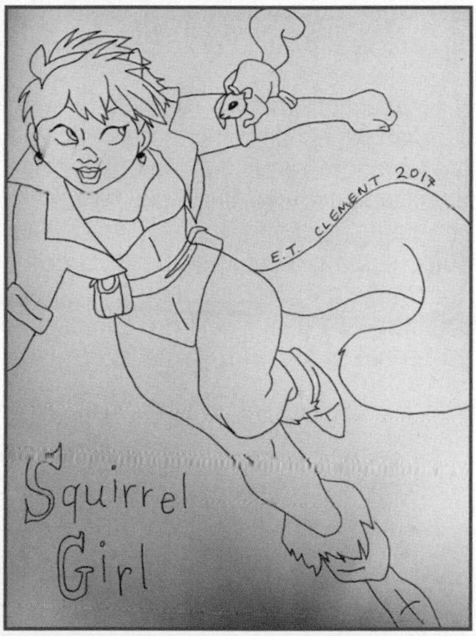
E.T. CLEMENT 2017
Squirrel
Girl

RYAN: Thanks, Emma! Great job on the art too! I was kinda close to going into computer engineering (my dad is an electrical engineer), but the computer engineering courses I took showed me that I was better at abstract ideas about computation than the actual implementation. But I was really glad I took the courses, because they made me feel like if I had to build a computer from scratch, I'd at least have SOMEWHAT of an idea of what I was doing?

ERICA: I LOVE IT. I'm glad we could make your last day of break a good time.

Ryan and Erica,

I'm 13, and I'm a huge fan of the series. My older brother, Roni, the arrogant computer science student who wrote the pseudocode letter published in issue #16, had already started teaching me about CS when I read issue #11. So, with your and his help, here's my review of USG #16 in the form of flattering pseudocode:

```
IF (they announce a 25th anniversary){
 I_want_to_read_it_immediately();
}
I_start_reading_it();
I_am_literally_laughing_out_loud();
IF (I do not stop laughing){
 My_family_asks_me_to_be_quiet();
}
WHILE (seeing Doreen as a kid){
 She_is_too_cute();
 I_want_a_series_about_her();
}
IF (Will Murray writes a part){
 I_am_surprised();
 WHILE (reading it){
 I_do_not_want_it_to_end();
 }
}
IF (I finish reading){
 veni_vidi_lovediti();
 It_is_my_favorite_issue();
 I_want_SG_as_Avengers_leader();
}
```

Oof, that's not easy...
Ryan, I hope that, as "a guy who knows things," you'll approve my pseudocode.
Erica, I hope that you'll enjoy my sorcery

Adam Kaufman

P.S. Actually, I began reading USG before my brother, so I was upset when he got his letter published first.

P.P.S. Hey, Roni here! It made my day when I saw my letter was in the special issue, but I also noticed I had made a mistake! I forgot a closing bracket at the end! So, I apologize and I ask every reader to correct it. Grab a pen and add the bracket at the end. Thank you. By the way, Adam, did you just call me arrogant?!

RYAN: Pseudocode: APPROVED. And everyone, yes, please update your past issues appropriately. Finally: a niggling syntax error that I'm NOT responsible for!! The 25th anniversary issue was a lot of fun, and I really enjoyed hanging out with 5-, 10-, and 15-year-old Doreen. (Also 25-year-old Doreen, which is TECHNICALLY a spoiler, but if that spoils you why are you reading comic books out of order? In this comic, we respect the "sequential" part of "sequential art"!!) I think you should continue your brotherly arguments over "who is the most x" in other comic books too. Argue over who is the smartest in the letters page of MOON GIRL AND DEVIL DINOSAUR! Argue who is the strongest in the letters page of THE TOTALLY AWESOME HULK! Argue over who is the best at petting cats in the letters page of HELLCAT! I see zero flaws in this plan.

ERICA: Oh no code. One of these days I'll sneak in a bunch of art history references so that Ryan can be the one out of the loop. Mwahaha.

Dear Erica and Ryan,

I just wanted to drop a quick line and thank you for all the great work you have been doing on UNBEATABLE SQUIRREL GIRL. It is a constant beacon of optimism I get to look forward to every month.

Man, do we need Squirrel Girl. It's been a difficult year, packed to the brim with a lot of anxiety and apprehension and uncertainty. Yet, whenever I find myself at odds with others who have differing viewpoints, I always think back to how Doreen handles conflict. Having conviction, looking for common ground, and accepting the truth of other's "lived experiences" (USG #9) are all lessons we can learn from the unbeatable super heroine.

Really appreciate the work you guys are doing, and I hope you keep it up.

Manuel

RYAN: Thank you, Manuel! I do like how optimistic Doreen is, and I think it's a point of view that's especially hopeful when things look bleak.

ERICA: It's been really important to me for the same reason. I'm glad that we've had the chance to share these stories, and it's always good to hear that it's helping other people.

Dear Team Squirrel Girl,

My 10- and 13-year-old sons and I love your comic. When I don't read it quickly enough, they follow me around with it, brandishing it menacingly and saying, "We want to share the jokes, Mom. Read it now!"

But one thing gets in the way of my enjoyment. I am 48 and wear bifocals, and I still struggle to read the tiny beige type at the bottom of the pages. I love the tiny beige type at the bottom of the pages. I love the tiny type! It's full of funniness! But reading USG sometimes gives me a literal headache. Can you help a gal out?

Please, can you make the ink darker so it contrasts more and is easier to read? And if there's a possibility that you could make it even a squirrel's hair bigger, that'd be cool too. I might still need to get out a magnifying glass to aid my aging eyes, but darker ink would help a lot for those of us readers with older peepers.

I also had two questions about issue #16: Is the corgi when Doreen is 10 related to the corgis (mer- and otherwise) from MOCKINGBIRD?

Then, when she's 20, she says that she saved Iron Man before she helped the Hulk. Did I miss that happening?

Many thanks for the terrific book, and hopes for many more years of Doreen and team.

Kristin Boldon
Minneapolis, MN

RYAN: You did miss that happening! But that's forgivable, because it's from a story that came out 25 years ago! In Squirrel Girl's first appearance she saved Iron Man from Doctor Doom, and the two of them have been pals ever since. (Iron Man and Doreen, I mean. The relationship between Doom and Doreen is a bit more complicated.) I do like that the text at the bottom is small – it makes it like a fun surprise – but we might be able to make it more readable! As for the corgi, I will defer to Erica, the Corgi Expert on this team.

ERICA: The corgi doesn't have to do with anything except that Ryan wrote in the script that it's a big vicious dog and I thought: 1. A corgi would be funnier and 2. I don't want to perpetuate any bully-breed myths.

P.S. Ryan, the text doesn't have to be that big of a secret.

Hello SQUIRREL GIRL writers,

I've noticed something...wrong.

In the letters page to #13, Erica tells us that "As a vegetarian, Doreen would have to be fairly conscious of her diet...[Squirrels] also need fungi, greens, fruits and insects ... So Doreen's vegetarianism is less about being like a squirrel and more about realizing that animals are sentient."

Okay, fair enough.

BUT, in GREAT LAKES AVENGERS #1, Doreen is seen eating lobster. You can even see the claw sticking out of her mouth.

Was it a lapse? Does she make an exception for seafood? (Many people do, and call themselves vegetarian.) Was it a shapeshifter in disguise? Why does somebody with the powers of a squirrel get bored in the woods? Maybe an android version of her?

Mik Bennett
Canberra, Australia

P.S. Sorry, issue 01011 doesn't contain the story of how I learned to count in binary on my fingers—I learned that from a girl when I was in, uh, grade 11 or 12. I actually go from thumb to pinky, where SG goes pinky to thumb. Either way, be very careful around the number 4.

RYAN: My pal Zac Gorman wrote that comic, so you'd have to ask him how to explain this APPARENT DISCREPANCY. But if I were to hazard a guess, I would say Zac would definitely 100% say that Doreen was actually eating a soy faux-lobster confit which was coated in a hard nut-derived shell colored red with vegetable-derived inks. Does this food exist in real life? Sadly, not yet. But given that there is already a market for vegetarian food that can pass as meat (I'm looking at you, veggie ground round), are we truly that far off from a vegetarian "lobster" whose claws you can stuff into your mouth? All I can say is: HOPEFULLY NOT.

ERICA: ZAAAAAAAAAAC!

Hello, Squirrel Girl Team!

I'm a reading tutor, and I've been sharing THE UNBEATABLE SQUIRREL GIRL with one of my little students as her end-of-lesson treat. She wanted to send you a note about how much she loves Squirrel Girl, but please be aware that the note is from her alter ego — a super hero with "all the powers" named SuperZoe! who fights a new villain every day. Thanks for all your great work, and the fun you've given us.

Best,
Ellie

(Here is SuperZoe!'s letter. All words and exclamation points are her own.)

Dear Ryan and Erica,

It is so awesome!!! My name is Zoe! I love Squirrel Girl! I love that she fights crime and it's really cool that she puts her tail in her pants. I would like if Squirrel Girl went to Hawaii and took a break and had a vacation. And then the super heroes can all come to Hawaii where they fight crime, and Squirrel Girl will say "Ahhh! What are you doing? I need a break!"

Please make more books about Squirrel Girl because she is amazing! MORE BOOKS PLEASE!!!!!!!!!!

From
SuperZoe!!!!!!!!!!!!!!!!!!
Age 7

RYAN: Hi Ellie, I love that you've been using our comic as a literacy treat! I think that's the greatest compliment you can give a piece of writing, so thank you so much! The rest of this is from Squirrel Girl to SuperZoe!, so please forward this letter accordingly.

ERICA: HI SUPERZOE! I wish we could take credit for the tail in the pants, but that's from forever ago! All the way back to 1992! I like your vacation idea. We could all use it!

SQUIRREL GIRL: Hi SuperZoe!!

Your letter was awesome and you are awesome. I've got squirrel powers but you've got ALL the powers, so should we team up sometime? I think the answer is: UM, YES PLEASE??

If I went on vacation I wouldn't mind if other super heroes joined me, but if they brought super villains with them then I would totally say "Ahhh! What are you doing? I need a break!" Preferably while sipping a vacation drink out of a coconut. Can it be a vacation without drinking out of a giant nut? I for one prefer not to find out.

Yours in justice,
Squirrel Girl

Next Issue:

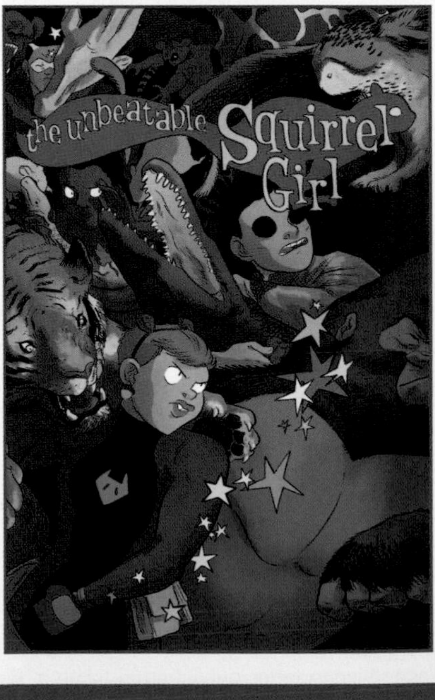
the unbeatable Squirrel Girl

Attention, Squirrel Scouts! Make sure to check out our production blog, **unbeatablesquirrelgirl.tumblr.com**, where we post behind-the-scenes stuff on how the book gets made, along with all sorts of cool things *you* make: fanart, cosplay, whatever!

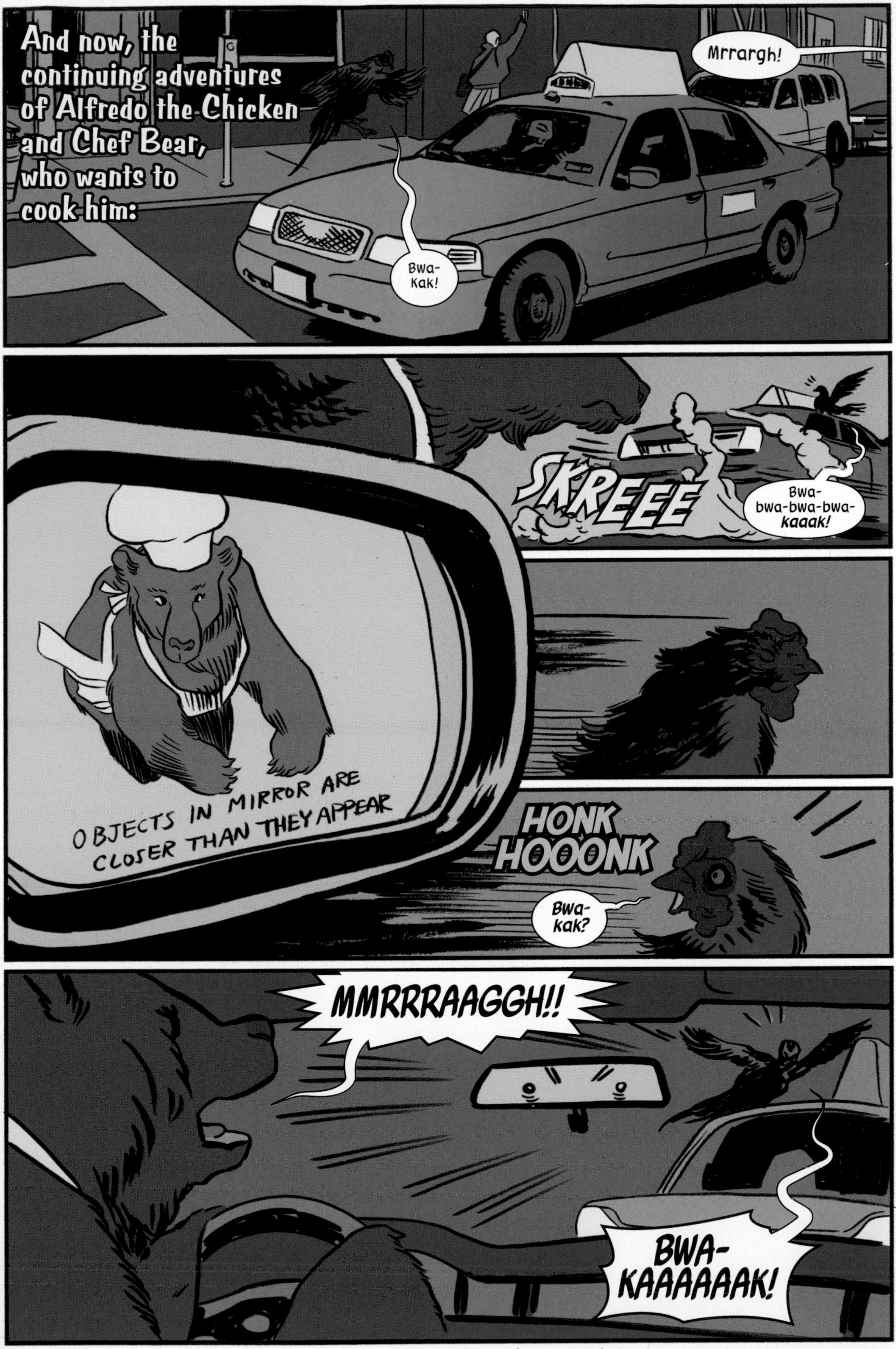

And now, the continuing adventures of Alfredo the Chicken and Chef Bear, who wants to cook him:
Mrrargh!
Bwa-Kak!
SKREEE
Bwa-bwa-bwa-bwa-kaaak!
OBJECTS IN MIRROR ARE CLOSER THAN THEY APPEAR
HONK HOOONK
Bwa-kak?
MMRRRAAGGH!!
BWA-KAAAAAAK!

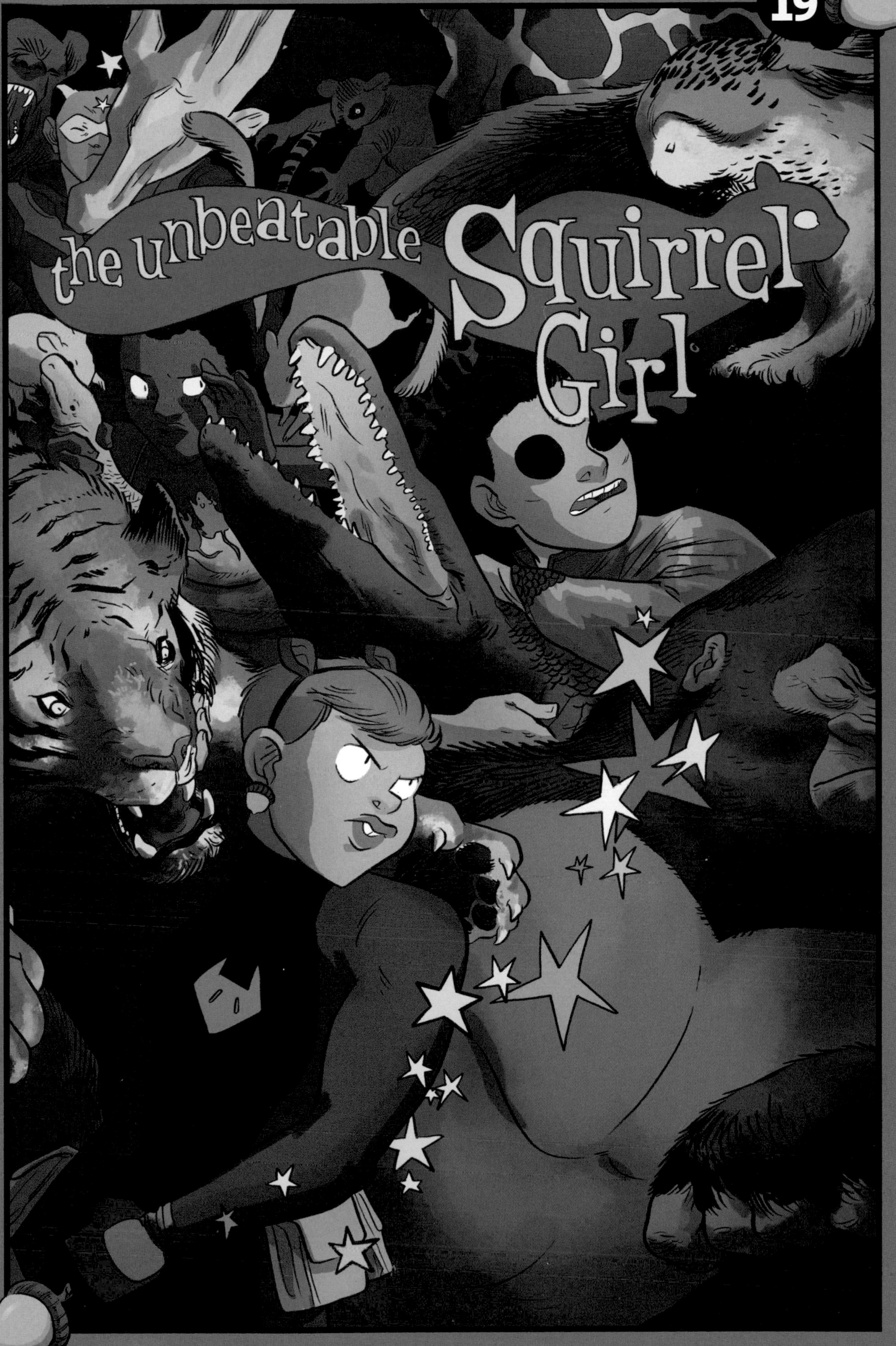
the unbeatable Squirrel Girl

Doreen Green isn't just a second-year computer science student: she secretly also has all the powers of both squirrel and girl! She uses her amazing abilities to fight crime ***and*** *be as awesome as possible. You know her as...* ***The Unbeatable Squirrel Girl!*** *Find out what she's been up to, with...*

Squirrel Girl *in a nutshell*

Squirrel Girl @unbeatablesg
Hey so remember how I was kinda bragging about the flying suit a new friend gave me a while back?? Remember how that was a thing?

Squirrel Girl @unbeatablesg
Remember how I was all "fav this if you're a criminal who isn't gonna do crimes anymore now that you know I'MMA FLY NOW"?

Squirrel Girl @unbeatablesg
Remember how I then went on to post how I was definitely gonna KEEP flying forever, b/c my new suit was great and definitely not sabotaged?

Squirrel Girl @unbeatablesg
Remember how all of those were posted in a manner that might, in retrospect, be described as "hubristic"??

Squirrel Girl @unbeatablesg
Well uh

Squirrel Girl @unbeatablesg
Turns out that Greek myth that warned us not to fly too close to the sun was NOT ENTIRELY OFF BASE, IN VERY LIMITED CIRCUMSTANCES??

Tony Stark @starkmantony
@unbeatablesg Icarus, right? Kid and his dad invent wings from wax and feathers, kid flies too close to the sun, wings melt, the end.

Tony Stark @starkmantony
@unbeatablesg Here's the thing about that. So Icarus and his dad invent AMAZING SUITS from SCRATCH while being held PRISONER--

Tony Stark @starkmantony
@unbeatablesg (an idea which, for obvious reasons, really appeals to me on a fundamental level)

Tony Stark @starkmantony
@unbeatablesg --and then one of them dies because he's TOO SUCCESSFUL at FLYING SUIT INVENTION, and that's supposed to teach us something?

Tony Stark @starkmantony
@unbeatablesg I'll tell you what it teaches me. It teaches me that whoever is telling it never studied science.

Tony Stark @starkmantony
@unbeatablesg There's a reason why Everest is snowy at the top instead of being covered in beach towels, sunglasses, and mojitos.

Tony Stark @starkmantony
@unbeatablesg In flight range, air pressure goes down as you go up, and gases under less pressure are slower and colder. Hence, freezing.

Tony Stark @starkmantony
@unbeatablesg In conclusion, it's a ridiculous myth, and in real life Icarus would've a) survived, and b) been lauded as a great engineer.

Tony Stark @starkmantony
@unbeatablesg And I would've hired him.

Tony Stark @starkmantony
@unbeatablesg Anyway. Don't feel bad that you trusted someone. That's what you DO, Squirrel Girl. What are you gonna do, not trust anyone?

Tony Stark @starkmantony
@unbeatablesg That's a horrible way to live your life. And it's not you.

Tony Stark @starkmantony
@unbeatablesg You did nothing wrong. And if there's anything I can do to help, you just let me know.

Tony Stark @starkmantony
@unbeatablesg I may be a disembodied AI in a computer now, but I still know who my friends are.

Squirrel Girl @unbeatablesg
@starkmantony AW TONY <3

Squirrel Girl @unbeatablesg
@starkmantony You're the greatest, holy crap

Squirrel Girl @unbeatablesg
@starkmantony Also it's cute how you keep claiming to be an AI even though that is CLEARLY NOT THE CASE

Squirrel Girl @unbeatablesg
@starkmantony

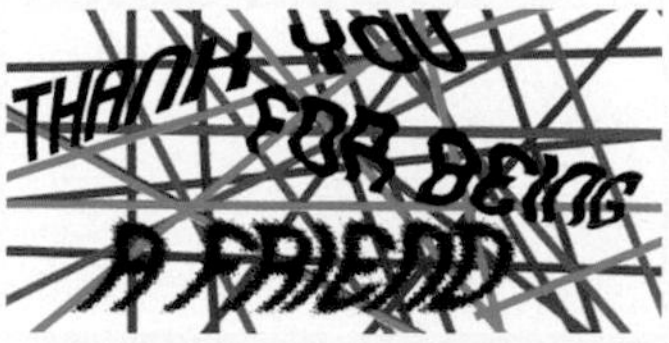
THANK YOU FOR BEING A FRIEND

Tony Stark @starkmantony
@unbeatablesg Listen, I keep telling you, I can still read those no problem so it's really not a big deal for me.

search!

#markII

#ascuteastheyaredeadly

#howardtheduck

#howardthesurlyguyonthestreet

#chefbear

#alfredothechicken

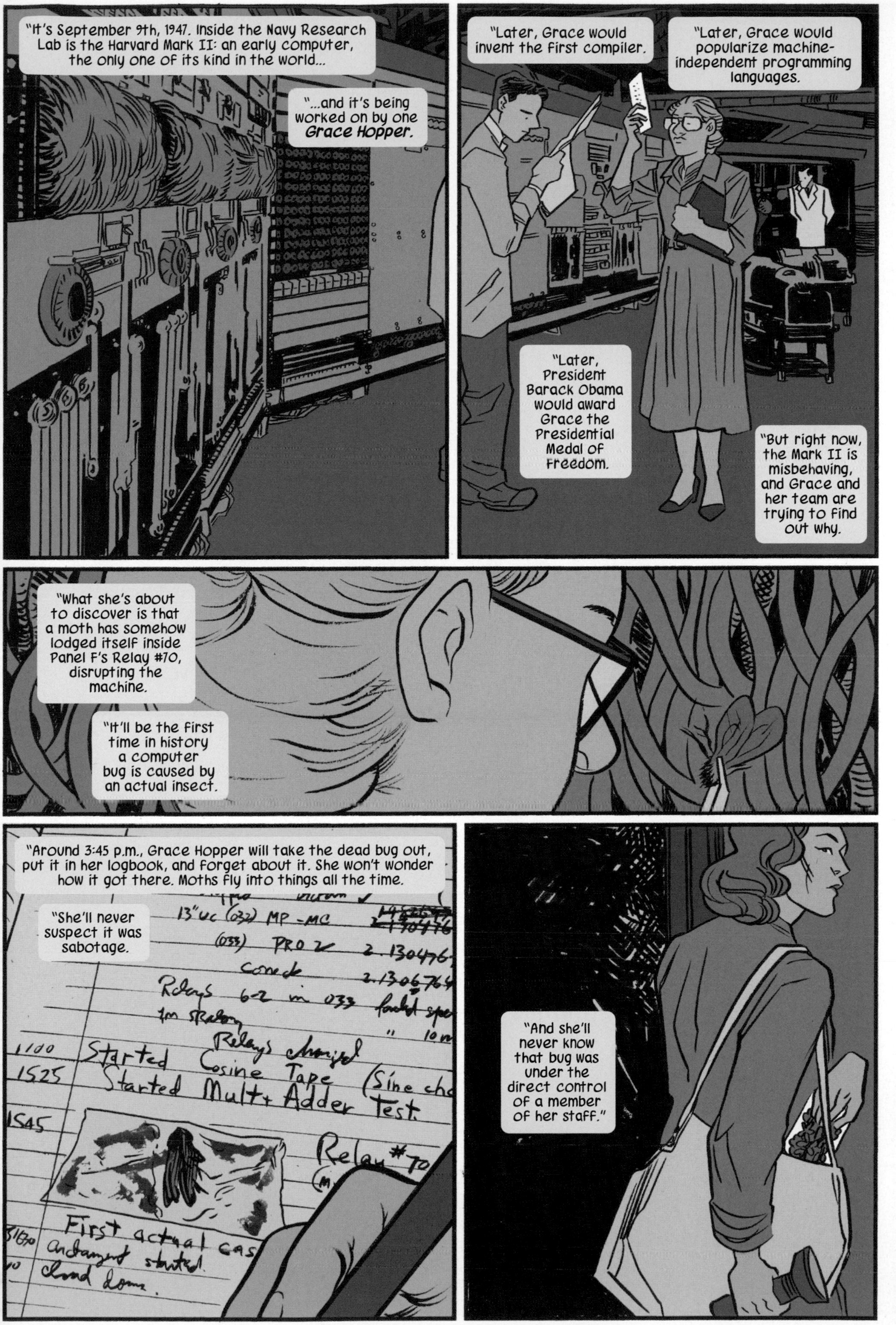
"It's September 9th, 1947. Inside the Navy Research Lab is the Harvard Mark II: an early computer, the only one of its kind in the world...
"...and it's being worked on by one *Grace Hopper.*
"Later, Grace would invent the first compiler.
"Later, Grace would popularize machine-independent programming languages.
"Later, President Barack Obama would award Grace the Presidential Medal of Freedom.
"But right now, the Mark II is misbehaving, and Grace and her team are trying to find out why.
"What she's about to discover is that a moth has somehow lodged itself inside Panel F's Relay #70, disrupting the machine.
"It'll be the first time in history a computer bug is caused by an actual insect.
"Around 3:45 p.m., Grace Hopper will take the dead bug out, put it in her logbook, and forget about it. She won't wonder how it got there. Moths fly into things all the time.
"She'll never suspect it was sabotage.
Relays changed
1100 Started Cosine Tape
1525 Started Mult+ Adder Test.
1545 Relay #70
First actual case
"And she'll never know that bug was under the direct control of a member of her staff."

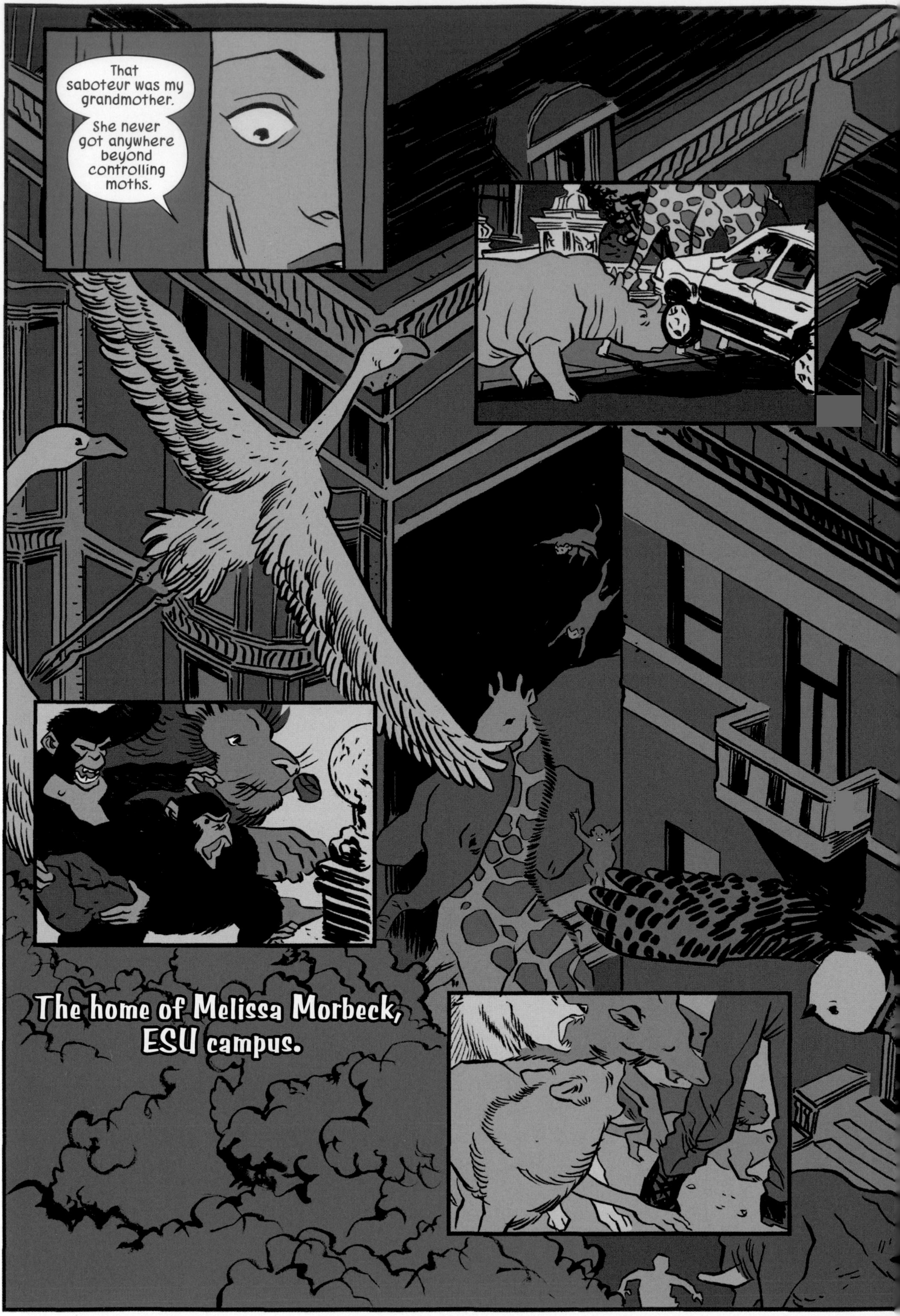
That saboteur was my grandmother.
She never got anywhere beyond controlling moths.
The home of Melissa Morbeck, ESU campus.

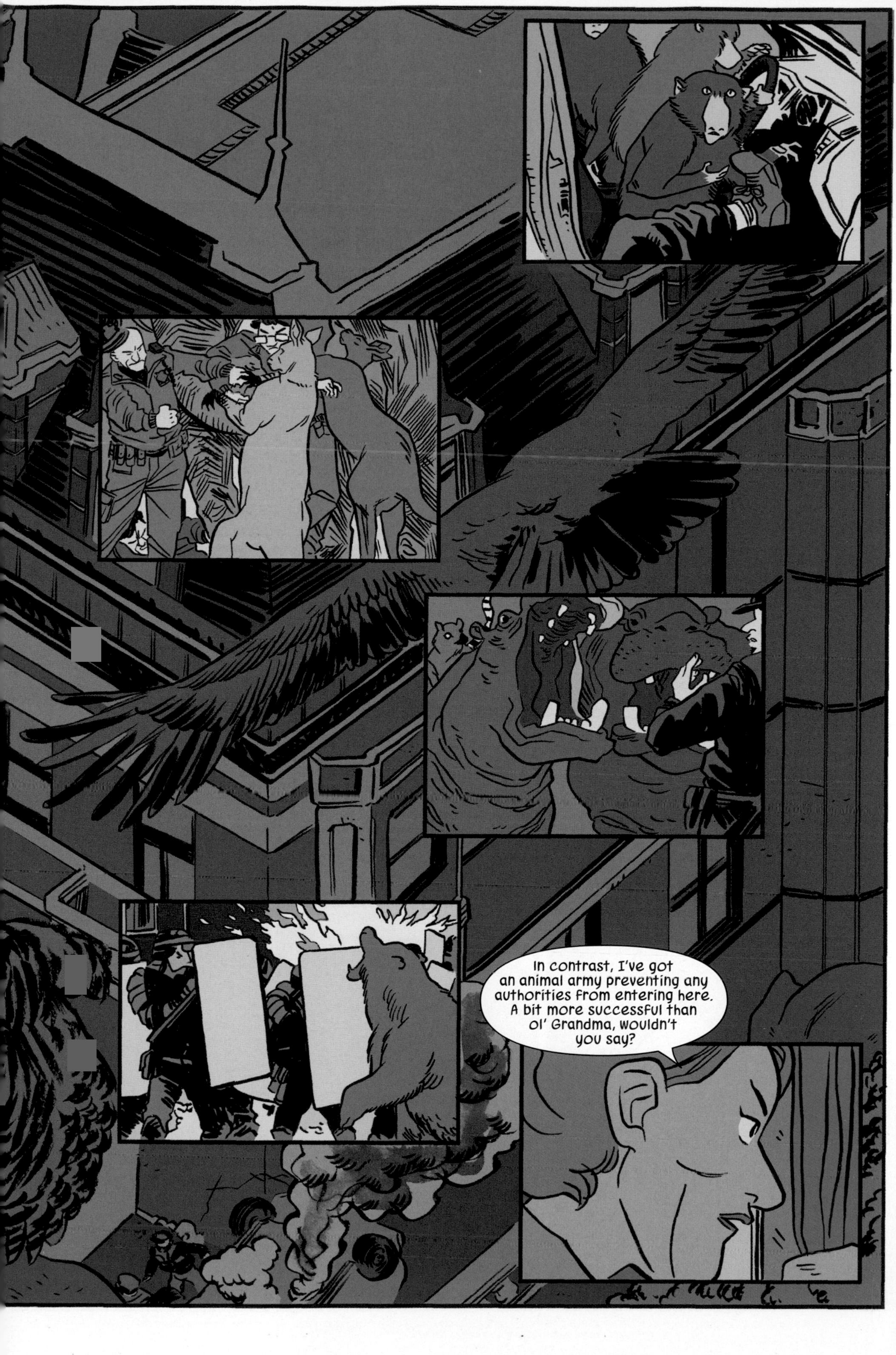
In contrast, I've got an animal army preventing any authorities from entering here. A bit more successful than ol' Grandma, wouldn't you say?

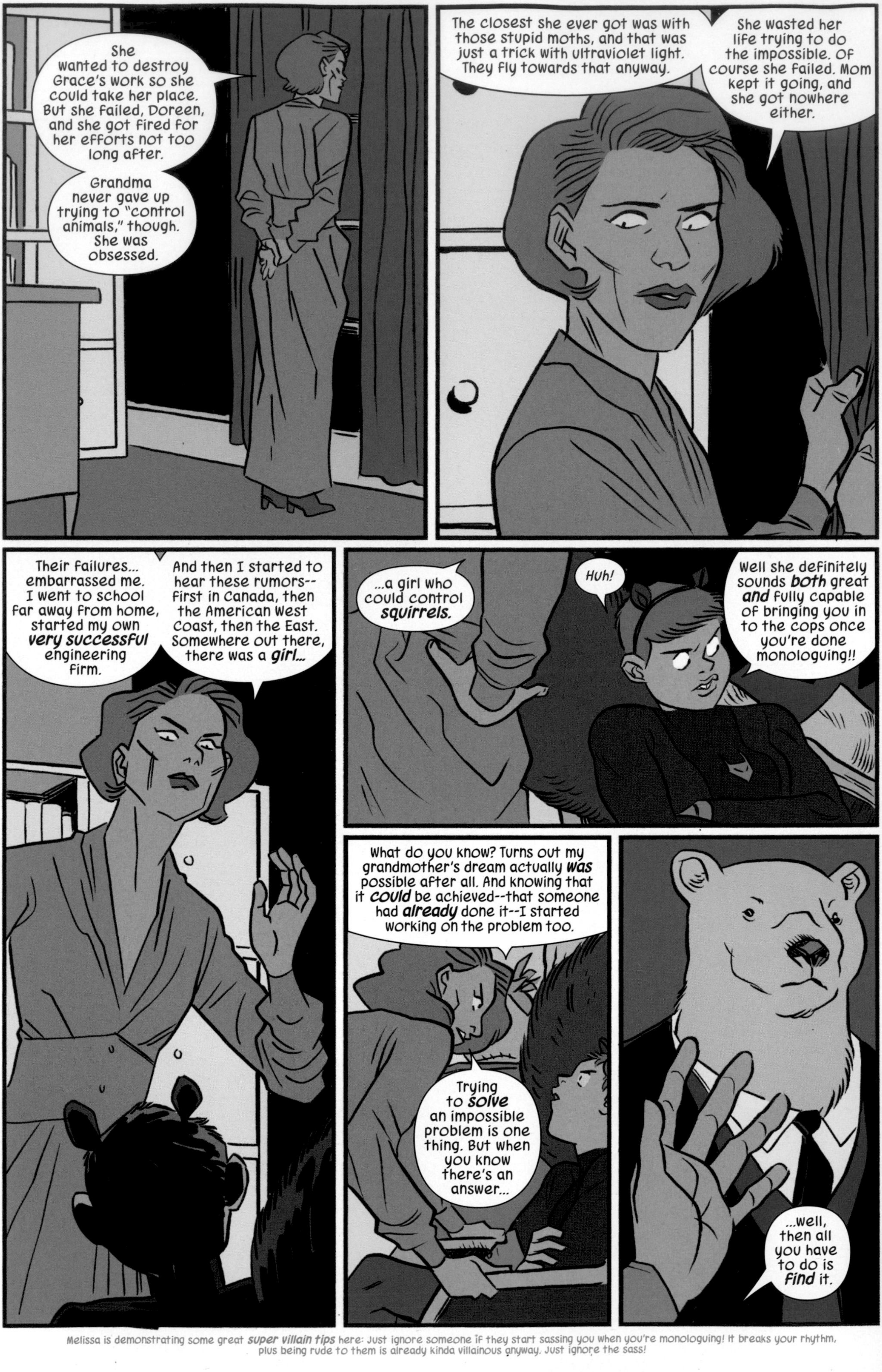
She wanted to destroy Grace's work so she could take her place. But she failed, Doreen, and she got fired for her efforts not too long after.
Grandma never gave up trying to "control animals," though. She was obsessed.
The closest she ever got was with those stupid moths, and that was just a trick with ultraviolet light. They fly towards that anyway.
She wasted her life trying to do the impossible. Of course she failed. Mom kept it going, and she got nowhere either.
Their failures... embarrassed me. I went to school far away from home, started my own **very successful** engineering firm.
And then I started to hear these rumors--first in Canada, then the American West Coast, then the East. Somewhere out there, there was a **girl...**
...a girl who could control **squirrels.**
Huh!
Well she definitely sounds **both** great **and** fully capable of bringing you in to the cops once you're done monologuing!!
What do you know? Turns out my grandmother's dream actually **was** possible after all. And knowing that it **could** be achieved--that someone had **already** done it--I started working on the problem too.
Trying to **solve** an impossible problem is one thing. But when you know there's an answer...
...well, then all you have to do is **find** it.

Melissa is demonstrating some great *super villain tips* here: Just ignore someone if they start sassing you when you're monologuing! It breaks your rhythm, plus being rude to them is already kinda villainous anyway. Just ignore the sass!

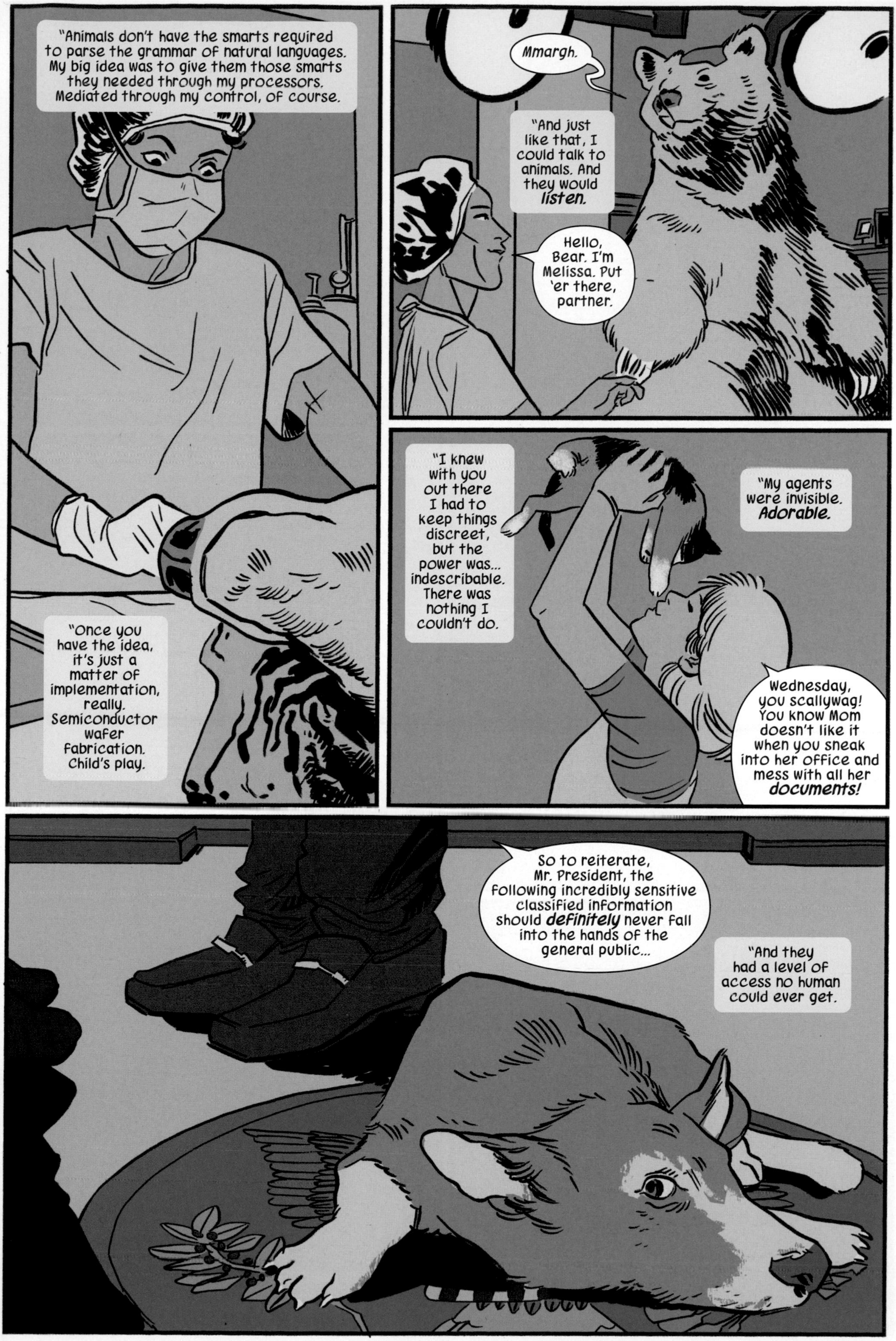
"Animals don't have the smarts required to parse the grammar of natural languages. My big idea was to give them those smarts they needed through my processors. Mediated through my control, of course.
"Once you have the idea, it's just a matter of implementation, really. Semiconductor wafer fabrication. Child's play.
Mmargh.
"And just like that, I could talk to animals. And they would *listen.*
Hello, Bear. I'm Melissa. Put 'er there, partner.
"I knew with you out there I had to keep things discreet, but the power was... indescribable. There was nothing I couldn't do.
"My agents were invisible. *Adorable.*
Wednesday, you scallywag! You know Mom doesn't like it when you sneak into her office and mess with all her *documents!*
So to reiterate, Mr. President, the following incredibly sensitive classified information should *definitely* never fall into the hands of the general public...
"And they had a level of access no human could ever get.

And here's a second *super villain tip*: Always turn the President's dog into a spy. What a great tip! Just don't lend this comic to any real-life super villains because these are some *primo tips!* Also: I'm beginning to think writing super villain tips in our comic *might* not be the brightest idea we've ever had??

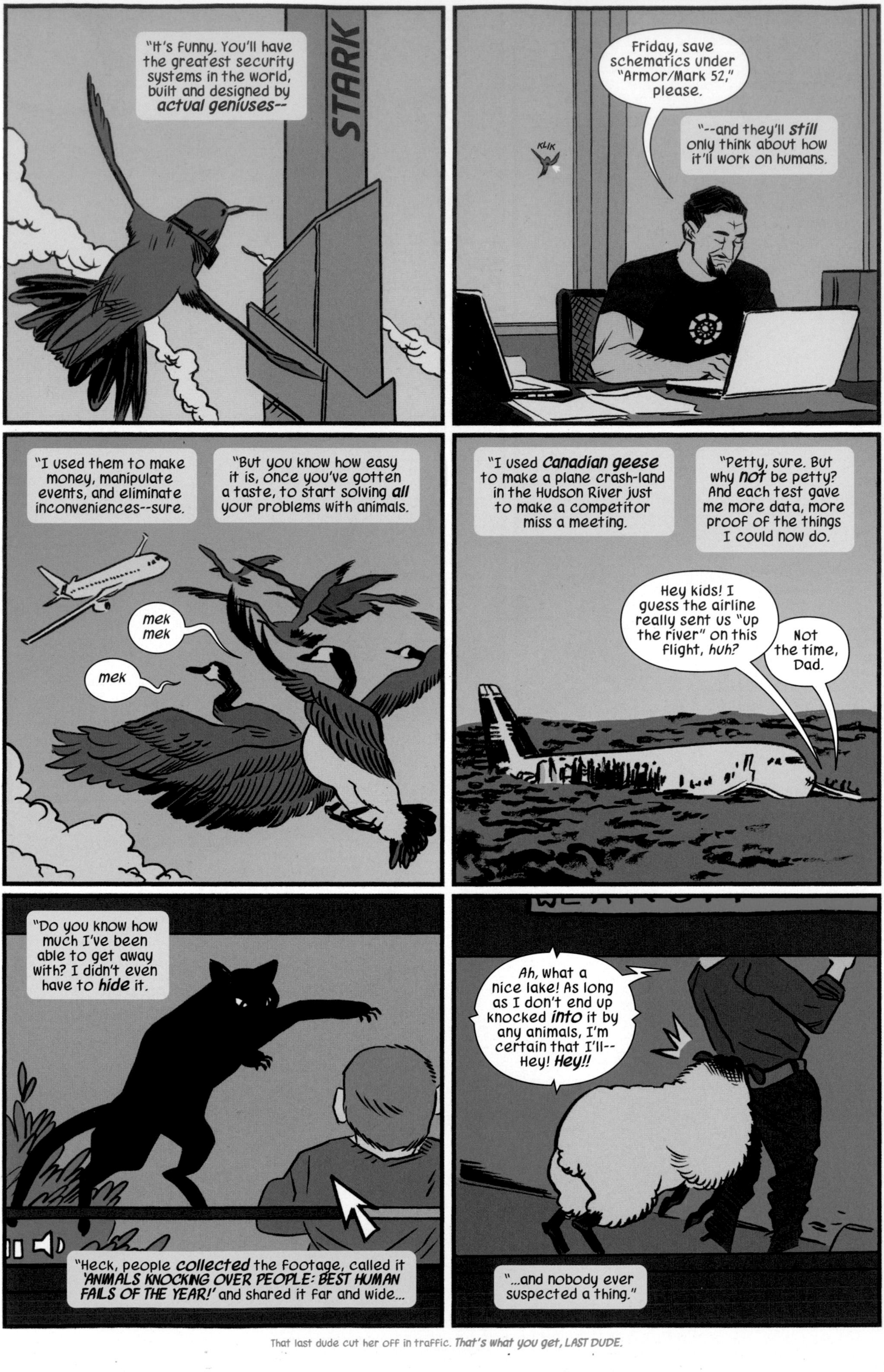
"It's funny. You'll have the greatest security systems in the world, built and designed by actual geniuses--
STARK
Friday, save schematics under "Armor/Mark 52," please.
KLIK
"--and they'll still only think about how it'll work on humans.
"I used them to make money, manipulate events, and eliminate inconveniences--sure.
"But you know how easy it is, once you've gotten a taste, to start solving all your problems with animals.
mek mek
mek
"I used Canadian geese to make a plane crash-land in the Hudson River just to make a competitor miss a meeting.
"Petty, sure. But why not be petty? And each test gave me more data, more proof of the things I could now do.
Hey kids! I guess the airline really sent us "up the river" on this flight, huh?
Not the time, Dad.
"Do you know how much I've been able to get away with? I didn't even have to hide it.
"Heck, people collected the footage, called it 'ANIMALS KNOCKING OVER PEOPLE: BEST HUMAN FAILS OF THE YEAR!' and shared it far and wide...
Ah, what a nice lake! As long as I don't end up knocked into it by any animals, I'm certain that I'll-- Hey! Hey!!
"...and nobody ever suspected a thing."

That last dude cut her off in traffic. *That's what you get, LAST DUDE.*

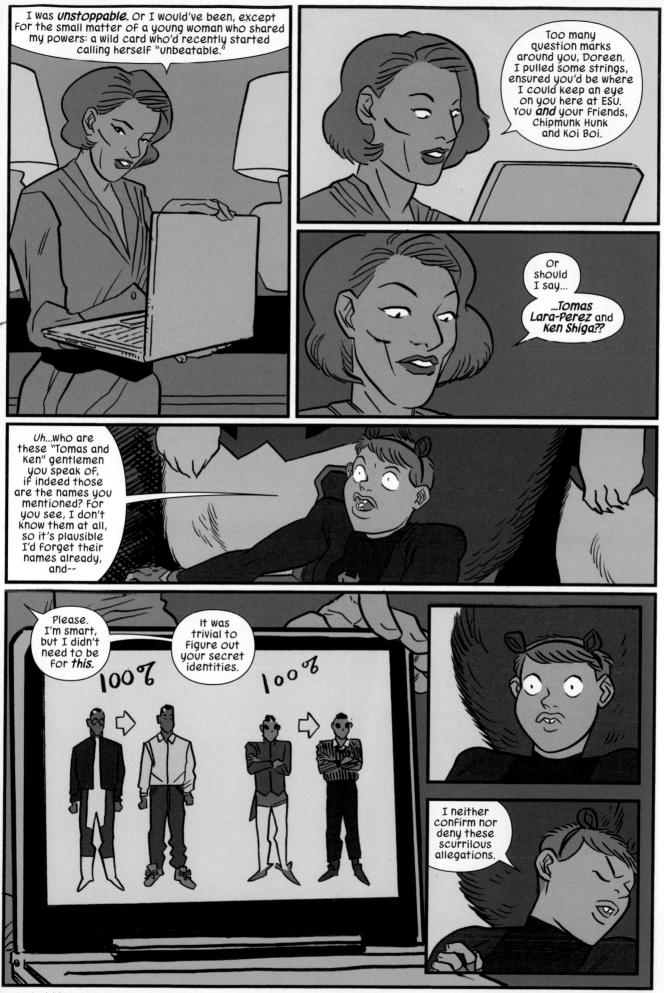

I was **unstoppable**. Or I would've been, except for the small matter of a young woman who shared my powers: a wild card who'd recently started calling herself "unbeatable."

Too many question marks around you, Doreen. I pulled some strings, ensured you'd be where I could keep an eye on you here at ESU. You **and** your friends, Chipmunk Hunk and Koi Boi.

Or should I say... ...*Tomas Lara-Perez* and *Ken Shiga??*

Uh...who are these "Tomas and Ken" gentlemen you speak of, if indeed those are the names you mentioned? For you see, I don't know them at all, so it's plausible I'd forget their names already, and--

Please. I'm smart, but I didn't need to be for *this*.

It was trivial to figure out your secret identities.

100% → 100%

I neither confirm nor deny these scurrilous allegations.

How hard did I resist the "squirrels are members of the 'Sciuridae' biological family, so instead of 'scurrilous allegations,' Doreen could say 'sciuridious allegations'" pun? *Not hard enough, it seems??*

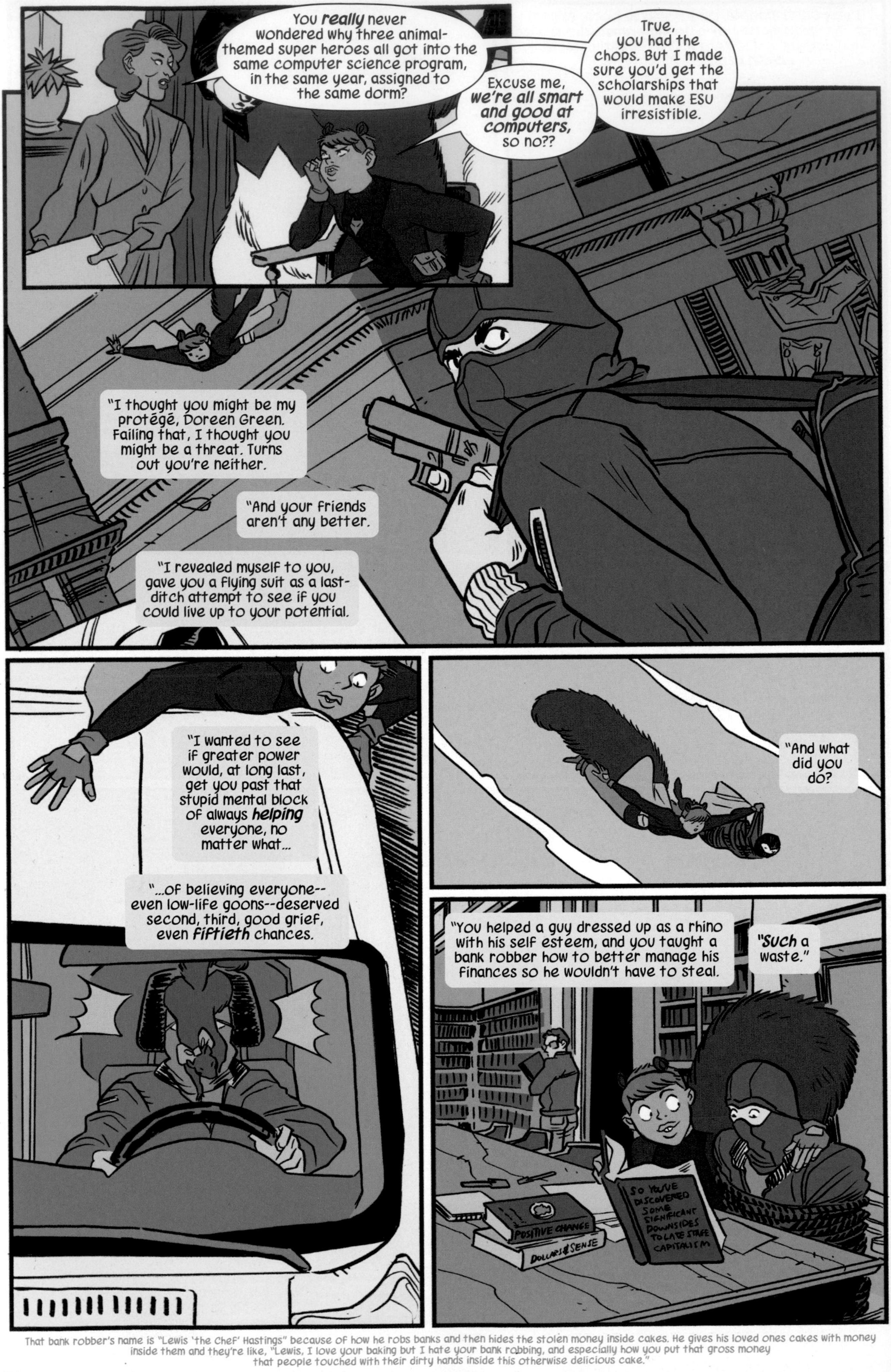
You really never wondered why three animal-themed super heroes all got into the same computer science program, in the same year, assigned to the same dorm?
Excuse me, we're all smart and good at computers, so no??
True, you had the chops. But I made sure you'd get the scholarships that would make ESU irresistible.
"I thought you might be my protégé, Doreen Green. Failing that, I thought you might be a threat. Turns out you're neither.
"And your friends aren't any better.
"I revealed myself to you, gave you a flying suit as a last-ditch attempt to see if you could live up to your potential.
"I wanted to see if greater power would, at long last, get you past that stupid mental block of always helping everyone, no matter what...
"...of believing everyone--even low-life goons--deserved second, third, good grief, even fiftieth chances.
"And what did you do?
"You helped a guy dressed up as a rhino with his self esteem, and you taught a bank robber how to better manage his finances so he wouldn't have to steal.
"Such a waste."
POSITIVE CHANGE
DOLLARS & SENSE
SO YOU'VE DISCOVERED SOME SIGNIFICANT DOWNSIDES TO LATE STAGE CAPITALISM

That bank robber's name is "Lewis 'the Chef' Hastings" because of how he robs banks and then hides the stolen money inside cakes. He gives his loved ones cakes with money inside them and they're like, "Lewis, I love your baking but I hate your bank robbing, and especially how you put that gross money that people touched with their dirty hands inside this otherwise delicious cake."

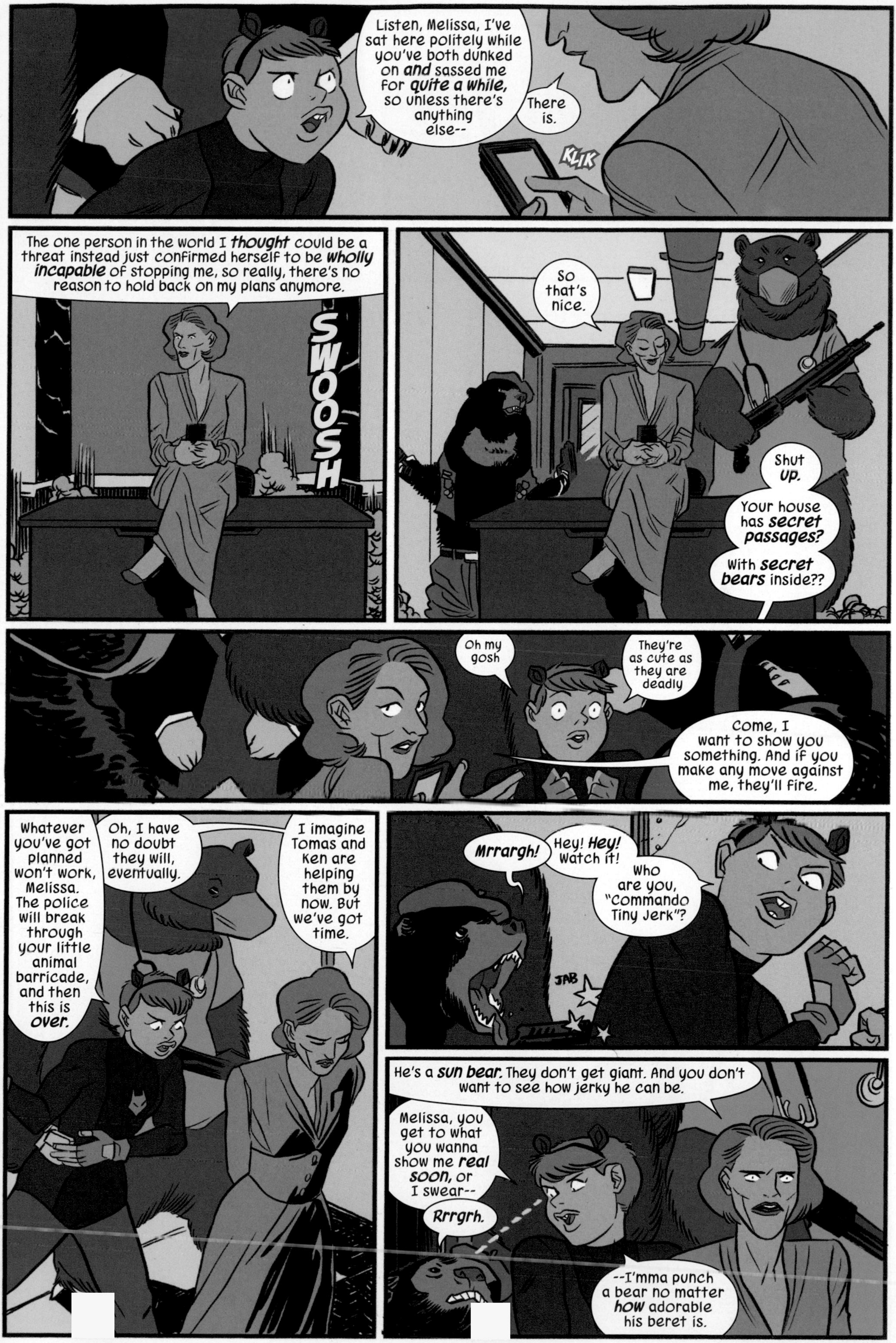
Listen, Melissa, I've sat here politely while you've both dunked on and sassed me for quite a while, so unless there's anything else--
There is.
KLIK
The one person in the world I thought could be a threat instead just confirmed herself to be wholly incapable of stopping me, so really, there's no reason to hold back on my plans anymore.
SWOOSH
So that's nice.
Shut up.
Your house has secret passages?
With secret bears inside??
Oh my gosh
They're as cute as they are deadly
Come, I want to show you something. And if you make any move against me, they'll fire.
Whatever you've got planned won't work, Melissa. The police will break through your little animal barricade, and then this is over.
Oh, I have no doubt they will, eventually.
I imagine Tomas and Ken are helping them by now. But we've got time.
Mrrargh!
Hey! Hey! Watch it!
Who are you, "Commando Tiny Jerk"?
JAB
He's a sun bear. They don't get giant. And you don't want to see how jerky he can be.
Melissa, you get to what you wanna show me real soon, or I swear--
Rrrgrh.
--I'mma punch a bear no matter how adorable his beret is.

They're not just as cute as they are deadly, Doreen: they're also as adorable as they are impatient with your stalling tactics!! And that is *by design.*

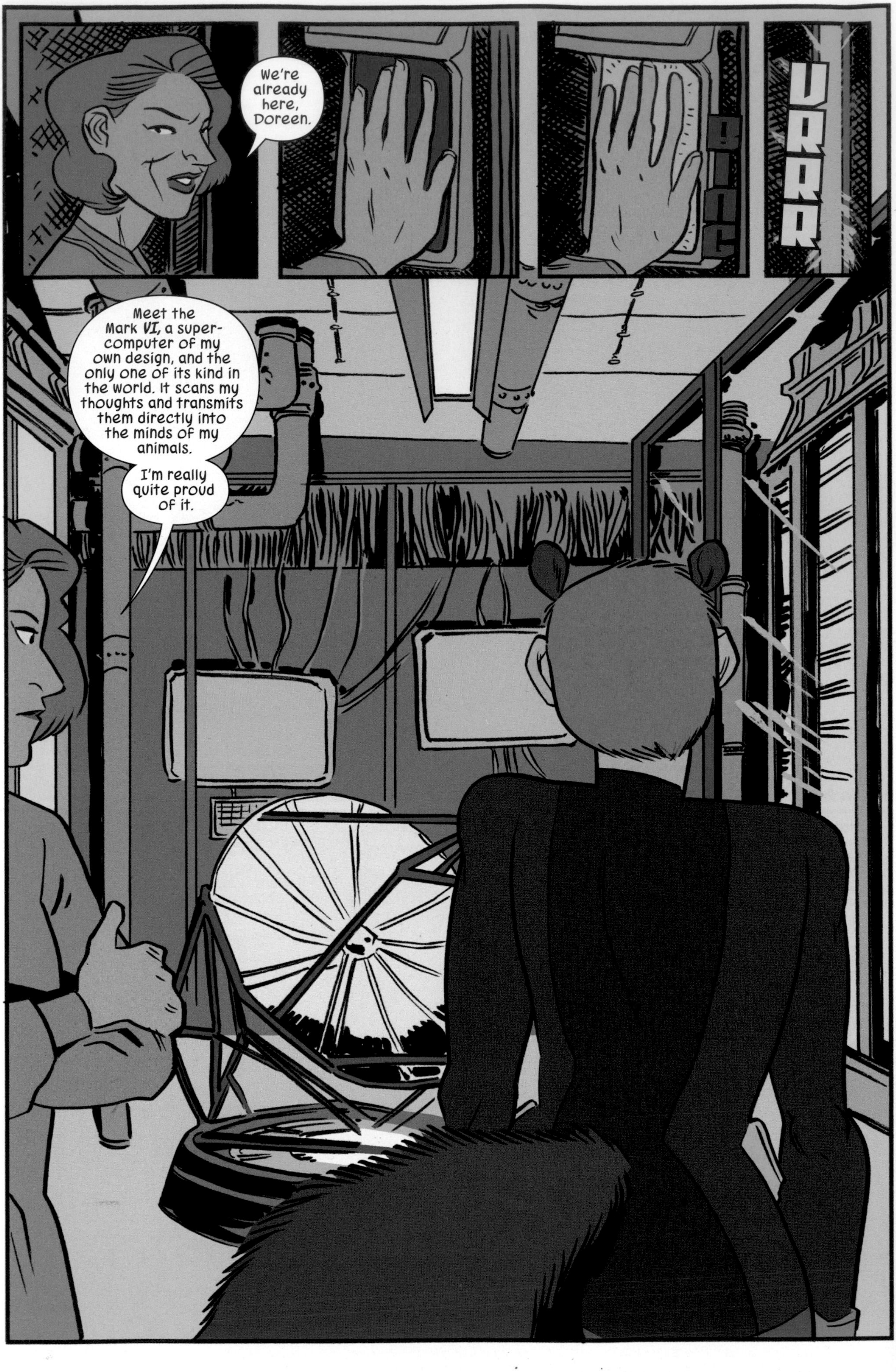
We're already here, Doreen.
BIING
VRRR
Meet the Mark VI, a super-computer of my own design, and the only one of its kind in the world. It scans my thoughts and transmits them directly into the minds of my animals.
I'm really quite proud of it.

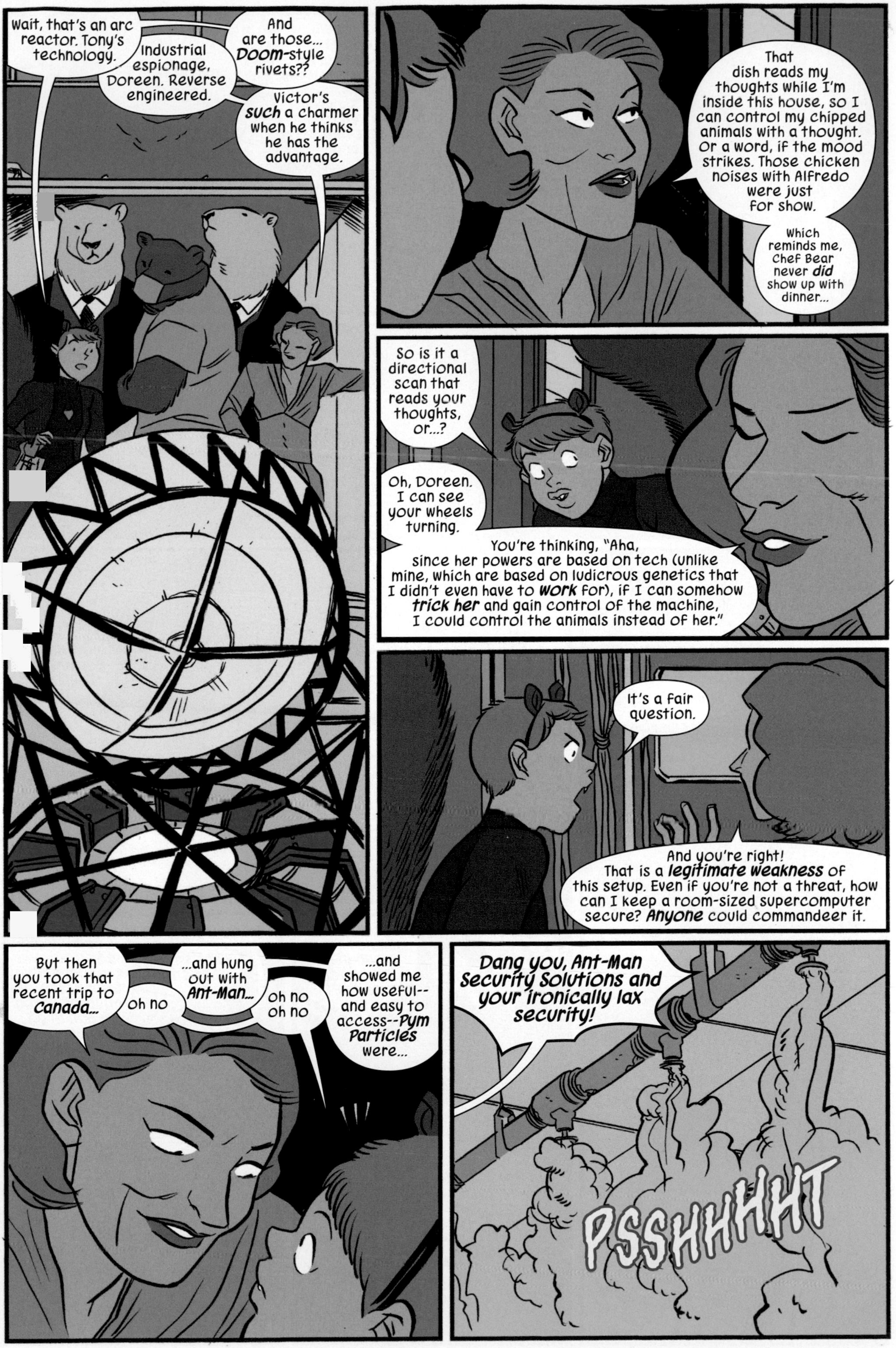
Wait, that's an arc reactor. Tony's technology.
And are those... DOOM-style rivets??
Industrial espionage, Doreen. Reverse engineered.
Victor's SUCH a charmer when he thinks he has the advantage.
That dish reads my thoughts while I'm inside this house, so I can control my chipped animals with a thought. Or a word, if the mood strikes. Those chicken noises with Alfredo were just for show.
Which reminds me, Chef Bear never did show up with dinner...
So is it a directional scan that reads your thoughts, or...?
Oh, Doreen. I can see your wheels turning.
You're thinking, "Aha, since her powers are based on tech (unlike mine, which are based on ludicrous genetics that I didn't even have to work for), if I can somehow trick her and gain control of the machine, I could control the animals instead of her."
It's a fair question.
And you're right! That is a legitimate weakness of this setup. Even if you're not a threat, how can I keep a room-sized supercomputer secure? Anyone could commandeer it.
But then you took that recent trip to Canada...
oh no
...and hung out with Ant-Man...
oh no oh no
...and showed me how useful--and easy to access--Pym Particles were...
Dang you, Ant-Man Security Solutions and your ironically lax security!
PSSHHHHT

I would 100% read a comic called *Dang You, Ant-Man Security Solutions And Your Ironically Lax Security.* Imagine what sorts of hilarious misadventures Ant-Man would get up to in that comic! Someone would steal his stuff, he'd shrink down to ant size so he can scream and kick things without causing a scene, then he'd come back up to normal size and try to continue his very important board meeting like nothing happened.

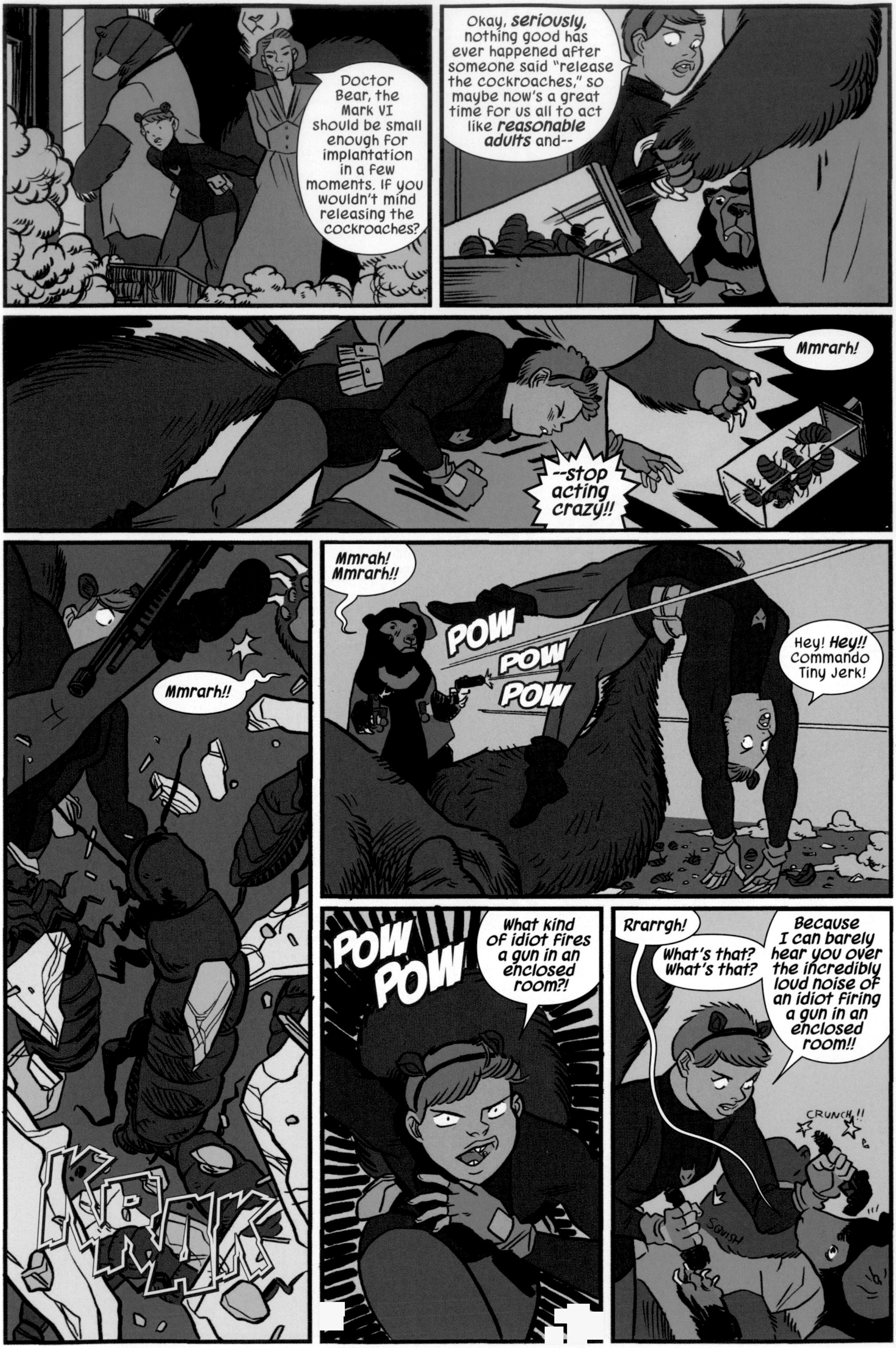
Doctor Bear, the Mark VI should be small enough for implantation in a few moments. If you wouldn't mind releasing the cockroaches?
Okay, seriously, nothing good has ever happened after someone said "release the cockroaches," so maybe now's a great time for us all to act like reasonable adults and--
Mmrarh!
--stop acting crazy!!
Mmrarh!!
KRAK
Mmrah! Mmrarh!!
POW
POW
POW
Hey! Hey!! Commando Tiny Jerk!
POW
POW
What kind of idiot fires a gun in an enclosed room?!
Rrarrgh!
What's that? What's that?
Because I can barely hear you over the incredibly loud noise of an idiot firing a gun in an enclosed room!!
CRUNCH!!
SQUISH

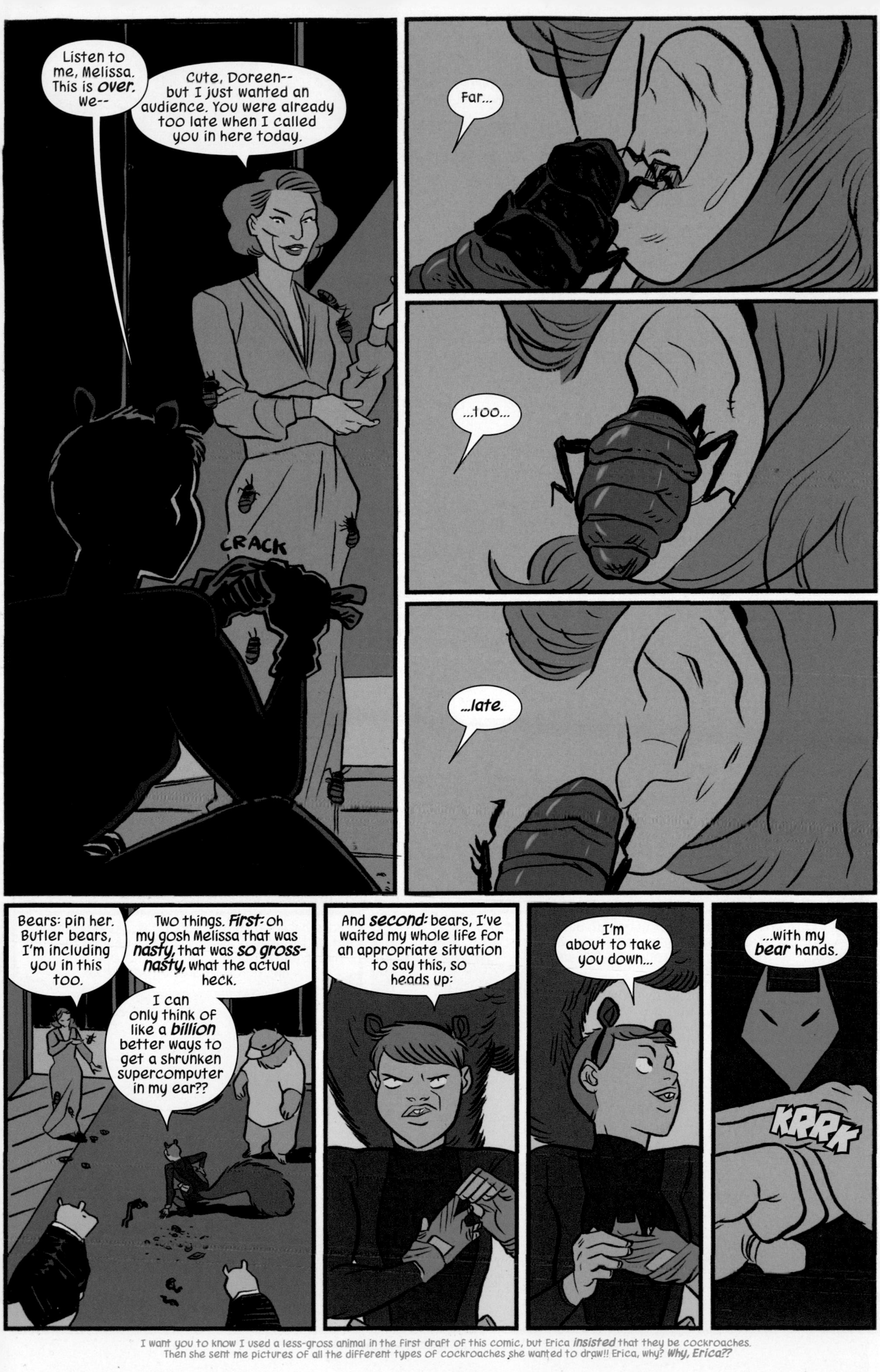
Listen to me, Melissa. This is *over.* We--
Cute, Doreen-- but I just wanted an audience. You were already too late when I called you in here today.
CRACK
Far...
...too...
...late.
Bears: pin her. Butler bears, I'm including you in this too.
Two things. ***First:*** Oh my gosh Melissa that was ***nasty,*** that was ***so gross-nasty,*** what the actual heck.
I can only think of like a ***billion*** better ways to get a shrunken supercomputer in my ear??
And ***second:*** bears, I've waited my whole life for an appropriate situation to say this, so heads up:
I'm about to take you down...
...with my ***bear*** hands.
KRRK

I want you to know I used a less-gross animal in the first draft of this comic, but Erica ***insisted*** that they be cockroaches. Then she sent me pictures of all the different types of cockroaches she wanted to draw!! Erica, why? ***Why, Erica??***

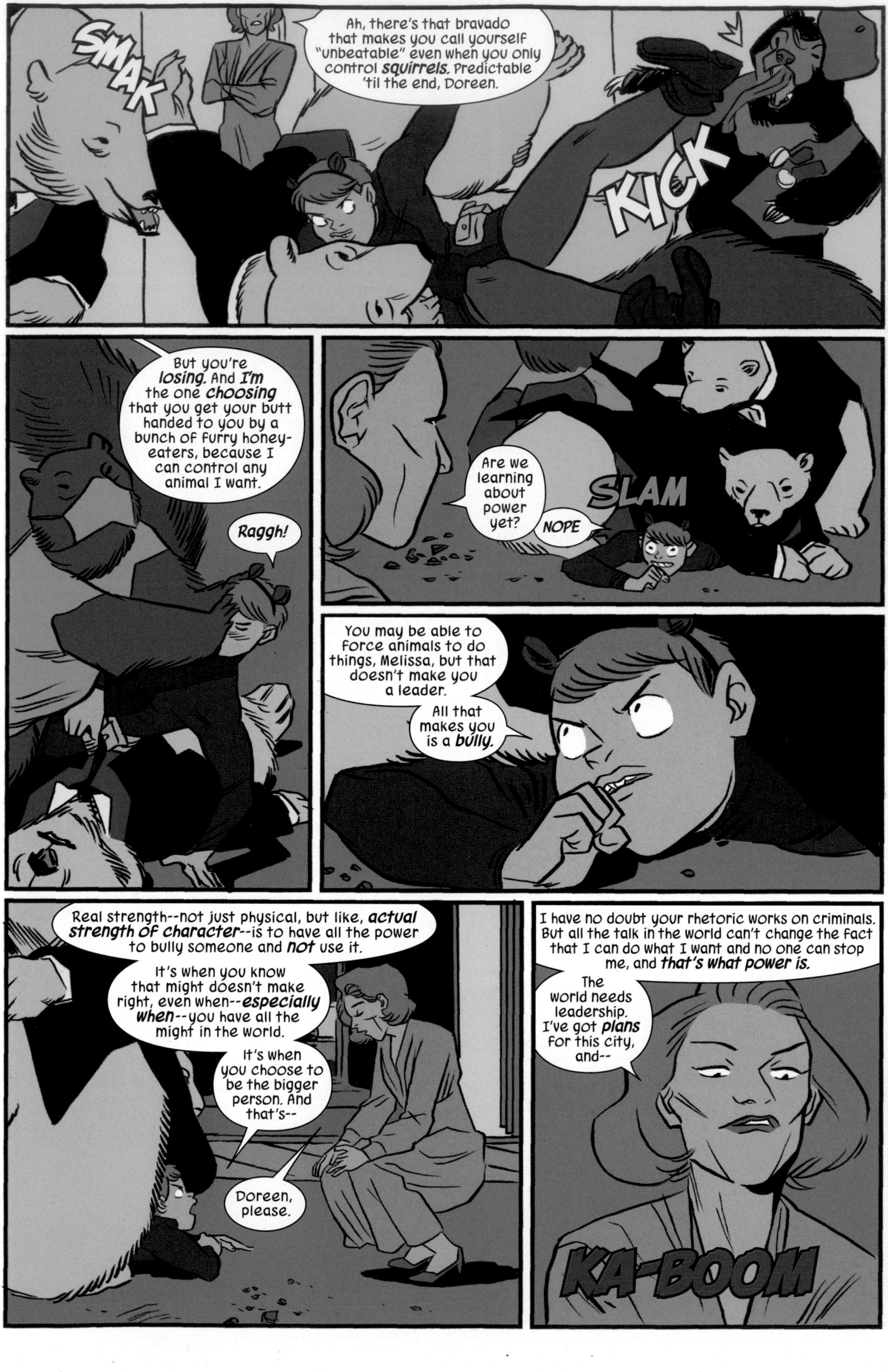
SMAK
Ah, there's that bravado that makes you call yourself "unbeatable" even when you only control squirrels. Predictable 'til the end, Doreen.
KICK
But you're losing. And I'm the one choosing that you get your butt handed to you by a bunch of furry honey-eaters, because I can control any animal I want.
Raggh!
Are we learning about power yet?
SLAM
NOPE
You may be able to force animals to do things, Melissa, but that doesn't make you a leader.
All that makes you is a bully.
Real strength--not just physical, but like, actual strength of character--is to have all the power to bully someone and not use it.
It's when you know that might doesn't make right, even when--especially when--you have all the might in the world.
It's when you choose to be the bigger person. And that's--
Doreen, please.
I have no doubt your rhetoric works on criminals. But all the talk in the world can't change the fact that I can do what I want and no one can stop me, and that's what power is.
The world needs leadership. I've got plans for this city, and--
KA-BOOM

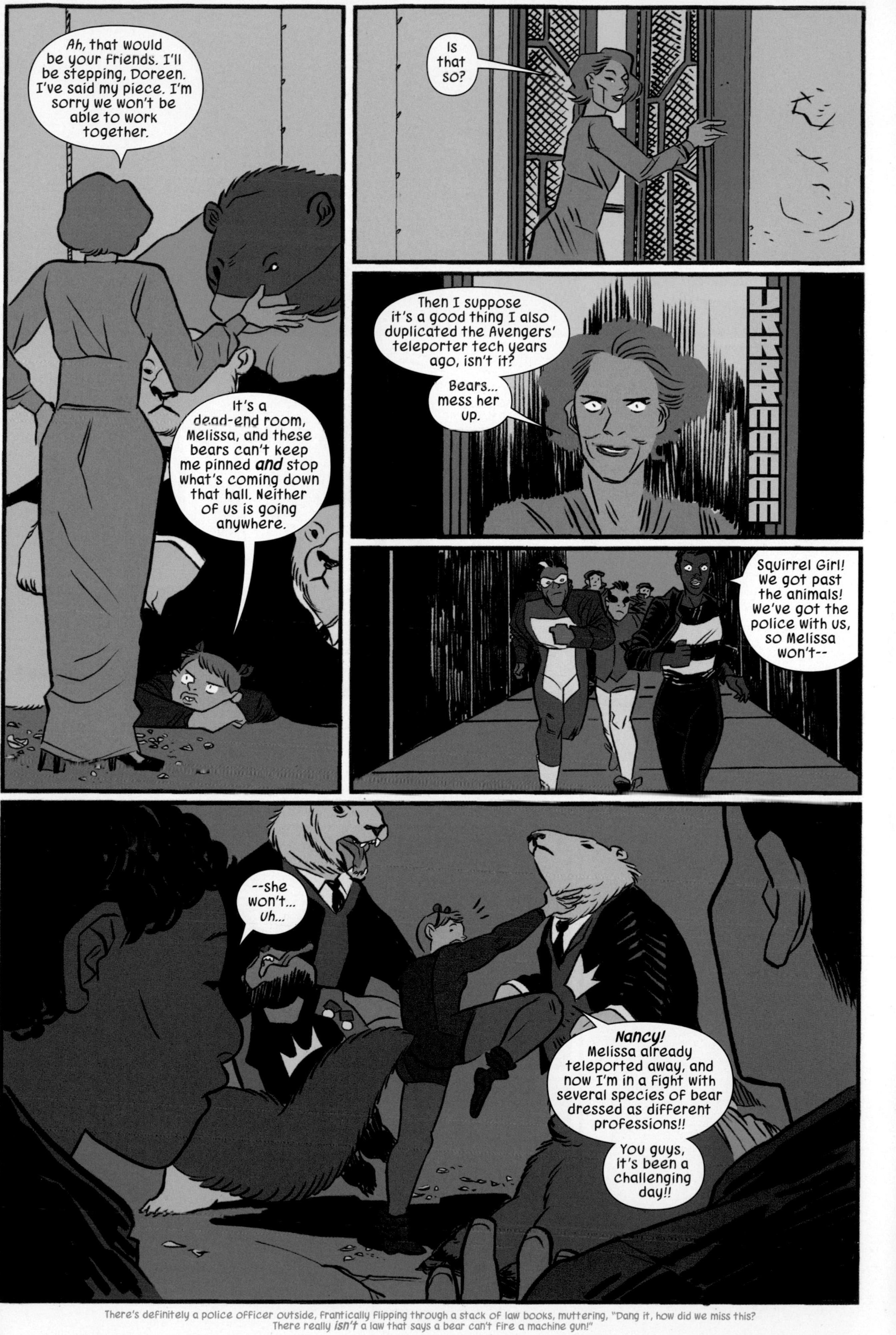
Ah, that would be your friends. I'll be stepping, Doreen. I've said my piece. I'm sorry we won't be able to work together.
It's a dead-end room, Melissa, and these bears can't keep me pinned and stop what's coming down that hall. Neither of us is going anywhere.
Is that so?
Then I suppose it's a good thing I also duplicated the Avengers' teleporter tech years ago, isn't it?
Bears... mess her up.
URRRMMMMM
Squirrel Girl! We got past the animals! We've got the police with us, so Melissa won't--
--she won't... uh...
Nancy! Melissa already teleported away, and now I'm in a fight with several species of bear dressed as different professions!!
You guys, it's been a challenging day!!

There's definitely a police officer outside, frantically flipping through a stack of law books, muttering, "Dang it, how did we miss this? There really *isn't* a law that says a bear can't fire a machine gun!"

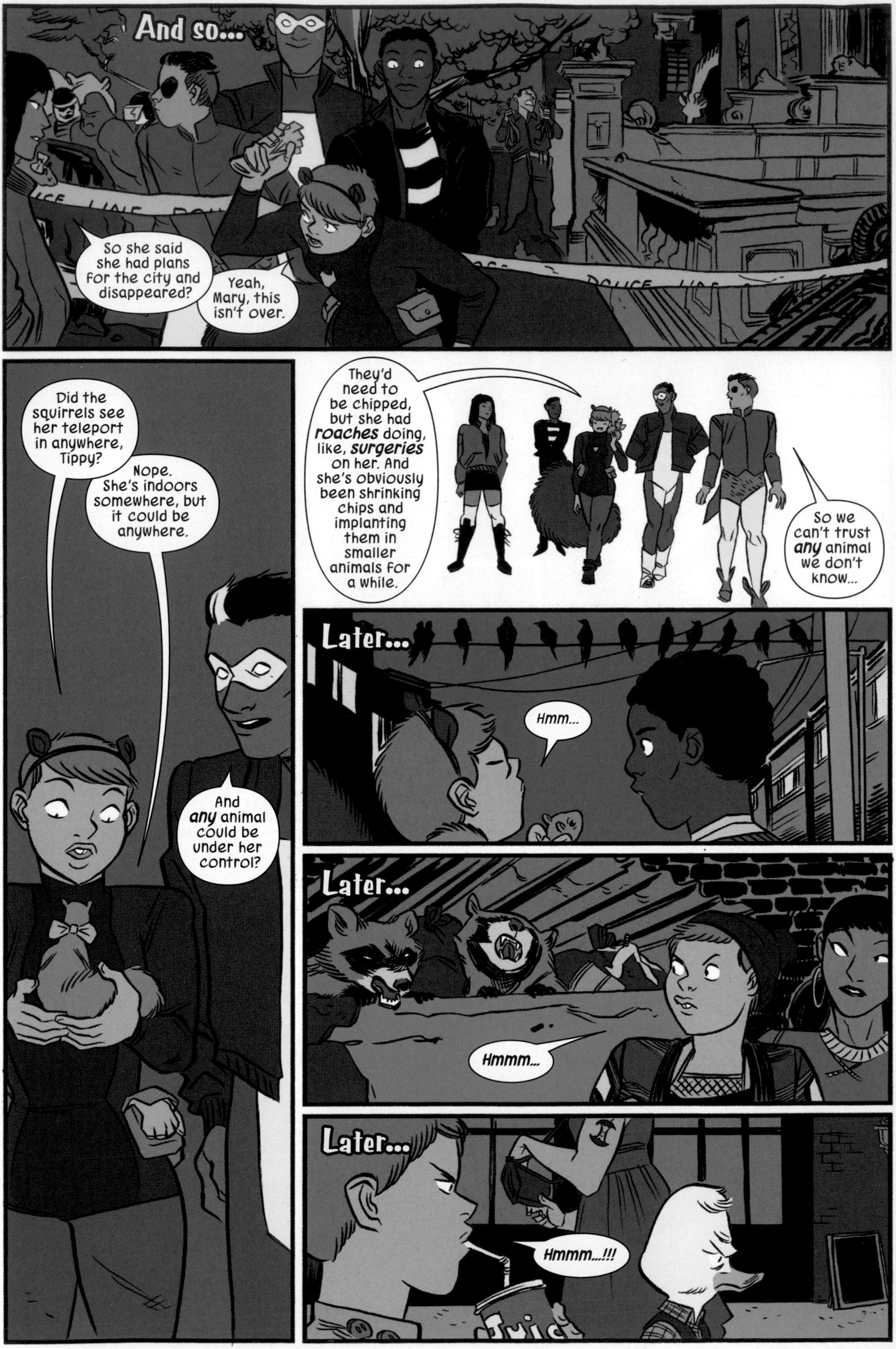
And so...
So she said she had plans for the city and disappeared?
Yeah, Mary, this isn't over.
Did the squirrels see her teleport in anywhere, Tippy?
Nope. She's indoors somewhere, but it could be anywhere.
And any animal could be under her control?
They'd need to be chipped, but she had roaches doing, like, surgeries on her. And she's obviously been shrinking chips and implanting them in smaller animals for a while.
So we can't trust any animal we don't know...
Later...
Hmm...
Later...
Hmmm...
Later...
Hmmm...!!!

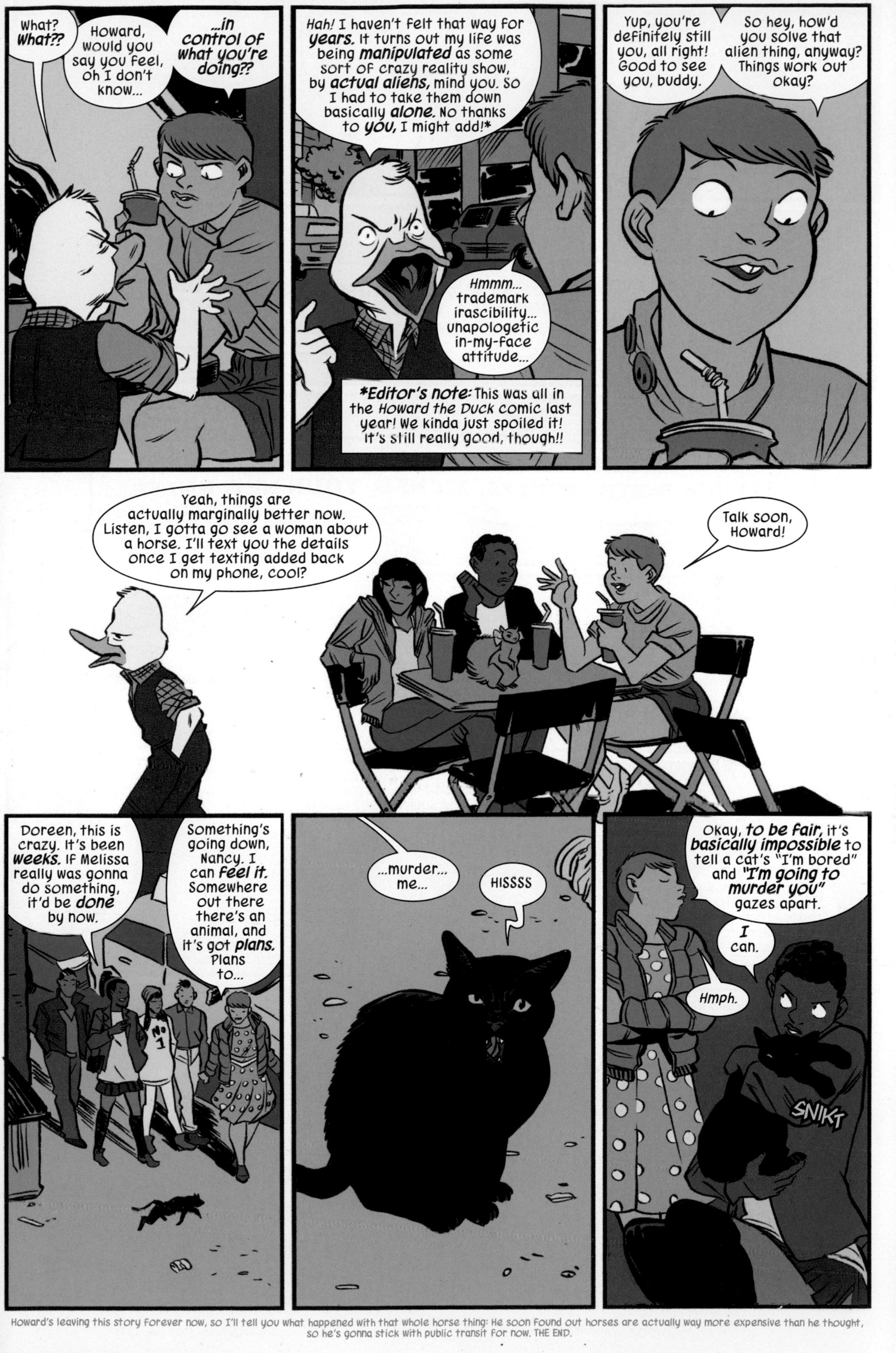
What? What??
Howard, would you say you feel, oh I don't know...
...in control of what you're doing??
Hah! I haven't felt that way for years. It turns out my life was being manipulated as some sort of crazy reality show, by actual aliens, mind you. So I had to take them down basically alone. No thanks to you, I might add!*
Hmmm... trademark irascibility... unapologetic in-my-face attitude...
*Editor's note: This was all in the Howard the Duck comic last year! We kinda just spoiled it! It's still really good, though!!
Yup, you're definitely still you, all right! Good to see you, buddy.
So hey, how'd you solve that alien thing, anyway? Things work out okay?
Yeah, things are actually marginally better now. Listen, I gotta go see a woman about a horse. I'll text you the details once I get texting added back on my phone, cool?
Talk soon, Howard!
Doreen, this is crazy. It's been weeks. If Melissa really was gonna do something, it'd be done by now.
Something's going down, Nancy. I can feel it. Somewhere out there there's an animal, and it's got plans. Plans to...
...murder... me...
HISSSS
Okay, to be fair, it's basically impossible to tell a cat's "I'm bored" and "I'm going to murder you" gazes apart.
I can.
Hmph.
SNIKT

Howard's leaving this story forever now, so I'll tell you what happened with that whole horse thing: He soon found out horses are actually way more expensive than he thought, so he's gonna stick with public transit for now. THE END.

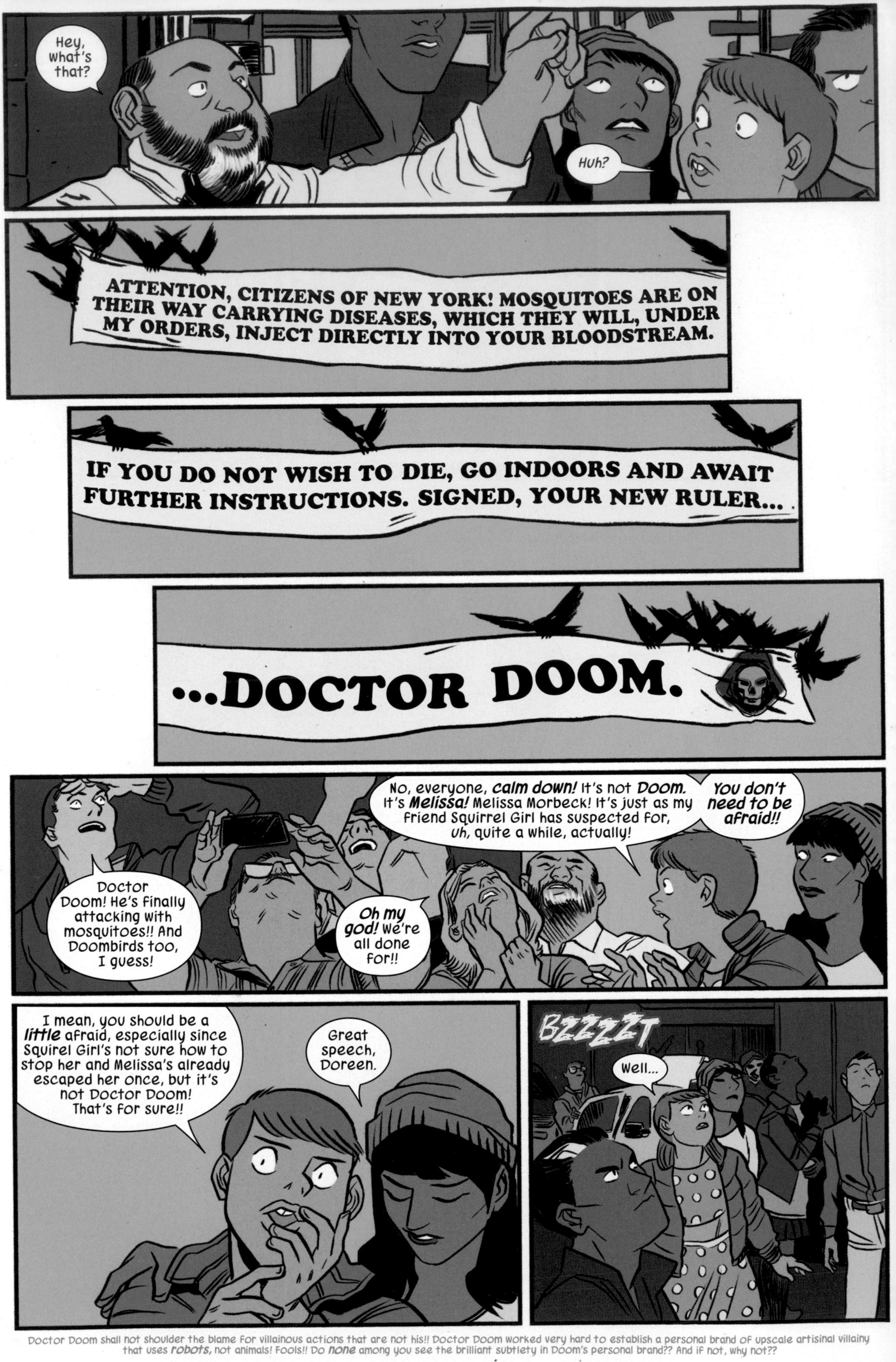
Hey, what's that?
Huh?
ATTENTION, CITIZENS OF NEW YORK! MOSQUITOES ARE ON THEIR WAY CARRYING DISEASES, WHICH THEY WILL, UNDER MY ORDERS, INJECT DIRECTLY INTO YOUR BLOODSTREAM.
IF YOU DO NOT WISH TO DIE, GO INDOORS AND AWAIT FURTHER INSTRUCTIONS. SIGNED, YOUR NEW RULER...
...DOCTOR DOOM.
Doctor Doom! He's finally attacking with mosquitoes!! And Doombirds too, I guess!
Oh my god! We're all done for!!
No, everyone, calm down! It's not Doom. It's Melissa! Melissa Morbeck! It's just as my friend Squirrel Girl has suspected for, uh, quite a while, actually!
You don't need to be afraid!!
I mean, you should be a little afraid, especially since Squirel Girl's not sure how to stop her and Melissa's already escaped her once, but it's not Doctor Doom! That's for sure!!
Great speech, Doreen.
BZZZZT
Well...

Doctor Doom shall not shoulder the blame for villainous actions that are not his!! Doctor Doom worked very hard to establish a personal brand of upscale artisinal villainy that uses *robots*, not animals! Fools!! Do *none* among you see the brilliant subtlety in Doom's personal brand?? And if not, why not??

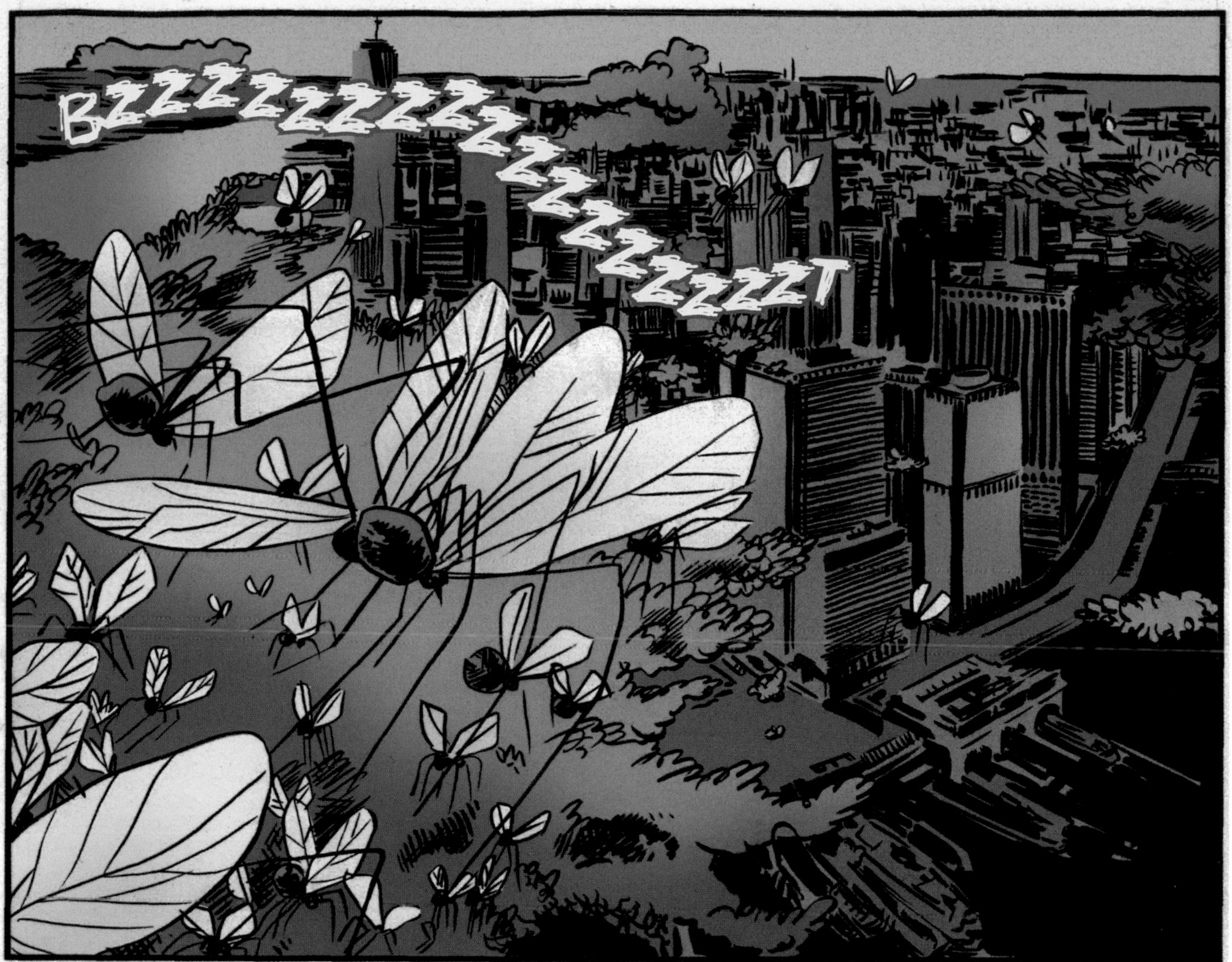
BZZZZZZZZZZZZZZZZZZZZZZZZT

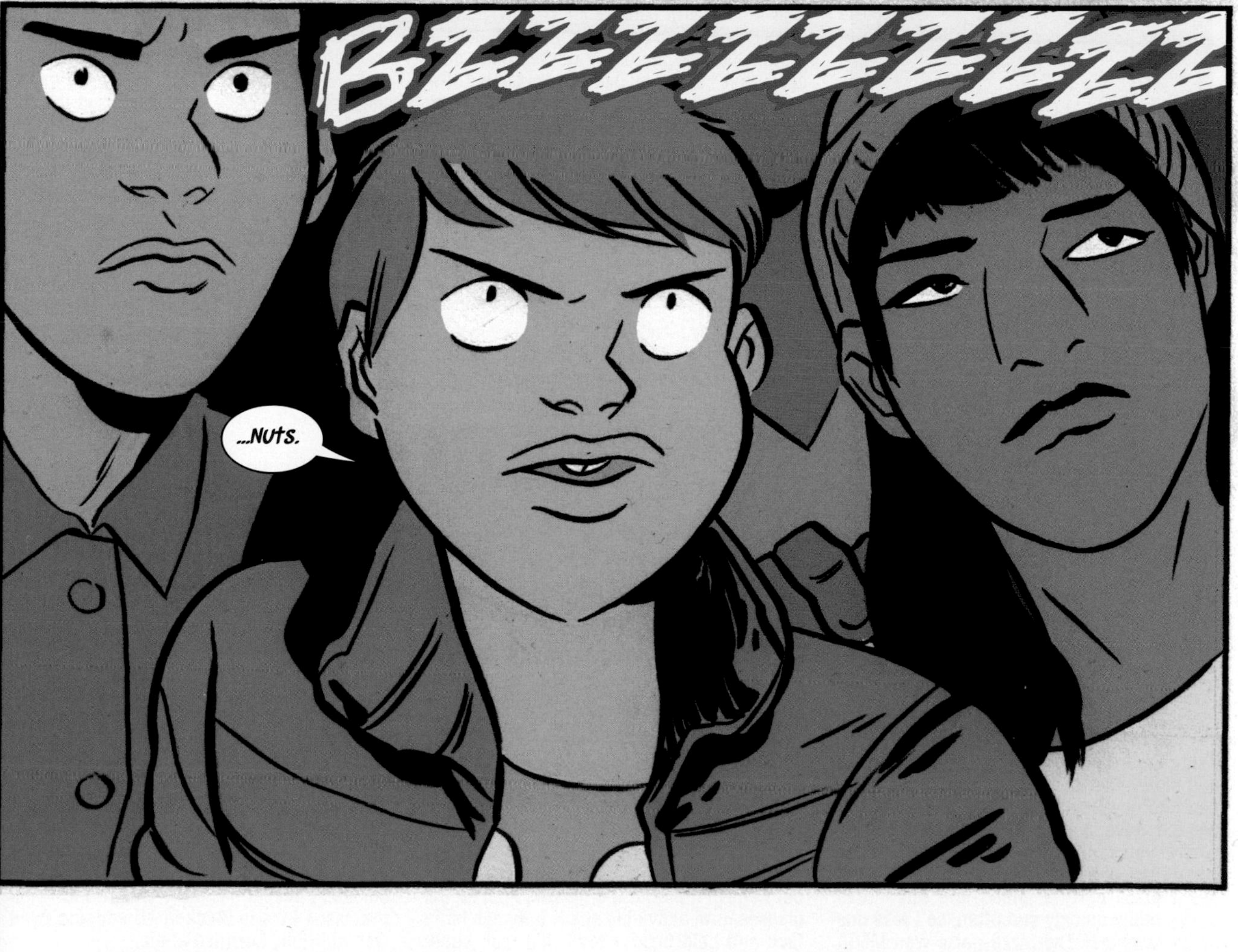
BZZZZZZZZZZZ
...NUTS.

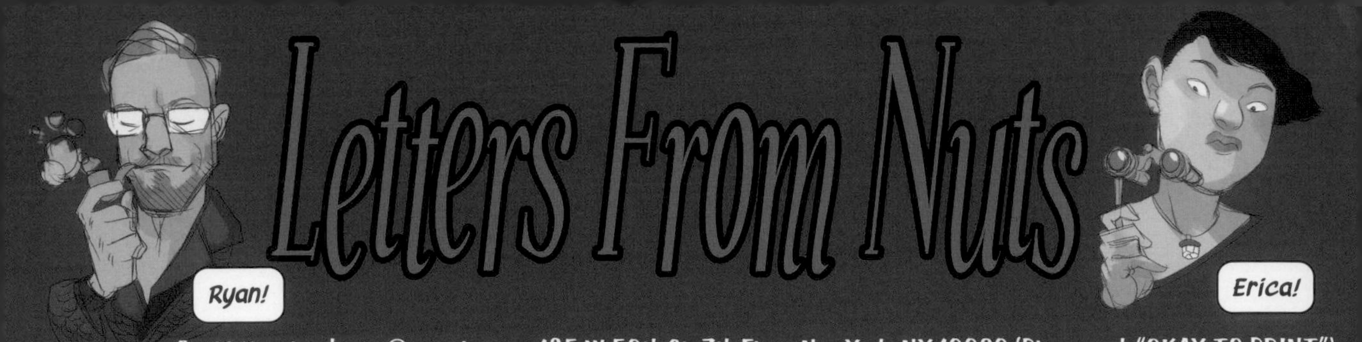
Letters From Nuts
Ryan!
Erica!

Send letters to mheroes@marvel.com or 135 W 50th St, 7th Floor, New York, NY 10020 (Please mark "OKAY TO PRINT")

Dear Erica and Ryan,

This is my daughter Emerson; she's 11--turning 12 next month. She's a super-huge fan of Squirrel Girl and wanted me to share the costume we made her for Literacy Day at school!

Emerson has been reading and re-reading the graphic novels ever since receiving them from her nerd uncle a few months ago. She got the new ones for Christmas and can't put them down. Tippy-Toe is her very favorite character!

Thanks for your time and your stories!

Abby from Canada!

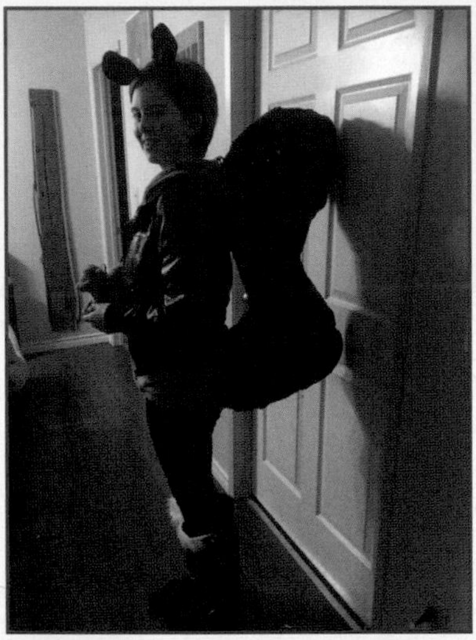

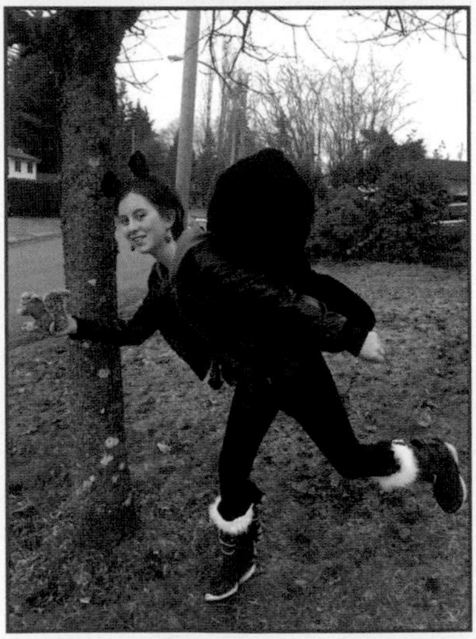

RYAN: Emerson is CLEARLY a woman of taste and skill—that costume is great! We never had Literacy Day when I was in school, but we did have a club at the school library where you could write down what books you'd read, and if you were in the top 2 you'd get a pizza party. I joined late but I read books really quickly and often, so I was one of the winners! The pizza party was MEGA DISAPPOINTING: it was just me and this other kid I didn't know hanging out at lunch hour when we wanted to be outside playing, and ever since then I've tended to read books for pleasure instead of pizza, and have become extremely suspicious of pizza-based bribery.

ERICA: I had neither of these things, or maybe I never noticed because I had zero extracurriculars because I too busy drawing and reading stuff. In my senior year though, the English department let me have the key to the secret other library where they kept the books they didn't teach anymore—JOY LUCK CLUB and A CLOCKWORK ORANGE aplenty! That is a great costume though. I like all the black. NEGA SQUIRREL GIRL.

P.S. Ryan, the next time I'm in town can I use your guest room? I'll bring a pizza.

Dear Ryan and Erica,

THE UNBEATABLE SQUIRREL GIRL is my favorite comic book! You can ask the community over at Destructoid!!! (It's a video game website where I profess my love for Squirrel Girl on a regular basis!) Even my parents know how much I absolutely LOVE Squirrel Girl!!! I just gave a presentation for one of my classes three days ago, where I explained that Squirrel Girl is 100% the biggest thing that influenced me to go back to school and pursue a degree in Computer Science! I'm a 29-year-old, large, bald, bearded man, and I am a huge fan of your work! Please, keep being amazing forever.

Sincerely,
Kevin
Richmond, VA

P.S. One of my friends at Destructoid even drew Squirrel Girl (and three of my other favorite characters of all time) on this lovely picture that they made for me as a Secret Santa gift!!!!

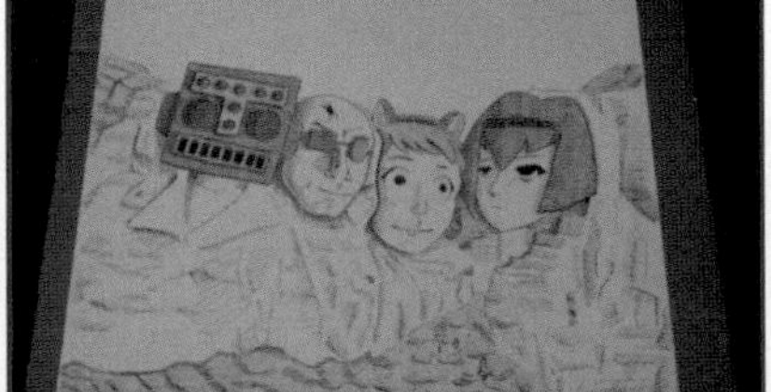

Pictured (from left to right): The Destructoid Robot (the site mascot), Spider Jerusalem (TRANSMETROPOLITAN), Squirrel Girl (!!!), and Dorothy (from the anime BIG O)

RYAN: Ahhh, this is great! I know 3/4s of those characters. Also: I am not a 3/4 bald man, but I'm really considering shaving my head. HERE'S THE PITCH: I keep my beard, but I shave it just at the glasses line, so the glasses form a dividing space between hairy face and bald head. I think it'd look super awesome, but I haven't taken the plunge yet. This is all to say: as a bald, bearded man, you are kinda living my (most recent) dream?? Also: congrats on going back to school as an adult! I have a friend who recently did that too, and she doesn't regret it at all now that she's graduated. Hooray for education!

ERICA: Ryan, I do not care how much hair you plan on having but please do not create tangents. Don't do it. Kevin, I'm glad you like the book! Fun fact: my first few jobs out of school were in video games. I was at Harmonix for the insanity that was THE BEATLES: ROCK BAND.

Hi Erica and Ryan,

I was so shocked when you told me that nice young woman Melissa was evil that I went into denial. However, after some reflection, I've accepted that a trans-reality crush is unlikely to redeem her, so I'm ready to move on to the remaining stages of grief. Oh comics, why do you hurt me when I love you SO much?!

I also want to tell you that you have upset the routine I have for reading comics. When I bought comics I'd sort them so I'd read any new series or one-offs first, and then least-anticipated (still pretty good; I'm a fussy reader) to most-anticipated new issue. I've been doing this for decades. My friends and family make jokes about how much I like routine. You've broken my system. For the last three months I have been unable to defer gratification in regards to reading SQUIRREL GIRL. Your comic's changed my life, guys.

Finally, and this is awkward because it's in a letter, so it looks manipulative, but I want to say it anyway, your letter pages are wonderful—a must-read part of your comic.

Best wishes,
David Morris

RYAN: Haha, I'm sorry, David! I've never been a combo breaker before, especially a decades-long streak. Doreen "The Exception" Green for the win! Also thanks for the props on our letters page: it's one of my favorite things (you all send in such nice words and great pictures), so I'm always happy when Marvel sends us the (virtual) mailbag for Letter Column Day.

ERICA: I don't know why letter columns ever went away! Anyway, I understand the need for routine. My routine is very important to me. I do my work in the back of the same cafe every day, and the baristas know my name and drink to the point where if I change my order, they'll call me over to make sure someone didn't write down the wrong thing. Also, since you brought up Melissa's reveal—while I was working on that issue I made Chicken Alfredo and Ryan was rightfully horrified at me.

Hi Squirrel People,

My cat, Moogle, would like to audition for the part of Cat-Thor in the movie that will inevitably get made once Nancy's genius is recognized. She's not quite worthy enough to lift the hammer yet, but has promised to get in moral shape in time for filming.

Thanks for your consideration. Stay awesome,

Matt

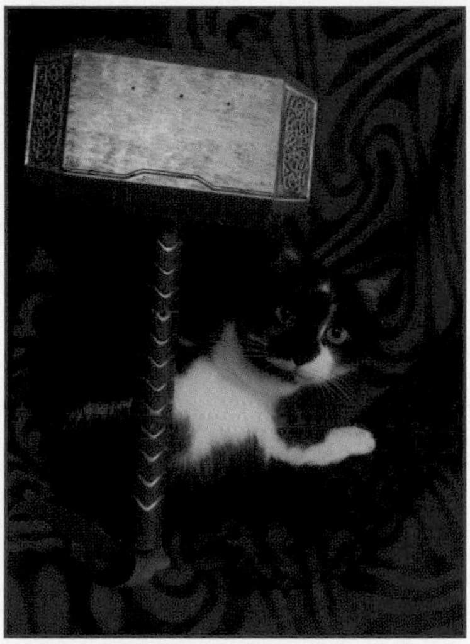

RYAN: I hereby greenlight this motion picture on the strength of this image alone. Make it happen, whoever is in charge of movies! Just because I don't know your name doesn't mean you shouldn't immediately do what I say!

ERICA: She doesn't have to lift it. She could be the Bill Bixby to a Maine Coon's Lou Ferigno, assuming that Cat-Thor works with traditional Thor rules and we work in a Donald Blake situation.

Dear Erica and Ryan,

I just want to say that Squirrel Girl has made my life so much better. Your secret formula mixes the right amount of humor, butt-kicking, computer science, puns, and awesome. While I don't know the whole formula, I know how much awesome there is: all of the awesome. Yep. 100% of the awesome is crammed into every panel. Now some people would be panicking at this thought, worried that there is no awesome left for anything else. But I know that one simply needs to think about Doreen, and then everything gets to bask in her reflected awesome. This allows me to shine awesome over everything in my life.

Please keep doing everything that you do,

Miguel Valdespino

RYAN: Miguel, thank you! Putting as many awesome things as we can into each panel is our secret goal, so it's super great that you noticed!

ERICA: Doreen is pretty awesome, which makes it easy to figure out the rest.

Hello,

I have just finished reading the first paperback of THE UNBEATABLE SQUIRREL GIRL, collecting the first four issues of the series. WOW, this comic book has given me hope for the future of comics! I thought they were all dark and violent nowadays, but I found SQUIRREL GIRL to be funny, creative, and exciting like old-school comics used to be!

Also, I love that you are printing the letters columns. They are fun and make me feel part of your community!

Keep up the good work!

Aaron
Santa Monica, CA

RYAN: More love for the letters page this month! AND IT'S THE ONE PAGE WE CAN'T FULLY TAKE THE CREDIT FOR.

ERICA: It's the most writing I ever have to do in one month though--unless someone on the internet is saying that ROBOCOP is not very good.

I am so excited to be writing to you guys. So excited, that I might pull a Doreen and ramble a bit.

First off, I would like to recount how I had found and eventually fell in love with everyone's favorite hero. It all started the way most things tend to in today's world. I was scrolling aimlessly on the internet, when I found a website that had all the Marvel characters and a power grid for comparison. Well, I found Onslaught, who had a full power grid, and decided to find all the characters with a full grid. Well, the next character I found was, of course, Squirrel Girl. I was dumbfounded. At first I thought "surely this is a mistake," and I decided to read what it said about her. In my defense, the article I read said nothing of Doctor Doom, Thanos, or any of that. All it said was that the other kids made fun of her "deformities" (there was no picture so I had no idea what she looked like; I wasn't smart enough to realize it meant her teeth and tail) and that she tried to kill a guy named Bug-Eyed Voice (literally the lamest sounding villain ever) in an effort to impress Iron Man. That was it. Nothing of her unbeatableness, none of the extensive list of vanquished foes, nada.

Many moons later, I found out who Thanos was. Then I discovered Squirrel Girl beat him. That's all it took for me. I went to a local comic-book store and found issue #2 (vol. 2, I later found out. That was very confusing). I read it, then thought of nothing but it until I could go back and get issues #3-5. I then checked out #1-5 of vol. 1 at the library (those places DO rock!). Then came issue #8 (back at vol. 2), and for Christmas, #9-15 (parents rock!). I starved myself until I could get issue #6 and #7, but since it never happened (got #6 of vol. 1 though; that's how I figured out there was two volumes), I just delved into #8 and on. Which is funny, it's like that one recap page on issue #9 you questioned printing was precisely put in for me because it filled exactly what I needed to bridge the gap. So thank you, and rest at ease, it was the right choice.

A few more random things: I noticed no one mentioned this, but the intro thing in issue #9 lists "Brotastic Brad" but shows a picture of Nancy (or someone—definitely not Brad). I don't mean to be tedious, but kept wondering if it was an honest mistake, an effort to get Brad to denounce his blogging, or (what I personally hope is going on) a secret sweepstakes contest thing where one special person gets a slightly edited copy of an issue and they have to spot it and mail it to you to claim their prize. And none of the rules or even the contest was announced, so you must wait and see if anyone noticed and wins. I really hope that's the case.

No matter what happens with that last point, I love your comic book. Keep it up guys! I'm glad we can have a high-spirited, clean-humored comic book to read. Plus, it is super educational! Tree lobsters are awesome!

From one Ryan to another (and to you too, Erica),

Your pal,
Ryan Lewis

P.S. I can't help but ask, who on this vast expanse of dirt we call Earth is Claude?! The guy on the cover of issue #8? I kept expecting him to show up. Thought he was Brad at first. I just don't understand. Who is that guy caressing Squirrel Girl? Why is he mentioned by name on the cover? And caressing? On the cover?!

RYAN: The Brad thing was a coloring error: he switches skin tones in that one page only because it turns out that we CAN make mistakes sometimes, just to mix things up! But I have been assured it'll be fixed for the trade. Hopefully–hopefully we remembered to fix it for the trade?? Claude is a made-up person who appeared because we tried to make the most romance-novel cover in the world, and needed the most romance-novel name in the world. Attention, all real-life Claudes who are reading this right now: feel confident! You got this, man!!

ERICA: Didn't we have a long e-mail thread going trying to figure out what his name should be? All the text on the (second) issue 8 cover was the result of four people going back and forth for what seemed like a day. Claude is low-rent Fabio. Since the theme of this letters page seems to be me sharing weird details that are only tangentially related: The first Fabio book cover I ever saw was the copy of THE TWO TOWERS I got from the library where he seemed to be Legolas.

Next Issue:

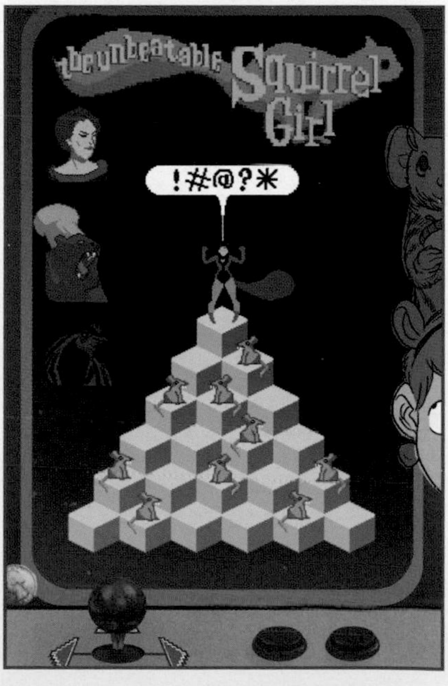
the unbeatable Squirrel Girl
!#@?*

Attention, Squirrel Scouts! Make sure to check out our production blog, **unbeatablesquirrelgirl.tumblr.com**, where we post behind-the-scenes stuff on how the book gets made, along with all sorts of cool things *you* make: fanart, cosplay, whatever!

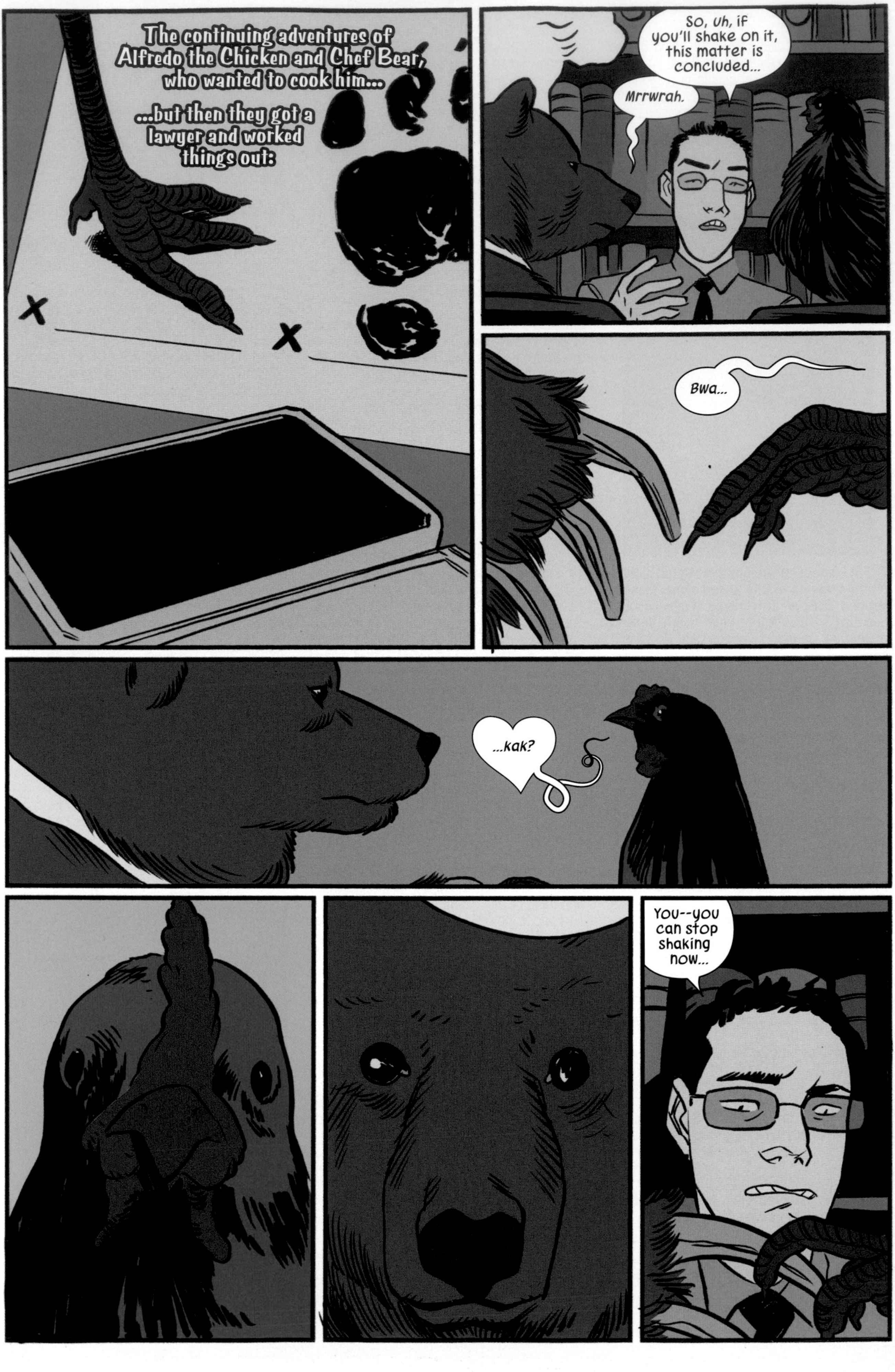
The continuing adventures of Alfredo the Chicken and Chef Bear, who wanted to cook him...
...but then they got a lawyer and worked things out:
X
X
So, uh, if you'll shake on it, this matter is concluded...
Mrrwrah.
Bwa...
...kak?
You--you can stop shaking now...

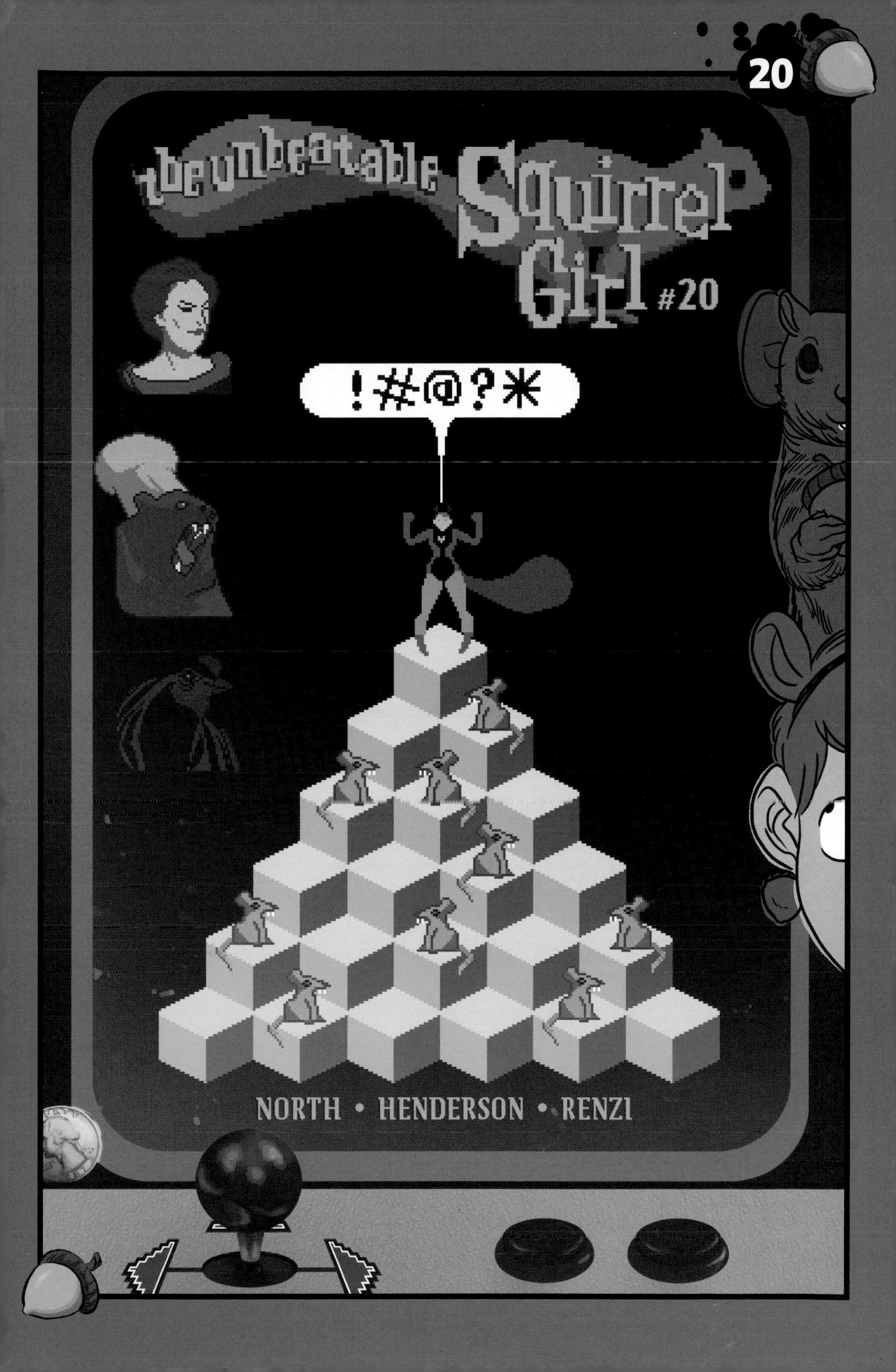
20
the unbeatable Squirrel Girl #20
!#@?*
NORTH • HENDERSON • RENZI

*Doreen Green isn't just a second-year computer science student: she secretly also has all the powers of both squirrel and girl! She uses her amazing abilities to fight crime **and** be as awesome as possible. You know her as...**The Unbeatable Squirrel Girl!** Find out what she's been up to, with...*

Squirrel Girl *in a nutshell*

Squirrel Girl @unbeatablesg
MELISSA MORBECK CALL-OUT POST

Squirrel Girl @unbeatablesg
She publicly acts like she's this kind tech billionaire lady with awesome teas, but it's not true! SHE'S AMASSING AN ANIMAL ARMY!!

Squirrel Girl @unbeatablesg
She controls them through microchips in their brains! It's gross! She made cockroaches put a shrunken computer in her EAR!!

Squirrel Girl @unbeatablesg
(Fun fact: when I got up this morning, I did not want to see cockroaches put a shrunken ANYTHING in ANYONE'S ear, but here we are)

Squirrel Girl @unbeatablesg
Anyway, that banner pulled by birds that says Doctor Doom is behind this? Don't believe it! It's her! IT'S ALWAYS HER.

Squirrel Girl @unbeatablesg
SHE'S the one who makes animals act like jerks! She's the one threatening the city with disease-carrying mosquitoes!!

Mosquito Man @skeetyman
Well met, @unbeatablesg! Sounds like you need the pest-repelling power... of MOSQUITO MAN!

Squirrel Girl @unbeatablesg
@skeetyman wait, for real?

Squirrel Girl @unbeatablesg
@skeetyman Okay this is awesome, I am always happy to meet another hero!

Squirrel Girl @unbeatablesg
@skeetyman Mosquito Man, I too fight for justice. If you can break the mosquitoes from Melissa's control, WE CAN SAVE THE DAY.

Squirrel Girl @unbeatablesg
@skeetyman Follow me so I can DM coordinates to meet up!

Mosquito Man @skeetyman
@unbeatablesg Our coordinates are your local Mosquito Man retailer! Say "bye" to bugs with over FOUR power-packed citronella scents!

Squirrel Girl @unbeatablesg
@skeetyman oh my god i thought you were a super hero but you're a brand of bugspray

Squirrel Girl @unbeatablesg
@skeetyman i can't believe we're in the middle of a city-wide crisis and you're selling bugspray and citronella candles on social media

Squirrel Girl @unbeatablesg
@skeetyman look up "disappointment" on Wikipedia and the entire article is just a screengrab of this convo

Mosquito Man @skeetyman
@unbeatablesg Don't forget to tell your followers we're the Bugspray That Bites Back™ for 10% off your next purchase!

Squirrel Girl @unbeatablesg
@skeetyman NO

Squirrel Girl @unbeatablesg
@skeetyman i will NOT

Tippy-Toe @yoitstippytoe
@unbeatablesg chtt cchttk ktttc

Squirrel Girl @unbeatablesg
@yoitstippytoe true enough Tippy, I should get back to saving the day instead of sassing #brands online

Tippy-Toe @yoitstippytoe
@unbeatablesg churrkt chrtt

Squirrel Girl @unbeatablesg
@yoitstippytoe also yes, I should change into my super-hero outfit real quick

Tippy-Toe @yoitstippytoe
@unbeatablesg cktt chutt!

Squirrel Girl @unbeatablesg
@yoitstippytoe i've never used phone booths?? every restaurant ever has a bathroom i can duck into no problem??

Mosquito Man @skeetyman
@unbeatablesg @yoitstippytoe Speaking of restaurants, are you a restaurateur with a patio? Mosquito Man can help keep the bugs at bay!

Squirrel Girl @unbeatablesg
@skeetyman OH MY GOD HAS THIS EVER WORKED

search!

#tippyshaircareregimen
#doomsgiantthirstymouth
#alfredothechicken
#chefbear
#lilbusta
#jjj

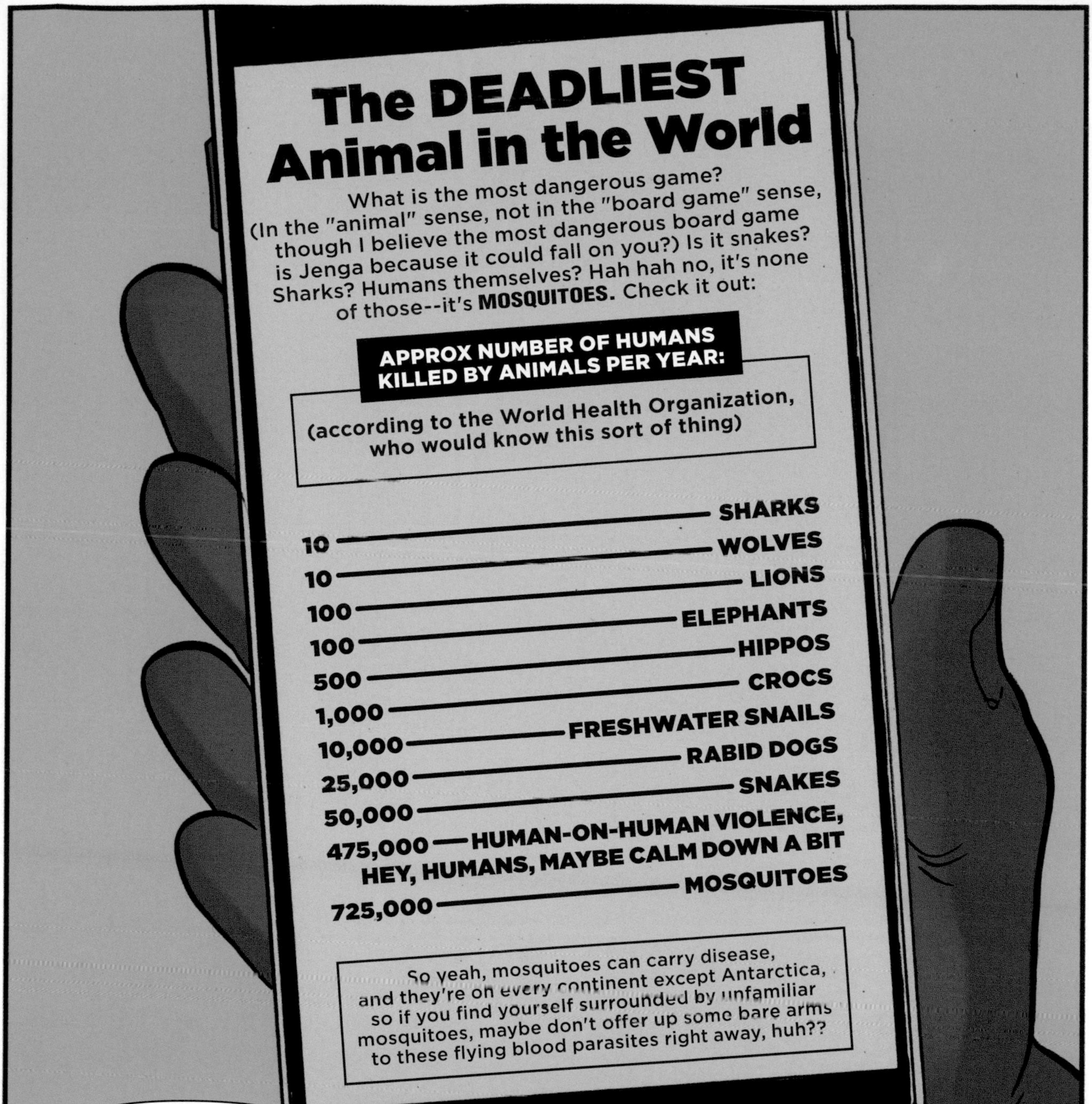

Snails: *Surprisingly* high up on that list, yeah? Turns out it's not the snails themselves that are a threat *(phew)*, but parasites they carry that can mess with humans too. Nice try, snails! You want everyone to think you're tough but now we all know you're just surprisingly unwell!!

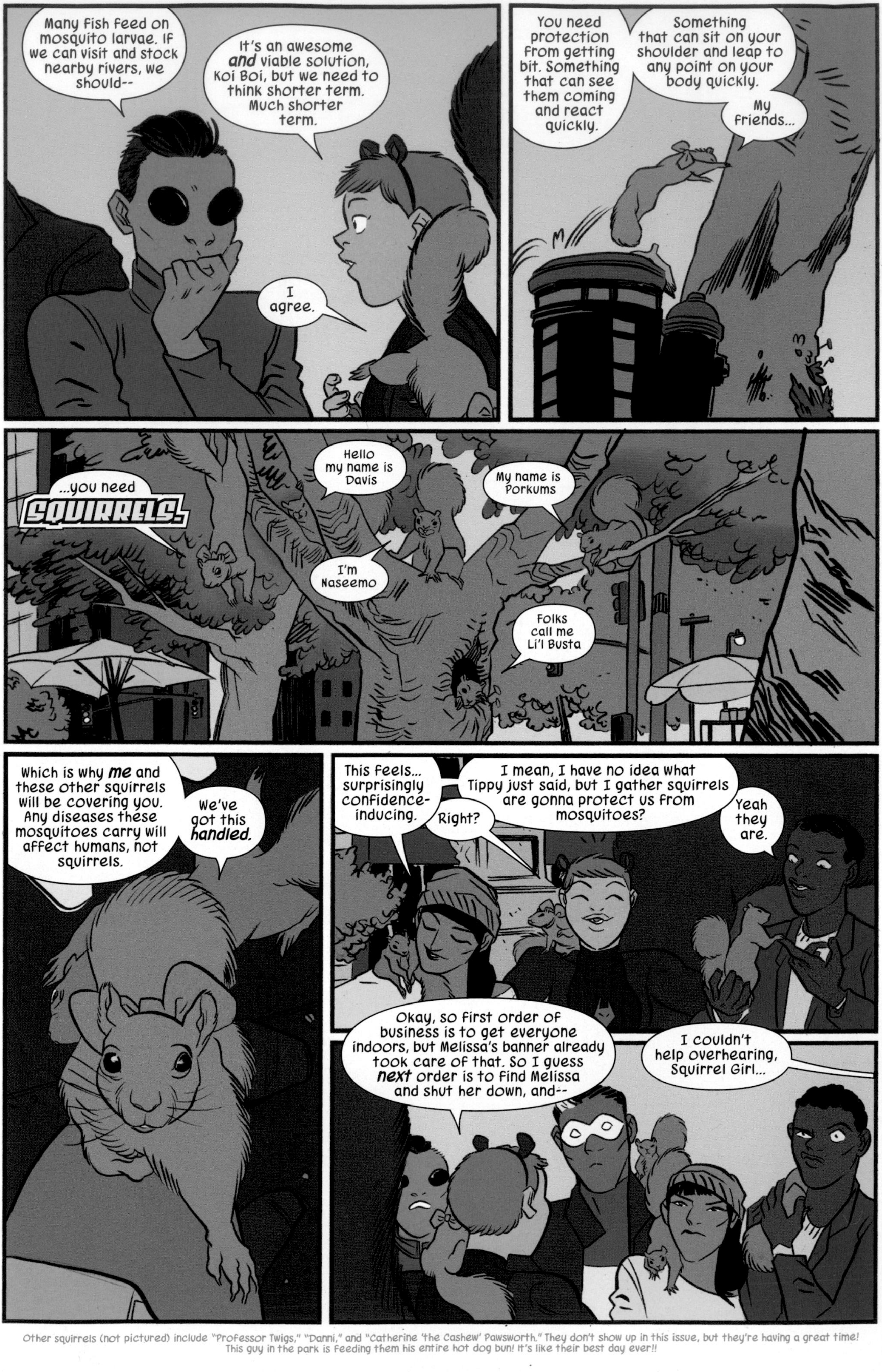
Many fish feed on mosquito larvae. If we can visit and stock nearby rivers, we should--
It's an awesome *and* viable solution, Koi Boi, but we need to think shorter term. Much shorter term.
I agree.
You need protection from getting bit. Something that can see them coming and react quickly.
Something that can sit on your shoulder and leap to any point on your body quickly.
My friends...
...you need SQUIRRELS.
Hello my name is Davis
My name is Porkums
I'm Naseemo
Folks call me Li'l Busta
Which is why *me* and these other squirrels will be covering you. Any diseases these mosquitoes carry will affect humans, not squirrels.
We've got this *handled.*
This feels... surprisingly confidence-inducing.
I mean, I have no idea what Tippy just said, but I gather squirrels are gonna protect us from mosquitoes?
Right?
Yeah they are.
Okay, so first order of business is to get everyone indoors, but Melissa's banner already took care of that. So I guess *next* order is to find Melissa and shut her down, and--
I couldn't help overhearing, Squirrel Girl...

Other squirrels (not pictured) include "Professor Twigs," "Danni," and "Catherine 'the Cashew' Pawsworth." They don't show up in this issue, but they're having a great time! This guy in the park is feeding them his entire hot dog bun! It's like their best day ever!!

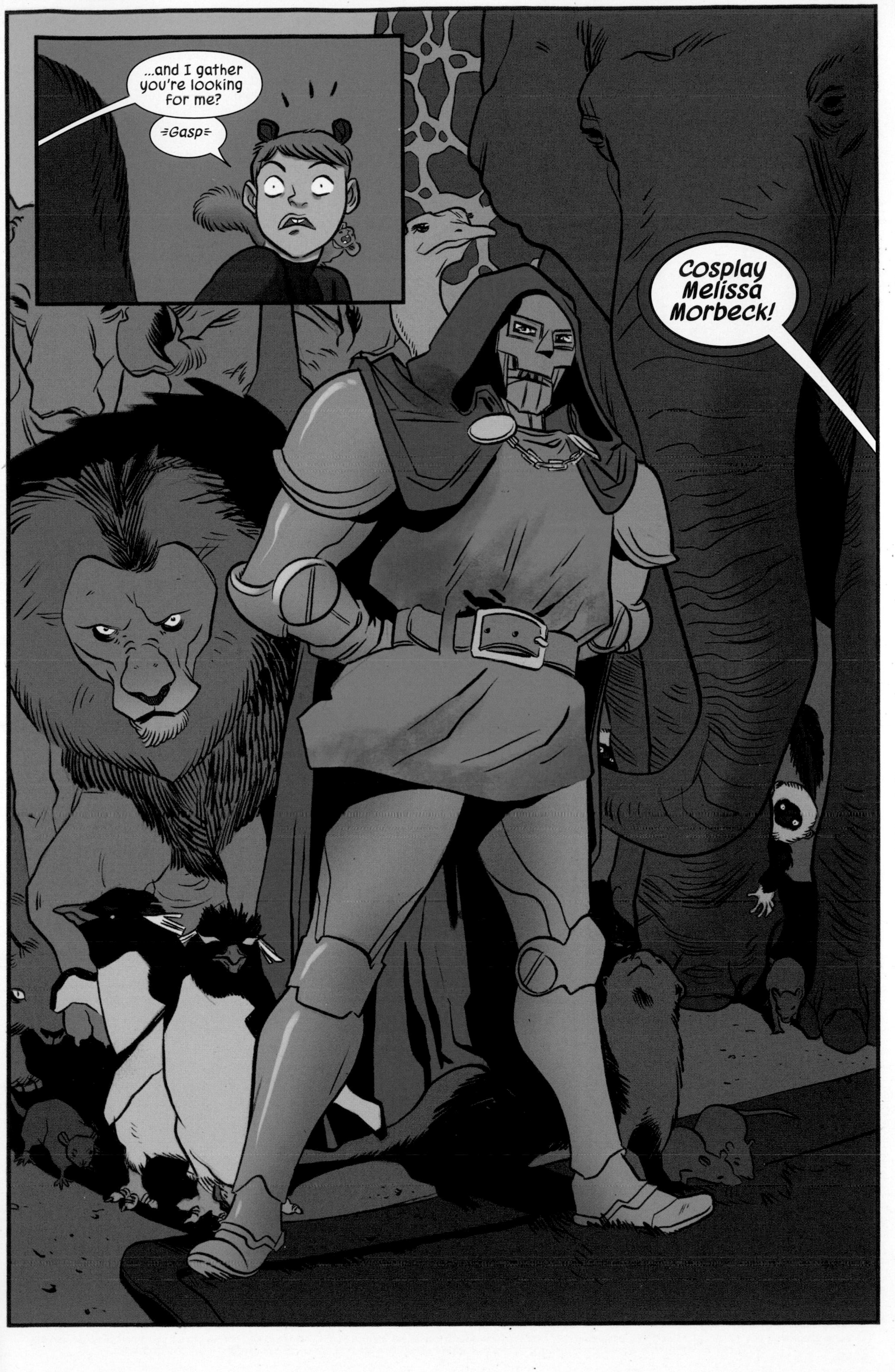
...and I gather you're looking for me?
=Gasp=
Cosplay Melissa Morbeck!

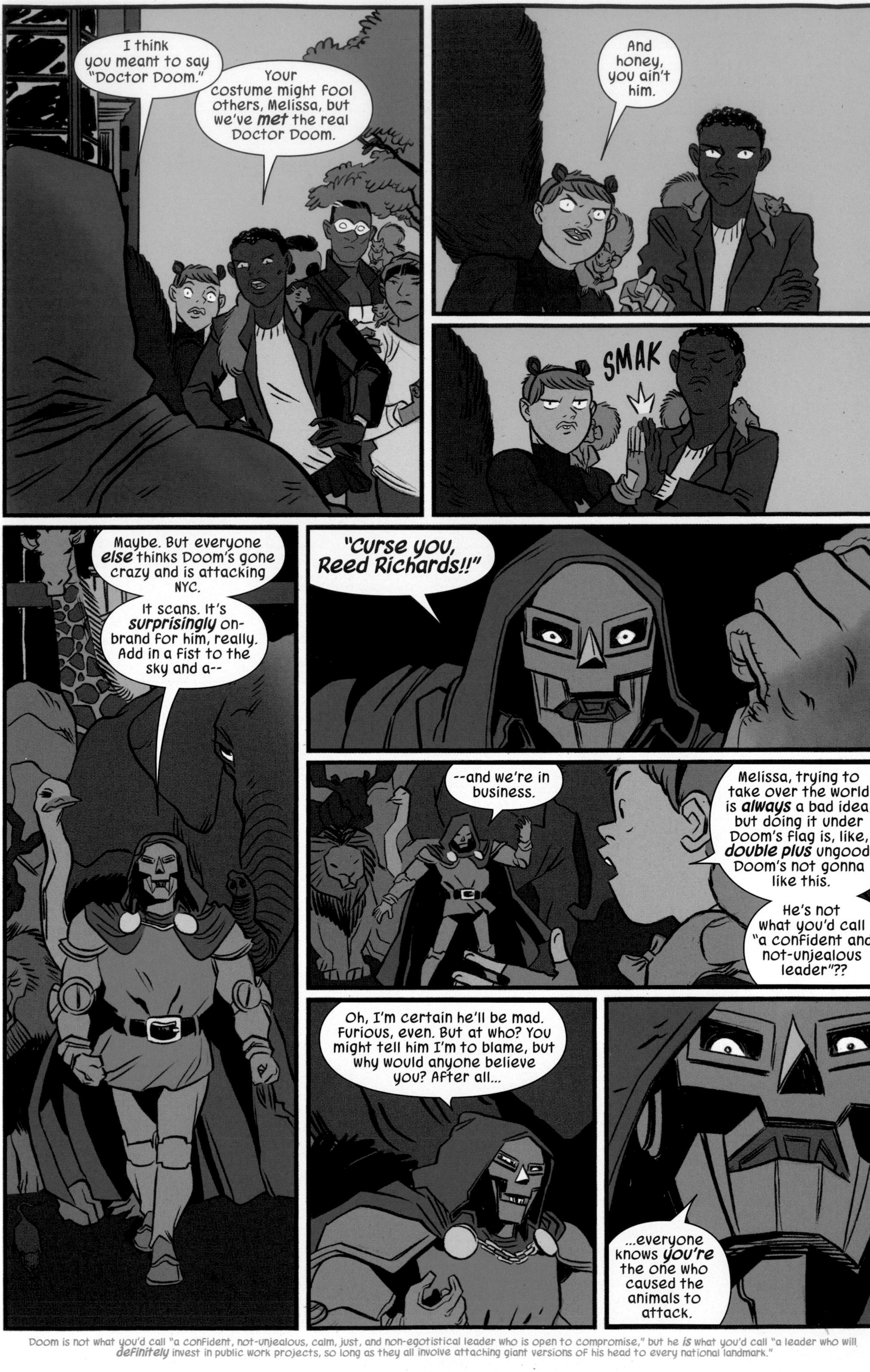
I think you meant to say "Doctor Doom."
Your costume might fool others, Melissa, but we've *met* the real Doctor Doom.
And honey, you ain't him.
SMAK
Maybe. But everyone *else* thinks Doom's gone crazy and is attacking NYC.
It scans. It's *surprisingly* on-brand for him, really. Add in a fist to the sky and a--
"Curse you, Reed Richards!!"
--and we're in business.
Melissa, trying to take over the world is *always* a bad idea, but doing it under Doom's flag is, like, *double plus* ungood. Doom's not gonna like this.
He's not what you'd call "a confident and not-unjealous leader"??
Oh, I'm certain he'll be mad. Furious, even. But at who? You might tell him I'm to blame, but why would anyone believe you? After all...
...everyone knows *you're* the one who caused the animals to attack.

Doom is not what you'd call "a confident, not-unjealous, calm, just, and non-egotistical leader who is open to compromise," but he *is* what you'd call "a leader who will *definitely* invest in public work projects, so long as they all involve attaching giant versions of his head to every national landmark."

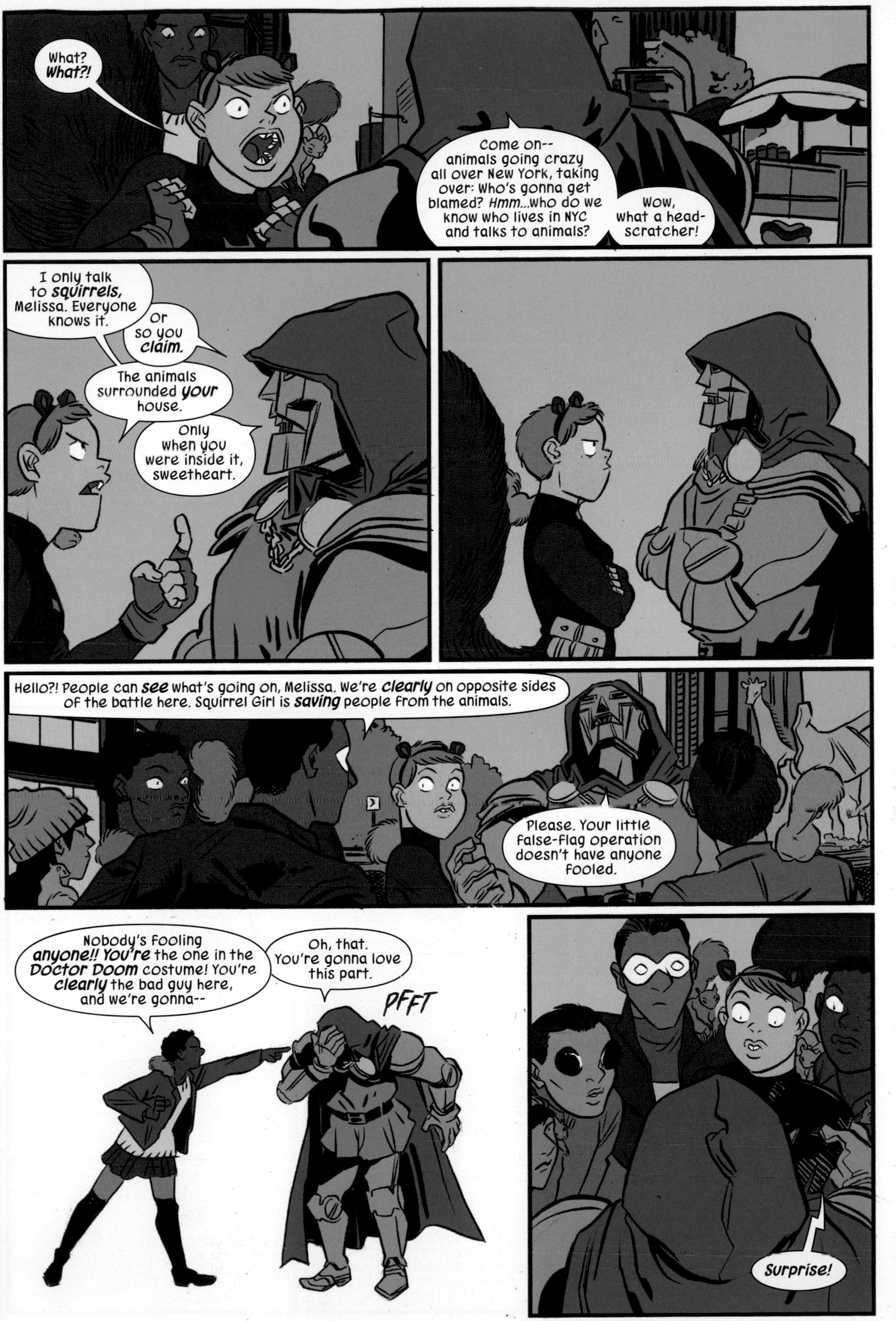
What? What?!
Come on-- animals going crazy all over New York, taking over: Who's gonna get blamed? Hmm...who do we know who lives in NYC and talks to animals?
Wow, what a head-scratcher!
I only talk to squirrels, Melissa. Everyone knows it.
Or so you claim.
The animals surrounded your house.
Only when you were inside it, sweetheart.
Hello?! People can see what's going on, Melissa. We're clearly on opposite sides of the battle here. Squirrel Girl is saving people from the animals.
Please. Your little false-flag operation doesn't have anyone fooled.
Nobody's fooling anyone!! You're the one in the Doctor Doom costume! You're clearly the bad guy here, and we're gonna--
Oh, that. You're gonna love this part.
PFFT
Surprise!

I'm sorry for mentioning "Doom attaching giant versions of his head to national landmarks" on the last page and then not having that show up, because now it's all you want to see! I understand. To satisfy your curiosity, please just imagine Mount Rushmore except everyone's in a Doom mask, the Washington Monument except with Doom's head on top, and Niagara Falls only with all the water tumbling down into Doom's giant thirsty mouth.

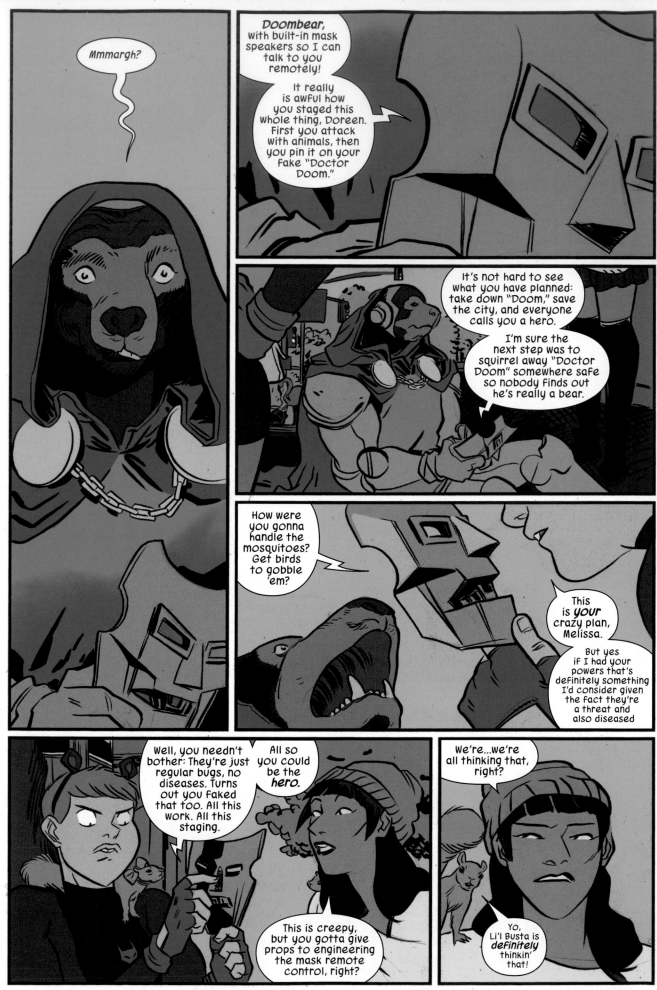

Mmmargh?

Doombear, with built-in mask speakers so I can talk to you remotely!

It really is awful how you staged this whole thing, Doreen. First you attack with animals, then you pin it on your fake "Doctor Doom."

It's not hard to see what you have planned: take down "Doom," save the city, and everyone calls you a hero.

I'm sure the next step was to squirrel away "Doctor Doom" somewhere safe so nobody finds out he's really a bear.

How were you gonna handle the mosquitoes? Get birds to gobble 'em?

This is **your** crazy plan, Melissa.

But yes if I had your powers that's definitely something I'd consider given the fact they're a threat and also diseased

Well, you needn't bother: They're just regular bugs, no diseases. Turns out you faked that too. All this work. All this staging.

All so you could be the **hero.**

This is creepy, but you gotta give props to engineering the mask remote control, right?

We're...we're all thinking that, right?

Yo, Li'l Busta is **definitely** thinkin' that!

I bet when Erica agreed to draw SQUIRREL GIRL, she didn't think she'd be drawing quite so many bears, especially in Doctor Doom costumes. I'm not apologizing, Erica!
Now that everyone knows "bears in Doom costumes" is an option, I bet other artists are gonna be adding them to the backgrounds of *every other Marvel comic!!*

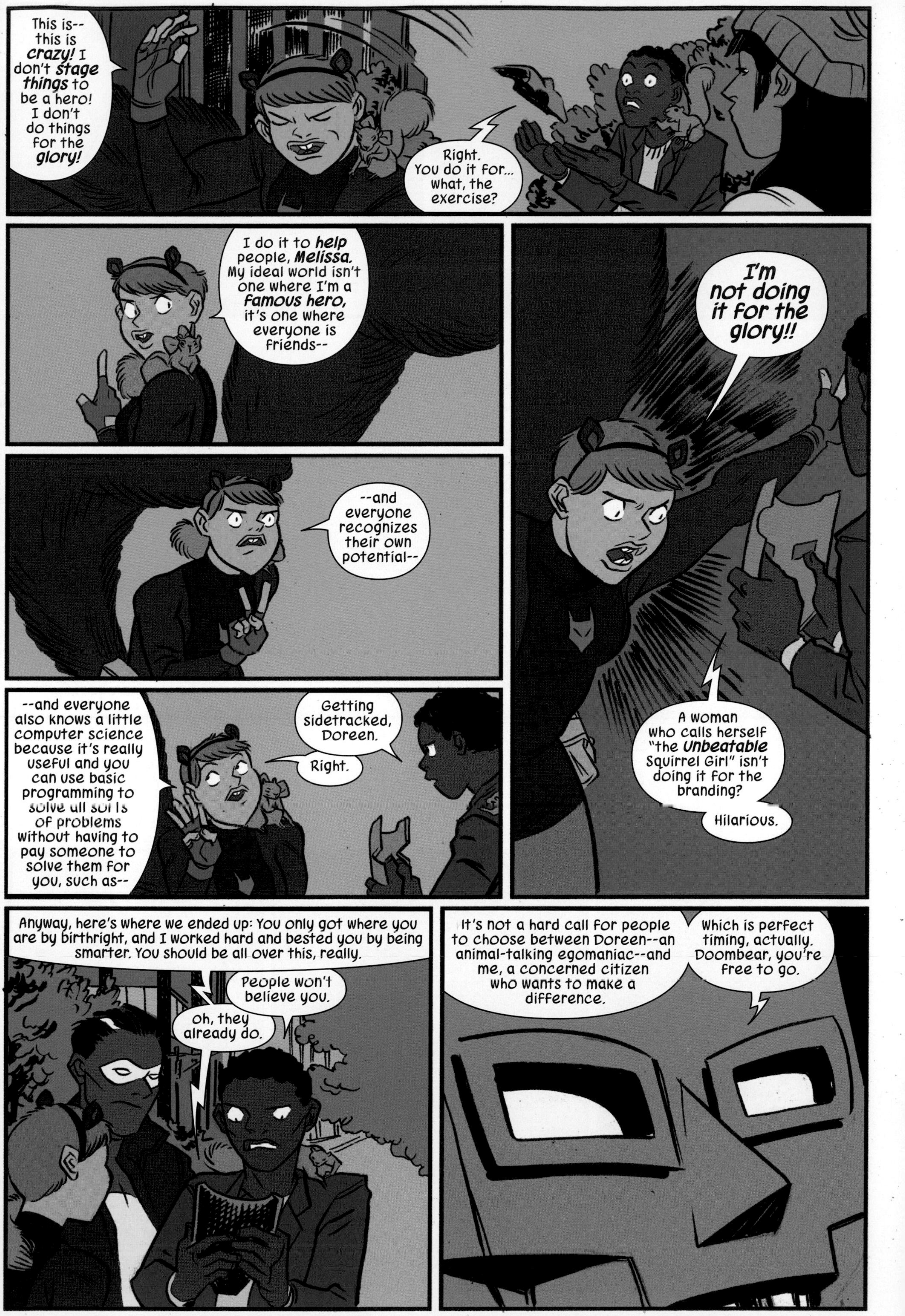
This is-- this is crazy! I don't stage things to be a hero! I don't do things for the glory!
Right. You do it for... what, the exercise?
I do it to help people, Melissa. My ideal world isn't one where I'm a famous hero, it's one where everyone is friends--
I'm not doing it for the glory!!
--and everyone recognizes their own potential--
--and everyone also knows a little computer science because it's really useful and you can use basic programming to solve all sorts of problems without having to pay someone to solve them for you, such as--
Getting sidetracked, Doreen.
Right.
A woman who calls herself "the Unbeatable Squirrel Girl" isn't doing it for the branding?
Hilarious.
Anyway, here's where we ended up: You only got where you are by birthright, and I worked hard and bested you by being smarter. You should be all over this, really.
People won't believe you.
Oh, they already do.
It's not a hard call for people to choose between Doreen--an animal-talking egomaniac--and me, a concerned citizen who wants to make a difference.
Which is perfect timing, actually. Doombear, you're free to go.

It's actually really lucky for Doombear that he found work that ties in to both his name *and* his interests so perfectly.

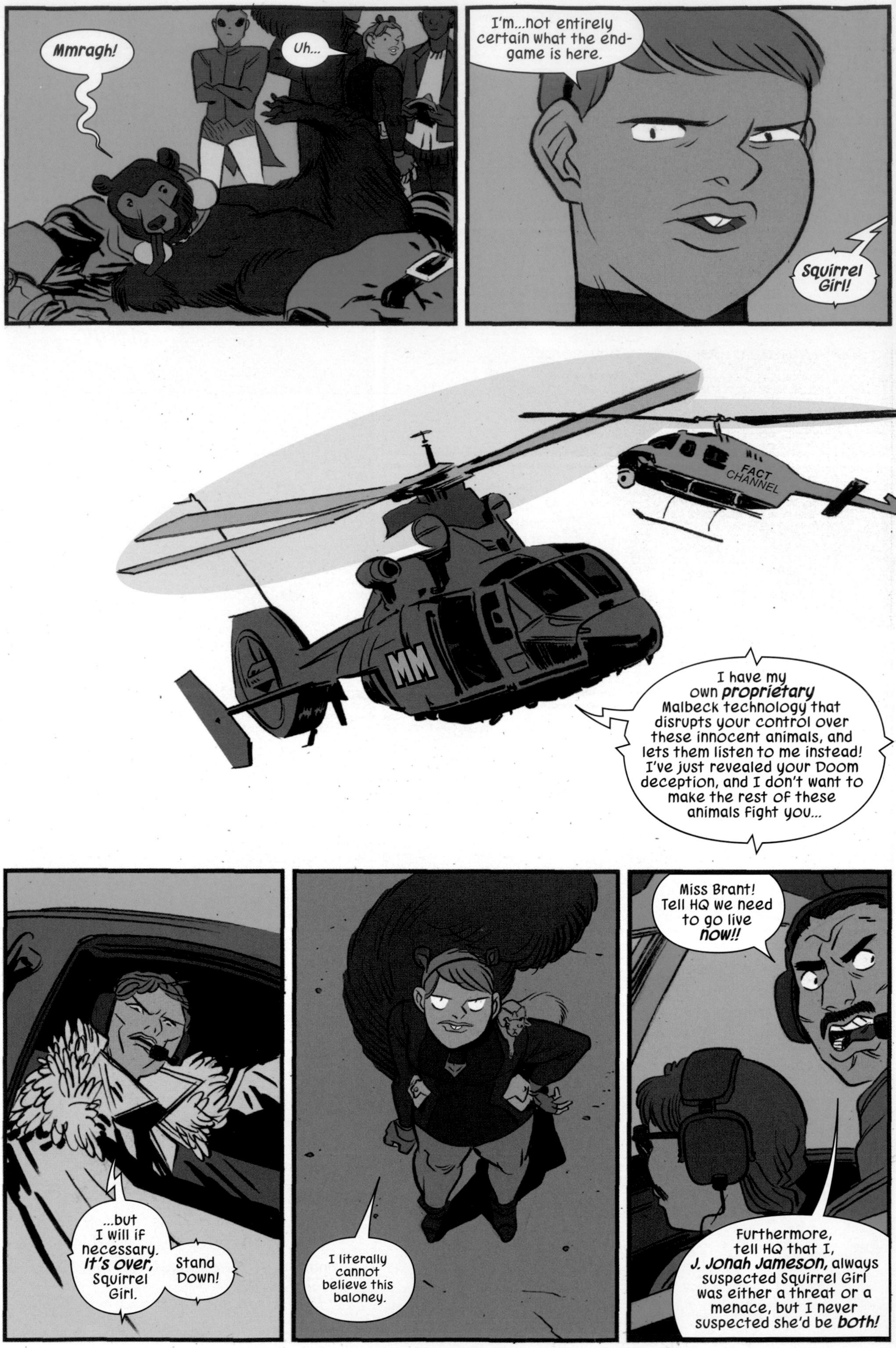
Mmragh!
Uh...
I'm...not entirely certain what the end-game is here.
Squirrel Girl!
FACT CHANNEL
MM
I have my own ***proprietary*** Malbeck technology that disrupts your control over these innocent animals, and lets them listen to me instead! I've just revealed your Doom deception, and I don't want to make the rest of these animals fight you...
...but I will if necessary. ***It's over,*** Squirrel Girl.
Stand Down!
I literally cannot believe this baloney.
Miss Brant! Tell HQ we need to go live ***now!!***
Furthermore, tell HQ that I, ***J. Jonah Jameson,*** always suspected Squirrel Girl was either a threat or a menace, but I never suspected she'd be ***both!***

Miss Brant! It's very kind of you to begin working for me again even though I've never actually taken the time to learn your first name! Wait...it's not "Miss," is it? Is it "Miss"? I'm just gonna assume it's "Miss," Miss Brant!

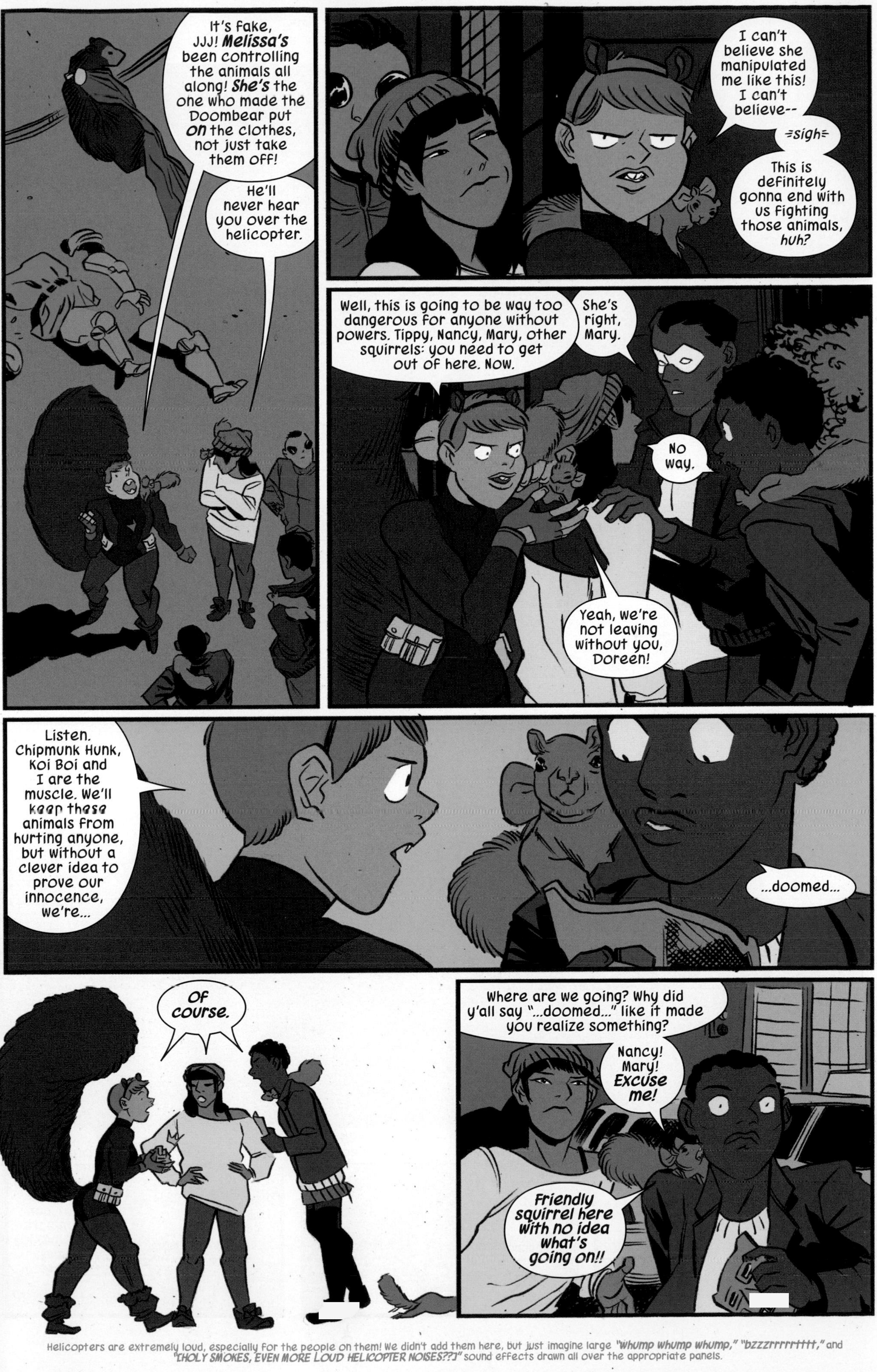

It's fake, JJJ! Melissa's been controlling the animals all along! She's the one who made the Doombear put ON the clothes, not just take them off!
He'll never hear you over the helicopter.
I can't believe she manipulated me like this! I can't believe--
=sigh=
This is definitely gonna end with us fighting those animals, huh?
Well, this is going to be way too dangerous for anyone without powers. Tippy, Nancy, Mary, other squirrels: you need to get out of here. Now.
She's right, Mary.
No way.
Yeah, we're not leaving without you, Doreen!
Listen. Chipmunk Hunk, Koi Boi and I are the muscle. We'll keep these animals from hurting anyone, but without a clever idea to prove our innocence, we're...
...doomed...
Of course.
Where are we going? Why did y'all say "...doomed..." like it made you realize something?
Nancy! Mary! Excuse me!
Friendly squirrel here with no idea what's going on!!

Helicopters are extremely loud, especially for the people on them! We didn't add them here, but just imagine large *"whump whump whump," "bzzzrrrrrtttt,"* and *"[HOLY SMOKES, EVEN MORE LOUD HELICOPTER NOISES??]"* sound effects drawn all over the appropriate panels.

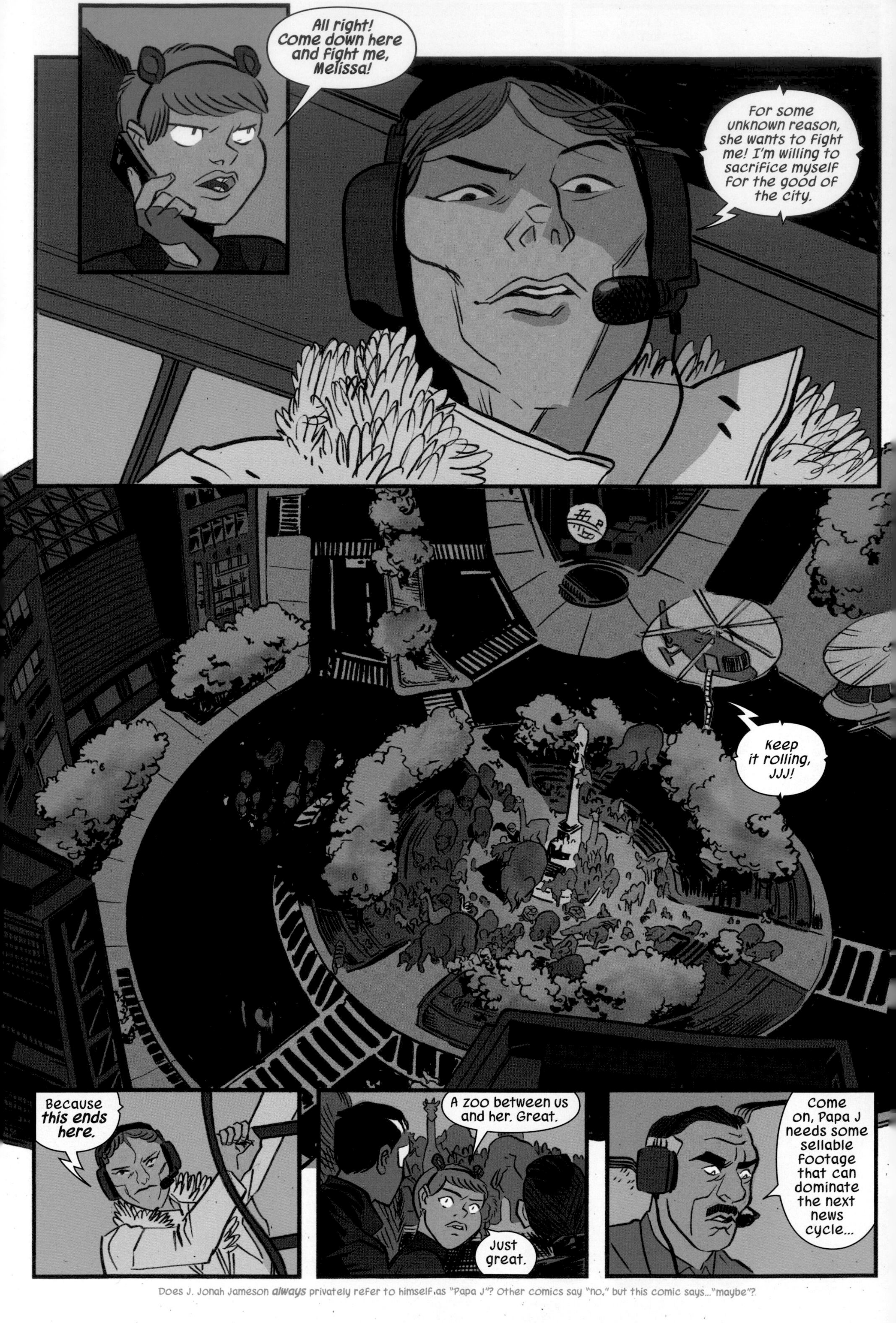

All right! Come down here and fight me, Melissa!
For some unknown reason, she wants to fight me! I'm willing to sacrifice myself for the good of the city.
Keep it rolling, JJJ!
Because this ends here.
A ZOO between us and her. Great.
Just great.
Come on, Papa J needs some sellable footage that can dominate the next news cycle...

Does J. Jonah Jameson *always* privately refer to himself as "Papa J"? Other comics say "no," but this comic says..."maybe"?

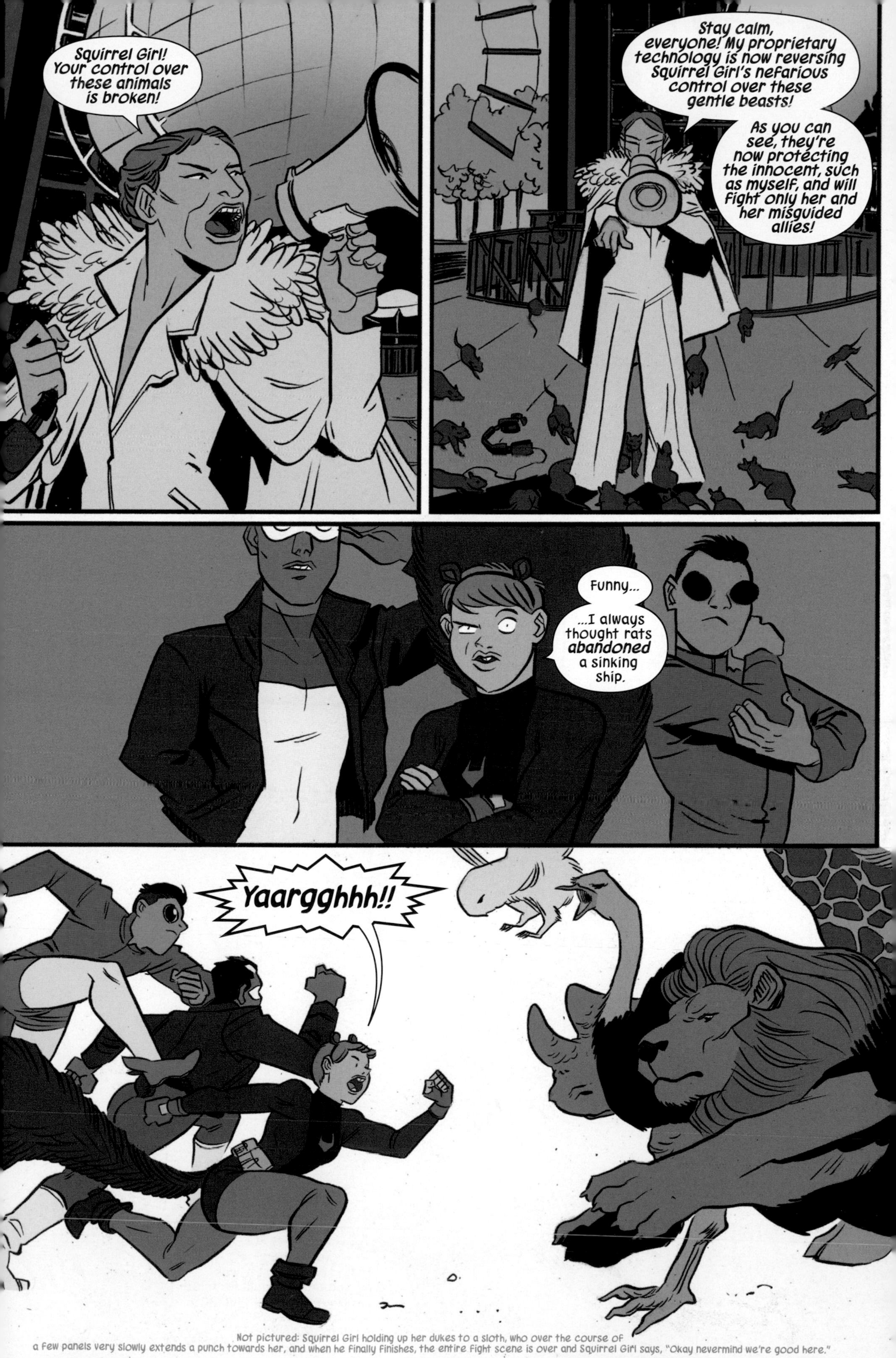
Squirrel Girl! Your control over these animals is broken!
Stay calm, everyone! My proprietary technology is now reversing Squirrel Girl's nefarious control over these gentle beasts!
As you can see, they're now protecting the innocent, such as myself, and will fight only her and her misguided allies!
Funny...
...I always thought rats *abandoned* a sinking ship.
Yaargghhh!!

Not pictured: Squirrel Girl holding up her dukes to a sloth, who over the course of a few panels very slowly extends a punch towards her, and when he finally finishes, the entire fight scene is over and Squirrel Girl says, "Okay nevermind we're good here."

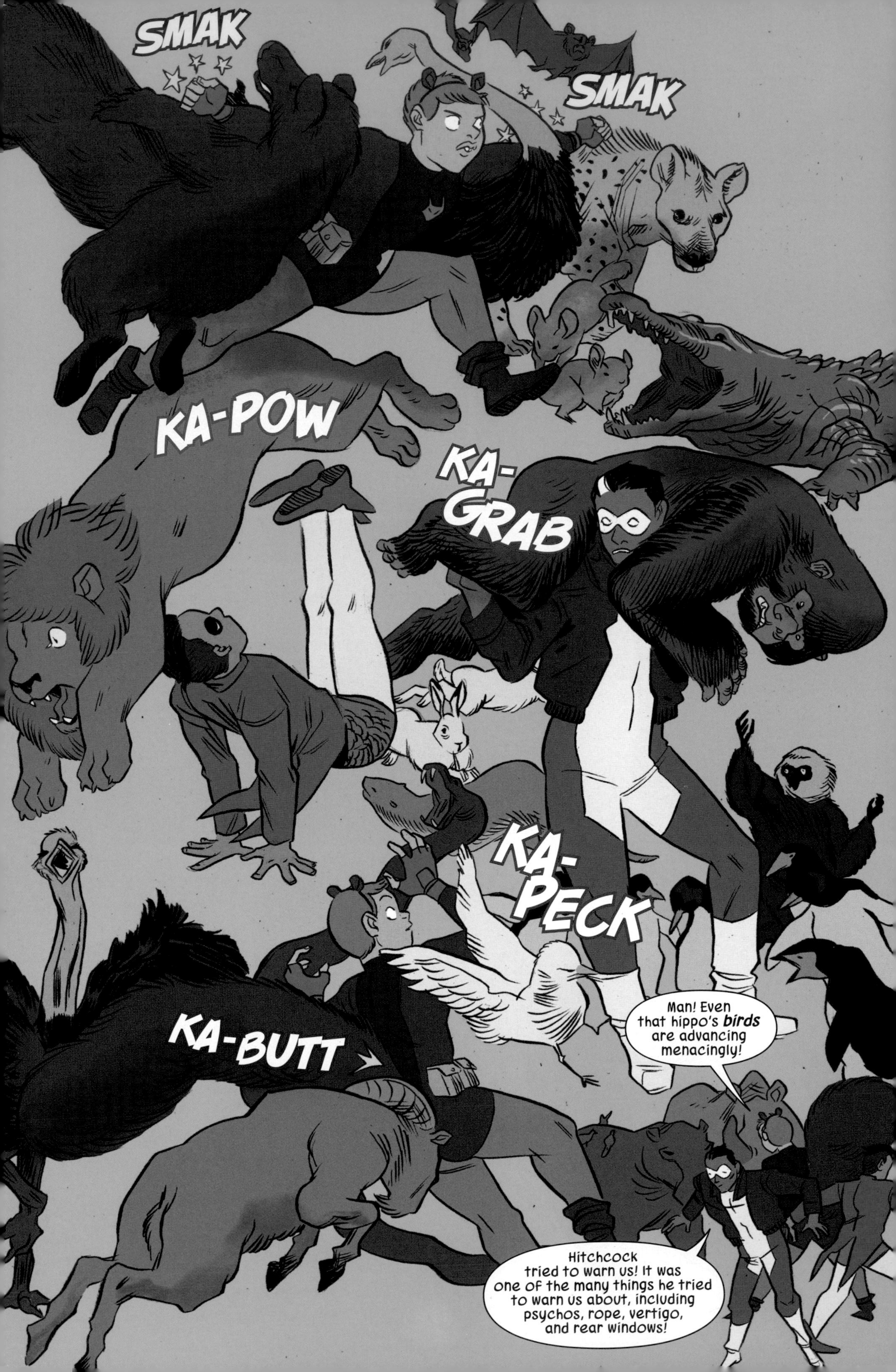
SMAK
SMAK
KA-POW
KA-GRAB
KA-PECK
KA-BUTT
Man! Even that hippo's *birds* are advancing menacingly!
Hitchcock tried to warn us! It was one of the many things he tried to warn us about, including psychos, rope, vertigo, and rear windows!

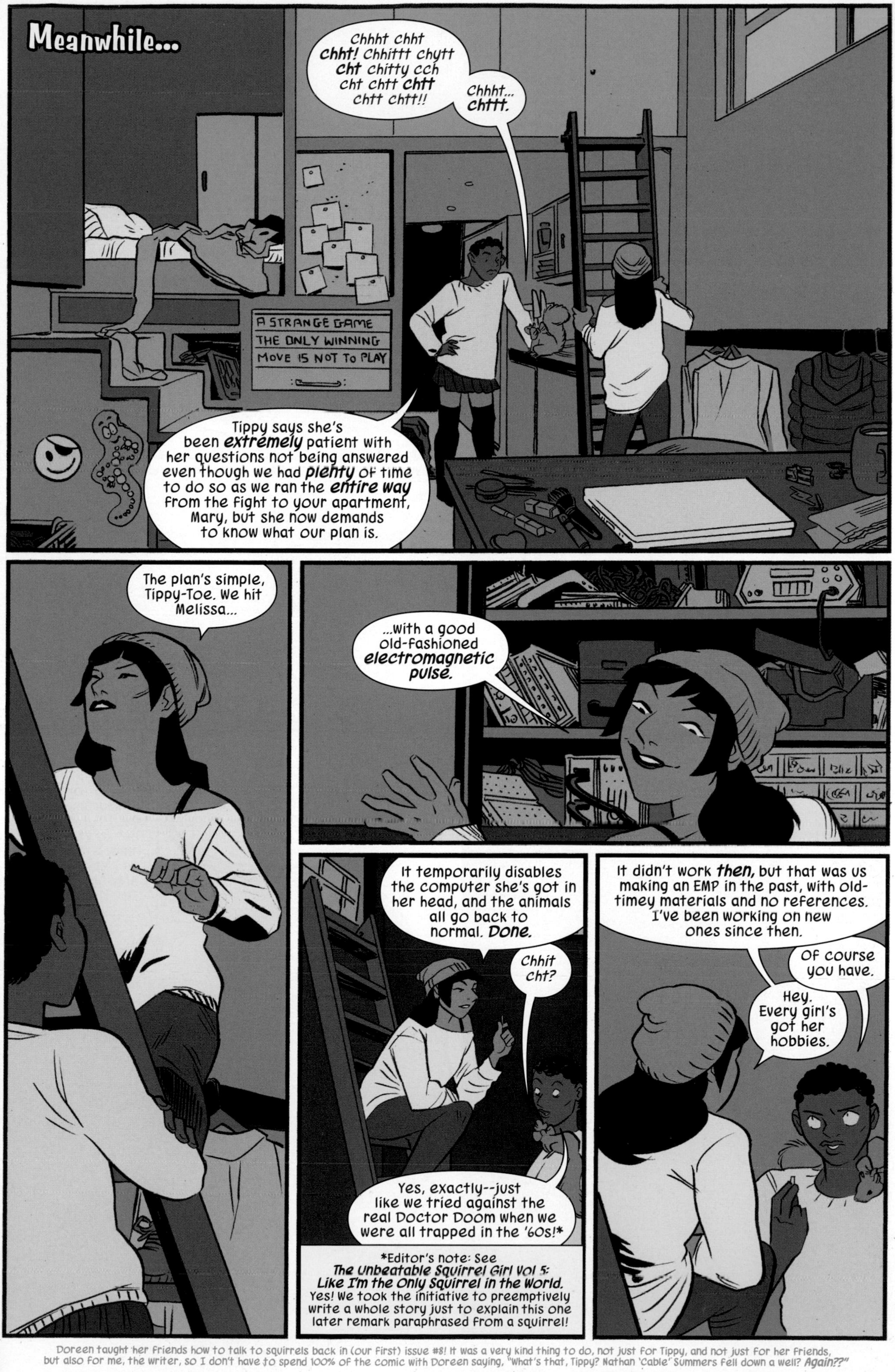
Meanwhile...
Chhht chht chht! Chhittt chytt cht chitty cch cht chtt chtt chtt chtt!!
Chhht... chttt.
A STRANGE GAME
THE ONLY WINNING
MOVE IS NOT TO PLAY
Tippy says she's been *extremely* patient with her questions not being answered even though we had *plenty* of time to do so as we ran the *entire way* from the fight to your apartment, Mary, but she now demands to know what our plan is.
The plan's simple, Tippy-Toe. We hit Melissa...
...with a good old-fashioned *electromagnetic pulse.*
It temporarily disables the computer she's got in her head, and the animals all go back to normal. *Done.*
Chhit cht?
Yes, exactly--just like we tried against the real Doctor Doom when we were all trapped in the '60s!*
*Editor's note: See *The Unbeatable Squirrel Girl Vol 5: Like I'm the Only Squirrel in the World.* Yes! We took the initiative to preemptively write a whole story just to explain this one later remark paraphrased from a squirrel!
It didn't work *then,* but that was us making an EMP in the past, with old-timey materials and no references. I've been working on new ones since then.
Of course you have.
Hey. Every girl's got her hobbies.

Doreen taught her friends how to talk to squirrels back in (our first) issue #8! It was a very kind thing to do, not just for Tippy, and not just for her friends, but also for me, the writer, so I don't have to spend 100% of the comic with Doreen saying, "What's that, Tippy? Nathan 'Cable' Summers fell down a well? *Again??*"

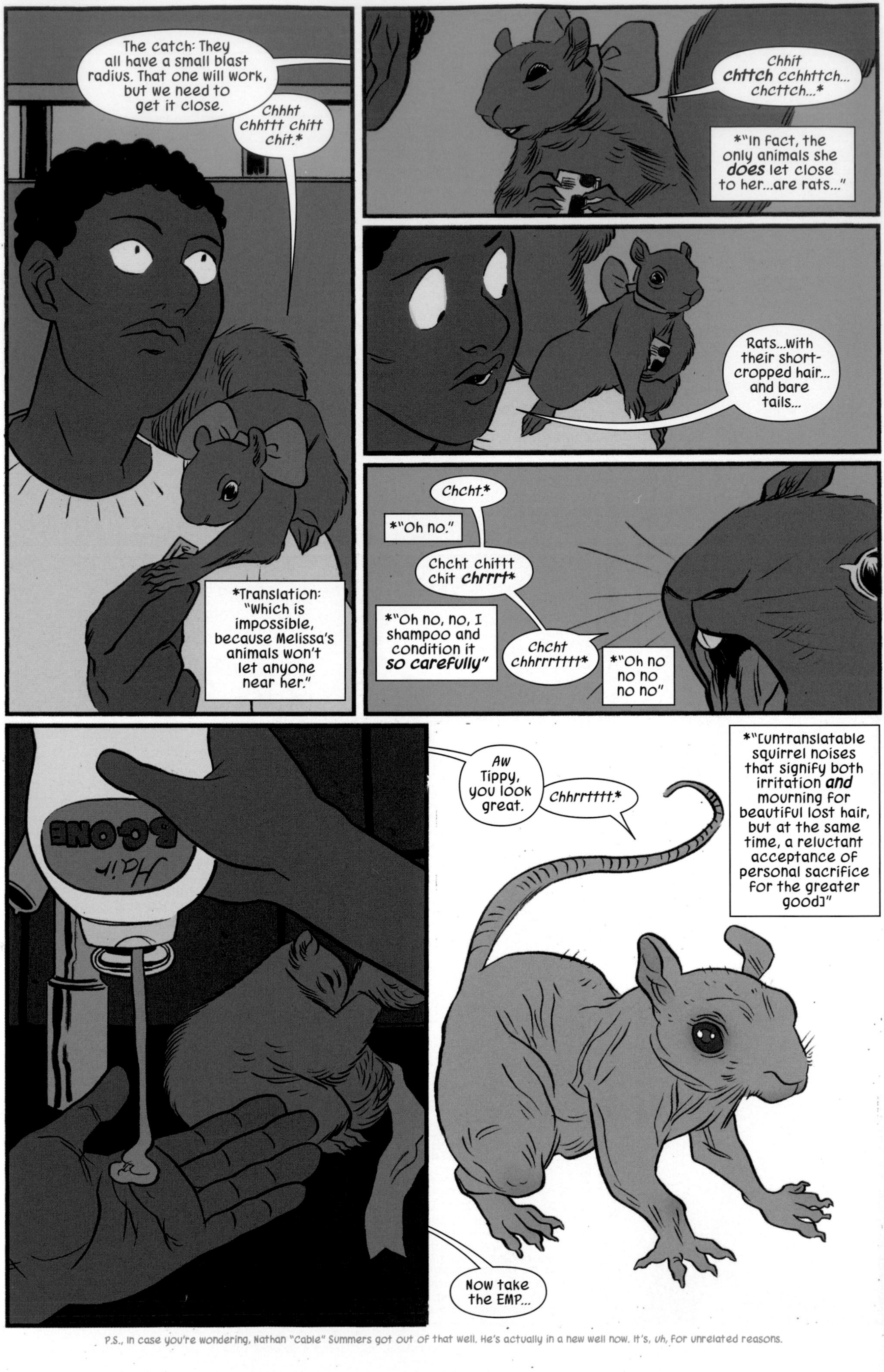
The catch: They all have a small blast radius. That one will work, but we need to get it close.
Chhht chhttt chitt chit.*
*Translation: "Which is impossible, because Melissa's animals won't let anyone near her."
Chhit chttch cchhttch... chcttch...*
*"In fact, the only animals she does let close to her...are rats..."
Rats...with their short-cropped hair... and bare tails...
Chcht.*
*"Oh no."
Chcht chittt chit chrrrt*
*"Oh no, no, I shampoo and condition it so carefully"
Chcht chhrrrtttt*
*"Oh no no no no no"
Aw Tippy, you look great.
Chhrrtttt.*
*"[untranslatable squirrel noises that signify both irritation and mourning for beautiful lost hair, but at the same time, a reluctant acceptance of personal sacrifice for the greater good]"
Now take the EMP...

P.S., in case you're wondering, Nathan "Cable" Summers got out of that well. He's actually in a new well now. It's, *uh*, for unrelated reasons.

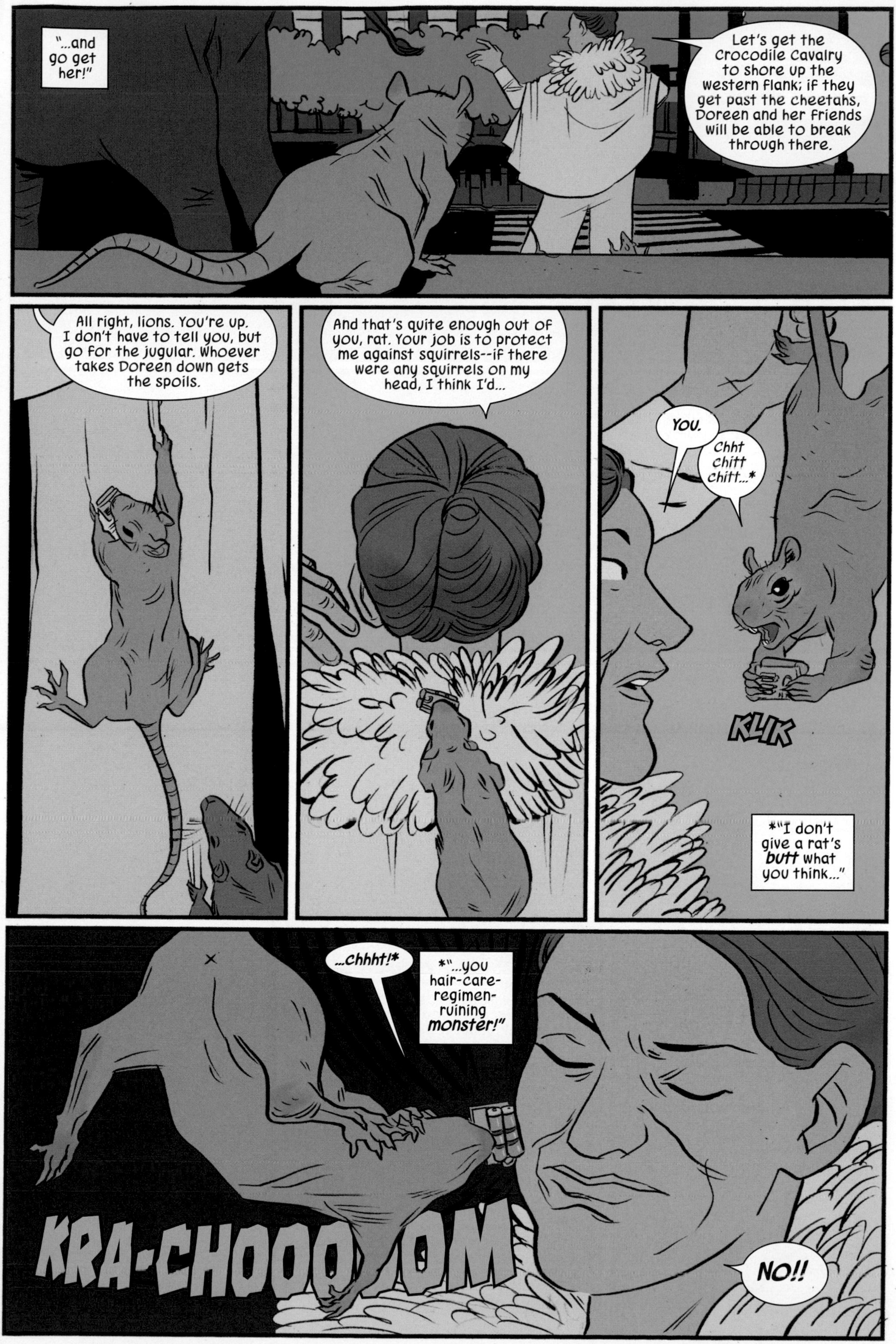

"...and go get her!"
Let's get the Crocodile Cavalry to shore up the western flank; if they get past the cheetahs, Doreen and her friends will be able to break through there.
All right, lions. You're up. I don't have to tell you, but go for the jugular. Whoever takes Doreen down gets the spoils.
And that's quite enough out of you, rat. Your job is to protect me against squirrels--if there were any squirrels on my head, I think I'd...
YOU.
Chht chitt chitt...*
KLIK
*"I don't give a rat's butt what you think..."
...chhht!*
*"...you hair-care-regimen-ruining monster!"
KRA-CHOOOOOM
NO!!

Normally EMPs are silent and invisible, but not in the Marvel Universe! The Marvel Universe is the world outside your window except for two changes: a) super powers, and b) visible EMP radiation that makes a *"kra-choooooom!"* sound in certain circumstances. Otherwise: *largely identical?*

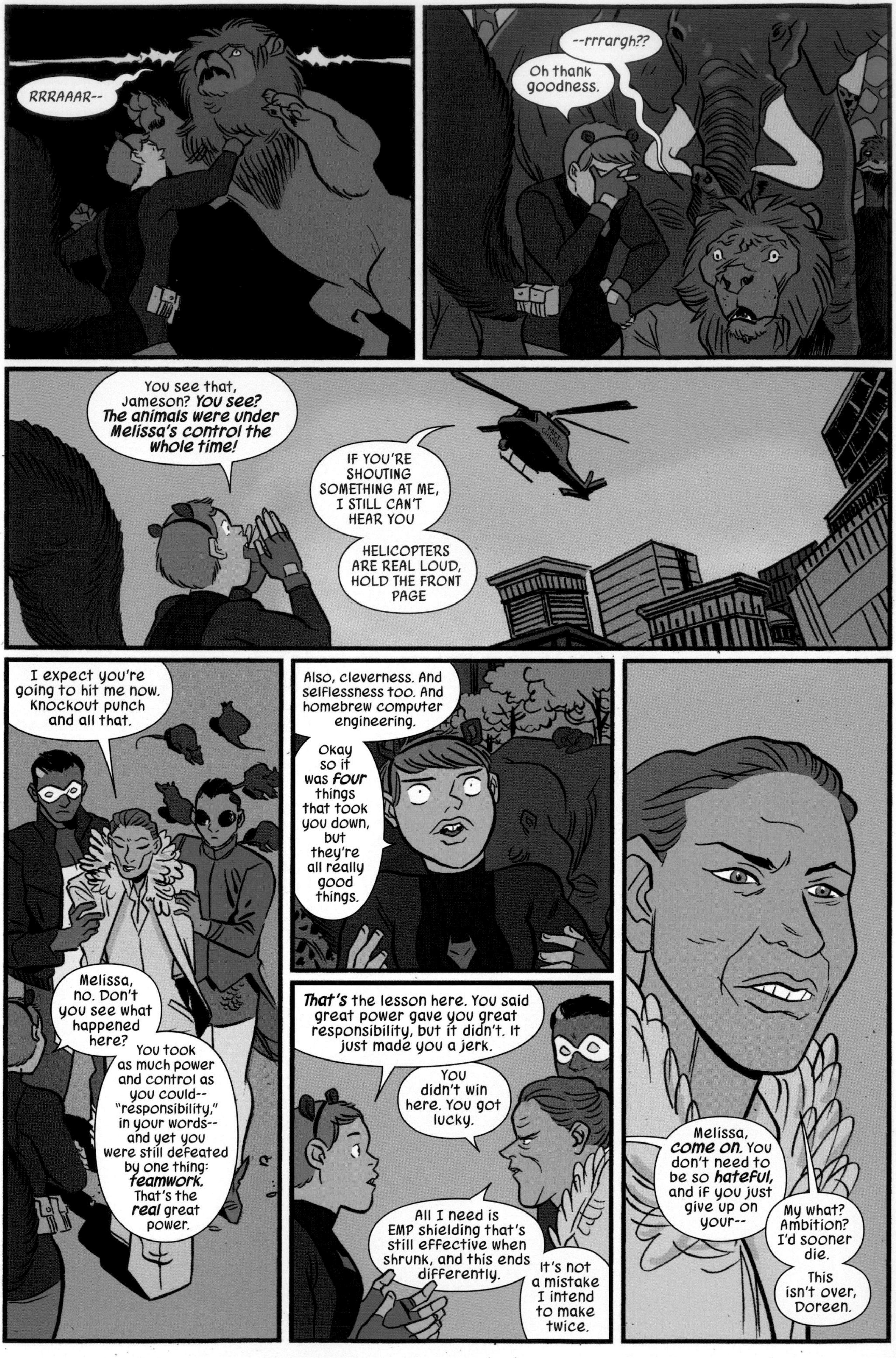
RRRAAAR--
--rrrargh??
Oh thank goodness.
You see that, Jameson? You see? The animals were under Melissa's control the whole time!
IF YOU'RE SHOUTING SOMETHING AT ME, I STILL CAN'T HEAR YOU
HELICOPTERS ARE REAL LOUD, HOLD THE FRONT PAGE
FACT CHANNEL
I expect you're going to hit me now. Knockout punch and all that.
Melissa, no. Don't you see what happened here?
You took as much power and control as you could-- "responsibility," in your words-- and yet you were still defeated by one thing: teamwork. That's the real great power.
Also, cleverness. And selflessness too. And homebrew computer engineering.
Okay so it was four things that took you down, but they're all really good things.
That's the lesson here. You said great power gave you great responsibility, but it didn't. It just made you a jerk.
You didn't win here. You got lucky.
All I need is EMP shielding that's still effective when shrunk, and this ends differently.
It's not a mistake I intend to make twice.
Melissa, come on. You don't need to be so hateful, and if you just give up on your--
My what? Ambition? I'd sooner die.
This isn't over, Doreen.

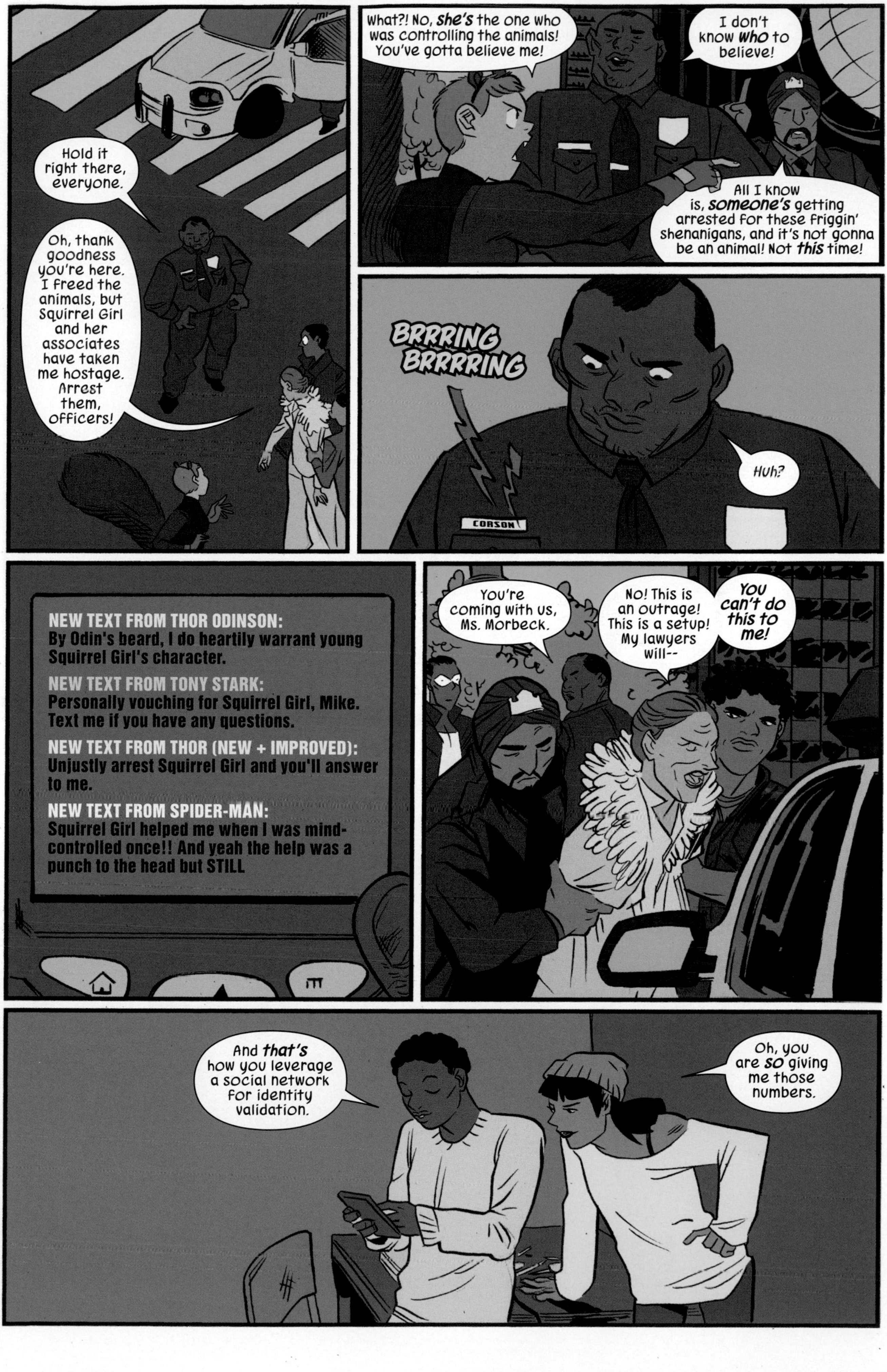
Hold it right there, everyone.
Oh, thank goodness you're here. I freed the animals, but Squirrel Girl and her associates have taken me hostage. Arrest them, officers!
What?! No, she's the one who was controlling the animals! You've gotta believe me!
I don't know who to believe!
All I know is, someone's getting arrested for these friggin' shenanigans, and it's not gonna be an animal! Not this time!
BRRRING BRRRRING
CORSON
Huh?
NEW TEXT FROM THOR ODINSON:
By Odin's beard, I do heartily warrant young Squirrel Girl's character.
NEW TEXT FROM TONY STARK:
Personally vouching for Squirrel Girl, Mike. Text me if you have any questions.
NEW TEXT FROM THOR (NEW + IMPROVED):
Unjustly arrest Squirrel Girl and you'll answer to me.
NEW TEXT FROM SPIDER-MAN:
Squirrel Girl helped me when I was mind-controlled once!! And yeah the help was a punch to the head but STILL
You're coming with us, Ms. Morbeck.
No! This is an outrage! This is a setup! My lawyers will--
You can't do this to me!
And that's how you leverage a social network for identity validation.
Oh, you are so giving me those numbers.

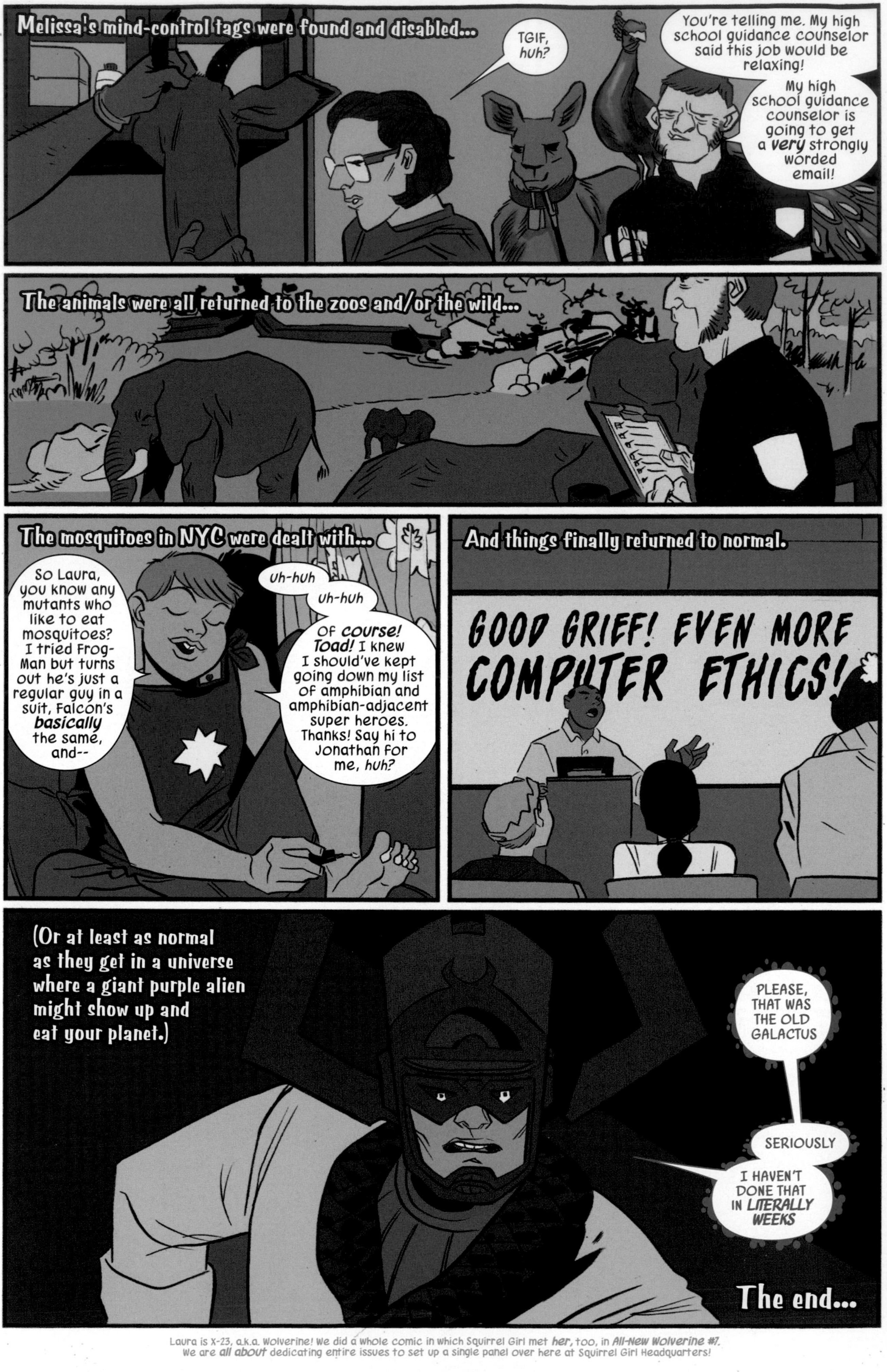
Melissa's mind-control tags were found and disabled...
TGIF, huh?
You're telling me. My high school guidance counselor said this job would be relaxing!
My high school guidance counselor is going to get a very strongly worded email!
The animals were all returned to the zoos and/or the wild...
The mosquitoes in NYC were dealt with...
So Laura, you know any mutants who like to eat mosquitoes? I tried Frog-Man but turns out he's just a regular guy in a suit, Falcon's basically the same, and--
Uh-huh
Uh-huh
Of course! Toad! I knew I should've kept going down my list of amphibian and amphibian-adjacent super heroes. Thanks! Say hi to Jonathan for me, huh?
And things finally returned to normal.
GOOD GRIEF! EVEN MORE COMPUTER ETHICS!
(Or at least as normal as they get in a universe where a giant purple alien might show up and eat your planet.)
PLEASE, THAT WAS THE OLD GALACTUS
SERIOUSLY
I HAVEN'T DONE THAT IN LITERALLY WEEKS
The end...

Laura is X-23, a.k.a. Wolverine! We did a whole comic in which Squirrel Girl met *her,* too, in ***All-New Wolverine #7.***
We are ***all about*** dedicating entire issues to set up a single panel over here at Squirrel Girl Headquarters!

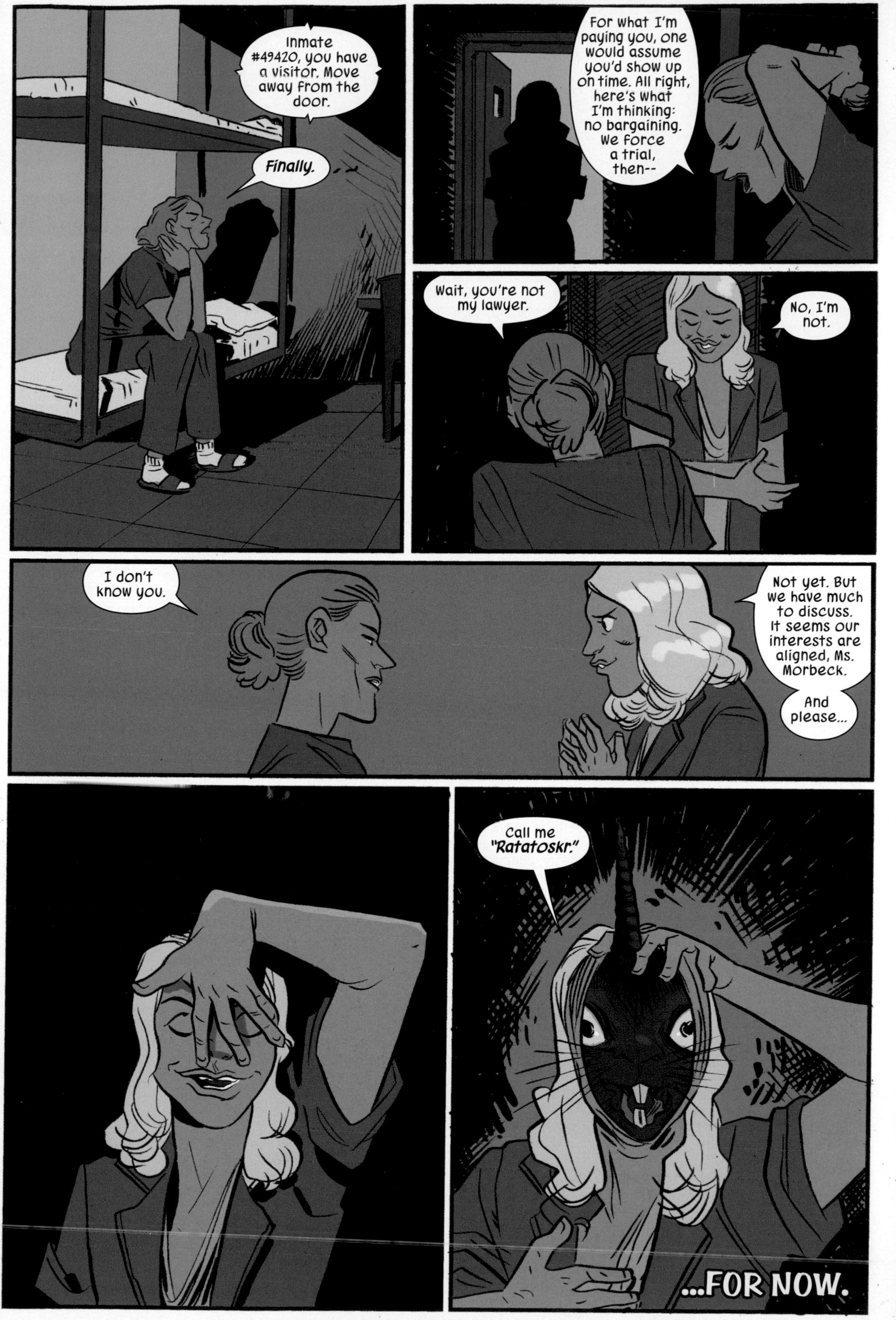
Inmate #49420, you have a visitor. Move away from the door.
Finally.
For what I'm paying you, one would assume you'd show up on time. All right, here's what I'm thinking: no bargaining. We force a trial, then--
Wait, you're not my lawyer.
No, I'm not.
I don't know you.
Not yet. But we have much to discuss. It seems our interests are aligned, Ms. Morbeck.
And please...
Call me "Ratatoskr."
...FOR NOW.

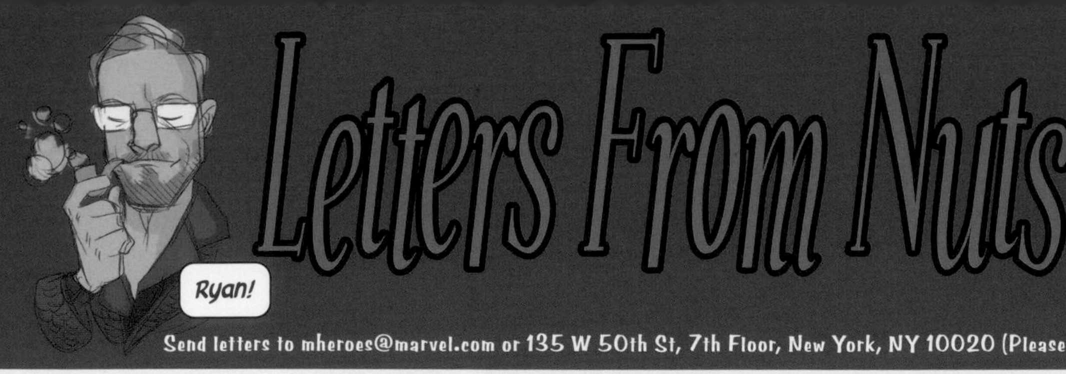
Ryan!

Letters From Nuts

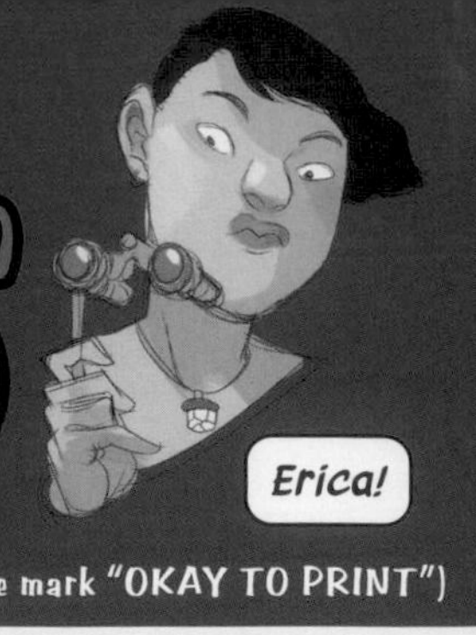
Erica!

Send letters to mheroes@marvel.com or 135 W 50th St, 7th Floor, New York, NY 10020 (Please mark "OKAY TO PRINT")

Ryan and Erica,

YOU GUYS ARE SO UNBELIEVABLY FABULOUS. I used to be an occasional comics reader, and then I discovered the SQUIRREL GIRL trades at my local library…and now I'm literally a RABID DEVOURER OF COMICS. In the reading sense, not the food sense. That'd be gross and most definitely not nutritious.

Anyway, I've got a question, and I'm hoping I won't get in trouble with Marvel for including a DC character in this, but…what's the deal with Mole Man wearing Captain Cold's glasses? (Totally not complaining. Snart is my heart).

Thank you thank you thank you for the amazing work you do. If I had half the talent and wit you have in your left pinkies, I'd be very fortunate indeed. :)

Amy Levenson
South Florida

P.S. My friends are planning on kidnapping me for my first convention in a few months, so of course I'm already planning my Nancy cosplay (also a first!). I'll send pictures if I manage to pull it off.

RYAN: I was going to say, "Mole Man first appeared in 1961 while Captain Cold first appeared afterwards," but I did a search and it turned out that Captain Cold first appeared in 1957! So what the heck, Mole Man? YOU ARE BITING THE STYLE OF ANOTHER PERSON FROM ANOTHER UNIVERSE.

But the real answer is, Mole Man lives underground and so can't see in bright light, so he uses those glasses to minimize the amount of light reaching his eyes. They're also used for snow blindness for the same reasons, so it makes sense that Captain Cold would wear them while he's, you know, in the Arctic colds he's apparently captaining, but I dunno why he wears them on the regular.

I think we are all on-record here in the SQUIRREL GIRL letters pages as being extremely pro-cosplay pictures, so send 'em in when they happen!!

ERICA: I need to see more Nancy cosplay! I know she's a tough one because she's a regular person without a uniform, which is why you don't see her a lot, but I want it!

Also, I didn't design Mole Man! I am all for his adult onesie with a structured cape look, though.

I've been enjoying your comics for the past few months, ever since I first managed to get my hands on them. Last night, I decided to introduce my littlest sister to them, and since I wanted to read them at the same time, we ended up both sitting on my bed looking at them while I read them out loud. I've never been much of a fan of reading comics out loud before, because they're so visual, but it worked surprisingly well with yours. I did voices, and it was a lot of fun. (I forgot that Kraven is Russian until after coming up with his voice, and so didn't give him a Russian accent, whoops.) In fact, it was so awesome that when I was done, my other little sister, who was in the room while we were reading, later asked to be able to read the comics too. Therefore, I have gotten both of my little sisters hooked on your comics. Thank you for bringing them into existence!

Also, I dressed up as Squirrel Girl for Halloween last year, and it was really fun. I even made a utility belt, in which I carried my phone and a bunch of almonds for snacking.

Sincerely, your fan,
Hannah Lerum

RYAN: THIS IS THE CUTEST STORY (AND THE GREATEST ASIDE MINI-STORY IN THE SECOND PARAGRAPH). Here is a secret: I do the voices too when I write, so every one of Kraven's lines gets read out loud in a horrible Canadian/Russian accent. This is also one of the reasons why I write only when nobody else is around.

ERICA: I work in cafes all the time, because at a certain point you just need to have other humans near you (also they make better coffee than I do), and I'm just picturing Ryan muttering to himself in bad Russian in that scenario.

To Ryan and Erica,

Hello from England! I just wanted to say that SG is my absolute favorite Marvel hero at the moment, and every second Wednesday of the month is brightened by her appearance in our local comic store. You guys are awesome, she's awesome—she has given me and my fellow comic fans, Sam Molly, Benji and Edgar plenty of awesome things to talk about! Like her, I'm a second-year university student (journalism posse!), so seeing her managing butt-kicking and essay writing is a great source of hype!

All the best,
Thomas L.

RYAN: Thanks, Thomas! This is super great to hear. As a Canadian, we share the same beautiful Queen, but also the same love of (correctly) putting the (absolutely necessary) letter "u" in places that Americans don't. I'm afraid they're going to edit them out of your letter, so I've restored them here: uuuuuuuuu. You're welcoume.

ERICA: English is a complicated enough language with rules that don't work across the board. There's no need to add letters to words that clearly don't need them.

Dear Erica and Ryan,

We want to thank you for your treatment of a population that is often victimized by prejudice: rats. We are pet rats, but write in solidarity with our wild brothers and sisters. Being controlled by super villains is a drag, but at least your magazine depicts rats with accuracy and respect.
We always thought of squirrels as annoying show-offs—with their *big eyes* and *bushy tails* that humans think are *so* cute—but now we are reassessing those fellow rodents. This is all thanks to Squirrel Girl and your wonderful magazine.

Is a redoubtable Rat Brat too much to hope for in the future?

Sincerely,

Floyd, Elmer, Martin, Jabberwocky, Stan, Ed, Mama Grace, Tillie, and Dora—via our human amanuensis, Bernadette Bosky

RYAN: Oh uh we kinda used some squirrel-positive and rat-negative imagery in this issue I'M SORRY ABOUT THAT!!! In my defense: I had a friend with a pet rat in high school, and it was the first rat I ever met, and she was great (the rat) (the friend was pretty great too, honestly) (just a great time all around at her house). Rat Brat was actually one of the things I considered way before our first issue (when Chipmunk Hunk was but a gleam in my eye), so in an alternate universe this is very close to your perfect comic magazine!

ERICA: Fun Erica trivia: I picked up a pet rat while he was fairly young because I really wanted a rat and told my boyfriend at the time that he was a mouse because he really DID NOT want a rat around. By the time he was full-sized it was too late! MWAHAHA.

Marvel staff,

I have been getting back into comic books after quite a long lapse. I was broke for a while, then I joined the military and couldn't keep print comics around for very long. I would pick them up here and there, but didn't have somewhere to put them. I'm still in the military, but I'm in a more stable situation. I got the Marvel Unlimited app and I started a pull list at my FLCS. It started with a couple of books I was interested in because of the creators' webcomics. (Wolverine was always my favorite, along with Punisher. And you killed them both! Where else was I going to turn?) Ryan North and Christopher Hastings are hilarious. So I picked up THE UNBEATABLE SQUIRREL GIRL and GWENPOOL. Man oh man, those are some of the best books out there. I love that Marvel has really encouraged these offbeat style books. I like the direction Marvel is going. Well, I did. I heard today that some of my favorite books are being canceled, and that my two current favorites, TUSG and GWENPOOL, might be on the chopping block. Well, if that happens, I might just put the comic hobby down again. I sincerely hope you don't cancel good books. I'm sorry if they're not making you the money you feel you need from them, but maybe think about the fact they don't have movies or TV shows to bump their fan base. Please keep making such good books!

Sincerely,
SGT Marc Muehling
G Co 113th FSC

RYAN: Chris Hastings and I have a history together (of really good friendship! He's great! I love that guy!), so I was stoked to hear that he was writing GWENPOOL. And, as YOU know because you read it, but as others might not, he even picked up on the adventures of Old Lady Squirrel Girl in the past in a GWENPOOL story! So I am the #1 fan of Chris Hastings over here. I don't get to decide which books get canceled (EXCEPT SQUIRREL GIRL, NOBODY CANCEL THAT BOOK), but if you haven't heard the news, let me tell you: a SQUIRREL GIRL and NEW WARRIORS TV show has just been announced for 2018! It'll be on Freeform, and it'll star the same Doreen Green we know and love. SQUIRREL GIRL IS COMING TO TV, AHHHHHHHHH.

ERICA: People have been saying we're canceled since issue #1—the first volume's #1—and if you're reading this you're holding the (ohmygod) 28th issue of SQUIRREL GIRL and there are five more outlined/almost finished so I'm not too worried??

P.S. I know it says issue 20, but remember how we had eight issues and then it rebooted eight months later? It was like two years ago.

Dear Erica, Ryan and the rest of the team,

This is what your comic has done to my brain:

I finally get around to going to the cinema to see *Logan*, and, as I sit there, watching the blood-soaked, R-rated carnage, this thought suddenly comes to me: "Truly, Wolverine was the best at what he did: He could count to 255 on one hand in binary.*"

May your wonderful talking squirrel comic—or talking human comic, as it is surely marketed in squirrel territories—long continue to skew my mind. And while I'm here, a big thanks to the—unfortunately now rather embattled—Sheffield Public Libraries for introducing me to it in the first place (I'm a university librarian myself; it never hurts to give other librarians a fillip for all the great stuff they do).

Yours Sincerely,
Sandy Buchanan,
Sheffield,
UK

*It might be a good idea for someone who doesn't have an arts background to check this fact.

RYAN: Sandy, your math is correct, well done! And that is an amazing thing to think during *Logan*. I am so happy and proud. And I am always happy to give a shout-out to libraries! I gave a talk at my local library (the Toronto Public Library) and I showed that scene during the Enigmos arc in which we gave librarians a shout-out in the text. I had to insist that it was real and not something I made up just to butter up the audience! Thank you to the Sheffield Public Library for reppin' our talking squirrel/talking human comic!

ERICA: I still haven't read issue #11. Always moving forward, never back! Although that means that people will keep referencing it and I will have to nod politely, so maybe I should, but every time I think I should I really just take a much-needed rest.

P.S. HOW GOOD WAS *LOGAN???* SO GOOD.

The wardrobes in our house just got so much cooler! I surprised my six-year-old twin daughters with THE UNBEATABLE SQUIRREL GIRL T-shirts, and they love them. We're super stoked to have official Erica Henderson gear that we can wear to show support for our favorite Marvel series. The girls have a bit of growing left before they fully fit in their shirts, but that'll just be something for them to look forward to.

Hopefully there are plans for more Squirrel Girl clothing in the near future!

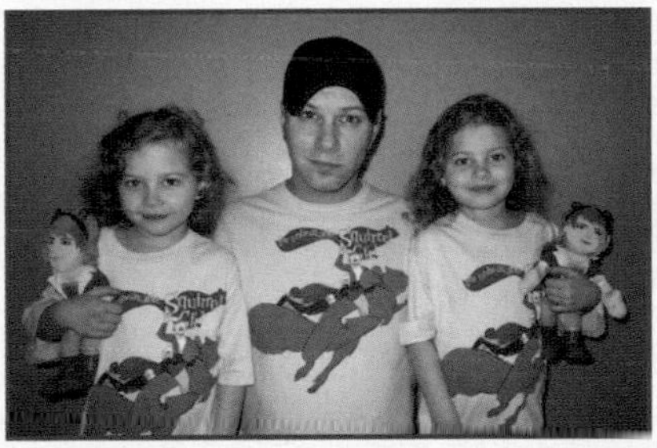

Darrick Patrick
Dayton, Ohio

P.S. I'm including a photograph of Logann, Nola, and I sporting our new attire.

RYAN: AHHHH I LOVE THIS, I LOVE THOSE SQUIRREL GIRL DOLLS, ABSOLUTELY EVERYTHING ABOUT THIS PHOTO IS A+++

ERICA: Unfortunately the shirts are all licensed out, but I'd keep checking that WeLoveFine site!

Dear Unbeatable Squirrel Warriors,

I have been reading for about half a year, and I absolutely LOVE this comic. I just recently discovered that Squirrel Girl will be on FREEFORM. I can't wait! Where was I going with this? Oh, right. Well, earlier today, I was sitting on my porch eating a peanut butter sandwich, in memory of Monkey Joe. I have corn hanging on my tree, so that squirrels will eat it. A squirrel was on a branch, near the corn, and it ripped the corn right out of the tree and stole it! Probably the weirdest thing I've seen this week. Now, I have a question. Could you come to my hometown of Kokomo, Indiana, possibly, for Kokomo-Con?

Bye for now, Unbeatable Squirrel Warriors!
Sarah King

RYAN: Sarah, around this time last year, some cartoonist friends and I were camping in the beautiful woods of Alaska with no cell phone signals or Internet, and we spent a long time—over an hour—arguing about whether "Kokomo" in the Beach Boys song was a real place. It's the kind of debate that could be settled today in two seconds, but with that option not available to us, all we could do was scour our memories for whatever Kokomo facts we had, and then rely on our skills in rhetoric to try to convince others. It was so much fun! My friend Jon recalled that the song mentioned Kokomo was "off the Florida Keys," which I thought was very convincing on the "it's real" side—why would the Boys of the Beach specify such an exact location for a fake place? I mention this because the first thing we ALL did when we got back was look up all the Kokomo information we could, and now I know all the Kokomo facts, which means I am more familiar with Kokomo, Indiana, than you might expect! And if Erica and I ever go down to Kokomo—we'll get there fast and then we'll take it slow—I'd be more than happy to share them.

ERICA: There is a strange old lady who lives in the strange house at the end of my street who leaves what appears to be an entire loaf of bread out every day for the birds (please don't do this as bread does not contain all the nutrition that animals need), and if I'm walking by right as she's just put it out, I can usually catch a squirrel or two stealing several slices from the birds and running off. They're pretty opportunistic and feisty.

P.S. Oh my god that song is in my head now—but the Muppets version.

P.P.S. Why would you hold a cartoonist retreat in a place with no internet? I don't understand. You did this on purpose, Ryan?

Next Issue:

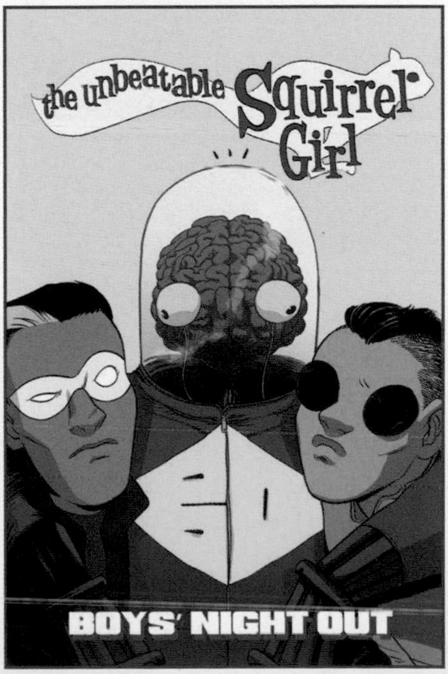
the unbeatable Squirrel Girl
BOYS' NIGHT OUT

Attention, Squirrel Scouts! Make sure to check out our production blog, **unbeatablesquirrelgirl.tumblr.com**, where we post behind-the-scenes stuff on how the book gets made, along with all sorts of cool things *you* make: fanart, cosplay, whatever!

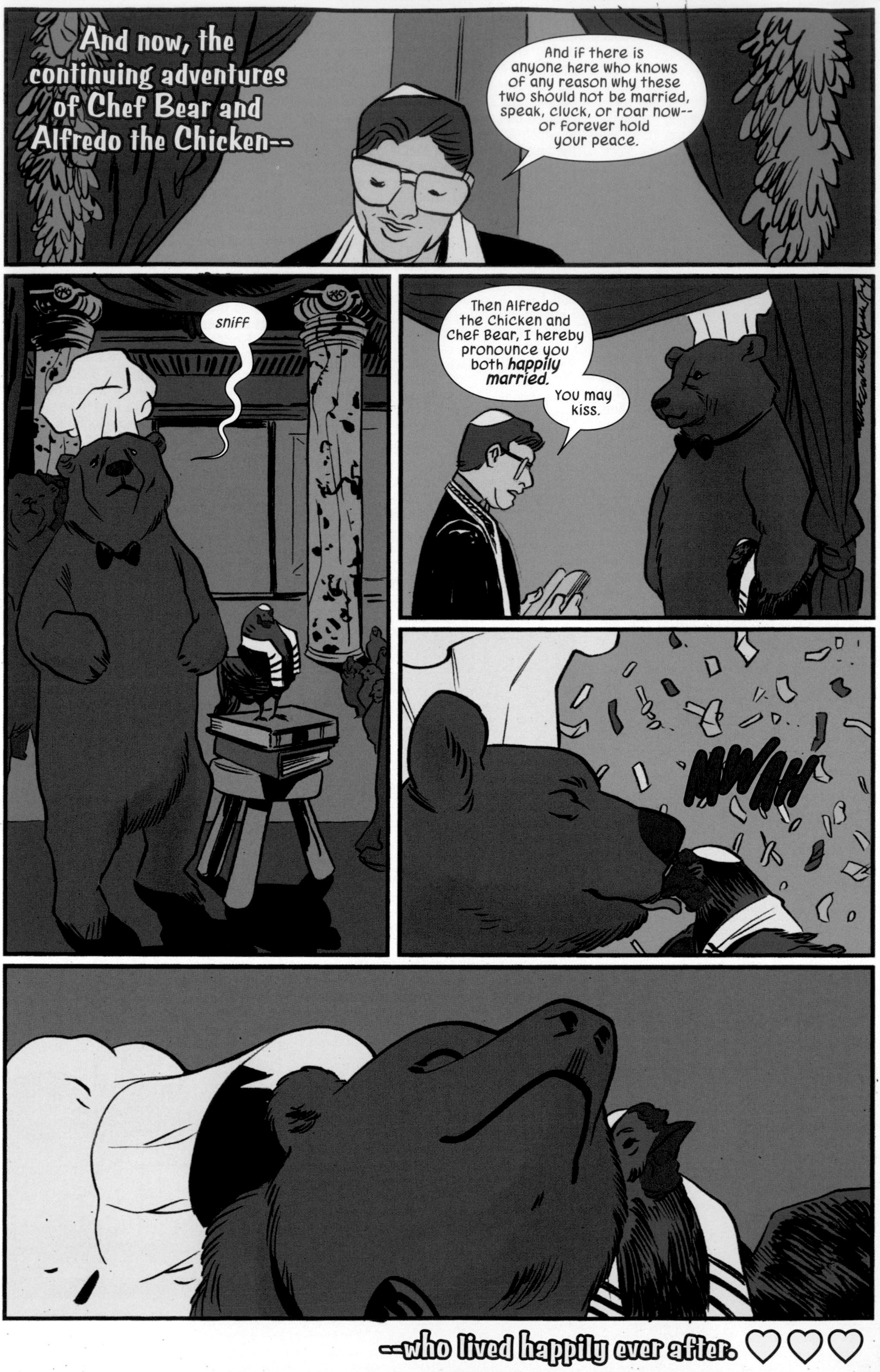

And now, the continuing adventures of Chef Bear and Alfredo the Chicken--
And if there is anyone here who knows of any reason why these two should not be married, speak, cluck, or roar now-- or forever hold your peace.
sniff
Then Alfredo the Chicken and Chef Bear, I hereby pronounce you both *happily married.*
You may kiss.
MWAH
--who lived happily ever after. ♡♡♡

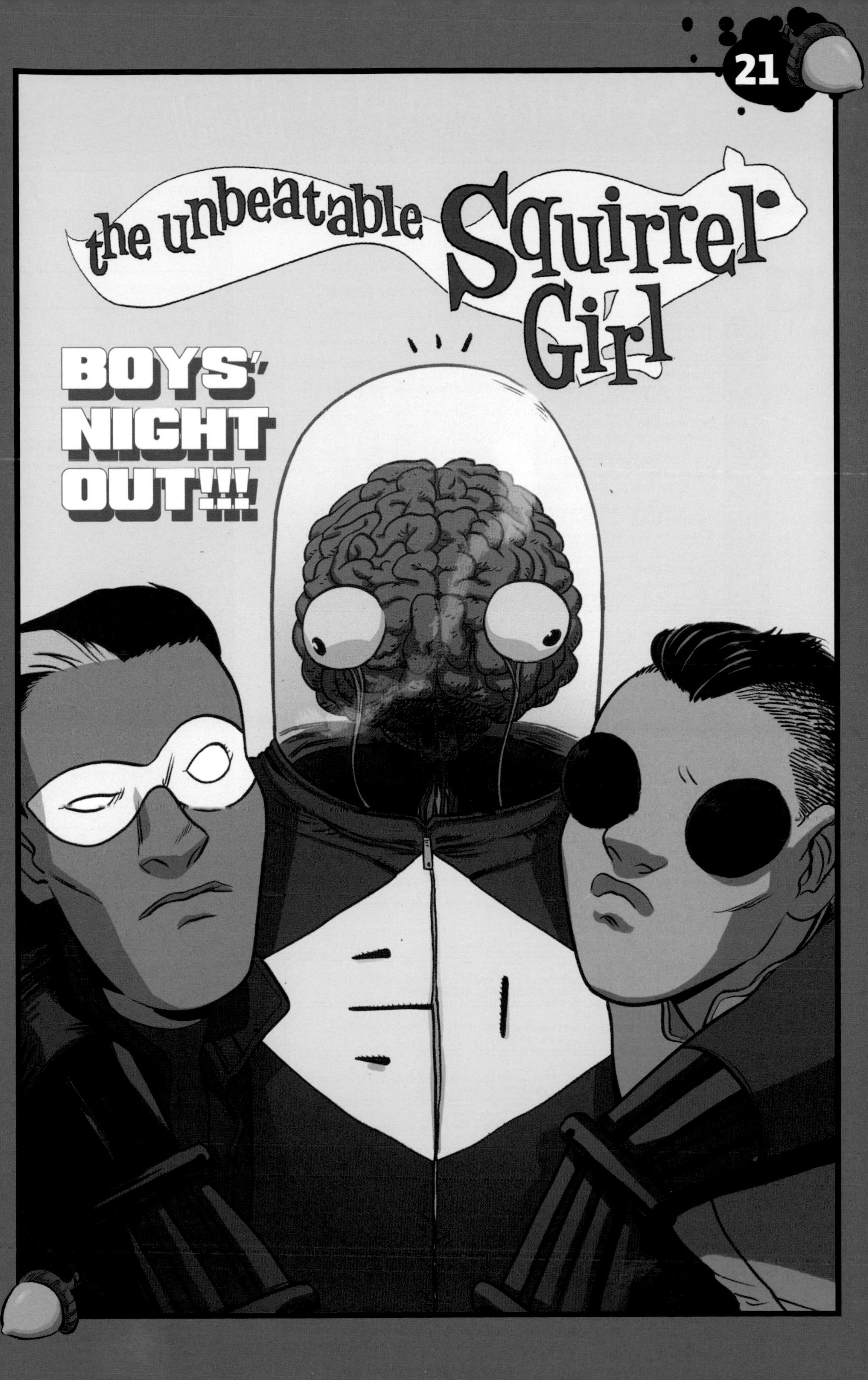
21
the unbeatable Squirrel Girl
BOYS' NIGHT OUT!!!

Doreen Green isn't just a second-year computer science student: she secretly also has all the powers of both squirrel and girl! She uses her amazing abilities to fight crime **and** be as awesome as possible. You know her as...**The Unbeatable Squirrel Girl!** Find out what she's been up to, with...

Squirrel Girl *in a nutshell*

search! 🔍

#braindrain

#chipmunkhunk

#koiboi

#itsfabulous

#diedandcamebackasfourguys

#theoctopals

Egg @imduderadtude
DOCTOR DOOM IS TAKNIG OVER NEW YORK CITY!!!!! PLEASE RT SO PPL KNO THAT DOC DOOM IS TAKNG OVER TEH CITY!!!!!!!

> **Squirrel Girl** @unbeatablesg
> @imduderadtude No it's not Doctor Doom, it's Melissa Morbeck! Also, me and my pals defeated her, so uh...we're good here

Egg @imduderadtude
DOCTOR DOOM IS GOING BY THE NAME "MELISSA MORBECK" NOW!!!!!! PLEASE RT!!!!!! #doctordoom

> **Squirrel Girl** @unbeatablesg
> @imduderadtude No, no, it was NEVER Doctor Doom, it was a NEW villain, Melissa Morbeck, who is COMPLETELY DIFFERENT from Doctor Doom!

> **Squirrel Girl** @unbeatablesg
> @imduderadtude Well, I mean, not COMPLETELY different. They both got that "take over the world" thing goin' on I guess

> **Squirrel Girl** @unbeatablesg
> @imduderadtude (also she briefly wore his clothes)

> **Squirrel Girl** @unbeatablesg
> @imduderadtude (or rather a bear under her control did)

> **Squirrel Girl** @unbeatablesg
> @imduderadtude (for reasons)

> **Squirrel Girl** @unbeatablesg
> @imduderadtude ANYWAY, point is, you don't need anyone to "please rt" anything, because the situation is under control!!

> **Egg** @imduderadtude
> @unbeatablesg wow it's almost like i said "please rt" and not "please @ me w fact checks"!!!!!

> **Egg** @imduderadtude
> @unbeatablesg OH WAIT I DID!!!!! blocked

Nancy W. @sewwiththeflo
@unbeatablesg whoooooo's up for a vacation?

> **Squirrel Girl** @unbeatablesg
> @sewwiththeflo Oh man! Negative Zone hangouts with Allene??

> **Tony Stark** @starkmantony ✅
> @unbeatablesg @sewwiththeflo Should you really be posting that you're leaving NYC undefended while you hang out in an alternate dimension?

> **Squirrel Girl** @unbeatablesg
> @starkmantony @sewwiththeflo Oh pfft it's not undefended. It's got YOU.

> **Tony Stark** @starkmantony ✅
> @unbeatablesg @sewwiththeflo I keep telling you, I'm a computer now. I put my consciousness into a computer. Because of course I did.

> **Squirrel Girl** @unbeatablesg
> @starkmantony @sewwiththeflo Tony I know you're trying to get me to make you another captcha pic but I'm busy packing for NEGAZONE TIMES

> **Squirrel Girl** @unbeatablesg
> @starkmantony @sewwiththeflo Besides, EVEN IF THAT WERE TRUE, Koi Boi, Chipmunk Hunk and Brain Drain are still gonna defend the city!!

> **Squirrel Girl** @unbeatablesg
> @starkmantony @sewwiththeflo I wonder what hilarious shenanigans THOSE crazy characters will get into! I, for one, would like to know!

> **Squirrel Girl** @unbeatablesg
> @starkmantony @sewwiththeflo And I WILL know, right after we return from visiting a friend in the Negative Zone SEE YOU LATER BYE

> **Tony Stark** @starkmantony ✅
> @unbeatablesg @sewwiththeflo Wait, are you there? Squirrel Girl?

> **Tony Stark** @starkmantony ✅
> @unbeatablesg @sewwiththeflo Squirrel Girl?

> **Tony Stark** @starkmantony ✅
> @unbeatablesg @sewwiththeflo Hello?

> **Tony Stark** @starkmantony ✅
> @unbeatablesg @sewwiththeflo ...

> **Tony Stark** @starkmantony ✅
> @unbeatablesg @sewwiththeflo You've been gone five minutes and the news is already reporting that a bear and a chicken got married

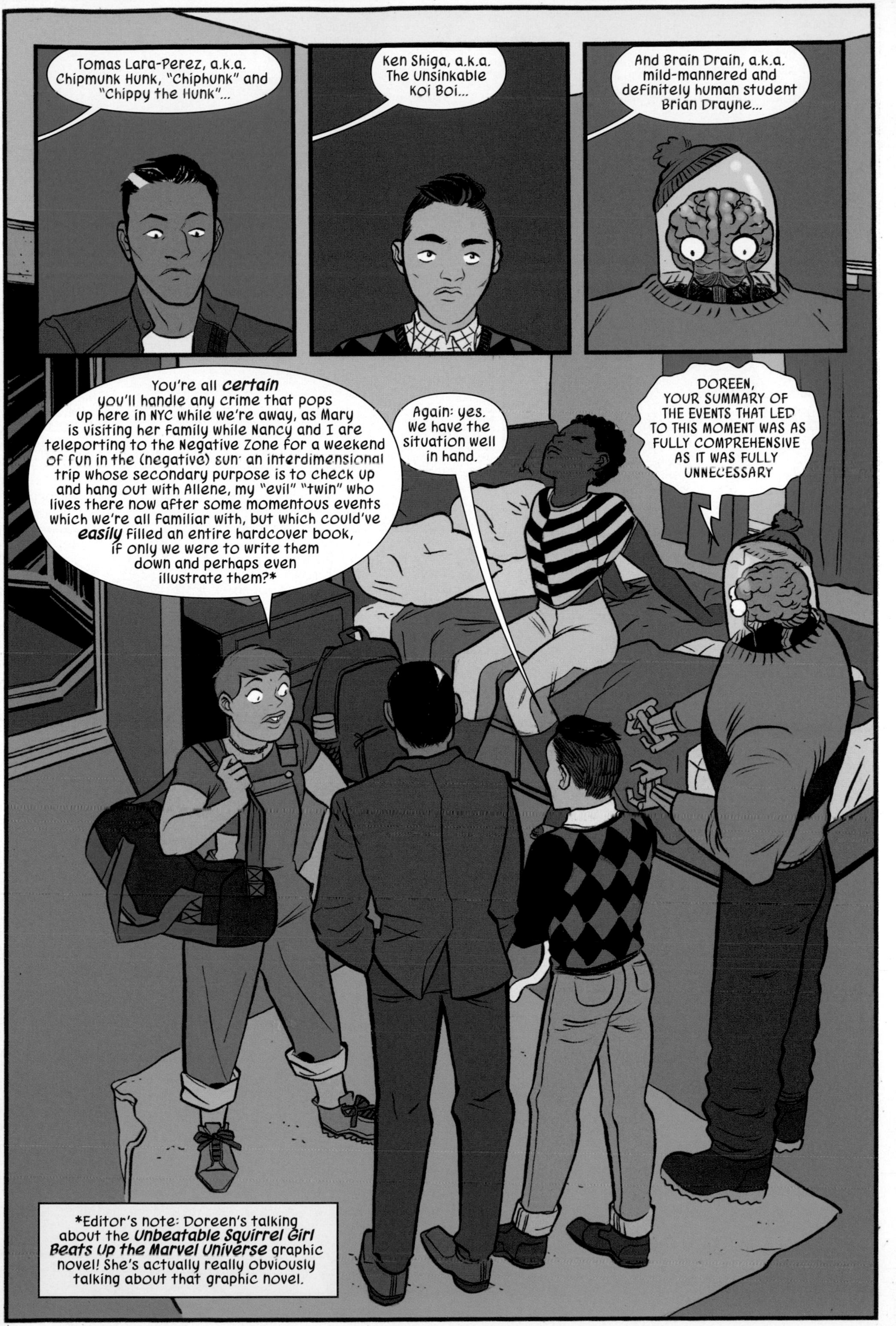
Tomas Lara-Perez, a.k.a. Chipmunk Hunk, "Chiphunk" and "Chippy the Hunk"...
Ken Shiga, a.k.a. The Unsinkable Koi Boi...
And Brain Drain, a.k.a. mild-mannered and definitely human student Brian Drayne...
You're all certain you'll handle any crime that pops up here in NYC while we're away, as Mary is visiting her family while Nancy and I are teleporting to the Negative Zone for a weekend of fun in the (negative) sun: an interdimensional trip whose secondary purpose is to check up and hang out with Allene, my "evil" "twin" who lives there now after some momentous events which we're all familiar with, but which could've easily filled an entire hardcover book, if only we were to write them down and perhaps even illustrate them?*
Again: yes. We have the situation well in hand.
DOREEN, YOUR SUMMARY OF THE EVENTS THAT LED TO THIS MOMENT WAS AS FULLY COMPREHENSIVE AS IT WAS FULLY UNNECESSARY
*Editor's note: Doreen's talking about the Unbeatable Squirrel Girl Beats Up the Marvel Universe graphic novel! She's actually really obviously talking about that graphic novel.

Doreen, if you are transforming the story of your life into some sort of "serialized illustrated picto-drama," then **heed my warning well:** it's actually really fun and I recommend it 100%!

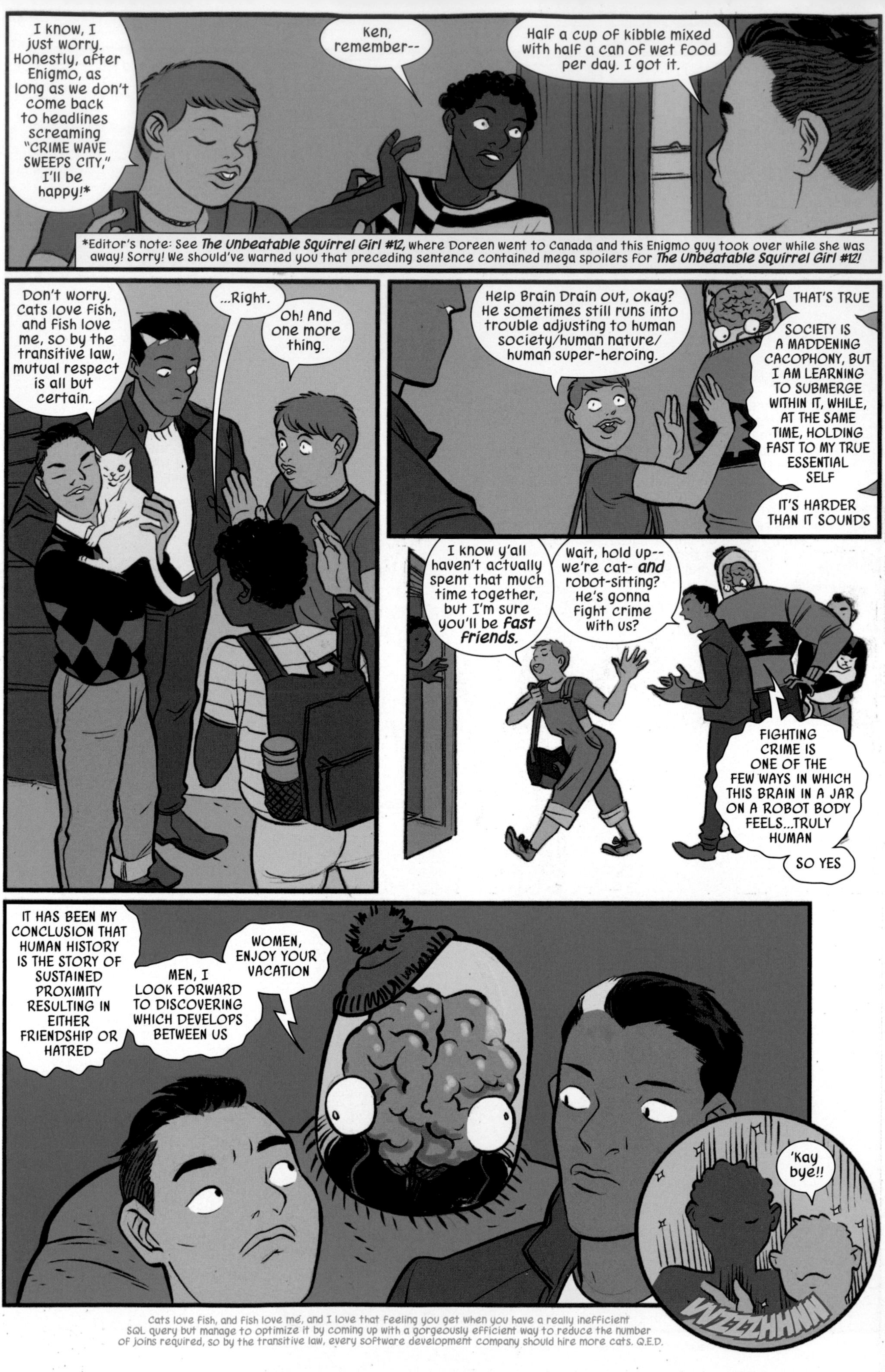
I know, I just worry. Honestly, after Enigmo, as long as we don't come back to headlines screaming "CRIME WAVE SWEEPS CITY," I'll be happy!*
Ken, remember--
Half a cup of kibble mixed with half a can of wet food per day. I got it.
*Editor's note: See *The Unbeatable Squirrel Girl #12*, where Doreen went to Canada and this Enigmo guy took over while she was away! Sorry! We should've warned you that preceding sentence contained mega spoilers for *The Unbeatable Squirrel Girl #12!*
Don't worry. Cats love fish, and fish love me, so by the transitive law, mutual respect is all but certain.
...Right.
Oh! And one more thing.
Help Brain Drain out, okay? He sometimes still runs into trouble adjusting to human society/human nature/ human super-heroing.
THAT'S TRUE
SOCIETY IS A MADDENING CACOPHONY, BUT I AM LEARNING TO SUBMERGE WITHIN IT, WHILE, AT THE SAME TIME, HOLDING FAST TO MY TRUE ESSENTIAL SELF
IT'S HARDER THAN IT SOUNDS
I know y'all haven't actually spent that much time together, but I'm sure you'll be **fast friends.**
Wait, hold up-- we're cat- **and** robot-sitting? He's gonna fight crime with us?
FIGHTING CRIME IS ONE OF THE FEW WAYS IN WHICH THIS BRAIN IN A JAR ON A ROBOT BODY FEELS...TRULY HUMAN
SO YES
IT HAS BEEN MY CONCLUSION THAT HUMAN HISTORY IS THE STORY OF SUSTAINED PROXIMITY RESULTING IN EITHER FRIENDSHIP OR HATRED
MEN, I LOOK FORWARD TO DISCOVERING WHICH DEVELOPS BETWEEN US
WOMEN, ENJOY YOUR VACATION
'Kay bye!!
VVZZZHHNNN

Cats love fish, and fish love me, and I love that feeling you get when you have a really inefficient SQL query but manage to optimize it by coming up with a gorgeously efficient way to reduce the number of joins required, so by the transitive law, every software development company should hire more cats. Q.E.D.

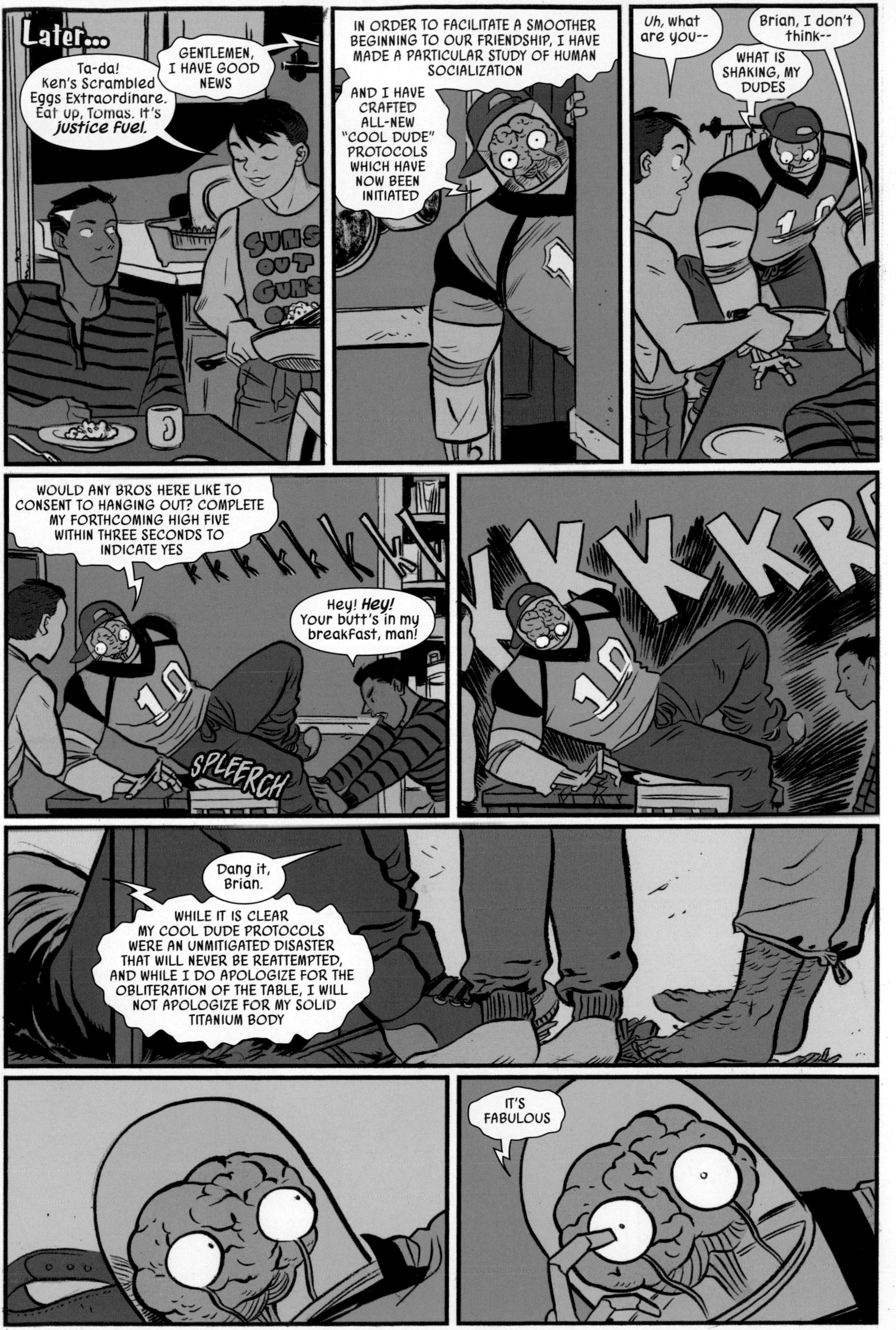
Later...
Ta-da! Ken's Scrambled Eggs Extraordinare. Eat up, Tomas. It's justice fuel.
GENTLEMEN, I HAVE GOOD NEWS
SUNS OUT GUNS
IN ORDER TO FACILITATE A SMOOTHER BEGINNING TO OUR FRIENDSHIP, I HAVE MADE A PARTICULAR STUDY OF HUMAN SOCIALIZATION
AND I HAVE CRAFTED ALL-NEW "COOL DUDE" PROTOCOLS WHICH HAVE NOW BEEN INITIATED
Uh, what are you--
Brian, I don't think--
WHAT IS SHAKING, MY DUDES
WOULD ANY BROS HERE LIKE TO CONSENT TO HANGING OUT? COMPLETE MY FORTHCOMING HIGH FIVE WITHIN THREE SECONDS TO INDICATE YES
Hey! Hey! Your butt's in my breakfast, man!
SPLEERCH
KKKR
Dang it, Brian.
WHILE IT IS CLEAR MY COOL DUDE PROTOCOLS WERE AN UNMITIGATED DISASTER THAT WILL NEVER BE REATTEMPTED, AND WHILE I DO APOLOGIZE FOR THE OBLITERATION OF THE TABLE, I WILL NOT APOLOGIZE FOR MY SOLID TITANIUM BODY
IT'S FABULOUS

Do eggs truly make a "spleerch" sound when you sit on a plate of them? This answer is generously left as an exercise for the reader.

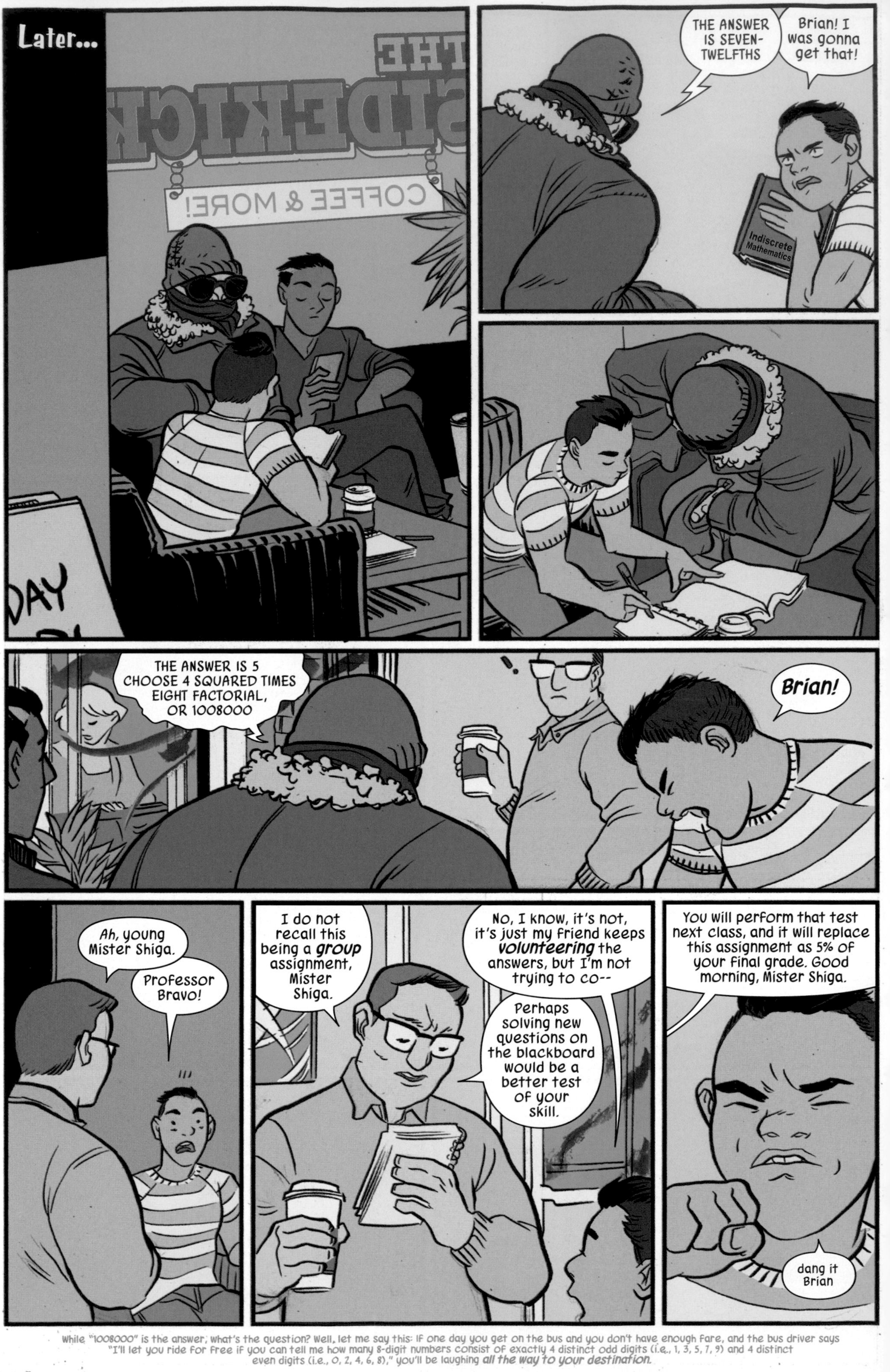
Later...
THE ANSWER IS SEVEN-TWELFTHS
Brian! I was gonna get that!
Indiscrete Mathematics
THE ANSWER IS 5 CHOOSE 4 SQUARED TIMES EIGHT FACTORIAL, OR 1008000
Brian!
Ah, young Mister Shiga.
Professor Bravo!
I do not recall this being a *group* assignment, Mister Shiga.
No, I know, it's not, it's just my friend keeps *volunteering* the answers, but I'm not trying to co--
Perhaps solving new questions on the blackboard would be a better test of your skill.
You will perform that test next class, and it will replace this assignment as 5% of your final grade. Good morning, Mister Shiga.
dang it Brian

While "1008000" is the answer, what's the question? Well, let me say this: If one day you get on the bus and you don't have enough fare, and the bus driver says "I'll let you ride for free if you can tell me how many 8-digit numbers consist of exactly 4 distinct odd digits (i.e., 1, 3, 5, 7, 9) and 4 distinct even digits (i.e., 0, 2, 4, 6, 8)," you'll be laughing ***all the way to your destination.***

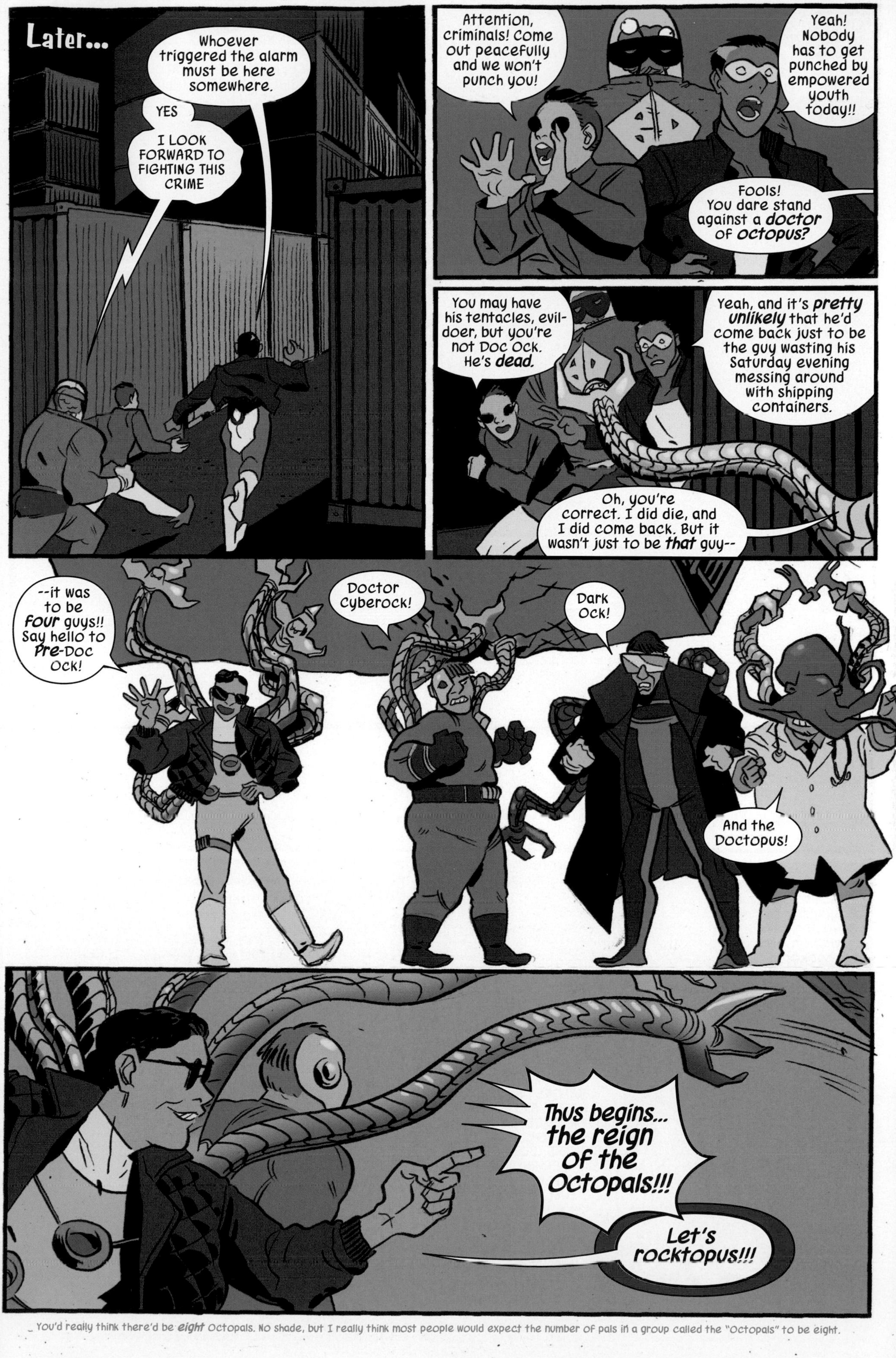
Later...
Whoever triggered the alarm must be here somewhere.
YES
I LOOK FORWARD TO FIGHTING THIS CRIME
Attention, criminals! Come out peacefully and we won't punch you!
Yeah! Nobody has to get punched by empowered youth today!!
Fools! You dare stand against a *doctor* of *octopus?*
You may have his tentacles, evildoer, but you're not Doc Ock. He's *dead.*
Yeah, and it's *pretty unlikely* that he'd come back just to be the guy wasting his Saturday evening messing around with shipping containers.
Oh, you're correct. I did die, and I did come back. But it wasn't just to be *that* guy--
--it was to be *four* guys!! Say hello to *Pre*-Doc Ock!
Doctor Cyberock!
Dark Ock!
And the Doctopus!
Thus begins... the reign of the Octopals!!!
Let's rocktopus!!!

_ You'd really think there'd be *eight* Octopals. No shade, but I really think most people would expect the number of pals in a group called the "Octopals" to be eight.

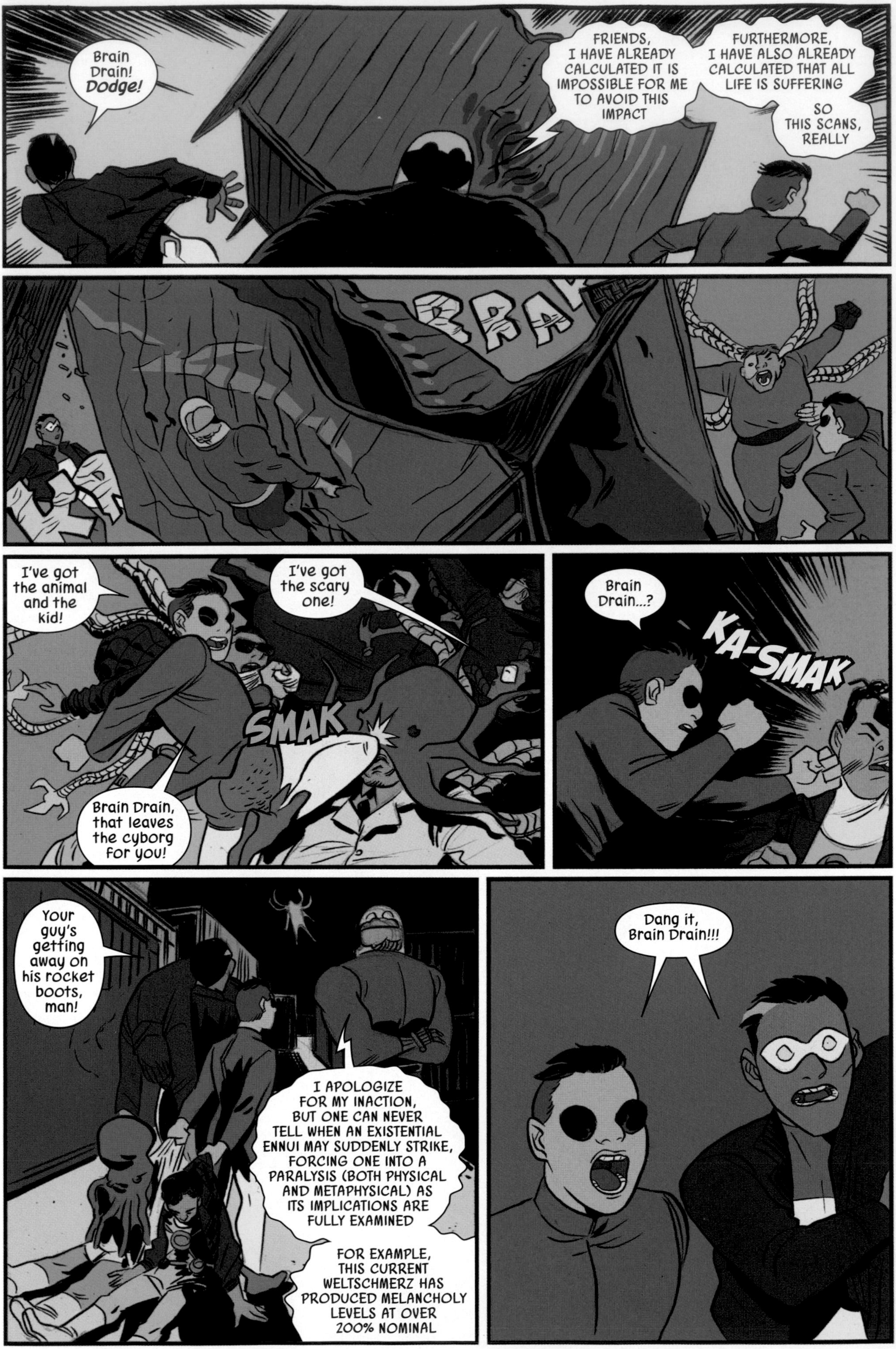
Brain Drain! Dodge!
FRIENDS, I HAVE ALREADY CALCULATED IT IS IMPOSSIBLE FOR ME TO AVOID THIS IMPACT
FURTHERMORE, I HAVE ALSO ALREADY CALCULATED THAT ALL LIFE IS SUFFERING
SO THIS SCANS, REALLY
BRA
I've got the animal and the kid!
I've got the scary one!
SMAK
Brain Drain, that leaves the cyborg for you!
Brain Drain...?
KA-SMAK
Your guy's getting away on his rocket boots, man!
I APOLOGIZE FOR MY INACTION, BUT ONE CAN NEVER TELL WHEN AN EXISTENTIAL ENNUI MAY SUDDENLY STRIKE, FORCING ONE INTO A PARALYSIS (BOTH PHYSICAL AND METAPHYSICAL) AS ITS IMPLICATIONS ARE FULLY EXAMINED
FOR EXAMPLE, THIS CURRENT WELTSCHMERZ HAS PRODUCED MELANCHOLY LEVELS AT OVER 200% NOMINAL
Dang it, Brain Drain!!!

"Weltschmerz" is a word English borrowed from German, and it refers to the world-weariness of someone who believes that the real world can never satisfy the demands of the mind! Feel free to use it whenever you feel that the real world can never satisfy your mind's demands, and remember the fun talking-squirrel comic book you learned it from!

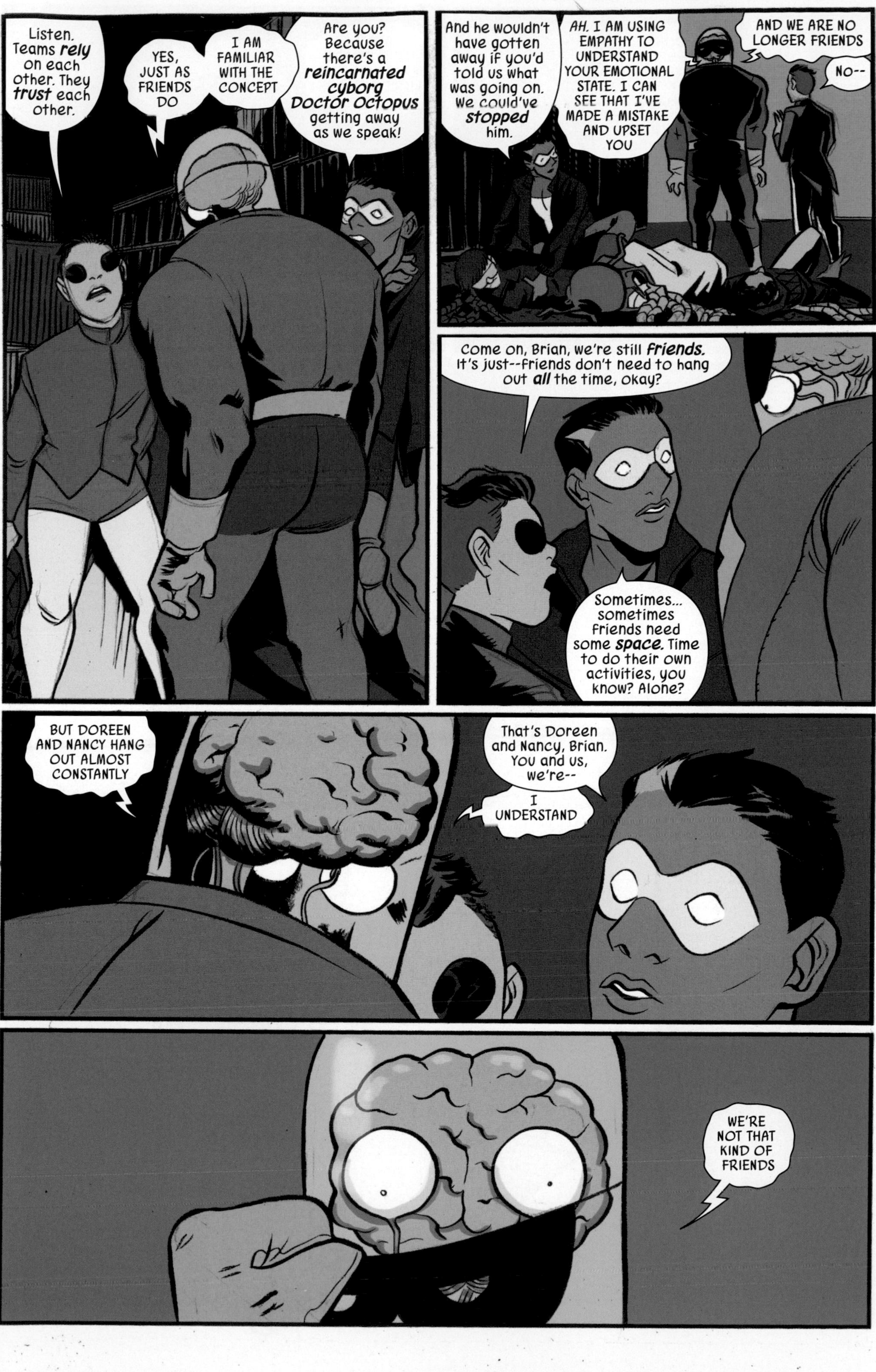
Listen. Teams rely on each other. They trust each other.
YES, JUST AS FRIENDS DO
I AM FAMILIAR WITH THE CONCEPT
Are you? Because there's a reincarnated cyborg Doctor Octopus getting away as we speak!
And he wouldn't have gotten away if you'd told us what was going on. We could've stopped him.
AH. I AM USING EMPATHY TO UNDERSTAND YOUR EMOTIONAL STATE. I CAN SEE THAT I'VE MADE A MISTAKE AND UPSET YOU
AND WE ARE NO LONGER FRIENDS
No--
Come on, Brian, we're still friends. It's just--friends don't need to hang out all the time, okay?
Sometimes... sometimes friends need some space. Time to do their own activities, you know? Alone?
BUT DOREEN AND NANCY HANG OUT ALMOST CONSTANTLY
That's Doreen and Nancy, Brian. You and us, we're--
I UNDERSTAND
WE'RE NOT THAT KIND OF FRIENDS

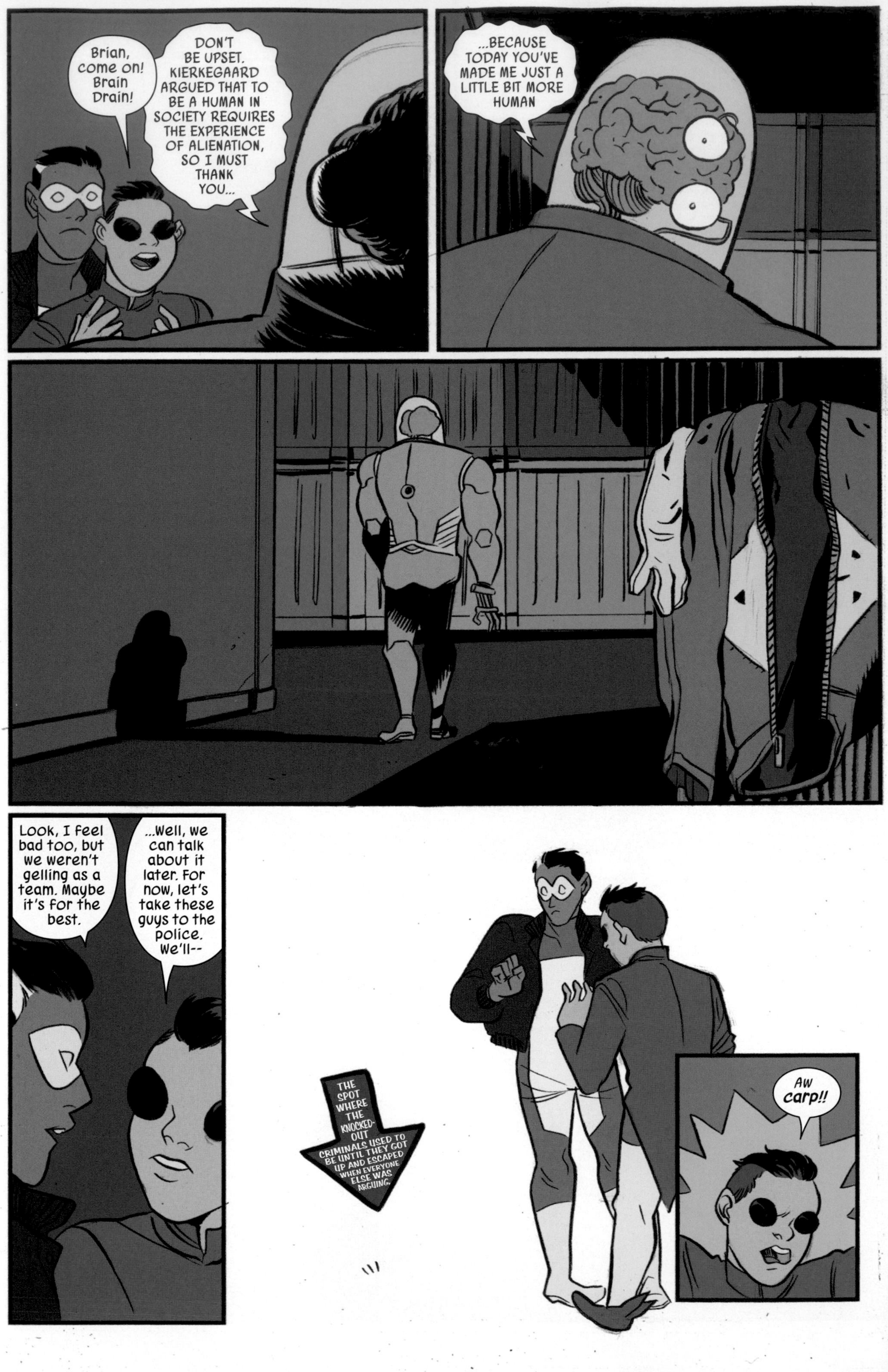
Brian, come on! Brain Drain!
DON'T BE UPSET. KIERKEGAARD ARGUED THAT TO BE A HUMAN IN SOCIETY REQUIRES THE EXPERIENCE OF ALIENATION, SO I MUST THANK YOU...
...BECAUSE TODAY YOU'VE MADE ME JUST A LITTLE BIT MORE HUMAN
Look, I feel bad too, but we weren't gelling as a team. Maybe it's for the best.
...Well, we can talk about it later. For now, let's take these guys to the police. We'll--
THE SPOT WHERE THE KNOCKED-OUT CRIMINALS USED TO BE UNTIL THEY GOT UP AND ESCAPED WHEN EVERYONE ELSE WAS ARGUING.
Aw carp!!

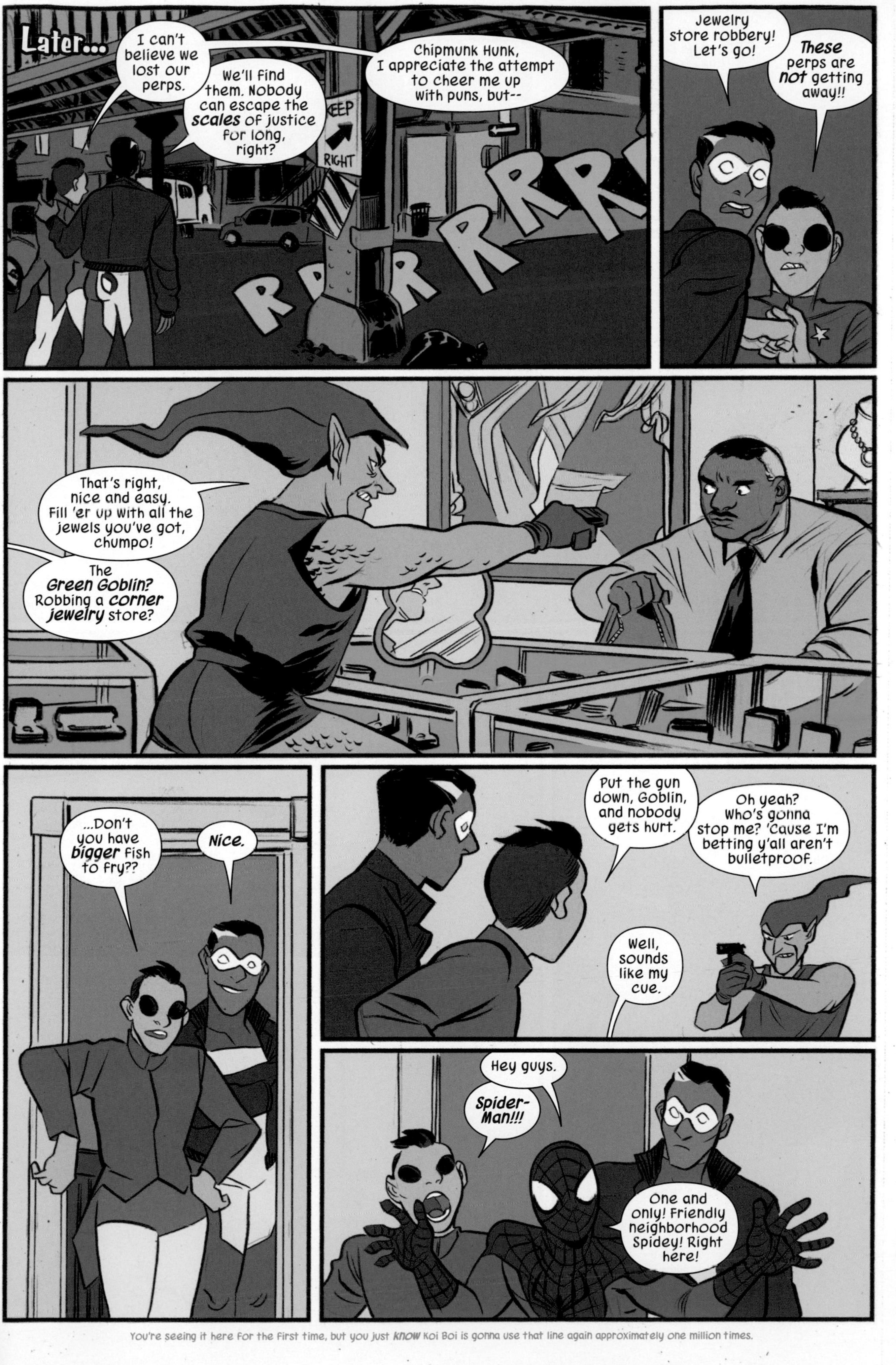
Later...
I can't believe we lost our perps.
We'll find them. Nobody can escape the scales of justice for long, right?
Chipmunk Hunk, I appreciate the attempt to cheer me up with puns, but--
KEEP RIGHT
RRRRRR
Jewelry store robbery! Let's go!
These perps are not getting away!!
That's right, nice and easy. Fill 'er up with all the jewels you've got, chumpo!
The Green Goblin? Robbing a corner jewelry store?
...Don't you have bigger fish to fry??
Nice.
Put the gun down, Goblin, and nobody gets hurt.
Oh yeah? Who's gonna stop me? 'Cause I'm betting y'all aren't bulletproof.
Well, sounds like my cue.
Hey guys.
Spider-Man!!!
One and only! Friendly neighborhood Spidey! Right here!

You're seeing it here for the first time, but you just *know* Koi Boi is gonna use that line again approximately one million times.

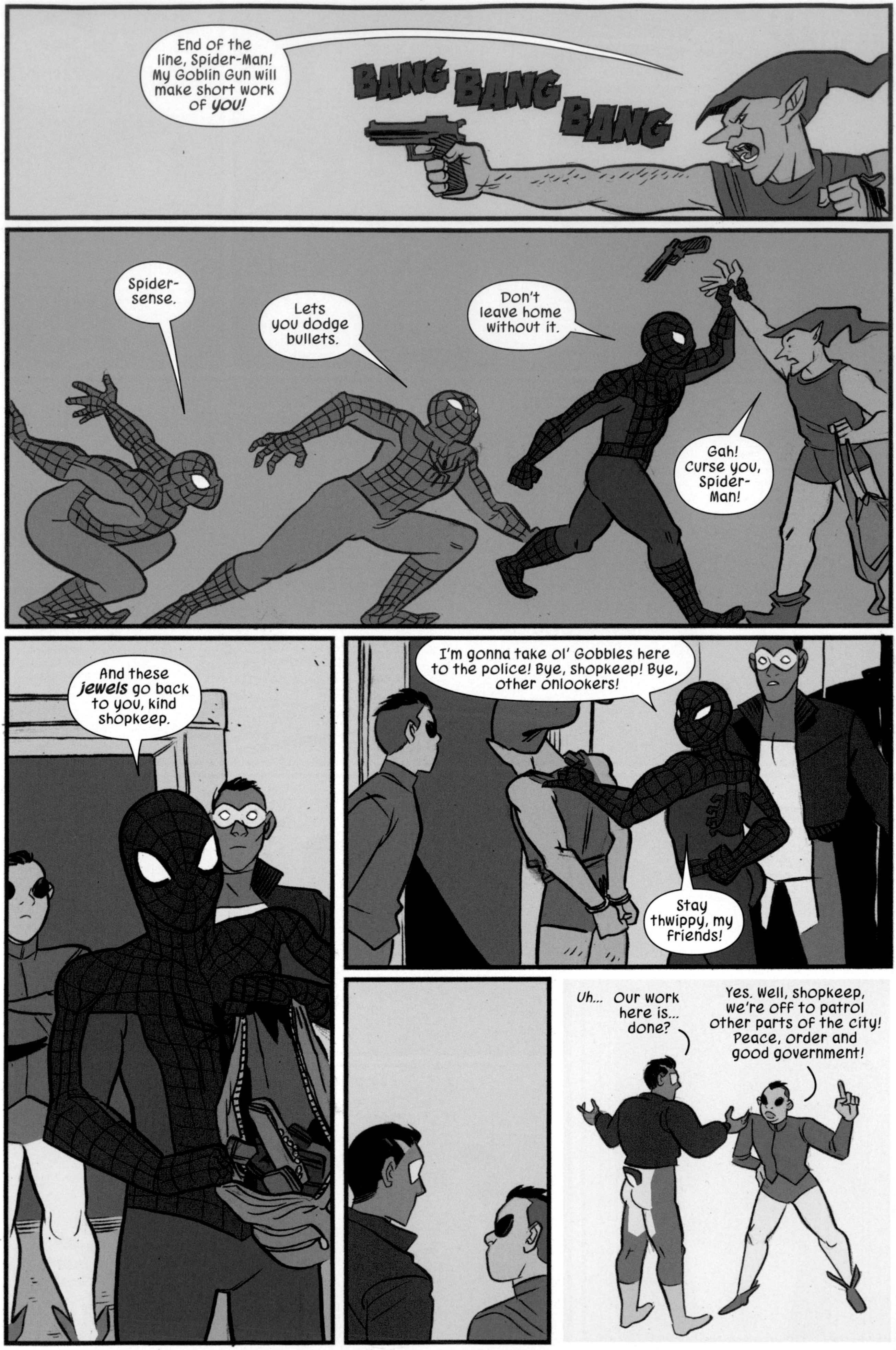
End of the line, Spider-Man! My Goblin Gun will make short work of *you!*
BANG BANG BANG
Spider-sense.
Lets you dodge bullets.
Don't leave home without it.
Gah! Curse you, Spider-Man!
And these *jewels* go back to you, kind shopkeep.
I'm gonna take ol' Gobbles here to the police! Bye, shopkeep! Bye, other onlookers!
Stay thwippy, my friends!
Uh... Our work here is... done?
Yes. Well, shopkeep, we're off to patrol other parts of the city! Peace, order and good government!

Spider-sense: Lets you dodge bullets, while also sensing if there are any cool spiders nearby. Honestly, I mostly only use the first part of it.

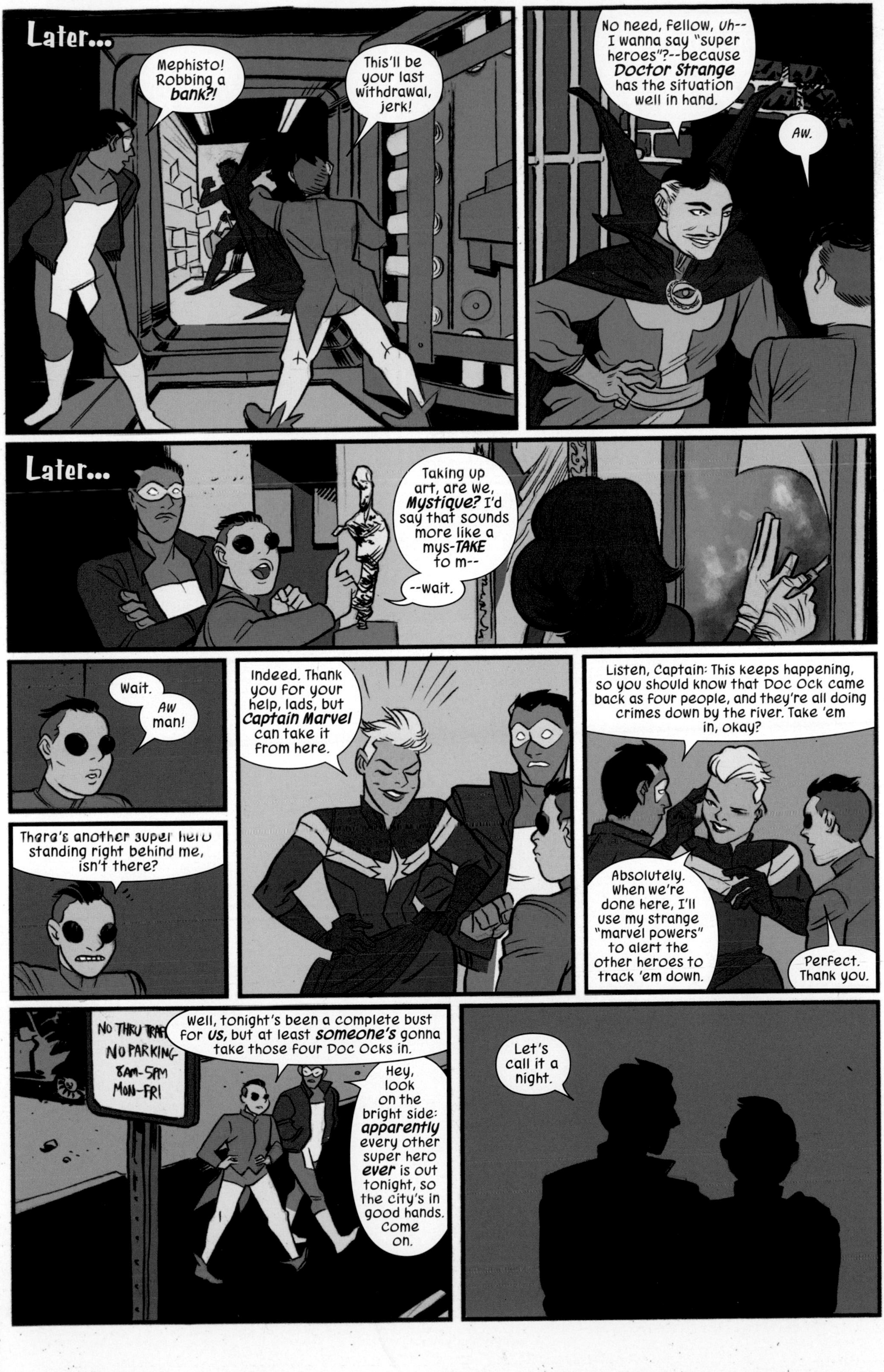
Later...
Mephisto! Robbing a bank?!
This'll be your last withdrawal, jerk!
No need, fellow, uh-- I wanna say "super heroes"?--because Doctor Strange has the situation well in hand.
AW.
Later...
Taking up art, are we, Mystique? I'd say that sounds more like a mys-TAKE to m--
--wait.
Wait.
Aw man!
Indeed. Thank you for your help, lads, but Captain Marvel can take it from here.
Listen, Captain: This keeps happening, so you should know that Doc Ock came back as four people, and they're all doing crimes down by the river. Take 'em in, okay?
There's another super hero standing right behind me, isn't there?
Absolutely. When we're done here, I'll use my strange "marvel powers" to alert the other heroes to track 'em down.
Perfect. Thank you.
NO PARKING
8AM-5PM
MON-FRI
Well, tonight's been a complete bust for us, but at least someone's gonna take those four Doc Ocks in.
Hey, look on the bright side: apparently every other super hero ever is out tonight, so the city's in good hands. Come on.
Let's call it a night.

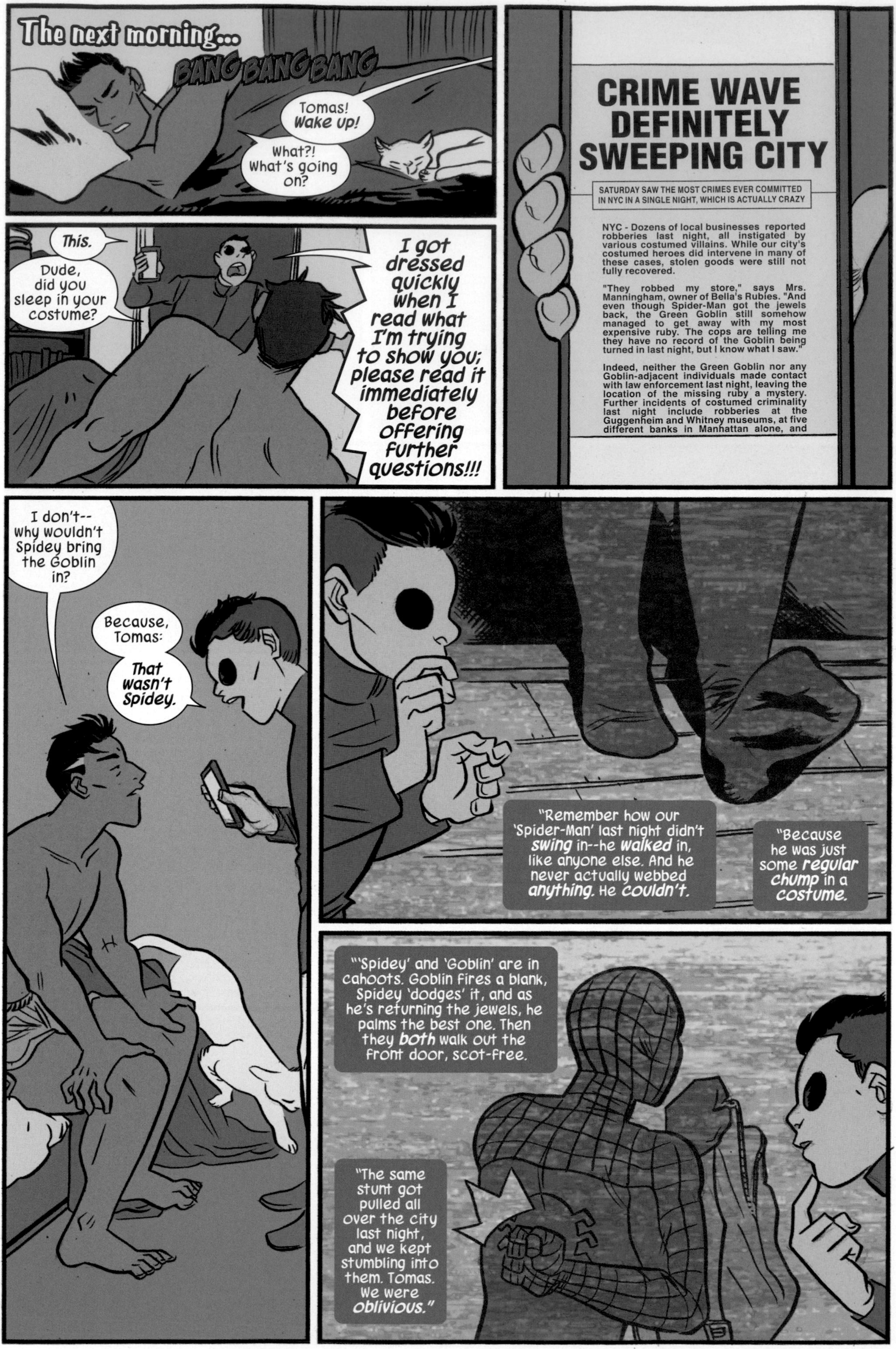
The next morning...
BANG BANG BANG
Tomas! Wake up!
What?! What's going on?
CRIME WAVE DEFINITELY SWEEPING CITY
SATURDAY SAW THE MOST CRIMES EVER COMMITTED IN NYC IN A SINGLE NIGHT, WHICH IS ACTUALLY CRAZY
NYC - Dozens of local businesses reported robberies last night, all instigated by various costumed villains. While our city's costumed heroes did intervene in many of these cases, stolen goods were still not fully recovered.
"They robbed my store," says Mrs. Manningham, owner of Bella's Rubies. "And even though Spider-Man got the jewels back, the Green Goblin still somehow managed to get away with my most expensive ruby. The cops are telling me they have no record of the Goblin being turned in last night, but I know what I saw."
Indeed, neither the Green Goblin nor any Goblin-adjacent individuals made contact with law enforcement last night, leaving the location of the missing ruby a mystery. Further incidents of costumed criminality last night include robberies at the Guggenheim and Whitney museums, at five different banks in Manhattan alone, and
This.
Dude, did you sleep in your costume?
I got dressed quickly when I read what I'm trying to show you; please read it immediately before offering further questions!!!
I don't-- why wouldn't Spidey bring the Goblin in?
Because, Tomas:
That wasn't Spidey.
"Remember how our 'Spider-Man' last night didn't swing in--he walked in, like anyone else. And he never actually webbed anything. He couldn't.
"Because he was just some regular chump in a costume.
"'Spidey' and 'Goblin' are in cahoots. Goblin fires a blank, Spidey 'dodges' it, and as he's returning the jewels, he palms the best one. Then they both walk out the front door, scot-free.
"The same stunt got pulled all over the city last night, and we kept stumbling into them. Tomas. We were oblivious."

It must be fun to be a headline writer in the Marvel Universe. I bet it's never boring. You probably get to use a 72pt font any time you want and don't even have to wait for a moon landing to give you the excuse.

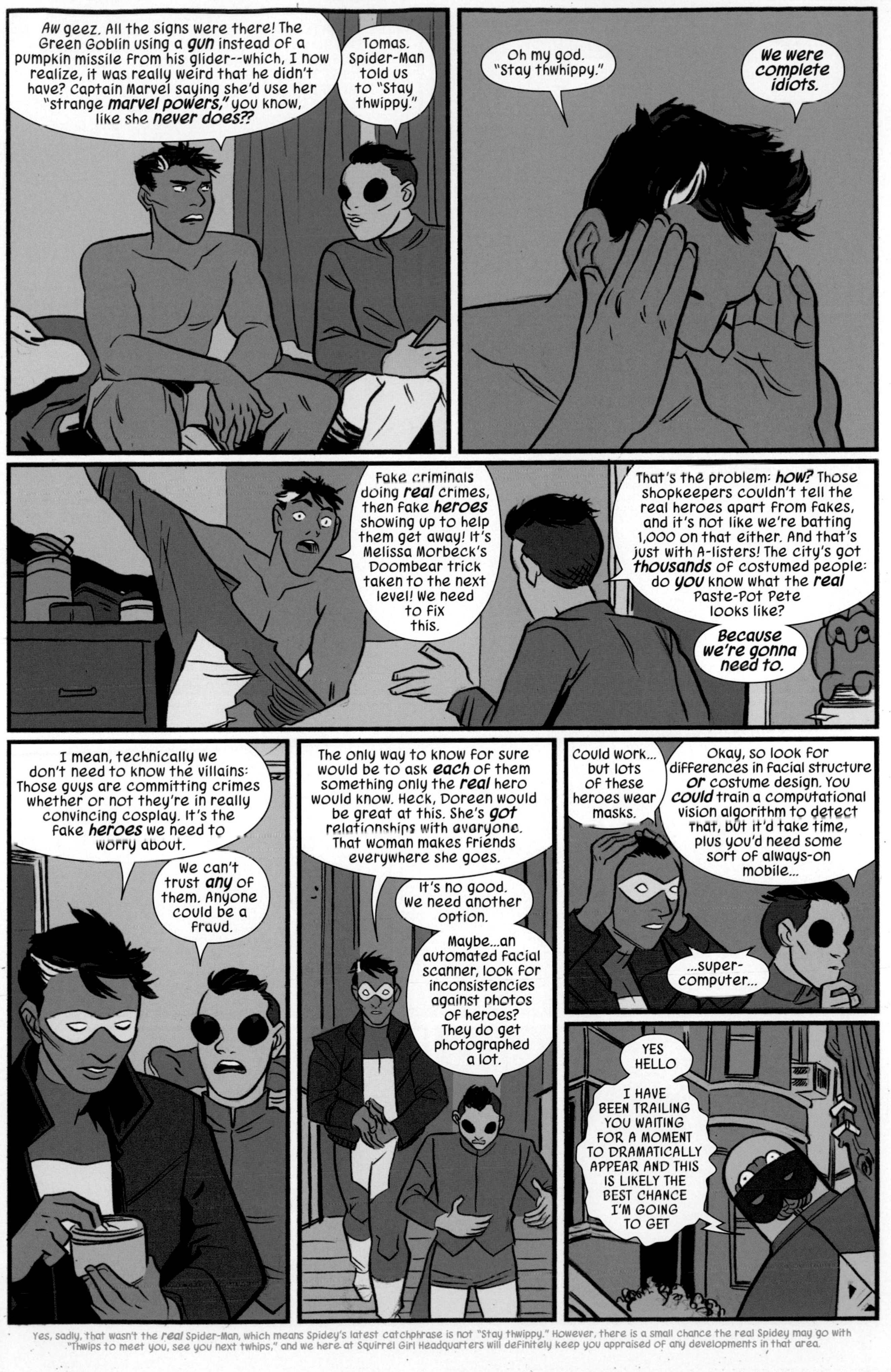
Aw geez. All the signs were there! The Green Goblin using a gun instead of a pumpkin missile from his glider--which, I now realize, it was really weird that he didn't have? Captain Marvel saying she'd use her "strange marvel powers," you know, like she never does??
Tomas. Spider-Man told us to "Stay thwippy."
Oh my god. "Stay thwhippy."
We were complete idiots.
Fake criminals doing real crimes, then fake heroes showing up to help them get away! It's Melissa Morbeck's Doombear trick taken to the next level! We need to fix this.
That's the problem: how? Those shopkeepers couldn't tell the real heroes apart from fakes, and it's not like we're batting 1,000 on that either. And that's just with A-listers! The city's got thousands of costumed people: do you know what the real Paste-Pot Pete looks like?
Because we're gonna need to.
I mean, technically we don't need to know the villains: Those guys are committing crimes whether or not they're in really convincing cosplay. It's the fake heroes we need to worry about.
We can't trust any of them. Anyone could be a fraud.
The only way to know for sure would be to ask each of them something only the real hero would know. Heck, Doreen would be great at this. She's got relationships with everyone. That woman makes friends everywhere she goes.
It's no good. We need another option.
Maybe...an automated facial scanner, look for inconsistencies against photos of heroes? They do get photographed a lot.
Could work... but lots of these heroes wear masks.
Okay, so look for differences in facial structure or costume design. You could train a computational vision algorithm to detect that, but it'd take time, plus you'd need some sort of always-on mobile...
...super-computer...
YES HELLO
I HAVE BEEN TRAILING YOU WAITING FOR A MOMENT TO DRAMATICALLY APPEAR AND THIS IS LIKELY THE BEST CHANCE I'M GOING TO GET

Yes, sadly, that wasn't the *real* Spider-Man, which means Spidey's latest catchphrase is not "Stay thwippy." However, there is a small chance the real Spidey may go with "Thwips to meet you, see you next twhips," and we here at Squirrel Girl Headquarters will definitely keep you appraised of any developments in that area.

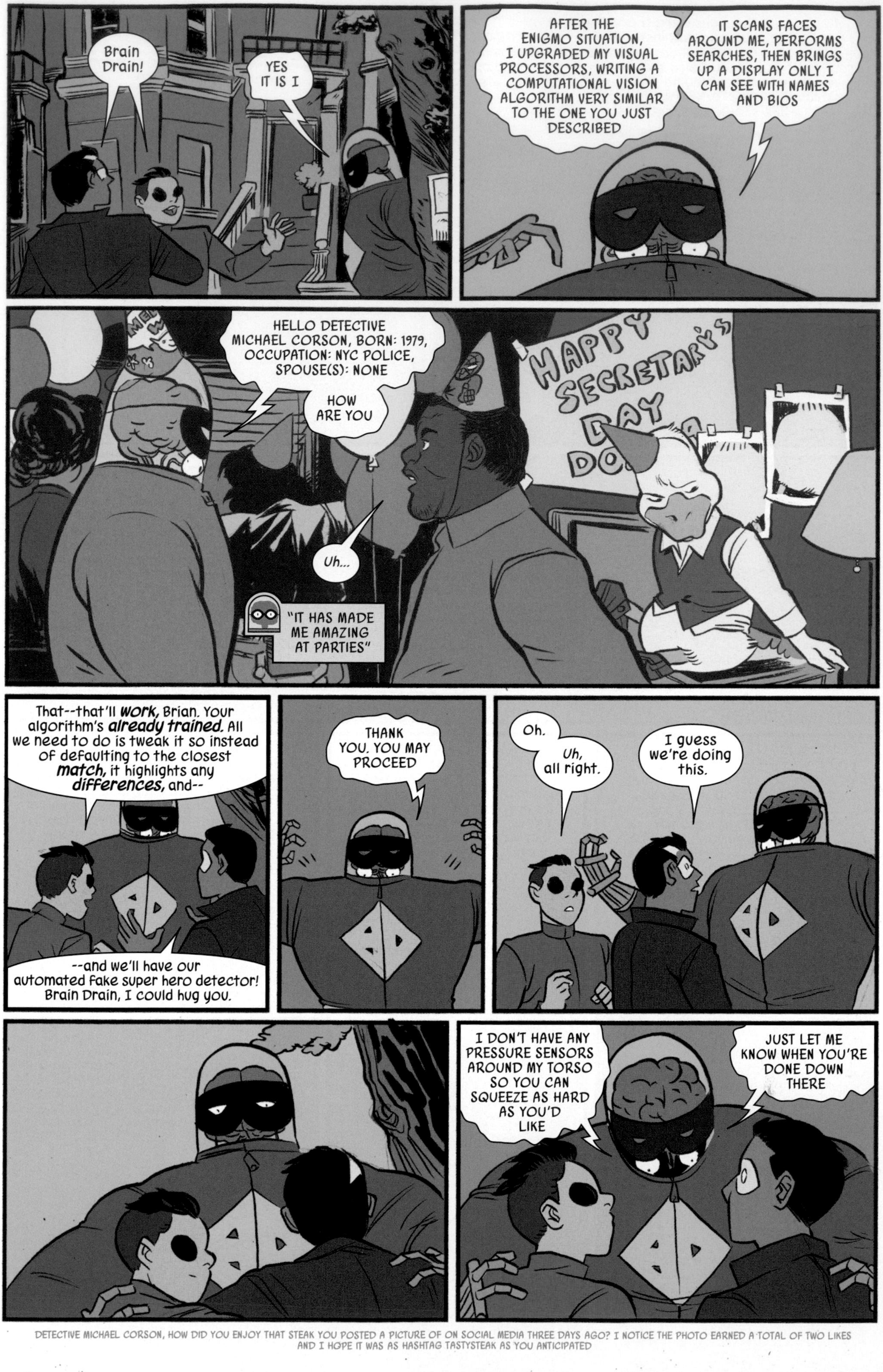
Brain Drain!
YES IT IS I
AFTER THE ENIGMO SITUATION, I UPGRADED MY VISUAL PROCESSORS, WRITING A COMPUTATIONAL VISION ALGORITHM VERY SIMILAR TO THE ONE YOU JUST DESCRIBED
IT SCANS FACES AROUND ME, PERFORMS SEARCHES, THEN BRINGS UP A DISPLAY ONLY I CAN SEE WITH NAMES AND BIOS
HELLO DETECTIVE MICHAEL CORSON, BORN: 1979, OCCUPATION: NYC POLICE, SPOUSE(S): NONE
HOW ARE YOU
HAPPY SECRETARY'S DAY
Uh...
"IT HAS MADE ME AMAZING AT PARTIES"
That--that'll work, Brian. Your algorithm's already trained. All we need to do is tweak it so instead of defaulting to the closest match, it highlights any differences, and--
--and we'll have our automated fake super hero detector! Brain Drain, I could hug you.
THANK YOU. YOU MAY PROCEED
Oh.
Uh, all right.
I guess we're doing this.
I DON'T HAVE ANY PRESSURE SENSORS AROUND MY TORSO SO YOU CAN SQUEEZE AS HARD AS YOU'D LIKE
JUST LET ME KNOW WHEN YOU'RE DONE DOWN THERE

DETECTIVE MICHAEL CORSON, HOW DID YOU ENJOY THAT STEAK YOU POSTED A PICTURE OF ON SOCIAL MEDIA THREE DAYS AGO? I NOTICE THE PHOTO EARNED A TOTAL OF TWO LIKES AND I HOPE IT WAS AS HASHTAG TASTYSTEAK AS YOU ANTICIPATED

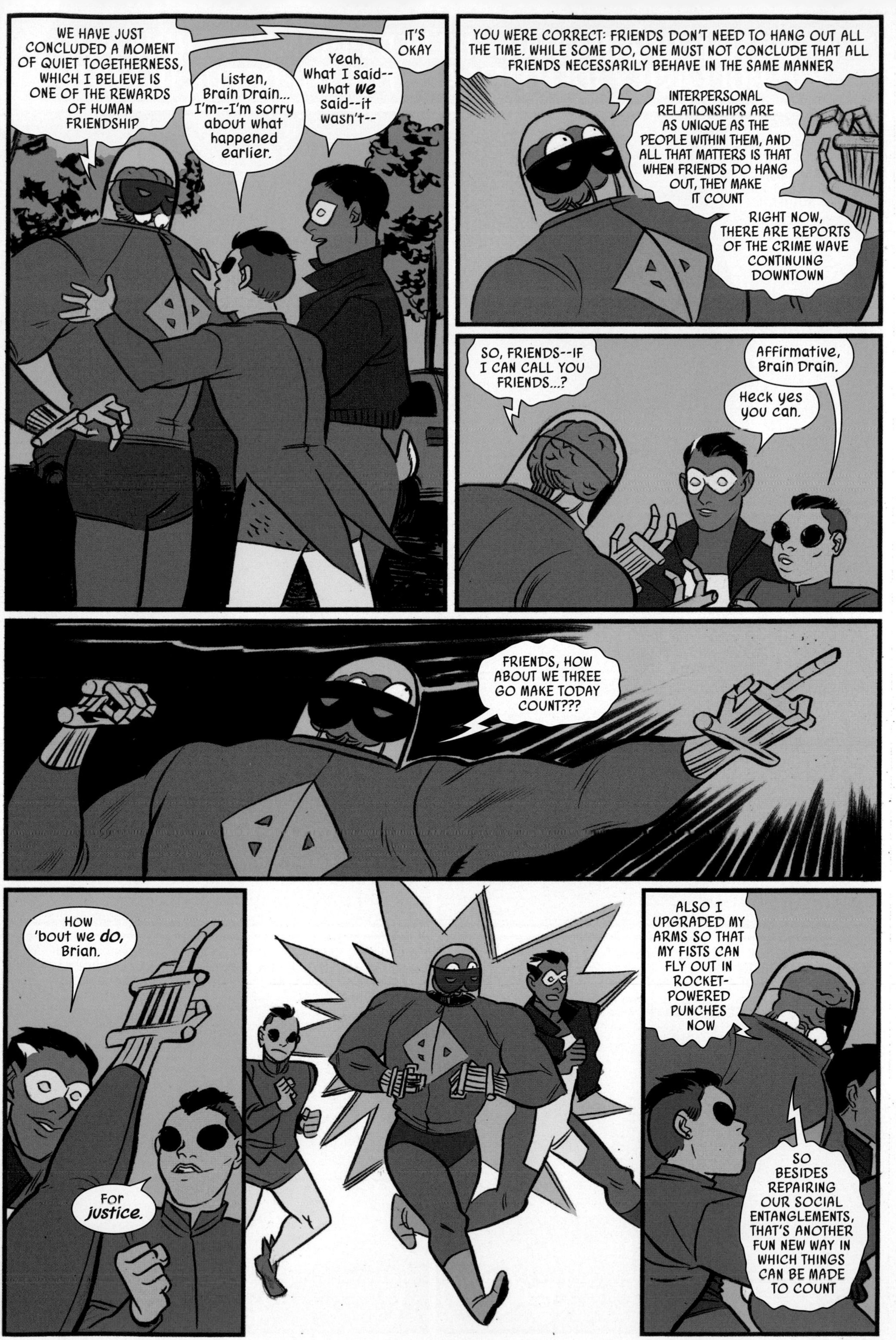
WE HAVE JUST CONCLUDED A MOMENT OF QUIET TOGETHERNESS, WHICH I BELIEVE IS ONE OF THE REWARDS OF HUMAN FRIENDSHIP
IT'S OKAY
Listen, Brain Drain... I'm--I'm sorry about what happened earlier.
Yeah. What I said--what we said--it wasn't--
YOU WERE CORRECT: FRIENDS DON'T NEED TO HANG OUT ALL THE TIME. WHILE SOME DO, ONE MUST NOT CONCLUDE THAT ALL FRIENDS NECESSARILY BEHAVE IN THE SAME MANNER
INTERPERSONAL RELATIONSHIPS ARE AS UNIQUE AS THE PEOPLE WITHIN THEM, AND ALL THAT MATTERS IS THAT WHEN FRIENDS DO HANG OUT, THEY MAKE IT COUNT
RIGHT NOW, THERE ARE REPORTS OF THE CRIME WAVE CONTINUING DOWNTOWN
SO, FRIENDS--IF I CAN CALL YOU FRIENDS...?
Affirmative, Brain Drain.
Heck yes you can.
FRIENDS, HOW ABOUT WE THREE GO MAKE TODAY COUNT???
How 'bout we do, Brian.
For justice.
ALSO I UPGRADED MY ARMS SO THAT MY FISTS CAN FLY OUT IN ROCKET-POWERED PUNCHES NOW
SO BESIDES REPAIRING OUR SOCIAL ENTANGLEMENTS, THAT'S ANOTHER FUN NEW WAY IN WHICH THINGS CAN BE MADE TO COUNT

I RECOVERED MY COSTUME FROM THE TRASH CAN I'D LEFT IT IN; IT IS LUCKY FOR ME THAT THIS CITY'S CUSTODIAL SERVICES ARE NOT AS RUTHLESSLY EFFICIENT AS, IN A MORE PERFECT WORLD, THEY COULD BE

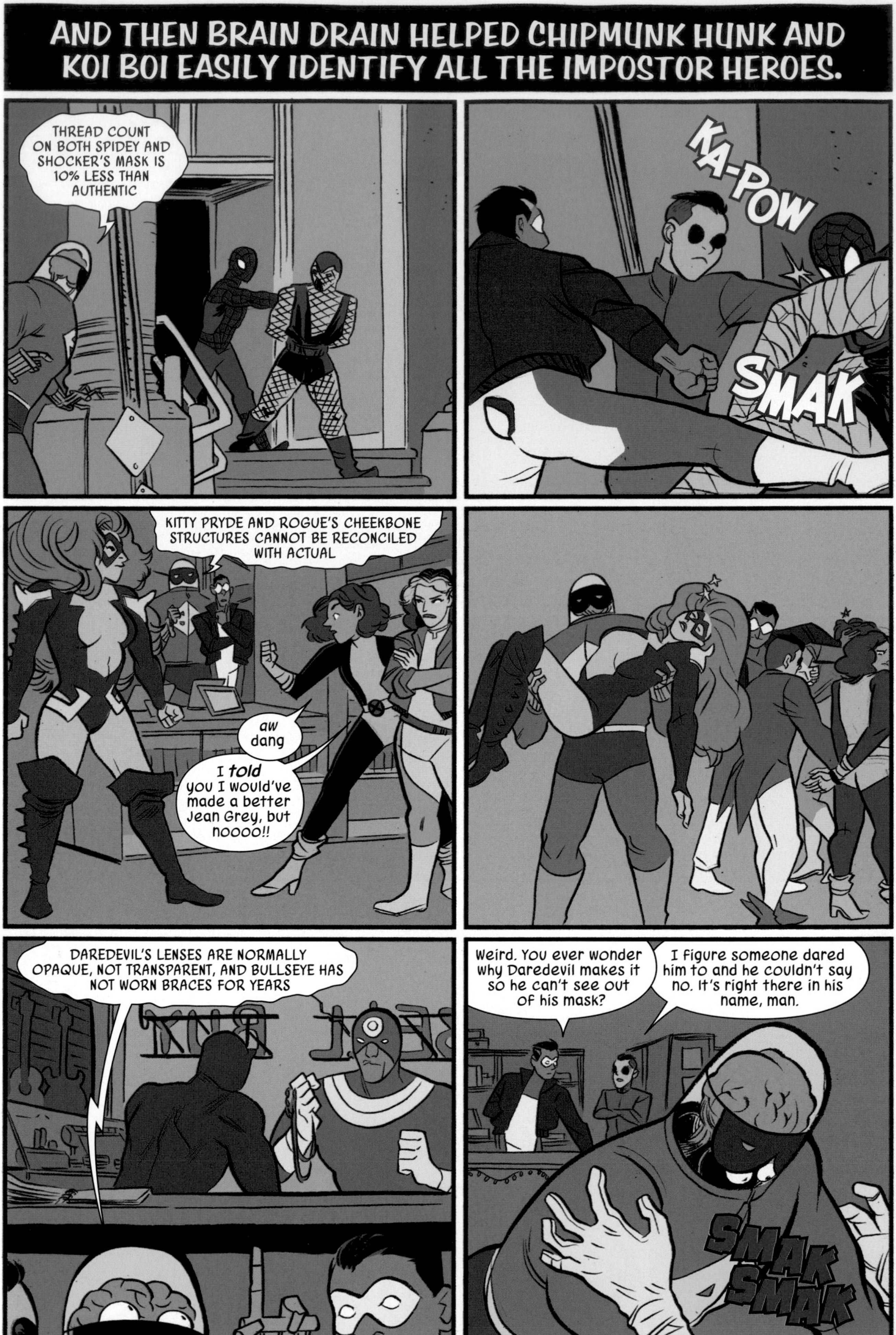
AND THEN BRAIN DRAIN HELPED CHIPMUNK HUNK AND KOI BOI EASILY IDENTIFY ALL THE IMPOSTOR HEROES.
THREAD COUNT ON BOTH SPIDEY AND SHOCKER'S MASK IS 10% LESS THAN AUTHENTIC
KA-POW
SMAK
KITTY PRYDE AND ROGUE'S CHEEKBONE STRUCTURES CANNOT BE RECONCILED WITH ACTUAL
aw dang
I *told* you I would've made a better Jean Grey, but noooo!!
DAREDEVIL'S LENSES ARE NORMALLY OPAQUE, NOT TRANSPARENT, AND BULLSEYE HAS NOT WORN BRACES FOR YEARS
Weird. You ever wonder why Daredevil makes it so he can't see out of his mask?
I figure someone dared him to and he couldn't say no. It's right there in his name, man.
SMAK SMAK

Is that ***truly*** the reason he's named "Daredevil"? Or is it more likely his ***real*** name is actually "Da Red Evil," but Daredevil has such horrible handwriting that all the words run together, and that, combined with crippling shyness about correcting anyone, means we never found out the truth...***until this very moment???***

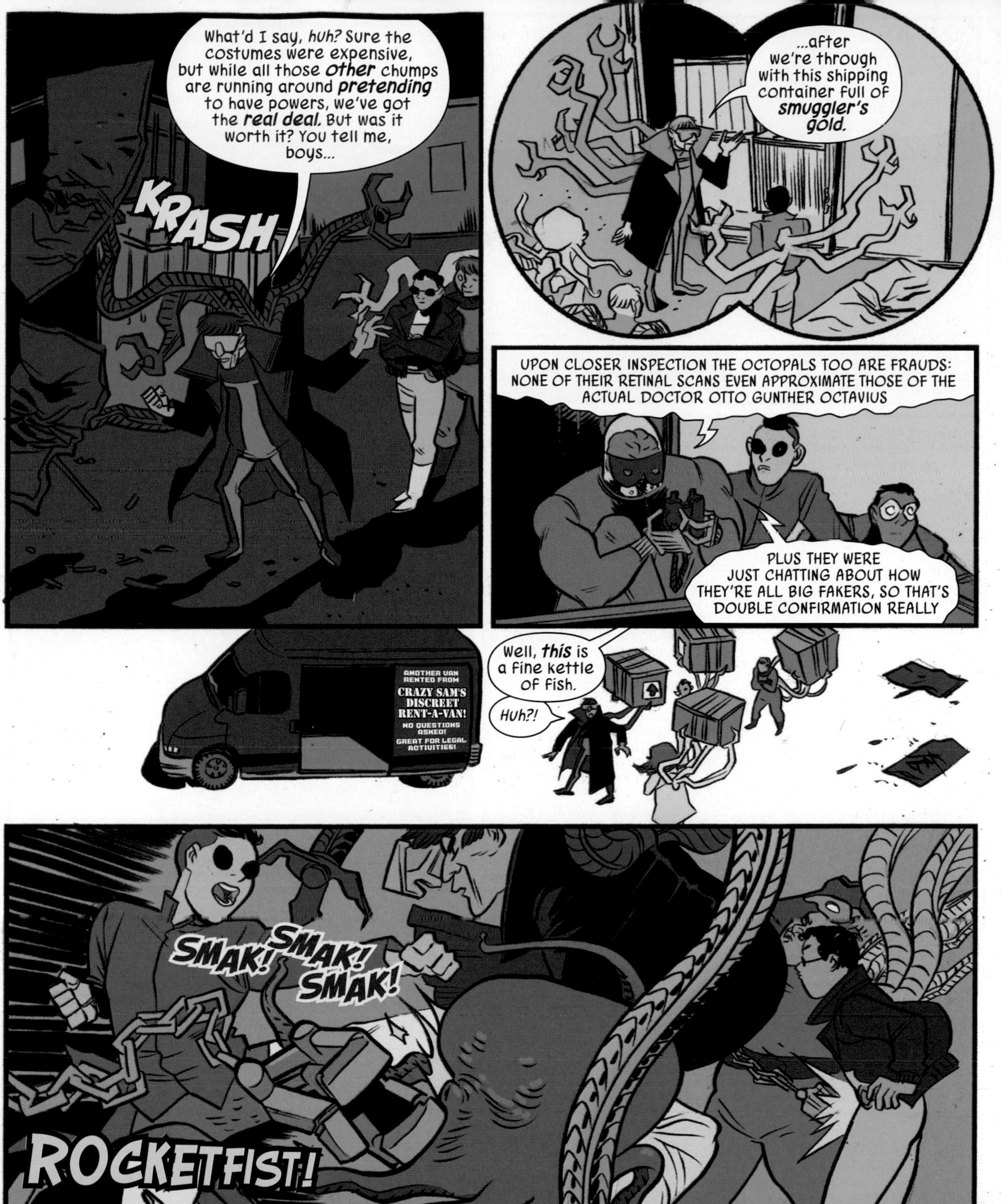
What'd I say, *huh?* Sure the costumes were expensive, but while all those ***other*** chumps are running around ***pretending*** to have powers, we've got the ***real deal.*** But was it worth it? You tell me, boys...
KRASH
...after we're through with this shipping container full of ***smuggler's gold.***
UPON CLOSER INSPECTION THE OCTOPALS TOO ARE FRAUDS: NONE OF THEIR RETINAL SCANS EVEN APPROXIMATE THOSE OF THE ACTUAL DOCTOR OTTO GUNTHER OCTAVIUS
PLUS THEY WERE JUST CHATTING ABOUT HOW THEY'RE ALL BIG FAKERS, SO THAT'S DOUBLE CONFIRMATION REALLY
ANOTHER VAN RENTED FROM CRAZY SAM'S DISCREET RENT-A-VAN! NO QUESTIONS ASKED! GREAT FOR LEGAL ACTIVITIES!
Well, ***this*** is a fine kettle of fish.
Huh?!
SMAK! SMAK! SMAK!
ROCKETFIST!
Gotta admit, Octopals: the rocket boots ***were*** impressive.
Yeah. None of the other criminals were as creative with ***their*** costumes, even if yours were all just ripping off an existing guy.
excuse me
"Pre-Doc Ock" is my own fully original character
do not steal

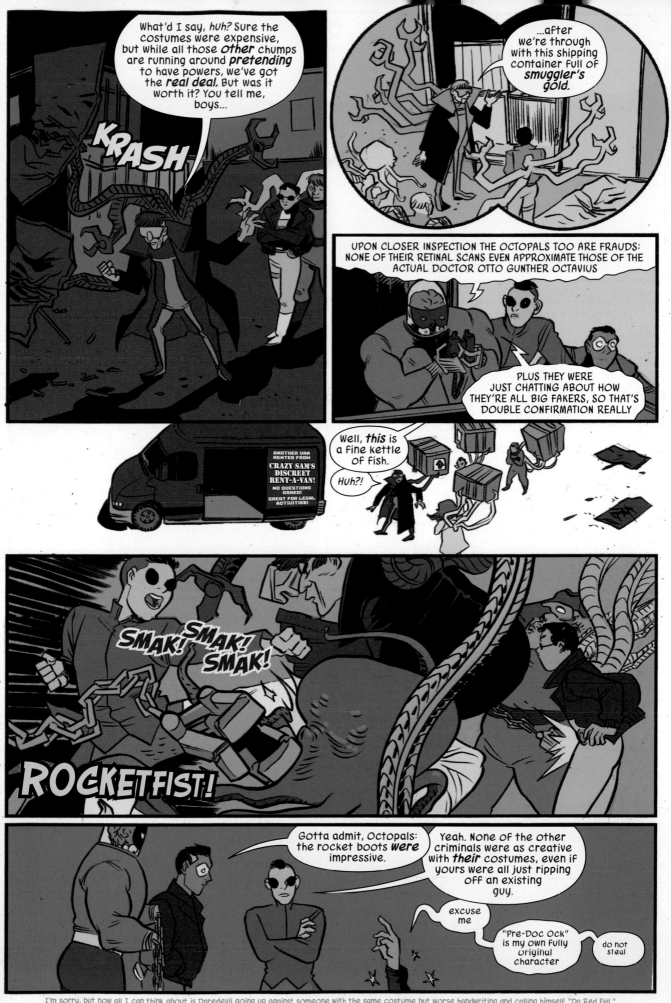

I'm sorry, but now all I can think about is Daredevil going up against someone with the same costume but worse handwriting and calling himself "Da Red Evil."
Attention, creators of the Daredevil TV series: I believe history may judge your next season harshly if you don't incorporate this extremely excellent idea??

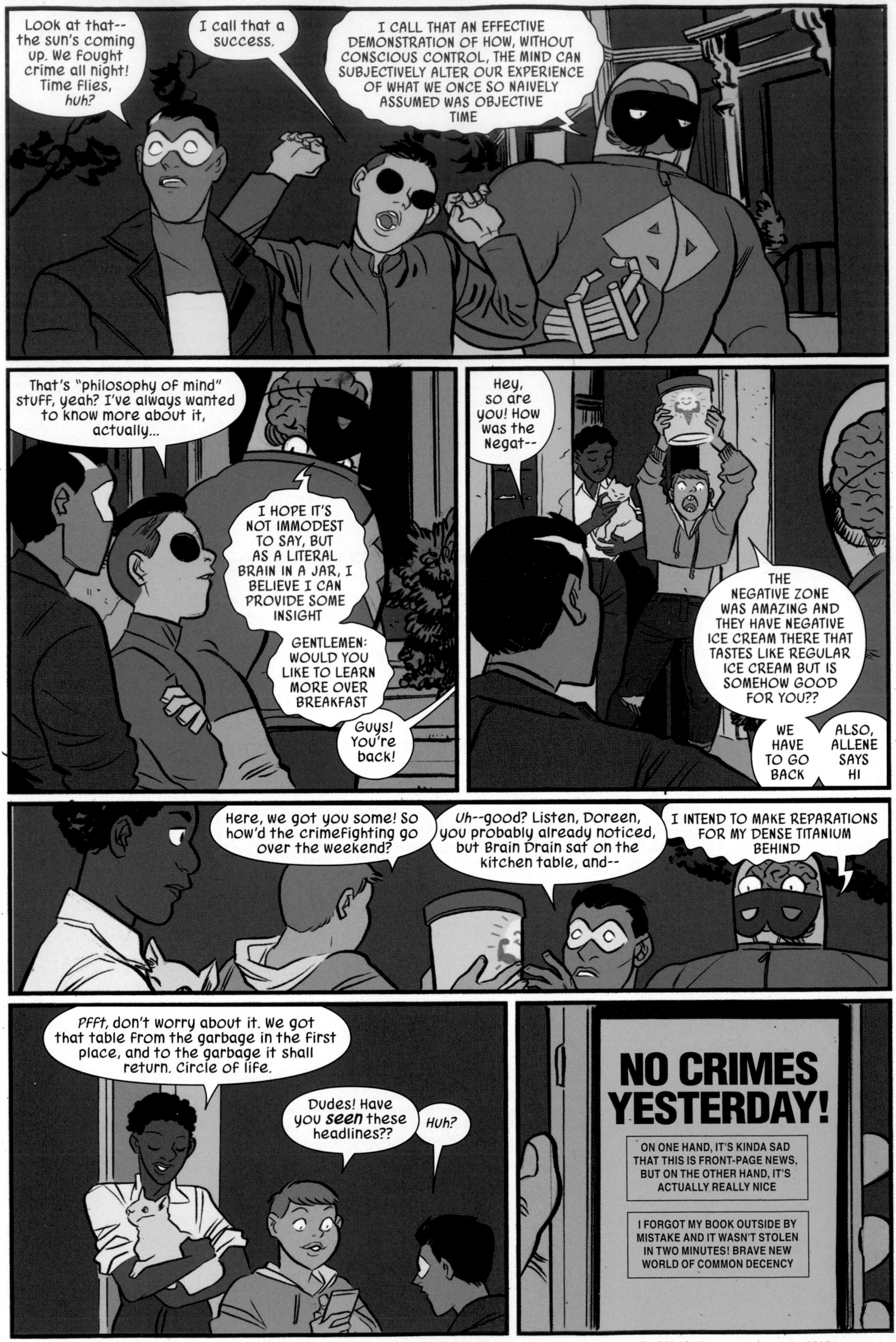
Look at that-- the sun's coming up. We fought crime all night! Time flies, huh?
I call that a success.
I CALL THAT AN EFFECTIVE DEMONSTRATION OF HOW, WITHOUT CONSCIOUS CONTROL, THE MIND CAN SUBJECTIVELY ALTER OUR EXPERIENCE OF WHAT WE ONCE SO NAIVELY ASSUMED WAS OBJECTIVE TIME
That's "philosophy of mind" stuff, yeah? I've always wanted to know more about it, actually...
I HOPE IT'S NOT IMMODEST TO SAY, BUT AS A LITERAL BRAIN IN A JAR, I BELIEVE I CAN PROVIDE SOME INSIGHT
GENTLEMEN: WOULD YOU LIKE TO LEARN MORE OVER BREAKFAST
Guys! You're back!
Hey, so are you! How was the Negat--
THE NEGATIVE ZONE WAS AMAZING AND THEY HAVE NEGATIVE ICE CREAM THERE THAT TASTES LIKE REGULAR ICE CREAM BUT IS SOMEHOW GOOD FOR YOU??
WE HAVE TO GO BACK
ALSO, ALLENE SAYS HI
Here, we got you some! So how'd the crimefighting go over the weekend?
Uh--good? Listen, Doreen, you probably already noticed, but Brain Drain sat on the kitchen table, and--
I INTEND TO MAKE REPARATIONS FOR MY DENSE TITANIUM BEHIND
Pfft, don't worry about it. We got that table from the garbage in the first place, and to the garbage it shall return. Circle of life.
Dudes! Have you seen these headlines??
Huh?
NO CRIMES YESTERDAY!
ON ONE HAND, IT'S KINDA SAD THAT THIS IS FRONT-PAGE NEWS, BUT ON THE OTHER HAND, IT'S ACTUALLY REALLY NICE
I FORGOT MY BOOK OUTSIDE BY MISTAKE AND IT WASN'T STOLEN IN TWO MINUTES! BRAVE NEW WORLD OF COMMON DECENCY

THIS REPORTER, FOR ONE, DOESN'T UNDERSTAND WHY PEOPLE KEPT STEALING HER BOOKS EVERY TIME SHE TURNS HER BACK IN THE FIRST PLACE! IF YOU GO TO THE LIBRARY, THEY HAVE A WAY BETTER SELECTION AND THEY'RE JUST AS FREE. PLUS THEY HAVE BLU-RAYS TOO

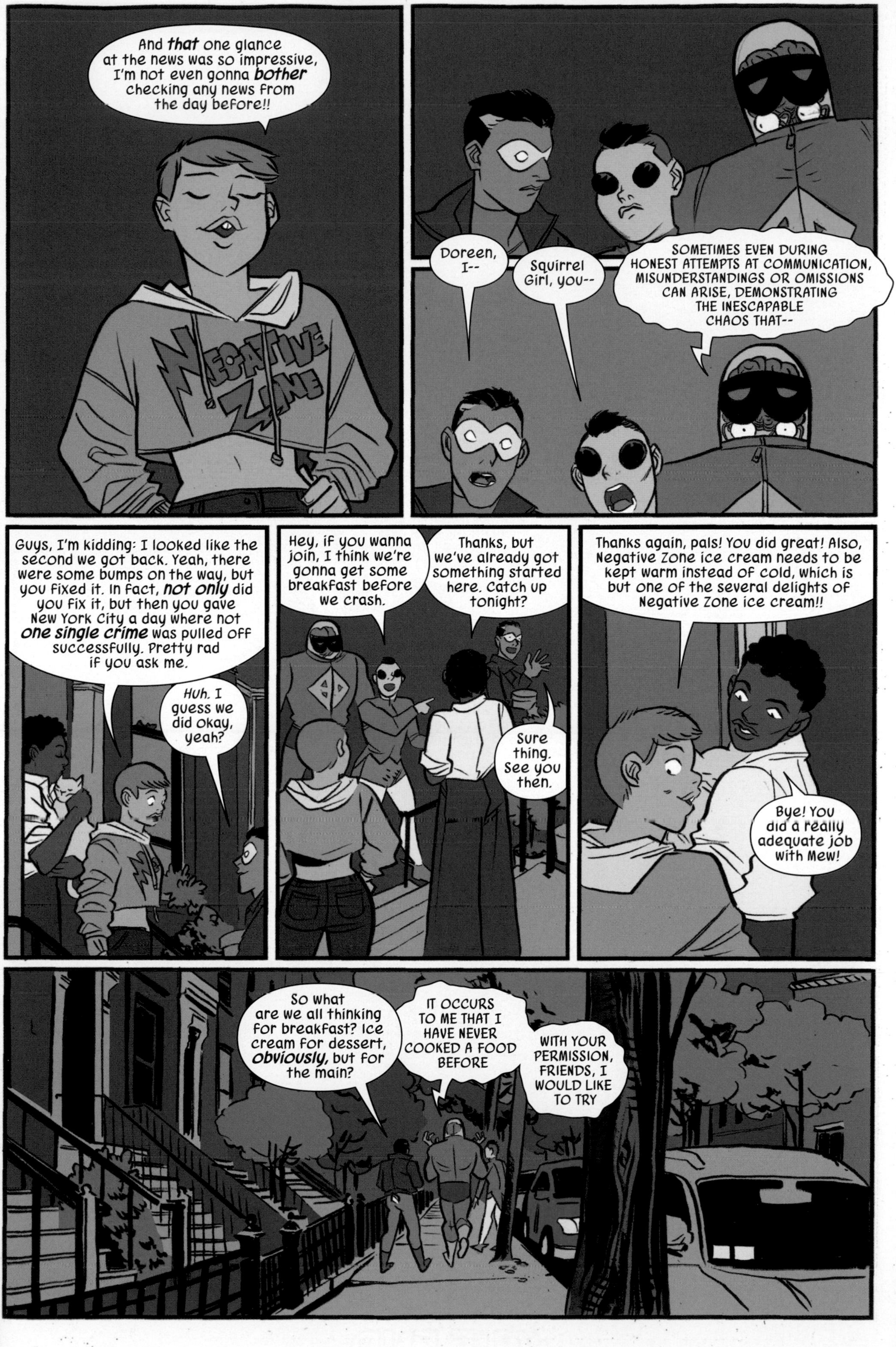
And that one glance at the news was so impressive, I'm not even gonna bother checking any news from the day before!!
Doreen, I--
Squirrel Girl, you--
SOMETIMES EVEN DURING HONEST ATTEMPTS AT COMMUNICATION, MISUNDERSTANDINGS OR OMISSIONS CAN ARISE, DEMONSTRATING THE INESCAPABLE CHAOS THAT--
Guys, I'm kidding: I looked like the second we got back. Yeah, there were some bumps on the way, but you fixed it. In fact, not only did you fix it, but then you gave New York City a day where not one single crime was pulled off successfully. Pretty rad if you ask me.
Huh. I guess we did okay, yeah?
Hey, if you wanna join, I think we're gonna get some breakfast before we crash.
Thanks, but we've already got something started here. Catch up tonight?
Sure thing. See you then.
Thanks again, pals! You did great! Also, Negative Zone ice cream needs to be kept warm instead of cold, which is but one of the several delights of Negative Zone ice cream!!
Bye! You did a really adequate job with Mew!
So what are we all thinking for breakfast? Ice cream for dessert, obviously, but for the main?
IT OCCURS TO ME THAT I HAVE NEVER COOKED A FOOD BEFORE
WITH YOUR PERMISSION, FRIENDS, I WOULD LIKE TO TRY

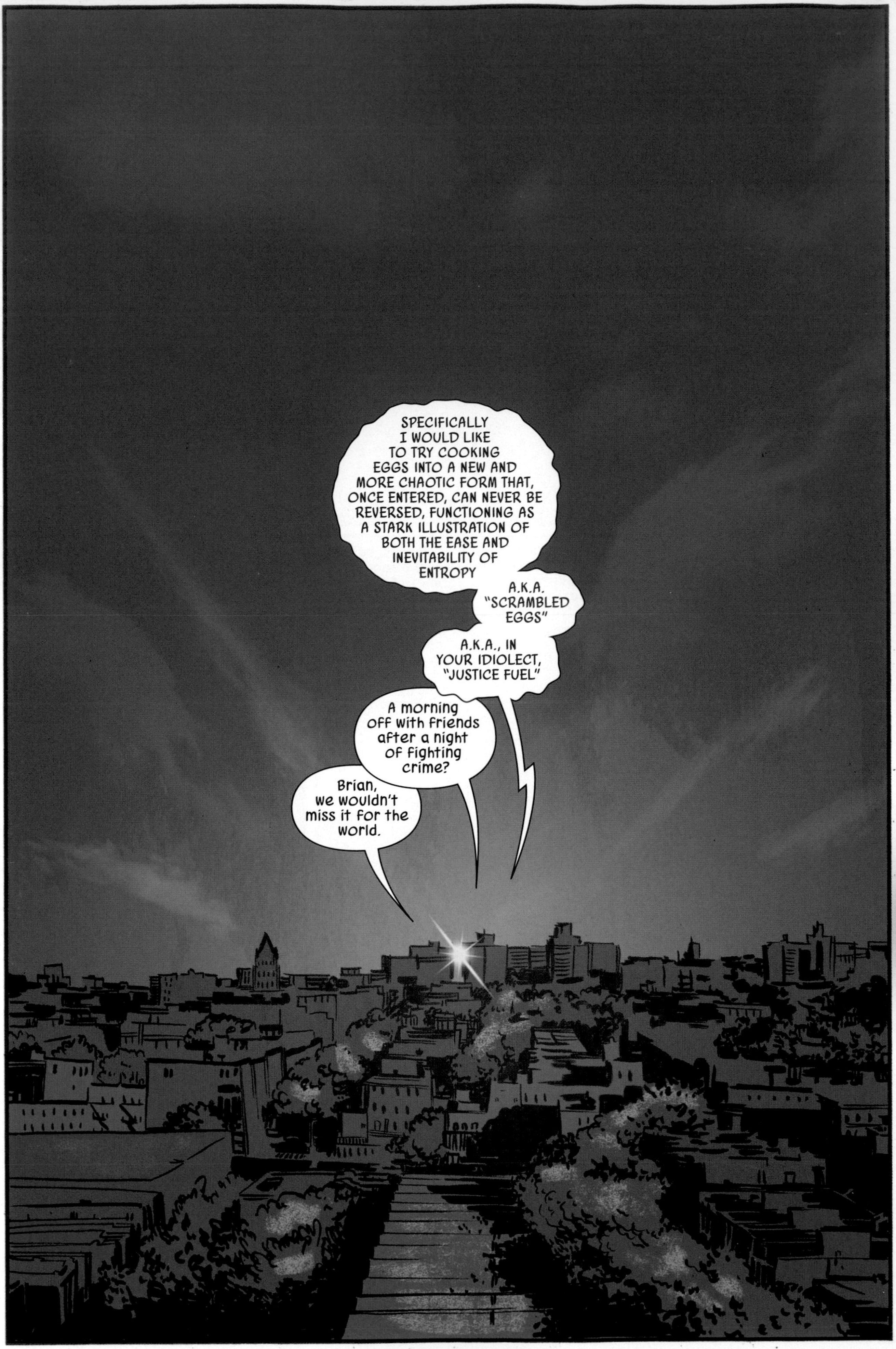
SPECIFICALLY I WOULD LIKE TO TRY COOKING EGGS INTO A NEW AND MORE CHAOTIC FORM THAT, ONCE ENTERED, CAN NEVER BE REVERSED, FUNCTIONING AS A STARK ILLUSTRATION OF BOTH THE EASE AND INEVITABILITY OF ENTROPY
A.K.A. "SCRAMBLED EGGS"
A.K.A., IN YOUR IDIOLECT, "JUSTICE FUEL"
A morning off with friends after a night of fighting crime?
Brian, we wouldn't miss it for the world.

THE END.

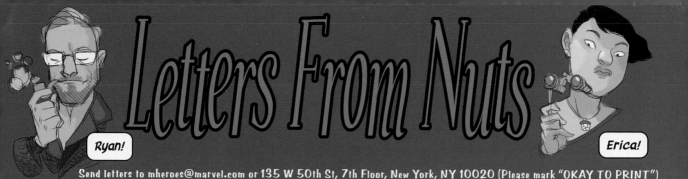

Letters From Nuts

Ryan!
Erica!

Send letters to mheroes@marvel.com or 135 W 50th St, 7th Floor, New York, NY 10020 (Please mark "OKAY TO PRINT")

How great is Brain Drain, y'all? (The correct answer is: MEGA great.)

So hey, the nominations for the 2017 Eisner Awards (which are like the Academy Awards, but for comics!) were recently announced, and THE UNBEATABLE SQUIRREL GIRL is up for Best Publication for Teens (ages 13-17)! Plus, the *JUGHEAD* series that Erica and Ryan both worked on is also up for Best Publication for Teens (ages 13-17) and for Best Humor Publication! That's right, Erica and Ryan have to prepare *three separate acceptance speeches!!!* (And by the way, if you're a fan of USG and you haven't read that *JUGHEAD* series, what are you waiting for?? It's crazy good!)

Will Eisner
Comic Industry Awards

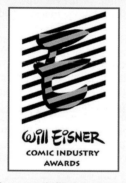

Also: We were thrilled to have Squirrel Girl co-creator Will Murray write a story in USG #16, the issue where we celebrated the 25th anniversary of Doreen's first appearance! Will did a signing at New England Comics back when issue #16 went on sale, and the real-life inspiration for Doreen--Doreen Greeley--was in attendance! How cool is that?? Here's a photo of Will and the IRL Doreen at the signing:

WILL MURRAY
CREATOR OF

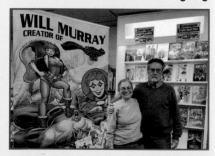

And to show you just how far Squirrel Girl's fan base now reaches, here's a photo of a Squirrel Girl that USG Executive Editor/Godfather Tom Brevoort took when he was a guest at the opening of "The Marvel Age of Heroes Exhibition" in Tokyo back in April:

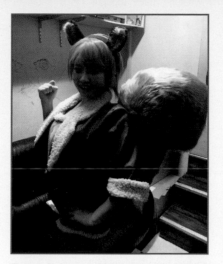

That tail is A+! Okay, now on to your letters, and Erica and Ryan's responses!!!

Dear Team Squirrel Girl,

The last time I sent a letter to Marvel was in the mid-'80s when I wanted to find out how I could find back issues of *ELFQUEST.* So it's been a while.

Happily, I've reached an age where I now understand how to find back issues of excellent comics, so I can focus this letter on what's really important: that y'all are awesome. I started picking up Squirrel Girl for my wife's cousin; I give her a stack of comics every year for Christmas, which is what my grandma used to do for me (back when JC Penney sold the 30-pack of Marvel comics out of their Christmas catalog, y'all need to find a way to bring that back). And the nice thing about giving the gift of comics is that you can read them before you wrap them up. No surprise, I was immediately hooked. You've heard it all before, but this book is so clever and intelligent and positive and lol funny.

But what prompted me to plunk down in front of my computer and send you an electronic message (did you hear that, '80s? We can send our mail electronically now!) was Alfredo the Chicken. When Ms. Morehead told Chef Bear to go cook Alfredo after Doreen left, I was caught off guard. It was a dark moment that was out of step for the book. I shouldn't have been worried, though. I was relieved and delighted to see that not only was Alfredo alive and well, but that he wasn't going down without a hilarious fight.

The Alfredo and Chef Bear subplot sums up how amazing this book is. In just a few pages, you got me to really care about a sentient chicken. I will allow you to use that blurb for any subsequent Squirrel Girl collections.

Keep up the amazing work.
Jason

RYAN: Thank you! The Alfredo backups in the Melissa arc ended up being one of my favorite parts, and they began life entirely for the reason you saw: I didn't want Alfredo to get eaten, and then the relationship with Chef Bear began to develop, and it was lots and lots of fun. I got a message from someone on Twitter once who was upset that Alfredo died and I got to say "keep reading!"--they had messaged before they'd even finished the book, assuming he was definitely 100% dead! BUT THAT NEVER HAPPENS IN COMICS, especially OUR talking-squirrel comics. And I'm glad Alfredo broke your 30-year drought of not writing in letters to comic books!

ERICA: I feel like given how much we've fallen for Alfredo, this isn't the last we've seen of him. P.S. ELFQUEST! That brings me back.

Heyo, Erica and Ryan!

So, first: I love love love this comic book! Sometimes my friends say, "Isn't a Squirrel Girl a joke character? And I say, "Have you ever been surrounded by a mob of angry squirrels? They can bite you, in places." So, let it be said: Squirrel Girl is the coolest, fiercest super hero with a tail ever!!

Second: I have a proposition. I just saw Squirrel Girl make a cameo in HOWARD THE DUCK (2016) #6, as well as PATSY WALKER, A.K.A. HELLCAT. So I was thinking, "Hey, I've seen a lot of Marvel cameos recently: Ms. Marvel cameos in MOON GIRL AND DEVIL DINOSAUR, Howard the Duck cameos in PATSY WALKER, A.K.A. HELLCAT, Squirrel Girl cameos in HOWARD THE DUCK, etc." So, what if we had a super ultimate amazing (you catch my drift) crossover? Specifically, between:

Squirrel Girl (and Chipmunk Hunk, Koi Boy, Nancy and Tippy-Toe), Moon Girl and Devil Dinosaur, America Chávez, Hellcat (and Telekinian, Attaché, Jubilee, and She-Hulk), Howard the Duck and Ms. Marvel (Kamala Khan).

Would that be great or what? (Rhetorical question. Of course it would). Maybe Loki could even join in on the fun. What would we call such an event? Something cool I hope. What would these guys do together? Maybe fight Black Cat, Casiolena, The Inventor, The Skrull, the Collector and Doctor Doom all at once! That would be interesting...

Peace out and tune in,
Claudine Gale
Tigard, Oregon

RYAN: Claudine, I see no problems with your ideas and would like to see this ultimate team-up happen. Now that Chip Zdarsky is writing PETER PARKER: THE SPECTACULAR SPIDER-MAN [First issue is on sale next week! – Chip] instead of HOWARD THE DUCK, we should probably throw Spidey in the mix too, so Chip doesn't feel left out. It's hard when you have to write a story about a man with gross spider-powers instead of a cool-talking duck, so we should all send our sympathies to him. [PP:TSS #2 on sale July 19! – Chip]

ERICA: How many of these people are in one place at a time?

Hi Ryan and Erica,

I'm a big fan of THE UNBEATABLE SQUIRREL GIRL and I'm enjoying the latest adventure, including the backup feature introducing us to the breakout creations of 2017: Alfredo the Chicken and Chef Bear. I had to let you know that there is a real (fake) Chef Bear here in San Diego! You can sign up for a special dinner at a secret location where an anonymous chef in a bear costume in a chef costume will serve you and your friends a five-course meal with wine pairings. I won't include it here, because I'm sure Marvel doesn't want plugs for other businesses in their letter columns, but I'm sure you can find the website, including video of Chef Bear, with your considerable computer finesse. Thanks for the great comics!

Chris Martin
San Diego, CA

RYAN: WHAT. WHAT EVEN IS THIS. Marvel, please send me and Erica to San Diego ON THE DOUBLE, because I didn't even know I wanted to be served dinner by an anonymous chef in a bear costume in a chef costume until this moment, and now it's the only thing I've ever wanted. CHEF BEAR IS REAL!!

ERICA: Ryan, I guess we have our night-before-SDCC plans set. There's no turning back on your destiny, Ryan. Ryan. We're doing this.

I've never written a letter to a comic before... But as I was reading the latest issue of SQUIRREL GIRL (#19), I noticed that Melissa called the geese "Canadian" geese. Funny enough, on the morning news today, they were watching a video of a goose attacking a man (which in retrospect is not too dissimilar to the videos of animals attacking people reference in the book as well) and one anchor said Canadian geese and the other corrected her with an off-camera affirmation that "Hey, they are called Canada geese, not 'Canadian.'" And on most occasions, after learning this, for someone to misname them wouldn't be a big deal, but for Melissa Morbeck to misname them seems out of place. She seems like someone who knows a lot about animals and wouldn't make this mistake. Just saying.

Funny thing is, if I read this yesterday, I wouldn't have thought twice about it.

Always reading,
Asher Humm

RYAN: I have lived in Canada my entire life and never distinguished between the two! But that may just be me not paying attention. Perhaps Melissa meant to say they were merely Canadian Canada geese and she just dropped out the "Canada" because it was redundant in that construction? Does that solve all the problems? Let's say it does, and I'll say "Canada goose" moving forward!

ERICA: I can say with full confidence that Melissa doesn't really care all that much about animals.

Hey hey Team Squirrel Girl!

I love this comic book so much, words fail me. Between Erica's anime-esque illustrations and Ryan's hilarious writing, you two combine to make an amazing series (it's almost like you're a Dynamic Duo, huh?). There is one little suggestion I have that would make this comic even more amazing: A Madcap adventure! You know, the purple-and-yellow harlequin who can't be hurt and likes to mind-control people for laughs? He's one of my favorite villains, and seeing Squirrel Girl and Co. take him on would be the best!

Stay squirrelly,
Lucy James
Wilsonville, Oregon

RYAN: Well, with Ratatoskr showing up in the last issue--who already has mind-control powers of her own--Doreen may have her hands full! That is, once she realizes Ratatoskr has returned, which she hasn't yet, because clearly that Norse Squirrel God is gathering her powers and hasn't tipped her hand, but something is going on there!

Erica, Ryan, Rico and the rest of the team:

Thanks for putting out what is consistently one of the funniest, most emotionally-compelling comics on the market. My daughter Thessaly and I anxiously await SQUIRREL GIRL every month, and it's always one of the first books we read together. I'm so incredibly thankful for this book and for the positive representation it provides for her and for other girls—Doreen is effortlessly awesome in two fields too-long dominated by men, she's not afraid to stand up for herself, and she always looks for (and helps people find) the best in others. Keep up the fantastic work, and may you be able to continue to make SQUIRREL GIRL until you've completely run out of nut-themed puns.

Charles Paul Hoffman (and Thessaly)
Indianapolis, Indiana

Oh, here's a picture Thessaly drew of Squirrel Girl. Thessaly met Erica at C2E2, which she said was her favorite part of the convention.

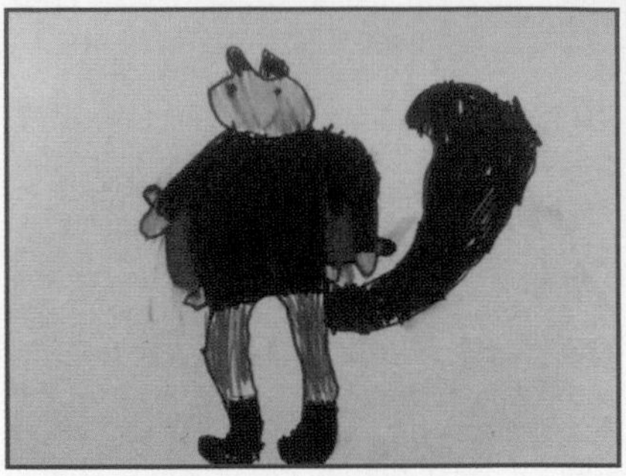

RYAN: LOVE IT. Thessaly's drawing is now officially my favorite part of this letters page too! Also: The idea of running out of nut-themed puns is terrifying. THEY'RE ALL I HAVE, AND I NEED MORE. Please send more.

ERICA: SHE'S THE FIRST (and only, but C2E2 wasn't that long ago) SQUIRREL GIRL COSPLAYER I'VE SEEN WITH THE NEW COSTUME WITH WINGS! It was amazing y'all. It's on my Twitter if you want to dig back several months (not recommended, I tweet A LOT). Anyway, letters like all of these--bringing families together and getting people back into the lost art of letter writing--makes it all worth it.

Next Issue:

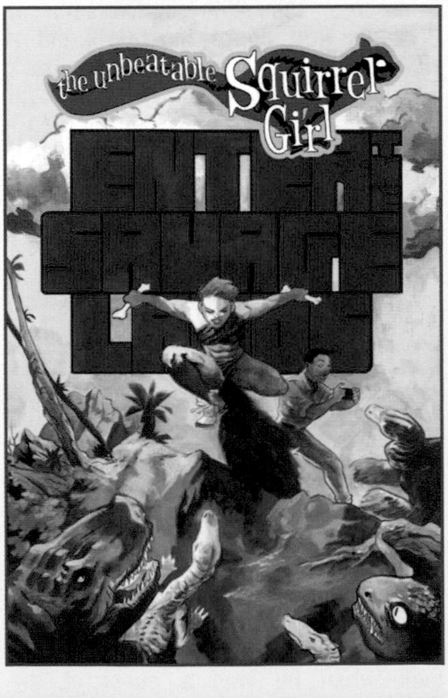
the unbeatable Squirrel Girl

Attention, Squirrel Scouts! Make sure to check out our production blog, **unbeatablesquirrelgirl.tumblr.com**, where we post behind-the-scenes stuff on how the book gets made, along with all sorts of cool things *you* make: fanart, cosplay, whatever!

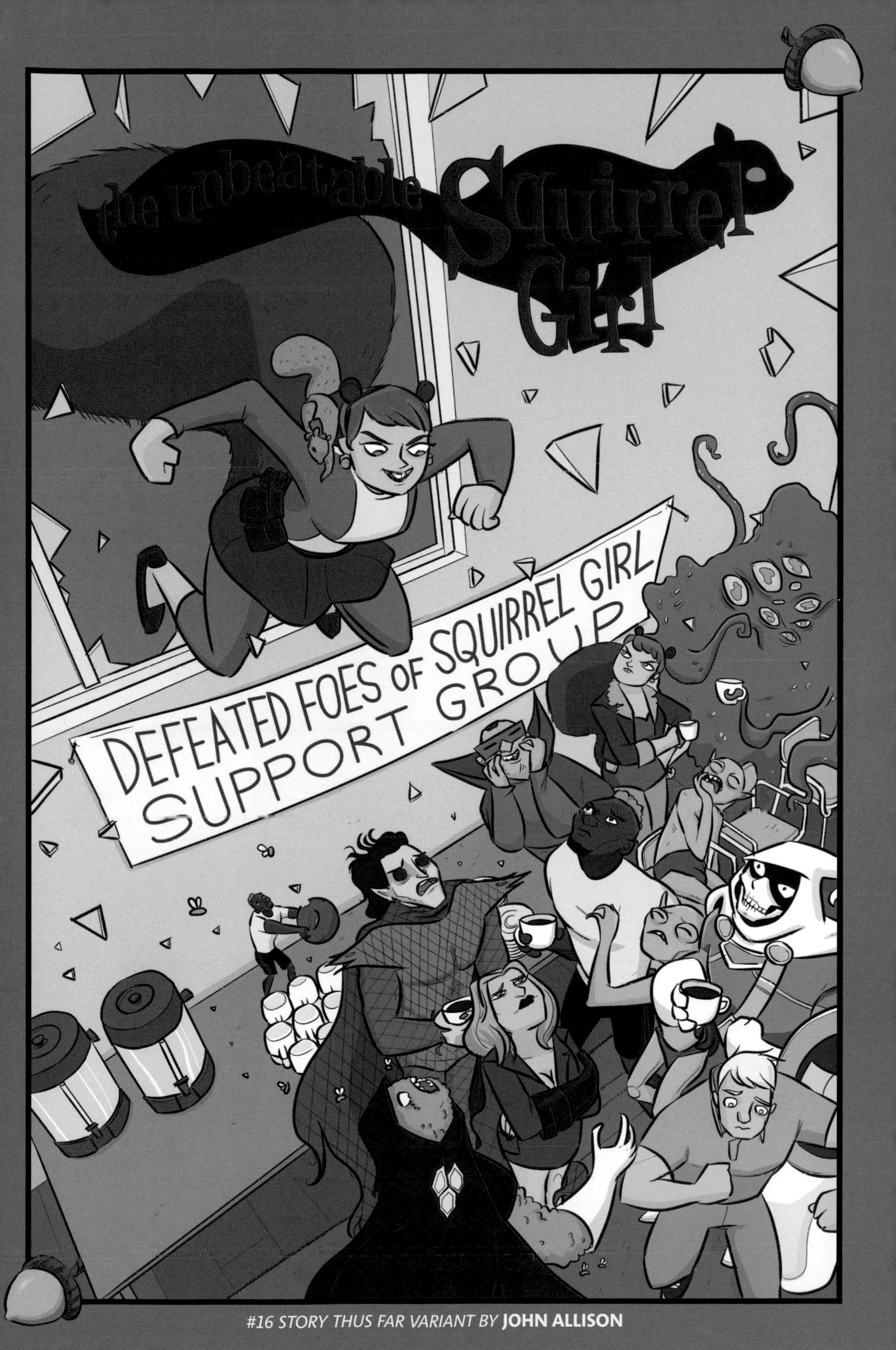
the unbeatable Squirrel Girl
DEFEATED FOES OF SQUIRREL GIRL
SUPPORT GROUP

#16 STORY THUS FAR VARIANT BY **JOHN ALLISON**

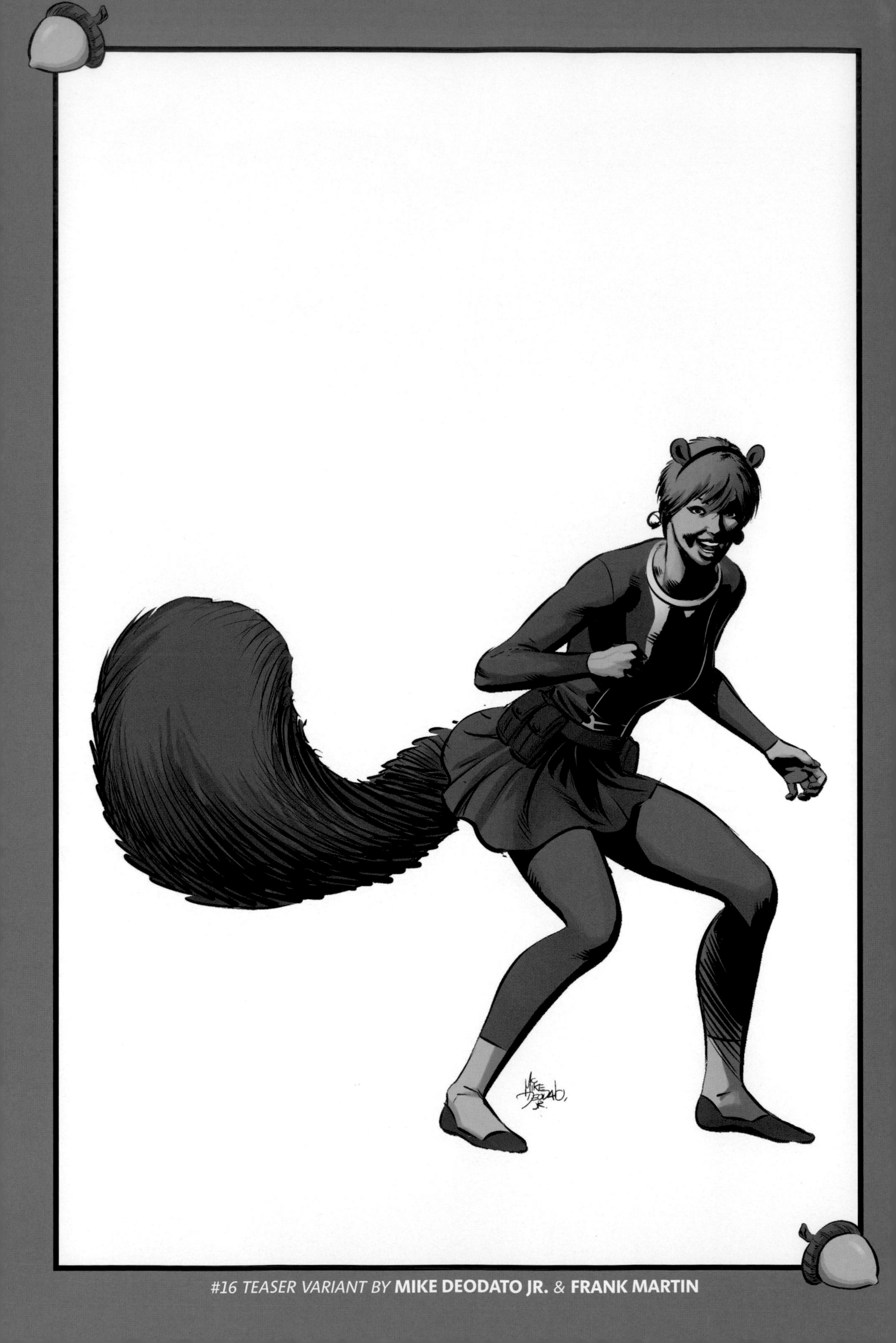

#16 TEASER VARIANT BY **MIKE DEODATO JR.** & **FRANK MARTIN**

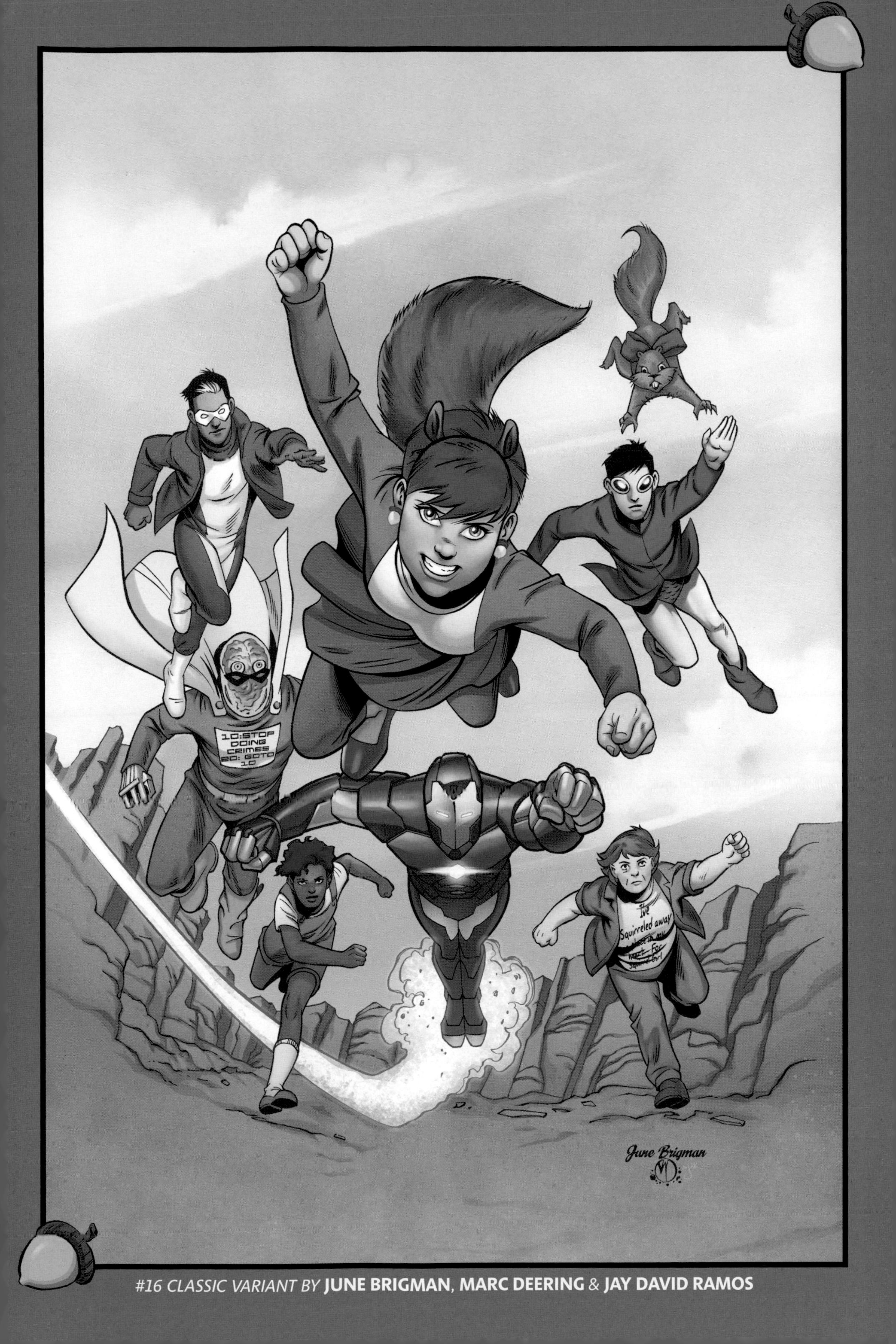
10:STOP DOING CRIMES 20: GOTO 10
June Brigman

#16 CLASSIC VARIANT BY **JUNE BRIGMAN**, **MARC DEERING** & **JAY DAVID RAMOS**

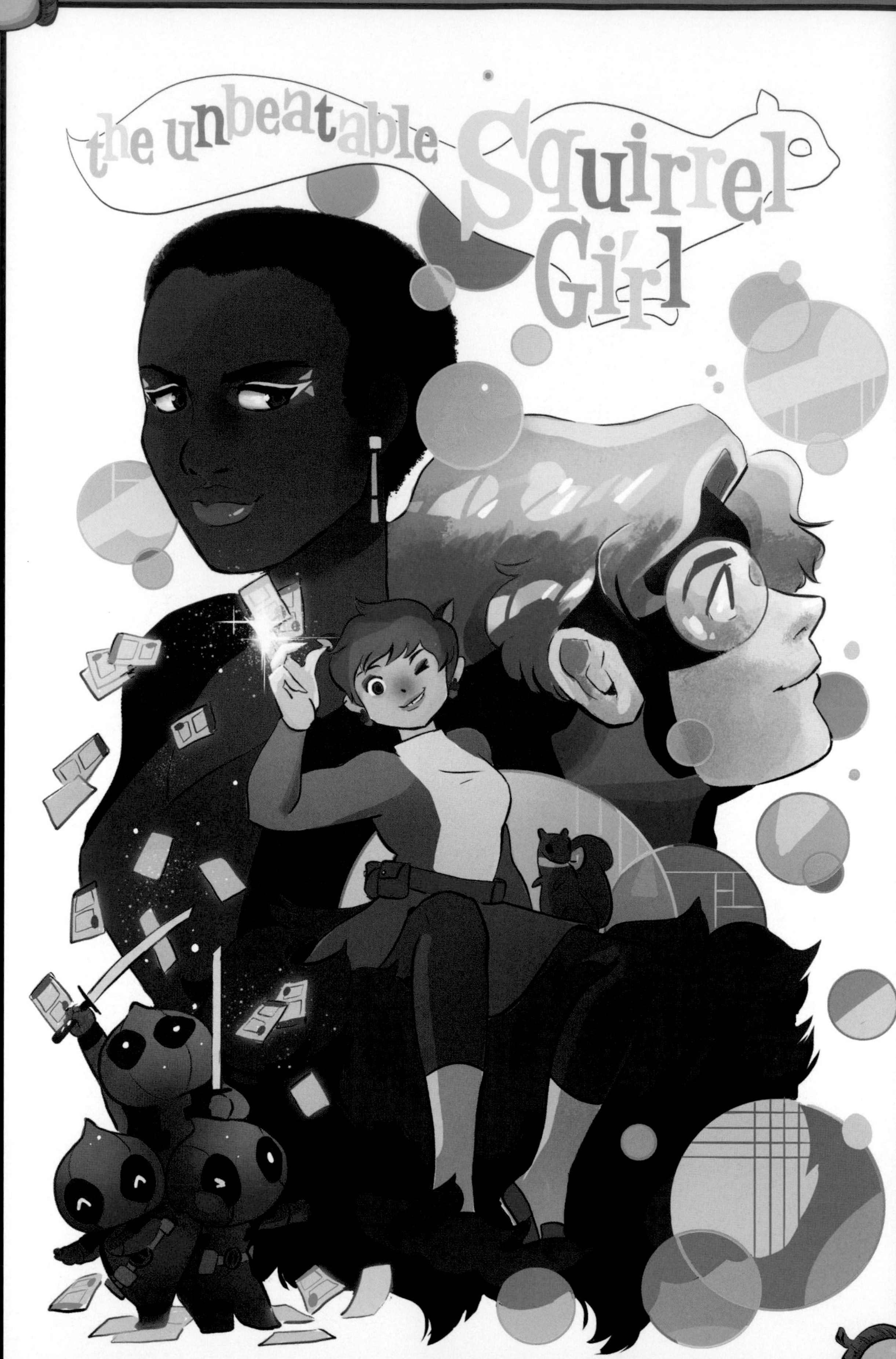
the unbeatable Squirrel Girl

#16 VARIANT BY **NATASHA ALLEGRI**

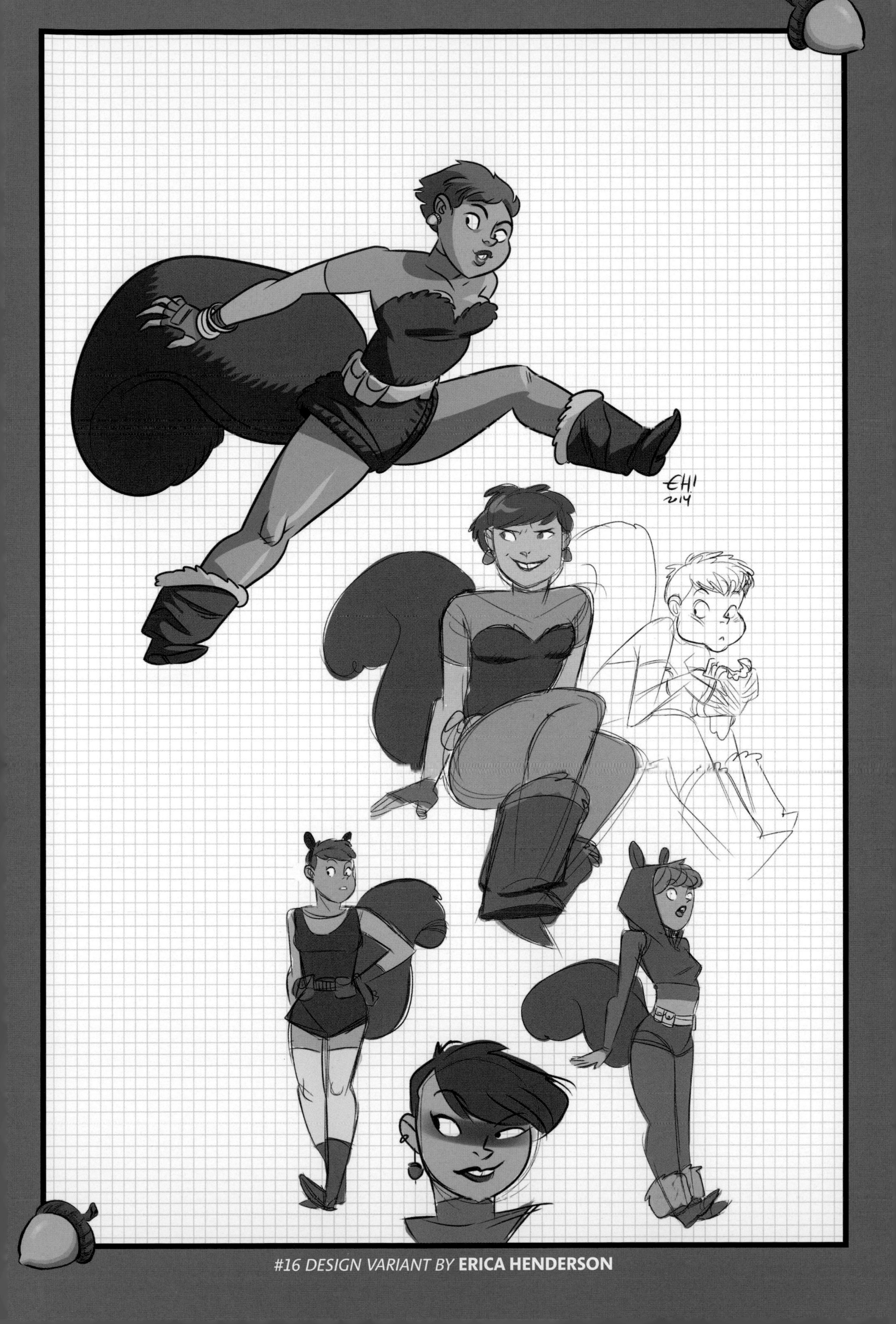
EH!
2014

#16 DESIGN VARIANT BY **ERICA HENDERSON**

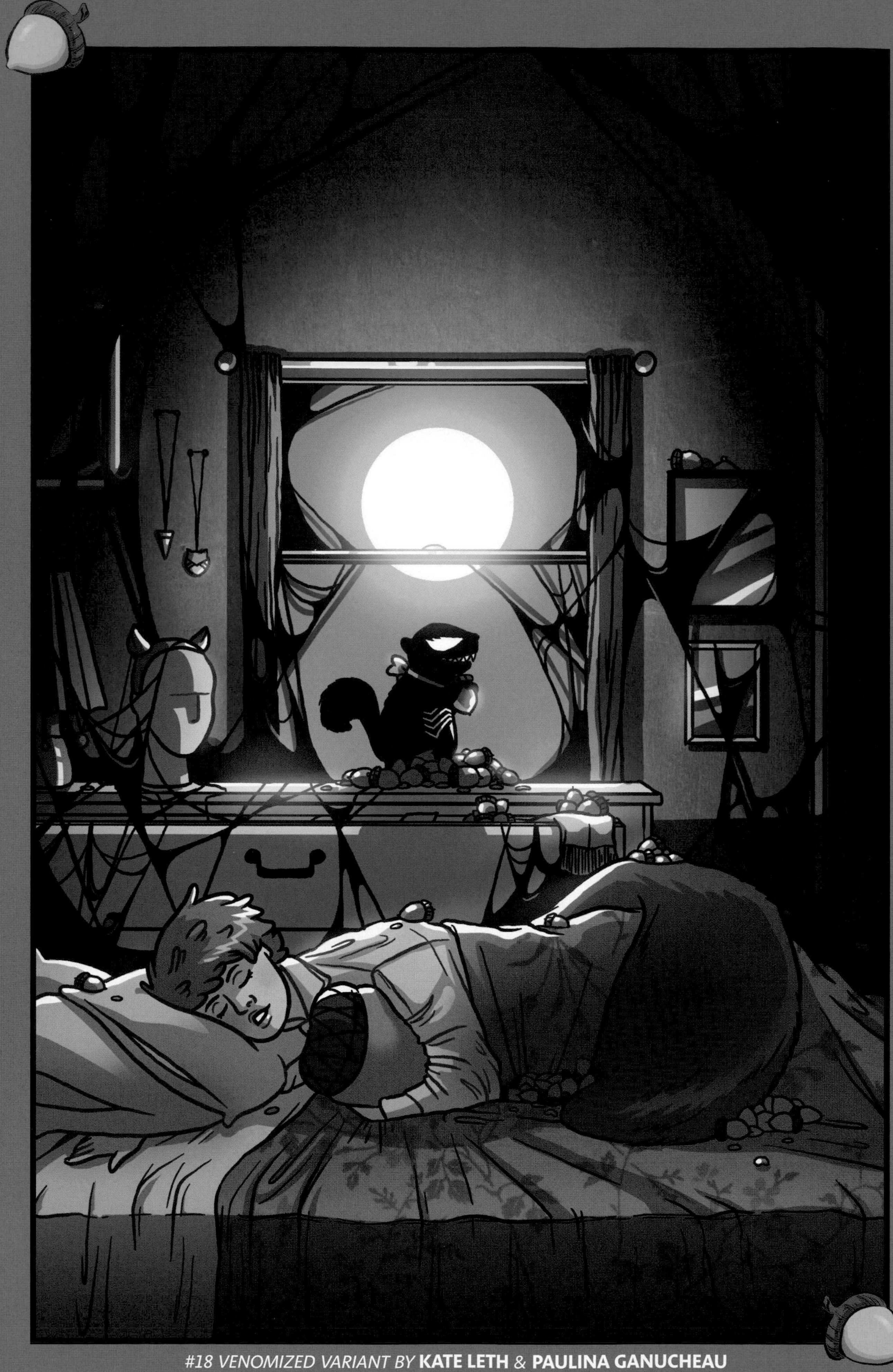

#18 VENOMIZED VARIANT BY **KATE LETH** & **PAULINA GANUCHEAU**

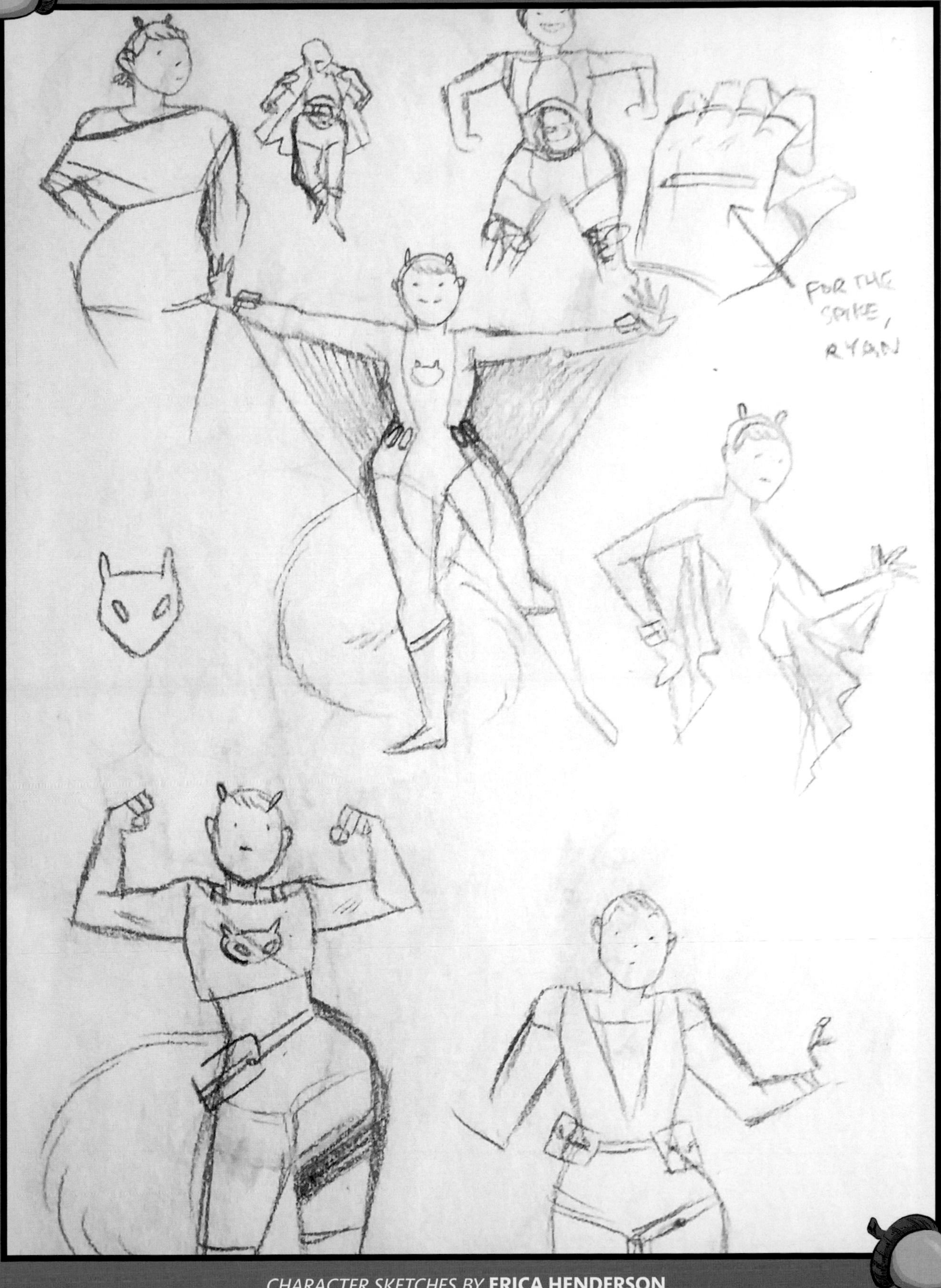
FOR THE SPIKE, RYAN

CHARACTER SKETCHES BY **ERICA HENDERSON**

FIGHT

FIGHT!

CH
K

#18 PAGES 1-3 LAYOUTS AND INKS BY **ERICA HENDERSON**

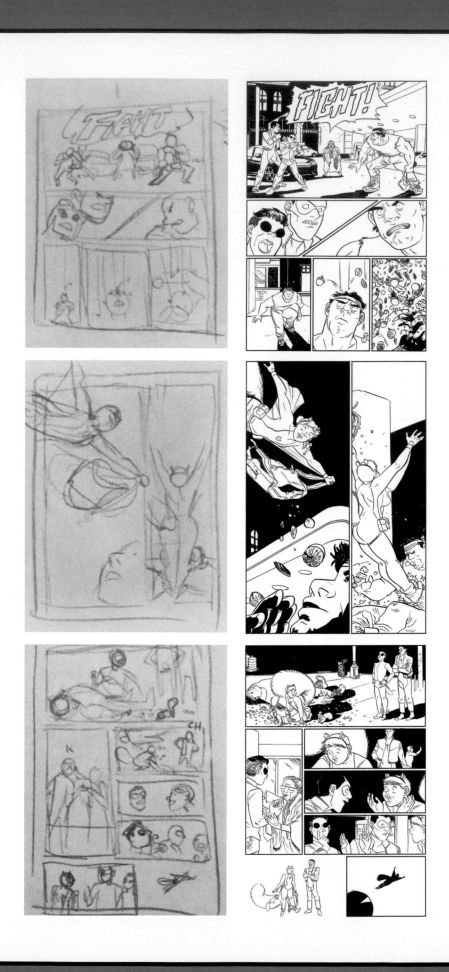

#18 PAGES 4-6 LAYOUTS AND INKS BY **ERICA HENDERSON**

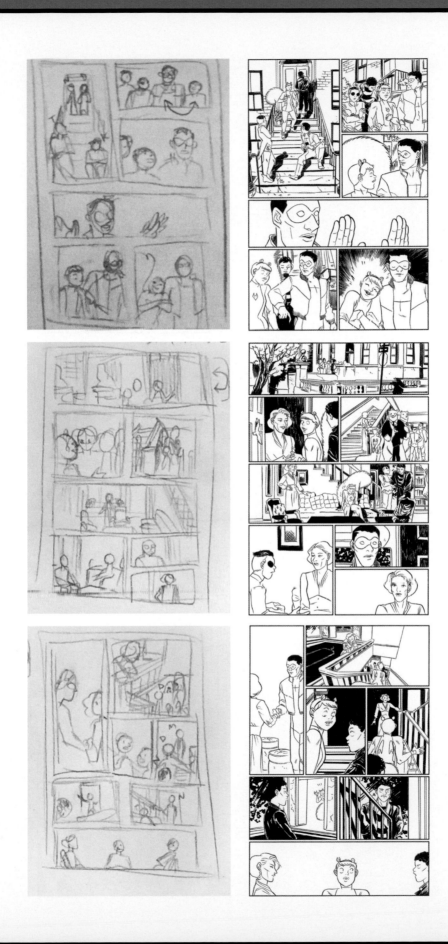

19

2 3

4

#19 PAGES 1-4 LAYOUTS AND INKS BY **ERICA HENDERSON**

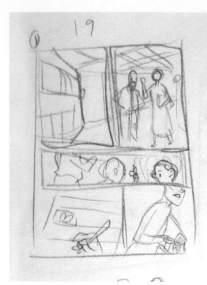

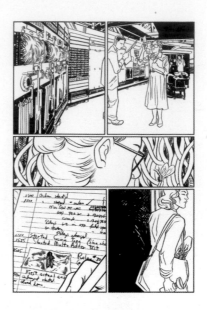

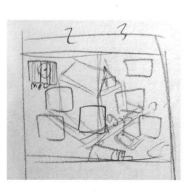

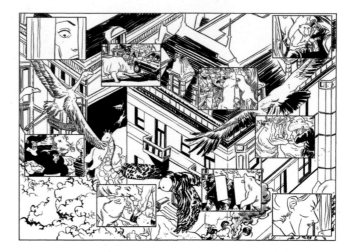

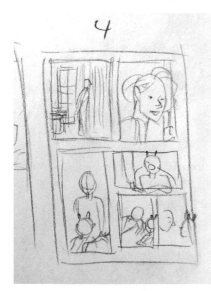

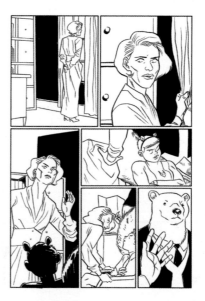

9
SUN BEARS

10

11
LAST LINE ??

#19 PAGES 9-11 LAYOUTS AND INKS BY **ERICA HENDERSON**

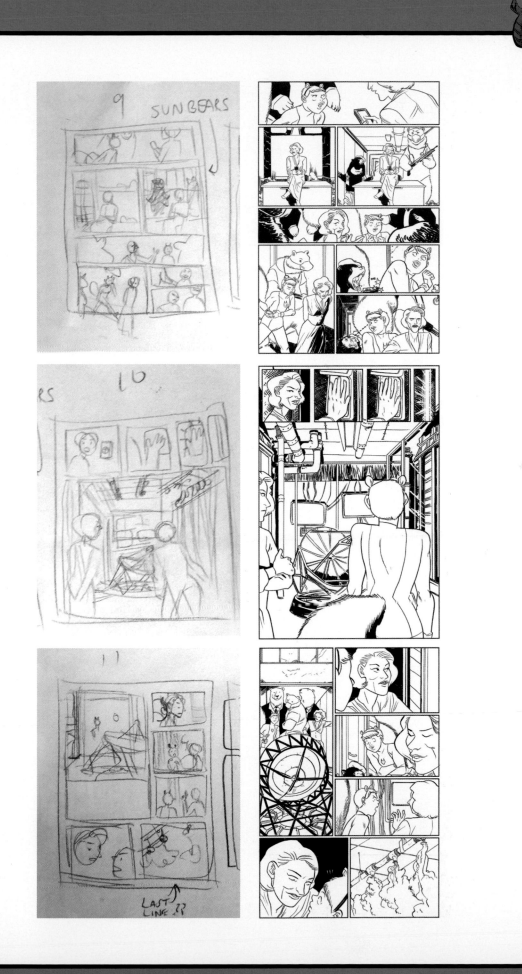

STUFF
DROP CEILING

4

#20 PAGES 13-15 LAYOUTS AND INKS BY **ERICA HENDERSON**

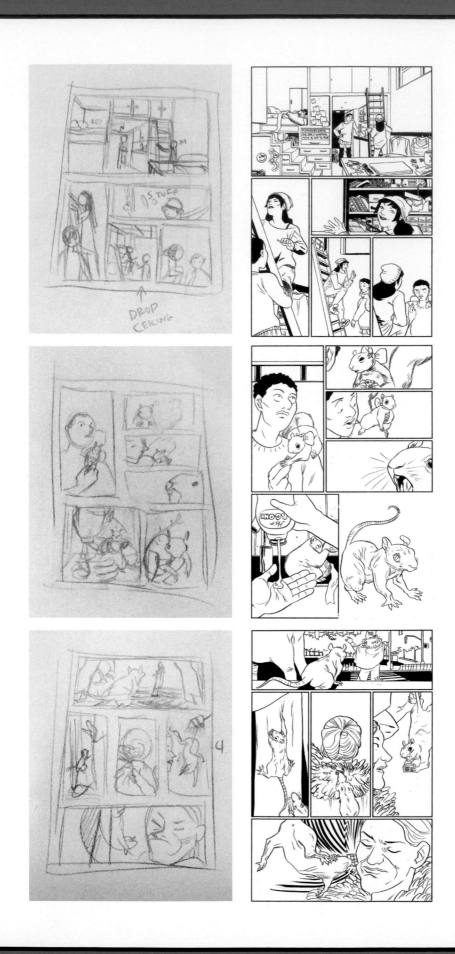